THE COMPLETE

CROSSWORD SOLVER

Fiona Ball

INDEX

Published by
Arcturus Publishing Limited
for Index Books Ltd
Henson Way, Kettering,
Northants, NN16 8PX

Published 2004

Copyright © Arcturus Publishing Limited
26/27 Bickels Yard
151–153 Bermondsey Street
London SE1 3HA

ISBN 1-84193-210-8

Printed in India

Contents

Arts and Literature

Antique Trade Terms

3

waf

4

cost
kite
lump
ring

5

aggro
folky
fresh
Lyle's
moody
repro
right
rough
run up
touch
trade
Vicky

6

looker
made-up
period
punter
runner
smalls
totter

7

breaker
call-out
cut down
knocker
Miller's

8

as bought
bent gear
bought in
chairman
down to me
estimate
follower
marriage
sclenter

9

clearance
inner ring
six and two

10

commercial
four and two
off the wall
old friends

11

eight and two
hammer price
out of the air
sight unseen

12

knocking down

14

collector's item

Architecture

3

bay
cap
die
eye
key

4

ambo
anta
apse
arch
band
bead
bell
boss
dado
dais
dome
fret
frog
fust
nave
pele
stoa

5

aisle
ambry
arris
attic
conge
crown
crypt
Doric
foils
gable
glyph
helix
inlay
ionic
lobby
newel
Roman
scape
shaft
shank
talon
tenia
Tudor

verge

6

abacus
access
alcove
arcade
atrium
attick
aumbry
belfry
bonnet
broach
canopy
chevet
column
corona
crenel
cupola
dagger
dentil
diaper
façade
fillet
finial
fleche
fresco
frieze
gablet
gazebo
Gothic
guttae
heroic
lesene
lintel
lintol
loggia
louvre
mantel ·
merlon
metope
mutule
Norman

oculus
pagoda
patera
plinth
pulpit
quadra
regula
rococo
scapus
scroll
sedile
soffit
trophy
urella
vestry
volute
wreath
xystus
zig-zag

7

annulet
arch rib
astylar
balcony
baroque
bastion
butment
capital
cavetto
chancel
chevron
cornice
crochet
crocket
distyle
echinus
encarpa
entasis
eustyle
festoon
fleuron
fluting

gadroon
Galilee
gallery
lacunar
lantern
lattice
lequear
lunette
narthex
nulling
obelisk
oratory
parvise
portail
portico
postern
pteroma
reeding
Regency
reredos
rosette
rotunda
roundel
scallop
Spanish
systyle
tessara
tondino
tracery
trumeau

8

abutment
acanthus
aedicula
apophyge
astragal
atlantes
baluster
bartizan
basilica
beak head
caryatid

cimborio
cincture
crenelle
cresting
cymatium
diastyle
dipteral
dog-tooth
edge roll
extrados
formeret
gargoyle
intrados
keel arch
keystone
lich gate
lych gate
miserere
pavilion
pedestal
pediment
pilaster
predella
pulpitum
rocaille
spandrel
spandril
torching
transept
triglyph
tympanum
verandah
vignette
wainscot

9

acropolis
antefixae
anthemion
apex stone
arch brick
archivolt
attic base

bird's beak
Byzantine
campanile
canephora
cartouche
caulicoli
cloisters
colonnade
composite
dripstone
foliation
grotesque
hexastyle
hypocaust
hypostyle
ingle nook
label stop
lacunaria
linenfold
mezzanine
mouldings
octastyle
Palladian
refectory
sgraffito
strapwork
stylobate
trabeated
triforium
trilithon
vestibule
zoophorus

10

acroterion
ambulatory
araeostyle
architrave
baldachino
ball flower
battlement
cinquefoil

colonnette
Corinthian
egg and dart
enrichment
hagioscope
Lady chapel
lancet arch
misericord
modillions
pietra dura
presbytery
pycnostyle
quatrefoil
Romanesque
rood screen
rose window
sexpartite
tetrastyle
trachelion

11

castellated
entablature
fan vaulting
harelip arch
leaded light
mantelpiece
mantelshelf
oriel window
Renaissance
reticulated

12

amphitheatre
blind tracery
cockle stairs
egg and tongue
lancet window
porte-cochere

13

amphiprostyle

14

angular capital
flying buttress
hypotrachelion

Art Methods, Terms etc

2 and 3

air
art
bur
del.
exc.
fec.
hue
inc.
inv.
key
mat
oil
op
pop
sit

4

airy
arts
base
body
burr
bust
cast
chic
dada
daub
draw
etch
flat
form

gild
halo
herm
icon
ikon
.kore
lime
line
lipo
mass
nude
pinx.
pose
size
term
tone
wash

5

batik
bloom
blush
board
brush
burin
cameo
chalk
couch
delin.
draft
easel
ember
Fauve
fecit
frame
genre
gesso
glaze
glory
gloss
grave
hatch
inert

japan
lay-in
lumia
magot
model
mount
mural
nabis
naive
paint
pieta
print
prime
putto
rebus
salon
scene
sculp
secco
sepia
shade
Stijl
study
stump
style
tondo
torso
trace
vertu
virtu

6

action
artist
ashcan
bistre
cachet
canvas
colour
crayon
cubism
depict
design

doctor
ectype
emblem
embos
enamel
engild
flambé
fresco
fylfot
gothic
ground
incavo
kitcat
kit-kat
kitsch
kouros
limner
maesta
mastic
medium
mobile
mosaic
niello
nimbus
object
ormolu
ox-gall
pastel
patina
pencil
pinxit
plaque
plaster
purism
reflex
relief
rhythm
rococo
school
sculpt.
shadow
shippo
sitter

sketch
statue
stucco
studio
stylus
tuscan
uncial
veduta
verism

7

abbozzo
academy
acrylic
atelier
amorino
archaic
atelier
aureole
baroque
Bauhaus
bitumen
bodegon
bottega
bachiru
biscuit
cabinet
camaieu
cartoon
carving
cissing
classic
collage
contour
cosmati
Dadaism
daubing
De Stijl
diagram
diptych
draught
drawing
ecorche

etching
excudit
faience
Fauvism
felt tip
gilding
glazing
gouache
graphic
hot tone
impaint
impasto
incidit
lacquer
lino-cut
lost wax
lunette
modello
montage
mordant
orphism
outline
painter
palette
picture
pigment
plastic
pochade
profile
realism
relievo
remodel
replica
reredos
rococco
scumble
sfumato
shading
sinopia
sketchy
stabile
stencil
stipple

support
surlace
tableau
tempera
texture
tracery
T-square
vanitas
varnish
vehicle
woodcut

8

abstract
academic
acid bath
acrolith
air-brush
allegory
anaglyph
ancients
aquatint
armature
arriccio
artistic
barbizon
blue four
bozzetto
carytid
charcoal
concours
cool tone
diaglyph
drolerie
drypoint
emulsion
engraver
figurine
fixative
freehand
frottage
Futurism
gargoyle

graffiti
grouping
hatching
half-tone
handling
idealism
intaglio
intonaco
luminist
majolica
makimono
mandorla
maquette
monotype
mounting
negative
oil paint
ornament
painting
panorama
pastiche
penumbra
plein air
pleurant
portrait
pouncing
predella
repousse
romantic
sculspit
seascape
seicento
staffage
statuary
symmetry
tachisme
tapestry
tectonic
tesserae
throwing
trecento
triglyph
triptych

Venetian
vignette
warm tone

9

aggregate
alla prima
anti-cerne
appliqué
aquarelle
aquatinta
arabesque
asymmetry
autograph
ball-point
has-relief
blockbook
bric-a-brac
brushwork
byzantine
capriccio
cartridge
cartouche
cloisonné
colourist
crow quill
damascene
damaskeen
dichroism
distemper
emblemata
embossing
encaustic
engraving
facsimile
geometric
gradation
grisaille
grotesque
highlight
hot colour
indelible
indian ink

intimisme
japanning
landscape
lay figure
lithotint
mahlstick
maulstick
mannerism
marquetry
maulstick
mezzotint
miniature
modelling
neo-gothic
oil colour
oleograph
painterly
phototype
polyptych
primitive
ready made
recession
sculpture
scumbling
serigraph
statuette
still-life
stippling
strapwork
stretcher
Symbolist
symbolism
tailpiece
tattooing
tenebrism
Totentanz
Vorticism
woodblock
xylograph

10

accidental
achromatic

altogether
anaglyphic
anaglyptic
arricciato
Art Nouveau
assemblage
atmosphere
automatism
avant-garde
background
biomorphic
body colour
caricature
cartellino
cerography
cire-perdue
classicism
cool colour
cornucopia
craquelure
dead colour
embossment
embroidery
fitch brush
flat colour
flotentine
foreground
full-length
hair pencil
half-length
India paper
Jugendstil
kinetic art
lithograph
metal point
mezzotinto
monochrome
morbidezza
naturalism
night piece
organic art
paint brush
pen and wash

pentimento
pencilling
photograph
pietra dura
plasticity
portcrayon
provenance
quadratura
Raphaelism
Raphaelite
repoussoir
Romanesque
serigraphy
silhouette
silk screen
Surrealism
synthesism
terracotta
turpentine
warm colour
xylography

11

academician
alto-relievo
aquatinting
bamboccanti
battle piece
biedermeier
calligraphy
carolingian
chiaroscuro
chinoiserie
chromograph
cinquecento
colour print
composition
concrete art
connoisseur
conte crayon
divisionism
draughtsman
eclecticism

electrotype
engravement
foreshorten
found object
french chalk
ground plane
heliochrome
heliochromy
iconography
illusionism
imprimatura
life drawing
lithography
marqueterie
masterpiece
neo-romantic
oil painting
pavement art
perspective
photography
picturesque
pointillism
portraiture
poster paint
primitivism
renaissance
restoration
retroussage
scenography
stylization
stained glass
stereochromy
suprematism
tessellation
tracing linen
tracing paper
tromp l'oeil
watercolour

12

acrylic paint
alkyd colours
anamorphosis

bird's eye view
cloisonnisme
contrapposto
counterproof
dare-obscure
illumination
illustration
palette knife
precisionism
quattrocento
scraper board
superrealism

13

architectonic
black and white
complementary
daguerreotype
decorative art
etching needle
expressionism
fete champetre
glass painting
Impressionism
Neo-Classicism
neoplasticism
papiers colles
Pre-Raphaelite
primary colour
social realism
tactile values
underpainting

14 and over

action painting (14)
cabinet picture (14)
chromatography (14)
constructivism (14)
conversation piece (17)
draughtsmanship (15)
foreshortening (14)
Neo-Impressionism (16)

Neo-Romanticism (14)
pavement artist (14)
picture gallery (14)
plaster of paris (14)
portrait painter (15)
Post-Impressionism (17)
representational (16)
socialist realism (16)
steel engraving (14)
vanishing point (14)
Ballet Terms

4

bras
demi
jete
plie
pose
saut
tutu
vole

5

arque
barre
battu
beats
brise
colle
coupe
décor
eleve
fondu
ligne
passé
piqué
pivot
porte
rosin
sauté
serre
tombe

6

aplomb
a terre
attack
baisse
ballon
cambre
chaine
change
chasse
croise
degage
detire
devant
ecarte
efface
elance
entrée
epaule
etendu
etoile
failli
jarret
monter
penche
pointe
releve
retire
voyage

7

allonge
arrondi
attaque
balance
danseur
deboite
echappe
emboite
etendre
fouette
jarrete

leotard
maillot
marquer
poisson
ramasse
retombe
sissone
soutenu
taquete

8

assemble
attitude
back bend
ballonne
ballotte
batterie
cabriole
cagneaux
coryphée
danseuse
deboules
derriere
detourne
glissade
pistolet
renverse
serpette
spotting
stulchik
tonnelet

9

arabesque
ballabile
cou de pied
developpe
elevation
entrechat
enveloppe
equilibre

hortensia
juponnage
limbering
marcheuse
pas de deux
pirouette
raccourci
reverence
revoltade

10

battements
enlevement
epaulement
soubresaut
taqueterie

11

contretemps
pas de basque

12

choreography
enchainement
gargouillade

13

choreographer
corps de ballet

14

closed position
divertissement
prima ballerina

15

autour de la salle

17

regisseur-generale

Characters from Jane Austen

Character	Novel
Allen Mr/Mrs	Northanger Abbey
Bates, Mrs	Emma
Bennet, Jane/Elizabeth/Catherine/Mary/Lydia	Pride and Prejudice
Benwick, Captain	Persuasion
Bertram, Lady Maria/Sir Thomas/Rev Edmund/ Maria/Julia	Mansfield Park
Bingley, Charles/Caroline/Louisa	Pride and Prejudice
Brandon, Colonel	Sense and Sensibility
Campbell, Colonel/Jane	Emma
Churchill, Frank	Emma
Clay, Mrs	Persuasion
Collins, Rev William	Pride and Prejudice
Crawford, Henry/Mary/Admiral	Mansfield Park
Croft, Admiral	Persuasion
Darcy, Fitzwilliam/Lady Anne/Georgiana	Pride and Prejudice
Dashwood, Henry/John/Fanny/Elinor/Marianne/ Margaret	Sense and Sensibility
De Bourgh, Lady Catherine	Pride and Prejudice
Dixon, Mr	Emma
Elton	Emma
Fairfax, Jane	Emma
Ferrars, Edward/Robert	Sense and Sensibility
Fitzwilliam, Colonel	Pride and Prejudice
Forster, Colonel/Harriet	Pride and Prejudice
Gardiner, Edward	Pride and Prejudice
Goddard, Mrs	Emma
Grant, Rev Dr	Mansfield Park
Harville, Captain	Persuasion
Hayter, Mrs	Persuasion
Hurst, Louisa	Pride and Prejudice
Jennings, Mrs	Sense and Sensibility
Knightly, George/John/Isabella	Emma
Lucas, Sir William/Charlotte/Marie	Pride and Prejudice
Martin, Robert	Emma
Middleton, Sir John	Sense and Sensibility
Morland, Catherine/James/Sarah/George/Harriet	Northanger Abbey
Musgrove, Mary/Richard/Charles/Henrietta/Laura	Persuasion
Norris, Mrs/Rev Mr	Mansfield Park

Character	Novel
Palmer, Mrs Charlotte	Sense and Sensibility
Perry	Emma
Phillips, Mrs	Pride and Prejudice
Price, Mrs Frances/Lieutenant/ Fanny/William/ Susan	Mansfield Park
Rushworth, Maria/James	Mansfield Park
Russell, Lady	Persuasion
Shepherd, John	Persuasion
Smith, Harriet	Emma
Smith, Mrs	Persuasion
Smith, Mrs	Sense and Sensibility
Steele, Anne/Lucy	Sense and Sensibility
Thorpe, Mrs/Isabella/John/Edward/William	Northanger Abbey
Tilney, Henry/Eleanor/General/Captain Fred	Northanger Abbey
Wentworth, Captain Frederick	Persuasion
Weston, Mrs	Emma
Wickham, George	Pride and Prejudice
Williams, Eliza	Sense and Sensibility
Willoughby, John	Sense and Sensibility
Woodhouse, Emma/Isabella	Emma
Yates, Hon John	Mansfield Park

Dickensian Characters

Character	Novel
2	
Jo	Bleak House
3	
Amy	Oliver Twist
Bet, Betsy	Oliver Twist
Bud, Rosa	Edwin Drood
Cly	A Tale of Two Cities
Gay, Walter	Dombey and Son
Joe	Pickwick Papers
Tox, Miss	Dombey and Son

Character	Novel
4	
Anne	Dombey and Son
Baps	Dombey and Son
Begs, Mrs Ridger	David Copperfield
Bray, Madeline	Nicholas Nickleby
Bray, Walter	Nicholas Nickleby
Dick, Mr	Oliver Twist
Duff	Oliver Twist
Fips, Mr	Martin Chuzzlewit
Fogg	Pickwick Papers
Gamp, Mrs Sarah	Martin Chuzzlewit
Grip	Barnaby Rudge
Hawk, Sir Mulberry	Nicholas Nickleby
Heep, Uriah	David Copperfield
Hugh	Barnaby Rudge
Jowl, Mat	The Old Curiosity Shop
Jupe, Cecilia	Hard Times
Kags	Oliver Twist
Knag, Miss	Nicholas Nickleby
List, Isaac	The Old Curiosity Shop
Mann, Mrs	Oliver Twist
Mary	Pickwick Papers
Mell, Charles	David Copperfield
Miff, Mrs	Dombey and Son
Omer	David Copperfield
Peak	Barnaby Rudge
Pell, Solomon	Pickwick Papers
Peps, Dr Parker	Dombey and Son
Pott, Minerva	Pickwick Papers
'Riah	Our Mutual Friend
Rugg, Anastasia	Little Dorrit
Tigg, Montague	Martin Chuzzlewit
Wade, Miss	Little Dorrit
Wegg, Silas	Our Mutual Friend
5	
Adams, Jack	Dombey and Son
Allen, Arabella/Benjamin	Pickwick Papers
Bates, Charley	Oliver Twist
Betsy	Pickwick Papers

Character	Novel
Brass, Sally/Sampson	The Old Curiosity Shop
Brick, Jefferson	Martin Chuzzlewit
Brown, Alice/Mrs	Dombey and Son
Buzuz, Sergeant	Pickwick Papers
Casby, Christopher	Little Dorrit
Chick, John/Louisa	Dombey and Son
Clare, Ada	Bleak House
Clark	Dombey and Son
Clive	Little Dorrit
Crowl	Nicholas Nickleby
Crupp, Mrs	David Copperfield
Daisy, Solomon	Barnaby Rudge
David	Nicholas Nickleby
Dawes, Mary	Dombey and Son
Dingo, Professor	Bleak House
Diver, Colonel	Martin Chuzzlewit
Donny, Mrs	Bleak House
Doyce, Daniel	Little Dorrit
Drood, Edwin	Edwin Drood
Dumps, Nicodemus	Pickwick Papers
Fagin	Oliver Twist
Flite, Miss	Bleak House
Giles	Oliver Twist
Gills, Solomon	Dombey and Son
Gowan, Harry	Little Dorrit
Green, Tom	Barnaby Rudge
Gride, Arthur	Nicholas Nickleby
Guppy, William	Bleak House
Hexam, Charlie/Jesse/Lizzie	Our Mutual Friend
Janet	David Copperfield
Jones, Mary	Barnaby Rudge
Krook	Bleak House
Lobbs, Maria/'Old'	Pickwick Papers
Lorry, Jarvis	A Tale of Two Cities
Lucas, Solomon	Pickwick Papers
Lupin, Mrs	Martin Chuzzlewit
Mealy	David Copperfield
'Melia	Dombey and Son
Miggs, Miss	Barnaby Rudge
Mills, Julia	David Copperfield
Molly	Great Expectations

Character	Novel
Mould	Martin Chuzzlewit
Nancy	Oliver Twist
Nandy, John Edward	Little Dorrit
Noggs, Newman	Nicholas Nickleby
Perch	Dombey and Son
Pinch, Ruth/Tom	Martin Chuzzlewit
Price, 'Tilda	Nicholas Nickleby
Pross, Miss/Solomon	A Tale of Two Cities
Quale	Bleak House
Quilp, Daniel	The Old Curiosity Shop
Rudge, Barnaby/Mary	Barnaby Rudge
Sally, Old	Oliver Twist
Scott, Tom	The Old Curiosity Shop
Sharp	David Copperfield
Sikes, Bill	Oliver Twist
Slurk	Pickwick Papers
Slyme, Chevy	Martin Chuzzlewit
Smike	Nicholas Nickleby
Snobb, The Hon	Nicholas Nickleby
Squod, Phil	Bleak House
Stagg	Barnaby Rudge
Toots, Mr P	Dombey and Son
Trabb	Great Expectations
Trent, Frederick/Nellie	The Old Curiosity Shop
Twist, Oliver	Oliver Twist
Venus, Mr	Our Mutual Friend
Watty	Pickwick Papers

6

Character	Novel
Badger, Dr Bayham/Laura/Malta/Matthew/Quebec/Woolwich	Bleak House
Bailey, Benjamin	Martin Chuzzlewit
Bailey, Captain	David Copperfield
Bamber, Jack	Pickwick Papers
Bantam, Angelo Cyrus	Pickwick Papers
Barker, Phil	Oliver Twist
Barkis	David Copperfield
Barley, Clara	Great Expectations
Barney	Oliver Twist
Bedwin, Mrs	Oliver Twist
Betsey, Jane	Dombey and Son

Character	Novel
Bitzer	Hard Times
Boffin, Henrietta/Nicodemus	Our Mutual Friend
Bonney	Nicholas Nickleby
Briggs	Dombey and Son
Bumble	Oliver Twist
Bunsby, Captain	Dombey and Son
Carker, Harriet/James/John	Dombey and Son
Carton, Sydney	A Tale of Two Cities
Cheggs, Alick	The Old Curiosity Shop
Clarke	Pickwick Papers
Codger, Mrs	Martin Chuzzlewit
Codlin, Thomas	The Old Curiosity Shop
Conway, General	Barnaby Rudge
Corney, Mrs	Oliver Twist
Curdle	Nicholas Nickleby
Cutler, Mr/Mrs	Nicholas Nickleby
Cuttle, Captain Ned	Dombey and Son
Darnay, Charles	A Tale of Two Cities
Dartle, Rosa	David Copperfield
Dennis, Ned	Barnaby Rudge
Dibabs, Mrs	Nicholas Nickleby
Dodson	Pickwick Papers
Dombey, Fanny/Florence/Louisa/Paul	Dombey and Son
Dorker	Nicholas Nickleby
Dorrit, Amy/Edward/Fanny/Frederick/William	Little Dorrit
Dowler, Captain	Pickwick Papers
Feeder	Dombey and Son
Feenix	Dombey and Son
Fizkin, Horatio	Pickwick Papers
Foliar	Nicholas Nickleby
George	The Old Curiosity Shop
George	Pickwick Papers
George, Mr	Bleak House
Gordon, Lord George	Barnaby Rudge
Graham, Mary	Martin Chuzzlewit
Groves, 'Honest' James	The Old Curiosity Shop
Gunter	Pickwick Papers
Harmon, John	Our Mutual Friend
Harris, Mrs	Martin Chuzzlewit

Character	Novel
Hawdon, Captain	Bleak House
Higden, Betty	Our Mutual Friend
Hominy, Major	Martin Chuzzlewit
Howler, Rev M	Dombey and Son
Jarley, Mrs	The Old Curiosity Shop
Jasper, Jack	Edwin Drood
Jingle, Alfred	Pickwick Papers
Kettle, La Fayette	Martin Chuzzlewit
Lammle, Alfred	Our Mutual Friend
Lobley	Edwin Drood
Lumley, Dr	Nicholas Nickleby
Magnus, Peter	Pickwick Papers
Malden, Jack	David Copperfield
Marley, Jacob	A Christmas Carol
Marton	The Old Curiosity Shop
Maylie, Harrie/Mrs/Rose	Oliver Twist
Merdle, Mr	Little Dorrit
Milvey, Rev Frank	Our Mutual Friend
Mivens	Pickwick Papers
Moddle, Augustus	Martin Chuzzlewit
Morfin	Dombey and Son
Mullet, Professor	Martin Chuzzlewit
Nipper, Susan	Dombey and Son
Pancks	Little Dorrit
Perker	Pickwick Papers
Phunky	Pickwick Papers
Pipkin, Nathaniel	Pickwick Papers
Pirrip, Philip	Great Expectations
Pocket, Herbert/Matthew/Sarah	Great Expectations
Pogram, Elijah	Martin Chuzzlewit
Raddle, Mr and Mrs	Pickwick Papers
Rigaud, Monsieur	Little Dorrit
Sapsea, Thomas	Edwin Drood
Sawyer, Bob	Pickwick Papers
Scaley	Nicholas Nickleby
Sleary, Josephine	Hard Times
'Sloppy'	Our Mutual Friend
Sownds	Dombey and Son
Strong, Dr	David Copperfield
Tacker	Martin Chuzzlewit
Tapley, Mark	Martin Chuzzlewit

Character	Novel
Tartar	Edwin Drood
Tippin, Lady	Our Mutual Friend
Tisher, Mrs	Edwin Drood
Toodle	Dombey and Son
Tupman, Tracey	Pickwick Papers
Varden, Dolly/Gabriel	Barnaby Rudge
Vholes	Bleak House
Vuffin	Curiosity Shop
Walker, Mick	David Copperfield
Wardle, Emily/Isabella/Mr/Rachel	Pickwick Papers
Weller, Sam/Tony	Pickwick Papers
Wilfer, Bella/Lavinia/Reginald	Our Mutual Friend
Willet, Joe/John	Barnaby Rudge
Winkle, Nathaniel	Pickwick Papers
Wopsle	Great Expectations

7

Baillie, Gabriel	Pickwick Papers
Bangham, Mrs	Little Dorrit
Barbara	The Old Curiosity Shop
Barbary, Miss	Bleak House
Bardell, Mrs Martha/Tommy	Pickwick Papers
Bazzard	Edwin Drood
Belling, Master	Nicholas Nickleby
Blimper, Dr	Dombey and Son
Blotton	Pickwick Papers
Bobster, Cecilia/Mr	Nicholas Nickleby
Boldwig, Captain	Pickwick Papers
Brogley	Dombey and Son
Brooker	Nicholas Nickleby
Browdie, John	Nicholas Nickleby
Bullamy	Martin Chuzzlewit
Charley	David Copperfield
Chester, Edward/Sir John	Barnaby Rudge
Chillip, Dr	David Copperfield
Chivery, John	Little Dorrit
Chollop, Hannibal	Martin Chuzzlewit
Chuffey	Martin Chuzzlewit
Cleaver, Fanny	Our Mutual Friend
Clennam, Arthur	Little Dorrit
Clubber, Sir Thomas	Pickwick Papers

Character	Novel
Crackit, Toby	Oliver Twist
Crawley, Young Mr	Pickwick Papers
Creakle	David Copperfield
Crewler, Mrs/Rev Horace/Sophy	David Copperfield
Crimple, David	Martin Chuzzlewit
Crookey	Pickwick Papers
Dawkins, Jack	Oliver Twist
Dedlock, Sir Leicester/Volumnia	Bleak House
Defarge, Madame	A Tale of Two Cities
Dolloby	David Copperfield
Drummle, Bentley	Great Expectations
Dubbley	Pickwick Papers
Durdles	Edwin Drood
Edmunds, John	Pickwick Papers
Estella	Great Expectations
Fleming, Agnes	Oliver Twist
Gabelle, Theophile	A Tale of Two Cities
Gargery Biddy/Joe/Pip	Great Expectations
Garland, Abel/Mrs/Mr	The Old Curiosity Shop
Gaspard	A Tale of Two Cities
Gazingi, Miss	Nicholas Nickleby
General, Mrs	Little Dorrit
Gilbert, Mark	Barnaby Rudge
Granger, Edith	Dombey and Son
Gridley	Bleak House
Grimwig	Oliver Twist
Grudden, Mrs	Nicholas Nickleby
Haggage, Dr	Little Dorrit
Heyling, George	Pickwick Papers
Jaggers	Great Expectations
Jellyby, Caddy/Mrs/Peepy	Bleak House
Jinkins	Martin Chuzzlewit
Jobling, Dr John	Martin Chuzzlewit
Jobling, Tony	Bleak House
Johnson, Mr	Nicholas Nickleby
Jorkins	David Copperfield
Kedgick, Captain	Martin Chuzzlewit
Kenwigs, Morleena	Nicholas Nickleby
Larkins, Mr	David Copperfield
Leeford, Edward	Oliver Twist
Lewsome	Martin Chuzzlewit

Character	Novel
Mallard	Pickwick Papers
Manette, Dr/Lucie	A Tale of Two Cities
Meagles	Little Dorrit
Minerva	Pickwick Papers
Mowcher, Miss	David Copperfield
Nadgett	Martin Chuzzlewit
Neckett, Charlotte/Emma/Tom	Bleak House
Nubbles, Christopher	The Old Curiosity Shop
Nupkins, George	Pickwick Papers
Pawkins, Major	Martin Chuzzlewit
Pilkins, Dr	Dombey and Son
Pipchin, Mrs	Dombey and Son
Podsnap, Georgina/Mr	Our Mutual Friend
Quinion	David Copperfield
Sampson, George	Our Mutual Friend
Scadder, Zephaniah	Martin Chuzzlewit
Scrooge, Ebenezer	A Christmas Carol
Simmons, William	Martin Chuzzlewit
Skewton, Hon Mrs	Dombey and Son
Skylark, Mr	David Copperfield
Slammer, Dr	Pickwick Papers
Slumkey, Hon Samuel	Pickwick Papers
Snagsby	Bleak House
Snawley	Nicholas Nickleby
Snubbin, Sergeant	Pickwick Papers
Spartsit, Mrs	Hard Times
Spenlow, Dora	David Copperfield
Squeers, Fanny/Wackford	Nicholas Nickleby
Startop	Great Expectations
Stryver, C J	A Tale of Two Cities
Tamaroo, Miss	Martin Chuzzlewit
Todgers, Mrs	Martin Chuzzlewit
Trotter, Job	Pickwick Papers
Trundle	Pickwick Papers
Wackles Jane/Melissa/Sophie	The Old Curiosity Shop
Watkins	Nicholas Nickleby
Wemmick	Great Expectations
Wickham, Mrs	Dombey and Son
Withers	Dombey and Son

Character	Novel
8	
Akersham, Sophronia	Our Mutual Friend
Bagstock, Major	Dombey and Son
Barnwell, B B	Martin Chuzzlewit
Billikin, Mrs	Edwin Drood
Blathers	Oliver Twist
Boythorn, Lawrence	Bleak House
Bravassa, Miss	Nicholas Nickleby
Brownlow, Mr	Oliver Twist
Claypole, Noah	Oliver Twist
Cluppins	Pickwick Papers
Craddock, Mrs	Pickwick Papers
Cratchit, Belinda/Bob/Tiny Tim	A Christmas Carol
Cripples, Mr	Little Dorrit
Crummles, Ninetta/Vincent	Nicholas Nickleby
Cruncher, Jeremiah/Jerry	A Tale of Two Cities
Crushton, Hon Mr	Pickwick Papers
Datchery, Dick	Edwin Drood
D'Aulnais	A Tale of Two Cities
Finching, Mrs Flora	Little Dorrit
Fledgeby, Old/Young	Our Mutual Friend
Gashford	Barnaby Rudge
Haredale, Emma/Geoffrey/Reuben	Barnaby Rudge
Havisham, Miss	Great Expectations
Hortense	Bleak House
Jarndyce, John	Bleak House
La Creevy, Miss	Nicholas Nickleby
Landless, Helena/Neville	Edwin Drood
Langdale	Barnaby Rudge
Lenville	Nicholas Nickleby
Littimer	David Copperfield
Losberne	Oliver Twist
Magwitch, Abel	Great Expectations
Mary Anne	David Copperfield
Matthews	Nicholas Nickleby
Micawber, Wilkins	David Copperfield
Mutanhead, Lord	Pickwick Papers
Nickleby, Godfrey/Kate/Nicholas/Ralph	Nicholas Nickleby
Peggotty, Clara/Daniel/Ham/Little Em'ly	David Copperfield

Character	Novel
Pickwick, Samuel	Little Dorrit
Potatoes	David Copperfield
Scadgers, Lady	Hard Times
Skiffins, Miss	Great Expectations
Skimpole, Arethusa/Harold/Kitty/ Laura	Bleak House
Skittles, Sir Barnet	Dombey and Son
Smiggers, Joseph	Pickwick Papers
Sparkler, Edmund	Little Dorrit
Stiggins	Pickwick Papers
Traddles, Tom	David Copperfield
Trotwood, Betsey	David Copperfield
Westlock, John	Martin Chuzzlewit
Wrayburn, Eugene	Our Mutual Friend

9	
Belvawney, Miss	Nicholas Nickleby
Berinthia	Dombey and Son
Blackpool, Stephen	Hard Times
Bounderby, Josiah	Hard Times
Charlotte	Oliver Twist
Cheeryble, Charles/Frank/Ned	Nicholas Nickleby
Chickweed, Conkey	Oliver Twist
Chuckster	The Old Curiosity Shop
Compeyson	Great Expectations
Fibbitson, Mrs	David Copperfield
Gradgrind, Louisa/Thomas	Hard Times
Gregsbury	Nicholas Nickleby
Grewgious	Edwin Drood
Harthouse, James	Hard Times
Headstone, Bradley	Our Mutual Friend
Lightwood, Mortimer	Our Mutual Friend
Lillyvick	Nicholas Nickleby
Mantalini, Mr	Nicholas Nickleby
Murdstone, Edward/Jane	David Copperfield
Old Barley	Great Expectations
Pardiggle, Francis/O A	Bleak House
Pecksniff, Charity/Mercy/Seth	Martin Chuzzlewit
Priscilla	Bleak House
Riderhood, Pleasant/Roger	Our Mutual Friend
Smallweed, Bartholomew/Joshua/	

Character	Novel
Judy	Bleak House
Smorltork, Count	Pickwick Papers
Snodgrass, Augustus	Pickwick Papers
Summerson, Esther	Bleak House
Swiveller, Richard	The Old Curiosity Shop
Tappertit, Simon	Barnaby Rudge
Veneering, Anastasia/Hamilton	Our Mutual Friend
Verisopht, Lord Frederick	Nicholas Nickleby
Wickfield, Agnes/Mr	David Copperfield
Witherden, Mr	The Old Curiosity Shop
Woodcourt, Allan	Bleak House

10

Character	Novel
Ayresleigh, Mr	Pickwick Papers
Chuzzlewit, Anthony/Diggory/ George/Jonas/Martin/Mrs/Ned/Toby	Martin Chuzzlewit
Crisparkle, Rev Septimus	Edwin Drood
Flintwich, Affery/Ephraim/ Jeremiah	Little Dorrit
Macstinger, Mrs	Dombey and Son
Rouncewell, Mrs	Bleak House
Snevellici, Miss	Nicholas Nickleby
Sowerberry	Oliver Twist
Stareleigh, Justice	Pickwick Papers
Steerforth, James	David Copperfield
Tattycoram	Little Dorrit
Turveydrop, Prince	Bleak House
Twinkleton, Miss	Edwin Drood
Waterbrook	David Copperfield
Wititterly, Julia	Nicholas Nickleby

11

Character	Novel
Copperfield, Clara/David	David Copperfield
'Dismal Jimmy'	Pickwick Papers
'Game Chicken', The	Dombey and Son
Marchioness, The	The Old Curiosity Shop
Pumblechook	Great Expectations
Spottletoes, Mrs	Martin Chuzzlewit
St Evremonde, Marquis de/ Marquise de	A Tale of Two Cities
Sweedlepipe, Paul	Martin Chuzzlewit

Character	Novel
Tulkinghorn	Bleak House

12

Character	Novel
Honeythunder, Luke	Edwin Drood
'Shiny William'	Pickwick Papers
Sweet William	The Old Curiosity Shop
Tite-Barnacle, Clarence/Ferdinand/ Junior/Lord Decimus/Mr	Little Dorrit

15

Character	Novel
Von Koeldwethout	Nicholas Nickleby

Fictional Characters

Character	Title	Author

3

Character	Title	Author
Fox, Brer	Uncle Remus	J.C. Harris
Gog	The Tower of London	W.H. Ainsworth
Hur, Judah	Ben Hur	L. Wallace
Jim, 'Lord'	Lord Jim	J. Conrad
Kim	Kim	Rudyard Kipling
Lee, General Robert E.	Abraham Lincoln	J. Drinkwater
Lee Lorelei	Gentleman Prefer Blondes	Anita Loos
Owl	Winnie the Pooh	A.A. Milne
Roo	Winnie the Pooh	A.A. Milne
Tom	The Water Babies	C. Kingsley
Tom, 'Uncle'	Uncle Tom's Cabin	Harriet B. Stowe

4

Character	Title	Author
Abel	Middlemarch	George Eliot
Cass, Eppie	Silas Marner	George Eliot
Casy, Rev. Jim	The Grapes of Wrath	J. Steinbeck
Cuff, Sergeant	The Moonstone	W. Collins
Dean, Ellen	Wuthering Heights	Emily Bronte
East	Tom Brown's Schooldays	T. Hughes
Easy, John	Mr Midshipman Easy	Captain Marryat
Eyre, Jane	Jane Eyre	Charlotte Bronte

Character	Title	Author
Fawn, Lord Frederic	Phineas Finn	A. Trollope
Fell, Dr Gideon	The Black Spectacles	J. Dickson Carr
Finn, Huckleberry	Huckleberry Finn, Tom Sawyer	M. Twain
Finn, Phineas	Phineas Finn	A. Trollope
Gray, Dorian	The Picture of Dorian Gray	Oscar Wilde
Gray, Nelly	Faithless Nelly Gray	T. Hood
Gunn, Ben	Treasure Island	R.L. Stevenson
Hook, Captain James	Peter Pan	J.M. Barrie
Judy	Wee Willie Winkie	R. Kipling
Lamb, Leonard	Middlemarch	George Eliot
Mole, Mr	The Wind in the Willows	K. Grahame
Nana	Peter Pan	J.M. Barrie
Nash, Richard (Beau)	Monsieur Beaucaire	Booth Tarkington
Puck (Robin Goodfellow)	Puck of Pook's Hill	R. Kipling
Rama (Tiger, Tiger)	The Jungle Book	R. Kipling
Reed, Mrs	Jane Eyre	Charlotte Bronte
Ridd, John	Lorna Doone	R.D. Blackmore
Seal, Basil	Put Out More Flags	E. Waugh
Smee	Peter Pan	J.M. Barrie
Toad, Mr	The Wind in the Willows	K. Grahame
Troy, Sergeant Francis	Far from the Madding Crowd	T. Hardy
Vane, Harriet	Strong Poison	Dorothy L. Sayers
Vane, Lady Isabel	East Lynne	Mrs Henry Wood
Wolf, 'Brer'	Uncle Remus	J.C. Harris

5

Character	Title	Author
Adler, Irene	The Adventures of Sherlock Holmes	A. Conan Doyle
Akela	The Jungle Book	R. Kipling
Alibi, Tom	Waverley	W. Scott
Athos	The Three Musketeers	Alexandre Dumas
Baloo	The Jungle Book	R. Kipling
Blake, Franklin	The Moonstone	W. Collins
Bones, Captain Billy	Treasure Island	R.L. Stevenson
Booby, Sir Thomas	Joseph Andrews	H. Fielding
Bruff	The Moonstone	W. Collins
Bulbo, Prince	The Rose and the Ring	W.M. Thackeray
Chant, Mercy	Tess of the D'Urbervilles	T. Hardy
Clack, Drusilla	The Moonstone	W. Collins
Clare, Angel	Tess of the D'Urbervilles	T. Hardy

Character	Title	Author
Darcy, Fitzwilliam	Pride and Prejudice	Jane Austen
Deans, Effie/Jeannie	The Heart of Midlothian	W. Scott
Dixon, James	Lucky Jim	K. Amis
Doone, Lorna	Lorna Doone	R.D. Blackmore
Eager, Rev. Cuthbert	Room with a View	E.M. Forster
Fanny	Fanny's First Play	G.B. Shaw
Flynn, Father James	The Dubliners	J. Joyce
Geste, Beau	Beau Geste	P.C. Wren
Gwynn, Nell	Simon Dale	A. Hope
Hands, Israel	Treasure Island	R.L. Stevenson
Hatch, Bennet	The Black Arrow	R.L. Stevenson
Jones, Tom	Tom Jones	H. Fielding
Kanga	Winnie the Pooh	A.A. Milne
Kipps, Arthur	Kipps	H.G. Wells
Leigh, Captain Sir Amyas	Westward Ho	C. Kingsley
Magog	The Tower of London	W.H. Ainsworth
March, Amy/Beth/	Little Women etc.	Louisa M. Alcott
Josephine (Jo)/Meg		
Mercy	Pilgrim's Progress	J. Bunyan
Mitty, Walter	The Secret Life of Walter Mitty	J. Thurber
Moore, Mrs	A Passage to India	E.M. Forster
O'Hara, Kimball	Kim	R. Kipling
O'Hara, Scarlett	Gone with the Wind	Margaret Mitchell
Otter, Mr	The Wind in the Willows	K. Grahame
Paget, Jean	A Town Like Alice	N. Shute
Polly, Alfred	The History of Mr Polly	H.G. Wells
Poole, Grace	Jane Eyre	Charlotte Bronte
Porgy	Porgy	Du Bose Heywood
Prism, Miss Laetitia	The Importance of Being Earnest	Oscar Wilde
Punch	Wee Willie Winkie	R. Kipling
Ready, Masterman	Masterman Ready	F. Marryat
Remus, Uncle	Uncle Remus series	J.C. Harris
Ryder, Charles	Brideshead Revisited	E. Waugh
Sally	Sally in our Alley	H. Carey
Sambo	Just So Stories	R. Kipling
Sharp, Rebecca (Becky)	Vanity Fair	W.M. Thackeray
Slope, Rev. Obadiah	Barchester Towers	A Trollope
Sloth	Pilgrim's Progress	J. Bunyan
Smith, Winston	1984	G. Orwell

Character	Title	Author
Snowe, Lucy	Villette	Charlotte Bronte
Tarka	Tarka the Otter	H. Williamson
Thumb, Tom	The Tale of Two Bad Mice	Beatrix Potter
Topsy	Uncle Tom's Cabin	Harriet B. Stowe
Uncas	The Last of the Mohicans	J. Fennimore Cooper

6

Character	Title	Author
Aitkin	Prester John	J. Buchan
Aramis	The Three Musketeers	Alexandre Dumas
Ayesha	She	H. Rider Haggard
Bennet, Catherine/ Elizabeth/Jane/Lydia/Mary	Pride and Prejudice	Jane Austen
Bessie	Jane Eyre	Charlotte Bronte
Binkie, Lady Grizzel	Vanity Fair	W.M. Thackeray
Bovary, Emma	Madame Bovary	G. Flaubert
Butler, Rhett	Gone with the Wind	Margaret Mitchell
Cackle	Vanity Fair	W.M. Thackeray
Crusoe, Robinson	Robinson Crusoe	D. Defoe
Dangle	The Critic	R.B. Sheridan
Eeyore	Winnie the Pooh	A.A. Milne
Elaine	Idylls of the King	Lord Tennyson
'Friday'	Robinson Crusoe	D. Defoe
Fritha	The Snow Goose	P. Gallico
Garter, Polly	Under Milk Wood	D. Thomas
Gatsby, Major Jay	The Great Gatsby	F. Scott Fitzgerald
George	Three Men in a Boat	J.K. Jerome
Gerard, Etienne	The Exploits of Brigadier Gerard	A. Conan Doyle
Gilpin, John	John Gilpin	W. Cowper
Glover, Catherine	The Fair Maid of Perth	W. Scott
Gordon, Squire	Black Beauty	A. Sewell
Grimes	The Water Babies	C. Kingsley
Hannay, Richard	The Thirty-Nine Steps	J. Buchan
Harker, Jonathan/Minna	Dracula	Bram Stoker
Harman, Joe	A Town like Alice	N. Shute
Harold, Childe	Childe Harold's Pilgrimage	Lord Byron
Hearts, King of/ Knave of/ Queen of	Alice in Wonderland	L. Carroll
Holmes, Mycroft	The Return of Sherlock Holmes	A. Conan Doyle
Holmes, Sherlock	A Study in Scarlet, The Sign	A. Conan Doyle

Character	Title	Author
	of Four, The Hound of the Baskervilles etc.	
Hooper, Fanny	Fanny by Gaslight	M. Sadleir
Jeeves	Thank You, Jeeves	P.G. Woodhouse
Jekyll, Henry	Dr Jekyll and Mr Hyde	R.L. Stevenson
Laurie	Little Women	Louisa M. Alcott
Laurie, Annie	Annie Laurie	Douglass
Legree, Simon	Uncle Tom's Cabin	Harriet B. Stowe
Linton, Edgar	Wuthering Heights	Emily Bronte
Mangan, Boss	Heartbreak House	G.B. Shaw
Manson, Dr Andrew	The Citadel	A.J. Cronin
Marple, Jane	A Pocketful of Rye etc.	Agatha Christie
Merlin	Idylls of the King	Lord Tennyson
Modred, Sir	Idylls of the King	Lord Tennyson
Moreau, Andre-Louis	Scaramouche	R. Sabatini
Moreau, Dr	The Island of Dr Moreau	H.G. Wells
Morgan, Angharad/Huw	How Green Was My Valley	R. Llewellyn
Morgan, Organ	Under Milk Wood	D. Thomas
Mowgli	The Jungle Book	R. Kipling
Nutkin, Squirrel	The Tale of Squirrel Nutkin	Beatrix Potter
Omnium, Duke of (Family name Palliser)	The Barsetshire series	Angela Thirkell
Pickle, Peregrine	Peregrine Pickle	T. Smollett
Piglet, Henry Pootel	Winnie the Pooh	A.A. Milne
Poirot, Hercule	The Mysterious Affair at Styles etc.	Agatha Christie
Rabbit	Winnie the Pooh	A.A. Milne
Rabbit, 'Brer'	Uncle Remus	J. C. Harris
Rabbit, The White	Alice in Wonderland	L. Carroll
Rivers, St John	Jane Eyre	Charlotte Bronte
Rustum	Sohrab and Rustum	M. Arnold
Sawyer, Tom	The Adventures of Tom Sawyer	M. Twain
Shandy, Tristram	Tristram Shandy	L. Sterne
Silver, Long John	Treasure Island	R.L. Stevenson
Simnel, Lambert	Perkin Warbeck	John Ford
Sohrab	Sohrab and Rustum	M. Arnold
Temple, Miss	Jane Eyre	Charlotte Bronte
Thorne, Dr Thomas	Doctor Thorne	A. Trollope
Thorpe, Isabella	Northanger Abbey	Jane Austen
Tilney, Henry	Northanger Abbey	Jane Austen

Character	Title	Author
Turner, Jim (Flint)	Swallows and Amazons	A. Ransome
Umpopa	King's Solomon's Mines	H. Ryder Haggard
Walker, John/Roger/ Susan/Titty/Vicky	Swallows and Amazons	A. Ransome
Weston, Mrs	Emma	Jane Austen
Wilkes, Ashley/India	Gone with the Wind	Margaret Mitchell
Wimsey, Lord Peter De'athBredon	Whose Body	Dorothy L. Sayers

7

Character	Title	Author
Aisgill, Alice	Room at the Top	J. Braine
Bagster	Middlemarch	George Eliot
Beesley	Lucky Jim	Kingsley Amis
Bingley, Charles	Pride and Prejudice	Jane Austen
Brandon, Colonel	Sense and Sensibility	Jane Austen
Candour, Mrs	The School for Scandal	R.B. Sheridan
Chesney, Jack	Charley's Aunt	Brandon Thomas
Collins, Rev. William	Pride and Prejudice	Jane Austen
Cypress, Mr	Nightmare Abbey	T.L. Peacock
Danvers, Mrs	Rebecca	Daphne du Maurier
Despair, Giant	Pilgrim's Progress	J. Bunyan
Dracula, Count	Dracula	Bram Stoker
Epicene	Epicene	B. Jonson
Fairfax, Gwendolen	The Importance of Being Earnest	Oscar Wilde
Fairfax, Jane	Emma	Jane Austen
Fairfax, Mrs	Jane Eyre	Charlotte Bronte
Fairlie, Frederick	Woman in White	W. Collins
Faustus	The History of Dr Faustus	C. Marlowe
Forsyte, Fleur/Irene/ Jolyon/Jon/Soames	The Forsyte Saga	J. Gallsworthy
Galahad	Idylls of the King	Lord Tennyson
Geraint	Idylls of the King	Lord Tennyson
Grantly, Bishop of Barchester	The Warden, Barchester Towers	A. Trollope
Hawkins, Jim	Treasure Island	R.L. Stevenson
Hentzau, Rupert of	The Prisoner of Zenda	A. Hope
Herries, Francis	Rough Herries	H. Walpole
Higgins, Henry	Pygmalion	G.B. Shaw
Ivanhoe, Wilfred,	Ivanhoe	W. Scott

Character	Title	Author
Knight of Jenkins, Rev Eli	Under Milk Wood	D. Thomas
Keeldar, Shirley	Shirley	Charlotte Bronte
Lampton, Joe	Room at the Top	J. Braine
Latimer, Darsie	Redgauntlet	W. Scott
Lawless	The Black Arrow	R.L. Stevenson
Lincoln, Abraham	Abraham Lincoln	J. Drinkwater
Lucifer	Faustus	C. Marlowe
Markham, Gilbert	The Tenant of Wildfell Hall	Anne Bronte
Messala	Ben Hur	L. Wallace
Michael, Duke of Strelsau	The Prisoner of Zenda	A. Hope
Miniver, Mrs Caroline	Mrs Miniver	Jan Struther
Morland, Catherine	Northanger Abbey	Jane Austen
Nokomis	Song of Hiawatha	H.W. Longfellow
Porthos	The Three Musketeers	Alexandre Dumas
Proudie, Dr/Mrs	Framley Parsonage	A. Trollope
Raffles, A.J.	Raffles series	E.W. Hornung
Randall, Rebecca	Rebecca of Sunnybrook Farm	Kate D. Wiggin
Rattler, Martin	Martin Rattler	R.M. Ballantyne
Rebecca	Rebecca	Daphne du Maurier
Rebecca	Rebecca of Sunnybrook Farm	Kate D. Wiggin
Red King	Alice Through the Looking Glass	L. Carroll
Robsart, Amy	Kenilworth	W. Scott
Sandars (Sandi)	Sanders of the River	E. Wallace
Shelton, Richard	The Black Arrow	R.L. Stephenson
Shipton, Mother	The Luck of Roaring Camp	Bret Harte
Smollet, Captain	Treasure Island	R.L. Stevenson
Sorrell, Christopher (Kit)	Sorrell and Son	W. Deeping
St Clare, Evangeline (Little Eva)	Uncle Tom's Cabin	Harriet B. Stowe
Tiddler, Tom	Adam's Opera	Clemence Dane
Warbeck, Perkin	Perkin Warbeck	John Ford
Western Mrs/Sophia /Squire	Tom Jones	H. Fielding
William	Just William	Richmal Crompton
Wooster, Bertie	Thank You, Jeeves	P.G. Woodhouse

Character	Title	Author
8		
Absolute, Sir Anthony	The Rivals	R.B. Sheridan
Angelica	The Rose and the Ring	W.M. Thackeray
Apollyon	Pilgrim's Progress	J. Bunyan
Armitage, Jacob	The Children of the New Forest	Captain Marryat
Backbite, Sir Benjamin	The School for Scandal	R.B. Sheridan
Bagheera	The Jungle Book	R. Kipling
Black Dog	Treasure Island	R.L. Stevenson
Carraway, Nick	The Great Gatsby	F. Scott Fitzgerald
Casaubon, Rev. Edward	Middlemarch	George Eliot
Crawfurd, David	Prester John	J. Buchan
Crichton, Bill	The Admirable Crichton	J.M. Barrie
Dashwood, Henry	Sense and Sensibility	Jane Austen
De Bourgh, Lady Catherine	Pride and Prejudice	Jane Austen
De Winter, Maximilian	Rebecca	Daphne du Maurier
Earnshaw, Catherine	Wuthering Heights	Emily Bronte
Everdene, Bathsheba	Far from the Madding Crowd	T. Hardy
Ffoulkes, Sir Andrew	The Scarlet Pimpernel	Baroness Orczy
Flanders, Moll	Moll Flanders	D. Defoe
Flashman	Tom Brown's Schooldays	T. Hughes
Gloriana	The Faerie Queen	E. Spenser
Gollantz, Emmanuel	Young Emmanuel	N. Jacob
Gulliver, Lemuel	Gulliver's Travels	J. Swift
Gunga Din	Barrack-room Ballads	R. Kipling
Hiawatha	The Song of Hiawatha	H.W. Longfellow
Knightly, George	Emma	Jane Austen
Lancelot, Sir	Idylls of the King	Lord Tennyson
Languish, Lydia	The Rivals	R.B. Sheridan
Laurence, Theodore	Little Women	Louisa M. Alcott
Lessways, Hilda	The Clayhanger Trilogy	Arnold Bennett
Lestrade, of Scotland Yard	A Study in Scarlet	A. Conan Doyle
Lockwood	Wuthering Heights	Emily Bronte
Macavity	Old Possum's Book of Practical Cats	T.S. Eliot
Malaprop, Mrs	The Rivals	R.B. Sheridan
Mary Jane	When We Were Very Young	A.A. Milne
Moriarty, Professor	Memoirs of	A. Conan Doyle

Character	Title	Author
James	Sherlock Holmes	
O'Ferrall, Trilby	Trilby	George du Maurier
Olifaunt, Nigel	The Fortunes of Nigel	W. Scott
O'Trigger, Sir Lucius	The Rivals	R.B. Sheridan
Palliser, Lady Glencora/		
Plantagenet	Phineas Finn	A. Trollope
Primrose, Dr Charles	The Vicar of Wakefield	O. Goldsmith
Quantock, Mrs Daisy	Queen Lucia	E.F. Benson
Red Queen	Alice Through the Looking Glass	L. Carroll
Shotover, Captain	Heartbreak House	G.B. Shaw
St Bungay, Duke of	Phineas Finn	A. Trollope
Svengali	Trilby	George du Maurier
Thatcher, Becky	The Adventures of Tom Sawyer	M. Twain
Tristram	Idylls of the King	Lord Tennyson
Tulliver, Maggie/Tom	The Mill on the Floss	George Eliot
Verinder, Lady Julia	The Moonstone	W. Collins
Water Rat (Ratty)	The Wind in the Willows	K. Grahame
Waverley, Edward	Waverley	W. Scott
Whiteoak (Family)	The Whiteoak Chronicles	Mazo de la Roche
White-Tip	Tarka the Otter	Henry Williamson
Whittier, Pollyanna	Pollyanna	Eleanor H. Porter
Williams, Percival William	Wee Willie Winkie	R. Kipling
Worthing, John	The Importance of Being Earnest	Oscar Wilde

9

Character	Title	Author
Abbeville, Horace	Cannery Row	J. Steinbeck
Ablewhite, Godfrey	The Moonstone	W. Collins
Allworthy, Squire	Tom Jones	H. Fielding
Babberley, Lord Fancourt	Charley's Aunt	Brandon Thomas
Barrymore	The Hound of the Baskervilles	A. Conan Doyle
Bracknell, Lady	The Importance of Being Earnest	Oscar Wilde
Bulstrode, Nicholas	Middlemarch	George Eliot
Chainmail	Crochet Castle	T.L. Peacock
Christian	Pilgrim's Progress	J. Bunyan
Churchill, Frank	Emma	Jane Austen
D'Artagnan	The Three Musketeers	Alexandre Dumas

Character	Title	Author
Doolittle, Eliza	Pygmalion	G.B. Shaw
Greystoke, Lord	Tarzan series	E.R. Burroughs
Guinevere	Idylls of the King	Lord Tennyson
Indian Joe	The Adventures of Tom Sawyer	M. Twain
Leicester, Earl of	Kenilworth	W. Scott
Macgregor, Robin	Rob Roy	W. Scott
March Hare, The	Alice in Wonderland	L. Carroll
Marchmain, Lady Cordelia/ Lady Julia/Lord Sebastian/ Marquis of Teresa/ The Earl of Brideshead	Brideshead Revisited	E. Waugh
Mehitabel, the cat	Archy and Mehitabel	D. Marquis
Merrilies, Meg	Guy Mannering	W. Scott
Minnehaha	The Song of Hiawatha	H.W. Longfellow
Moncrieff, Algernon	The Importance of Being Earnest	Oscar Wilde
Pendennis, Arthur (Pen)	Pendennis	W.M. Thackeray
Percivale	Idylls of the King	Lord Tennyson
Red Knight	Alice Through the Looking Glass	L. Carroll
Rochester, Bertha/ Edward Fairfax	Jane Eyre	Charlotte Bronte
Shere Khan (Lungri)	The Jungle Book	R. Kipling
Southdown, Earl of	Vanity Fair	W.M. Thackeray
Tamerlane	Tamerlane	N. Rowe
Tanqueray, Aubrey	The Second Mrs Tanqueray	A.W. Pinero
Tiger Lily	Peter Pan	J.M. Barrie
Trelawney, Rose	Trelawney of the Wells	A.W. Pinero
Trelawney, Squire	Treasure Island	R.L. Stevenson
Twitchett, Mrs Tabitha	The Tale of Tom Kitten	Beatrix Potter
Virginian, The	The Virginian	O. Wister
Waynflete, Lady Cecily	Captain's Brassbound's Conversion	G.B. Shaw
Woodhouse, Emma/Isabella	Emma	Jane Austen

10

Abrams Moss	Pendennis	W.M. Thackeray
Allan-a-Dale	Ivanhoe	W. Scott
Arrowpoint	Daniel Deronda	George Eliot
Belladonna	Vanity Fair	W.M. Thackeray

Character	Title	Author
Challenger, Professor	The Lost World	A. Conan Doyle
Crimsworth, William	The Professor	Charlotte Bronte
Evangeline	Evangeline	H.W. Longfellow
Fauntleroy, Lord Cedric	Little Lord Fauntleroy	F.H. Burnett
Goodfellow, Robin	St Ronan's Well	W Scott
Heathcliff	Wuthering Heights	Emily Bronte
Hornblower, Horatio	The Hornblower series	C.S. Forester
Hunca Munca	The Tale of Two Bad Mice	Beatrix Potter
Hunter-Dunn, Joan	A Subaltern's Love Song	J Betjaman
Jackanapes	Jackanapes	Juliana H. Ewing
Lethbridge, Daphne	The Dark Tide	Vera Brittain
Man in Black	A Citizen of the World	O. Goldsmith
Mauleverer, Lord	Cranford	Mrs Gaskell
Mock Turtle, The	Alice in Wonderland	L. Carroll
Puddleduck, Jemima	The Tale of Jemima Puddleduck	Beatrix Potter
Quatermain, Allan	King Solomon's Mines	H. Rider Haggard
Rassendyll, Rudolf	The Prisoner of Zenda	A. Hope
Starkadder, Judith/Old Mrs	Cold Comfort Farm	Stella Gibbons
Tinkerbell	Peter Pan	J.M. Barrie
Tweedledee/ Tweedledum	Alice Through the Looking Glass	L. Carroll
Undershaft, Barbara	Major Barbara	G.B. Shaw
Willoughby, John	Sense and Sensibility	Jane Austen
Windermere, Lord Arthur/ Margaret	Lady Windermere's Fan	Oscar Wilde

I I

Character	Title	Author
Addenbrooke, Bennett	Raffles	E.W. Hornung
Durbeyfield, Tess	Tess of the D'Urbervilles	T. Hardy
Jabberwocky	Alice Through the Looking Glass	L. Carroll
Maccrochet	Crochet Castle	T.L. Peacock
Montmorency, the dog	Three Men in a Boat	J.K. Jerome
Redgauntlet, Sir Arthur	Redgauntlet	W. Scott
Tamburlaine	Tamburlaine	C. Marlowe
Tam O'Shanter	Tam O'Shanter	R Burns
Tiggywinkle, Mrs	The Tale of Mrs Tiggywinkle	Beatrix Potter
Tittlemouse, Mrs Thomasina	The Tale of Mrs Tittlemouse	Beatrix Potter

Character	Title	Author
Trumpington, Lady	The Virginians	W.M. Thackeray

12

Brocklehurst	Jane Eyre	Charlotte Bronte
Captain Flint	Swallows and Amazons	A. Ransome
Frankenstein, Victor	Frankenstein	Mary Shelley
Humpty-Dumpty	Alice Through the Looking Glass	L. Carroll
Pennyfeather, Paul	Decline and Fall	E. Waugh

13

Winnie-the-Pooh (Edward Bear)	Winnie-the-Pooh	A.A. Milne

14

Mephistopheles	Doctor Faustus	C. Marlowe
Rikki-Tikki-Tavi	The Jungle Book	R. Kipling
Samuel Whiskers	The Tale of	
Samuel Whiskers	Beatrix Potter	
Worldly-Wiseman	Pilgrim's Progress	J. Bunyan

15

Ogmore-Pritchard, Mrs	Under Milk Wood	D. Thomas
Valiant-for-Truth	Pilgrim's Progress	J. Bunyan
Violet Elizabeth	Just William	Richmal Crompton

Fictional Detectives

Character	Creator
Martin Ainsworth	Michael Underwood
Superintendent Roderick Alleyn	Ngaio Marsh
Inspector Enrique Alvarez	Roderic Jeffries
Sir John Appleby	Michael Innes
Sergeant Nick Attwell	Michael Underwood
Inspector Bill Aveyard	James Frazer
Professor Andrew Basnett	E. X. Ferrars
Superintendent Battle	Agatha Christie
Sergeant William Beef	Leo Bruce
Tommy and Tuppence Beresford	Agatha Christie

Character	Creator
Colonel Peter Blair	J. R. L. Anderson
Inspector Bland	Julian Symons
Dr William Blow	Kenneth Hopkins
Inspector Salvador Borges	John and Emery Bonett
Dame Beatrice Bradley	Gladys Mitchell
Constable John Bragg	Henry Wade
Miles Bredon	Ronald A. Knox
Ernst Brendel	J. C. Masterman
Inspector John Brentford	S. B. Hough
Ronald Briercliffe	Francis Breeding
Inspector David Brock	R. J. White
Superintendent John Brock	John Bingham
Father Brown	G. K. Chesterton
Jane and Dagobert Brown	Delano Ames
Inspector Thomas Brunt	John Buxton Hilton
Inspector Burnivel	Edward Candy
Brother Cadfael	Ellis Peters
Inspector Thomas Cadover	Michael Innes
Ronald Camberwell	J.S. Fletcher
Albert Campion	Margery Allingham
John Carlyle	Henry Calvin
Superintendent Charlesworth	Christianna Brand
Ambrose Chitterwick	Anthony Berkeley
Joshua Clunk	H.C. Bailey
Inspector Cockrill	Christianna Brand
Mrs Craggs	H. R. F. Keating
Inspector Crambo	Julian Symons
Professor Thea Crawford	Jessica Mann
Sergeant Cribb	Peter Lovesey
Tessa Crichton	Anna Morice
Sergeant Cuff	Wilkie Collins
Superintendent Adam Dalgliesh	P.D. James
Professor Daly	Ellis Dillon
Superintendent Andrew Dalziel	Reginald Hill
Charmain Daniels	Jennie Melville
Dr R.V. Davie	V.C. Clinton-Baddeley
Carolus Deene	Leo Bruce
Inspector Piet Deventer	J. R. L. Anderson
Superintendent Ditteridge	E. X. Ferrars
Kenneth Ducane	John Bingham
Superintendent Duffy	Nigel FitzGerald

Character	Creator
Toby Dyke	E. X. Ferrars
Rosa Epton	Michael Underwood
Major Faide	Henry Wade
Kate Fansler	Amanda Cross
Gideon Fell	John Dixon Carr
Superintendent George, Dominic and Bunty Felse	Ellis Peters
Gervase Fen	Edmund Crispin
Inspector Finch (Rudd)	June Thompson
Inspector Septimus Finch	Margaret Erskine
Reggie Fortune	H.C. Bailey
Superintendent Francis Fox	Lionel Black
Virginia Freer	E.X. Ferrars
Inspector Joseph French	Freeman Wills Crofts
Dr Henry Frost	Josephine Bell
Inspector Matthew Furnival	Stella Phillips
Inspector Robert Fusil	Michael Alding
Superintendent George Gently	Alan Hunter
Colonel Anthony Gethryn	Philip MacDonald
Inspector Ganesh Ghote	H.R.F. Keating
Lindsay Gordon	Val McDermid
Colonel Alister Granby	Francis Beeding
Inspector Alan Grant	Gordon Daviot
Celia Grant	John Sherwood
Dr Patrick Grant	Margaret Yorke
Cordelia Gray	P.D. James
Emma Greaves	Lionel Black
Sid Halley	Dick Francis
Superintendent Hannasyde	Georgette Heyer
Paul Harris	Gavin Black
Jimmie Haswell	Herbert Adams
Inspector Hazlerigg	Michael Gilbert
Inspector Hemingway	Georgette Heyer
Sherlock Holmes	Arthur Conan Doyle
Charles Honeybath	Michael Innes
Tamara Hoyland	Jessica Mann
Inspector Harry James	Kenneth Giles
Inspector Benjamin Jurnet	S.T. Haymon
Superintendent Richard Jury	Martha Grimes
Inspector Kelsey	Emma Page
Inspector Mike Kenny	Ellis Dillon

Character	Creator
Superintendent Simon Kenworthy	John Buxton Hilton
Inspector Don Kerry	Jeffrey Ashford
Inspector Kyle	Roy Vickers
Gerald Lee	Kenneth Hopkins
Corporal Juan Llorca	Delano Ames
Inspector Henry Lott	Henry Wade
Lovejoy	Jonathan Gash
Adam Ludlow	Simon Nash
Superintendent MacDonald	E.C.R. Lorac
Maigret	George Simenon
Antony Maitland	Sarah Woods
Dan Mallett	Frank Parrish
Inspector Mallett	Cyril Hare
Professor Gideon Manciple	Kenneth Hopkins
Professor Mandrake	John and Emery Bonett
Superintendent Simon Manton	Michael Underwood
Miss Jane Marple	Agatha Christie
Inspector George Martin	Francis Beeding
Perry Mason	Erle Stanley Gardner
Superintendent George Masters	Douglas Clark
Kinsey Millhouse	Sue Grafton
Superintendent Steven Mitchell	Josephine Bell
Inspector Montero	Simon Nash
Inspector Morse	Colin Dexter
Ariadne Oliver	Agatha Christie
Dai Owen	Henry Calvin
Charles Paris	Simon Brent
Inspector Peter Pascoe	Reginald Hill
Amelia Peabody	Elizabeth peters
Douglas Perkins	Marian Babson
Sergeant Patrick Petrella	Michael Gilbert
Mikael Petros	James Anderson
Francis Pettigrew	Cyril Hare
Superintendent James Pibble	Peter Dickinson
Superintendent Arnold Pike	Philip Macdonald
Miss Melinda Pink	Gwen Moffat
Inspector Thomas and Charlotte E. Pitt	Anne Perry
Inspector Pointer	A. Fielding
Hercule Poirot	Agatha Christie
Superintendent Tom Pollard	Elizabeth Lemarchand
Inspector John Pool	Henry Wade

Character	Creator
Thomas Preston	Francis Beeding
Dr Lancelot Priestly	John Rhode
Inspector Walter Purbright	Colin Watson
Dr Henry Pym	W.J. Burley
Inspector Douglas Quantrill	Sheila Radley
Colonel Race	Agatha Christie
Superintendent George Rogers	Jonathan Ross
Inspector Rudd	June Thompson
Alan Russell	Nigel FitzGerald
Dr Kay Scarpetta	Patricia Cornwell
Roger Sheringham	Anthony Berkeley
Jemima Shore	Antonia Fraser
Maud Silver	Patricia Wentworth
Inspector C.D. Sloan	Catherine Aird
Superintendent Ben Spence	Michael Allen
Matthew Stock	Leonard Tourney
Nigel Strangeways	Nicholas Blake
Professor Hilary Tamar	Sarah Caudwell
Inspector Luke Thanet	Dorothy Simpson
Kate Theobald	Lionel Black
Lizzie Thomas	Anthony Oliver
Dr John Thorndyke	R. Austin Freeman
Superintendent George Thorne	John Penn
Superintendent Henry and Emily Tibbit	Patricia Moyes
Mark Treasure	David Williams
Philip Trent	E.C. Bentley
Superintendent Perry Trethowan	Robert Barnard
Miss Amy Tupper	Josephine Bell
V.I. Warshawski	Sara Paretsky
Malcolm Warren	C.H.B. Kitchin
Claud Warrington-Reeve	Josephine Bell
John Webber	Anthony Oliver
Inspector Reginald Wexford	Ruth Rendell
Inspector Wilkins	James Anderson
Inspector Wilkins	Francis Beeding
Lord Peter Wimsey	Dorothy L. Sayers
Dr David Wintringham	Josephine Bell
Nero Wolfe	Rex Stout
Superintendent Charles Wycliffe	W.J. Burley

Literary Terms

3

ode
wit

4

epic
foot
iamb
myth

5

elegy
fable
genre
ictus
irony
lyric
metre
novel
octet
prose
rhyme
style
theme
verse

6

ballad
bathos
cesura
cliché
dactyl
hubris
lament
monody
octave
parody
pathos
satire
school

septet
sestet
simile
sonnet
stanza
stress
symbol

7

caesure
conceit
couplet
diction
elision
epigram
epistle
epitaph
euphony
fabliau
humours
imagery
nemesis
paradox
prosody
Pyrrhic
realism
spondee
subplot
tragedy
trochee

8

allegory
anapaest
augustan
didactic

elements
exemplum
eye rhyme

metaphor
oxymoron
pastoral
quatrain
rhetoric
scansion
syllable
trimeter

9

ambiguity
assonance
burlesque
catharsis
classical
euphemism
free verse
half rhyme
hexameter
hyperbole
monometer
octameter
pararhyme

10

blank verse
caricature
denouement
epic simile
heptameter
mock heroic
naturalism
pentameter
picaresque
Spoonerism
subjective
tetrameter

11

anachronism
courtly love

end stopping
enjambement
Gothic novel
Horatian ode
malapropism
noble savage
objectivity
tragicomedy

12

alliteration
onomatopoeia

13

anthropomorph
heroic couplet
internal rhyme

14

existentialism
feminine ending
Miltonic sonnet
romantic poetry
sentimentality

15

masculine ending
pathetic fallacy
personification

16

Petrarchan sonnet

18

metaphysical poetry
negative capability
omniscient narrator

20+

stream of consciousness

Music

Musical Terms

Term	Definition	Term	Definition
1 and 2		largo	very slow
f	loud	lento	slowly
ff	very loud	mesto	sad, mournful
mf	half loud	mezzo	half
p	soft	molto	very much
pp	very soft	mosso	moving, fast
sf	strongly accented	piano	soft
		quasi	almost, as if
3		segno	sign
bis	repeat	senza	without
dim	becoming softer	soave	sweet; gentle
ped.	(abbreviation for) pedal	stark	strong, loud (German)
Piu	more	tacet	instrument is silent
piz	plucked	tanto	so much
rfz	accentuated	tempo	the speed of a composition
rit	slowing down, holding back	tutti	all
sfz	strongly accented	zoppa	in syncopated rhythm
ten	held		
vif	lively (French)	**6**	
		adagio	slow
4		al fine	to the end
coda	final part of a movement	chiuso	stopped (of a note); closed
moto	motion	da capo	from the beginning
rall	slowing down	dehors	outside; prominent
sino	up to; until	divisi	divided
tief	deep; low (German)	doppio	double
		facile	easy, fluent
5		legato	bound, tied (of notes), smoothly
ad lib	at will	marcia	march
assai	very	niente	nothing
buffo	comic	nobile	noble
dolce	sweet	retenu	held back
forte	loud	sempre	always, still
		subito	immediately

Term	Definition	Term	Definition
tenuto	held	maestoso	majestic
		moderato	moderately
7		portando	carrying one note into the next
agitato	agitated; rapid tempo		
allegro	lively, brisk	ritenuto	slowing down, holding back
al segno	as far as the sign		
amoroso	loving, emotional	sourdine	mute (French)
animato	spirited	staccato	detached
attacca	attack; continue without a pause	vivement	lively (French)
calando	ebbing; lessening of tempo	**9**	
codetta	small coda; to conclude a passage	adagietto	quite slow
		cantabile	in a singing fashion
con brio	with vigour	cantilena	lyrical, flowing
dolente	sorrowful	crescendo	becoming louder
estinto	extremely softly, almost without tone	fioritura	decoration of a melody
		glissando	sliding scale played on instrument
giocoso	merry; playful	meno mosso	slower pace
marcato	accented	mezza voce	at half power
morbido	soft, delicate	obbligato	not to be omitted
pesante	heavily, firmly	piuttosto	somewhat
schnell	fast (German)	pizzicato	plucked
sfogato	effortless; in a free manner	schneller	faster (Germany)
		sforzando	strongly accented
sordino	mute	sin'al fine	up to the end
stretto	accelerating or intensifying; overlapping of entry of fugue	slentando	slowing down
		sostenuto	sustained
		sotto voce	quiet subdued tone
8		**10**	
a battuta	return to strict time	affettuoso	tender
a piacere	as you please	alla caccia	in hunting style
brilliant	brilliant	allargando	broadening; more dignified
col canto	accompaniment to follow solo line		
		allegretto	quite lively, brisk
col legno	to strike strings with stick of the bow	diminuendo	becoming softer
		fortissimo	very loud
con fuoco	fiery; vigorous	mezzoforte	half loud
dal segno	from the sign	nobilmente	nobly
in modo di	in the manner of	perdendosi	dying away gradually

Term	Definition	Term	Definition
pianissimo	very soft	affrettando	hurrying
portamento	carrying one note into the next	minacciando	menacing
		rallentando	slowing down
ravvivando	quickening	rinforzando	accentuated
ritardando	slowing down, holding back		

12

scherzando	joking; playing	alla cappella	in church style
schleppend	dragging; fluent	leggeramente	lightly
stringendo	tightening; intensification		

13

leggieramente	lightly

11

accelerando   accelerating

Tonic Sol-Fa

doh
ray
me
fah
soh
lah
te

Musical Instruments

2

ud (lute)
yu (scraper)

3

bin (vina)
kit (fiddle)
lur (horn)
oud (ud)
saz (lute)
sho (mouth organ)

tar (drum; lute)
uti (lute)

4

bata (drum)
biwa (lute)
ch'in (zither)
drum
fife
fuye (flute)
gong
harp
horn
kena (quena)
khen (mouth organ)
koto (zither)
lira (fiddle)
lute
lyra (lyre)
lyre
mu yu (drum)
mvet (zither)
oboe
outi (lute)
p'i p'a (lute)

pipe
rote (lyre)
ruan (lute)
sona (shawm)
tro-u (fiddle)
urua (clarinet)
vina (stringed instrument related to sitar)
viol
whip (percussion)
zobo (mirliton)

5

auloi (shawn)
banjo
bells
bhaya (kettledrum)
bugle
bumpa (clarinet)
cello
chang (dulcimer)
chime
clave
cobza (lute)

cornu (trumpet)
crwth (lyre)
dauli (drum)
dhola (drum)
dobro (guitar)
erh-hu (fiddle)
fidel (fiddle)
fidla (zither)
flute
gaita (bagpipe)
gajdy (bagpipe)
gusle (fiddle)
huruk (drum)
kakko (drum)
kanun (qanun)
kazoo (mirliton)
kerar (lyre)
ko-kiu (fiddle)
mbila (xylophone)
ngoma (drum)
nguru (flute)
okedo (drum)
organ
piano
pi nai (shawm)
pu-ilu (clappers)
qanun (zither)
quena (flute)
raspa (scraper)
rebab (fiddle)
rebac (fiddle)
saron (metallophone)
shawn
sheng (mouth organ)
sitar (lute)
tabla (drum)
tabor (drum)
taiko (drum)
tibia (shawn)
tiple (shawn)
ti-tzu (flute)
tudum (drum)
tumyr (drum)

tupan (drum)
viola
yun lo (gong)
zurla (shawm)
zurna (shawm)

6

alboka (hornpipe)
arghul (clarinet)
bagana (lyre)
biniou (bagpipe)
carynx (trumpet)
chakay (zither)
cha pei (lute)
cornet
curtal (double reed)
darbuk (drum)
fandur (fiddle)
fiddle
fujara (flute)
gekkin (lute)
gender (metallophone)
gongue (percussion)
guitar
hu ch'in (fiddle)
hummel (zither)
kenong (gong)
kissar (lyre)
koboro (drum)
lirica (fiddle)
lirone (fiddle)
lituus (trumpet)
lontar (clappers)
mayuri (lute)
moropi (drum)
nakers (drums)
naqara (drums)
ntenga (drum)
o-daiko (drum)
ombgwe (flute)
p'ai pan (clappers)
pommer (shawm)
racket (double reed)

ramkie (lute)
rattle
santir (dulcimer)
shaing (horn)
shaker
shanai (shawm)
shield (percussion)
shofar (horn)
sopile (shawm)
spinet
spoons (clappers)
sralay (shawm)
surnaj (shawm)
switch (percussion)
syrinx (panpipe)
tam-tam (gong)
tom-tom (drum)
txistu (flute)
valiha (zither)
vielle (fiddle)
violin
yangum (dulcimer)
zither

7

adenkum (stamping
tube)
alphorn (trumpet)
anklung (rattle)
atumpan (kettledrum)
bagpipe
baryton (viol)
bassoon
bodhran (drum)
bonnang (gong)
bow harp
box lyre
buccina (trumpet)
buisine (trumpet)
bumbass
celeste
changko (drum)
cittern

cornett
cowbell
crotals (percussion)
cymbals
da-daiko (drum)
diplice (clarinet)
dugdugi (drum)
enzenze (zither)
fithele (fiddle)
gadulka (fiddle)
gittern
gling-bu (flute)
hula ipu (percussion)
ingungu (drum)
isigubu (drum)
kachapi (zither)
kalungu (talking drum)
kamanje (fiddle)
kantele (zither)
kemanak (clappers)
kithara (lyre)
komungo (zither)
machete (lute)
mandola (lute)
maracas (percussion)
masenqo (fiddle)
migyaun (zither)
mokugyo (drum)
murumbu (drum)
musette (shawm)
musette (bagpipe)
obukano (lyre)
ocarina (flute)
octavin (wind)
orphica (piano)
pandora (cittern)
panpipe
pianino
pibcorn (hornpipe)
piccolo
puffaro (shawm)
quinton (viol)
reshoto (drum)

rinchik (cymbals)
sackbut (trombone)
salpinx (trumpet)
samisen (lute)
santoor (dulcimer)
sarangi (fiddle)
sarinda (fiddle)
saw-thai (fiddle)
saxhorn
saxtuba
serpent
shiwaya (flute)
sistrum (rattle)
sordine (kit)
sordone (double reed)
spagane (clappers)
tam am la (gong)
tambura (lute)
terbang (drum)
theorbo (lute)
tiktiri (clarinet)
timpani
trumpet
tsuzumi (drum)
ujusini (flute)
ukulele
vihuela (guitar)
violene (viol)
whistle
yun ngao (gong)
zummara (clarinet)

8

alghaita (shawm)
altohorn
autoharp
bandoura (lute)
bass drum
bass horn
bombarde (shawm)
bouzouki (lute)
bowl lyre
buzz disk

calliope (mechanical organ)
carillon
chine bar
cimbalom (dulcimer)
capactli (flute)
clappers
clarinet
clavicor (brass family)
claw bell
courtaut (double reed)
crecelle (cog rattle)
crumhorn (double reed)
dulcimer
dvoynice (flute)
gong drum
handbell
hand horn
hawkbell
jew's harp
kayakeum (zither)
khumbgwe (flute)
langleik (zither)
langspil (zither)
lap organ (melodeon)
mandolin (lute)
melodeon
melodica
mirliton (kazoo)
mridanga (drum)
oliphant (horn)
o-tsuzumi (drum)
ottavino (virginal)
p'ai hsiao (panpipe)
penorcon (cittern)
pochette (kit)
psaltery (zither)
putorino (trumpet)
recorder
rkan-dung (trumpet)
rkan-ling (horn)
roneat-ek (xylophone)

san hsien (lute)
side drum
slit drum
sonajero (rattle)
springara (fiddle)
surbahar (lute)
talambas (drum)
tarabuka (drum)
tarogato (clarinet; shawm)
timbales (drum)
triangle
tro-khmer (fiddle)
trombone
violetta (viol)
virginal
yangchin (dulcimer)
yueh ch'in (lute)
zampogna (bagpipe)

9

accordion
angle harp
arpanetta (zither)
balalaika (lute)
bandurria (lute)
banjolele
bassonore (bassoon)
bombardon (tuba)
castanets
chalumeau (clarinet)
cog rattle
componium (mechanical organ)
cornemuse (bagpipe)
cornopean (brass family)
daibyoshi (drum)
darabukke (drum)
djunadjan (zither)
dudelsack (bagpipes)
dvojachka (flute)
euphonium (brass family)
flageolet (flute)
flexatone (percussion)
gong ageng
hackbrett (dulcimer)
harmonica
harmonium
hydraulis (organ)
kelontong (drum)
konighorn (brass family)
launeddas (clarinet)
mandobass (lute)
mandolone (lute)
morin-chur (fiddle)
orpharion (cittern)
picco pipe (flute)
pien ch'ing (lithophone)
rommelpot (drum)
saxophone
tallharpa (lyre)
totombito (zither)
tuba-dupre
wood block
Wurlitzer
xylophone
xylorimba (xylophone)

10

banana drum
barrel drum
bassanello (double reed)
basset horn
bible regal (organ)
bicitrabin (vina)
bird scarer
bongo drums
bull-roarer
chengcheng (cymbals)
chitarrone (lute)
clavichord
claviorgan
colascione (lute)
contrabass (double bass)
cor anglais
didgeridoo (trumpet)
flugelhorn
French horn
geigenwerk (mechanical harpsichord)
gong chimes
grand piano
handle drum
hurdy gurdy
kettledrum
lithophone (percussion)
mandocello (lute)
mellophone (horn)
moshupiane (drum)
mouth organ
ophicleide (brass family)
ranasringa (horn)
saxotromba
shakuhachi (flute)
sousaphone
spitzharfe (zither)
symphonium (mouth organ)
tambourine (drum)
teponaztli (drum)
thumb piano (jew's harp)
tin whistle
tlapiztali (flute)
tsuri daiko (drum)

11

Aeolian harp
angel chimes
barrel organ
bell cittern
bivalve bell
bladder pipe
board zither
clapper bell

fipple flute
gambang kaya
(xylophone)
guitar-banjo
hand trumpet
harpsichord
heckelphone (oboe)
nyckelharpa
paimensarvi (horn)
panhuehuetl (drum)
saron demong
(metallophone)
sleigh bells
spike fiddle
theorbo-lute
uchiwa daiko (drum)
viola d'amore (viol)
violincello

12

diplo-kithara (zither)
gansa gambang
(metallophone)
gansa jongkok
(metallophone)
glockenspiel
(metallophone)

guitar-violin
hi-hat cymbals
kanteleharpe (lyre)
mandolinetto (ukulele)
peacock star (lute)
rauschpfeife (double
reed)
sarrusophone (brass)
shoulder harp
stock-and-horn
hornpipe)
Tippoo's tiger (organ)
tubular bells
viola da gamba (viol)
whistle flute

13

cocktail drums
contrabassoon
double bassoon
(contrabassoon)
hardangerfele (fiddle)
heckelclarina (clarinet)
Savernake-horn
schrillpfeife (flute)
slide trombone
viola bastarda (viol)

14

clarinet d'amore
clavicytherium
(harpsichord)
cythara anglica (harp)
jingling johnny
tlapanhuehuetl (drum)
triccaballacca (clappers)

15

classical guitar
Moog synthesizer
Turkish crescent
(jingling johnny)

16

Chine wood block
chitarra battente
(guitar)
cylindrical drums
Deutsche schalmei
(double reed)
strumento di porco
(zither)

Novel Titles

Novel	Author
3	
She	H Rider Haggard
4	
Dr No	Ian Fleming
Emma	Jane Austin
Gigi	Colette
Nana	Emile Zola

Novel	Author
5	
Cheri	Colette
Kipps	H G Wells
Scoop	Evelyn Waugh
Sybil	Benjamin Disraeli
Zadig	Voltaire
6	
Amelia	Henry Fielding
Ben Hur	Lew Wallace
Chocky	John Wyndham
Lolita	Vladimir Nabokov
Pamela	Henry Fielding
Rob Roy	Walter Scott
7	
Camilla	Fanny Burney
Candide	Voltaire
Cecilia	Fanny Burney
Dracula	Bram Stoker
Erewhon	Samuel Butler
Evelina	Fanny Burney
Ivanhoe	Walter Scott
Rebecca	Daphne du Maurier
Shirley	Charlotte Bronte
The Fall	Albert Camus
Ulysses	James Joyce
8	
Adam Bede	George Eliot
Cranford	Mrs Gaskell
Jane Eyre	Charlotte Bronte
Lucky Jim	Kingsley Amis
Swan Song	John Galsworthy
The Idiot	Fyodor Mikhailovich Dostoevsky
The Magus	John Fowles
The Rebel	Albert Camus
Tom Jones	Henry Fielding
Villette	Charlotte Bronte
Waverley	Walter Scott

Novel	Author

9

Novel	Author
Agnes Grey	Anne Bronte
Billy Liar	Keith Waterhouse
Coningsby	Benjamin Disraeli
Dubliners	James Joyce
Glenarvon	Lady Caroline Lamb
Hard Times	Charles Dickens
I Claudius	Robert Graves
Kidnapped	Robert Louis Stevenson
Love Story	Erich Segal
Rogue Male	Geoffrey Household
The Chimes	Charles Dickens
The Devils	Fyodor Mikhailovich Dostoevsky
The Heroes	Charles Kingsley
The Hobbit	J R R Tolkien
The Plague	Albert Camus
Vice Versa	F Anstey

10

Novel	Author
Animal Farm	George Orwell
Bleak House	Charles Dickens
Cancer Ward	Alexander Solzhenitsyn
Clayhanger	Arnold Bennett
Don Quixote	Cervantes
Goldfinger	an Fleming
In Chancery	ohn Galsworthy

Novel	Author
Kenilworth	Walter Scott
Lorna Doone	R D Blackmore
Persuasion	Jane Austen
The Rainbow	D H Lawrence
Titus Alone	Mervyn Peake
Titus Groan	Mervyn Peake
Vanity Fair	William Makepeace Thackeray

11

Novel	Author
Black Beauty	Anna Sewell
Burmese Days	George Orwell

Novel	Author
Cakes and Ale	W Somerset Maugham
Cousin Bette	Honore de Balzac
Daisy Miller	Henry James
Gormenghast	Mervyn Peake
Little Women	Louisa M Alcott
Lost Horizon	James Hilton
Middlemarch	George Eliot
Mrs Dalloway	Virginia Woolf
Oliver Twist	Charles Dickens
Silas Marner	George Eliot
The Big Sleep	Raymond Chandler
The Outsider	Albert Camus
War and Peace	Leo Tolstoy
Women in Love	D H Lawrence

12

Anna Karenina	Leo Tolstoy
A Severed Head	Iris Murdoch
Barnaby Rudge	Charles Dickens
Brighton Rock	Graham Green
Casino Royale	Ian Fleming
Dombey and Son	Charles Dickens
Frankenstein	Mary Shelley
Guy Mannering	Walter Scott
Headlong Hall	Thomas Love Peacock
Little Dorrit	Charles Dickens
Madame Bovary	Gustave Flaubert
Moll Flanders	Daniel Defoe
Of Mice and Men	John Steinbeck
Rogue Justice	Geoffrey Household
Room at the Top	John Braine
The Decameron	Boccaccio
The Go-Between	L P Hartley
The Lost World	Arthur Conan Doyle
The Moonstone	Wilkie Collins
The Professor	Charlotte Bronte

13

A Kind of Loving	Stan Barstow
A Modern Comedy	John Galsworthy
Brave New World	Aldous Huxley

Novel	Author
Daniel Deronda	George Eliot
Doctor Zhivago	Boris Pasternak
Fanny and Zooey	J D Salinger
Jacob Faithful	Captain Marryat
Just-So Stories	Rudyard Kipling
Les Miserables	Victor Hugo
Live and Let Die	Ian Fleming
Liza of Lambeth	W Somerset Maugham
Mansfield Park	Jane Austen
North and South	Mrs Gaskell
Pincher Martin	William Golding
Sketched by Boz	Charles Dickens
Smiley's People	John le Carre
Sons and Lovers	D H Lawrence
Tarka the Otter	Henry Williamson
The Blue Lagoon	H de Vere Stacpoole
The Chrysalids	John Wyndham
The Golden Bowl	Henry James
The History Man	Malcolm Bradbury
The Last Tycoon	F Scott Fitzgerald
Therese Raquin	Emile Zola
Zeleika Dobson	Max Beerbohm

14

A Man of Property	John Galsworthy
A Room of One's Own	Virginia Woolf
A Room with a View	E M Forster
A Town Like Alice	Neville Shute
Changing Places	David Lodge
Cider with Rosie	Laurie Lee
Crochet Castle	Thomas Love Peacock
Death on the Nile	Agatha Christie
Decline and Fall	Evelyn Waugh
Goodbye, Mr Chips	James Hilton
Jude the Obscure	Thomas Hardy
Lord of the Flies	William Golding
Nightmare Abbey	Thomas Love Peacock
Our Man in Havana	Graham Greene
Pickwick Papers	Charles Dickens
Rites of Passage	William Golding
Robinson Crusoe	Daniel Defoe

Novel	Author
The Ambassadors	Henry James
The Coral Island	R M Ballantyne
The First Circle	Alexander Solzhenitsyn
The Forsyth Saga	John Galsworthy
The Great Gatsby	F Scott Fitzgerald
The Kraken Wakes	John Wyndham
The Long Goodbye	Raymond Chandler
The Secret Agent	Joseph Conrad
The Silver Spoon	John Galsworthy
The Time Machine	H G Wells
The Water-Babies	Charles Kingsley
The White Monkey	John Galsworthy
The Woodlanders	Thomas Hardy
Treasure Island	Robert Louis Stevenson
Tristram Shandy	Laurence Sterne
What Maisie Knew	Henry James

15

A Christmas Carol	Charles Dickens
A Farewell to Arms	Ernest Hemingway
A Passage to India	E M Forster
Cold Comfort Farm	Stella Gibbons
Eustace and Hilda	L P Hartley
Gone with the Wind	Margaret Mitchell
Goodbye to Berlin	Christopher Isherwood
Northanger Abbey	Jane Austen
Our Mutual Friend	Charles Dickens
Portrait of a Lady	Henry James
Portrait of Clare	Francis Brett Young
Strait is the Gate	Andre Gide
The Country Girls	Edna O'Brien
The Invisible Man	H G Wells
The Secret Garden	Frances Hodgson Burnett
The Silmarillion	J R R Tolkien
The Trumpet Major	Thomas Hardy
The White Company	Arthur Conan Doyle
The Woman in White	Wilkie Collins
Three Men in a Boat	Jerome K Jerome

16

A Clockwork Orange	Anthony Burgess

Novel	Author
A Tale of Two Cities	Charles Dickens
David Copperfield	Charles Dickens
Gulliver's Travels	Jonathan Swift
Martin Chuzzlewit	Charles Dickens
Mr Midshipman Easy	Captain Marryat
Nicholas Nickleby	Charles Dickens
Tender is the Night	F Scott Fitzgerald
Ten Little Niggers	Agatha Christie
The Grapes of Wrath	John Steinbeck
The Plumed Serpent	D H Lawrence
The Scarlet Letter	Nathaniel Hawthorne
Wuthering Heights	Emily Bronte

17

Novel	Author
Alice in Wonderland	Lewis Carroll
Dr Jekyll and Mr Hyde	Robert Louis Stevenson
Great Expectations	Charles Dickens
King Solomon's Mines	H Rider Haggard
My Brother Jonathan	Francis Brett Young
Point Counter Point	Aldous Huxley
Pride and Prejudice	Jane Austen
The Devils of Loudun	Aldous Huxley
The Diary of a Nobody	G and W Grossmith
The Lord of the Rings	J R R Tolkien
The Midwich Cuckoos	John Wyndham
The Mill on the Floss	George Eliot
The War of the Worlds	H G Wells
The Wings of the Dove	Henry James
Wives and Daughters	Mrs Gaskell

18

Novel	Author
A High Wind in Jamaica	Richard Hughes
Anna of the Five Towns	Arnold Bennett
Crime and Punishment	Fyodor Mikhailovich Dostoevsky
Nineteen Eighty-Four	George Orwell
Swallows and Amazons	Arthur Ransome
The Catcher in the Rye	J D Salinger
The Moon and Sixpence	W Somerset Maugham
The Old Man and The Sea	Ernest Hemingway
The Prisoner of Zenda	Anthony Hope
The Thirty-Nine Steps	John Buchan

Novel	Author
The Three Musketeers	Alexandre Dumas

19

Brideshead Revisited	Evelyn Waugh
For Whom the Bell Tolls	Ernest Hemingway
Sense and Sensibility	Jane Austen
The Day of the Triffids	John Wyndham
The Gulag Archipelago	Alexander Solzhenitsyn
The History of Mr Polly	H G wells
The Man in the Iron Mask	Alexandre Dumas
The Old Curiosity Shop	Charles Dickens
The Pilgrim's Progress	John Bunyan
The Riddle of the Sands	Erskine Childers
The Scarlet Pimpernel	Baroness Orczy
The Screwtape Letters	C S Lewis
The Vicar of Wakefield	Oliver Goldsmith
The Wind in the Willows	Kenneth Graham
Tom Brown's Schooldays	Thomas Hughes

20+

A Connecticut Yankee in King Arthur's Court	Mark Twain
A Dance to the Music of Time	Anthony Powell
As I Walked Out One Midsummer's Morning	Laurie Lee
Children of the New Forest	Captain Marryat
Far From the Madding Crowd	Thomas Hardy
John Halifax, Gentleman	Mrs Craik
Keep the Aspidistra Flying	George Eliot
Lady Chatterley's Lover	D H Lawrence
Lark Rise to Candleford	Flora Thompson
Little Lord Fauntleroy	Frances Hodgson Burnett
Murder on the Orient Express	Agatha Christie
Out of the Silent Planet	C S Lewis
Around the World in Eighty Days	Jules Verne
Tess of the D'Urbervilles	Thomas Hardy
The Adventures of Huckleberry Finn	Mark Twain
The Adventures of Tom Sawyer	Mark Twain
The Beautiful and the Damned	F Scott Fitzgerald
The Bride of Lammermoor	Walter Scott
The Brothers Karamazov	Fyodor Mikhailovich Dostoevsky

The Cricket on the Hearth	Charles Dickens
The French Lieutenant's Woman	John Fowles
The Heart of Midlothian	Walter Scott
The History of Henry Esmond	William Makepeace Thackeray
The Honourable Schoolboy	John Le Carre
The Innocence of Father Brown	G K Chesterton
The Island of Doctor Moreau	H G Wells
The Last of the Mohicans	James Fenimore Cooper
The Memoirs of Sherlock Holmes	Arthur Conan Doyle
The Mysteries of Udolpho	Mrs Radcliffe
The Mysterious Affair at Styles	Agatha Christie
The Mystery of Edwin Drood	Charles Dickens
The Picture of Dorian Gray	Oscar Wilde
The Prime of Miss Jean Brodie	Muriel Spark
The Red Badge of Courage	Stephen Crane
The Return of the Native	Thomas Hardy
The Tenant of Wildfell Hall	Anne Bronte
Tinker, Taylor, Soldier, Spy	John Le Carre
Twenty Thousand Leagues Under The Sea	Jules Verne
Two Years Before the Mast	Richard Henry Dana
Under the Greenwood Tree	Thomas Hardy

Play Titles

Title	Playwright
4	
Loot	Joe Orton
Ross	Terence Rattigan
5	
Caste	T W Robertson
Faust	Goethe
Medea	Euripides
Roots	Arnold Wesker
6	
Ghosts	Henrik Ibsen
Hamlet	William Shakespeare
Henry V	William Shakespeare
Phedre	Jean Racine
Plenty	David Hare

Title	Playwright
Strife	John Galsworthy

7

Amadeus	Peter Shaffer
Athalie	Jean Racine
Candida	George Bernard Shaw
Electra	Sophocles
Galileo	Bertolt Brecht
Henry IV	William Shakespeare
Henry VI	William Shakespeare
Jumpers	Tom Stoppard
Macbeth	William Shakespeare
Othello	William Shakespeare
The Lark	Jean Anouilh
The Room	Harold Pinter
Volpone	Ben Johnson
Antigone	Sophocles
Hay Fever	Noel Coward
King John	William Shakespeare
King Lear	William Shakespeare
Pericles	William Shakespeare
Peter Pan	J M Barrie
Tartuffe	Moliere
The Birds	Aristophanes
The Frogs	Aristophanes
The Miser	Moliere

9

All My Sons	Arthur Miller
Billy Liar	Willis Hall and Keith Waterhouse
Cavalcade	Noel Coward
Cymbeline	William Shakespeare
Dr Faustus	Christopher Marlowe
Flare Path	Terence Rattigan
Golden Boy	Clifford Odets
Happy Days	Samuel Beckett
Henry VIII	William Shakespeare
Pygmalion	George Bernard Shaw
Richard II	William Shakespeare
Saint Joan	George Bernard Shaw
The Circle	W Somerset Maugham

Title	Playwright
The Critic	Sheridan
The Devils	John Whiting
The Rivals	Sheridan

10

All For Love	John Dryden
Andromaque	Jean Racine
Aureng-Zebe	John Dryden
Coriolanus	William Shakespeare
I Am A Camera	John Van Druten
Oedipus Rex	Sophocles
Richard III	William Shakespeare
The Bacchae	Euripides
The Balcony	Jean Genet
The Hostage	Brendan Behan
The Seagull	Anton Chekov
The Tempest	William Shakespeare
Uncle Vanya	Anton Chekov

11

A Doll's House	Henrik Ibsen
As You Like It	William Shakespeare
Journey's End	R C Sherriff
Love for Love	William Congreve
Pandora's Box	Frank Wedekind
Rookery Nook	Ben Travers
The Bankrupt	Alexander Ostrovsky
The Contrast	Royall Tyler
The Crucible	Arthur Miller
The Wild Duck	Henrik Ibsen

12

After the Fall	Arthur Miller
Anna Christie	Eugene O'Neill
Bedroom Farce	Alan Ayckbourn
Blithe Spirit	Noel Coward
Blood Wedding	Garcia Lorca
Charley's Aunt	Brandon Thomas
Duel of Angels	Jean Giraudoux
Julius Caesar	William Shakespeare
Major Barbara	George Bernard Shaw

Title	Playwright
Private Lives	Noel Coward
The Alchemist	Ben Jonson
The Anatomist	James Bridie
The Apple Cart	George Bernard Shaw
The Broken Jug	Heinrich von Kleist
The Caretaker	Harold Pinter
The Mousetrap	Agatha Christie
Three Sisters	Anton Chekov
Twelfth Night	William Shakespeare

13

Arms and the Man	George Bernard Shaw
A Taste of Honey	Shelagh Delaney
Hobson's Choice	Harold Brighouse
Le Misanthrope	Moliere
Quality Street	J M Barrie
The Acharnians	Aristophanes
The Dumb Waiter	Harold Pinter
The Jew of Malta	Christopher Marlowe
The Linden Tree	J B Priestley
The Magistrate	Pinero
The Matchmaker	Thornton Wilder
The White Devil	John Webster
The Winslow Boy	Terence Rattigan
Timon of Athens	William Shakespeare
Under Milk Wood	Dylan Thomas

14

An Ideal Husband	Oscar Wilde
Man and Superman	George Bernard Shaw
Romeo and Juliet	William Shakespeare
Separate Tables	Terence Rattigan
The Corn is Green	Emlyn Williams
The Country Girl	Clifford Odets
The Deep Blue Sea	Terence Rattigan
The Fire-Raisers	Max Frisch
The Ghost Sonata	August Strindberg
The Old Bachelor	William Congreve
The Philanderer	George Bernard Shaw
The Trojan Woman	Euripides
The Winter's Tale	William Shakespeare

Title	Playwright
This Happy Breed	Noel Coward
Bartholomew Fair	Ben Jonson
Dangerous Corner	J B Priestley
Design for Living	Noel Coward
Heartbreak House	George Bernard Shaw
Look Back In Anger	John Osborne
Marriage a la Mode	John Dryden
Present Laughter	Noel Coward
The Constant Wife	W Somerset Maugham
The Iceman Cometh	Eugene O'Neill
Titus Andronicus	William Shakespeare
Two Noble Kinsman	William Shakespeare
Venice Preserved	Thomas Otway
Waiting for Godot	Samuel Beckett

16

A Cuckoo in the Nest	Ben Travers
An Inspector Calls	J B Priestley
Cat on a Hot Tin Roof	Tennessee Williams
Death of a Salesman	Arthur Miller
Love's Labour's Lost	William Shakespeare
Pillars of Society	Henrik Ibsen
Ring Round the Moon	Jean Anouilh
The Adding Machine	Elmer Rice
The American Dream	Edward Albee
The Birthday Party	Harold Pinter
The Cherry Orchard	Anton Chekov
The Cocktail Party	T S Eliot
The Family Reunion	T S Eliot
The Master Builder	Henrik Ibsen
What The Butler Saw	Joe Orton

17

A Man For All Seasons	Robert Bolt
An Italian Straw Hat	Eugene Labiche
Arsenic and Old Lace	Joseph Kesselring
Barefoot in the Park	Neil Simon
Juno and the Paycock	Sean O'Casey
Measure for Measure	William Shakespeare
Romanoff and Juliet	Peter Ustinov
The Beaux Stratagem	George Farquhar

Title	Playwright
The Comedy of Errors	William Shakespeare
The Devil's Disciple	George Bernard Shaw
The Doctor's Dilemma	George Bernard Shaw
The Duchess of Malfi	John Webster
The Glass Menagerie	Tennessee Williams
The Good-Natured Man	Oliver Goldsmith
The School for Wives	Moliere
The Suppliant Woman	Aeschylus
'Tis Pity She's A Whore	John Ford

18

An Enemy of the People	Henrik Ibsen
Antony and Cleopatra	William Shakespeare
Caesar and Cleopatra	George Bernard Shaw
Five Finger Exercise	Peter Shaffer
French Without Tears	Terence Rattigan
Lady Windermere's Fan	Oscar Wilde
She Stoops To Conquer	Oliver Goldsmith
Suddenly Last Summer	Tennessee Williams
The Browning Version	Terence Rattigan
The Romans in Britain	Howard Brenton
Triolus and Cressida	William Shakespeare

19

Androcles and the Lion	George Bernard Shaw
Chips With Everything	Arnold Wesker
Much Ado About Nothing	William Shakespeare
Tamburlaine the Great	Christopher Marlowe
The Merchant of Venice	William Shakespeare
The School for Scandal	Sheridan
The Taming of the Shrew	William Shakespeare
What Every Woman Knows	J M Barrie

20+

Accidental Death of an Anarchist	Dario Fo
All God's Chillun Got Wings	Eugene O'Neill
All's Well That Ends Well	William Shakespeare
A Midsummer Night's Dream	William Shakespeare
A Streetcar Named Desire	Tennessee Williams
A Woman of No Importance	Oscar Wilde
Captain Brassbound's Conversion	George Bernard Shaw

Entertaining Mr Sloane	Joe Orton
Inadmissible Evidence	John Osborne
Mourning Becomes Electra	Eugene O'Neill
Murder in the Cathedral	T S Eliot
Rozencrantz and Guildenstern are Dead	Tom Stoppard
The Admirable Crichton	J M Barrie
The Barretts of Wimpole Street	Rudolf Besier
The Causican Chalk Circle	Bertolt Brecht
The Government Inspector	Nikolai Gogol
The Importance of Being Earnest	Oscar Wilde
The Lady's Not For Burning	Christopher Fry
The Merry Wives of Windsor	William Shakespeare
The Second Mrs Tanqueray	Pinero
The Two Gentlemen of Verona	William Shakespeare
Who's Afraid of Virginia Woolf?	Edward Albee

Pottery and Porcelain

3 and 4
Ault
bow
Ming
tang

5
Delft
Derby
imari
Spode

6
bisque
bretby
Canton
Minton
parian
Ruskin
Sevres

7
belleek

biscuit
Bristol
Chelsea
Doulton
faience
Italian
meissen
moulded
new hall
redware
Satsuma
Toby jug

8
caneware
Caughley
chaffers
coalport
fairings
maiolica
majolica
nantgarw
Plymouth
Salopian
slipware
Wedgwood

9
agate ware
china clay
crackling
creamware
Davenport
hard paste
linthorpe
Liverpool
Lowestoft
Moorcroft
pearlware
Prattware
soft paste
stoneware
Worcester

10
Canton ware
china stone
lustre ware
martinware
Pilkington
polychrome
Rockingham
salt-glazed

stone china	Longton Hall	willow pattern
terracotta	pate-sur-pate	
		15
11	**12**	Asiatic pheasant
black basalt	blue and white	Cambrian pottery
capodimonte	Nagasaki ware	
earthenware		**20**
famille rose	**13**	Mason's ironstone china
famille vert	Staffordshire	

Shakespearean Characters

Character	Play
2	
Hal	Henry IV Part I
Nym	Henry V, The Merry Wives of Windsor
4	
Adam	As You Like It
Ajax	Troilus and Cressida
Eros	Antony and Cleopatra
Ford, Mistress	The Merry Wives of Windsor
Grey	Henry V
Hero	Much Ado About Nothing
Iago	Othello
Iras	Antony and Cleopatra
Lear	King Lear
Page, Mistress	The Merry Wives of Windsor
Peto	Henry IV Part 2
Puck	A Midsummer Night's Dream
Snug	A Midsummer Night's Dream
5	
Aaron	Titus Andronicus
Ariel	The Tempest
Belch, Sir Toby	Twelfth Night
Blunt	Henry IV Part 2
Caius, Doctor	The Merry Wives of Windsor
Celia	As You Like It
Cleon	Pericles
Corin	As You Like It

Character	Play
Diana	All's Well that Ends Well
Edgar	King Lear
Elbow	Measure for Measure
Feste	Twelfth Night
Flute	A Midsummer Night's Dream
Froth	Measure for Measure
Gobbo, Launcelot	The Merchant of Venice
Julia	The Two Gentlemen of Verona
Lafew	All's Well that Ends Well
Maria	Love's Labour's Lost, Twelfth Night
Paris	Troilus and Cressida
Percy	Henry IV Part 1
Phebe	As You Like It
Pinch	The Comedy of Errors
Poins	Henry IV Part 1, Henry IV Part 2
Priam	Troilus and Cressida
Regan	King Lear
Romeo	Romeo and Juliet
Snout	A Midsummer Night's Dream
Timon	Timon of Athens
Titus	Titus Andronicus
Viola	Twelfth Night

6

Character	Play
Aegeon	The Comedy of Errors
Alonso	The Tempest
Angelo	Measure for Measure
Antony	Antony and Cleopatra
Arcite	The Two Noble Kinsmen
Armado	Love's Labour's Lost
Audrey	As You Like It
Banquo	Macbeth
Bianca	The Taming of the Shrew, Othello
Bottom	A Midsummer Night's Dream
Brutus	Coriolanus, Julius Caesar
Cassio	Othello
Chiron	Titus Andronicus
Cloten	Cymbeline
Dennis	As You Like It
Dromio	The Comedy of Errors
Dumain	Love's Labour's Lost

Character	Play
Duncan	Macbeth
Edmund	King Lear
Emilia	Othello, The Two Noble Kinsmen
Fabian	Twelfth Night
Fenton	The Merry Wives of Windsor
Fulvia	Antony and Cleopatra
Hamlet	Hamlet
Hecate	Macbeth
Hector	Troilus and Cressida
Helena	A Midsummer Night's Dream, All's Well that Ends Well
Hermia	A Midsummer Night's Dream
Imogen	Cymbeline
Juliet	Romeo and Juliet, Measure for Measure
Lucius	Titus Andronicus
Marina	Pericles
Mutius	Titus Andronicus
Oberon	A Midsummer Night's Dream
Oliver	As You Like It
Olivia	Twelfth Night
Orsino	Twelfth Night
Oswald	King Lear
Pistol	Henry IV Part 2, Henry V, The Merry Wives of Windsor
Pompey	Measure for Measure, Antony and Cleopatra
Portia	The Merchant of Venice
Quince	A Midsummer Night's Dream
Rumour	Henry IV Part 2
Silvia	The Two Gentlemen of Verona
Tamora	Titus Andronicus
Thasia	Pericles
Thurio	The Two Gentlemen of Verona
Tybalt	Romeo and Juliet
Verges	Much Ado About Nothing

7

Adriana	The Comedy of Errors
Aemilia	The Comedy of Errors
Agrippa	Antony and Cleopatra
Alarbus	Titus Andronicus
Antonio	The Merchant of Venice, The Tempest
Berowne	Love's Labour's Lost

Character	Play
Bertram	All's Well that Ends Well
Calchas	Troilus and Cressida
Caliban	The Tempest
Capulet	Romeo and Juliet
Cesario	Twelfth Night
Claudio	Much Ado About Nothing, Measure for Measure
Costard	Love's Labour's Lost
Dionyza	Pericles
Douglas	Henry IV Part I
Escalus	Measure for Measure
Flavius	Timon of Athens
Fleance	Macbeth
Goneril	King Lear
Gonzalo	The Tempest
Horatio	Hamlet
Hotspur	Henry IV Part I
Iachimo	Cymbeline
Jacques	As You Like It
Jessica	The Merchant of Venice
Laertes	Hamlet
Lavinia	Titus Andronicus
Leontes	The Winter's Tale
Lorenzo	The Merchant of Venice
Luciana	The Comedy of Errors
Macbeth	Macbeth
Macduff	Macbeth
Malcolm	Macbeth
Mariana	Measure for Measure, All's Well that Ends Well
Martius	Titus Andronicus
Miranda	The Tempest
Nerissa	The Merchant of Venice
Octavia	Antony and Cleopatra
Ophelia	Hamlet
Orlando	As You Like It
Othello	Othello
Palamon	The Two Noble Kinsmen
Paulina	The Winter's Tale
Perdita	The Winter's Tale
Pisanio	Cymbeline
Proteus	The Two Gentlemen of Verona
Quickly, Mistress	Henry IV Part I, Henry IV Part 2, The Merry

Character	Play
	Wives of Windsor
Quintus	Titus Andronicus
Shallow, Justice	Henry IV Part 2, The Merry Wives of Windsor
Shylock	The Merchant of Venice
Silence	Henry IV Part 2
Silvius	As You Like It
Slender	The Merry Wives of Windsor
Solinus	The Comedy of Errors
Theseus	A Midsummer Night's Dream, The Two Noble Kinsmen
Titania	A Midsummer Night's Dream
Troilus	Troilus and Cressida
Ulysses	Troilus and Cressida
William	As You Like It

8

Achilles	Troilus and Cressida
Aufidius	Coriolanus
Baptista	The Taming of the Shrew
Bardolph	Henry IV, Henry V, The Merry Wives of Windsor
Bassanio	The Merchant of Venice
Beatrice	Much Ado About Nothing
Belarus	Cymbeline
Benedick	Much Ado About Nothing
Benvolio	Romeo and Juliet
Charmian	Antony and Cleopatra
Claudius	Hamlet
Cominius	Coriolanus
Cordelia	King Lear
Cressida	Troilus and Cressida
Diomedes	Antony and Cleopatra, Troilus and Cressida
Dogberry	Much Ado About Nothing
Don Pedro	Much Ado About Nothing
Falstaff	The Merry Wives of Windsor, Henry IV
Florizel	The Winter's Tale
Gertrude	Hamlet
Gratiano	The Merchant of Venice
Hermione	The Winter's Tale
Isabella	Measure for Measure
Lucentio	The Taming of the Shrew
Lysander	A Midsummer Night's Dream

Character	Play
Malvolio	Twelfth Night
Menenius	Coriolanus
Mercutio	Romeo and Juliet
Montague	Romeo and Juliet
Mortimer	Henry IV Part I
Octavius	Antony and Cleopatra
Pandarus	Troilus and Cressida
Parolles	All's Well that Ends Well
Pericles	Pericles
Philoten	Pericles
Polonius	Hamlet
Prospero	The Tempest
Roderigo	Othello
Rosalind	As You Like It
Rosaline	Love's Labour's Lost
Sicinius	Coriolanus
Stephano	The Tempest
Trinculo	The Tempest
Violenta	All's Well that Ends Well
Volumnia	Coriolanus

9

Aguecheek, Sir Andrew	Twelfth Night
	Antiochus Pericles
Arviragus	Cymbeline
Bassianus	Titus Andronicus
Brabantio	Othello
Cambridge	Henry V
Cleopatra	Antony and Cleopatra
Cymbeline	Cymbeline
Demetrius	A Midsummer Night's Dream, Antony and Cleopatra, Titus Andronicus
Desdemona	Othello
Enobarbus	Antony and Cleopatra
Ferdinand	Love's Labour's Lost, The Tempest
Glendower. Owen	Henry IV Part I
Guiderius	Cymbeline
Helicanus	Pericles
Hippolyta	A Midsummer Night's Dream, The Two Noble Kinsmen
Hortensio	The Taming of the Shrew

Character	Play
Katherina	The Taming of the Shrew
Katherine	Henry V, Love's Labour's Lost
Mamillius	The Winter's Tale
Patroclus	Troilus and Cressida
Petruchio	The Taming of the Shrew
Polixenes	The Winter's Tale
Sebastian	The Tempest, Twelfth Night
Tearsheet, Doll	Henry IV Part 2
Valentine	The Two Gentlemen of Verona
Vincentio	Measure for Measure, The Taming of the Shrew

10

Alcibiades	Timon of Athens
Antopholus	The Comedy of Errors
Coriolanus	Coriolanus
Fortinbras	Hamlet
Jaquenetta	Love's Labour's Lost
Longaville	Love's Labour's Lost
Lysimachus	Pericles
Posthumous	Cymbeline
Saturninus	Titus Andronicus
Touchstone	As You Like It

11

Rozencrantz	Hamlet

12

Guildenstern	Hamlet

14

Christopher Sly	The Taming of the Shrew

Theatrical Terms

2
op
SM

3
act

arc
ASM
box
gel
ham
leg
pit
run
set

4
blue
book
boom
drop
exit
flat
gaff

gobo
gods
grid
iris
leko
mask
olio
pipe
prop
rail
rake
sock
tabs
tail
wing

5

above
actor
ad lib
agent
apron
arena
aside
below
brace
cloth
cloud
flies
float
foyer
gauze
glory
halls
heavy
hoist
inset
lyric
manet
odeum
perch
scene
scrim

skene
slips
slote
sound
stage
stall
stile
traps
truck
uppet
visor

6

barrel
batten
boards
border
box set
bridge
busker
cellar
centre
circle
critic
dimmer
geggie
groove
make-up
neumes
old man
poster
return
runway
scruto
sea row
teaser
telari
toggle
walk-on

7

acct drop
actress

aulaeum
balcony
benefit
call boy
catwalk
circuit
curtain
diorama
flipper
gallery
jornada
manager
matinee
on stage
pinspot
rain box
roll-out
rostrum
royalty
scenery
sky dome
spot bar
tableau
top drop
trilogy
tumbler
two-fold
upstage
valance

8

audition
blackout
book flat
book wing
call door
chairman
cut-cloth
designer
director
dumb show
elevator
epilogue

fauteuil
fox wedge
juvenile
lashline
libretto
lighting
off stage
old woman
panorama
paradiso
parallel
pass door
platform
playbill
producer
prologue
prompter
scenario
set piece
sill iron
siparium
sky cloth
star trap
vamp trap
wardrobe

9

acoustics
backcloth
backstage
boat truck
box office
call board
carpet cut
cyclorama
downstage
fan effect
footlight
grave trap
green room
groundrow
hand-props
hemp house

light pipe
limelight
loft block
noises off
open stage
orchestra
penny gaff
periaktoi
projector
promenade
provinces
reflector
rehearsal
repertory
rod-puppet
rope house
sand-cloth
scene dock
set waters
sight line
sky border
slapstick
slip stage
soubrette
spotlight
stage crew
stage door
stage prop
stage rake
three-fold
throwline
thyristor
tormentor
traveller
trickwork
water rows

10

anti-masque
auditorium
avant-garde
built stuff
corner trap

curtain set
drag artist
floodlight
follow spot
ghost glide
hall keeper
house light
impresario
inner stage
lycopodium
marionette
pipe batten
prompt side
saddle-iron
sciopticon
show portal
spectatory
stage cloth
strip light
thunder run
tree border
understudy

11

backing flat
book ceiling
border light
bristle trap
curtain call
dress circle
falling flap
formal stage
fresnel spot
light batten
low comedian
off-Broadway
profile spot
rise-and-sink
roll ceiling
scene relief
spieltreppe
stage-keeper
strobe light

switchboard
tritagonist
upper circle
waggon stage
wind machine

12

actor-manager
amphitheatre
author's night
cauldron trap
ceiling cloth
choreography
concert party
Corsican trap
costume drama
curtain-music
flying effect
front of house
light console
lobsterscope
masking piece
pepper's ghost
profile board
reverberator
rundhorizont
scissor cross
sound effects
stage manager
stage setting
stereopticon
stichomythia
stock company
thundersheet
transparency
twopenny gaff

13

detail scenery

deus ex machina
improvisation
laterna magica
mazarine floor
platform stage
portal opening
safety curtain
stage lighting
supernumerary
word rehearsal

14

contour curtain
courtroom drama
drapery setting
dress rehearsal
footlights trap
general utility
jack-knife stage
kuppelhorizont
mezzanine floor
off-off-Broadway
pageant lantern
private theatre
proscenium arch
revolving stage
stage direction

15

barn door shutter
flexible staging
hand worked house
incidental music
multiple setting
proscenium doors
quick-change room
stage-door-keeper
traverse curtain

16

alienation effect
asphaleian system
composite setting
dramatis personae
drawing-room drama
proscenium border
touring companies

17

cup-and-saucer drama

18

bespeak performance
carbon arc spotlight
drum-and-shaft system
female impersonator
grandmaster control
linsenscheinwer fer
technical rehearsal

19

counterweight system
simultaneous setting
transformation scene

20+

advertisement curtain
assistant stage manager
carriage-and-frame
system
chariot-and-pole system
promenade productions
silicon controlled
rectifier
synchronous winch
system

Business and Professions

Business, Trade and Commerce Terms

2

A I
C.A.
H.P.
r.d.

3

bid
B.O.T.
buy
C.O.D.
cut
dun
E.C.U.
E.E.C.
fee
F.O.B.
G.N.P.
I.O.U.
job
lot
Ltd
net
owe
par
pay
rig
S.E.T.
sum
tax
tip
V.A.T.

4

agio
back
bail
bank
bear
bill
bond
boom
bull
call
cash
cess
chip
coin
cost
deal
dear
debt
deed
dole
dues
dump
duty
earn
easy
E.F.T.A.
even
fine
firm
fisc
free
fund
gain
G.A.T.T.
gild
gilt
giro
glut
gold
good
hire
idle
I.O.U.S.
kite
lend
levy
lien
loan
long
loss
mart
mint
nett
note
owed
paid
P.A.Y.E.
poll
pool
post
puff
punt
ramp
rate
rent
ring
risk
sale
scot
sell
sink
sold
spot
stag
tare
term
turn
vend
wage

5

agent
angel
asset
at par
audit
award
batch
bears
bid up

block	owing	amount
board	panic	assets
bonds	paper	assign
bonus	payee	at cost
brand	payer	avails
bribe	pound	bailee
bulls	price	bailor
buyer	proxy	banker
buy in	quota	barter
buy up	quote	bearer
by-law	rally	borrow
cargo	rates	bought
cheap	remit	bounce
check	repay	bounty
chips	rider	bourse
clear	score	branch
clerk	scrip	broker
costs	share	bubble
cover	shark	budget
crash	short	burden
cycle	sight	buying
debit	slump	buy out
draft	stock	by-laws
entry	talon	cartel
ex cap.	taxes	cheque
ex div.	teind	change
float	tight	client
folio	tithe	corner
funds	token	coupon
gilts	trade	credit
goods	trend	crisis
gross	trust	cum. div
hedge	usury	dealer
'House'	value	deal in
index	wages	debtor
issue	worth	defray
labor	yield	demand
lease		dicker
limit	**6**	docket
money	accept	drawee
notes	accrue	drawer
offer	advice	equity
order	agency	estate

excise	output	staple
expend	packet	stocks
export	parity	strike
factor	pay-day	supply
figure	paying	surety
fiscal	pay-off	surtax
freeze	pay out	syndic
go down	pledge	tariff
growth	plunge	taxman
hammer	policy	teller
holder	profit	tender
honour	public	ticket
import	punter	tithes
in cash	quorum	trader
income	racket	tycoon
in debt	rating	unload
indent	realty	unpaid
insure	rebate	usance
jobber	recoup	usurer
job lot	redeem	valuta
labour	refund	vendor
ledger	remedy	vendue
lender	rental	volume
liable	rentes	wampan
Lloyd's	report	wealth
lock-up	resale	wind up
margin	retail	
market	return	**7**
mark-up	salary	account
mature	sample	actuary
merger	save up	advance
minute	saving	allonge
nem. com.	sell in	annuity
notice	sell up	arrears
octroi	set off	at sight
office	settle	auction
on call	shares	auditor
on cost	shorts	average
option	silver	backing
one off	simony	bad debt
outbid	specie	balance
outlay	spiral	banking
outlet	spread	bargain

bidding	forward	pension
bonanza	freight	per cent
bullion	funding	pre-empt
buy back	futures	premium
cambist	gearing	prepaid
capital	haulage	pricing
cashier	hedging	product
ceiling	holding	profits
certify	imports	promote
charter	imprest	pro rate
company	indorse	pyramid
consols	inflate	realize
convert	in funds	receipt
crossed	insured	reissue
customs	interim	renewal
cut-rate	invoice	reserve
damages	jobbers	returns
day book	kaffirs	revenue
dealing	killing	rigging
declare	lay days	royalty
default	leasing	salvage
deficit	lending	selling
deflate	limited	sell-out
deposit	lockout	service
douceur	lottery	sold out
draw out	lump sum	solvent
dumping	manager	spinoff
duopoly	mint par	squeeze
economy	minutes	stipend
embargo	name day	storage
endorse	nest egg	subsidy
engross	net gain	surplus
entrust	no funds	swindle
ex bonus	on offer	takings
expense	on order	tax free
exploit	package	tonnage
exports	partner	trade in
factory	payable	trading
failure	pay cash	traffic
fall due	payment	trustee
feedback	pay rise	utility
finance	payroll	vending
flutter	pay slip	venture

war bond
war loan
warrant
way bill
wound up
write up

8

above par
acceptor
accounts
act of God
after tax
agiotage
amortize
ante-date
appraise
assignee
assigner
auditing
back bond
bailment
bank bill
bankbook
bank giro
bank loan
banknote
bank rate
bankrupt
barratry
basic pay
below par
berthage
blue chip
book debt
borrower
bottomry
business
buying in
carriage
cashbook
cash down
cash sale

clearing
commerce
consumer
contango
contract
creditor
credit to
cum bonus
currency
customer
cut-price
dealings
defrayed
delivery
director
disburse
discount
dividend
drawings
dry goods
earnings
embezzle
employee
employer
emporium
endorsee
endorser
entrepot
equities
estimate
evaluate
exchange
expenses
exporter
ex gratia
ex rights
finances
fine gold
flat rate
gold pool
goodwill
gratuity
hallmark

hammered
hard cash
hard sell
hot money
importer
in arrear
increase
indebted
industry
interest
in the red
investor
lame duck
manifest
mark down
markings
maturing
maturity
merchant
monetary
monopoly
mortgage
net price
novation
on credit
on demand
on strike
operator
ordinary
overhead
overtime
par value
passbook
pin money
poundage
price cut
price war
proceeds
producer
property
purchase
quit rent
rack rent

receipts
receiver
recovery
reinvest
reserves
retailer
retainer
scarcity
schedule
security
shipment
sinecure
solvency
spending
spot cash
sterling
straddle
supertax
swindler
takeover
taxation
tax dodge
taxpayer
trade gap
transfer
Treasury
turnover
undercut
unquoted
wage rate
warranty
windfall
write off

9

actuarial
ad valorem
aggregate
allotment
allowance
annuitant
ante-dated
anti-trust

appraisal
appraiser
arbitrage
arrearage
assurance
averaging
bank stock
blank bill
book value
bordereau
borrowing
brokerage
by-product
call money
call price
carry over
certified
chartered
charterer
clearance
closing bid
commodity
cost price
cum rights
death duty
debenture
debit note
deck cargo
deduction
defaulter
deflation
demurrage
depletion
depositer
directors
dishonour
easy money
easy terms
economics
economies
economize
emolument
exchequer

executive
extortion
face value
fair price
fair trade
fiat money
fiduciary
financial
financier
fine paper
firm offer
firm price
first call
first cost
flotation
franchise
free trade
fully paid
garnishee
gilt-edged
going rate
guarantee
guarantor
hard money
import tax
in arrears
incentive
income tax
indemnity
indenture
inflation
insolvent
insurance
inventory
leasehold
liability
list price
long-dated
mail order
marketing
middleman
mortgagee
mortgagor

near money
negotiate
net income
order book
outgoings
overdraft
overdrawn
overheads
packaging
pari passu
paymaster
pecuniary
petty cash
piecework
portfolio
preferred
price list
price ring
price rise
prime cost
principal
profiteer
promotion
purchaser
put option
quittance
quotation
ratepayer
ready cash
recession
redundant
reflation
reimburse
repayable
repayment
resources
restraint
reversion
royalties
sell short
shift work
short bill
sold short

speculate
spot price
stamp duty
statement
stock list
stockpile
subscribe
subsidize
surcharge
syndicate
tax return
ticket day
trade fair
trademark
trade name
tradesman
traveller
treasurer
undersell
unit trust
utilities
valuation
vendition
viability
wage claim
warehouse
wealth tax
wholesale
winding up
work force
work sheet
work study
World Bank

10

acceptance
accountant
account day
accounting
accumulate
active bond
adjustment
advice note

appreciate
assessment
assignment
attachment
auctioneer
automation
average out
bank credit
bank return
bankruptcy
bear market
bearer bond
bill broker
bill of sale
block grant
bondholder
bonus issue
bonus share
bookkeeper
bucket shop
bulk buying
bull market
calculator
call option
capitalism
capitalist
capitalize
capitation
chain store
chequebook
closed shop
collateral
colporteur
commercial
commission
compensate
consortium
contraband
conversion
credit bank
credit card
credit note
credit slip

cumulative	marketable	recompense
defalcator	mass market	redeemable
del credere	mercantile	redemption
depreciate	money order	redundancy
depression	monopolist	remittance
direct cost	monopolize	remunerate
dirty money	moratorium	rock bottom
drawn bonds	negotiable	sales force
elasticity	non-payment	scrip issue
encumbered	no par value	second-hand
engrossing	note of hand	securities
ergonomics	obligation	selling out
evaluation	open cheque	settlement
excise duty	open credit	serial bond
ex dividend	opening bid	share index
first offer	open market	short bonds
fiscal year	open policy	short-dated
fixed charge	option rate	sole agency
fixed costs	overcharge	speculator
fixed price	paper money	statistics
fixed trust	pawnbroker	stockpiles
free market	percentage	stock split
floor price	plough back	subscriber
forwarding	pre-emption	tape prices
funded debt	preference	tax evasion
gross value	prepayment	ticker tape
ground rent	price index	tight money
growth area	price level	trade cycle
honorarium	production	trade price
import duty	profitable	trade union
income bond	profits tax	ultra vires
industrial	prospector	underwrite
insolvency	prospectus	unemployed
instalment	prosperity	upset price
investment	prosperous	wage freeze
joint stock	provide for	Wall Street
lighterage	purchasing	wholesaler
liquidator	pure profit	working day
living wage	pyramiding	work to rule
long period	quarter day	written off
loss leader	ready money	
management	real estate	*11*
marked down	real income	account book

accountancy
acquittance
advance note
advertising
arbitration
asking price
auction ring
auction sale
average bond
bank account
bank balance
bank holiday
bank of issue
bear squeeze
beneficiary
big business
bill of entry
billionaire
bimetallism
black market
blank cheque
bonded goods
bonus scheme
book-keeping
budget price
businessman
capital gain
cash account
central bank
certificate
circulation
commitments
competition
comptometer
commodities
common stock
competitive
consignment
consumption
co-operative
corporation
counterfeit
cum dividend

customs duty
days of grace
defence bond
demand curve
demand draft
deposit rate
deposit slip
devaluation
discounting
dishonoured
distributor
dividend tax
double entry
down payment
economic law
economic man
endorsement
expenditure
fixed assets
fixed charge
fixed income
fluctuation
foreclosure
free on board
freight note
Gresham's Law
gross income
high finance
hypothecate
income stock
indemnified
indirect tax
industrials
job analysis
joint return
legal tender
liquidation
loan capital
manufacture
market overt
market price
mass produce
merchandise

middle price
millionaire
minimum wage
money-lender
negotiation
net interest
net receipts
open account
option price
outstanding
overpayment
overtrading
package deal
partnership
pay on demand
physiocrats
point of sale
postal order
poverty line
premium bond
price fixing
price freeze
property tax
purchase tax
Queer street
raw material
realization
reinsurance
reserve bank
revaluation
rights issue
risk capital
safe deposit
sales ledger
savings bank
seigniorage
sell forward
selling day
shareholder
single entry
sinking fund
small trader
sold forward

speculation
stockbroker
stockjobber
stock market
stockpiling
stocktaking
subsistence
supermarket
syndicalism
take-home pay
takeover bid
time deposit
transaction
undercharge
undervalued
underwriter
with profits

12

above the line
account payee
ad valorem tax
amalgamation
amortization
appreciation
assembly line
balance sheet
banker's draft
banker's order
bargain price
below the line
bill of lading
board meeting
Board of Trade
bond creditor
bonded stores
bottomry bond
branch office
bridging loan
buyer's market
callable bond
capital gains
capital goods

capital stock
carrying over
carry-over day
cash and carry
caveat emptor
charter party
clearing bank
closing price
common market
compensation
consumer goods
contract note
cost of living
credit rating
current price
current ratio
customs union
Defence Bonds
denomination
depreciation
differential
direct labour
disbursement
discount rate
disinflation
distribution
Dutch auction
earned income
embezzlement
econometrics
economy drive
entrepreneur
exchange rate
export credit
first refusal
fiscal policy
fixed capital
floating debt
frozen assets
going concern
gold standard
hard currency
hire purchase

indirect cost
interest rate
invoice clerk
irredeemable
joint account
keep accounts
labour market
laissez-faire
life interest
liquid assets
manufacturer
marginal cost
mass-produced
maturity date
mercantilism
merchant bank
mixed economy
monetization
money changer
national bank
national debt
nearest offer
nominal price
nominal value
official list
opening price
overcapacity
pay as you earn
pay in advance
paying-in-slip
policy holder
present worth
price ceiling
price control
price current
price rigging
productivity
profiteering
profit margin
profit motive
profit talking
public sector
rate of growth

raw materials
redeployment
remuneration
remunerative
reserve price
rig the market
rising prices
running costs
sale or return
sales manager
salesmanship
severance pay
share capital
shareholding
sliding scale
social credit
soft currency
specie points
statistician
sterling area
stock in trade
stockjobbery
stockjobbing
surplus value
tax avoidance
tax collector
tax exemption
terms of trade
trade balance
trading stamp
transfer deed
treasury bill
treasury bond
treasury note
trial balance
trustee stock
underwriting
valued policy
welfare state
works council

13

acceptilation

allotment note
appropriation
articled clerk
average clause
backwardation
bank statement
blank transfer
bullion market
business cycle
clearing house
contract curve
credit account
credit control
credit squeeze
crossed cheque
current assets
discount house
dividend yield
dollar premium
Dow-Jones index
exchequer bill
free trade area
futures market
gross receipts
guarantee fund
incomes policy
interim report
issued capital
livery company
Lombard Street
long-dated bill
making-up price
non-cumulative
not negotiable
ordinary share
outside broker
overhead price
paid-up capital
par of exchange
participating
premium income
private sector
profitability

profit sharing
public company
quote sampling
rateable value
sales forecast
settlement day
share transfer
specification
Stock Exchange
switch selling
taxable income
trade discount
value added tax
vendor's shares
wasting assets
wheeler-dealer
works council

14

account current
advance freight
apprenticeship
balance of trade
bearer security
bill of exchange
blocked account
break-even point
bureau de change
capital account
capital gearing
capitalization
consumer credit
convertibility
corporation tax
current account
current balance
debenture stock
decimalization
deferred rebate
deferred shares
deposit account
discount market
economic growth

featherbedding
fiduciary issue
finance company
floating charge
founders' shares
fringe benefits
full employment
garnishee order
general average
general manager
half-commission
holder for value
holding company
hyperinflation
infrastructure
inscribed stock
invisible trade
joint stock bank
letter of credit
limited company
liquidity ratio
Lloyd's Register
loan conversion
macro-economics
managing agents
market research
micro-economics
monthly accounts
mortgage broker
new issue market
nominal capital
option dealings
ordinary shares
oversubscribed
preferred stock
progress chaser
promissory note
quality control
random sampling
rate of exchange
rate of interest
receiving order
revenue account

short-term gains
social security
superannuation
surrender value
trading account
uberrimae fidei
unearned income
working capital

15

average adjuster
bonded warehouse
building society
capital employed
commission agent
consignment note
dividend warrant
exchange control
ex-gratia payment
foreign exchange
interim dividend
investment trust
labour-intensive
liquidity ratios
marine insurance
nationalization
non-contributory
political science
preference bonds
preference share
preferred shares
preference stock
public ownership
public relations
purchasing power
rationalization
redemption yield
reducing balance
secured creditor
sleeping partner
sterling balance
unissued capital

Occupations, Professions and Trades

2 and 3

doc
don
G.P.
gyp
M.D.
M.O.
P.A.
P.M.
pro
P.R.O.
rep
spy
vet

4

alma
ayah
babu
bard
boss
char
chef
cook
crew
diva
dyer
gang
hack
hand
head
herd
hind
lead
magi
maid
mali
mate

mime
page
peon
poet
ryot
seer
serf
syce
thug
tout
ward
whip

5

actor
ad-man
agent
augur
avoue
baker
bonze
boots
bosun
caddy
choir
clerk
clown
coach
comic
crier
crimp
curer
daily
egger
envoy
extra
fakir
fence
fifer
filer
finer
flier
gager

gipsy
gluer
groom
guard
guide
guild
hakim
harpy
helot
hirer
hiver
hoppo
lamia
leech
luter
mason
medic
miner
navvy
nurse
oiler
owler
pilot
piper
plyer
pupil
quack
quill
rabbi
rater
reeve
ruler
scout
sewer
shoer
slave
smith
sower
staff
swami
sweep
tamer
tawer

taxer
thief
tiler
tuner
tutor
tyler
usher
valet
viner

6

airman
archer
artist
aurist
author
bagman
bailee
bailer
bailor
balker
bandit
banker
barber
bargee
barker
barman
batman
bearer
beggar
binder
boffin
bookie
bowman
brewer
broker
bugler
bursar
busker
butler
cabbie
cabman
calker

canner	flayer	lackey
carman	forger	lander
carter	fowler	lascar
carver	framer	lawyer
casual	fuller	lector
censor	gaffer	lender
clergy	ganger	loader
cleric	gaoler	logman
codist	gaucho	lumper
coiner	gauger	magian
comber	gigolo	marker
conder	gilder	master
con man	gillie	matron
coolie	glazer	medico
cooper	glover	mender
copper	graver	menial
co-star	grocer	mentor
coster	guider	mercer
cowboy	guidon	milker
cowman	gunman	miller
critic	gunner	minter
cutler	harper	monger
cutter	hatter	morisk
dacoit	hawker	mummer
dancer	healer	mumper
dealer	heaver	mystic
digger	hodman	nailer
docker	hooper	notary
doctor	horner	nurser
dowser	hosier	oboist
draper	hunter	oilman
drawer	intern	orator
driver	issuer	ostler
drover	jailer	packer
editor	jailor	parson
fabler	jobber	pastor
factor	jockey	patrol
farmer	joiner	pavier
fellah	jowter	pavior
feller	jurist	pedant
fictor	keeler	pedlar
fisher	keeper	penman
fitter	killer	picker

pieman
pirate
pitman
plater
player
porter
potboy
potter
priest
pruner
purser
querry
rabbin
ragman
ranger
ratter
reader
reaper
reaver
rector
regent
relief
renter
rigger
ringer
robber
roofer
rooter
sacker
sailor
salter
salvor
sapper
sartor
sawyer
scribe
sea-dog
sealer
seaman
seiner
seizor
seller
server

setter
sexton
shroff
singer
sircar
skivvy
slater
slaver
slavey
sleuth
snarer
socman
sorter
souter
spicer
squire
stager
stoker
storer
sutler
tabler
tailor
tamper
tanner
tasker
taster
teller
termer
tester
tiller
tinker
tinman
tinner
toller
touter
toyman
tracer
trader
troupe
tubman
turner
tycoon
typist

usurer
vacher
valuer
vamper
vanman
vassal
vendor
verger
verser
viewer
waiter
walker
waller
warden
warder
warper
washer
weaver
weeder
welder
whaler
worker
wright
writer

7

abacist
abigail
acolyte
acolyth
acrobat
actress
actuary
alewife
almoner
alnagar
analyst
ancient
apposer
Arabist
arbiter
artisan
artiste

assayer	coalman	flunkey
assizer	cobbler	flutist
assured	cockler	footboy
assurer	collier	footman
auditor	co-pilot	footpad
aviator	copyist	foreman
awarder	coroner	founder
bailiff	corsair	friseur
bandman	counsel	frogman
barmaid	courier	fueller
bedeman	cowherd	furrier
bellboy	cowpoke	gateman
bellhop	crofter	girdler
birdman	cropper	glazier
blaster	curator	gleaner
blender	currier	gleeman
boatman	custode	glosser
bondman	danseur	graffer
bookman	dentist	grafter
bottler	dialist	grainer
bouncer	dietist	granger
brigand	ditcher	grantee
builder	dominie	grantor
burglar	doorman	grazier
butcher	dragman	grinder
buttons	drapier	gymnast
callboy	drawboy	hackler
cambist	drayman	harpist
carrier	dredger	haulier
caseman	dresser	helotry
cashier	drogman	herbist
cateran	drummer	herdman
caterer	dustman	heritor
caulker	exegete	higgler
cellist	famulus	hogherd
chanter	farrier	hostler
chapman	fascist	indexer
chemist	faunist	inlayer
chorist	fiddler	ironist
cleaner	fireman	janitor
clicker	fish-fag	juggler
clippie	flesher	junkman
co-agent	florist	juryman

keelman	pleader	spinner
knacker	plumber	spotter
knitter	poacher	stainer
laborer	poetess	stamper
laceman	postboy	stapler
lockman	postman	statist
lombard	presser	steerer
mailman	prestor	steward
maltman	printer	surgeon
manager	puddler	swabber
mangler	rancher	sweeper
marbler	realtor	taborer
marcher	refiner	tallier
mariner	riveter	tapster
marshal	roadman	taxi-man
matador	roaster	teacher
matelot	rustler	tipster
mealman	sacrist	tracker
meatman	saddler	trainer
matayer	sampler	trapper
metrist	samurai	trawler
midwife	scourer	trimmer
milkman	scraper	trucker
modiste	servant	trustee
moneyer	settler	tumbler
monitor	sharper	turnkey
mootman	shearer	vintner
moulder	shipper	violist
newsboy	shopboy	wagoner
oculist	shopman	waister
officer	showman	warrior
orderer	shunter	waterer
orderly	silkman	webster
packman	simpler	weigher
pageboy	skinner	wheeler
painter	skipper	whetter
palmist	slipper	wireman
pantler	smelter	woodman
peddler	snipper	woolman
painist	socager	workman
picador	soldier	wrapper
planner	soloist	
planter	spencer	_8_____

adscript	claqueur	exporter
aeronaut	clothier	fabulist
algerine	coachman	factotum
analyser	codifier	falconer
annalist	coistril	famulist
aphorist	collator	farmhand
apiarist	comedian	ferryman
apron-man	compiler	figurant
arborist	composer	filmstar
armourer	conclave	finisher
armorist	conjurer	fishwife
arrester	conveyer	flatfoot
arrestor	coryphée	flautist
assessor	courtier	fletcher
attorney	cow-leech	fodderer
bagmaker	coxswain	forester
bagpiper	croupier	forgeman
ballader	cutpurse	fugleman
bandsman	dairyman	gangster
bargeman	danseuse	gardener
bearherd	deckhand	gavelman
bearward	defender	gendarme
bedesman	designer	glassman
bedmaker	director	goatherd
bit-maker	dog-leech	godsmith
bleacher	domestic	gossiper
boatsman	doughboy	governer
bondmaid	dragoman	guardian
bondsman	druggist	gunsmith
boniface	editress	hammerer
botanist	educator	handmaid
bowmaker	embalmer	handyman
boxmaker	emissary	hatmaker
brewster	employee	haymaker
broacher	employer	headsman
busheler	engineer	head cook
cabin boy	engraver	helmsman
cellarer	enroller	henchman
ceramist	epic poet	herdsman
chandler	essayist	hired man
choirboy	essoiner	hireling
co-author	exorcist	histrion
ciderist	explorer	home help

hotelier	minstrel	publican
houseboy	mistress	pugilist
huckster	modeller	purveyor
huntsman	muleteer	quarrier
importer	muralist	raftsman
improver	musician	ranchero
inkmaker	neatherd	rapperee
inventor	newshawk	receiver
japanner	novelist	recorder
jet pilot	onion-man	regrater
jeweller	operator	relessee
jongleur	optician	relessor
kipperer	ordainer	repairer
labourer	ordinand	reporter
landgirl	organist	resetter
landlady	outrider	restorer
landlord	overseer	retailer
lapidary	pargeter	retainer
larcener	parodist	reviewer
larderer	penmaker	rewriter
Latinist	perfumer	rivetter
leadsman	peterman	romancer
lecturer	pewterer	rugmaker
linesman	picaroon	rumourer
lumberer	picklock	salesman
magician	pinmaker	satirist
magister	plagiary	sawbones
maltster	plougher	scullion
manciple	polisher	sculptor
masseuse	portress	seamster
measurer	postiler	sea-rover
mechanic	potmaker	seasoner
medalist	preacher	seedsman
melodist	prefacer	sempster
mercator	preluder	servitor
merchant	pressman	shearman
messager	probator	shepherd
metal-man	procurer	ship's boy
milkmaid	promoter	shipmate
millgirl	prompter	shopgirl
millhand	prosaist	showgirl
milliner	provider	sidesman
minister	psalmist	simplist

sketcher
smuggler
soldiery
spaceman
spearman
speedcop
spurrier
starcher
stitcher
stockman
storeman
stripper
strummer
stuntman
supplier
surveyor
swindler
tabourer
tallyman
taverner
teamster
thatcher
thespian
thresher
tin miner
tinsmith
tipstaff
torturer
toymaker
tripeman
truckman
turncock
turnspit
tutoress
unionist
valuator
vintager
virtuoso
vocalist
volumist
waitress
walker-on
wardress

warrener
watchman
waterman
wet nurse
whaleman
whitener
whitster
wigmaker
winnower
wool-dyer
workfolk

9

alchemist
alluminor
anatomist
annotator
announcer
arbitress
arborator
archeress
architect
archivist
art critic
art dealer
artificer
astronaut
attendant
authoress
balladeer
balladist
ballerina
bank agent
barrister
barrow boy
beefeater
beekeeper
beemaster
berserker
biologist
boanerges
boatswain
bodyguard

boilerman
bondslave
bondwoman
bookmaker
bootblack
bootmaker
buccaneer
bus driver
burnisher
cab driver
café owner
cameraman
car driver
caretaker
carpenter
casemaker
catechist
cellarman
chanteuse
charwoman
chauffeur
cheapjack
chorister
clarifier
clergyman
clinician
clogmaker
coalminer
coalowner
collector
columnist
colourist
comprador
concierge
conductor
conserver
cosmonaut
cost clerk
costumier
courtesan
couturier
cowfeeder
cowkeeper

cracksman
craftsman
crayonist
cymbalist
dactypist
daily help
dairymaid
decorator
decretist
desk clerk
detective
dice-maker
die-sinker
dietetist
dietician
directrix
dispenser
dissector
distiller
doctoress
draftsman
dramatist
drawlatch
drum major
drum-maker
drysalter
ecologist
embezzler
enameller
engineman
engrosser
epitomist
errand boy
estimator
examinant
excavator
excerptor
exchanger
executive
exercitor
exciseman
exorciser
eye doctor

fabricant
fandancer
fashioner
felt-maker
figurante
financier
film actor
film extra
film-maker
fire-eater
fish-curer
fisherman
fish-woman
flag-maker
flax-wench
flyfisher
freelance
freighter
fripperer
fruiterer
furbisher
furnisher
galvanist
gasfitter
gazetteer
gem-cutter
geologist
gladiator
gluemaker
goldsmith
gondolier
gospeller
governess
groundman
guardsman
guerrilla
guitarist
gun-runner
harlequin
harmonist
harpooner
harvester
Hellenist

herbalist
herbarian
herborist
herb-woman
hired hand
hired help
homeopath
historian
hog-ringer
hop-picker
hosteller
housemaid
housewife
hygienist
hypnotist
incumbent
ingrafter
innholder
innkeeper
inscriber
inspector
intendant
ironsmith
itinerant
jack-smith
job-master
kennel-man
lacemaker
lacquerer
lady's maid
lampooner
land agent
landreeve
larcenist
launderer
laundress
law writer
legionary
librarian
linotyper
liontamer
liveryman
loan agent

lockmaker	part-timer	railmaker
locksmith	pasquiler	recruiter
log-roller	paymaster	reformist
lumberman	pedagogue	rehearser
machinist	performer	ribbonman
magnetist	physician	roadmaker
majordomo	physicist	romanticist
male model	pitsawyer	ropemaker
male nurse	planisher	roundsman
man-at-arms	plasterer	ruddleman
mannequin	ploughboy	rum-runner
mechanist	ploughman	sacristan
medallist	pluralist	safemaker
memoirist	poetaster	sailmaker
mendicant	pointsman	scarifier
mercenary	policeman	scavenger
mesmerist	pontonier	scenarist
messenger	pop artist	scholiast
metallist	porteress	schoolman
metrician	portrayer	scientist
middleman	portreeve	scrivener
mill-owner	postilion	scytheman
modelgirl	postwoman	sea-robber
mortician	poulterer	secretary
muffin-man	practiser	ship's mate
musketeer	precentor	shipowner
musketoon	predicant	shoeblack
myologist	preceptor	shoemaker
navigator	prelector	sightsman
negotiant	priestess	signalman
neologian	privateer	sinologue
neologist	professor	soapmaker
newsagent	profilist	solicitor
nursemaid	provedore	sonneteer
odd job man	publicist	sopranist
office boy	publisher	sorceress
operative	pulpiteer	soubrette
orchestra	puppeteer	space crew
ordinator	pythoness	spiderman
osteopath	qualifier	stableboy
otologist	quarryman	stableman
outfitter	quirister	stagehand
pantaloon	racketeer	stationer

stay-maker
steersman
stevedore
subeditor
subworker
succentor
sur-master
swan-upper
swineherd
switchman
swordsman
syndicate
synoptist
tablemaid
tactician
tailoress
tap dancer
teataster
tentmaker
test pilot
therapist
theurgist
throwster
timberman
toolsmith
top sawer
town clerk
town crier
tradesman
tragedian
traveller
treasurer
trepanner
tributary
trumpeter
tympanist
usherette
varnisher
versifier
vetturino
vexillary
violinist
volcanist

voltigeur
wadsetter
warrantee
warranter
washerman
waxworker
whitester
winemaker
wood-reeve
workwoman
zookeeper
zoologist
zootomist

10

able seaman
accomptant
accoucheur
accountant
acolothist
adelantado
advertiser
aerologist
agrologist
agronomist
air hostess
air steward
algebraist
amanuensis
apothecary
apple-woman
apprentice
arbalister
arbitrator
astrologer
astronomer
atmologist
auctioneer
audit clerk
ballet girl
balloonist
ballplayer
bandmaster

bank robber
baseballer
bassoonist
beadswoman
beautician
bell-hanger
bell-ringer
bibliopole
bill-broker
billposter
biochemist
biographer
blacksmith
blockmaker
bluejacket
bombardier
bondswoman
bonesetter
bookbinder
bookholder
bookkeeper
bookseller
bootlegger
bricklayer
brickmaker
brushmaker
bureaucrat
butterwife
caravaneer
career girl
cartoonist
cartwright
cash-keeper
cat breeder
cat burglar
ceramicist
chair-maker
chargehand
charioteer
chirurgeon
chorus girl
chronicler
chucker-out

circuiteer	doorkeeper	gold-digger
claim agent	dramaturge	gold-washer
clapperboy	dressmaker	governante
clockmaker	drummer-boy	grammarian
clog dancer	dry cleaner	gunslinger
cloth maker	emblazoner	hackney-man
coachmaker	emboweller	hall porter
coal-backer	enamellist	handmaiden
coal-fitter	ephemerist	harvestman
coalheaver	epitaphist	hatcheller
coal-master	epitomizer	head porter
co-assessor	evangelist	head waiter
coastguard	examinator	hierophant
collocutor	explorator	highwayman
colloquist	eye-servant	horn player
colporteur	fell-monger	horologist
comedienne	fictionist	horsecoper
compositor	file-cutter	horse-leech
compounder	fillibuster	house agent
concordist	film editor	huckstress
contractor	firemaster	husbandman
controller	fire-worker	inoculator
copyholder	fishmonger	institutor
copywriter	flight crew	instructor
cordwainer	flowergirl	interagent
cotton lord	fluvialist	ironmonger
counsellor	folk-dancer	ironworker
crow-keeper	folk-singer	journalist
cultivator	forecaster	journeyman
customs man	frame-maker	lady doctor
cytologist	freebooter	land holder
delineator	fund raiser	land jobber
directress	fustianist	land waiter
disc jockey	gamekeeper	land worker
discounter	game warden	laundryman
discoverer	geisha girl	law officer
dishwasher	gear-cutter	legislator
dispatcher	geneticist	librettist
distrainer	geographer	lighterman
distrainor	glee-singer	lime-burner
dockmaster	glossarist	linotypist
dog breeder	glue-boiler	liquidator
dog-fancier	gold-beater	lobsterman

lock-keeper
lumberjack
magistrate
management
manageress
manicurist
manservant
matchmaker
meat-hawker
medical man
militiaman
millwright
mineralist
ministress
mintmaster
missionary
moonshiner
naturalist
nautch girl
negotiator
news editor
newscaster
newsvendor
newswriter
night nurse
nosologist
nurseryman
obituarist
oil painter
orchardist
osteologer
overlooker
panegyrist
pantrymaid
park-keeper
park-ranger
pasquilant
pastry-cook
pathfinder
pawnbroker
pearl-diver
pediatrist
pedicurist

peltmonger
penologist
perruquier
pharmacist
philologer
piano tuner
pickpocket
platelayer
playwright
politician
portionist
postillion
postmaster
prescriber
prima donna
private eye
procurator
programmer
pronouncer
proprietor
prospector
protractor
proveditor
puncturist
pyrologist
quiz-master
railwayman
rat catcher
recitalist
researcher
ringmaster
roadmender
ropedancer
roughrider
safe blower
sales force
saleswoman
schoolmarm
scrutineer
sculptress
sea-captain
seamstress
second mate

seminarist
serving-man
sexologist
ship-broker
ship-holder
shipmaster
shipwright
shopfitter
shopkeeper
shopwalker
signwriter
silentiary
silk-mercer
silk-weaver
sinologist
skirmisher
slop seller
sneak thief
soap-boiler
specialist
staff nurse
steersmate
stewardess
stipulator
stocktaker
stone-borer
stonemason
strategist
street-ward
supercargo
superviser
surcharger
surface-man
swan-keeper
symphonist
tally clerk
taskmaster
taxi-dancer
taxi-driver
tea-blender
tea planter
technician
technocrat

theogonist
theologian
theologist
threnodist
timekeeper
tractarian
trade union
traffic sop
trafficker
tram-driver
transactor
translator
trawlerman
treasuress
troubadour
typesetter
undertaker
veterinary
victualler
vinegrower
vivandiere
vocabulist
wage-earner
wainwright
warrioress
watchmaker
waterguard
wharfinger
wholesaler
whitesmith
winegrower
wine-waiter
wireworker
woodcarver
woodcutter
wood-monger
woodworker
wool-carder
wool-comber
wool-driver
wool-grower
wool-sorter
wool-trader

wool-winder
wool-worker
work-fellow
working man
workmaster
work people
yardmaster
zinc-worker
zoographer
zymologist

II

accompanist
accoucheuse
acoustician
adjudicator
allopathist
annunciator
antiquarian
apple-grower
arbitratix
army officer
arquebusier
artillerist
audio typist
auscultator
bag-snatcher
ballad-maker
bank cashier
bank manager
bargemaster
basketmaker
batti-wallah
battologist
beachcomber
bell-founder
Benedictine
bill-sticker
bird-catcher
bird fancier
bird watcher
boatbuilder
body servant

boilermaker
boilersmith
bondservant
boot-catcher
broadcaster
bullfighter
businessman
butterwoman
candlemaker
car salesman
cattle thief
cat's-meat man
chair-mender
chalk-cutter
chambermaid
chiffonnier
chirologist
chiromancer
chiropodist
choirmaster
chronologer
cinder-wench
cinder-woman
clock-setter
cloth worker
coal-whipper
coffin-maker
cognoscente
collar-maker
common-crier
condisciple
condottiere
conductress
confederate
congressman
consecrator
conservator
constituent
conveyancer
coppersmith
cosmogonist
cosmologist
crane driver

crimewriter
cub reporter
cypher clerk
day-labourer
delivery man
demographer
dispensator
draughtsman
duty officer
electrician
emblematist
embroiderer
entertainer
estate agent
ethnologist
etymologist
executioner
extortioner
face-painter
factory hand
faith healer
fancy-monger
fourbisseur
fringe-maker
fruit picker
funambulist
galley-slave
genealogist
ghostwriter
glass-bender
glass-blower
glass-cutter
glass-worker
grass-cutter
grave-digger
greengrocer
haberdasher
hagiologist
hairdresser
hair stylist
hardwareman
harvest lord
head foreman

head workman
hedge-priest
hedge-writer
hierologist
histologist
horse doctor
horse jockey
horse-keeper
horse trader
hospitaller
hotel-keeper
housekeeper
housemaster
housemother
hymnologist
illuminator
illusionist
illustrator
infantryman
institutist
interpreter
interviewer
iron-founder
ivory-carver
ivory-turner
ivory-worker
kennelmaid
kitchenmaid
lamplighter
land steward
laundrymaid
leading lady
ledger clerk
lifeboatman
lightkeeper
linen draper
lithologist
lithotomist
lorry driver
madrigalist
maidservant
mammalogist
master baker

mechanician
medicine man
merchantman
memorialist
metal worker
miniaturist
money-broker
money-lender
monographer
mule-spinner
music critic
music master
myographist
mysteriarch
necrologist
necromancer
needlewoman
neurologist
neurotomist
night porter
night sister
nightworker
nomenclator
numismatist
office staff
onion-seller
opera singer
ophiologist
orientalist
orthopedist
osteologist
pamphleteer
panel-beater
pantomimist
paperhanger
parish clerk
parlourmaid
pathologist
pattenmaker
pearlfisher
pedobaptist
penny-a-liner
petrologist

pettifogger	silversmith	waiting-maid
philatelist	slaughterer	washerwoman
philologist	slave-driver	watchkeeper
piece worker	slave-holder	water-doctor
phytologist	smallholder	water gilder
phonologist	sociologist	wax-chandler
polyphonist	stage-driver	wheel-cutter
pork butcher	stage-player	wheelwright
portraitist	stake-holder	whitewasher
preceptress	steeplejack	witch-doctor
print-seller	stereotyper	wool-stapler
probationer	stipendiary	xylophonist
promulgator	stockbroker	zoographist
proofreader	stockjobber	
property man	stonecutter	*12*
proprietrix	storekeeper	accordionist
quacksalver	stripteaser	actor manager
questionary	sundriesman	ambulance man
radiologist	system-maker	anaesthetist
rag merchant	taxidermist	animalculist
representer	telegrapher	archeologist
republisher	telephonist	artilleryman
rhetorician	ticket agent	artist's model
roadsweeper	toastmaster	bagpipe-maker
safebreaker	tobacconist	ballad singer
sandwich man	tooth-drawer	ballet dancer
Sancritist	topographer	ballet master
saxophonist	torch-bearer	bantam weight
scoutmaster	town planner	bellows-maker
scrapdealer	toxophilite	bibliologist
scrip-holder	tragedienne	bibliopegist
secret agent	train-bearer	bibliopolist
seditionary	transcriber	body-snatcher
servant girl	transporter	booking clerk
serving-maid	travel agent	bus conductor
share-broker	type-founder	cabinet-maker
sheepfarmer	typographer	calligrapher
shepherdess	underbearer	caricaturist
shipbreaker	underletter	carpet-bagger
shipbuilder	underwriter	carpet-fitter
ship's master	upholsterer	cartographer
shopsteward	versemonger	cataclysmist
silk-thrower	vine-dresser	cerographist

cheesemonger	first officer	lexicologist
chief cashier	flying doctor	lithographer
chimney-sweep	footplateman	longshoreman
chiropractor	geometrician	loss adjuster
chronologist	geriatrician	lumber-dealer
churchwarden	glass-grinder	maitre d'hotel
circuit rider	glossologist	make-up artist
civil servant	greasemonkey	malacologist
clarinettist	guild brother	man of letters
clerk of works	gymnosophist	manual worker
cloth-shearer	gynecologist	manufacturer
coach-builder	hagiographer	mass producer
coleopterist	haliographer	meat-salesman
commissioner	harness-maker	mezzo soprano
conchologist	head gardener	metallurgist
confectioner	headshrinker	microscopist
corn chandler	homeopathist	mineralogist
cosmographer	horse-breaker	miscellanist
costermonger	horse-courser	money-changer
crafts-master	horse-knacker	monographist
craniologist	hotel manager	morris-dancer
cryptogmatist	housebreaker	mosaic-artist
dance hostess	housepainter	mosaic-worker
deep-sea diver	house steward	mythographer
demonologist	house surgeon	newspaperman
demonstrator	hydographer	notary public
dendrologist	hydropathist	nutritionist
dramaturgist	hypothecator	obstetrician
ecclesiastic	immunologist	office junior
Egyptologist	instructress	oneirocritic
elecutionist	invoice clerk	orchestrator
engastrimuth	jerry-builder	organ-builder
engine-driver	joint-trustee	organ-grinder
entomologist	jurisconsult	orthodonist
entomotomist	juvenile lead	orthographer
entrepreneur	king's counsel	ovariotomist
escapologist	knife-grinder	paper-stainer
ethnographer	knife-thrower	papyrologist
experimenter	labouring man	pattern-maker
family doctor	land surveyor	pediatrician
farm labourer	lath-splitter	phonographer
film director	leader-writer	photographer
film producer	legal adviser	phrenologist

physiologist
plant manager
ploughwright
plumber's mate
plyer-for-hire
postmistress
practitioner
press officer
prestigiator
prison warder
prize-fighter
professional
propagandist
proprietress
psychiatrist
psychologist
publicity man
pupil-teacher
puppet-player
pyrotechnist
quarry master
racing driver
radiographer
receptionist
remembrancer
restaurateur
riding-master
right-hand man
rubber grader
sales manager
scene-painter
scene-shifter
school master
screenwriter
scullery-maid
seafaring man
seed-merchant
seismologist
sharecropper
sharpshooter
ship chandler
ship's husband
shoe-repairer

silver-beater
slaughterman
snake charmer
social worker
soil mechanic
special agent
speechwriter
spice blender
sportscaster
sportswriter
stage manager
statistician
steel erector
stenographer
stonebreaker
stonedresser
stonesquarer
street-trader
street-walker
sugar-refiner
tax-collector
technologist
telegraph boy
telegraphist
test engineer
therapeutist
thief-catcher
ticket-porter
timber trader
toll-gatherer
tourist agent
toxicologist
tradespeople
transplanter
trichologist
undermanager
veterinarian
waiting-woman
water diviner
warehouseman
wine merchant
wood-engraver
woollen-draper

works manager
zincographer

13

administrator
agriculturist
antique dealer
arachnologist
archaeologist
arithmetician
articled clerk
Assyriologist
barber-surgeon
bibliographer
calico-painter
campanologist
cartographist
chartographer
chicken-farmer
chirographist
choreographer
chronographer
civil engineer
clearstarcher
coffee-planter
cometographer
contrabandist
contortionist
cotton-spinner
counter-caster
counterfeiter
cranioscopist
cryptographer
dancing master
deipnosophist
dermatologist
diagnostician
diamond-cutter
draughtswoman
drawing-master
dress designer
drill sergeant
electroplater

electrotypist
emigrationist
entozoologist
epigrammatist
estate manager
exhibitionist
family butcher
fencing-master
fortune-teller
freight-broker
galvanologist
game-preserver
gastriloquist
glossographer
glyphographer
ground-bailliff
gynaecologist
harbour master
hieroglyphist
horse-milliner
hospital nurse
icthyologist
industrialist
intelligencer
joint-executor
letter-carrier
letter-founder
lexicographer
lighthouseman
maid-of-all-work
master-builder
master mariner
mathematician
melodramatist
metaphysician
meteorologist
metoposcopist
music mistress
night-watchman
old-clothes-man
ornithologist
orthographist
park attendant

periodicalist
pharmaceutist
physiognomist
physiographer
posture-master
poultry farmer
privateersman
process-server
psalmographer
psychoanalyst
pteridologist
public speaker
queens counsel
racing-tipster
revolutionary
revolutionist
rubber-planter
sailing master
schoolteacher
science master
shop assistant
silk-throwster
singing-master
station-master
stenographist
stereoscopist
stethoscopist
street-sweeper
sub-contractor
superintender
supernumerary
thaumaturgist
thimble-rigger
toll collector
trade unionist
tram conductor
tramcar-driver
ventriloquist
violoncellist
window-cleaner
window-dresser
writing-master

14

administratrix
anthropologist
autobiographer
bacteriologist
ballet mistress
billiard-marker
billiard-player
chamber-counsel
chimney-sweeper
citizen-soldier
classics master
colour sergeant
commissionaire
dancing partner
discount-broker
educationalist
ecclesiologist
encyclopaedist
exchange-broker
grammaticaster
handicraftsman
heresiographer
horticulturist
house decorator
house furnisher
language master
leather-dresser
manual labourer
market-gardener
medical officer
merchant-tailor
miscellanarian
money-scrivener
mother-superior
music publisher
naval pensioner
painter-stainer
pharmacologist
pneumatologist
psalmographist
reception clerk
representative

schoolmistress
ship's-carpenter
siderographist
spectacle-maker
spectroscopist
superintendent
systems analyst
tallow chandler
water-colourist
weather prophet

15

arboriculturist
assistant master
Bow Street runner
crossing-sweeper
crustaceologist
dancing mistress
diamond merchant
domestic servant
forwarding agent
gentleman-farmer
hackney coachman
heart specialist
helminthologist
hierogrammatist
historiographer
instrumentalist
insurance broker
jack-of-all-trades
musical director
numismatologist
ophthalmologist
palaeontologist
platform-speaker
portrait-painter
professional man
programme seller
provision dealer
railway engineer
resurrectionist
scripture-reader
sleeping partner

stretcher-bearer
ticket collector
tightrope walker
tonsorial artist

Official Positions and Religious Titles

2 and 3

aga
beg
bey
cid
dey
don
jam
J.P.
M.C.
M.P.
ras
rex
sir

4

abbe
agha
aide
amir
amma
babu
beak
cadi
cham
cure
czar
dean
doge
duce
duke
earl

emir
foud
graf
head
imam
inca
khan
king
lady
lama
lord
miss
naib
naik
page
papa
peer
pope
rani
rank
shah
sire
tsar
tzar
ward
whip
zaim

5

abbot
agent
ameer
baboo
baron
bedel
begum
board
boyar
canon
chief
Clare
count
dewan

divan	state	exarch
donna	suite	fecial
doyen	synod	Fuhrer
edile	thane	gauger
elder	vakil	harman
emeer	vicar	herald
envoy	wazir	hetman
ephor		judger
friar	**6**	kaiser
hakam	abbess	kavass
imaum	aedile	keeper
judge	alcade	knight
junta	archon	legate
junto	ataman	lictor
jurat	avener	mikado
kalif	avenor	misses
laird	bailie	mister
laity	barony	mullah
liege	bashaw	notary
macer	beadle	nuncio
mahdi	begaum	police
mayor	bigwig	prefat
mufti	bishop	pretor
nabob	brehon	primus
nawab	bursar	prince
nizam	caesar	puisne
noble	caliph	rabbin
pacha	cantor	ranger
pasha	censor	rector
padre	cherif	regent
porte	childe	sachem
prior	consul	satrap
queen	curate	sbirro
rabbi	custos	senate
rajah	datary	sexton
ranee	deacon	sheikh
reeve	deputy	shogun
ruler	despot	sirdar
sagan	donzel	squire
sahib	duenna	sultan
sheik	dynast	syndic
sophi	eparch	tanist
staff	ephori	umpire

verger
vestry
vizier
warden
warder

7

alcalde
apostle
armiger
asiarch
attaché
bailiff
baronet
bellman
bencher
burgess
cacique
caloyer
cazique
commere
compere
consort
coroner
council
curator
custode
custrel
czarina
dapifer
dauphin
dogeate
donship
dowager
duchess
dukedom
duumvir
dynasty
earldom
effendi
elector
embassy
emperor

empress
enactor
eparchy
equerry
equites
esquire
estafet
exactor
fidalgo
Fuehrer
gabeler
gaekwar
Gestapo
grandee
hangman
head boy
headman
hidalgo
infanta
infante
jemadar
jerquer
justice
khalifa
khedive
kinglet
maestro
magnate
mahatma
majesty
marquis
marshal
monarch
muezzin
navarch
nomarch
notable
officer
orderer
padisha
paladin
paritor
peerage

peeress
podesta
pontiff
praetor
prefect
prelate
premier
primacy
primate
proctor
prophet
provost
questor
referee
regency
retinue
royalty
sea-king
sea-lord
senator
senatus
shereef
sheriff
signior
skipper
speaker
steward
subadar
sub-dean
sultana
supremo
Tammany
toparch
tribune
tsarina
tzarina
vavasor
viceroy
vaivode
voivode

8

alderman

antistes
archduke
autocrat
banneret
baroness
baronial
Black Rod
blazoner
blindman
brevetcy
burgrave
canoness
cardinal
carnifex
caudillo
chafewax
chairman
chaplain
cicerone
co-bishop
cofferer
consular
co-regent
cursitor
czarevna
deaconry
deanship
deemster
delegate
diaconal
dictator
diocesan
diplomat
director
douanier
dukeling
dukeship
emeritus
emmisary
enthrone
ethnarch
genearch
guardian

head girl
headship
headsman
heptarch
hierarch
highness
hospodar
imperial
imperium
interrex
kingling
ladyship
laureate
lawgiver
lawmaker
lay elder
legation
licenser
life peer
lordling
lordship
maharaja
manciple
mandarin
margrave
marquess
marquise
martinet
mayoress
minister
ministry
monarchy
monocrat
myriarch
myrmidon
nobility
nobleman
noblesse
official
oligarch
optimacy
overlord
overseer

palatine
placeman
pontifex
princess
priorate
prioress
provisor
quaestor
recorder
regality
register
resident
sagamore
seigneur
seignior
squireen
summoner
suzerain
synarchy
talukdar
tetrarch
tipstaff
treasury
triarchy
tribunal
triumvir
tsarevna
tzarevna
verderer
viscount
wardmote
zemindar

9

ale-conner
ale-taster
archdruid
archducal
archduchy
authority
baronetcy
beglerbeg
bodyguard

bretwalda
bumbledom
burggrave
caliphate
captaincy
carmelite
cartulary
castellan
catchpole
celebrant
cellarist
centurion
chevalier
chieftain
chief whip
chilliarch
commander
commodore
constable
cordelier
court fool
cupbearer
custodian
Dalai Lama
darbyites
deaconess
decemviri
despotism
diaconate
dictatrix
dignitary
diplomate
directory
dominator
drum major
eldership
electress
envoyship
ephoralty
escheator
estafette
exarchate
exciseman

executive
exequatur
ex-officer
fort-major
goldstick
grand duke
high court
incumbent
inspector
Jack Ketch
judgeship
justiciar
knightage
landgrave
lifeguard
liveryman
lord mayor
magnifico
maharajah
majordomo
mandatary
mandatory
mayoralty
moderator
monocracy
monsignor
oligarchy
ombudsman
Orangeman
palsgrave
patriarch
patrician
pendragon
pentarchy
policeman
polyarchy
polycracy
portfolio
portreeve
potentate
precentor
presbyter
president

pretender
princedom
principal
proconsul
registrar
reichstrat
rural dean
sacristan
secretary
seneschal
seraskier
sovereign
statesman
sub-beadle
sub-deacon
suffragan
sultaness
timocracy
town clerk
town crier
treasurer
vestryman
viscounty
vizierate
waldgrave
whipper-in
zemindari

10

agonothete
aide-de-camp
ambassador
appanagist
archbishop
archdeacon
archflamen
archimagus
archpriest
areopagite
autocrator
bergmaster
borsholder
bumbailiff

bursarship
camerlengo
carabineer
catechumen
catholicos
censorship
chancellor
chaplaincy
chartulary
chatellany
cimeliarch
cloisterer
cloistress
commandant
commissary
consulship
controller
corporator
corregidor
coryphaeus
councillor
councilman
covenanter
crown agent
czarevitch
dauphiness
deaconship
delegation
designator
dock-master
doorkeeper
enomotarch
enumerator
episcopate
excellency
fire-master
headmaster
heraldship
high master
high priest
Home Office
incumbency
inquisitor

institutor
justiciary
king-at-arms
knighthood
lay brother
legateship
legislator
lieutenant
lower house
mace-bearer
magistracy
magistrate
margravine
marquisate
mayor-elect
midshipman
ministrant
mint-master
monarchism
noblewoman
ochlocracy
officially
oligarchal
opposition
parliament
plutocracy
postmaster
prebendary
presbytery
presidency
proclaimer
procurator
prolocutor
proscriber
proveditor
pursuivant
rectorship
regentship
sachemship
sea captain
sextonship
shrievalty
sign manual

squirehood
squireship
statecraft
state paper
sultanship
suzerainty
tithing-man
unofficial
upper house
vice-counsul
vicegerent
vice-master
vice-regent
war council
whiggarchy

11

adelantado
archdapifer
archduchess
archdukedom
aristocracy
assay-master
autocratrix
burgess-ship
burgomaster
cardinalate
catercousin
chamberlain
chieftaincy
comptroller
corporation
county court
court jester
cross-bearer
crossbowman
crown lawyer
crown prince
diplomatist
directorate
directorial
earl-marshal
ecclesiarch

electorship
executioner
flag officer
functionary
good templar
grand master
grand vizier
gymnasiarch
headborough
intercessor
internuncio
justiceship
landgravine
legislatrix
legislature
lieutenancy
lord provost
marchioness
marshalship
ministerial
monarchical
monseigneur
officialdom
officiating
papal legate
papal nuncio
policewoman
pontificate
pound-keeper
praepositor
premiership
primateship
prince royal
preconsular
proctorship
protocolist
protonotary
provostship
puisne judge
queen-mother
questorship
referendary
school board

senatorship
speakership
squirearchy
stadtholder
stratocracy
subordinate
sword-bearer
tax assessor
tax gatherer
thesmothete
town council
tribuneship
triumvirate
vestry clerk
vice-regency
viceroyalty
viscountess
wreckmaster

12

agent-general
ambassadress
armour-bearer
avant-courier
bound-bailiff
carpet knight
chairmanship
chief justice
chief of staff
churchwarden
civil servant
civil service
commendatory
commissioner
constabulary
crown-equerry
dictatorship
ecclesiastic
enfranchiser
enthronement
field officer
guardianship
headmistress

heir apparent
House of Lords
inspectorate
internuncius
jack-in-office
laureateship
legislatress
lord-temporal
maid of honour
mastersinger
metropolitan
muster-master
notary public
office-bearer
parish priest
peace officer
poet laureate
prince-bishop
Privy Council
quaestorship
queen-consort
queen-dowager
queen-regnant
quindecemvir
recordership
remembrancer
sheriff-clerk
staff officer
tax collector
Trinity house
unauthorized
uncovenanted
vicar-general
viscountship
water-bailiff
witenagemote

13

administrator
archidiaconal
archimandrite
archpresbyter
archtreasurer

army commander
barrack-master
borough-master
chieftainship
chorepiscopus
color sergeant
consul-general
count palatine
county council
district judge
generalissimo
grand-seigneur
gubernatorial
high constable
inspectorship
judge-advocate
lord-spiritual
mounted police
parliamentary
prime minister
Prince of Wales
Princess Royal
public trustee
state function
states-general
statesmanship
vice-president

vigintivirate

14

archchancellor
archiepiscopal
auditor-general
chancellorship
chief constable
colour sergeant
crown solicitor
dowager-duchess
lord of the manor
gentleman-usher
high court judge
House of Commons
king's messenger
lord chancellor
lord lieutenant
lords-spiritual
medical officer
parochial board
political agent
provost marshal
revenue officer
superintendent
town councillor
vicar-apostolic

vice-chancellor

15

advocate-general
archchamberlain
archiepiscopacy
archiepiscopate
astronomer-royal
attorney-general
cabinet minister
chamberlainship
charge d'affaires
district officer
election auditor
governor-general
heir-presumptive
lords lieutenant
messenger-at-arms
parliamentarian
plenipotentiary
privy councillor
queen's messenger
sheriff's officer
suffragen bishop
surveyor-general
vice-chamberlain
vice-chancellors

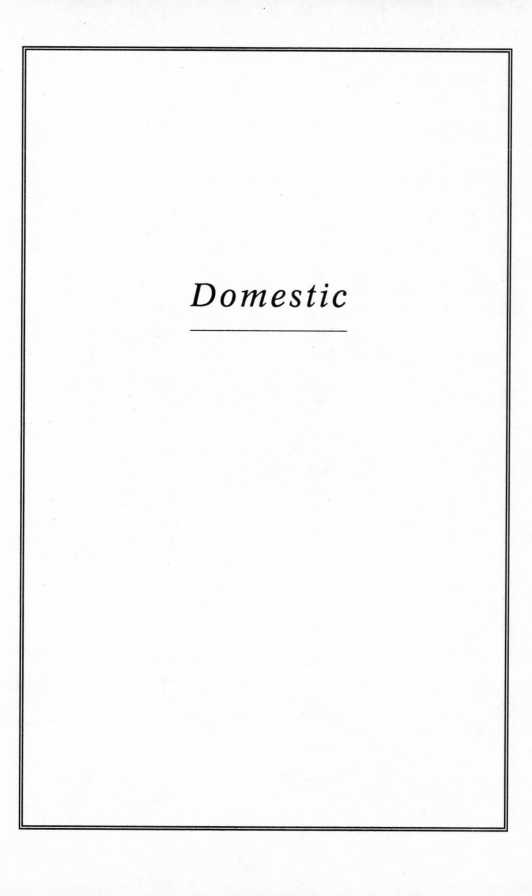

Domestic

Clothes and Material

3

aba
abb
alb
bag
bas
bat
bib
boa
bra
bur
cap
fez
fur
hat
hem
jam
kid
kit
lap
lei
mac
net
obi
PVC
rag
rep
sox
tam
tie
wig
zip

4

abba
agal
alba
apex
band
baft

baju
barb
batt
beck
belt
benn
boot
bota
brim
burr
busk
cack
calf
capa
cape
clog
coat
coif
cony
cope
cote
cowl
cuff
daps
dido
disk
down
drab
drag
duck
duds
felt
frog
garb
gear
geta
gimp
gown
gros
haik
hemp
hide
hood

hose
inro
izar
jama
jute
kepi
kilt
lace
lame
lawn
leno
list
mask
maud
maxi
mesh
midi
mini
mink
mitt
moff
muff
mule
mull
pelt
poke
pulu
pump
repp
robe
ruff
sack
sari
sark
sash
saya
shag
shoe
silk
skin
slip
slop
sock

spat
spur
stud
suit
tabi
toga
togs
topi
tutu
vamp
veil
vest
wool
wrap
yarn

5

abaya
abnet
acton
aegis
amice
amid
ampyx
apron
arcan
armet
armor
ascot
baize
barbe
barry
batik
beige
benjy
beret
bezan
blake
bluey
boina
boots
braid
budge

burka
busby
cabas
cadet
camis
capoc
cappa
caxon
chale
chaps
chino
choga
choli
cloak
clogs
cloth
clout
cordy
cotta
cotte
crape
crash
crepe
crest
crown
cuban
curch
cylas
cymar
denim
derby
dhoti
dicky
dress
drill
ephod
ermin
fanon
fichu
finos
floss
fogle
foule

frill
frock
gansy
gauze
get-up
gilet
gippo
glove
guimp
gunny
habit
haick
heels
hulls
ihram
imrah
inkle
jabot
jamah
jasey
jeans
jelab
jippo
jupon
jussi
kamik
kapok
khaki
lacet
lammy
lapel
Levis
linen
liner
lisle
loden
lungi
middy
mitre
mitts
moiré
mufti
mungo

mutch	spats	angola
ninon	stays	angora
nubia	stock	anklet
nylon	stola	anorak
orlon	stole	aridas
orris	straw	artois
pagne	stuff	baftas
pagri	suede	balkan
palla	surah	banian
pants	tabby	banyan
parka	tails	barege
pilch	talma	barret
pirny	tammy	barvel
pique	tanga	basque
plaid	teddy	bautta
pleat	terai	beanie
plume	terry	beaver
plush	tiara	bengal
pumps	toile	bequin
quoif	tongs	berlin
rayon	topee	bertha
romal	toque	bicorn
ruche	train	bietle
rumal	trews	bikini
sable	tulle	biggin
sabot	tunic	birrus
sagum	tweed	bishop
saree	twill	bliaud
saṭin	vamps	blazer
sayon	visor	blouse
scarf	vizor	boater
serge	V-neck	bob-wig
shako	voile	bodice
shash	weeds	bolero
shawl	welly	bonnet
shift		bonten
shirt	**6**	bootee
simar	abolla	boucle
sisal	achkan	bowler
skirt	almuce	bow tie
slops	alpaca	boxers
smock	anadem	braces
snood	analav	bragas

breton	cloche	frieze
briefs	coatee	fringe
brogan	cobcab	gaiter
brogue	cocket	gansey
buckle	collar	garter
burlap	collet	gillie
burnet	cornet	girdle
buskin	corset	gloria
bustle	cossas	grogan
button	cothum	guimpe
byrrus	cotton	gurrah
byssus	cravat	gusset
cabaan	crepon	halter
cabeca	cyprus	hankie
caftan	dacron	helmet
calash	damask	humhum
calcei	diadem	hennininsole
calico	diaper	jacket
caliga	dickey	jerkin
calpac	dimity	jersey
camail	dirndl	joseph
camisa	dolman	jubbah
camise	domett	jumper
camlet	domino	juppon
canvas	dornic	kabaya
capoch	dorsel	kaftan
capote	dowlas	kersey
capuce	duffel	kimono
caputi	duster	kirtle
caraco	ear-cap	kittel
casque	edging	lammie
castor	ermine	lampas
catgut	fabric	lappet
cestus	fag-end	lining
chadar	faille	linsey
chimer	fedora	livery
chinos	ferret	loafer
chintz	fibule	lungee
chiton	fillet	madras
choker	flares	magyar
chrome	fleece	mantee
cilice	forfar	mantle
claque	foxfur	mantua

marmot
melton
memo
mitten
mobcap
mohair
moreen
mundil
muslin
nutria
nylons
outfit
Oxford
panama
patten
pegtop
peltry
peplos
peplum
peruke
pileus
pinner
pleats
pompom
poncho
pongee
poplin
pugree
puttee
PVC mac
raglan
ratine
rebato
reefer
riband
ribbon
rigout
rochet
rubber
ruffle
russet
samite
sandal

sarong
satara
sateen
saxony
sendal
sequin
serape
sheath
shimmy
shoddy
shorts
shroud
sissol
slacks
sleeve
smalls
sontag
soneri
stamin
step-in
sunhat
tabard
tamine
tartan
thibet
ticken
tights
tinsel
tippet
tissue
tobine
toison
top-hat
topper
toquet
torque
toupee
toupet
tricot
trilby
trunks
T-shirt
tucker

turban
tussah
tuxedo
tweeds
ulster
undies
uplist
vampay
velure
velvet
visite
waders
wampum
weeper
whites
wimple
wincey
witney
woolly
zonnar
zouave

7

abb wool
acrilan
acrylic
alamode
alepine
amictus
apparel
arisard
arm band
art-silk
baboosh
baldric
balteus
bandana
bandeau
barbute
baroque
bashlyk
basinet
batiste

bay-yam	chevron	fake fur
beveren	chimere	fallals
beretta	chip hat	falsies
betsies	chlamys	fanchon
biretta	chopine	fashion
blanket	chrisom	felt hat
blucher	chuddar	felting
bocking	chudder	filibeg
bottine	civvies	fish net
box cape	clobber	flannel
box coat	clothes	flat cap
brimmer	coating	flat hat
brocade	cockade	floroon
brogans	coronet	flounce
buckram	corsage	foulard
burnous	cossack	frislet
busskin	costume	frounce
bycoket	cow-hide	fur coat
byssine	coxcomb	fur felt
cagoule	crepida	fustian
calecon	crispin	gaiters
calotte	crochet	galloon
camblet	crounet	gantlet
cambric	cut-away	garment
camouro	delaine	gaskins
capuche	djibbah	genappe
canezou	doeskin	ghillie
cantoon	dogskin	gingham
cape hat	dollman	grogram
capuche	dopatta	guipure
capulet	dornock	G-string
cassock	doublet	gum boot
casuals	drabbet	gum shoe
catskin	drawers	gym shoe
cerevis	drip-dry	gymslip
challis	dulband	handbag
chalwar	earmuff	hat-band
chamois	egrette	hessian
chapeau	epaulet	hoggers
chaplet	ermelin	hogskin
chechia	eton cap	holland
chemise	everett	homburg
chenille	faconne	hopsack

hosiery
jaconet
jap silk
jodphur
klompen
lasting
latchet
layette
leather
legging
leghorn
leotard
liberty
loafers
lockram
Mae West
maillot
malines
maniple
manteau
mantlet
matting
mechlin
minever
miniver
montero
morocco
muffler
nacarat
nankeen
necktie
nightie
oilskin
olivers
organza
orleans
orphrey
ottoman
overall
oxfords
paisley
paletot
pallium

panties
parasol
partlet
pattens
pattern
pelisse
percale
periwig
petasus
pierrot
pigskin
pillbox
pugaree
purflew
puttees
pyjamas
raiment
regalia
rompers
rosette
sacking
sarafan
sarsnet
satinet
scarlet
silesia
silk hat
singlet
ski-boot
slip-ons
slipper
sneaker
soutane
spattee
spencer
sporran
stammel
stetson
suiting
sultane
sunsuit
surcoat
surtout

sweater
tabaret
tabinet
taffeta
taffety
tank top
tatting
textile
ticking
tie silk
tiffany
top boot
top coat
top-knot
traheen
tricorn
tunicle
turn-ups
tussore
twinset
uniform
vandyke
veiling
velours
vesting
vesture
viscose
viyella
watteau
webbing
wedgies
wellies
wetsuit
whittle
wiggery
wing tie
woollen
worsted
yashmak
y-fronts
zimarra

8

abbe cape	calf skin	deerskin
aigrette	cameline	diamante
all-in-one	camisole	djellaba
appliqué	canotier	dom pedro
art linen	cape coat	dress tie
babouche	capeline	drilling
baffetas	capriole	duchesse
baldrick	capucine	dungaree
balmoral	caputium	dust coat
bandanna	carcanet	footwear
barathea	cardigan	earmuffs
barracan	carlisle	ecru silk
bathrobe	cashmere	ensemble
baudekin	catercap	eolienne
bearskin	Celanese	Fair Isle
bed linen	chagreen	faldetta
bedsocks	chaperon	fatigues
benjamin	chaqueta	fillibeg
biggonet	chasuble	fingroms
blancard	chausses	flannels
bloomers	chenille	flimsies
bluchers	chesible	florence
boat-neck	chongsam	fontange
bobbinet	cloaking	footwear
body-belt	cloth cap	frilling
body coat	clothing	frippery
bombards	coiffure	frontlet
bombasin	collaret	froufrou
bonelace	colobium	furbelow
boot hose	copatain	gabarage
bootikin	corduroy	galoshes
bottines	cordwain	gambeson
box cloth	corporal	gambroon
breeches	corselet	gauntlet
brocatel	couch hat	glad rags
brodekin	coverall	goatskin
buckskin	cracowes	gold lace
buffskin	cretonne	gold lame
Burberry	crush hat	gold wire
burgonet	culottes	gossamer
burnoose	dagswain	gumboots
bycocket	dance set	gymshoes
cabasset	dandy hat	half slip

hall-hose
headband
headgear
hipsters
homespun
jackboot
Jacquard
jodhpurs
judo coat
jump suit
kerchief
knickers
knitwear
lambskin
larrigan
lava-lava
leggings
lingerie
lustrine
lustring
mackinaw
mantelet
mantilla
marcella
material
menswear
moccasin
moleskin
moquette
muffetee
muslinet
musquash
nainsook
neckband
necklace
negligee
nightcap
oilcloth
opera hat
organdie
osnaburg
overalls
overcoat

overshoe
pabouche
paduasoy
parament
peasecod
peignoir
pelerine
piccadil
pinafore
playsuit
plimsoll
plumelet
polo-neck
ponyskin
prunella
prunello
pullover
pure silk
raincoat
rose-knot
sandshoe
sarsenet
sealskin
scapular
shagreen
shalloon
Shantung
sheeting
shirring
shirting
shoelace
shot silk
skiboots
skipants
skullcap
slipover
slippers
smocking
sneakers
snowshoe
sombrero
soutache
stitchel

stocking
straw hat
sundress
sunshade
surplice
swanskin
swimsuit
tabbinet
taglioni
tailcoat
tapestry
tarboosh
tarlatan
terai-hat
Terylene
Thai silk
trainers
trencher
tricorne
trimming
trousers
two-piece
umbrella
valencia
vallancy
vestment
wardrobe
wax cloth
whipcord
woollens
woollies
wristlet
zebeline
zoot suit

9

alpargata
Alice band
Alpine hat
ankle-boot
astrakhan
baby linen
balaclava

ball·dress	dress suit	justi-coat
bambin hat	duffle bag	kid gloves
bandolier	dungarees	knee socks
barcelona	dunstable	lambswool
beachwear	escoffian	levantine
bedjacket	epaulette	linen mesh
beegum hat	fermillet	loincloth
bell skirt	fingering	longcloth
billycock	fleshings	long dress
blond lace	flipflops	long skirt
blousette	floss silk	long socks
blue jeans	forage cap	macintosh
body linen	frockcoat	millinery
bombazine	full dress	miniskirt
bowler hat	full skirt	moiré silk
brassiere	fur collar	muffette
broadbrim	gaberdine	nightgown
brunswick	galoshes	nightwear
bushshirt	gambadoes	neckcloth
calamanco	garibaldi	nightgown
camelhair	gauntlets	organzine
caparison	georgette	outerwear
cape dress	Glengarry	overdress
cape stole	greatcoat	overshirt
cassimere	grenadine	overshoes
cerecloth	grosgrain	overskirt
chantilly	haircloth	panama hat
charmeuse	hairshift	pantalets
chaussure	hairpiece	pantaloon
cheongsam	headdress	pantyhose
clump boot	headscarf	paramatta
coat dress	headpiece	patchwork
coat shirt	helmet cap	pea jacket
cocked hat	high heels	peaked cap
comforter	hoop skirt	percaline
copintank	horsehair	petersham
Courtelle	housecoat	petticoat
crinoline	huckaback	pina cloth
Cuban heel	hula skirt	pixie hood
dalmatica	Inverness	plimsolls
décolleté	jack boots	plus-fours
dog collar	jockey cap	point lace
dress coat	juliet cap	polonaise

pourpoint
polyester
press stud
Quaker hat
quoiffure
redingote
round-neck
sackcloth
sack dress
safety pin
sailcloth
sailor cap
sailor hat
sanbenito
satinette
scapulary
school cap
scoop-neck
separates
shaksheer
sharkskin
sheepskin
shovel hat
shower cap
silk serge
sloppy joe
slouch hat
snowshoes
sou'wester
spun rayon
stockinet
stockings
stomacher
strapless
strouding
suede coat
sunbonnet
swansdown
sweatband
sword belt
tarpaulin
tent dress
thigh boot

towelling
track suit
trilby hat
trousseau
undercoat
undergown
undervest
underwear
velveteen
vestments
victorine
waistband
waistcoat
watch coat
wedge heel
wide-awake
wristband
zucchetto

10

angora wool
ankle socks
apron tunic
baby bonnet
balbriggan
ballet shoe
bathing cap
beaverteen
beer jacket
Berlin wool
bishop's-cap
blanketing
bobbin lace
bobbysocks
boiler suit
bombazette
bosom shirt
brigandine
broadcloth
brocatello
bushjacket
buttonhole
calzoneras

candlewick
canonicals
canvas shoe
cape collar
cassinette
chatelaine
chemisette
chinchilla
cossack cap
court dress
court shoes
coverchief
crepe soles
cricket cap
cummerbund
dance dress
deshabille
dinner suit
diving suit
drainpipes
dress plaid
dress shirt
dress shoes
duffel coat
embroidery
espadrille
epauletted
Eton collar
Eton jacket
fancy dress
fearnought
feather boa
florentine
flying suit
foot mantle
foresleeve
fustanella
gold thread
grass cloth
grass skirt
habiliment
halterneck
harem skirt

Havana pelt
hodden-gray
hodden-grey
horsecloth
Irish linen
jersey silk
jersey wool
kerseymere
khaki drill
lounge suit
lumberjack
mackintosh
mess jacket
middy skirt
mock velvet
mousseline
needlecord
new clothes
nightdress
nightshirt
old clothes
opera cloak
overblouse
Oxford bags
Oxford gown
pantalettes
pantaloons
party dress
persiennes
piccadilly
pillow lace
pilot-cloth
pith helmet
plastic mac
pork pie hat
print dress
rabbitskin
riding-hood
roquelaure
sailorsuit
scratch wig
seersucker
service cap

shoebuckle
shoe string
slingbacks
sportscoat
sportswear
string vest
Sunday best
suspenders
sweatshirt
tablecloth
table linen
three-piece
thrown silk
toilinette
trench coat
trousering
turtle-neck
tussah silk
underdress
underlinen
underpants
undershirt
underskirt
waterproof
windjammer
Windsor tie
wing collar
wraparound

II

Arran sweater
bathing suit
battledress
bellbottoms
best clothes
bib-and-brace
black patent
boxer shorts
breechcloth
cancan dress
candystripe
canvas shoes
cap and bells

cavalier hat
chapel de fer
cheesecloth
clodhoppers
cloth-of-gold
combination
cowboy boots
crash-helmet
deerstalker
dinner dress
diving dress
Dolly Varden
dreadnought
empire skirt
espadrilles
evening gown
evening slip
farthingale
flannelette
flared skirt
football cap
formal dress
hammer cloth
hand-me-downs
Harris tweed
herringbone
hunting boot
Honiton lace
Kendal green
leather coat
leatherette
leopardskin
mechlin lace
morning coat
mortarboard
neckerchief
netherlings
nettlecloth
Norfolk suit
overgarment
panty girdle
Phrygian cap
pilot jacket

pinstripes
ready-to-wear
regimentals
riding habit
running shoe
Russian boot
sewing apron
shoe leather
shoulder bag
slumberwear
stiff collar
stockinette
suede jacket
tam-o'-shanter
tennis dress
tennis skirt
torchon lace
trencher cap
trouser suit
tussore silk
Tyrolean hat
undergirdle
underthings
walking shoe
watered silk
wedding gown
wedding veil
wellingtons
widow's weeds
windbreaker
windcheater
yachting cap

12

antigropelos
asbestos suit
balloon skirt
baseball boot
bathing dress
billycock hat
body stocking
bolting cloth
business suit

cardinal's hat
cavalier boot
cavalry twill
chastity belt
chemise dress
circassienne
chesterfield
collar and tie
college scarf
crepe-de-chine
dinner jacket
divided skirt
donkey jacket
dress clothes
dressing gown
Easter bonnet
evening dress
evening shoes
football boots
galligaskins
handkerchief
headkerchief
Indian cotton
knee breeches
leather skirt
lumber jacket
mandarin coat
moiré antique
monkey jacket
morning dress
pedal pushers
plain clothes
pleated skirt
Quaker bonnet
service dress
shirtwaister
sleeping suit
sportsjacket
stockingette
stovepipe hat
tailored suit
ten-gallon hat
underclothes

undergarment
wedding dress
Welsh flannel

13

Anthony Eden
Bermuda shorts
cashmere shawl
chinchilla fur
football scarf
Hawaiian skirt
leather jacket
mourning dress
Norfolk jacket
patent leather
pinafore dress
platform soles
princess dress
Russia leather
smoking jacket
spatterdashes
sports clothes
suspender-belt
swaddling band
underclothing

14

artificial silk
bathing costume
chamois leather
dressing jacket
Egyptian sandal
Fair Isle jumper
knickerbockers
Morocco leather
riding breeches
Shetland jumper
shooting jacket
shoulder strap
swaddling cloth
undress uniform

15

chevalier bonnet
Fair Isle sweater
montgomery beret
maribou feathers
mourning clothes
ostrich feathers
tarpaulin jacket

Food and Drink

Cookery Terms

4

bard
beat
bleu (au)
boil
bone
chop
coat
hang
hash
lard
pipe
rare
toss

5

baste
berny
blanc (a)
blanc (au)
broil
brown
brule
carve
chill
crown
daube
drain
dress
glaze

grill
knead
melba
pluck
poach
point (a)
prove
puree
reine (a la)
roast
rub in
sauté
scald
steam
sweat
truss

6

aurore
braise
confit
creole (a la)
decant
desalt
diable (a la)
fillet
fondue
gratin
grease
maison
mignon
nature
reduce
simmer
zephyr

7

al dente
arrêter
blanche
blondir
chemise (en)
colbert

crouton
deglaze
emincer
flamber
grecque (a la)
marengo
medicis
nicoise (a la)
refresh
supreme
tartare (a la)

8

allonger
Anglaise (a la)
appareil
assation
barbecue
bellevue (en)
bretonne (a la)
Catalane (a la)
chambord
chasseur
chemiser
crudities
dauphine (a la)
devilled
Duchesse (a la)
emulsion
escalope
flamande (a la)
infusion
julienne
macerate
marinate
meuniere (a la)
pistache
pot-roast
surprise (en)

9

acidulate
bake blind

canelling
detailler
dieppoise (a la)
espagnole (a la)
fricassee
knock back
liegeoise (a la)
lyonnaise (a la)
mariniere (a la)
medallion
Milanaise (a la)

10

antillaise (a l')
ballottine
blanquette
bonne femme
bordelaise (a la)
boulangere (a la)
chaud-froid
Dijonnaise (a la)
Florentine (a la)
Provencale (a la)

11

belle-Hélène
bourguignon
charcuterie
dauphinoise (a la)
hollandaise (a la)

13

bourguignonne (a la)
clarification
deep-fat frying

Baking

3

bap
bun
cob
far

pie

4

baba
cake
chou
flan
pave
rusk
tart

5

bagel
baton
bread
crepe
flute
icing
plait
sable
scone
stick
toast

6

cookie
cornet
éclair
leaven
muffin
oublie
rocher
tourte
waffle

7

baklava
bannock
biscuit
bloomer
brioche
chapati
cottage

cracker
crumpet
ficelle
fritter
galette
palmier
pancake
praline
pretzel
stollen
strudel
tartine
tartlet

8

amandine
baguette
barm cake
batonnet
biscotte
doughnut
duchesse
dumpling
empanada
frosting
grissini
sandwich
split tin
tortilla
turnover

9

allumette
barquette
croissant
feuillete
friandise
kugelhopf
petit four
vol-au-vent

10

crispbread

frangipane
patisserie
puff pastry
religieuse
shortbread
sponge cake

11

choux pastry
linzertorte
petit-beurre
profiterole

12

langue-de-chat
pumpernickel
sponge finger

13

Genoese sponge

14

pain au chocolat

15

Savoy sponge cake

Cereals

3

rye

4

bran
corn
oats
rice

5

maize
spelt
wheat

6

barley
bulgur
meteil
millet

7

burghul
froment
sorghum

9

buckwheat

12

cracked wheat

Cheeses

4

brie (France)
curd
edam (Netherlands)
feta (Greece)
tome (France)

5

banon (France)
brick (USA)
caboc (Scotland)
comte (France)
danbo (Denmark)
Derby (England)
fetta (Greece)
Gouda (Netherlands)
herve (Belgium)
Leigh (England)
molbo (Denmark)
murol (France)
niolo (Corsica)
tamie (France)

6

asiago (Italy)
bagnes (Switzerland)
bresse (France)
cachet (France)
cantal (France)
cendre (France)
Dunlop (Scotland)
fourme (France)
Gapron (France)
Gerome (France)
halumi (Greece)
Hramsa (Scotland)
leiden (Netherlands)
morven (Scotland)
Olivet (France)
pourly (France)
rollot (France)
salers (France)
samsoe (Denmark)
Sbrinz (Switzerland)
Surati (India)
Tilsit (Switzerland)
venaco (Corsica)

7

bondard (France)
brinzen (Hungary)
broccio (Corsica)
brocciu (Corsica)
bryndza (Hungary)
cabecou (France)
cheddar (England)
crowdie (Scotland)
dauphin (France)
demi-sel (France)
fontina (Italy)
gaperon (France)
Gjetost (Norway)
Gruyere (France;
Switzerland)
jonchee (France)
langres (France)

levroux (France)
limburg (Belgium)
livarot (France)
macquee (France)
Mont-d'Or (France)
morbier (France)
Munster (France)
nantais (France)
picodon (France)
quargel (Austria)
ricotta (Italy)
sapsago (Switzerland)
Stilton (England)
vendome (France)

8

Auvergne (France)
Ayrshire (Scotland)
Beaufort (France)
bel paese (Italy)
bergkase (Austria)
boulette (France)
chaource (France)
Cheshire (England)
edelpilz (Germany)
emmental (Switzerland)
epoisses (France)
manchego (Spain)
parmesan (Italy)
pecorino (Italy)
pelardon (France)
remoudou (Belgium)
scamorze (Italy)
Tallegio (Italy)
vacherin (Switzerland)
Valency (France)

9

Appenzell (Switzerland)
Broodkaas
(Netherlands)
Caithness (Scotland)
cambozola (Italy;

Germany)
camembert (France)
chabichou (France)
chevreton (France)
emmenthal
(Switzerland)
excelsior (France)
gammelost (Norway)
La bouille (France)
Leicester (England)
limburger (Belgium)
maroilles (France)
mimolette (France)
pave d'Auge (France)
Port-Salut (France)
provolone (Italy)
reblochon (France)
Roquefort (France)

10

Caerphilly (Wales)
Danish blue (Denmark)
dolcelatte (Italy)
Gloucester (England)
gorgonzola (Italy)
Lancashire (England)
mozzarella (Italy)
Neufchatel
(Switzerland)
pithiviers (France)
red Windsor (England)
saingorlon (France)
stracchino (Italy)

11

carre de l'est (France)
Coeur de Bray (France)
coulommiers (France)
Katshkawalj (Bulgaria)
petit-Suisse (France)
Pont-l'Eveque (France)
Saint-Maure (France)
Saint-Paulin (France)

Schabzieger
(Switzerland)
Tete-de-Moine
(Switzerland)
Weisslacker (Germany)
Wensleydale (England)

12

Caciocavallo (Italy)
Red Leicester (England)
Soumaintrain (France)

13

Saint-Nectaire (France)
Selles-sur-Cher
(France)

14

brillat-savarin (France)
feuille de Dreux
(France)
laguiole-aubrac (France)
Saint-Florentin (France)
Saint-Marcellin (France)
trappistenkase
(Germany)

15

Bouton-de-Culotte
(France)

16

Double Gloucester
(England)

17

Rigotte de Pelussin
(France)

18

chevrotin des Aravis
(France)
crottin de Chavignol

(France)

19
Pouligny-Saint-Pierre
(France)

Herbs and Spices

3-5

anise
balm
basil
bay
chive
cive
clary
clove
cress
cumin
dill
grass
mace
mint
myrrh
rape
rue
sage
senna
tansy
thyme
woad

6

bennet
betony
borage
burnet
capers
cecily
chilli
chives
cloves
endive

fennel
galega
garlic
ginger
hyssop
isatis
lovage
lunary
nutmeg
orpine
pepper
savory
sesame
simple
sorrel

7

aconite
boneset
burdock
caraway
catmint
cayenne
chervil
chicory
comfrey
dittany
frasera
gentian
henbane
juniper
lettuce
milfoil
mustard
oregano
panicum
paprika
parsley
perilla
pimento
pot herb
rampion
saffron

salsify
spignel
succory
Tabasco
vanilla

8

agrimony
allspice
angelica
camomile
cardamom
cardamon
cinnamon
dropwort
feverfew
hog's-bean
lavender
lungwort
marigold
marjoram
mouse ear
origanum
plantain
purslane
reedmace
rosemary
samphire
spicknel
tarragon
turmeric
waybread
wormwood

9

baneberry
bear's foot
chamomile
chickweed
coriander
coronopus
eyebright
fenugreek

finocchio
goose foot
groundsel
hellebore
horehound
liquorice
sea fennel
spearmint
sweet herb
tormentil

10

asafoetida
cassumunar
hyoscyamus
lemon thyme
motherwort
oyster plant
penny royal
peppermint
watercress
willow herb

11

dog's cabbage
dragon's head
hedge hyssop
herb of grace
horseradish
pot marigold
pot marjoram
sweet rocket
swine's cress
winter green

12

adder's tongue
hottentot fig
southernwood
summer savory
thoroughwort
winter savory

13

mournful widow
sweet marjoram

14

black-eyed Susan
Florence fennel
medicinal herb

15

mustard and cress
vegetable oyster

Joints of Meat

Beef

brisket
chuck
fillet steak
flank
fore rib
leg
neck
rib
rolled ribs
rump
shin
silverside
sirloin
T-bone
topside
undercut teak

Pork

belly
blade
hand
hock
leg
leg fillet

loin
shoulder
spare rib
tenderloin
trotter

Lamb

best end of neck
breast
chump
chump chops
leg
loin
scrag-end
shoulder

Pasta

4

pipe

5

penne

6

bigoli
ditali
risoni
rotini

7

capelli
fusilli
lasagne
lumache
noodles
ravioli
rotelle

8

bucatini

ditaloni
farfalle
fettucce
fidelini
gramigna
linguine
macaroni
rigatoni
stelline
taglioni
trenette

9

agnolotti
annellini
manicotti
spaghetti
tuffoloni

10

cannelloni
conchiglie
cravattine
farfalline
fettuccine
tagiolini
tortellini
tortelloni
vermicelli

11

cappelletti
orecchiette
pappardelle
spaghettini
spaghettone
tagliatelle
tortiglioni

12

paglia e fieno

Drink

Wines and Aperitifs

4

fino
hock
port

5

byrhh
crepy
fitou
Medoc
rioja
tavel
tokay

6

Alsace
bandol
barolo
barsac
beaune
cahors
cassis
chinon
claret
frangy
graves
Malaga
Saumur
sherry
volnay

7

aligote
Campari
Chablis
Chianti
clairet
cremany

falerno
caillac
Madeira
margaux
Marsala
martini
Moselle
Orvieto
Pommard
retsina
vouvray

8

Bordeaux
brouilly
Dubonnet
gigondas
mercurey
montagny
montilla
muscadet
pauillac
Riesling
rosé wine
Sancerre
satenay
valencay
vermouth
vin jaune

9

bourgueil
champagne
clairette
Cote-rotie
hermitage
lambrusco
meursault
montlouis
Sauternes

10

barbaresco

Beaujolais
Bull's Blood
manzanilla
montrachet
richebourg
rivesaltes
vinho verde

11

aloxe-corton
amontillado
monbazillac
Pouilly-fume
Saint Julien
vin de paille

12

Cotes-du-Rhone
Romanee-Conti
Saint Emilion
Saint Estephe
valpolicella
vosne-Romanee

13

Chateau d'Yquem
Chateau Lafite
Chateau Latour
entre-deux-mers
Pouilly-Fuisse

14

Chateau Margaux
Cotes-du-Ventoux
Gewurztraminer
Lacrima Christi

15

Cotes-de-Provence
Cotes-du-Vivarais
Crozes-Hermitage
Morey-Saint-Denis

16

Chambolle-Musigny
Chateau Haut-Brion
Gevrey-Chambertin
Savigny-les-Beaune

17

Corton-Charlemagne
Cotes-du-Roussillon
Nuits-Saint-Georges

18

Blanquette de Limoux

19

Chassagne-Montrachet

20+

Chateau Mouton-
Rothschild

Beers and Beverages

3

ale

4

mead
mild

5

cider
kvass
lager
perry
stout

6

bitter
lambic

shandy

8

Guinness
hydromel

10

barley beer
barley wine

Spirit

3

gin
rum

4

arak
marc
ouzo

5

choum
vodka
boukha
brandy
chicha
Cognac
grappa
kirsch
mescal
metaxa
pastis
Pernod
pulque
whisky

7

akvavit
aquavit
Bacardi

boukhra
bourbon
schnaps
tequila
whiskey

8

Armagnac
calvados
falernum
schnapps

9

slivovica
slivovitz

10

rye whiskey

11

aguardiente

Liqueurs

4

sake
saki

5

anise
anram

6

cassis
kummel
meliss
qetsch
scubac
strega

7

alcamas
allasch
Baileys
curacao
escubac
ratafia
sambuca

8

absinthe
Advocaat
anisette
Drambuie
persicot
prunelle

9

arquebuse
Cointreau
framboise
guignolet
mirabelle
triple sec

10

brou de noix
chartreuse
maraschino

11

Benedictine
Trappistine

12

cherry brandy
crème de cacao
Grand Marnier

13

crème de menthe

15

Southern Comfort

17

Amaretto di Saranno

Non-alcoholic drinks

3

cha (tea)
tea

4

char (tea)
coke
cola
mate
soda
milk

5

cocoa
juice
lassi
water

6

Bovril
coffee
orgeat
Ribena
squash
tisane

7

beef tea
cordial
diabolo
limeade
seltzer

8

coca-cola
espresso

green tea
lemonade

9

barley-pop
chocolate
ginger-ale
ginger-pop
grenadine
iced water
Indian tea
limejuice
milkshake
orangeade
soda water

10

café-au-lait
cappuccino
ginger beer
malted milk
tonic water

11

barleywater
souchong tea
spring water
tomato juice

12

ice-cream soda
mineral water
orange squash
sarsaparilla

Furniture, fittings and
personal effects

*(See also Kitchen utensils,
requisites and tableware)*

3

bag
bar
bed
bin
can
cot
fan
hod
ink
mat
nib
nog
pad
ped
pen
pew
pin
rug
urn
vat

4

ambo
bath
bowl
bunk
butt
case
cask
cist
comb
cott
crib
desk
door
etui
form
gong
hi-fi
lamp
mull
oven

poke
rack
sack
safe
seal
seat
sofa
tank
tape
till
trap
tray
trug
vase
wick
z-bed

5

apron
arras
basin
bench
berth
besom
bidet
blind
board
broom
chair
chest
china
cigar
clock
cloth
coign
coppy
couch
cover
crate
creel
crock
cruet
cruse

diota	suite	drawer
divan	swing	duster
doily	table	fender
dosel	tache	fly-net
doser	tapis	forfex
duvet	tongs	fridge
flask	tools	geyser
flisk	torch	goblet
futon	towel	goglet
glass	traps	hamper
globe	trunk	hat-box
grill	twine	hearth
guard	vesta	heater
jesse	watch	hookah
joram		hoppet
jorum	**6**	hussif
label	air-bed	ink-pot
laver	ash-bin	ice-box
leash	ash-can	ladder
light	awning	keeler
linen	basket	kit-bag
mural	beaker	kurkee
paper	bicker	locker
paten	bucket	log bin
patin	bunker	loofah
piano	bureau	lowboy
pouch	camera	mangle
purse	carafe	mirror
quill	carboy	mobile
quilt	carpet	napery
radio	carver	napkin
razor	casket	needle
scrip	castor	noggin
shade	cheval	oilcan
shelf	chowry	pallet
skeel	coffer	patera
slate	consol	patine
spill	cooker	pelmet
stall	cradle	pencil
stand	day-bed	piggin
stool	dishes	pillow
stoup	dosser	plaque
strop	drapet	pomade

posnet
pottle
pouffe
punkah
punnet
red ink
rocker
saddle
salver
scales
sconce
scovel
screen
settee
settle
shovel
shower
siphon
sponge
starch
string
syphon
tablet
teapot
tea set
tea urn
thread
throne
tiller
tin box
tinder
toy box
trevet
tripod
trivet
trophy
tureen
valise
wallet
window
wisket
zip-bag

7

adaptor
aerator
almirah
amphora
andiron
armoire
ash-tray
baggage
bath mat
bathtub
bedding
beeswax
bellows
blanket
blotter
bolster
brasier
brazier
broiler
bunk bed
cabinet
camp bed
canteen
cassone
chalice
chamois
chopper
cistern
cobiron
coir-mat
commode
compact
costrel
counter
cue-rack
cutlery
curtain
cushion
door-mat
down-bed
drapery
dresser

drugget
dustbin
dust-pan
epergne
flacket
flasket
fly-rail
fuse-box
gas-fire
gas ring
goggles
griddle
hair-oil
hammock
hassock
highboy
hip bath
holdall
horn-cup
ink-horn
knocker
lagging
lantern
lectern
lighter
matches
matting
monocle
netsuke
oil-lamp
ottoman
padlock
pannier
percher
pianino
pianola
picture
pillion
pin-case
playpen
pomatum
pottager
pot-hook

roaster
rundlet
rush-mat
saccule
sadiron
samovar
sampler
sand-box
satchel
scraper
shelves
shoebox
show-box
skimmer
soap-box
sofa-bed
steamer
stopper
stopple
syringe
tallboy
tambour
tankard
tea-cosy
tea-tray
tent-bed
thermos
thimble
tin-case
toaster
tobacco
tool kit
trammel
trolley
truckle
tumbler
tun-dish
twin bed
valance
wardian
wash-tub
what-not
whisket

wine-bag
woodcut
work-bag
workbox
wringer
yule-log

8

ale bench
angel bed
armchair
baluster
banister
barbecue
bar stool
bassinet
bed cover
bed linen
bed quilt
bedstaff
bedstead
bed-straw
bird-bath
bird-cage
bookcase
bookends
borachio
box chair
camp-bath
card-case
cashbook
cathedra
causeuse
cellaret
chair-bed
chattels
clay pipe
coat-hook
colander
coverlet
credenza
crockery
cupboard

curtains
cuspidor
decanter
demi-john
ditty-box
dog-chain
doorbell
doorknob
door-step
egg-timer
end table
endirons
eyeglass
fauteuil
field-bed
firewood
flock-bed
fly paper
foot-bath
fuse wire
gallipot
gasalier
handbell
hangings
hat-brush
hatstand
heirloom
hip flask
holdfast
inkstand
jalousie
knapsack
lamp-wick
lanthorn
latchkey
linoleum
lipstick
loo table
love seat
matchbox
mattress
nail-file
note-book

oak chest
oilcloth
ornament
penknife
pianette
pipe-rack
postcard
press-bed
quill-pen
radiator
recliner
reticule
road-book
saddlery
scissors
sea chest
shoehorn
shoelace
show-case
sink unit
sitz-bath
slop bowl
slop pail
snuffbox
snuffers
soap dish
speculum
spittoon
stair-rod
standish
steel pen
suitcase
sun-blind
table-mat
tabouret
tantalus
tape-line
tapestry
tea-board
tea-caddy
tea-chest
tea-cloth
tea-table

trencher
tridarne
triptych
tweezers
umbrella
vestiary
vestuary
wall-safe
wardrobe
watch-key
water bed
water-can
water-pot
water tap
wax cloth
wax light
wineskin
wireless

9

barometer
bathtowel
bedspread
black-jack
bookshelf
book-stand
boot-brush
bric-a-brac
cakestand
camp-chair
camp-stool
cane-chair
cantharus
card-table
carpet-bag
carpeting
case-knife
casserole
china bowl
chinaware
cigarette
clack-dish
clasplock

club chair
coffee-cup
coffee-pot
comb-brush
container
corkscrew
crumb-tray
cullender
cushionet
davenport
deck chair
devonport
directory
dishcloth
dish-clout
dish-cover
dog-basket
dog-collar
dog-kennel
double bed
dust-brush
dust-sheet
Dutch oven
easy chair
egg boiler
eiderdown
Empire bed
equipment
face towel
faldstool
fire-board
fire-brush
fire-grate
fire-guard
fire-irons
fireplace
fish-knife
fish-plate
flower-pot
food-mixer
foot-board
footstool
flying-pan

gas-burner
gas-cooker
gas-geyser
girandole
gold-plate
gout-stool
hairbrush
hair tonic
hall table
hand-towel
haversack
high chair
hope chest
horsewhip
housewife
ink-bottle
ink-holder
inventory
jack-towel
jewel case
kitchener
lamp-shade
lampstand
letter-box
light bulb
loving-cup
marquetry
master-key
mouse-trap
muffineer
music book
nail brush
newspaper
nick-nacks
nipperkin
notepaper
ornaments
paillasse
palliasse
paper clip
paper-rack
parchment
pepper-pot

perdonium
pewter pot
pier-glass
pier-table
piggy-bank
plate-rack
porringer
portfolio
port glass
pot-hanger
pot-pourri
pounce-box
powder-box
punchbowl
punkah-fan
quail-pipe
radiogram
rush-light
safety-pin
scrutoire
secretary
serviette
shakedown
shoe-brush
shower-cap
sideboard
side-chair
side-light
side-table
single bed
slop-basin
spin-drier
sponge-bag
sprinkler
stair rods
stamp-case
steel wool
stopwatch
string-box
sword-cane
table bell
table hook
table lamp

tableware
tea-kettle
telephone
timepiece
timetable
tinder-box
tin-opener
toothpick
underfelt
vanity-box
wall-clock
wallpaper
wall-light
wash-basin
wash-board
wash-stand
water-butt
water-tank
wax candle
wax polish
window-box
wine glass
wing chair
work table

10

air-cushion
alarm clock
alarm watch
bedclothes
biscuit-box
boot polish
broomstick
brown paper
buck-basket
bucket seat
cabbage net
calefactor
candelabra
canterbury
ceiling fan
chandelier
chessboard

chiffonier	hair lotion	saddle-bags
choir stall	hair pomade	salt-cellar
chopsticks	jardinière	scatter rug
clamp-irons	knife-board	sealing-wax
clothes peg	langesettle	secretaire
clothes pin	lead pencil	shower-bath
coal bucket	letter-rack	soda syphon
coal bunker	loose cover	spectacles
coat hanger	marking ink	spirit lamp
crumb-brush	musical box	stamp-album
crumb cloth	music-stand	stationery
curtain rod	music-stool	step-ladder
dandy-brush	napkin ring	strip light
deep-freeze	needle-book	tablecloth
disfurnish	needle-case	table linen
dishwasher	needlework	tablespoon
down pillow	night-light	television
dumb-waiter	nutcracker	time-keeper
elbow-chair	opera glass	time-switch
escritoire	overmantel	tobacco-jar
featherbed	pack-saddle	toilet roll
finger-bowl	pack-thread	toothbrush
fire-basket	paper-knife	toothpaste
fire-bucket	paper-stand	truckle-bed
fire-escape	pencil-case	trug-basket
firescreen	peppermill	trundlebed
fire-shovel	persian mat	typewriter
fish-basket	persian rug	upholstery
fish-carver	pewter dish	vapour-bath
fish-kettle	photograph	warming-pan
fish-trowel	pianoforte	wash basket
flesh-brush	piano stool	wassail-cup
floor-cloth	pile carpet	watch-chain
flower-bowl	pillowcase	watch-glass
fly-catcher	pillowslip	watch-guard
fly-swotter	pincushion	watch-light
foot-warmer	plate-glass	watch-stand
fourposter	pocket-book	window-seat
garbage-can	prayer-book	wine-bottle
gas-bracket	rattan-cane	wine-cooler
gas-lighter	razor-strop	work basket
gramophone	riding-whip	wrist-watch
grand piano	rolling-pin	

11

account book
address book
airing horse
alarum clock
alarum watch
attaché case
barrel chair
basket chair
bed-hangings
billiard-cue
bolster-case
book matches
boot-scraper
braising-pan
butter-print
butter-stamp
button-stick
candelabrum
candlestick
canopied bed
carver chair
centrepiece
chafing-dish
cheese board
cheval-glass
chiffonnier
clothes-hook
clothes-line
coal-scuttle
coffee table
coir-matting
colonial bed
counterpane
curtain hook
curtain rail
curtain ring
despatch-box
dining chair
dining-table
dinner-table
dispatch-box
dredging-box

dripping-pan
Dutch carpet
finger-glass
fire-lighter
first-aid box
floor polish
flour-dredge
foldaway bed
footcushion
foot-scraper
fountain-pen
gaming-table
garden chair
hearth brush
king-size bed
knick-knacks
lamp-chimney
leather case
linen basket
lounge chair
minute glass
minute watch
morris chair
mosquito-net
nut-crackers
ormolu clock
panelled bed
paper-basket
paperweight
picture-rail
pipe-lighter
pocket flask
pocket-glass
pocket-knife
porridge-pot
portmanteau
primus stove
pumice-stone
reading desk
reading lamp
roll-top desk
saddle-cloth
safety-razor

scuffle-cask
shaker chair
shopping bag
siphon-stand
slate-pencil
stair-carpet
straw pillow
studio couch
swivel chair
syphon-stand
table napkin
table-runner
tape-measure
tea-canister
thermometer
tin-lined box
tissue paper
tobacco pipe
toilet-cover
toilet-table
tooth-powder
vacuum flask
vinaigrette
waffle-irons
washing line
wash-leather
wassail-bowl
waste-basket
water heater
watering-can
watering-pot
window blind
wooden chair
writing-desk

12

adhesive tape
antimacassar
bedside light
bedside table
blotting book
boston rocker
bottle-opener

bottom drawer
bucking stool
camp-bedstead
candleholder
candle-sconce
carpet beater
chaise longue
chesterfield
china cabinet
churchwarden
clothes-brush
clothes drier
clothes-horse
console table
cottage piano
cup and saucer
despatch-case
dessert-spoon
dispatch-case
dressing-case
drinking-horn
Dutch dresser
electric bulb
electric fire
electric iron
electric lamp
fan regulator
field-glasses
fish-strainer
flour-dredger
flower-basket
folding chair
folding stool
gate-leg table
gladstone bag
Grecian couch
hot-water tank
bubble-bubble
ironing board
ironing table
judgment-seat
kitchen table
kneehole desk

knife-cleaner
leather chair
library table
looking-glass
lucifer match
milking stool
nail-scissors
nursing chair
nutmeg-grater
opera-glasses
packing cloth
packing paper
packing sheet
paraffin lamp
picnic basket
picnic hamper
playing cards
porridge-bowl
postage stamp
queen-size bed
reading glass
record-player
refrigerator
roasting-rack
rocking chair
rocking horse
slant-top desk
slope top desk
standard lamp
straw bolster
sweating-bath
table lighter
table service
tallow-candle
tape recorder
thermos flask
tin-lined case
toasting fork
tobacco pouch
toilette case
trestle table
turkey carpet
visitors' book

upright piano
walking-staff
walking stick
washing board
water pitcher
Welsh dresser
wicker basket
Windsor chair
wine decanter
writing table
writing paper

13

bentwood chair
billiard balls
billiard table
blotting paper
captain's chair
carpet sweeper
chopping block
chopping knife
cribbage board
double dresser
dressing-table
drinks cabinet
drop-leaf table
electric clock
electric stove
feather pillow
feeding bottle
filing cabinet
florence flask
folding screen
four-poster bed
liquor cabinet
medicine glass
mirror cabinet
netting needle
newspaper rack
packing needle
pedestal table
Pembroke table
Persian blinds

Persian carpet
petrol-lighter
ping-pong table
quizzing-glass
razor-stropper
roulette table
sewing-machine
Sheraton chair
smoothing-iron
sounding-board
straight chair
straw mattress
styptic pencil
turnover table
umbrella stand
vacuum cleaner
visiting-cards
washhand-stand
window curtain
witney blanket

14

anglepoise lamp
billiard marker
chamber-hanging
chest-of-drawers
cocktail-shaker
corner cupboard
eiderdown quilt
electric cooker
electric geyser
electric kettle
feather bolster
glove-stretcher
hot water bottle
kitchen dresser
meerschaum pipe
panel-back chair
Queen-Anne chair
reclining chair
tobacco stopper
Venetian blinds
washing machine

wheel-back chair

15

cocktail cabinet
convertible sofa
electric blanket
feather mattress
garden furniture
gate-legged table
Japanese lantern
knitting needles
ladder-back chair
mosquito curtain
pestle and mortar
photograph album
photograph frame

16

pneumatic pillow
upholstered chair

Furniture Terms

3

ear

4

bail
bulb
husk
ogee
swag

5

apron
bevel
bombe
cleat
dowel
frets
gesso

inlay
loper
ovolo
shell
skirt
splat
squab
stile

6

daiper
figure
fillet
finial
fly-leg
frieze
lining
muntin
ormolu
patera
patina
plinth
rebate
runner
scroll
veneer
volute

7

amorini
banding
beading
blister
bun foot
carcase
castors
chamfer
cornice
en suite
fluting
gallery
hipping
lozenge

lunette
pad foot
paw foot
reeding
roundel
saltire
tambour
turning

8

acanthus
arcading
astragal
baluster
bow foot
cabochan
dovetail
hoop back
lion mask
moulding
pediment
pie crust
pilaster
ram's head
sabre leg
sunburst
swan-neck
terminal
wainscot

9

anthemion
arabesque
blind fret
cameo back
cartouche
drop front
fall front
guilloche
linenfold
marquetry
medallion
parquetry

rule joint
shoe-piece
spade foot
spoon back
strapwork
stretcher
striation
stringing

10

boulle work
break-front
egg-and-dart
escutcheon
gadrooning
key pattern
ladder back
mitre joint
monopodium
quartering
serpentine
shield-back
under-brace

11

ball-and-claw
balloon back
bracket foot
cabriole leg
chip-carving
cockbeading
cup-and-cover
latticework
spiral twist

12

cresting rail
dished corner
fielded panel
oyster veneer

13

bobbin turning

column turning

14

broken pediment

15

channel moulding
mortise-and-tenon

16

barley-sugar twist

Kitchen Utensils, Requisites and Tableware

3

bin
can
cup
hob
jar
jug
lid
mop
mug
pan
pot
tap
tin
tub
urn
wok

4

bowl
coal
cosy
dish
ewer

fork
grid
hook
iron
lard
mill
oven
pail
peel
rack
salt
sink
soap
soda
spit
suet
trap
tray

5

airer
bahut
basin
besom
board
broom
broth
brush
caddy
china
chope
churn
cover
crock
cruet
doily
dough
drier
flour
flute
glass
grate
grill

gruel
hatch
herbs
jelly
joint
knife
ladle
match
mixer
mould
paste
pelle
plate
poker
press
range
russe
sauce
scoop
shelf
sieve
spice
spoon
steel
stock
stove
straw
sugar
table
timer
tongs
towel
whisk
wiper
yeast

6

ash-pan
basket
beaker
beater
boiler
bottle

bucket
burner
butter
candle
carafe
carver
caster
cloche
cooker
cooler
crible
cupful
diable
drawer
duster
eggbox
eggcup
fender
filter
flagon
funnel
gas-jet
geyser
goblet
gradin
grater
grease
haybox
heater
ice-box
jugful
juicer
kettle
larder
mangle
mincer
mortar
muslin
pantry
pastry
pepper
pestle
pichet

pickle
pitter
poelon
polish
pot-lid
posnet
primus
recipe
salver
saucer
scales
shaker
shears
shovel
sifter
siphon
skewer
slicer
starch
string
tajine
tea-cup
tea-pot
tea-urn
toupin
trivet
tureen

vessel

7

alembic
attelet
basting
blender
bluebag
broiler
butlery
caisses
cake-tin
cambrel
canteen
chinois
chip pan

chopper
coal-bin
coal-box
cocotte
cuisine
cutlery
dishmat
dishmop
drainer
dredger
dresser
dust-bin
dust-pan
ecuelle
freezer
griller
grinder
infuser
kneader
kneeler
marmite
milk-jug
panikin
pie-dish
pitcher
platter
potager
ramekin
rondeau
sapples
saltbox
samovar
scuffle
seether
skillet
skimmer
spatula
steamer
stew-pan
syringe
tat-vin
tea-cosy
tea-tray

terrine
toaster
tumbler
vinegar
wash-tub

8

bread bin
canister
caquelon
cauldron
clapdish
colander
covercle
cream-jug
crepe pan
crockery
cupboard
daubiere
dish rack
egg-slice
eggspoon
egg timer
eggwhisk
fish fork
flan ring
flat-iron
gas stove
gridiron
hotplate
matchbox
mazagran
meatsafe
mouvette
oilcloth
oilstove
patty pan
saucepan
saute pan
scissors
shoe box
slop bowl
stockpot

strainer
tart ring
taste-vin
tea caddy
teacloth
teaplate
teaspoon
trencher
water jug

9

alcarraza
autoclave
bain-marie
baking tin
cafetiere
can opener
casserole
chinaware
coffee-cup
coffee pot
compotier
corkscrew
crumb tray
decoupoir
dishcloth
dish cover
egg beater
egg boiler
firegrate
fire-irons
fireplace
fish-knife
fish-plate
fish-slice
flue brush
frying-pan
gas burner
gas cooker
gas geyser
gravy boat
kilner jar
mandoline

mijoteuse
muffineer
pastry bag
pepper-box
pepper-pot
piping bag
plate-rack
porringer
ring mould
salad bowl
sauceboat
sharpener
slop basin
soupspoon
steak batt
sugar bowl
tea kettle
tin opener
tisaniere
tourtiere
wineglass

10

apple corer
biscuit box
bread board
bread knife
broomstick
butter dish
caissettes
chopsticks
coffee mill
cook's knife
cruet stand
dipping pin
dishwasher
egg poacher
fish carver
fish kettle
floor cloth
flour crock
gas lighter
ice freezer

jelly mould
knife board
liquidizer
milk boiler
mustard pot
pan scourer
pepper mill
percolator
rolling pin
rotisserie
salamander
salt cellar
salting tub
slow cooker
sterilizer
tablecloth
tablespoon
waffle iron

11

baking sheet
braising pan
bread grater
butter knife
candissoire
chafing dish
cheesecloth
coalscuttle
coffee maker
dinner plate
dough trough
dripping pan
flour dredge
fruit stoner
gargoulette
jambonniere
meat chopper
nutcrackers
paring knife
pastry brush
pastry wheel
porridge pot
pudding bowl

serving dish
sugar dredge
tea canister
thermometer
water filter
yogurt-maker

12

breakfast-cup
carving knife
deep-fat fryer
dessertspoon
double boiler
fishstrainer
flour dredger
hot cupboard
ironing board
kitchen range
knife cleaner
knife machine
measuring cup
measuring jug

nutmeg grater
palette knife
pastry cutter
porridge bowl
potato masher
potato peeler
pudding basin
pudding cloth
refrigerator
thermos flask
toasting fork
turbot kettle

13

butcher's block
chopping board
coffee grinder
food processor
ice-cream maker
kitchen scales
larding needle
lemon squeezer

microwave oven
preserving jar
saccharometer
saucepan brush
vegetable dish
water softener

14

crockery washer
fuelless cooker
galvanized pail
juice extractor
kneading trough
knife sharpener
mincing machine
pressure cooker
scrubbing brush
trussing needle

15

meat-carving tongs
vegetable cutter

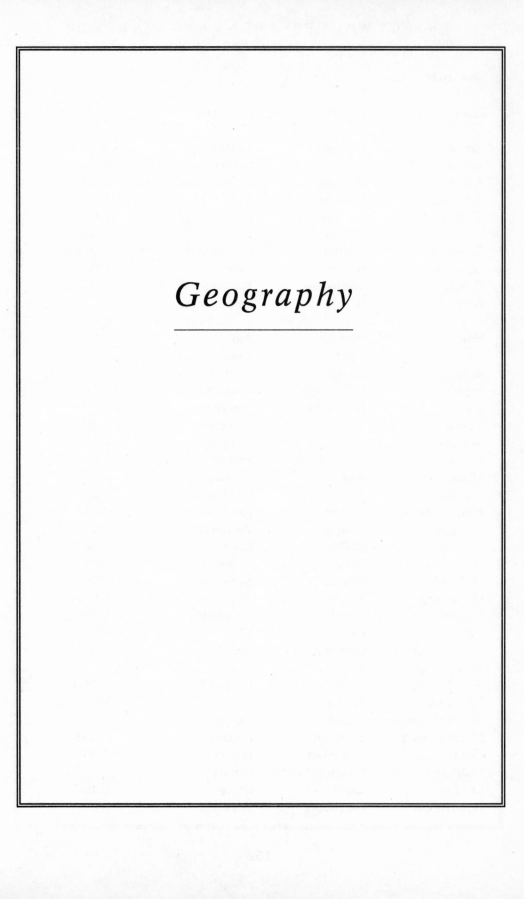

Geography

American States

State	Capital	Nickname	Abbreviation
Alabama	Montgomery	Cotton	ALA
Alaska	Juneau	Last Frontier	ALAS
Arizona	Phoenix	Grand Canyon	ARIZ
Arkansas	Little Rock	Land of Opportunity	ARK
California	Sacramento	Golden	CAL
Colorado	Denver	Centennial	COLO
Connecticut	Hartford	Constitution	CONN
Delaware	Dover	First	DEL
Florida	Tallahassee	Sunshine	FLA
Georgia	Atlanta	Empire State of the South	GA
Hawaii	Honolulu	Aloha	HA
Idaho	Boise	Gem	IDA
Illinois	Springfield	Land of Lincoln	ILL
Indiana	Indianapolis	Hoosier	IND
Iowa	Des Moines	Hawkeye	IA
Kansas	Topeka	Sunflower	KAN
Kentucky	Frankfort	Bluegrass	KY
Louisiana	Baton Rouge	Pelican	LA
Maine	Augusta	Pine Tree	ME
Maryland	Annapolis	Old Line	MD
Massachusetts	Boston	Bay	MASS
Michigan	Lansing	Wolverine	MICH
Minnesota	St. Paul	Gopher	MINN
Mississippi	Jackson	Magnolia	MISS
Missouri	Jefferson City	Show Me	MO
Montana	Helena	Treasure	MONT
Nebraska	Lincoln	Cornhusker	NEBR
Nevada	Carson City	Silver	NEV
New Hampshire	Concord	Granite	NH
New Jersey	Trenton	Garden	NJ
New Mexico	Santa Fe	Land of Enchantment	N MEX
New York	Albany	Empire	NY
North Carolina	Raleigh	Tarheel	NC
North Dakota	Bismarck	Flickertail	NDAK
Ohio	Columbus	Buckeye	OH
Oklahoma	Oklahoma City	Sooner	OKLA
Oregon	Salem	Beaver	OREG
Pennsylvania	Harrisburg	Keystone	PA

State	Capital	Nickname	Abbreviation
Rhode Island	Providence	Ocean	RI
South Carolina	Columbia	Palmetto	SC
South Dakota	Pierre	Sunshine	S DAK
Tennessee	Nashville	Volunteer	TENN
Texas	Austin	Lone Star	TEX
Utah	Salt Lake City	Beehive	UT
Vermont	Montpelier	Green Mountain	VT
Virginia	Richmond	Old Dominion	VA
Washington	Olympia	Evergreen	WASH
West Virginia	Charleston	Mountain	W VA
Wisconsin	Madison	Badger	WIS
Wyoming	Cheyenne	Equality	WYO

Capital Cities

Capital	Country
Abu Dhabi	United Arab Emirates
Abuja	Nigeria
Accra	Ghana
Addis Ababa	Ethiopia
Aden	Yemen
Agana	Guam
Ajman	Ajman
Algiers	Algeria
Amman	Jordan
Amsterdam	Netherlands
Andorra la Vella	Andorra
Ankara	Turkey
Antananarivo	Madagascar
Apia	Western Samoa
Ashkhabad (or Ashgabat)	Turkmenistan
Asmara	Eritrea
Astana	Kazakhstan
Asuncion	Paraguay
Athens	Greece
Baghdad	Iraq
Baku	Azerbaijan
Bamako	Mali
Bandar Seri Begawan	Brunei

Capital	Country
Bangkok	Thailand
Bangui	Central African Republic
Banjul	The Gambia
Basseterre	Saint Kitts and Nevis
Beijing	China
Beirut	Lebanon
Belgrade	Yugoslavia
Belmopan	Belize
Berlin	Germany
Bern	Switzerland
Bishkek	Kyrgyzstan
Bissau	Guinea-Bissau
Bogota	Columbia
Brasilia	Brazil
Bratislava	Slovakia
Brazzaville	Congo-Brazzaville
Bridgetown	Barbados
Brunei	Brunei
Brussels	Belgium
Bucharest	Romania
Budapest	Hungary
Buenos Aires	Argentina
Bujumbura	Burundi
Cairo	Egypt
Canberra	Australia
Cape Town	South Africa
Caracas	Venezuela
Castries	Saint Lucia
Chisinau	Moldova
Colombo	Sri Lanka
Conakry	Guinea
Copenhagen	Denmark
Dacca	Bangladesh
Dakar	Senegal
Dalap-Uliga-Darrit	Marshall Islands
Damascus	Syria
Dhaka	Bangladesh
Djibouti	Djibouti
Dodoma	Tanzania
Doha	Qatar
Douglas	Isle of Man

Capital	Country
Dublin	Ireland, Republic of
Dushanbe	Tajikstan
Fongafale	Tuvalu
Freetown	Sierra Leone
Gaborone	Botswana
Georgetown	Guyana
Guatemala City	Guatemala
Hanoi	Vietnam
Harare	Zimbabwe
Havana	Cuba
Helsinki	Finland
Hobart	Tasmania
Honiara	Solomon Islands
Islamabad	Pakistan
Jakarta	Indonesia
Jerusalem	Israel
Kabul	Afghanistan
Kampala	Uganda
Kathmandu	Nepal
Khartoum	Sudan
Kiev	Ukraine
Kigali	Rwanda
Kingston	Jamaica
Kingstown	Saint Vincent and the Grenadines
Kinshasa	Congo, Democratic Republic of
Kishinev	Moldova
Koror	Belau
Kuala Lumpur	Malaysia
Kuwait City	Kuwait
Lagos	Nigeria
La Paz	Bolivia
Lefkosia	Cyprus
Libreville	Gabon
Lilongwe	Malawi
Lima	Peru
Lisbon	Portugal
Ljubljana	Slovenia
Lome	Togo
London	United Kingdom
Luanda	Angola
Lusaka	Zambia

Capital	Country
Luxembourg	Luxembourg
Madrid	Spain
Macao	Macao
Majuro	Marshall Islands
Malabo	Equatorial Guinea
Male	Maldives
Managua	Nicaragua
Manama	Bahrain
Manila	Philippines
Maputo	Mozambique
Maseru	Lesotho
Masquat	Oman
Mbabane	Swaziland
Mexico City	Mexico
Minsk	Belarus
Mogadishu	Somalia
Monaco	Monaco
Monrovia	Liberia
Montevideo	Uruguay
Moroni	Comoros Islands
Moscow	Russia
Muscat	Oman
Nairobi	Kenya
Nassau	Bahamas
N'Djamena	Chad
New Delhi	India
Naimey	Niger
Nicosia	Cyprus
Nouakchott	Mauritania
Nuku'alofa	Tonga
Oslo	Norway
Ottawa	Canada
Ougadougou	Burkina Faso
Palikir	Micronesia
Panama City	Panama
Paramaribo	Suriname
Paris	France
Peking	China
Phnom Penh	Cambodia
Plymouth	Monserrat
Port-au-Prince	Haiti

Capital	Country
Port Vila	Vanuatu
Port Louis	Mauritius
Port Moresby	Papua New Guinea
Port of Spain	Trinidad and Tobago
Porto-Novo	Benin
Prague	Czech Republic
Praia	Cape Verde
Pretoria	South Africa
Pyongyang	North Korea
Quito	Ecuador
Rabat	Morocco
Rangoon	Burma
Reykjavik	Iceland
Riga	Latvia
Riyadh	Saudi Arabia
Rome	Italy
Roseau	Dominica
St George's	Grenada
St Helier	Jersey
St Peter Port	Guernsey
Saint John's	Antigua and Barbuda
Sana'a	Yemen
San Jose	Costa Rica
San Marino	San Marino
San Salvador	El Salvador
Santiago	Chile
Santo Domingo	Dominican Republic
Sao Tome	Sao Tome and Principe
Sarajevo	Bosnia and Herzegovina
Seoul	South Korea
Singapore	Singapore
Skopje	Macedonia
Sofia	Bulgaria
Stanley	Falkland Islands
Stockholm	Sweden
Sucre	Bolivia
Suva	Fiji
Taipei	Taiwan
Tallinn	Estonia
Tarawa	Kiribati
Tashkent	Uzbekistan

Capital	Country
Tblisi	Georgia
Tegucigalpa	Honduras
Tehran	Iran
Thimphu (or Thimbu)	Bhutan
Tirana (or Tirane)	Albania
Tokyo	Japan
Tripoli	Libya
Tunis	Tunisia
Ulaanbaatar (or Ulan Bator)	Mongolia
Vaduz	Liechtenstein
Valetta	Malta
Vatican City	Vatican City State
Victoria	Seychelles
Vienna	Austria
Vientiane	Laos
Vila	Vanuatu
Vilnius	Lithuania
Warsaw	Poland
Washington D.C.	United States of America
Wellington	New Zealand
Windhoek	Namibia
Yamoussoukro	Ivory Coast (Cote d'Ivoire)
Yangon	Myanmar
Yaounde	Cameroon
Yaren	Nauru
Yerevan	Armenia
Zagreb	Croatia
Zomba	Malawi

Former Names of Capital and Major Cities

Current Name	Former Name(s) (most recent first)
Almaty	Alma-ata
	Verny
Antananarivo	Tananarive
Astana	Akmola
Bander Seri Begawan	Brunei Town
Banjul	Bathurst
Beijing (or Peking)	Pei-P'ing (or Beibing)

Current Name	Former Name(s) (most recent first)
	Ta-Tu
Bishkek (or Pishpek)	Frunze
Bogota	Bacata
Bujumbura	Usumbura
Cairo	El Qahira
	El Fustat
Caracas de Caracas	Santiago de Leon
Charlotte Amalie	Saint Thomas
Constantine	Cirta
Dhaka	Dacca
Dnepropetrovsk	Ekaterinoslav
Donetsk	Stalino
	Yuzovka
Dun Laoghaire	Kingstown
	Dunleary
Dushanbe	Stalinabad
	Dyushambe
Ekaterinburg	Sverdlovsk
East London	Port Rex
Faisalabad	Lyallpur
Fort-de-France	Fort Royal
Gaberone	Gaberones
Harare	Salisbury
Ho Chi Minh City	Saigon
Istanbul	Constantinople
	Byzantium
Izmar	Smyrna
Jakarta	Batavia
Kanpur	Cawnpore
Kinshasa	Leopoldville
Kirov	Vyatka
Koror	Corrora
Luanda	Sao Paulo de Loanda
Malabo	Santa Isabel
Maputo	Lourenco Marques
Mexico City	Tenochtitlan
Montreal	Ville-Marie
Mumbai	Bombay
Naberezhnye Chelny	Breshnev
	Chelny
Naples	Neapolis

Current Name	Former Name(s) (most recent first)
N'djamena	Fort Lamy
Nizhny Novgorod	Gorky (or Gorki)
Noumea	Port-de-France
Nuuk	Godthaab
Ottawa	Bytown
Oslo	Kristiania
Pago Pago	Pango Pango
Palikir	Kolonia
Perm	Molotov
Samara	Kuybyshev
Santo Domingo	Ciudad Trujillo
Sofia	Serdica
St Petersburg	Leningrad
	Petrograd
T'blisi	Tiflis
Thessaloniki	Salonika
	Thessalonica
Tokyo	Edo
Tripoli	Oea
Ujang Pandang	Macassar (or Makasar)
Ulaanbaatar	Urga
Vadodara	Baroda
Volgograd	Stalingrad
	Tsaritsyn

Towns and Cities in the United Kingdom

England

3

Ely
Eye
Rye
Wem

4

Bath
Bray
Bude

Bury
Clun
Deal
Diss
Eton
Holt
Hove
Hull
Hyde
Ince
Leek
Looe
Lydd

Ross
Ryde
Shap
Ware
Wark
Yarm
York

5

Acton
Alton
Bacup
Blyth

Bourn
Calne
Chard
Cheam
Colne
Cowes
Crewe
Derby
Dover
Egham
Epsom
Filey
Fowey

Frome	Bognor	Neston	Witney
Goole	Bolton	Newark	Wooler
Hawes	Bootle	Newent	Yeovil
Hedon	Boston	Newlyn	
Hurst	Bruton	Newton	**7**
Hythe	Bungay	Norham	Alnwick
Leeds	Burton	Oakham	Andover
Leigh	Buxton	Oldham	Appleby
Lewes	Castor	Ormsby	Arundel
Louth	Cobham	Ossett	Ashford
Luton	Cromer	Oundle	Aylsham
March	Darwen	Oxford	Bampton
Olney	Dudley	Penryn	Banbury
Otley	Durham	Pewsey	Barking
Poole	Ealing	Pinner	Beccles
Reeth	Eccles	Pudsey	Bedford
Ripon	Epping	Putney	Belford
Risca	Exeter	Ramsey	Berwick
Rugby	Goring	Redcar	Bewdley
Sarum	Hanley	Ripley	Bexhill
Selby	Harlow	Romney	Bickley
Stoke	Harrow	Romsey	Bilston
Stone	Havant	Rugely	Bourton
Tebay	Henley	Seaham	Bowfell
Thame	Hexham	Seaton	Brandon
Tring	Howden	Selsey	Bristol
Truro	Ilford	Settle	Brixham
Wells	Ilkley	Snaith	Bromley
Wigan	Ilsley	St Ives	Burnham
	Jarrow	Strood	Burnley
6	Kendal	Stroud	Burslem
Alford	Leyton	Sutton	Caistor
Alston	London	Thirsk	Catford
Ashton	Ludlow	Thorne	Cawston
Barnet	Lynton	Totnes	Charing
Barrow	Lytham	Walton	Chatham
Barton	Maldon	Watton	Cheadle
Batley	Malton	Weston	Chedder
Battle	Marlow	Whitby	Chesham
Bawtry	Masham	Widnes	Chester
Bedale	Morley	Wigton	Chorley
Belper	Naseby	Wilton	Clacton
Bodmin	Nelson	Witham	Clifton

Crawley	Molesey	Taunton	Bromyard
Croydon	Moreton	Telford	Broseley
Darsley	Morpeth	Tenbury	Camborne
Datchet	Mossley	Tetbury	Carlisle
Dawlish	Newbury	Thaxted	Caterham
Devises	Newport	Tilbury	Chertsey
Dorking	Norwich	Torquay	Clevedon
Douglas	Oldbury	Twyford	Clovelly
Dunster	Overton	Ventnor	Coventry
Elstree	Padstow	Walsall	Crediton
Enfield	Penrith	Waltham	Daventry
Everton	Poulton	Wantage	Debenham
Evesham	Prescot	Wareham	Dedworth
Exmouth	Preston	Warwick	Deptford
Fareham	Rainham	Watchet	Dewsbury
Farnham	Reading	Watford	Egremont
Feltham	Redhill	Wembley	Eversley
Glossop	Redruth	Wickwar	Fakenham
Gosport	Reigate	Winslow	Falmouth
Grimsby	Retford	Winster	Foulness
Halifax	Romford	Wisbeck	Grantham
Hampton	Rossall	Worksop	Grantown
Harwich	Royston		Hadleigh
Haworth	Runcorn	*8*	Hailsham
Helston	Salford	Abingdon	Halstead
Heywood	Saltash	Alfreton	Hastings
Hitchin	Sandown	Alnmouth	Hatfield
Honiton	Saxelby	Amesbury	Helmsley
Hornsea	Seaford	Ampthill	Hereford
Hornsey	Shifnal	Axbridge	Herne Bay
Horsham	Shipley	Aycliffe	Hertford
Ipswich	Shipton	Bakewell	Hinckley
Ixworth	Silloth	Barnsley	Holbeach
Keswick	Skipton	Berkeley	Hunmanby
Kington	Spilsby	Beverley	Ilkeston
Lancing	Staines	Bicester	Keighley
Langton	Stilton	Bideford	Kingston
Ledbury	St Neots	Bolsover	Lavenham
Leyburn	Sudbury	Brackley	Lechlade
Lincoln	Sunbury	Bradford	Liskeard
Malvern	Swanage	Brampton	Longtown
Margate	Swindon	Bridport	Lynmouth
Matlock	Swinton	Brighton	Maryport

Midhurst	Thetford	Clitheroe	Maidstone
Minehead	Thornaby	Congleton	Mansfield
Nantwich	Tiverton	Cranborne	Middleton
Newhaven	Tunstall	Cranbrook	Newcastle
Nuneaton	Uckfield	Crewkerne	Newmarket
Ormskirk	Uxbridge	Cricklade	New Romney
Oswestry	Wallasey	Cuckfield	Northwich
Penzance	Wallsend	Dartmouth	Otterburn
Pershore	Wanstead	Devonport	Pembridge
Peterlee	Westbury	Doncaster	Penistone
Petworth	Wetheral	Donington	Penkridge
Pevensey	Wetherby	Droitwich	Penyghent
Plaistow	Weymouth	Dronfield	Pickering
Plymouth	Woodford	Dungeness	Rochester
Ramsgate	Woolwich	Dunstable	Rotherham
Redditch	Worthing	Ellesmere	Salisbury
Richmond	Yarmouth	Faversham	Saltfleet
Ringwood		Fleetwood	Sevenoaks
Rochdale	_9_	Gateshead	Sheerness
Rothbury	Aldeburgh	Godalming	Sheffield
Saltburn	Aldershot	Gravesend	Sherborne
Sandgate	Allendale	Greenwich	Smethwick
Sandwich	Alresford	Grinstead	Southgate
Sedbergh	Ambleside	Guildford	Southport
Shanklin	Ashbourne	Harrogate	Southwell
Shelford	Ashburton	Haslemere	Southwold
Shipston	Avonmouth	Haverhill	Starcross
Sidmouth	Aylesbury	Hawkhurst	St Austell
Skegness	Blackburn	Holmfirth	Stevenage
Sleaford	Blackpool	Ilchester	Stockport
Southend	Blandford	Immingham	Stokesley
Spalding	Blisworth	Kettering	Stourport
Stafford	Bracknell	King's Lynn	Stratford
St Albans	Braintree	Kingswear	Tarporley
Stamford	Brentford	Lambourne	Tavistock
Stanhope	Brentwood	Lancaster	Tenterden
Stanwell	Brighouse	Leicester	Tonbridge
St Helens	Broughton	Lichfield	Towcester
Stockton	Cambridge	Liverpool	Tynemouth
Stratton	Carnforth	Longridge	Ulverston
Surbiton	Castleton	Lowestoft	Upminster
Swaffham	Chesilton	Lyme Regis	Uppingham
Tamworth	Chingford	Lymington	Uttoxeter

Wainfleet
Wakefield
Warkworth
Weybridge
Whernside
Whithaven
Wimbledon
Wincanton
Wokingham
Woodstock
Worcester
Wymondham

10

Accrington
Aldborough
Altrincham
Barnstaple
Bedlington
Bellingham
Billericay
Birkenhead
Birmingham
Bridgnorth
Bridgwater
Bromsgrove
Broxbourne
Buckingham
Canterbury
Carshalton
Chelmsford
Cheltenham
Chichester
Chippenham
Chulmleigh
Coggeshall
Colchester
Cullompton
Darlington
Dorchester
Dukinfield
Eastbourne
Eccleshall

Farningham
Folkestone
Freshwater
Gillingham
Gloucester
Halesworth
Hartlepool
Haslingdon
Heathfield
Horncastle
Hornchurch
Hungerford
Hunstanton
Huntingdon
Ilfracombe
Kenilworth
Kingsclere
Kirkoswald
Launceston
Leamington
Leominster
Littleport
Maidenhead
Malmesbury
Manchester
Mexborough
Micheldean
Middlewich
Mildenhall
Nailsworth
Nottingham
Okehampton
Orfordness
Pangbourne
Patrington
Peacehaven
Pontefract
Portishead
Portsmouth
Potter's Bar
Ravenglass
Rockingham
Saxmundham

Shepperton
Sheringham
Shrewsbury
Stalbridge
St Leonards
Stowmarket
Sunderland
Teddington
Teignmouth
Tewkesbury
Thamesmead
Torrington
Trowbridge
Twickenham
Walsingham
Warminster
Warrington
Washington
Wednesbury
Wellington
Westward Ho
Whitchurch
Whitstable
Whittlesey
Willenhall
Winchelsea
Winchester
Windermere
Windlesham
Wirksworth
Withernsea
Woodbridge
Workington

11

Basingstoke
Bearminster
Bognor Regis
Bournemouth
Bridlington
Buntingford
Cleethorpes
Cockermouth

East Retford
Glastonbury
Great Marlow
Guisborough
Haltwhistle
Hampton Wick
Hatherleigh
High Wycombe
Ingatestone
Leytonstone
Littlestone
Ludgershall
Lutterworth
Mablethorpe
Manningtree
Market Rasen
Marlborough
Much Wenlock
New Brighton
Newton Abbot
Northampton
Petersfield
Pocklington
Rawtenstall
Scarborough
Shaftesbury
Southampton
South Molton
Stalybridge
St Margaret's
Stourbridge
Tattershall
Wallingford
Walthamstow
Westminster
Whitechurch
Woodhall Spa

12

Attleborough
Bexhill-on-Sea
Castle Rising
Chesterfield

Christchurch
Gainsborough
Great Grimsby
Great Malvern
Huddersfield
Ingleborough
Long Stratton
Loughborough
Macclesfield
Milton Keynes
Morecambe Bay
North Berwick
North Shields
North Walsham
Peterborough
Shoeburyness
Shottesbrook
South Shields
Stoke-on-Trent

13

Barnard Castle
Berkhampstead
Bishop's Castle
Boroughbridge
Brightlingsea
Burton-on-Trent
Bury St Edmunds
Chipping Ongar
Finchampstead
Godmanchester
Great Yarmouth
Higham Ferrers
Kidderminster
Kirkby Stephen
Knaresborough
Littlehampton
Lytham St Annes
Market Deeping
Market Drayton
Melcombe Regis
Melton Mowbray
Middlesbrough

Northallerton
Saffron Walden
Shepton Mallet
Wolverhampton
Wootton Basset

14

Berwick-on-Tweed
Bishop Auckland
Bishops Waltham
Chipping Barnet
Chipping Norton
Hemel Hempstead
Kirkby Lonsdale
Market Bosworth
Mortimer's Cross
Stockton-on-Tees
Stony Stratford
Sutton Courtney
Tunbridge Wells
Wellingborough
West Hartlepool

15+

Ashton-under-Lyne
Barrow-in-Furness
Bishop's Stortford
Burnham-on-Crouch
Castle Donington
Leighton Buzzard
Newcastle-on-Tyne
St Leonards-on-Sea
Stratford-on-Avon
Sutton Coldfield
Welwyn Garden City
Weston-Super-Mare

Northern Ireland

5

Doagh
Glynn
Keady
Larne
Newry
Omagh
Toome

6

Antrim
Armagh
Augher
Bangor
Belcoo
Beragh
Comber
Lurgan
Raphoe

7

Belfast
Belleek
Caledon
Clogher
Crumlin
Dervock
Dromore
Finaghy
Fintona
Gilford

Glenarm
Kilkeel
Lisburn
Pomeroy

8

Ahoghill
Annalong
Dungiven
Hilltown
Holywood
Limavady
Portrush
Strabane
Trellick

9

Ballintra
Ballymena
Ballymore
Ballynure
Banbridge
Bushmills
Carnlough
Coleraine
Cookstown
Craigavon
Cushendun
Dungannon
Kircubbin
Lisnaskea
Moneymore
Newcastle
Portadown
Rasharkin
Rostrevor
Tandragee
Tovermore

10

Aldergrove
Aughnacloy
Ballyclare

Ballygowan
Ballymoney
Ballyroney
Castlederg
Coalisland
Cushendall
Donaghadee
Markethill
Portaferry
Saintfield
Strangford
Tanderagee

11

Ballycastle
Ballygawley
Carrickmore
Crossmaglen
Downpatrick
Draperstown
Enniskillen
Londonderry
Magherafelt
Newtownards
Portglenone
Portstewart
Randlestown
Rathfriland
Warrenpoint

12

Ballyhalbert
Ballynahinch
Castle Dawson
Castlewellan
Fivemiletown
Hillsborough
Stewartstown

13

Brooke-Borough
Carrickfergus
Crawfordsburn

Derrygonnelly

14

Newtown
Stewart

Scotland

3

Ayr
Uig

4

Alva
Barr
Duns
Elie
Kirn
Luss
Nigg
Oban
Reay
Rona
Stow
Wick

5

Alloa
Annan
Appin
Avoch
Ayton
Banff
Beith
Brora
Bunaw
Busby
Ceres
Clova
Clune
Crail
Cupar
Denny

Downe
Elgin
Ellon
Errol
Fyvie
Govan
Insch
Islay
Keiss
Keith
Kelso
Lairg
Largo
Leith
Nairn
Perth
Salen
Troon

6

Aboyne
Alford
Barvas
Beauly
Bervie
Biggar
Bo' ness
Buckie
Carron
Cawdor
Comrie
Crieff
Cullen
Culter
Dollar
Drymen
Dunbar
Dundee
Dunlop
Dunnet
Dunoon
Dysart
Edzell

Findon
Forfar
Forres
Girvan
Glamis
Hawick
Huntly
Irvine
Killin
Kilmun
Lanark
Lauder
Leslie
Linton
Lochee
Meigle
Moffat
Pladda
Reston
Rhynie
Rosyth
Rothes
Shotts
Thurso
Tongue
Wishaw
Yarrow

7

Airdrie
Balfron
Balloch
Banavie
Bowmore
Braemar
Brechin
Brodick
Canobie
Cantyre
Carbost
Cargill
Carluke
Crathie

Culross
Cumnock
Denholm
Douglas
Dunkeld
Dunning
Evanton
Fairlie
Falkirk
Galston
Gifford
Glasgow
Glencoe
Golspie
Gourock
Granton
Guthrie
Halkirk
Kenmore
Kessock
Kilmory
Kilsyth
Kinross
Kintore
Lamlash
Larbert
Lybster
Macduff
Maybole
Meldrum
Melrose
Melvich
Methven
Milmuir
Monikie
Muthill
Newport
Paisley
Peebles
Polmont
Poolewe
Portree
Portsoy

Renfrew
Saddell
Sarclet
Scourie
Selkirk
Stanley
Strathy
Tarbert
Tarland
Tayport
Tranent
Tundrum
Turriff
Ullster
Yetholm

8

Aberdeen
Aberlady
Abington
Arbroath
Armadale
Arrochar
Auldearn
Ballater
Banchory
Barrhill
Beattock
Blantyre
Burghead
Canisby
Carnwath
Creetown
Cromarty
Dakeith
Dalmally
Dingwall
Dirleton
Dufftown
Dumfries
Dunbeath
Dunblane
Dunscore

Earlston
Eyemouth
Findhorn
Fortrose
Giffnock
Glenluce
Greenlaw
Greenock
Hamilton
Inverary
Inverury
Jeantown
Jedburgh
Kilbride
Kilniver
Kilrenny
Kinghorn
Kirkwall
Langholm
Latheron
Leuchars
Loanhead
Markinch
Marykirk
Moniaive
Montrose
Monymusk
Muirkirk
Neilston
Newburgh
Newmilns
Penicuik
Pitsligo
Pooltiel
Quiraing
Rothesay
St Fergus
Stirling
Strichen
Talisker
Taransay
Traquair
Ullapool

Whithorn
Woodside

9

Aberfeldy
Aberfoyle
Ardrossan
Berridale
Bettyhill
Blacklarg
Bracadale
Braeriach
Broadford
Broughton
Buckhaven
Cairntoul
Callander
Carstairs
Dumbarton
Edinburgh
Ferintosh
Fochabers
Inchkeith
Inveraray
Inverness
Johnstone
Kildrummy
Kingussie
Kirkcaldy
Leadhills
Lochgelly
Lochnivar
Lochnagar
Lockerbie
Logierait
Mauchline
Milngavie
Peterhead
Pitlochry
Port Ellen
Prestwick
Riccarton
Ronaldsay

Rothiemay
Saltcoats
Shieldaig
Slamannan
St Andrews
Stewarton
St Fillans
Stranraer
Strathdon
Strontian
Thornhill
Tobermory
Tomintoul

10

Abbotsford
Achnasheen
Anstruther
Applecross
Ardrishaig
Auchinleck
Ballantrae
Blackadder
Carnoustie
Carsphairn
Castletown
Coatbridge
Coldingham
Coldstream
Dalbeattie
Drumlithie
East Linton
Galashiels
Glenrothes
Johnshaven
Kilcreggan
Killenaule
Kilmainham
Kilmalcolm
Kilmarnock
Kilwinning
Kincardine
Kingsbarns

Kirkmaiden
Kirkoswald
Kirriemuir
Lennoxtown
Lesmahagow
Livingston
Milnathort
Motherwell
Pittenweem
Portobello
Rutherglen
Stonehaven
Stonehouse
Stoneykirk
Strathhaven
Strathmore
Tweedmouth
West Calder
Wilsontown

11

Aberchirder
Balquhidder
Bannockburn
Blair Atholl
Blairgowrie
Cambeltown
Charlestown
Cumbernauld
Drummelzier
Dunfermline
Ecclefechan
Fettercairn
Fort William
Fraserburgh
Helensburgh
Invergordon
Kirkmichael
Lossiemouth
Lostwithiel
Maxwelltown
Musselburgh
Port Glasgow

Port Patrick
Prestonpans
Pultneytown
Strathblane

12

Auchterarder
Ballachulish
East Kilbride
Fort Augustus
Garelochhead
Innerleithen
Kinlochleven
Lawrence Kirk
Lochgilphead
Portmahomack
Strathpeffer
Tillicoultry

13

Auchermuchty
Castle Douglas
Cocksburnspath
Dalmellington
Inverkeithing
Inverkeithnie
Kirkcudbright
Kirkintilloch
Newton Stewart
Rothiemurchus

Wales

3

Usk

4

Bala
Holt
Mold
Pyle
Rhyl

5

Barry
Chirk
Flint
Neath
Nevin
Tenby
Towyn

6

Amlwch
Bangor
Brecon
Builth
Conway
Margam
Ruabon
Ruthin

7

Carbury
Cardiff
Cwmbran
Denbigh
Maesteg
Newport
Newtown
St Asaph
Swansea
Wrexham

8

Aberavon
Aberdare
Abergele
Barmouth
Bridgend
Caerleon
Cardigan
Chepstow
Dolgelly
Ebbw Vale

	9	10	
Hawarden	Aberaeron	Cader Idris	Presteigne
Holyhead	Aberdovey	Caernarfon	
Holywell	Aberffraw	Caernarvon	**11**
Kidwelly	Beaumaris	Capel Curig	Abergavenny
Knighton	Bodlondeb	Carmarthen	Aberystwyth
Lampeter	Carnarvon	Crickhowel	Clydach Vale
Llanelli	Criccieth	Ffestiniog	Machynlleth
Llanelly	Festiniog	Llandovery	Oystermouth
Llanrwst	Fishguard	Llanfyllin	
Monmouth	Llanberis	Llangadock	**12**
Pembroke	Llandudno	Llangollen	Llandilofawr
Rhayader	New Radnor	Llanidloes	Llantrissant
Skerries	Pontypool	Montgomery	Ystrad Mynach
Skifness	Porthcawl	Plinlimmon	
Talgarth	Portmadoc	Pontypridd	**13**
Tredegar	Pwhllheli	Porth Nigel	Haverfordwest
Tregaron	Welshpool	Port Talbot	Merthyr Tydfil

US Towns and Cities

4	6		Lincoln
Gary	Albany	St Paul	Madison
Lima	Austin	Tacoma	Memphis
Reno	Bangor	Toledo	Modesto
Troy	Biloxi	Topeka	New York
Waco	Boston	Tucson	Norfolk
York	Camden	Urbana	Oakland
	Canton		Orlando
5	Dallas	**7**	Phoenix
Akron	Dayton	Abilene	Raleigh
Boise	Denver	Anaheim	Reading
Bronx	Duluth	Atlanta	Roanoke
Butte	El Paso	Boulder	Saginaw
Flint	Eugene	Buffalo	San Jose
Miami	Fresno	Chicago	Seattle
Omaha	Lowell	Concord	Spokane
Ozark	Mobile	Detroit	St Louis
Salem	Nassau	Hampton	Wicitha
Selma	Newark	Hoboken	Yonkers
Tulsa	Oxnard	Houston	**8**
Utica	Peoria	Jackson	Berkeley
		Key West	

Brooklyn
Columbus
Dearborn
Green Bay
Hannibal
Hartford
Honolulu
Lakeland
Las Vegas
New Haven
Oak Ridge
Palo Alto
Pasadena
Portland
Richmond
San Diego
Santa Ana
Savannah
Stamford
Stockton
Syracuse
Wheeling

9

Anchorage
Annapolis
Arlington
Baltimore
Bethlehem
Cambridge

Champaign
Charlotte
Cleveland
Des Moines
Fairbanks
Fort Wayne
Fort Worth
Galveston
Hollywood
Johnstown
Kalamazoo
Lancaster
Lexington
Long Beach
Manhattan
Milwaukee
Nashville
New London
Northeast
Princeton
Riverside
Rochester
Waterbury
Worcester
Ypsilanti

10

Atomic City
Baton Rouge
Birmingham

Charleston
Cincinnati
Evansville
Greensboro
Greenville
Harrisburg
Huntsville
Jersey City
Kansas City
Little Rock
Long Branch
Los Angeles
Louisville
Miami Beach
Montgomery
New Bedford
New Orleans
Pittsburgh
Providence
Sacramento
Saint Louis
San Antonio
Washington
Youngstown

11

Albuquerque
Cedar Rapids
Chatanooga
Grand Rapids

Minneapolis
Newport News
Palm Springs
Schenectady
Springfield

12

Atlantic City
Beverley Hills
Fayetteville
Independence
Indianapolis
Jacksonville
New Brunswick
Niagara Falls
Oklahoma City
Philadelphia
Poughkeepsie
Salt Lake City
San Francisco
Santa Barbara

13

Corpus Christi
St Petersburgh

14

Fort Lauderdale

15

Colorado
Springs

Towns and Cities

Afghanistan

5

Herat
Kabul

8

Kandahar

Albania

6

Tirana
Tirane

Algeria

4

Oran

7

Algiers
Angola

6

Huambo
Lobito
Luanda

Argentina

7

Cordoba
La Plata
Rosario

9

La Matanza

11
Bahia Blanca
Buenos Aires

Australia
5
Perth
6
Darwin
Hobart
Sydney
8
Adelaide
Brisbane
Canberra
9
Melbourne
Newcastle
12
Alice Springs

Austria
6
Vienna
8
Salzburg
9
Innsbruck

Azerbaijan
4
Baku

Bangladesh
5
Dhaka

10
Chittagong

Belarus
5
Brest
Minsk

Belgium
5
Ghent
Liege
Namur
Ypres
6
Bruges
Dinant
Ostend
7
Antwerp
Malines
8
Brussels

*Bosnia and
Herzegovina*
5
Tuzla
6
Mostar
8
Sarajevo
9
Banja Luka

Brazil

5
Belem
6
Manaus
Recife
8
Brasilia
Salvador
Sao Paolo
11
Porto Alegre
12
Rio de Janeiro
13
Belo Horizonte

Bulgaria
5
Sofia
Varna

Burma
3
Ava

Canada
6
Ottawa
Quebec
Regina
7
Calgary
Halifax
St John's
Toronto
8

Edmonton
Hamilton
Kingston
Montreal
Victoria
Winnipeg
9
Vancouver
Saskatoon
10
Thunder Bay
11
Fredericton
12
Niagara Falls
13
Charlottetown

Chile
8
Santiago
10
Valparaiso

China
4
Luta
Sian
5
Wuhan
6
Anshan
Canton
Dairen
Fushun
Harbin

Mukden
Peking
Tsinan

7

Beijing
Kunming
Lanchow
Nanking
Taiyuan

8

Shanghai
Shenyang
Tientsin

9

Changchun
Chungking

10

Port Arthur

Columbia

4

Cali

6

Bogota

8

Medellin

9

Cartagena

12

Barranquilla

15

Santa Fe De
Bogota

*Congo, Democratic
Republic of*

6

Bokavu

8

Kinshasa

10

Lubumbashi

Croatia

5

Split

6

Zagreb

Cuba

6

Havana

14

Santiago de Cuba

Czech Republic

4

Brno

6

Prague

Denmark

5

Arhus

6

Odense

10

Copenhagen

Ecuador

5

Quito

9

Guayaquil

Egypt

4

Giza
Suez

5

Aswan
Cairo
Luxor
Tanta

6

Thebes

7

Mansura
Memphis
Zagazig

8

Ismailia
Port Said

10

Alexandra

Eritrea

6

Asmara
Asmera

Estonia

7

Tallinn

France

3

Aix
Pau

4

Albi
Caen
Laon
Lyon
Metz
Nice
Tour

5

Arles
Arras
Brest
Dijon
Evian
Lille
Lyons
Macon
Nancy
Nimes
Paris
Reims
Rouen
Tours
Tulle

6

Amiens
Bayeux
Calais
Cannes
Dieppe
Le Mans
Nantes
Orange
Rheims
St Malo
Toulon
Verdun

7

Ajaccio
Alencon
Avignon
Bayonne
Dunkirk
Le Havre
Limoges
Lourdes
Orleans

8

Besancon
Biarritz
Bordeaux
Boulogne
Chartres
Grenoble
Soissons
St Tropez
Toulouse

9

Abbeville
Cherbourg
Dunkerque
Marseille
Montauban
Perpignan
St Etienne

10

Marseilles
Montelimar
Strasbourg
Versailles

11

Armentieres
Montpellier

15

Clermont-
Ferrand

Germany

4

Bonn
Gera
Kiel
Koln
Suhl

5

Essen
Halle
Mainz
Trier
Worms

6

Aachen
Berlin
Bochum
Bremen
Cassel
Erfurt
Kassel
Lubeck
Munich
Treves

7

Coblenz
Cologne
Cottbus
Dresden
Hamburg
Hanover
Homburg
Koblenz
Leipzig
Munchen
Potsdam
Rostock
Spandau

8

Augsburg

Dortmund
Hannover
Mannheim
Nurnberg
Schwerin

9

Brunswick
Darmstadt
Frankfurt
Magdeburg
Nuremberg
Stuttgart
Wiesbaden
Wuppertal

10

Baden Baden
Bad Homburg
Dusseldorf
Heidelberg

11

Brandenburg
Saarbrucken

13

Aic-la-Chapelle
Karl-Marx-Stadt

Greece

6

Athens
Sparta
Thebes

7

Corinth
Mycenae
Piraeus

11

Thessalonki

Hungary

4

Pecs
Pune

8

Budapest

India

4

Agra

5

Ajmer
Alwar
Delhi
Kotah
Patna
Poona
Simla
Surat

6

Bhopal
Bombay
Howrah
Imphal
Indore
Jaipur
Jhansi
Kalyan
Kanpur
Kohima
Madras
Meerut
Mumbai
Mysore
Nagpur
Rampur

7

Benares
Gwalior

Jodhpur
Lucknow

8

Agartala
Amritsar
Calcutta
Cawnpore
Jamalpur
Ludhiana
Shillong
Srinagar
Vadodara
Varanasi

9

Ahmadabad
Allahabad
Bangalore
Hyderabad

10

Chandigarh
Darjeeling
Jamshedpur
Trivandrum

11

Bhubaneswar

Indonesia

5

Medan

7

Bandung
Jakarta

8

Semarang
Surabaja

9

Palembang

Iran

6

Abadan
Shiraz
Tabriz
Tehran

7

Isfahan
Mashhad

Iraq

5

Basra
Mosul

6

Kirkuk

7

Baghdad
Karbala

Ireland, Republic of

4

Bray
Cobh
Cork
Muff
Naas
Trim
Tuam

5

Balla
Boyle
Cavan
Clare
Ennis
Kells
Sligo

6

Arklow
Bantry
Callan
Carlow
Carney
Cashel
Dublin
Galway
Shrule
Tralee

7

Athlone
Blarney
Carrick
Clonmel
Donegal
Dundalk
Dunmore
Kildare
Lifford
Shannon
Wexford
Wicklow
Youghal

8

Ballybay
Buncrana
Clontarf
Drogheda
Kilkenny
Limerick
Listowel
Longford
Maynooth
Monaghan
Rathdrum

9

Castlebar
Connemara
Killarney

Mullingar
Roscommon
Tipperary
Tullamore
Waterford
Castlefinn
Kilconnell
Shillelagh
Skibbereen
Stranorlar

11

Letterkenny

12

Dun Laoghaire

13

Castleblayney
Innishtrahull
Portalaoighise

16

Carrick-on-
Shannon

Israel

4

Gaza

5

Haifa
Jaffa

7

Tel Aviv

9

Beersheba
Jerusalem

Italy

4

Bari

Pisa
Rome

5 —————

Genoa
Milan
Ostia
Padua
Parma
Siena
Turin

6 —————

Modena
Naples
Reggio
Trento
Venice
Verona

7 —————

Bologna
Bergamo
Brescia
Catania
Ferrara
Messina
Palermo
Perugia
Pescara
Pompeii
Ravanna
Salerno
San Remo
Trieste
Vatican

8 —————

Cagliari
Florence
Syracuse

9 —————

Agrigento

Japan

4 —————

Fugi
Kobe

5 —————

Kyoto
Osaka
Tokyo

6 —————

Nagoya
Toyota

7 —————

Fukuoka
Hitachi
Sapporo

8 —————

Kawasaki
Nagasaki
Yokohama

9 —————

Hiroshima

10 —————

Kitakyushu

Kazakhstan

6 —————

Almaty

9 —————

Karaganda

Kenya

4 —————

Lamu

7 —————

Mombasa

Nairobi

Korea, North

9 —————

Pyongyang

Korea, South

7 —————

Seoul

9 —————

Panmunjon

Kyrgyzstan

7 —————

Bishpek
Pishpek

Latvia

4 —————

Riga

Lebanon

4 —————

Tyre

5 —————

Sidon

6 —————

Beirut

Libya

4 —————

Homs

6 —————

Tobruk

7 —————

Tripoli

Lithuania

7 —————

Vilnius

Macedonia

6 —————

Skopje

Mali

6 —————

Bamako

8 —————

Timbuktu

Mexico

6 —————

Juarez
Peubla

8 —————

Acapulco
Veracruz

9 —————

Monterrey

10 —————

Mexico City

11 —————

Guadalajara

Moldova

8 —————

Chisina
Kishnev

Morocco

3
Fez

5
Rabat

6
Agadir
Meknes

7
Tangier

8
Tangiers

9
Marrakech
Marrakesh

10
Casablanca

Myanmar

3
Ava

6
Yangon

7
Rangoon

8
Mandalay

Netherlands

5
Breda
Hague

6
Arnhem
Leiden

Leyden

7
Utrecht

8
The Hague

9
Amsterdam
Dordrecht
Eindhoven
Rotterdam

10
Maastricht

New Zealand

6
Napier
Nelson

7
Dunedin

8
Auckland

10
Wellington

12
Christchurch

Nigeria

4
Kano

5
Abuja
Enugu
Lagos

6
Ibadan

Norway

4
Oslo

6
Bergen

9
Trondheim

Pakistan

6
Lahore
Multan
Quetta

7
Karachi

8
Peshawar

9
Hyperabad
Islamabad

10
Faisalabad
Gujranwala
Rawalpindi

Peru

4
Lima

5
Cuzco

Philippines

6
Manila

10

Quezon City

Poland

4
Lodz

5
Posen

6
Danzig
Gdansk
Krakow
Lublin
Warsaw

7
Breslau

8
Przemysl

Portugal

6
Lisbon
Oporto

Russia

3 and 4
Ufa
Omsk
Perm
Tver

5
Kazan
Pskov

6
Moscow
Samara

7

Irkutsk
Yakutsk
8
Novgorod
Smolensk
9
Astrakhan
Kalingrad
Volgograd
11
Chelyabinsk
Novosibirsk
Vladisvostock
12
Ekaterinburg
Rostov-na-Donu
14
Nizhy Novgorod

Saudi Arabia
5
Mecca
6
Jeddah
Medina
Riyadh

Slovakia
10
Bratislava

Slovenia
9
Ljubljana

South Africa

6
Durban
Soweto
8
Cape Town
Mafeking
Pretoria
9
Kimberley
Ladysmith
10
Alexandria
East London
Simonstown
11
Grahamstown
Sharpeville
12
Bloemfontein
Johannesburg
13
Port Elizabeth
16
Pietermaritzberg

Spain
4
Vigo
5
Cadiz
6
Bilbao
Madrid
Malaga
7
Badajoz

Cordoba
Granada
Seville
8
Alicante
Pamplona
Valencia
Zaragoza
9
Barcelona
Cartagena
Las Palmas
Santander
Saragossa
12
San Sebastian

Sri Lanka
5
Galle
Kandy
7
Colombo
11
Trincomalee

Sudan
6
Berber
7
Dongola
8
Khartoum
Omdurman

Sweden

5
Malmo
7
Uppsala
8
Goteborg
9
Stockholm
10
Gothenburg
11
Helsingborg

Switzerland
4
Bale
Bern
5
Basel
Basle
6
Geneva
Zurich
7
Lucerne
8
Lausanne

Syria
4
Homs
5
Aleppo
7

Palmyra
8 _____
Damascus

Taiwan
6 _____
Taibei
Taipei
9 _____
Kao-Hsuing

Tajakstan
8 _____
Dushanbe

Tanzania
6 _____
Dodoma
8 _____
Zanzibar
11 _____
Dar Es Salaam

Turkey
5 _____
Adana
Izmir
6 _____
Ankara
Smyrna
7 _____
Erzerum
8 _____
Istanbul
9 _____
Byzantium
14 _____
Constantinople

Turkmenistan
9 _____
Ashkhabad

Ukraine
4 _____
Kiev
Lvov

5 _____
Yalta
6 _____
Odessa
7 _____
Donetsk

Uzbekistan
8 _____
Tashkent
9 _____
Samarkand

Venezuela
7 _____
Caracas
9 _____
Maracaibo

Vietnam
3 _____
Hue
6 _____

Danang

Yemen
4 _____
Aden
San'a
5 _____
Sana'a

Yugoslavia
3 _____
Nis
7 _____
Novi Sad
8 _____
Belgrade
9 _____
Podgorica

Zimbabwe
6 _____
Harare
8 _____
Bulawayo

Counties and Local Authorities   *(* indicates a former region or county)*

England

Authority	Administrative Centre
* Avon	Bristol
Bath and North East Somerset	Bath
Bedfordshire	Bedford
Berkshire	Reading
Buckinghamshire	Aylesbury

Authority	Administrative Centre
Calderdale	Halifax
Cambridgeshire	Cambridge
Cheshire	Chester
* Cleveland	Middlesbrough
Cornwall	Truro
* Cumberland	Carlisle
Cumbria	Carlisle
Derbyshire	Matlock
Devon	Exeter
Dorset	Dorchester
Durham	Durham
East Riding (of Yorkshire)	Beverley
East Sussex	Lewes
Essex	Chelmsford
Gloucestershire	Gloucester
Greater London	London
Greater Manchester	Manchester
Halton	Runcorn
Hampshire	Winchester
* Hereford and Worcester	Worcester
Herefordshire	Hereford
Hertfordshire	Hertford
* Humberside	Beverley
* Huntingdonshire	Huntingdon
Isle of Wight	Newport, Isle of Wight
Kent	Maidstone
Kirklees	Huddersfield
Lancashire	Preston
Leicestershire	Leicester
Lincolnshire	Lincoln
Medway	Gillingham
Merseyside	Liverpool
Norfolk	Norwich
Northamptonshire	Northampton
North-East Lincolnshire	Grimsby
North Lincolnshire	Scunthorpe
North Somerset	Weston-super-Mare
* North Riding (of Yorkshire)	Middlesbrough
North Tyneside	Wallsend
Northumberland	Morpeth
North Yorkshire	Northallerton

Authority	Administrative Centre
Nottinghamshire	Nottingham
Oxfordshire	Oxford
Redcar and Cleveland	Redcar
Rutland	Oakham
Salop	(Name for Shropshire between 1974 and 1980)
Shropshire	Shrewsbury
Somerset	Taunton
South Gloucestershire	Thornbury
South Tyneside	South Shields
South Yorkshire	Barnsley
Staffordshire	Stafford
Suffolk	Ipswich
Surrey	Guildford
Sussex	Lewes
Telford and Wrekin	Telford
Tyne and Wear	Newcastle-upon-Tyne
Warwickshire	Warwick
West Berkshire	Newbury
West Midlands	Birmingham
* Westmoreland	Kendal
* West Riding (of Yorkshire)	Wakefield
West Sussex	Chichester
West Yorkshire	Wakefield
Wiltshire	Trowbridge
Wirral	Birkenhead
Worcestershire	Worcester

Wales

*Anglesey	Llangefni
Blaenau Gwent	Ebbw Vale
* Breconshire	Brecon
* Caernarfonshire	Caernarfon
* Cardiganshire	Aberystwyth
Ceredigion	Aberaeron
*Clwyd	Mold
Conwy	Bodlondeb
Denbighshire	Ruthin
* Dyfed	Carmarthen
Flintshire	Mold
* Glamorgan	Cardiff

Authority	Administrative Centre
* Gwent	Cwmbran
Gwynedd	Caernarfon
* Merioneth	Dolgellan
* Mid Glamorgan	Cardiff
Monmouthshire	Cwmbran
Montgomeryshire	Welshpool
Neath Port Talbot	Port Talbot
Pembrokeshire	Haverfordwest
Powys	Llandridnod Wells
*Radnorshire	Llandridnod Wells
Rhondda Cynon Taff	Clydach Vale
* South Glamorgan	Cardiff
Swansea	Swansea
Torfaen	Pontypool
Vale of Glamorgan	Barry
* West Glamorgan	Swansea
Wrexham	Wrexham
Aberdeenshire	Aberdeen
Angus	Forfar
Argyll and Bute	Lochgilphead
* Argyll	Lochgilphead
* Ayrshire	Ayr
* Banff	Banff
* Berwick	Duns
* Bute	Rothesey
* Caithness	Wick
* Central	Stirling
Clackmannanshire	Alloa
Dumfries and Galloway	Dumfries
* Dumfries	Dumfries
* Dunbartonshire	Dumbarton
East Ayrshire	Kilmarnock
East Dunbartonshire	Kirkintilloch
East Lothian	Haddington
East Renfrewshire	Giffnock
Fife	Glenrothes
* Grampian	Aberdeen
Highland	Inverness
Inverclyde	Greenock
* Inverness-shire	Inverness
* Kincardineshire	Stonehaven

Authority	Administrative Centre
* Kinross	Kinross
* Kirkudbright	Kircudbright
* Lanarkshire	Hamilton
* Lothian	Edinburgh
Midlothian	Dalkeith
Moray	Elgin
* Nairn	Nairn
North Ayrshire	Irvine
North Lanarkshire	Motherwell
Orkney	Kirkwall
* Peebles	Peebles
Perth and Kinross	Perth
* Perthshire	Perth
Renfrewshire	Paisley
* Ross and Cromarty	Dingwall
* Roxburgh	Newton St. Boswells
Scottish Borders	Newton St. Boswells
* Selkirk	Selkirk
Shetland	Lerwick
South Ayrshire	Ayr
South Lanarkshire	Hamilton
Stirling	Stirling
* Strathclyde	Glasgow
* Sutherland	Golspie
* Tayside	Dundee
West Dunbartonshire	Dumbarton
Western Isles	Lewis
West Lothian	Livingston
* Wigtownshire	Stranraer
Zetland	(Former name for Shetland)

Provinces and Counties of Ireland (** *indicates counties of Northern Ireland*)

Province

County	*County Town*

Connacht

Mayo	Castlebar
Sligo	Sligo
Galway	Galway
Leitrim	Carrick-on-Shannon
Roscommon	Roscommon

Leinster

Louth	Dundalk
Meath	Trim
Carlow	Carlow
Dublin	Dublin
Offaly	Tullamore
Kildare	Naas
Wexford	Wexford
Wicklow	Wicklow
Kilkenny	Kilkenny
Laoighis (or Laois or Leix)	Portlaoighise or Portlaoise
Longford	Longford
Westmeath	Mullingar

Munster

Cork	Cork

Province

Clare	Ennis
Kerry	Tralee
Limerick	Limerick
Tipperary	Clonmel
Waterford	Waterford

Ulster

** Down	Downpatrick

County	County Town
Cavan	Cavan
** Armagh	Armagh
** Antrim	Belfast
** Tyrone	Omagh
Donegal	Lifford
Monaghan	Monaghan
** Fermanagh	Enniskillen
** Londonderry	Londonderry

Deserts

3

Gila
Gobi
Thar

4

Namib
Nefud
Negev
Olmos
Ordos
Sinai
Sturt

6

Arunta
Gibson

Mojave
Nubian
Sahara
Syrian
Ust-Urt

7

Alashan
Arabian
Atacama
Kara Kum
Morrope
Painted
Sechura
Simpson

8

Colorado
Kalahari
Kyzyl Kum
Muyunkum
Vizcaino

9

Black Rock
Dasht-I-Lut

Dzungaria

10

Australian
Bet-Pak-Dala
Great Sandy
Patagonian

Rub'al Khali 11
Dasht-I-Kavir
Dasht-I-Margo
Death Valley

13

Great Salt Lake

Great Victoria
Bolson de
Mapimi

16

Turfan
Depression

Geographical Terms

2 and 3

iat
alp
as
bay
ben
bog
cay

col
cwm
dam
dun
ea
fen
geo
lea

lin
map
nek
ria
sea
tor
voe

4

aber
bank
beck
berg
bill
burn
cape

city	pond	combe	oasis
comb	port	copse	ocean
cove	race	creek	plain
crag	reef	crest	point
croy	reen	croft	polar
dale	rill	delta	poles
dell	road	donga	reach
dene	rock	downs	rhine
dike	sike	drift	ridge
dyke	sima	duchy	river
doab	spit	esker	sands
dune	sudd	fault	scarp
east	syke	field	shelf
eyot	tarn	fiord	shire
ford	town	fjord	shoal
gapo	tump	firth	shore
glen	vale	fiett	slade
gulf	vega	ghaut	sound
hill	wadi	glade	south
holm	weir	globe	speos
holt	west	gorge	state
inch	wind	grove	swale
isle	wold	haven	swamp
kaim	wood	heath	swang
kame	wynd	hithe	sward
lake	zone	hurst	weald
land		hythe	yarfa
lane	**5**	inlet	
linn	abyss	islet	**6**
loam	alley	karoo	alpine
loch	atlas	kloof	arctic
lock	atoll	kopje	boreal
marl	Banat	knoll	canada
mead	Bayou	lande	canton
mere	bight	llano	canyon
mesa	brook	loess	circar
moor	canal	lough	clough
mull	chart	marsh	colony
naze	chasm	monte	colure
ness	chine	mound	common
pass	cliff	mount	county
peak	clime	mouth	cranny
pole	coast	north	crater

cuesta
defile
desert
diapir
dingle
divide
domain
empery
empire
eyalet
forest
geyser
glacis
hamlet
harbor
inland
inning
island
isobar
jungle
karroo
lagoon
maidan
meadow
morass
nullah
orient
pampas
parish
polder
rapids
ravine
region
riding
rillet
runlet
runnel
seaway
sierra
skerry
spinny
spruit
steppe

strait
strath
stream
street
suburb
summit
talook
tropic
tundra
upland
valley
warren
yarpha

7

airport
alluvia
austral
bogland
channel
clachan
commune
compass
contour
country
cutting
deltaic
drought
eastern
enclave
eparchy
equator
estuary
euripus
exclave
georama
glacier
habitat
harbour
highway
hillock
hilltop
hommock

hornito
hummock
hundred
iceberg
ice-floe
insular
isthmus
kingdom
lakelet
lowland
midland
new town
oceanic
platueat
polders
prairie
rivulet
rosland
satrapy
savanna
seaport
seaside
spurway
straits
thicket
torrent
tropics
village
volcano
western

8

affluent
alluvial
alluvium
altitude
brooklet
cantonal
cataract
crevasse
currents
district
dominion

downland
easterly
eastward
eminence
eminency
environs
foreland
frontier
headland
highland
high road
hillside
home-park
interior
isthmian
landmark
latitude
littoral
lowlands
mainland
midlands
moorland
mountain
neap-tide
northern
occident
oriental
post-town
province
quagmire
republic
salt lake
seaboard
seacoast
seashore
sheading
snow-line
southern
sub-polar
toparchy
township
tropical
volcanic

westerly
westward
wild land
woodland

9

antarctic
antipodal
antipodes
backwater
backwoods
cadastral
capricorn
catchment
cisalpine
coastline
continent
coral reef
fleet-dike
foothills
heathland
highlands
landslide
longitude
marshland
monticule
north-east
northerly
northward
north-west
peninsula
precipice
rockbound
salt-marsh
sandbanks
shoreline
south-east
southerly
southmost
southward
south-west
stewartry

streamlet
sub-alpine
tableland
territory
tetrarchy
trade wind
tributary
wapentake
waterfall
watershed
waterside
westwards

10

co-latitude
county town
equatorial
escarpment
fluviatile
frigid zone
garden city
geographer
Gulf Stream
hemisphere
interfluve
land-locked
margravate
market town
meridional
metropolis
mountainet
no-mans-land
occidental
palatinate
peninsular
plantation
polar-angle
population
presidency
projection
promontory
quicksands

sandy beach
south downs
spring tide
table-shore
tidal creek
torrid zone
water table
wilderness

11

archipelago
bergschrund
circumpolar
cisatlantic
continental
conurbation
coral island
countryside
equinoctial
morningland
mountainous
northwardly
polar circle
polar region
river course
septentrion
subtropical
territorial
tetrarchate
tidal waters
transalpine
transmarine
trout stream
ultramarine
watercourse

12

equitorially
landgraviate
magnetic pole
northeastern
northwestern

principality
protectorate
southeastern
southernmost
southwestern
stratosphere
ultramontane
virgin forest

13

deltafication
extratropical
intertropical
magnetic north
Mediterranean
mother country
neighbourhood
northeasterly
northeastward
northwesterly
northwestward
polar distance
septentrional
southeasterly
southeastward
southwesterly
southwestward
temperate zone
transatlantic
virgin country
watering place

14+

acclimatization
circummeridian
circumnavigate
irrigation canal
magnetic equator
Mercator's chart
north frigid zone
south frigid zone
tropic of cancer

Islands

3

Rum

4

Aran
Bali
Bute
Cebu
Coll
Cuba
Edge
Eigg
Faro
Fiji
Guam
Iona
Java
Jura
Mull
Oahu
Sark
Skye

5

Arran
Banks
Capri
Ceram
Clare
Corfu
Crete
Devon
Ellis
Haiti
Ibiza
Islay
Lewis
Leyte
Lundy

Luzon
Malta
Panay
Rhode
Samar
Timor

6

Azores
Baffin
Borneo
Canary
Cyprus
Easter
Flores
Hainan
Harris
Hawaii
Honshu
Jersey
Kodiak
Kyushu
Lesbos
Limmos
Madura
Negros
Orkney
Penang
Puffin
Rhodes
Scilly
Sicily
Tahiti
Taiwan
Tobago
Virgin

7

Antigua
Bahamas

Bahrain
Barents
Bermuda
Celebes
Channel
Corsica
Curacao
Formosa
Gotland
Grenada
Iceland
Ireland
Jamaica
Madeira
Majorca
Mindoro
Okinawa
Orkneys
Palawan
Phoenix
Rathlin
Reunion
Rockall
Shikoku
Solomon
St Kitts
St Lucia
Sumatra
Wrangel

8

Alderney
Anglesey
Antilles
Barbados
Canaries
Dominica
Fair Isle
Falkland
Guernsey

Hokkaido
Hong Kong
Malagasy
Mallorca
Melville
Mindanao
Pitcairn
Sakhalin
Sardinia
Shetland
Somerset
Sri Lanka
St Helena
Sulawesi
Tasmania
Tenerife
Trinidad
Unalaska
Victoria
Vitu Levu
Windward
Zanzibar

9

Anticosti
Ascension
Australia
Benbecula
Ellesmere
Falklands
Galapagos
Greenland
Halmahera
Isle of Man
Manhattan
Mauritius
Nantucket
New Guinea
Polynesia
Santa Cruz

Santorini
Shetlands
Singapore
St Vincent
Vancouver

10

Cape Breton
Grenadines
Guadeloupe
Hispaniola
Holy Island
Isle of Skye
Isle of Dogs
Long Island
Madagascar
Martinique
Monserrat

New Britain
New Ireland
New Zealand
Puerto Rico
Saint Kitts
Saint Lucia
Seychelles
West Indies

11

Axel Heiberg
Cook Islands
Grand Canary
Guadalcanal
Isle of Pines
Isle of Wight
Monte Cristo
New Hebrides

Philippines
Scilly Isles

12

Bougainville
Easter Island
Great Britain
Isle of Thanet
New Caledonia
Newfoundland
Novaya Zemlya
Saint Vincent
Turk's Islands

13

Isle of Sheppey
Norfolk Island
North East Land

Prince of Wales
Prince Patrick
Santa Catalina

14

South Shetlands
Thursday Island
Tierra del Fuego

15

Martha's
Vineyard
West
Spitsbergen

18

Prince Edward
Island

Largest Waterfalls

Waterfall	Country
Churchill	Canada
Gavarnie	France
Giessbach	Switzerland
Guaira	Brazil
Hamilton	Canada
Krimmler	Australia
Multnomah	U.S.A.
Niagara	Canada-U.S.A.
Ribbon	U.S.A.
Roraima	Guyana
Salto Angel	Venezuela
Sete Quedas	Brazil
Stanley	Ziare
Sutherland	New Zealand
Trummelbach	Switzerland
Vettisfos	Norway
Victoria	Zambia, Zimbabwe
Yosemite, Upper	U.S.A.

National Parks

Park	Location	Special Feature
Abisko	Sweden	
Abruzzo	Italy	
Altos de Campana	Panama	
Amazonia	Brazil	
Angkor	Kampuchea	Khmer civilisation remains
Arusha	Tanzania	
Atitlan	Guatemala	
Awash	Ethiopia	
Babiogorski	Poland	
Banff	Alberta, Canada	hot springs at Sulphur Mountains
Bayarischer Wald	Bavaria, West Germany	
Belovezhskaya	Belorussia	
Bailowieski	Poland	
Cabo de Hornos	Chile	automatically operated lighthouse
Canaima	Venezuela	Salto Angel
Canon del Rio Blanco	Mexico	
Canyonlands	Utah, United States	landforms carved in red sandstone
Carlsbad Caverns	New Mexico	largest area of caverns in the world
Carnarvon	Queensland	
Chobe	Botswana	
Corbett	Uttar Pradesh, India	
Cradle Mountain - Lake Saint Clair	Tasmania, Australia	
Daisetsuzan	Japan	
Danali	Alaska, United States	Mt. McKinley
Djung-kulon	Indonesia	
Etosha	Namibia	
Everglades	Florida, United States	
Fiordland	New Zealand	
Franklin D. Roosevelt	Uruguay	
Fray Jorge	Chile	
Fuji-Hakone-Izu	Japan	

Park	Location	Special Feature
Fundy	New Brunswick, Canada	
Galapagos	Ecuador	giant iguanas and giant tortoises
Gemsbok	Botswana	
Gir Lion	Gujurat, India	
Glacier	Montana, United States	
Gorongosa	Mozambique	
Grand Canyon	Arizona, United States	
Gran Paradiso	Italy	
Great Smoky Mountains	North Carolina & Tennessee, United States	
Hawaii Volcanoes	Hawaii, United States	
Henri Pittier	Venezuela	
Hohe Tauern	Austria	Krimmler Waterfall
Hortobagyl	Hungary	
Huascaran	Peru	
Nevado	Huascaran	
Iguacu	Brazil	Iguacu Falls
Iguazu	Argentina	Iguazu River cliffs, Iguazu Falls
Isle Royale	Michigan, United States	
Ixtacihuatl-Popocatepetl	Mexico	
Jasper	Alberta, Canada	Columbia Icefield
Kabalega	Uganda	Kabalega Falls
Kafue	Zambia	
Kaieteur	Guyana	Kaieteur Falls
Kalahari Gemsbok	Cape of Good Hope, South Africa	
Katatepe-Asiantas	Turkey	Hittite, Roman, and Phoenician civilizations ruins
Katmai	Alaska, United States	
Kaziranga	Assam, India	
Khao Yai	Thailand	
Kilimanjaro	Tanzania	
Komoe	Ivory Coast	

Park	Location	Special Feature
Kosciusko	New South Wales, Australia	Mt. Kosciusko
Kruger	Transvaal, South Africa	
Lake District	England	Lake Windermere
Los Glaciares	Argentina	glacial landforms
Monovo-Gounda-Saint Floris	Central African Republic	
Manu	Peru	
Mayon Volcano	Philippines	Mayon Volcano
Mesa Verde	Colorado,	remains of cliff dwellings of pre-United States Columbian Indians
Mocamedes Reserva	Angola	
Mount Apo	Philippines	
Mount Aspiring	New Zealand	Mt. Aspiring
Mount Carmel	Israel	
Mount Cook	New Zealand	Mt Cook; Tasman Glacier
Nahuel Huapi	Argentina	Mt. Tronador
Nairobi	Kenya	
Namib Desert	Namibia	
Odzala	Congo	
Olympic	Washington, United States	
Olympus	Greece	
Pellas-Ounastunturi	Finland	
Pembrokeshire Coast	Wales	
Petrified Forest	Arizona United States	forests of petrified trees
Pfalzerwald	Rheinland-Pfalz, West Germany	
Pico de Orizaba	Mexico	Citlaltepetl volcano
Plitvicka, Jezera	Croatia	
Purace	Columbia	
Pyrenees Occidentales	France	
Rapa Nui	Chile	sites of an ancient civilisation
Redwood	California, United States	
Retezat	Romania	

Park	Location	Special Feature
Rocky Mountain	Colorado, United States	
Rondane	Norway	
Ruwenzori	Uganda	
Sarek	Sweden	
Schweizerische	Switzerland	
Serengeti	Tanzania	
Setto-Naikai	Japan	
Sierra Nevada de Merida	Venezuela	
Skaftafell Thingvellir	Iceland	
Snowdonia	Wales	Snowdon Peak
Stirling Range	Western Australia, Australia	
Stolby Zapovednik	Russia	
Tatransky Narodni	Slovakia	
Tatrzanski	Poland	
Teberdinsky Zapovednik	Russia	
Tikal	Guatemala	ruins of Mayan city
Totruguero	Costa Rica	green sea turtles
Toubkal	Morocco	
Triglavski Narondi	Slovenia	Kanjavec Peak; Savica Waterfalls
Tsavo	Kenya	
Uluru	Northern Territory, Australia	Mt. Olga; Ayers Rock
Valle de Ordesa	Spain	
Vanoise	France	
Veluwezoom, Het	Netherlands	
Victoria Falls	Zimbabwe & Zambia	Victoria Falls
Virunga	Zaire	
Volcanoes	Rwanda	
Wankie	Zimbabwe	
Waterton Lakes	Alberta, Canada	
Waza	Cameroon	
Wood Buffalo	Alberta & Northwest Territories, Canada	reserve for bison herds
W. Parc	Benin, Niger & Burkina Faso	
Yellowstone	Wymoing, Montana & Idaho,	Old Faithful

Park	Location	Special Feature
Yoho	United States British Columbia, Canada	Takakkaw Falls
Yorkshire Dales	England	
Yosemite	California, United States	Yosemite Falls
Zion	Utah, United States	

Oceans and Seas

3 and 4
Aral (Sea)
Azov (Sea of)
Dead (Sea)
Java (Sea)
Red (Sea)
Ross (Sea)
Sava (Sea)

5
Banda (Sea)
Black (Sea)
China (Sea)
Coral (Sea)
Irish (Sea)
Japan (Sea of)
North (Sea)
Timor (Sea)
White (Sea)

6
Aegean (Sea)
Artic (Ocean)
Baltic (Sea)
Bering (Sea)
Celtic (Sea)
Indian (Ocean)
Inland (Sea)
Ionian (Sea)

Laptev (Sea)
Nanhai (Sea)
Tasman (Sea)
Yellow (Sea)

7
Andaman (Sea)
Arabian (Sea)
Arafura (Sea)
Barents (Sea)
Behring (Sea)
Caspian (Sea)
Dong Hai (Sea)
Galilee (Sea of)
Marmara (Sea of)
Okhotsk (Sea of)
Pacific (Ocean)
Weddell (Sea)

8
Adriatic (Sea)
Amundsen (Sea)
Atlantic (Ocean)
Beaufort (Sea)
Huang Hai (Sea)
Ligurian (Sea)
Sargasso (Sea)
Tiberias (Sea of)

9
Antarctic (Ocean)

Caribbean (Sea)
East China (Sea)
Greenland (Sea)

10
Philippine (Sea)
Seto-Naikai (Sea)
South China (Sea)

13
Mediterranean (Sea)

14
Bellingshausen (Sea)

Bays

3
Ise (Japan)
Mal (Republic of Ireland)
Tor (England)

4
Acre (Israel)
Clew (Republic of Ireland)
Luce (Scotland)
Lyme (England)
Pigs (Cuba)

Vigo (Spain)
Wick (Scotland)

5

Algoa (South Africa)
Cadiz (Spain)
Casco (USA)
Dvina (Russia)
Fundy (Canada)
Hawke (New Zealand)
James (Canada)
Milne (New Guinea)
Omura (Japan)
Osaka (Japan)
Sligo (Republic of Ireland)
Table (South Africa)
Tampa (USA)
Tokyo (Japan)
Urado (Japan)
Vlore (Albania)
Abukir (Egypt)
Alaska (USA)
Ariake (Japan)
Baffin (Baffin Island, Greenland)
Bantry (Republic of Ireland)
Bengal (India, Bangladesh, Myanmar (Burma))
Biscay (France, Spain)
Botany (Australia)
Calloa (Peru)
Colwyn (Wales)
Dingle (Republic of Ireland)
Galway (Republic of Ireland)
Gdansk (Poland)
Hudson (Canada)
Jervis (Australia)
Lobito (Angola)

Manila (Philippines)
Mobile (USA)
Naples (Italy)
Newark (USA)
Plenty (New Zealand)
Ramsey (Isle of Man)
Tasman (New Zealand)
Toyama (Japan)
Tralee (Republic of Ireland)
Ungava (Canada)
Vyborg (Finland)
Walvis (Namibia)
Wigton (Scotland)

7

Aboukir (Egypt)
Brittas (Republic of Ireland)
Cape Cod (USA)
Delagoa (Mozambique)
Dundalk (Republic of Ireland)
Florida (USA)
Kavalla (Greece)
Killala (Republic of Ireland)
Montego (Jamaica)
Moreton (Australia)
New York (USA)
Poverty (New Zealand)
Setubal (Portugal)
Swansea (Wales)
Thunder (Canada)
Trinity (Canada)
Walfish (Namibia)
Wexford (Republic of Ireland)
Youghal (Republic of Ireland)

8

Bideford (England)

Biscayne (USA)
Buzzards (USA)
Campeche (Mexico)
Cardigan (Wales)
Delaware (USA)
Dunmanus (Republic of Ireland)
False Bay (South Africa)
Georgian (Canada)
Gweebara (Republic of Ireland)
Hangzhou (China)
Jianzhou (China)
Plymouth (USA)
Quiberon (France)
San Pedro (USA)
Santiago (Cuba)
St Brides (Wales)
St Michel (France)
Tremadog (Wales)

9

Bombetoka (Madagascar)
Discovery (Australia)
Encounter (Australia)
Famagusta (Cyprus)
Frobisher (Canada)
Gibraltar (Gibraltar, Spain)
Guanabara (Brazil)
Inhambane (Mozambique)
Liverpool (England)
Magdalena (Mexico)
Morecambe (England)
Placentia (Canada)
St Austell (England)
White Park (Northern Ireland)

10

Ballyheige (Republic of

Ireland)
Ballyteige (Republic of
Ireland)
Barnstaple (England)
Bridgwater (England)
Caernarfon (Wales)
Caernarvon (Wales)
Carmarthen (Wales)
Chesapeake (USA)
Cienfuegos (Cuba)
Guantanamo (Cuba)

11

Bridlington (England)
Lutzow-Holme
(Antarctica)
Port Philip (Australia)
Trincomalee (Sri Lanka)

12

Narragansett (USA)
San Francisco (USA)

13

Corpus Christi (USA)
Espirito Santo (Brazil)
Massachusetts (USA)
Passamaquoddy
(Canada, USA)

Straits

4

Bass (Australia,
Tasmania)
Cook (New Zealand)
Palk (India, Sri Lanka)

5

Canso (Canada)

Davis (Canada,
Greenland)
Dover (England, France)
Kerch (Ukraine, Russia)
Korea (South Korea,
Japan)
Menai (Wales)
Sumba (Indonesia:
Sumba, Flores)
Sunda (Indonesia:
Sumatra, Japan)
Tatar (Russia)
Tiran (Egypt, Saudi
Arabia)

6

Bangka (Indonesia:
Bangka, Sumatra)
Bering (Alaska, Russia)
Hainan (China)
Hormuz (Iran, Oman)
Hudson (Canada)
Johore (Malaysia,
Singapore)
Lombok (Indonesia:
Bali, Lombak)
Soemba (Indonesia:
Sumba, Flores)
Taiwan (Taiwan, China)
Torres (Australia, New
Guinea)

7

Basilan (Philippines:
Basilan, Mindanao)
Denmark (Greenland,
Iceland)
Florida (USA, Cuba)
Formosa (Taiwan,
China)
Georgia (Canada)
Makasar (Borneo,

Sulawesi)
Malacca (Peninsular
Malaysia, Sumatra)
Messina (Sicily, Italy)
Otranto (Italy, Albania)
Soendra (Indonesia:
Sumba, Java)
Tsugaru (Japan)

8

Clarence (Australia)
Macassar (Borneo,
Sulawesi)
Mackinac (Straits of;
USA)
Magellan (Chile, Tierra
del Fuego)
Makassar (Borneo,
Sulawesi)
Surabaya (Indonesia:
Java, Madura)

9

Belle Isle (Canada)
Gibraltar (Gibraltar,
Spain, Morocco)
La Perouse (Japan,
Russia)
Seorabaja (Indonesia:
Java, Madura)

10

Golden Gate (USA)
Juan de Fuca (Canada,
USA)

13

San Bernardino
(Philippines: Luzon,
Samar)

Lakes, Lochs and Loughs

3

Awe (Scotland)
Van (Turkey)

4

Aral (Kazahkstan, Uzbekistan)
Bala (Wales)
Chad (West Africa)
Como (Italy)
Erie (Canada, USA)
Eyre (Australia)
Kivu (Congo, Rwanda)
Nemi (Italy)
Ness (Scotland)
Tana (Ethiopia)

5

Foyle (Ireland)
Garda (Italy)
Great (Australia)
Great (USA, Canada)
Huron (USA, Canada)
Kioga (Uganda)
Kyoga (Uganda)
Leman (Switzerland, France)
Leven (Scotland)
Lochy (Scotland)
Maree (Scotland)
Neagh (Northern Ireland)
Nyasa (Malawi, Tanzania, Mozambique)
Onega (Russia)
Taupo (New Zealand)
Urmia (Iran)

6

Albert (Congo, Democratic Republic of, Uganda)
Baikal (Russia)
Edward (Congo, Democratic Republic of, Uganda)
Geneva (Switzerland, France)
Kariba (Zambia, Zimbabwe)
Ladoga (Russia)
Lomond (Scotland)
Lop Nor (China)
Malawi (Malawi, Tanzania, Mozambique)
Mobutu (Congo, Democratic Republic of, Uganda)
Nasser (Egypt)
Natron (Tanzania)
Peipus (Estonia, Russia)
Poyang (China)
Rudolf (Kenya, Ethiopia)
Saimaa (Finland)
Vanern (Sweden)

7

Balaton (Hungary)
Belfast (Northern Ireland)
Derwent (England)
Katrine (Scotland)
Koko Nor (China)
Lucerne (Switzerland)
Nu Jiang (China, Burma)
Ontario (Canada, USA)
Qinghai (China)
St Clair (USA, Canada)
Torrens (Australia)
Turkana (Kenya, Ethiopia)

8

Balkhash (Kazakhstan)
Chiemsee (Germany)
Coniston (England)
Dongting (China)
Grasmere (England)
Issyk Kul (Kyrgyzstan)
Maggiore (Italy, Switzerland)
Mazurian (Poland)
Menindee (Australia)
Michigan (USA)
Neusiedl (Austria, Hungary)
Superior (USA, Canada)
Titicaca (Peru, Bolivia)
Tonle Sap (Cambodia)
Tung-T-ing (China)
Victoria (Uganda, Tanzania, Kenya)
Winnipeg (Canada)

9

Athabasca (Canada)
Bangweulu (Zambia)
Champlain (USA)
Constance (Germany)
Ennerdale (England)
Great Bear (Canada)
Great Salt (USA)
Maracaibo (Venezuela)
Thirlmere (England)
Trasimeno (Italy)
Ullswater (England)
Wast Water (England)

10

Buttermere (England)
Great Slave (Canada)
Ijsselmeer (Netherlands)
Okeechobee (USA)
Strangford (Northern

Ireland)
Tanganyika (Burundi, Congo, Democratic Republic of, Tanzania, Zambia)
Windermere (England)

12

Kara-Bogaz-Gol (Turkmenistan)

18

Vierwaldstattersee (Switzerland)

Rivers

2

Ob (Russia)
Po (Italy)

3

Ain (France)
Aln (England)
Bug (Ukraine, Poland, Germany)
Cam (England)
Dee (Scotland, Wales, England)
Don (Russia, Scotland, England, France, Australia)
Ems (Germany, Netherlands)
Esk (Australia)
Exe (England)
Fal (England)
Fly (Papua New Guinea)
Han (China)

Kwa (Congo, Democratic Republic of)
Lea (England)
Lee (Republic of Ireland)
Lot (France)
Red (USA)
Rur (Germany)
Rye (England)
Tay (Scotland)
Ure (England)
Usk (Wales, England)
Wey (England)
Wye (Wales, England)
Yeo (England)

4

Adda (Italy)
Adur (England)
Aire (England, France)
Amur (Mongolia, Russia, China)
Arno (Italy)
Arun (Nepal)
Aube (France)
Avon (England)
Bann (Northern Ireland)
Beas (India)
Bure (England)
Cher (France)
Coln (England)
Dart (England)
Doon (Scotland)
Ebro (Spain)
Eden (England, Scotland)
Elbe (Germany, Czech Republic)
Emba (Kazakhstan)
Isis (England)
Juba (East Africa)

Kama (Russia)
Kura (Turkey, Georgia, Azerbaijan)
Lahn (Germany)
Lech (Germany, Austria)
Lena (Russia)
Lune (England)
Maas (Netherlands)
Main (Germany, Northern Ireland)
Mino (Spain)
Mole (England)
Nile (Sudan, Egypt)
Oder (Germany, Czech Republic, Poland)
Ohio (USA)
Oise (France)
Ouse (England)
Oxus (Turkmenistan, Uzbekistan)
Peel (Australia, USA)
Ravi (India, Pakistan)
Rede (England)
Ruhr (Germany)
Saar (Germany, France)
Spey (Scotland)
Taff (Wales)
Tajo (Spain)
Tarn (France)
Tawe (Wales)
Tawi (India)
Tees (England)
Tejo (Brazil)
Test (England)
Tyne (Scotland, England)
Ural (Russia, Kazakhstan)
Vaal (South Africa)
Wear (England)
Yare (England)

5

Adige (Italy)

Aisne (France)
Allen (Scotland, Syria)
Aller (Spain, Germany)
Annan (Scotland)
Benue (Nigeria)
Brent (England)
Camel (England)
Chari (Cameroon, Chad)
Clyde (Scotland, Canada)
Colne (England)
Congo (Congo, Democratic Republic of)
Dnepr (Russia, Belarus, Ukraine)
Doubs (France, Switzerland)
Douro (Spain, Portugal)
Dovey (Wales)
Drava (Italy, Austria, Yugoslavia, Hungary)
Duero (Spain)
Dvina (Russia)
Forth (Scotland)
Foyle (Northern Ireland)
Frome (Australia)
Indus (India, Pakistan, China)
James (USA, Australia)
Jumna (India)
Jurua (Brazil)
Kafue (Zambia)
Kasai (Angola, Congo, Democratic Republic of)
Kuban (Russia)
Lagan (Northern Ireland)
Lippe (Germany)
Loire (France)

Marne (France)
Maros (Indonesia)
Meuse (France, Belgium)
Minho (Spain, Portugal)
Mures (Romania, Hungary)
Negro (Spain, Brazil, Argentina, Bolivia, Paraguay, Uruguay, Venezuela)
Neman (Belarus, Lithuania)
Niger (Nigeria, Mali, Guinea)
Otter (England)
Peace (Canada, USA)
Pearl (USA, China)
Pecos (USA)
Piave (Italy)
Purus (Brazil)
Rance (France)
Rhine (Switzerland, Germany, Netherlands)
Saale (Germany)
Saone (France)
Seine (France)
Slave (Canada)
Snake (USA)
Somme (France)
Stour (England)
Swale (England)
Tagus (Portugal, Spain)
Tamar (England)
Tiber (Italy)
Trent (England)
Tweed (England, Scotland)
Volga (Russia, USA)
Volta (Ghana)
Weser (Germany)
Xingu (Brazil)
Zaire (Congo, Democratic Republic of)

6

Allier (France)
Amazon (Peru, Brazil)
Angara (Russia)
Bio-Bio (Chile)
Chenab (Pakistan)
Clutha (New Zealand)
Cooper (Australia)
Coquet (England)
Crouch (England)
Danube (Germany, Austria, Romania, Hungary, Slovakia, Bulgaria)
Dnestr (Ukraine, Moldova)
Escaut (Belgium, France)
Fraser (Canada)
Gambia (The Gambia, Senegal)
Ganges (India)
Glomma (Norway)
Hudson (USA)
Hunter (Australia)
Irtysh (China, Kazakhstan, Russia)
Itchen (England)
Japura (Brazil)
Jordan (Israel, Jordan)
Kolyma (Russia)
Liffey (Republic of Ireland)
Loddon (Australia, England)
Mamore (Brazil, Bolivia)
Medina (USA)
Medway (England)
Mekong (Laos, China)
Mersey (England)
Monnow (England,

Wales)
Murray (Australia, Canada)
Neckar (Germany)
Neisse (Poland, Germany)
Ogooue (Gabon)
Orange (South Africa)
Orwell (England)
Parana (Brazil)
Platte (USA)
Ribble (England)
St John (Liberia, USA)
Salado (Argentina, Cuba, Mexico)
Severn (England)
Sutlej (Pakistan, India, China)
Thames (England)
Ticino (Italy, Switzerland)
Tigris (Iraq, Turkey)
Tugela (South Africa)
Ussuri (China, Russia)
Vienne (France)
Vltava (Czech Republic)
Wabash (USA)
Weaver (England)
Yellow (China, USA, Papua New Guinea)

7

Bermejo (Argentina)
Cauvery (India)
Damodar (India)
Darling (Australia)
Derwent (England)
Durance (France)
Garonne (France)
Gironde (France)
Helmand (Afghanistan)
Hooghly (India)
Huang Ho (China)

Lachlan (Australia)
Limpopo (South Africa, Zimbabwe, Mozambique)
Lualaba (Congo, Democratic Republic of)
Madeira (Brazil)
Maranon (Brazil, Peru)
Maritsa (Bulgaria)
Moselle (Germany)
Orontes (Syria)
Pechora (Russia)
Potomac (USA)
Salween (Myanmar, China)
Scheldt (Belgium)
Senegal (Senegal)
Shannon (Republic of Ireland)
Songhua (Vietnam, China)
Sungari (China)
Suwannee (USA)
Uruguay (Uruguay, Brazil)
Vistula (Poland)
Waikato (New Zealand)
Xi Jiang (China)
Yenisei (Russia)
Zambezi (Zambia, Angola, Zimbabwe, Mozambique)

8

Amu Darya (Turkmenistan, Uzbekistan)
Araguaia (Brazil)
Arkansas (USA)
Canadian (USA)
Charente (France)

Colorado (USA)
Columbia (USA)
Demerara (Guyana)
Dordogne (France)
Godavari (India)
Manawatu (New Zealand)
Menderes (Turkey)
Missouri (USA)
Paraguay (Paraguay)
Putumayo (Ecuador)
Rio Bravo (Mexico)
Saguenay (Canada)
Syr Darya (Uzbekistan, Kazakhstan)
Torridge (England)
Tunguska (Russia)
Volturno (Italy)
Wansbeck (England)
Windrush (England)

9

Athabasca (Canada)
Churchill (Canada)
Essequibo (Guyana)
Euphrates (Iraq)
Great Ouse (England)
Hsi Chiang (China)
Irrawaddy (Burma)
Mackenzie (Australia)
Magdalena (Columbia)
Rio Grande (Jamaica)
Tennessee (USA)

10

Chang Jiang (China)
Chao Phraya (Thailand)
Coppermine (Canada)
Hawkesbury (Australia)
Shenandoah (USA)
St Lawrence (USA)

11

Assiniboine (Canada)
Brahmaputra (China, India)
Mississippi (USA)
Susquehanna (USA)

Yellowstone (USA)

12

Guadalquivir (Spain)
Murrumbidgee

(Australia)
Rio de la Plata (Argentina, Uruguay)
Saskatchewan (Canada)

Mountains and Hills (*Note: Mt = Mountain, Mts = Mountains*)

3

Aso (Mt) (Japan)
Ida (Mt) (Turkey)

4

Alps (France, Switzerland, Italy, Austria)
Blue (Mts) (Australia)
Cook (Mt) (New Zealand)
Etna (Mt) (Sicily)
Harz (Mts) (Germany)
Jaya (Mt) (Indonesia)
Jura (Mts) (France, Switzerland)
Ossa (Mt) (Australia)
Rigi (Switzerland)
Ural (Mts) (Russia)

5

Altai (Mts) (Russia, China, Mongolia)
Andes (South America)
Athos (Mt) (Greece)
Atlas (Mts) (Morocco, Algeria)
Black (Mts) (Wales)
Coast (Mts) (Canada)
Eiger (Switzerland)
Elgon (Mt) (Uganda, Kenya)
Ghats (India)
Kamet (Mt) (India)
Kenya (Mt) (Kenya)
Lenin (Peak) (Russia)
Logan (Mt) (Canada)
Pelee (Mt) (Martinique)
Rocky (Mts) (USA, Canada)

Sayan (Mts) (Russia)
Snowy (Mts) (Australia)
Tatra (Mts) (Poland, Slovakia)
Weald (The) (England)

6

Antrim (Hills) (Northern Ireland)
Ararat (Mt) (Turkey)
Balkan (Mts) (Bulgaria)
Carmel (Mt) (Israel)
Egmont (Mt) (New Zealand)
Elbert (Mt) (USA)
Elbrus (Mt) (Russia, Georgia)
Elburz (Mt) (Iran)
Erebus (Mt) (Antarctica)
Hermon (Mt) (Syria, Lebanon)
Hoggar (Mts) (Algeria)
Kunlun (Mts) (China)
Ladakh (Range) (India)
Matopo (Hills) (Zimbabwe)
Mendip (Hills) (England)
Mourne (Mts) (Northern Ireland)
Olives (Mt of) (Israel)
Pamirs (Tajikistan, China, Afghanistan)
Pindus (Mts) (Greece, Albania)
Taurus (Mts) (Turkey)
Vosges (France)
Zagros (Mts) (Iran)

7

Ahaggar (Mts) (Algeria)
Bernina (Switzerland)
Brocken (Germany)

Cheviot (Hills) (United Kingdom)
Chianti (Italy)
Everest (Mt) (Nepal, China)
Olympus (Mt) (Greece)
Palomar (Mt) (USA)
Rainer (Mt) (USA)
Roraima (Mt) (Brazil, Guyana, Venezuela)
Ruapehu (Mt) (New Zealand)
Skiddaw (England)
Slemish (Northern Ireland)
Snowdon (Wales)
Sperrin (Mts) (Northern Ireland)
St Elias (Mts) (Alaska, Yukon)
Tibesti (Mts) (Chad, Libya)
Wicklow (Mts) (Republic of Ireland)

8

Ardennes (Luxembourg, Belgium, France)
Ben Nevis (Scotland)
Cambrian (Mts) (Wales)
Caucasus (Mts) (Georgia, Azerbaijan, Armenia)
Cevennes (France)
Chiltern (Hills) (England)
Cotopaxi (Ecuador)
Cotswold (Hills) (England)
Flinders (Range) (Australia)
Fujiyama (Japan)
Hymettus (Mt) (Greece)
Jungfrau (Switzerland)
Kaikoura (Ranges) (New Zealand)
Musgrave (Ranges) (Australia)
Pennines (England)
Pyrenees (France, Spain)
Stanovoi (Range) (Russia)
Tian Shan (Tajikistan, China, Mongolia)
Vesuvius (Italy)

9

Aconcagua (Mt) (Argentina)

Allegheny (Mts) (USA)
Annapurna (Mt) (Nepal)
Apennines (Italy)
Cairngorm (Mts) (Scotland)
Dolomites (Italy)
Dunsinane (Scotland)
Grampians (Scotland)
Hamersley (Range) (Australia)
Helvellyn (England)
Himalayas (South Asia)
Hindu Kush (Central Asia)
Huascaran (Peru)
Karakoram (Range) (Chins, India, Pakistan)
Kosciusko (Mt) (Australia)
Mont Blanc (France, Italy)
Nanda Devi (Mt) (India)
Pacaraima (Mts) (Brazil, Venezuela, Guyana)
Parnassus (Mt) (Greece)
Ruwenzori (Mts) (Congo, Democratic Republic of, Uganda)
Tirich Mir (Mt) (Pakistan)
Zugspitze (Germany)

10

Adirondack (Mts) (USA)
Cader Idris (Wales)
Cantabrian (Mts) Spain)
Carpathian (Mts) (Slovakia, Poland, Romania, Hungary, Ukraine, Moldova)
Chimborazo (Mt) (India)
Dhaulagiri (Mt) (Nepal)
Erzgebirge (Czech Republic, Germany)
Kebnekaise (Sweden)
Lammermuir (Hills) (Scotland)
MacDonnell (Ranges) (Australia)
Majuba Hill (South Africa)
Matterhorn (Switzerland, Italy)
Middleback (Range) (Australia)
Monserrat (Spain)
Mount Lofty (Ranges) (Australia)

11

Anti-Lebanon (Mts) (Lebanon, Syria)
Appalachian (Mts) (USA)
Drakensberg (Mts) (South Africa)
Jotunheimen (Norway)
Kilimanjaro (Mt) (Tanzania)
Monadhliath (Mts) (Scotland)
Nanga Parbat (Mt) (Pakistan)
Scafell Pike (England)
Sierra Madre (Mexico)

12

Citlaltepetl (Mexico)
Godwin Austen (Mt) (Pakistan)
Golan Heights (Syria)
Gran Paradiso (Italy)
Ingleborough (England)
Kanchenjunga (Mt) (Nepal)
Peak District (England)
Popocatepetl (Mt) (Mexico)

Siding Spring (Mt) (Australia)
Sierra Morena (Spain)
Sierra Nevada (Spain, USA)
Slieve Donard (Northern Ireland)
Warrumbungle (Range) (Australia)

13

Carrantuohill (Republic of Ireland)
Communism Peak (Tajikistan)
Grossglockner (Austria)
Kangchenjunga (Mt) (Nepal)
Kommunizma Pik (Tajikistan)
Ojos del Salado (Argentina, Chile)
Sierra Maestra (Cuba)

14

Fichtelgebirge (Germany)
Finsteraarhorn (Switzerland)
Shire Highlands (Malawi)

Ports

Algeria

4

Oran

6

Skikda

7

Algiers

9

Port Arzew

Angola

6

Lobito
Luanda

Argentina

7

La Plata

11

Buenos Aires

Australia

6

Sydney

7

Dampier
Geelong

8

Adelaide
Brisbane

9

Melbourne

Newcastle

10

Freemantle

11

Port Jackson

12

Port Adelaide

Belgium

6

Ostend

7

Antwerp

9

Zeebrugge

Benin

7

Cotonou

9

Porto Novo

Brazil

4

Para

5

Belem

6

Recife
Santos

7

Tobarao
10
Pernambuco
12
Rio de Janeiro

Bulgaria
5
Varna

Burma
5
Akyab
6
Sittwe
7
Rangoon
8
Moulmein

Cameroon
6
Douala

Canada
7
Halifax
Kitimat
8
Montreal
9
Churchill
Esquimalt
Owen Sound
Vancouver

11
Three Rivers

Channel Islands
8
St Helier
11
Saint Helier
St Peter Port

Chile
5
Arica
8
Coquimbo
10
Valparaiso

China
4
Amoy
6
Chefoo
Hankow
Swatow
Weihai
7
Foochow
Yingkow
8
Shanghai
Tientsin
10
Port Arthur

Columbia

9
Cartagena
12
Barranquilla
Buenaventura

Congo, Democratic Republic of
6
Matadi
9
Mbuji-Mayi

Corsica
6
Bastia
7
Ajaccio

Cuba
6
Havana
14
Santiago de Cuba

Cyprus
7
Larnaca
8
Limassol

Denmark
6
Odense

7
Aalborg
Horsens
8
Elsinore
9
Helsingor
10
Copenhagen
13
Frederikshavn

Ecuador
9
Guayaquil

Egypt
4
Suez
8
Damietta
Port Said
10
Alexandria

England
4
Hull
5
Dover
6
London
7
Chatham

Grimsby
Harwich
Tilbury

8

Falmouth
Newhaven
Penzance
Plymouth
Portland
Sandwich
Weymouth

9

Avonmouth
Devonport
Gravesend
King's Lynn
Liverpool
Newcastle
Sheerness

10

Barnstaple
Colchester
Felixstowe
Folkestone
Hartlepool
Portsmouth
Sunderland
Teignmouth
Whitstable

11

Cinque Ports
Southampton

12

North Shields
Port Sunlight

13

Middlesbrough

Finland

8

Helsinki

France

5

Brest

6

Calais
Cannes
Dieppe
Toulon

7

Dunkirk
Le Havre

8

Bordeaux
Boulogne
Honfleur

9

Cherbourg
Fos-sur-Mer
Marseille

10

La Rochelle
Marseilles

French Guiana

7

Cayenne

Germany

4

Kiel

5

Emden

6

Bremen
Wismar

7

Hamburg
Rostock

8

Cuxhaven

9

Flensburg

11

Travemunde

13

Wilhelms-Haven

Ghana

4

Tema

8

Takoradi

Greece

5

Canea

Corfu

6

Patras
Rhodes

7

Piraeus

8

Navarino

10

Hermopolis

11

Hermoupolis

Hawaii

8

Honolulu

11

Pearl Harbor

Hungary

8

Budapest

India

6

Bombay
Cochin
Haldia
Kandla
Madres

8

Calcutta
Cocanada
Kakinada

11

Masulipatam
Pondicherry

12

Masulipatnam

Indonesia

6

Padang

7

Jakarta

8

Macassar
Paradeep

Iran

6
———————
Abadan

7
———————
Bushire

Iraq

5
———————
Basra

Ireland

4
———————
Cobh
Cork

7
———————
Donegal
Dundalk
Youghal

12
———————
Dun Laoghaire

Israel

4
———————
Acre
Akko
Elat

5
———————
Eilat
Haifa

6
———————
Ashdod

Italy

4
———————
Bari

5
———————
Gaeta
Genoa
Ostia
Trani

6
———————
Ancona
Naples
Venice

7
———————
Leghorn
Marsala
Messina
Palermo
Salerno
Trapani
Trieste

8
———————
Brindisi

Ivory Coast

7
———————
Abidjan

Jamaica

8
———————
Kingston

9
———————
Port Royal

10
———————
Montego Bay

Japan

4
———————
Kobe

5
———————
Kochi
Osaka

8
———————
Hakodate
Nagasaki
Yokohama

9
———————
Hiroshima
Kagoshima

11
———————
Shimonoseki

Kenya

7
———————
Mombasa

Kuwait

12
———————
Mina al-Ahmadi

Lebanon

6
———————
Beirut

Libya

7
———————
|Tripoli

8
———————
Benghazi

Madagascar

8
———————
Tamatave

Malaysia

6
———————
Penang

9
———————
Port Klang

10
———————
George Town

12
———————
Kotakinabulu

Mauritania

10
———————
Nouakchott

Mauritius

9
———————
Port Louis

Mexico

7
———————
Guaymas

8
———————
Veracruz

Morocco

4
———————
Safi

5
———————
Ceuta
Rabat

6
———————
Agadir
Tetuan

7
———————

Melilla
Mogador
Tangier
9
_____

Essaouira
10
_____

Casablanca
14
_____

Mina Hassan Tani

Mozambique
5
_____

Beira
6
_____

Maputo

Netherlands
5
_____

Delft
8
_____

Flushing
9
_____

Amsterdam
Europoort
Rotterdam
10
_____

Vlissingen

New Zealand
6
_____

Nelson
8
_____

Auckland
Gisborne
9
_____

Lyttleton

Nigeria
5
_____

Lagos
12
_____

Port Harcourt

Northern Ireland
5
_____

Larne
7
_____

Belfast

Norway
4
_____

Oslo
6
_____

Bergen
Larvik
Narvik
Tromso
9
_____

Stavanger
Trondheim
10
_____

Hammerfest
Kristiania
12
_____

Kristiansand

Pakistan
6
_____

Chalna
7
_____

Karachi

Panama
5
_____

Colon
6
_____

Balboa
9
_____

Cristobal

Papua New Guinea
11
_____

Port Moresby

Peru
3
_____

Ilo
6
_____

Callao
8
_____

Matarini
10
_____

San Juan Bay

Philippines
4
_____

Cebu
6
_____

Manila

Poland
6
_____

Danzig
Gdansk

Gdynia
7
_____

Stettin
8
_____

Szczecin
9
_____

Kolobrzeg

Portugal
6
_____

Lisbon
Oporto

Puerto Rico
7
_____

San Juan

Romania
10
_____

Constantsa

Russia
8
_____

Pechenga
Taganrog
9
_____

Archangel
11
_____

Vladivostock
12
_____

St Petersburg

Saudi Arabia
6
_____

Jeddah

Scotland

4
Tain
Wick

5
Leith
Scapa

6
Dunbar
Dundee

8
Greenock

9
Ardrossan
Scapa Flow
Stornaway

11
Grangemouth
Port Glasgow

Senegal

5
Dakar

Sierra Leone

8
Freetown

South Africa

6
Durban

8
Cape Town

9
Mossel Bay
Port Natal

10
East London
Simonstown

11
Richard's Bay

13
Port Elizabeth

South Korea

5
Pusan

Spain

5
Palma
Palos

6
Bilbao
Ferrol
Malaga

7
Corunna
Funchal

8
Alicante
Arrecife
La Coruna

9
Algeciras
Barcelona
Cartagena
Las Palmas
Port Mahon

Sri Lanka

5
Galle

7
Colombo
Sudan

6
Suakin

9
Port Sudan

Sweden

5
Lulea
Malmo
Wisby
Ystad

6
Kalmar

8
Goteborg
Halmstad
Nykoping

9
Stockholm

10
Gothenburg

11
Helsingborg

Taiwan

6
Tainan

7
Keelung

9
Kao-Hsiung

Tanzania

6
Mtwara

11
Dar es Salaam

Trinidad and Tobago

11
Port-of-Spain

Turkey

5
Izmir

6
Smyrna

8
Istanbul

14
Constantinople

Uruguay

10
Montevideo

USA

4
Erie

7
Detroit
Houston
New York
Norfolk
Seattle

8
New Haven

9

Baltimore
Galveston
Nantucket
Pensacola

10

Bridgeport
Charleston
Jersey City
Los Angeles
New Bedford
New Orleans
Perth Amboy
Portsmouth

11

Rock Harbour

12

San Francisco

Venezuela

8

La Guiara

12

Puerto Hierro

13

Puerto Cabello

Wales

7

Cardiff
Swansea

8

Holyhead
Llanelli
Pembroke

9

Portmadoc

12

Milford Haven

Yemen

4

Aden

5

Mocha

6

Ahmedi

7

Hodeida

Yugoslavia

3

Bar

5

Kotor

7

Cattaro

Territories and Dependencies

Australian States and Territories

Australian Capital Territory
New South Wales
Northern Territory
Queensland
South Australia
Tasmania
Victoria
Western Australia

New Zealand Islands and Territories

Cook Islands
Niue
North Island
Ross Dependency
South Island
Tokelau

Canadian Provinces and Territories

Province/Territory	Abbreviation
Alberta	AB
British Columbia	BC
Manitora	MB
New Brunswick	NB
Newfoundland and Labrador	NF
Northwest Territories	NT
Nova Scotia	NS
Nunavut	-
Ontario	ON
Prince Edward Island	PE
Quebec	QC
Saskatchewan	SK
Yukon Territory	YT

European Union

State	Year Of Accession
Austria	1995
Belgium	1958
Denmark	1973
Finland	1995
France	1958
Germany	1958
Greece	1981
Ireland	1973
Italy	1958
Luxembourg	1958
Netherlands	1958
Portugal	1986
Spain	1986
Sweden	1995
United Kingdom	1973

Dependencies

Australia

Ashmore and Cartier Islands
Australian Antarctic Territory
Christmas Island
Principle Settlement: Flying Fish Cove
Cocos (Keeling) Islands
Principle Settlement: West Island
Heard Island and McDonald Island
Norfolk Island
Capital: Kingstown

Denmark

Faroe Islands
Capital: Torshavn

Greenland

Capital: Nuuk (Godthab)

France

French Guiana
Capital: Cayenne
French Polynesia
Capital: Papeete
Guadeloupe
Capital: Basse-Terre
Martinique
Capital: Fort-de-France
Mayotte
Capital: Dzaoudzi
New Caledonia
Capital: Noumea
Reunion
Capital: Saint-Denis
Saint Pierre and Miquelon
Capital: Saint-Pierre
Wallis and Futuna
Capital: Mata-Utu

The Netherlands

Aruba
Capital: Oranjestad
Netherlands Antilles
Capital: Willemstad

New Zealand

Cook Islands
Capital: Avarua
Niue
Capital: Alofi
The Ross Dependency
Tokelau

Norway

Bouvet Island
Jan Mayen
Peter the First Island
Princess Ragnhild Land
Queen Maud Land
Svalbard
Principle Settlement: Longyearbyen

Portugal

Macau
Capital: Macau

United Kingdom

Anguilla
Capital: The Valley
Bermuda
Capital: Hamilton
British Antarctic Territory
British Indian Ocean Territory
British Virgin Islands
Capital: Road Town
Cayman Islands
Capital: George Town
Falkland Islands
Capital: Stanley
Gibraltar
Capital: Gibraltar
Guernsey
Capital: St Peter Port
Isle of Man
Capital: Douglas

Jersey
Capital: St Helier
Monserrat
Capital: Plymouth
Pitcairn Islands
Sole town: Adamstown
Saint Helena
Capital: Jamestown
South Georgia and the South
Sandwich Islands
Turks and Caicos Islands
Capital: Cockburn Town

United States

American Samoa
Capital: Pago Pago
Guam
Capital: Agana
Northern Mariana Islands
Principle Settlement: Saipan
Puerto Rico
Capital: San Juan
United States Virgin Islands
Capital: Charlotte Amalie

Volcanoes

3

Aso (Japan)
Awu (Indonesia)

4

Etna (Sicily
Fogo (Cape Verde
Islands)
Gede (Indonesia)
Kaba (Indonesia)
Laki (Iceland)
Nila (Indonesia)
Poas (Costa Rica)
Siau (Indonesia)
Taal (Phillipines)

5

Agung (Indonesia)
Asama (Japan)
Askja (Iceland)
Dempo (Indonesia)
Fuego (Guatemala)
Hekla (Iceland)
Katla (Iceland)
Manam (Papua New
Guinea)
Mayon (Philippines)
Noyoe (Iceland)
Okmok (U.S.A.)
Paloe (Indonesia)

Pelee (Martinique)
Spurr (U.S.A.)

6

Alcedo (Galapagos
Islands)
Ambrim (Vanuatu)
Big Ben (Heard Island)
Buleng (Indonesia)
Colima (Mexico)
Dukono (Indonesia)
Izalco (El Salvador)
Katmai (U.S.A.)
Lascar (Chile)
Lassen (U.S.A.)

Llaima (Chile)
Lopevi (Vanuatu)
Marapi (Indonesia)
Martin (U.S.A.)
Meakan (Japan)
Merapi (Indonesia)
Mihara (Japan)
O'Shima (Japan)
Osorno (Chile)
Pacaya (Guatemala)
Pavlof (U.S.A.)
Purace (Columbia)
Sangay (Equador)
Semeru (Indonesia)
Slamat (Indonesia)
Tacana (Guatemala)
Unauna (Indonesia)

7

Atitlan (Guatemala)
Barcena (Mexico)
Bulusan (Philippines)
Didicas (Philippines)
El Mistri (Peru)
Galeras (Columbia)
Jorullo (Mexico)
Kilauea (U.S.A.)
Ometepe (Nicaragua)
Puyehue (Chile)
Ruapehu (New
Zealand)
Sabrina (Azores)
Soputan (Indonesia)
Surtsey (Iceland)
Ternate (Indonesia)
Tjareme (Indonesia)
Tokachi (Japan)
Torbert (U.S.A.)

Trident (U.S.A.)
Vulcano (Italy)

8

Bogoslof (U.S.A.)
Cameroon (Cameroon)
Cotopaxi (Ecuador)
Demavend (Iran)
Fonualei (Tonga Islands)
Fujiyama (Japan)
Hualalai (U.S.A.)
Kerintji (Indonesia)
Krakatau (Indonesia)
Krakatoa (Indonesia)
Muana Loa (U.S.A.)
Niuafo'ou (Tonga)
Rindjani (Indonesia)
Sangeang (Indonesia)
Tarawera (New
Zealand)
Vesuvius (Italy)
Yakedake (Japan)

9

Amburombu
(Indonesia)
Bandai-San (Japan)
Cleveland (U.S.A.)
Coseguina (Nicaragua)
Cotacachi (Ecuador)
Gamkonora (Indonesia)
Grimsvotn (Iceland)
Momotombo
(Nicaragua)
Myozin-Syo (Japan)
Ngauruhoe (New
Zealand)
Paricutin (Mexico)

Rinanahue (Chile)
Santorini (Greece)
Stromboli (Italy)
Tongariro (New
Zealand)
Acatenango
(Guatemala)
Capelinhos (Azores)
Cerro Negro
(Nicaragua)
Guallatiri (Chile)
Hibok Hibok
(Philippines)
Long Island (Papua New
Guinea)
Miyakejima (Japan)
Nyamiagira (Congo,
Democratic Republic
of)
Santa Maria
(Guatemala)
Shishaldin (U.S.A.)
Tungurahua (Ecuador)
Villarrica (Chile)

11

Great Sitkin (U.S.A.)
Kilimanjaro (Tanzania)
La Soufriere (Saint
Vincent and the
Grenadines)
Tupungatito (Chile)
White Island (New
Zealand)

12

Huainaputina (Peru)
Popocatepetl (Mexico)

Weather

3
dry
fog
hot
icy
sun
wet

4
calm
cold
cool
damp
dark
dull
east
gale
gust
hail
haze
hazy
heat
mild
mist
rain
smog
snow
tide
veer
warm
west
wind

5
cirri
cloud
dusty
eurus
flood
foggy
frost

gusty
light
misty
muggy
north
rainy
sleet
snowy
south
storm
sunny
windy

6
arctic
auster
bright
chilly
clouds
cloudy
colder
deluge
floods
freeze
frosty
hot day
lowery
meteor
mizzle
mizzly
nimbus
normal
shower
simoon
squall
starry
stormy
sultry
torrid
trades
vortex

warmer
wet day
winter
wintry
zephyr

7
backing
blowing
climate
clouded
cold day
coldish
cyclone
drizzle
drought
dry-bulb
fogbank
freshen
fresher
freshet
hailing
hottish
icy-cold
muggish
rainbow
raining
set fair
showery
snowing
squally
summery
sunspot
tempest
thunder
tornado
typhoon
veering
warm day
warmish
wintery

8
autumnal
blizzard
cold snap
cyclonic
dead-calm
doldrums
downpour
easterly
east wind
eddy wind
fireball
freezing
heatwave
hot night
hurlwind
landwind
lowering
meteoric
nubilous
overcast
rainfall
rainless
scirocco
snowfall
sunlight
thundery
tropical
westerly
west wind
wet night
windless

9
cold night
drift wind
drizzling
dry season
hailstorm
hard frost

hoarfrost
hurricane
lightning
moonlight
northeast
northerly
northwest
north wind
nor'-wester
raincloud
sea breeze
snow-storm
southeast
southerly
southwest
south wind
sou'-wester
starlight
tidal wave
trade wind
unclouded
unsettled
warm night
whirlwind
zephyrous

10

arctic cold
black frost
changeable
depression
freshening
frostbound
hot climate
hot weather
land breeze
March winds
monsoonish
pouring-wet
Scotch mist
storm-cloud
waterspout
wet weather

white frost

11

anticyclone
cats and dogs
cold climate
cold weather
dull weather
etesian wind
foul weather
hard weather
lowering sky
mackerel sky
meteorology
mild weather
rain or shine
rainy season
stiff breeze
storm signal
summer cloud
temperature
tempestuous
thunderbolt
thunderclap
warm weather
wind backing
wind veering

12

anticyclonic
April showers
atmospherics
easterly wind
equinoctials
freezing rain
mackerel gale
shooting star
storm brewing
thundercloud
thunderstorm
tropical heat
tropical rain
weather glass
westerly wind

windy weather

13

autumn weather
frosty weather
northeast wind
northerly wind
northwest wind
southeast wind
southerly wind
southwest wind
summer weather
thunder-shower
weather report
wintry weather

14

aurora borealis
meteorological
moonlight night
sheet lightning
starlight night
torrential rain
weather prophet

15

forked lightning
meteoric
showers
prevailing winds
summer lightning
tropical climate

Clouds

altocumulus
altostratus
cirrocumulus
cirrostratus
cirrus
cumulonimbus
cumulostratus
cumulus

currocumulus
currostratus
nimbostratus
stratocumulus
stratus

Notable Winds

4

berg
bise
bora
fohn

5

buran
foehn
gibli
zonda

6

austru
ghibli
haboob
kamsin
saniel
simoom
solano

7

chinook
etesian
gregale
khamsin
meltemi
mistral
monsoon
pampero
sirocco

8

levanter
libeccio

papagayo
santa ana
williwaw

9 _____

harmattan

libecchio
snow eater

10 _____

cape doctor
euroclydon

tramontana
tramontane
wet chinook
willy-willy

11 _____

tehuantepec

12 _____

brickfielder

15 _____

southerly buster

Geology

Gems and Jewellery

3 _____

gem
jet

4 _____

bead
clip
gaud
jade
onyx
opal
ring
ruby
sard
stud
torc
unio
ural

5 _____

agate
aglet
amber
badge
beads
beryl
bezel
bijou
brait
bugle

cameo
carat
clasp
coral
crown
ivory
jewel
lapis
links
nacre
paste
pearl
tiara
topaz
union
watch

6 _____

albert
amulet
anklet
armlet
augite
bangle
bauble
brooch
corals
diadem
earring
enamel

fibula
garnet
gewgaw
iolite
ligure
locket
olivet
pearls
pyrope
quartz
signet
sphere
spinel
telesm
tiepin
torque
turkis
wampum
zircon

7 _____

abraxas
adamant
annulet
armilla
asteria
axinite
cat's eye
chaplet
coronet

crystal
diamond
eardrop
emerald
espinel
euclase
faceted
filigree
jacinth
jewelry
olivine
pendant
peridot
regalia
ringlet
rubicel
sardine
sardius
sceptre
smaragd
spangle
telesia
trinket
yu-stone

8 _____

adularia
aigrette
amethyst
armillet

bracelet
carcanet
cardiace
corundum
diopside
gemmeous
hallmark
hyacinth
intaglio
liginite
necklace
pectoral
rock ruby
sapphire
sardonyx
scarf-pin
shirt-pin
sparkler
sunstone
topazine

9

balas ruby
black onyx
black opal
breast-pin
brilliant

carbuncle
carnelian
cornelian
cufflinks
foil-stone
gold watch
jadestone
jewellery
marcasite
medallion
moonstone
morganite
moss-agate
paillette
phenacite
press stud
pyreneite
rubellite
seed pearl
solitaire
starstone
thumbring
trinketry
turquoise
uvarovite

10

adderstone
amber beads
andalusite
aquamarine
black pearl
bloodstone
chalcedony
chrysolite
coral beads
glass beads
madrepearl
Mocha stone
rhinestone
signet ring
topazolite
tourmaline
watch-chain
watchstrap
water opal
wristwatch

11

aiguillette
alexandrite
bostrychite
cameo brooch
chalcedonyx

chrysoberyl
chrysophrase
colophonite
crocidolite
lapis lazuli
slave bangle
wedding-ring

12

bead necklace
eternity ring
grossularite
link bracelet

13

chain bracelet
coral necklace
mother-of-pearl
mourning ring
pearl necklace
precious stone

14

engagement ring
mourning brooch

15

crystal necklace

Minerals, Ores and Rocks

Minerals and Rocks

3

jet
tin
wad

4

alum
bort
cauk

clay
coal
gold
grit
iron
jade
lead
lias
mawl
mica
onyx
opal

rock
ruby
sard
spar
talc
tufa
wadd
zinc

5

agate
albin
alloy

amber
argil
argon
baria
beryl
borax
boron
brass
chalk
chert
emery
erbia

flint
fluor
frass
invar
macle
magma
nitre
ochre
pitch
prase
shale
silex
slate
spalt
steel
topaz
tutty
yeode

6

albite
aplome
augite
barium
bargyta
basalt
blende
cerite
cherty
cobalt
copper
davina
dipyre
doggar
egeran
erbium
gabbro
galena
garnet
glance
gneiss
gypsum
humite

indium
iolite
jargon
jasper
kaolin
kunkur
marble
mesole
mundic
nappal
nickel
nosean
ophite
ormolu
pewter
pinite
plasma
potash
pumice
pyrite
pyrope
quartz
radium
rutile
schorl
silica
silver
sinter
sodium
speiss
sphene
thoria
tombac
xylite
yenite
zircon

7

adamant
alumina
alunite
amianth
anatase

apatite
aphrite
arsenic
asphalt
axilite
azurite
barytes
bauxite
biotime
biotite
bismuth
bitumen
bornite
breccia
cadmium
calcite
calcium
caliche
calomel
cat's-eye
cuprite
cyprine
desmine
diamond
diorite
edelite
emerald
epidote
epigene
erinite
euclase
fahlerz
fahlore
felsite
felspar
fuscite
gassoul
granite
greisen
helvine
hessite
hyalite
ice spar

iridium
jargoon
kainite
kyanite
lignite
lithium
macadam
mellite
mercury
nacrite
olivine
peridot
petzite
pycnite
pyrites
realgar
romeine
sahlite
sinoper
sinople
sulphur
syenite
talcite
thorite
thorium
thulite
tripoli
uranium
wolfram
wurgite
yttrium
zeolite
zeuxite
zincite
zoisite
zorgite
zurlite

8

achirite
adularia
aerolite
amethyst

andesite
antimony
aphanite
asbestos
blue John
boracite
bronzite
brookite
calamine
calc-spar
cast iron
chabasie
chlorite
chromite
chromium
cinnabar
corundum
cryolite
dendrite
diallage
diopside
dioptase
dolerite
dolomite
embolite
epsomite
essonite
feldspar
felstone
fireclay
fluorite
graphite
hematite
hyacinth
idocrase
ilmenite
jasponyx
konilite
laterite
lazulite
ligurite
limonite
lirocone

litharge
lomonite
magnesia
massicot
meionite
melanite
melilite
mesolite
mesotype
micanite
mimetene
monazite
napolite
nemalite
nephrite
obsidian
orpiment
pagodite
pea stone
petalite
platinum
plumbago
porphyry
prehnite
psammite
pyroxene
ragstone
reussite
rhyolite
rock cork
rock salt
rock soap
rock wood
sagenite
sanidine
sapphire
sardonyx
selenite
siberite
siderite
smaltine
sodalite
spinelle

steatite
stellite
stibnite
stilbite
thallium
tin stone
titanium
trachyte
trap-rock
triphane
tungsten
turmalin
vesuvian
voltzite
weissite
wood opal
wood rock
worthite
wurtzite
xanthite
xylonite
yanolite
zirconia

9

alabaster
allophane
almandine
aluminium
alum shale
alum slate
amianthus
amphibole
anamesite
anglesite
anhydrite
anomalite
anorthite
aphrisite
argentite
argillite
aromatite
arquifoux

asphaltum
austerite
baikalite
basaltine
boltonite
brick-clay
brown-coal
brown-spur
byssolite
carbonado
carbuncle
carnelian
carnalite
casholong
cat-silver
cerussite
ceylanite
chabasite
chabazite
chalybite
cobaltine
columbite
cornelian
corn stone
earth flax
elaeolite
elaterite
erythrine
erythrite
eudyalite
eukairite
firestone
fluorspar
galactite
gmelinite
granitite
granulite
graystone
graywacke
greensand
grenatite
greystone
greywacke

haematite
heavy spar
horn slate
hornstone
indianite
ironstone
ittnerite
johannite
killinite
latrobite
laumonite
lenzinite
limbilite
limestone
lodestone
magnesite
magnesium
magnetite
malachite
manganese
marcasite
margarite
marmatite
melaphyre
mellitite
meteorite
mica slate
mispickel
moonstone
moorstone
muscovite
nagyagite
natrolite
necrolite
necronite
needletin
nepheline
niccolite
noumeaite
omphacite
ozokerite
pargasite
pearl spar

pectolite
pegmatite
periclase
petroleum
phenacite
phonolite
physalite
pleonaste
plinthite
potassium
proustite
pyrophane
quartzite
raphilite
rhodonite
rhombspar
rubellite
sandstone
satin spar
scapolite
scheelite
scolecite
soapstone
spinthere
spodumene
streamtin
strontium
sylvanite
tantalite
tautalite
tellurium
torbanite
torrelite
tremolite
tridymite
turnerite
turquoise
uvarovite
veinstone
vulcanite
wavellite
wernerite
willemite

withamite
witherite
woodstone
wulfenite
xanthocon
zinc bloom
zirconite

10

actinolite
amianthoid
amygdaloid
anthracite
aquamarine
aventurine
azure stone
batrachite
bergmanite
beudantite
bismuthite
bloodstone
calaverite
cannel coal
carnallite
cervantite
chalcedony
chalybeate
chonikrite
chrysolite
clinkstone
constantan
cross-stone
diallogite
dyscrasite
eagle stone
false topaz
floatstone
gabbronite
garnierite
glauberite
glauconite
glottalite
greenstone

heterosite
heulandite
hornblende
hornsilver
hydrophane
hyperstene
indicolite
iridosmine
iron glance
karpholite
Kentish rag
kieselguhr
koupholite
lead glance
lepidolite
malacolite
meerschaum
melaconite
mica schist
mocho stone
molybdenum
monelmetal
nussierite
nuttallite
orthoclase
osmiridium
paranthine
phosphorus
picrosmine
polyhalite
pyrochlore
pyrolusite
rathoffite
redruthite
retinalite
rock butter
rose quartz
sapphirine
sardachate
saussurite
schalstein
serpentine
sismondine

smaragdite
sparry iron
sphalerite
stalactite
stalagmite
staurolite
stephanite
talc schist
thomsonite
topazolite
tourmaline
vanadinite
villarsite
websterite
zinc blende

11

alexandrite
amblygonite
amphibolite
amphiboloid
Babbit metal
black silver
brewsterite
cassiterite
chlorophane
chondrodite
chromic iron
chrysoberyl
cobalt bloom
crichtonite
crocidolite
dendrachate
diving stone

epistilbite
ferrachrome
figure stone
franklinite
hypersthene
Iceland spar
iron pyrites
lapis lazuli
libethenite
milky quartz
molybdenum
Muller glass
muschel kalk
napoleonite
needlestone
octahedrite
phillipsite
pitchblende
polymignite
psilomelane
pyrallolite
pyrargyrite
pyrosmalite
rock crystal
sillimanite
smithsonite
smoky quartz
sordavalite
sphaerulite
tetradymite
thumerstone
titanic iron
yttrocerite

12

aerosiderate
artvedsonite
chalcopyrite
cobalt glance
copper glance
forest marble
fuller's earth
greyweathers
jeffersonite
kupfernickel
mineral black
mineral green
mineral resin
montmartrite
mountain cork
mountain flax
mountain milk
mountain soap
murchisonite
oriental ruby
puddingstone
pyrargillite
pyromorphite
quartz schist
silver glance
somervillite
Spanish chalk
specular iron
speisscobalt
sprig crystal
strontianite
tetrahedrite
woolastonite

13

agaric mineral
anthophyllite
chlorophaeite
cinnamon stone
cleavelandite
copper pyrites
emerald copper
kerosene shale
needle zeolite

14

antimony glance
bituminous coal
britannia metal
brown haematite
Cairngorm stone
chlorite schist
elastic bitumen
graphic granite
quartz porphyry

15

arkose sandstone
hydromica schist
mountain leather

16

galenabismuthite
orthoferrosilite
pharmacosiderite

17

hydrogrossularite
tellurobismuthite

Ores

Element	Ore	Element	Ore
3		gallium	bauxite
tin	cassiterite	hafnium	zircon
4		holmium	monazite
iron	haematite, magnetite	iridium	lithium lepidolite, spodumene
lead	galena	mercury	cinnabar
zinc	sphalerite, smithsonite, calamine	niobium	columbite-tantalite, pyrochlore, euxenite
5		rhenium	molybdenite rhodium
boron	kernite	silicon	silica
6		thorium	monazite
barium	barite, witherite	thulium	monazite
cerium	monazite, bastnaesite	uranium	pitchblende, uraninite, carnotite
cobalt	cobaltite, smaltite, erythrite	yttrium	monazite
copper	malachite, azurite, chalcopyrite, bornite, cuprite	**8**	
		antimony	stibnite
erbium	monazite, bastnaesite	chromium	chromite
indium	sphalerite, smithsonite, calamine	lutetium	monazite
		platinum	sperrylite
nickel	pentlandite, pyrrhotite	rubidium	lepidolite
osmium	iridosime	samarium	monazite, bastnaesite
radium	pitchblende, carnotite	scandium	thortveitite, davidite
		selenium	pyrites
silver	argentite, horn silver	tantalum	columbite-tantalite
sodium	salt	thallium	pyrites
7		titanium	rutile, ilmenite, sphere
arsenic	realgar, orpiment, arsenopyrite	tungsten	wolframite, scheelite
		vanadium	carnotite, roscoelite, vanadinite
cadmium	greenocktite	**9**	
caesium	lepidolite, pollucite	aluminium	bauxite
calcium	limestone, gypsum, fluorite	beryllium	beryl
		germanium	germanite, argyrodite

Element	Ore	Element	Ore
lanthanum	monazite, bastnaesite	**10**	
magnesium	magnesite, dolomite	dysprosium	monazite, bastnaesite
neodymium	monazite, bastnaesite	gadolinium	monazite, bastnaesite
palladium		molybdenum	molybdenite, wulfenite
potassium	sylvite, carnalite, polyhalite	phosphorous	apatite
ruthenium	pentlandite, pyroxinite	**12**	
strontium	celestite, strontianite	praseodymium	monazite, bastnaesite
tellurium		protactinium	pitchblende
ytterbium	monazite		

Languages phrases and words

Foreign and Latin Words and Phrases

and

French	et
German	und
Italian	e, ed
Spanish	e
Latin	et

but

French	mais
German	aber
Italian	ma
Spanish	pero
Latin	sed

for

French	pour
German	fur
Italian	per
Spanish	para, por
Latin	per

to

French	a
German	auf, nach
Italian	a
Spanish	a
Latin	ad

with

French	avec
German	mit
Italian	con
Spanish	con
Latin	cum

Mister, Mr

French	Monsieur, M.
German	Herr, Hr., Hrn.
Italian	Signor, Sr.

Spanish	Senor, Sr.
Latin	Dominus

Madame, Mrs

French	Madame, Mme.
German	Frau, French.
Italian	Signora, Sig.A., Sig.Ra.
Spanish	Senora, Sra
Latin	Domina

Miss, Ms

French	Mademoiselle, Mlle
German	Fraulein, Frl.
Italian	Signorina, Sig.Na
Spanish	Senorita, Srta.

from

French	de
German	aus, von
Italian	da
Spanish	de
Latin	ab

of

French	de
German	von
Italian	di
Spanish	de
Latin	de

girl

French	fille
German	madchen
Italian	ragazza
Spanish	chica, nina
Latin	puella

boy

French	garcon

German	junge
Italian	ragazzo
Spanish	chico, nino
Latin	puer

big

French	grand
German	gross
Italian	grande
Spanish	grande
Latin	magnus

little

French	petit
German	klein
Italian	piccolo
Spanish	pequeno, chico, poco
Latin	paucus

very

French	tres
German	sehr
Italian	molto
Spanish	mucho

fashionable

French	a la mode
German	modisch
Italian	di moda
Spanish	de moda

gentleman

French	monsieur
German	herr
Italian	signore
Spanish	caballero
Latin	dominus

lady

French	dame
German	dame
Italian	signora

Spanish	senora
Latin	domina

man

French	homme
German	mann
Italian	uomo
Spanish	hombre
Latin	homo

woman

French	femme
German	frau
Italian	donna
Spanish	dona
Latin	mulier

who

French	qui
German	wer
Italian	chi
Spanish	quien, que
Latin	quis

I

French	je
German	ich
Italian	io
Spanish	yo
Latin	ego

you

French	tu, vous
German	du, sie, ihr
Italian	tu, voi, lei
Spanish	tu, vosotros, vosotras
Latin	tu, vos

what

French	quoi, quel
German	was,
Italian	che, cosa

Spanish	que	Spanish	casa
Latin	quod	Latin	villa, domus

he		*street*	
French	il	French	rue
German	er	German	strasse
Italian	egli	Italian	strada
Spanish	el	Spanish	calle
Latin	is	Latin	via

she		*road*	
French	elle	French	route
German	sie	German	weg
Italian	ella	Italian	via
Spanish	ella	Spanish	camino
Latin	ea	Latin	via

we		*by*	
French	nous	French	par
German	wir	German	bei
Italian	noi	Italian	per
Spanish	nosotros/as	Spanish	por
Latin	nos	Latin	per

they		*before*	
French	ils, elles	French	avant
German	sie	German	vor
Italian	essi/e, loro	Italian	prima
Spanish	ellos, ellas	Spanish	(del) ante
Latin	ei, eae	Latin	ante

at home		*after*	
French	chez nous or a la maison	French	après
		German	nach
German	zu hause	Italian	dopo
Italian	a casa	Spanish	despues
Spanish	en casa	Latin	post
Latin	domo		

house		*under*	
French	maison	French	sous
German	haus	German	unter
Italian	casa	Italian	sotto
		Spanish	(de) bajo

Latin	sub

over

French	sur
German	ober
Italian	sopra, su
Spanish	sobre
Latin	super

near

French	pres de
German	nahe, bei
Italian	vicino
Spanish	cerca
Latin	prope

out

French	dehors
German	aus
Italian	via, fuori
Spanish	fuera
Latin	ex

in

French	dans
German	in
Italian	in
Spanish	en
Latin	in

how

French	comment
German	wie
Italian	come
Spanish	como
Latin	quo modo

why

French	pourquoi
German	warum
Italian	perche
Spanish	por que
Latin	cur

the

French	le, la, les
German	der, die, das
Italian	il, lo, la, I, gli, le
Spanish	el, la, lo, los, las
Latin	ille

a

French	un, une
German	ein, eine
Italian	un, uno, una
Spanish	un, una
Latin	unus

red

French	rouge
German	rot
Italian	rosso
Spanish	rojo
Latin	ruber

blue

French	bleu
German	blau
Italian	azzurro
Spanish	azul
Latin	caeruleus

yellow

French	jaune
German	gelb
Italian	giallo
Spanish	amarillo
Latin	fulvus

green

French	vert
German	grun
Italian	verde
Spanish	verde
Latin	virdis

black		white	
French	noir	French	blanc or blanche
German	schwarz	German	weiss
Italian	nero	Italian	bianco
Spanish	negro	Spanish	blanco
Latin	niger	Latin	albus

French Phrases

5

mêlée – brawl

on dit – piece of gossip, rumour

6

de trop – unwelcome

7

a la mode – fashionable

a propos – to the point

cap-a-pie – from head to foot

de regle - customary

en masse – all together

en route – on the way

8

bete noir – person or thing particularly disliked

idée fixe – obsession

mal de mar – seasickness

mot juste – the appropriate word

9

de rigueur – required by custom

en passant – by the way

en rapport – in harmony

entré nous – between you and me

10

a bon marche – cheap

billet doux – love letter

dernier cri – latest fashion, the last word

nom de plume – writer's assumed name

pense a bien – think for the best

11

amour propre – self esteem

gardez la foi – keep the faith

lese majeste – treason

nom de guerre – assumed name

raison d'etre – justification for existence

savoir faire – address, tact

tour de force – feat or accomplishment of great strength

12

force majeure – irresistible force or compulsion

hors de combat – out of the fight, disabled

sans dieu rien – nothing without God

ventre a terre – at great speed

double entendre – double meaning

enfant terrible – child who causes embarrassment

noblesse oblige – privilege entails responsibility

preux chevalier – gallant knight

verite sans peur – truth without fear

15

amende honorable – reparation
chercez la femme – look for the woman

17

piece de resistance – most outstanding item; main dish at a meal

20+

autre temps, autres moeurs – other times, other manners

Latin Phrases

4

fiat – let it be dome or made
in re – concerning
stet – let it stand

5

ad hoc – for this special purpose
ad lib – to speak of the cuff, without notes
ad rem – to the point
circa – about
fecit – he did it

6

ad usum – as is customary
in situ – in its original situation
in toto – entirely
in vivo – in life, describing biological occurrences within living bodies
pro tem – temporary, for the time being

7

ad finem – to the end
a priori – by deduction
cui bono? – whom does it benefit?
de facto – in fact
fiat lux – let there be light
in vitro – in glass, describing biological experiments outside a body
peccavi – a confession of guilt (I have sinned)
per diem – by the day
sine die – without a day being appointed
una voce – with one voice, unanimously

8

alter ego – another
bona fide – in good faith
emeritus – one retired from active official duties
mea culpa – an acknowledgement of guilt (I am to blame)
nota bene – observe or note well
pro forma – for the sake of form

9

ad interim – meanwhile
ad literam – to the letter
ad nauseam – to a disgusting, sickening degree
Dei gratia – by the grace of God
et tu, Brute – and you, Brutus
excelsior – still higher
ex officio – by right of position or office
hic et nunc – here and now
inter alia – amongst other things

pro patria – for one's country

status quo – the existing situation or state of affairs

sub judice – under consideration

vice versa – the terms being exchanged, the other way round

vox populi – popular opinion

10

anno domini – in the year of our Lord

Deo gratias – thanks be to God

ex cathedra – with authority

in extremis – in dire straits, at the point of death

in memoriam – to the memory of

loco citato – in the place quoted

post mortem – after death

prima facie – at first sight

sine qua non – something indispensable

terra firma – solid ground

11

ad infinitum – endlessly, to infinity

animo et fide – by courage and faith

de die in diem – from day to day

de profundis – from the depths of misery

ex post facto – after the event

gloria Patri – glory to the Father

locus standi – the right to be heard (in a law case)

non sequitur – an unwarranted conclusion

pax vobiscum – peace be with you

tempus fugit – time flies

12

ante meridiem – before noon

caveat emptor – let the buyer beware

compos mentis – of sane mind

festina lente – hasten slowly, be quick without impetuosity

jacta est alea – the die is cast

perseverando – by perseverance

post meridiem – after noon

servabo fidem – I will keep faith

veni, vidi, vici – I came, I saw, I conquered

volo non valeo – I am willing but unable

13

corpus delicti – body of facts that constitute an offence

dum spiro, spero – while I breathe, I hope

in vino veritas – there is a truth in wine, this is, the truth comes out

modus operandi – a method of operating

ne fronti crede – trust not to appearances

vincit veritas – truth conquers

virtutis amore – by love of virtue

14

ceteris paribus – other things being equal

editio princeps – the original edition

in loco parentis – in place of a parent

nil desperandum – never despair

pro bono publico – for the public good

15

amino non astutia – by courage not be craft

fortiter et recte – courageously and

honourably

fortuna sequatur – let fortune follow

infra dignitatem – beneath one's dignity

non compos mentis – mentally unsound

omnia vincit amor – love conquers all things

persona non grata – an unacceptable person

16

gloria in excelsis – glory to God in the highest

17

labor ipse voluptas – labour itself is pleasure

nunquam non paenitet – honesty repents not

probum non semper viret – Spring does not always flourish

18

nec temere nec timide – neither rashly nor timidly

pro rege, lege, et grege – for the king, the law and the people

reductio ad absurdum – reducing to absurdity

19

candide et constanter – fairly and firmly

sola nobilitas virtus – virtue alone is true nobility

virtuti non armis fido - I trust to virtue and not to arms

20+

de mortuis nil nisi bonum – speak only good of the dead

dulce et decorum est pro patria mori – it is sweet and seemly to die for one's country

fortuna favet fortibus – fortune favours the brave

patria cara carior libertas – my country is dear, but liberty is dearer

quod erat demonstrandum – which was to be demonstrated

sic transit gloria mundi – thus passes the glory of the world

timeo danaos et dona ferentis – I fear the Greeks, even when bearing gifts

vivit post funera virtus – virtue survives the grave

Numbers

	Roman Numerals	French	German	Italian	Spanish
1	I	un	ein	uno	uno
2	II	deux	zwei	due	dos
3	III	trois	drei	tre	tres
4	IV	quatre	vier	quattro	cuatro
5	V	cinq	funf	cinque	cinco
6	VI	six	sechs	sei	seis
7	VII	sept	seiben	sette	siete
8	VIII	huit	acht	otto	ocho
9	IX	neuf	neun	nove	neuve
10	X	dix	zehn	dieci	diez
20	XX	vingt	zwanzig	venti	veinte
30	XXX	trente	dreissig	trenta	treinta
40	XL	quarante	vierzig	quaranta	cuarenta
50	L	cinquante	funfzig	cinquanta	cincuenta
60	LX	soixante	sechzig	sessanta	setenta
70	LXX	soixante-dix	siebzig	settanta	sesenta
80	LXXX	quatre-vingt	achtzig	ottanta	ochenta
90	XC	quatre-vingt-dix	neunzig	novanta	noventa
100	C	cent	hundert	cento	cien(ciento)
500	D	cinq cents	funfhundert	cinquecento	quinientos
1000	M	mille	tausend	mille	mil

Languages and Alphabets

Languages of the World

2

Wu

3

Min

4

Urdu

5

Dutch
Greek
Hindi
Irish
Malay
Oriya
Tamil
Welsh

6

Arabic
Bihari
Breton
Danish
French
Gaelic
German
Korean
Pahari
Polish
Romany

Sindhi
Slovak
Telugu

7

Bengali
Catalan
English
Frisian
Italian
Latvian
Marathi
Punjabi
Russian
Slovene
Sorbian
Spanish
Swedish
Turkish

8

Assamese
Gujarati
Japanese
Javanese
Kashmiri
Mandarin
Romansch
Rumanian
Ukrainian

9

Afrikaans
Bulgarian
Cantonese
Icelandic
Norwegian
Sinhalese

10

Lithuanian
Portuguese
Rajasthani

Serbo-Croat

The Greek Alphabet

alpha
beta
gamma
delta
epsilon
zeta
eta
theta
iota
kappa
lambda
mu
nu
xi
omicron
pi
rho
sigma
tau
upsilon
phi
chi
psi
omega

Hebrew Alphabet

aleph
beth
gimel
daleth
he
vain/zayin
cheth/heth
teth
jod /yod
caph/kaph
lamed
mem
nun

samech/samekh
ain/ayin
pe
tzaddi/zade
koph
resh
schin/shin
tau/tav/taw

Words

Palindromes

3

aba
aga
aha
ama
ana
asa
ava
bab
bib
bob
bub
dad
did
dod
dud
eke
ere
eve
ewe
eye
gag
gig
gog
hah
huh
heh

mam

mim

mom

mum

nan

non

nun

oho

oxo

pap

pep

pip

pop

pup

sis

s.o.s.

tat

tit

TNT

tot

tut

wow

zuz

4

abba

anna

boob

deed

dood

ecce

keek

kook

ma'am

noon

otto

peep

poop

sees

toot

5

alula

anana

civic

kayak

level

madam

minim

put-up

radar

refer

rotor

sagas

sexes

shahs

sohos

solos

tenet

6

denned

hallah

hannah

marram

pull-up

redder

terret

tut-tut

7

deified

reifier

repaper

reviver

rotator

9

malayalam

rotavator

19

able was I ere I saw elba

Back Words

ah –ha

am –ma

at – ta

eh – he

ha – ah

he – eh

ho – oh

it – ti

ma – am

MP - PM

ta – at

ti – it

3

and – dna

bad – dab

bag – gab

ban – nab

bat – tab

bin – nib

bog – gob

boy – yob

bud – dub

bun – nub

bus – sub

but – tub

dab – bad

dam – mad

dew – wed

dim – mid

dna – and

dog – god

doh – hod

don – nod

dot – tod

dub – bud

ell – lee

gab – bag

gal – lag

gas – sag

gel – leg

gob – bog

god – dog
got – tog
gum – mug
gut – tug
hod – doh
jar – raj
lag – gal
lap – pal
lee – eel
leg – gel
mad – dam
mar – ram
may – yam
mid – dim
mug – gum
nab – ban
nap – pan
net – ten
nib – bin
nip – pin
nit – tin
nod – don
not – ton
now – won
nub – bun
pal – lap
pan – nap
par – rap
pat – tap
pay – yap
per – rep
pin – nip
pit – tip
pot – top
pus – sup
raj – jar
ram – mar
rap – par
rat – tar
raw – war
rep – per
rot – tor
sag – gas

sub – bus
sup – pus
tab – bat
tap – pat
tar – rat
ten – net
tin – nit
tip – pit
tod – dot
tog – got
ton – not
top – pot
tor – rot
tub – but
tug – gut
war – raw
way – yaw
wed – dew
won – now
yam – may
yap – pay
yaw – way
yob – boy

4

able – elba
abut – tuba
bard – drab
bats – stab
brag – garb
buns – snub
buts – stub
deer – reed
dial – laid
doom – mood
door – rood
drab – bard
draw – ward
dray – yard
dual – laud
edam – made
edit – tide
elba – able

emir – rime
emit – time
ergo – ogre
et al – late
evil – live
flog – golf
flow – wolf
gals – slag
garb – brag
gnat – tang
golf – flog
gulp – plug
gums – smug
guns – snug
hoop – pooh
keel – leek
keep – peek
laid – dial
lair – rial
late – et al
laud – dual
leek – keel
leer – reel
liar – rail
live – evil
loop – pool
loot – tool
macs – scam
made – edam
maps – spam
maws – swam
meet – teem
mood – doom
moor – room
naps – span
nips – spin
nuts – stun
ogre – ergo
pals – slap
pans – snap
part – trap
paws – swap
peek – keep

pets – step
pins – snip
plug – gulp
pooh – hoop
pool – loop
pots – stop
rail – liar
raps – spar
rats – star
reed – deer
reel – leer
rial – lair
rime – emir
rood – door
room – moor
scam – macs
slag – gals
slap – pals
smug – gums
snap – pans
snip – pins
snot – tons
snub – buns
snug – guns
spam – maps
span – naps
spar – raps
spat – taps
spay – yaps
spin – nips
spit – tips
spot – tops
stab – bats
star – rats
step – pets
stew – wets
stop – pots
stub – buts
stun – nuts
swam – maws
swap – paws
sway – yaws
swot – tows

tang – gnat
taps – spat
teem – meet
tide – edit
time – emit
tips – spit
tons – snot
tool – loot
tops – spot
tort – trot
tows – swot
trap – part
trot – tort
tuba – abut
ward – draw
wets – stew
wolf – flow
yaps – spay
yard – dray
yaws – sway

5

annam – manna
atlas – salta
cares – serac
daraf – farad
decal – laced
denim – mined
devil – lived
farad – daraf
fires – serif
keels – sleek
laced – decal
lager – regal
leper – repel
lever – revel
lived – devil
loops – spool
manna – annam
mined – denim
pacer – recap
parts – strap
pools – sloop

ports – strop
rebut – tuber
recap – pacer
regal – lager
remit – timer
repel – leper
revel – lever
salta – atlas
serac – cares
serif – fires
sleek – keels
sloop – pools
smart – trams
snips – spins
spins – snips
spool – loops
spots – stops
stops – spots
strap – parts
straw – warts
strop – ports
timer – remit
trams – smart
tuber – rebut
warts – straw

6

animal – lamina
delian – nailed
denier – reined
diaper – repaid
drawer – reward
harris – sirrah
lamina – animal
looter – retool
nailed – delian
pupils – slip–up
recaps – spacer
reined – denier
rennet – tenner
repaid – diaper
retool – looter
reward – drawer

serves – sevres
sevres – serves
sirrah – harris
slip–up – pupils
snoops – spoons
spacer – recaps
spoons – snoops
tenner – rennet

8

desserts – stressed
stressed – desserts

Homophones

accessary – accessory
accessory – accessary
aerial – ariel
aerie – airy
ail – ale
air – aire, e'er, ere, Eyre,
   heir
aire – air, e'er, ere, Eyre,
   heir
airship – heirship
airy – aerie
aisle – I'll, isle
ait – eight, ate
ale – ail
all – awl, orle
alms – arms
altar – alter
amah – armour
ante – anti
anti – ante
arc – ark
aren't – aunt
ares – Aries
ariel – aerial
Aries – ares
ark – arc
armour – amah
arms – alms

ascent – assent
assent – ascent
ate – ait, eight
auk – orc
aunt – aren't
aural – oral
austere – ostia
away – aweigh
awe – oar, o'er, ore
aweigh – away
awl – all – orle
axel – axle
axle – axel
ay – aye, eye, I
ayah – ire
aye – ay, eye, I
ayes – eyes

baa – bah, bar
baal – Basle
bah – baa, bar
bail – bale
bale – bail
ball – bawl
balm – barm
balmy – barmy
bar – baa, bah
bare – bear
barm – balm
barmy – balmy
baron – barren
barren – baron
base – bass
Basle – baal
bass – base
baud – bawd, board
bawd – baud, board
bawl – ball
bay – bey
beach – beech
bean – been
bear – bare
beat – beet

beater – beta
beau – boh, bow
beech – beach
been – been
beer – bier
beet – beat
bel – bell, belle
bell – bel, belle
belle – bel, bell
berry – bury
berth – birth
beta – beater
bey – bay
bhai – bi, buy, by, bye
bi – bhai, buy, by, bye
bier – beer
bight – bite, byte
birth – berth
bite – bight, byte
blew – blue
blue – blew
boar – Boer, boor, bore
board – baud, bawd
boarder – border
boart – bought
Boer – boar, boor, bore
boh – beau, bow
bole – bowl
bolt – boult
boor – boar, Boer, boor
born – borne
borne – born
bough – bow
bought – boart
boult – bolt
bow – beau, boh
bow – bough
bowl – bole
boy – buoy
brake – break
bread – bred
break – brake
bred – bread

brede – breed, breid
breed – brede, breid
breid – brede, breed
bridal – bridle
bridle – bridal
broach – brooch
brooch – broach
bunion – bunyan
bunyan – bunion
buoy – boy
burger – burgher
burgher – burger
bury – berry
bus – buss
buss – bus
buy – bhai, bi, by, bye
buyer – byre
by – bhai, bi, buy, bye
bye – bhai, bi, buy, by
byre – buyer
byte – bight, bite

cache – cash
cachou – cashew
cain – cane, kain
call – caul
callas – callous, callus
callous – callas, callus
callus – callas, callous
canapé – canopy
cane – cain, kain
canopy – canapé
carat – carrot, karat
carrot – carat, karat
cart – carte, kart
carte – cart, kart
cash – cache
cashew – cachou
cashmere – Kashmir
cast – caste, karst
caste – cast, karst
caught – court
caul – call

caw – cor, core, corps
cedar – seeder
cede – seed
ceil – seel, seal
cell – sell, szell
cellar – seller
censer – censor, sensor
censor – censer, sensor
cent – scent, sent
cere – sear, seer
cereal – serial
cession – session
chaw – chore
cheap – cheep
check – cheque, Czech
cheep – cheap
cheque – check, Czech
choir – quire
choler – collar
chord – cord
chore – chaw
chott – shot, shott
chou – shoe, shoo
chough – chuff
chuff – chough
chute – shoot, shute
cite – sight, site
clack – claque
claque – clack
climb – clime
clime – climb
coal – cole, kohl
coarse – corse, course
cole – coal, kohl
collar – choler
colonel – kernel
colour – culler
come – cum
complementary –
complimentary
complimentary –
complementary
coo – coup

coop – coupe
cor – caw, core, corps
cord – chord
core – caw, cor, corps
cornflour – cornflower
cornflower – cornflour
corps – caw, cor, core
corse – coarse, course
council – counsel
counsel – council
coup – coo
coupe – coop
course – coarse, corse
court – caught
creak – creek
creek – creak
culler – colour
cum – come
curb – kerb
currant – current
current – currant
cygnet – signet
cymbal – symbol
Czech – check, cheque

dam – damn
damn – dam
daw – door, dor
days – daze
daze – days
dear – deer
deer – dear
descent – dissent
desert – dessert
dessert – desert
dew – due
dinah – diner
dine – dyne
diner – dinah
dissent – descent
doe – doh, dough
doh – doe, dough
done – donne, dun

donne – done, dun
door – daw, dor
dor – daw, door
dost – dust
dough – doe, doh
draft – draught
draught – draft
droop – drupe
drupe – droop
dual – duel
ducks – dux
due – dew
duel – dual
dun – done, donne
dust – dost
dux – ducks
dyeing – dying
dying – dyeing
dyne – dine

earn – urn
eaten – Eton
e'er – air, aire, ere, Eyre, heir
eerie – eyrie
eider – ida
 eight – ait, ate
eire – eyra
elation – illation
elicit – illicit
elude – illude
elusory – illusory
emerge – immerge
emersed – immersed
emersion – immersion
ere – air, aire, e'er, Eyre, heir
erk – irk
err – ur
Ester – Esther
Esther – Ester
Eton – eaten
ewe – yew, you

eye – ay, aye, I
eyed – I'd ide
eyelet – islet
eyes – ayes
eyra – Eire
Eyre – air, aire, e'er ere, heir
eyrie – eerie

fa – far
fain – fane, feign
faint – feint
fair – fare
fane – fain, feign
far – fa
fare – fair
faro – pharaoh
farther
father
fate – fete
father – farther
faugh – for, four, fore
faun – fawn
fawn – faun
faze – phase
feat – feet
feet – feat
feign – fain, fane
feignt – faint
felloe – fellow
fellow – felloe
felt – veld, veldt
feta – fetter
fete – fate
fetter – feta
feu – few, phew
few – feu, phew
fir – fur
fisher – fissure
fissure – fisher
fizz – phiz
flair – flare
flare – flair

flaw – floor
flea – flee
flee – flea
flew – flu, flue
floe – flow
floor – flaw
flour – flower
flow – floe
flower – flour
flu – flew, flue
flue – flew, flu
for – faugh, four, fore
fore – faugh, for, four
fort – fought
forte – forty
forth – fourth
forty – forte
fought – fort
foul – fowl
four – faugh, for, fore
fourth – forth
fowl – foul
friar – frier
frier – friar
fur – fir

Gail – gale
gait – gate
gale – Gail
gallop – Gallup
Gallup – gallop
gamble – gambol
gambol – gamble
gate – gait
gawky – Gorky
gene – jean
gin – jinn
gladden – gladdon
gladdon – gladden
gnash – nash
gnat – nat
gnaw – nor
Gorky – gawky

grater – greater
greater – grater
groan – grown
grown – groan

hae – hay, heh, hey
hail – hale
hair – hare
hale – hail
hare – hair
hale – hail
hall – haul
Handel – handle
handle – Handel
hangar – hanger
hanger – hangar
hare – hair
hart – heart
haud – hoard, horde
haul – hall
haw – hoare, whore
hay – hae, heh, hey
hear – here
heart – hart
heh – hae, hay, hey
heir – air, aire, e'er, ere, Eyre
heirship – airship
here – hear
heroin – heroine
heroine – heroin
hew – hue
hey – hae, hay, heh
hie – high
high – hie
higher – hire
him – hymn
hire – higher
ho – hoe
hoar – haw, whore
hoard – haud, horde
hoarse – horse
hoe – ho

hole – whole
hoo – who
horde – haud, hoard
horse – hoarse
hour – our
hours – ours
hue – hew
hymn – him

I – ay, aye, eye
I'd – eyed, ide
ida – eider
ide – eyed, I'd
idle – idol
idol – idle
I'll – aisle, isle
illation – elation
illicit – elicit
illude – elude
illusory – elusory
immerge – emerge
immersed – emersed
immersion – emersion
in – inn
incite – insight
indict – indite
indite – indict
inn – in
insight – incite
insole – insoul
insoul – insole
ion – iron
ire – ayah
irk – erk
iron – ion
isle – aisle, I'll
islet – eyelet

jam – jamb, jambe
jamb – jam, jambe
jambe – jam, jamb
jean – gene
jinks – jinx
jinn – gin

jinx – jinks

kain – cain, cane
karat – carat, carrot
karst – cast, caste
kart – cart, carte
Kashmir – cashmere
kerb – curb
kernel – colonel
Kew – kyu, queue
key – quay
knave – nave
knead – need
knew – new, nu
knight – night
knightly – nightly
knit – nit
know – noh, no
knows – noes, nose
kohl – coal, cole
kyu – Kew, queue

lacker – lacquer
lacquer – lacker
lain – lane
lance – launce
lane – lain
laud – lord
launce – lance
law – lore
lay – lei, ley
lays – laze
laze – lays
lead – led
leaf – lief
Leah – lear, leer, lehr
leak – leek
leant – lent
lear – Leah, leer, lehr
led – lead
leek – leak
leer – Leah, lear, lehr
lehr – Leah, lear, leer
lei – lay, ley

leman – lemon
lemon – leman
lent – leant
lessen – lesson
ley – lay, lei
liar – lyre
lief – leaf
Lincs – links, lynx
links – Lincs, lynx
load – lode
loan – lone
lode – load
lone – loan
lord – laud
lore – law
lumbar – lumber
lumber – lumbar
lynx – Lincs, links
lyre – liar

ma – maar, mar
maar – ma, mar
made – maid
maid – made
mail – male
main – Maine, mane
Maine – main, mane
maize – maze
male – mail
mall – maul
mane – main, Maine
manna – manner, manor
manner – manna, manor
manor – manna, manner
maquis – marquee
mar – ma, maar
marc – mark, marque
mare – mayor
mark – marc, marque
marque – marc, mark
marquee – maquis

maul – mall
maw – mor, more, moor
mayor – mare
maze – maize
mean – mesne, mien
meat – meet, mete
medal – meddle
meddle – medal
meet – meat, mete
mesne – mien, mean
metal – mettle
mete – meat, meet
mettle – metal
mews – muse
mien – mesne, mean
might – mite
miner – minor
minor – miner
mite – might
moan – mown
moat – mote
mocha – mocker
mocker – mocha
moor – maw, more, moor
moose – mousse
mor – maw, more, moor
more – maw, mor, moor
morn – mourn
morning – mourning
mote – moat
mourn – morn
mourning – morning
mousse – moose
mown – moan
muscle – mussel
muse – mews

nae – nay, neagh, neigh, ney

nash – gnash
nat – gnat
naught – nought
naval – navel
nave – knave
navel – naval
nay – nae, neagh, neigh, ney
neagh – nae, nay, neigh, ney
need – knead
neigh – nae, nay, neagh, ney
neuk – nuke
new – knew, nu
ney – nae, nay, neagh, neigh
nigh – nye
night – knight
nightly – knightly
nit – knit
no – know, noh
noes – knows, nose
noh – know, no
none – nun
nor – gnaw
nose – knows, noes
nought – naught
nu – knew, new
nuke – neuk
nye – nigh

oar – awe, o'er, ore
o'er – awe, oar, ore
offa – offer
offer – offa
oh - owe
oral – aural
orc – auk
ore – awe, oar, o'er
orle – all, awl
ostia – austere
our – hour

ours – hours
out – owt
ova – over
over – ova
owe – oh
owt – out

pa – pah, par, parr, pas
packed – pact
pah – pa, par, parr, pas
pail – pale
pair – pare, pear
palate – palette, pallet
pale – pail
palette – palate, pallet
pallet – palate, palette
panda – pander
pander – panda
par – pa, pah, par, pas
pas – pa, pah, par, parr
paw – poor, pore, pour
pawky – porky
pawn – porn
pea – pee
peace – piece
peak – pique, peake, peek, peke
peal – peel
pear – pair, pare
pearl – purl
pearler – purler
pedal – peddle
peddle – pedal
pee – pea
peek – peak, peake, peke, pique
peel – peal
peke – peak, peake, peek, pique
per – purr
petrel
pharaoh – faro
phase – faze

phew – feu, few
phiz – fizz
pi – pie, pye
pie – pi, pye
piece – peace
Pilate – pilot
pilot – Pilate
pique – peak, peake, peek, peke
place – plaice
plaice – place
plain - plane
plane – plain
pole – poll
poll – pole
pomace – pumice
pommel – pummel
poor – paw, pore, pour
populace – populous
populous – populace
pore – paw, poor, pour
porky – pawky
porn – pawn
pour – paw, poor, pore
pray – prey
prey – pray
principal – principle
principle – principal
profit – prophet
prophet – profit
psalter – salter
pucka – pucker
pucker – pucka
pumice – pomace
pummel – pommel
purl – pearl
purler – pearler
purr – per
pye – pi, pie

quay – key
queue – Kew, kyu
quire – choir

rack – wrack
racket – racquet
racquet – racket
rain – reign, rein
rains – reins
raise – rase
rap – wrap
rapt – wrapped
rase – raise
raw – roar
read – rede, reed
reck – wreck
rede – read, reed
reed – read, rede
reek – wreak
reign – rain, rein
rein – rain, reign
reins – rains
rennes – wren
retch – wretch
revere – revers
revers – revere
rheum – room
rheumy – roomy
rho – roe, row
Rhone – roan, rone
right – rite, wright, write
ring – wring
ringer – wringer
rite – right, wright, write
roam – Rome
roan – Rhone, rone
roar – raw
roe – rho, row
role – roll
roll – role
Rome – roam
rone – roan, Rhone
rood – rude
room – rheum
roomy – rheumy

roose – ruse
root – route
rort – wrought
rote – wrote
rough – ruff
route – root
row – rho, roe
rude – rood
ruff – rough
rung – wrung
ruse – roose
rye – wry

sail – sale
sain – sane, Seine
sale – sail
salter - psalter
sane – sain, Seine
sauce – source
saut – sort, sought
saw – soar, sore
sawn – sorn
scene – seen
scent – cent, sent
scull – skull
seal – ceil, seel
seam – seem
sear – cere, seer
seed – cede
seeder - cedar
seek – seik, Sikh
seel – ceil, seal
seem – seam
seen – scene
seer – cere, sear
seik – seek, Sikh
Seine – sain, sane
sell – cell, szell
seller – cellar
sensor – censer, censor
sent – cent, scent
serf – surf
serge – surge

serial – cereal
session – cession
sew – so, soh, sow
sewn – sone, sown
shake – sheik
sheik – shake
shier – shyer, shire
shire – shier, shyer
shoe – chou, shoo
shoot – chute, shute
shot – chott, shott
shott – chot, shot
shute – chute, shoot
shyer – shier, shire
sight – cite, site
sign – syn
signet – cygnet
Sikh – seek, seik
Sioux – sou
site – cite, sight
skull – scull
sky – Skye
Skye – sky
slay – sleigh
sleave – sleeve
sleeve – sleave
sleigh – slay
sloe – slow
slow – sloe
so – sew, soh, sow
soar – saw, sore
soh – sew, so, sow
sole – soul
some – sum
son – sun, sunn
sone – sewn, sown
sonny – Sunni, sunny
sore – saw, soar
sorn – sawn
sort – saut, saught
sou – Sioux
sought – saut, sort
soul – sole

source – sauce
sow – sew, so, soh
sown – sewn, sone
stair – stare
stake – steak
stalk – stork
stare – stair
steak – stake
steal – steel
steel – steal
storey – story
stork – stalk
story – storey
suite – sweet
sum – some
sun – son, sunn
sundae – Sunday
Sunday – sundae
sunn – son, sun
Sunni – sonny, sunny
sunny – sonny, Sunni
surf – serf
surge – serge
swat – swot
sweet – suite
swot – swat
symbol – cymbal
syn – sign
szell – cell, sell

tacit – tasset
tai – taille, Thai, tie
tail – tale
taille – tai, Thai, tie
tale – tail
talk – torc, torque
tare – tear
tasset – tacit
taught – taut, tort, torte
taut – taught, tort, torte
tea – tee, ti
team – teem
tear – rate

tee – tea, ti
teem – team
tenner – tenor
tenor – tenner
terne – turn
Thai – tai, taille, tie
thaw – Thor
their – there, they're
there – their, they're
they're – their, there
Thor – thaw
threw – through, thru
throe – throw
throne – thrown
through – threw, thru
throw – throe
thrown – throne
thru – threw, through
thyme – time
ti – tea, tee
tic – tick
tick – tic
tide – tied
tie – tai, taille, Thai
tied – tide
tier – tire, tyre
tighten – Titan
timber – timbre
timbre – timber
time – thyme
tire – tyre
Titan – tighten
to - too, two
toad – toed, towed
toe – tow
toed – toad, towed
too – to, two
tor – tore
torc – talk, torque
tore – tor
torque – talk, torc
tort – taught, taut, torte

torte – taught, taut, tort
tow – toe
towed – toad, toed
troop – troupe
troupe – troop
tuna – tuner
tuner – tuna
turn – terne
two – to, too
tyre – tire

ur – err
urn – earn

vail – vale, veil
vain – vane, vein
vale – vail, veil
vane – vain, vein
veil – vail, vale
vein – vain, vane
veld – felt, veldt
veldt – felt, veld

wae – way, whey
wail – whale
wain – wane, Wayne
waist – waste
wait – weight
waive – wave
wane – wain, Wayne
war – Waugh, waw, wore
ware – wear, where
warn – worn
waste – waist
watt – what, wot
Waugh – war, waw, wore
wave – waive
waw – war, Waugh, wore
way – wae, whey
Wayne – wain, wane
weak – week

weakly – weekly
wear – ware, where
weave – we've
we'd – weed
weed – we'd
week – weak
weekly – weakly
weel – we'll, wheal, wheel
weight – wait
we'll – weel, wheal, wheel
wen – when
were – whirr
we've – weave
whale – wail
what – watt, wot
wheal – weel, we'll, wheel
wheel – weel, we'll, wheal
when – wen
where – ware, wear
whey – wae, way
which – witch
whine – wine
whirr – were
white – Wight, wite
whither – wither
who – hoo
whoa – wo, woe
whole – hole
whore – haw, hoar
Wight – white, wite
wine – whine
witch – which
wite – white, Wight
wither – whither
wo – whoa, woe
woe – whoa, wo
wore – war, Waugh, waw
worn – warn

wot – watt, what
wrack – rack
wrap – rap
wrapped – rapt
wreak – reek
wreck – reck
wren – rennes
wretch – retch
wright – right, rite,
write
wring – ring
wringer – ringer
write – right, rite,
wright
wrote – rote
wrought – rort
wrung – rung
wry – rye

yaw – yore, your
yaws – yours
yew – ewe, you
yoke – yolk
yolk – yoke
yore – yaw, your
you – ewe, yew
you'll – Yule
your – yaw, yore
yours – yaws
Yule – you'll

Similes

as bald as a coot
as black as pitch
as black as the ace of
spades
as blind as a bat
as blind as a mole
as bold as brass
as bright as a button
as busy as a bee
as calm as a millpond

as cheap as dirt
as chirpy as a cricket
as clean as a whistle
as clear as a bell
as clear as crystal
as clear as mud
as cold as charity
as common as muck
as cool as a cucumber
as cross as two sticks
as daft as a brush
as dead as a dodo
as dead as a doornail
as dead as mutton
as deaf as a post
as different as chalk and
cheese
as drunk as a lord
as dry as a bone
as dry as dust
as dull as dishwater
as easy as falling off a
log
as easy as pie
as fit as a flea
as flat as a pancake
as free as the wind
as fresh as a daisy
as good as gold
as green as grass
as happy as a lark
as happy as a sandboy
as happy as Larry
as happy as the day is
long
as hard as nails
as keen as mustard
as large as life
as light as a feather
as like as two peas in a
pod
as lively as a cricket
as mad as a hatter

as mad as a March hare
as meek as a lamb
as merry as a cricket
as neat as a new pin
as nutty as a fruitcake
as obstinate as a mule
as old as the hills
as pale as death
as plain as a pikestaff
as plain as the nose on
your face
as pleased as Punch
as poor as a church
mouse
as poor as Lazarus
as pretty as a picture
as proud as a peacock
as pure as the driven
snow
as quick as a flash
as quick as lightening
as quick as thought
as quiet as a mouse
as quiet as the grave
as red as a beetroot
as regular as clockwork
as rich as Croesus
as right as rain
as safe as houses
as sharp as a needle
as sick as a dog
as simple as falling off a
log
as slippery as an eel
as snug as a bug in a
rug
as sound as a bell
as steady as a rock
as stiff as a board
as stiff as a poker
as stiff as a ramrod
as straight as a die
as straight as an arrow

as stubborn as a mule
as sure as eggs is eggs
as sure as hell
as thick as thieves
as thick as two short planks
as thin as a lath
as thin as a rake
as thin as a stick

as tough as nails
as tough as old boots
as ugly as sin
as warm as toast
as weak as a kitten
as weak as dishwater
as welcome as the flowers in May
as white as a sheet

Measurement

Coins, Currency and Money

1

d
l
p
s

2

as

3

bit
bob
cob
dam
ecu
far
fin
kup
lac
lat
leu
lev
mag
mil
mna
oof
ore
pie
red
ree
rei
sen
sho
sol
sou
tin
won
yen

zac
zuz

4

anna
baht
beka
biga
buck
cash
cent
chip
daum
dawm
dime
doit
euro
geld
joey
kick
kran
kyat
lakh
lira
lire
loot
mail
mark
merk
mina
mite
note
obol
para
peag
peak
peso
pice
pony
quid
rand
real

rial
riel
ryal
tael
taka
unik
yuan
zack

5

agora
angel
asper
aurei
belga
betso
boole
brass
bread
broad
chiao
colon
conto
copec
crore
crown
daric
dinar
dough
ducat
eagle
franc
grand
groat
haler
koban
kopek
krona
krone
liard
libra
litas

livre
locho
lolly
louis
lucre
medio
mohar
mohur
moola
noble
obang
ochre
oncer
paolo
pence
pengo
penny
plack
pound
qursh
ready
rhino
ruble
rupee
sceat
scudi
scudo
semis
soldi
soldo
stica
styca
sucre
sugar
sycee
tical
ticcy
tizzy
toman
uncia
unite
zloty

6

amania
aureus
balboa
baubee
bawbee
bezant
bezart
bodole
boodle
condor
copang
copeck
change
copper
couter
deaner
décime
denier
dirhem
doblon
dollar
escudo
florin
forint
fuorte
gourde
guinea
gulden
heller
kobang
kopeck
lepton
markka
monkey
nickel
obolus
pagoda
pagode
peseta
rosser
rouble

rupiah
sceatt
sequin
shekel
souran
stater
stiver
talari
talent
tanner
tester
teston
thaler
tickey
tizzie
tomaun
valuta
zechin

7

angelot
bolivar
carolus
centava
centavo
centime
cordoba
crusado
denarii
drachma
guilder
jacobus
lempira
manilla
milreis
moidore
ngusang
pfennig
piastre
pistole
quarter
ringgit

sextans
stooter
testoon
testril
thrymsa
unicorn

8

ambrosin
denarius
didrachm
doubloon
ducatoon
farthing
florence
groschen
half anna
half mark
imperial
johannes
kreutzer
louis d'or
maravedi
megabuck
napoleon
new pence
new penny
picayune
portague
quadrans
quetzale
sesterce
shilling
sixpence
stotinka

9

boliviano
cuartillo
didrachma
dupondius

gold broad
gold noble
gold penny
half ackey
half angel
half broad
half crown
half groat
halfpenny
lilang-eni
pistareen
rixdollar
rose-noble
schilling
sestertii
sovereign
spur royal
two mohars
two mohurs
yellow boy

10

broad piece
crown piece
double pice
easterling
emalangeni
first brass
gold stater
half florin
half guinea
half laurel
quadrussis
sestertium
silverling
stour-royal
threepence
threepenny
tripondius
venezolano

11

Briton crown
double crown
double eagle
george noble
guinea piece
half guilder
half thistle
silver penny
spade guinea
tetradrachm
twelvepenny
two guilders

12

antoninianus
double sequin
hail farthing
mill sixpence
quarter angel
quarter noble
shinplaster
silver-stater
tetradrachma
tribute penny

13

half rose-noble
half sovereign
quarter dollar
quarter form
quarter laurel
sixpenny piece
threepenny bit
twenty dollars
twopenny piece
two-pound piece

14

barbadoes penny
five-pound piece

Hong Kong dollar	15	16
quarter guilder	five-guinea piece	threepenny piece
three farthings	twenty shillings	
two-guinea piece	two-guilder piece	

Currencies

(Including former currencies of countries which now use the euro. Also noted is where currency from one country is used elsewhere – e.g. US Dollar)

Currency	Country
Afghani	Afghanistan
Agora	Israel
Agorot	Israel
Agoroth	Israel
At	Laos
Aurar	Iceland
Austral	Argentina
Baht	Thailand
Baiza	Oman
Balboa	Panama
Ban	Moldova, Romania
Bani	Moldova, Romania
Birr	Ethiopia, Eritrea
Bolivar	Venezuela
Boliviano	Bolivia
Butet	The Gambia
Cauris	Guinea
Cedi	Ghana
Cent	Antigua and Barbuda, Australia, The Bahamas, Barbados, Belau, Belize, Canada, Cyprus, Dominica, Eritrea, Estonia, Ethiopia, Fiji, Grenada, Guyana, Jamaica, Kenya, Kiribati, Liberia, Malaysia, Malta, Marshall Islands, Mauritius, Micronesia, Namibia, Nauru, Netherlands, New Zealand, Panama, Saint Kitts and Nevis, Saint Lucia, Saint Vincent and the Grenadines, Seychelles, Sierra Leone, Singapore, Soloman Islands, Somalia, South Africa, Sri Lanka, Suriname, Swaziland, Taiwan, Tanzania, Trinidad and Tobago, Tuvalu, Uganda, United States of America, Zimbabwe

Currency	Country
Cént	Peru
Centai	Lithuania
Centas	Lithuania
Centavo	Bolivia, Brazil, Cape Verde, Chile, Columbia, Cuba, Dominican Republic, Ecuador, El Salvador, Guatemala, Honduras, Mexico, Mozambique, Nicaragua, Philippines, Portugal
Centesimi	Italy, San Marino, Vatican City
Centesimo	Italy, San Marino, Vatican City
Centésimo	Panama, Uruguay
Centime	Algeria, Andorra, Belgium, Benin, Burkina Faso, Burundi, Cameroon, Central African Republic, Chad, Comoros, Congo, Côte d'Ivoire (Ivory Coast), Djibouti, Equatorial Guinea, France, Gabon, Guinea, Haiti, Liechtenstein, Luxembourg, Madagascar, Mali, Monaco, Morocco, Niger, Rwanda, Senegal, Switzerland, Togo, Vanuatu
Céntimo	Andorra, Costa Rica, Paraguay, Spain, Venezuela
Centimo	São Tomé and Príncipe
CFA Franc	Benin, Burkina Faso, Cameroon, Central African Republic, Chad, Comoros, Congo, Côte d'Ivoire (Ivory Coast), Equatorial Guinea, Gabon, Guinea-Bissau, Mali, Niger, Senegal, Togo
Chetrum	Bhutan
Chon	South Korea
Chun	South Korea
Colon	Costa Rica
Colón	El Salvador
Colones	Costa Rica, El Salvador
Colons	Costa Rica, El Salvador
Copeck	Belarus, Russia
Copek	Belarus, Russia, Tajikstan
Córdoba	Nicaragua
Cruzeiro Real	Brazil
Dalasi	The Gambia
Deutsche Mark	Germany
Deutschmark	Germany
Dinar	Algeria, Bahrain, Bosnia & Herzegovina, Iraq, Jordan, Kuwait, Libya, Macedonia, Sudan, Tunisia, Yugoslavia
Dirham (Dirhem)	Libya, Morocco, Qatar, United Arab Emirates
Dobra	São Tomé and Príncipe

Currency	Country
Dollar	Australia, The Bahamas, Barbados, Belize, Bermuda, Brunei, Canada, Cayman Islands, Fiji, Guyana, Hong Kong, Jamaica, Liberia, Malaysia, Namibia, New Zealand, Singapore, Solomon Islands, Taiwan, Trinidad and Tobago, Tuvalu, United States of America, Zimbabwe
Dollar (Australian)	Australia, Christmas Island, Cocos (Keeling) Islands, Heard and McDonald Islands, Kiribati, Nauru, Norfolk Island, Tuvalu
Dollar (East Caribbean)	Anguilla, Antigua and Barbuda, British Virgin Islands, Dominica, Grenada, Monserrat, Saint Kitts, (Christopher) and Nevis, Saint Lucia, Saint Vincent and the Grenadines
Dollar (New Zealand)	Cook Islands, New Zealand, Niue, Pitcairn Islands, Tokelau
Dollar (US)	American Samoa, British Virgin Islands, Ecuador, Federated States of Micronesia, Guam, Marshall Islands, Northern Mariana Islands, Palau, Panama (with Balboa), Puerto Rico, Turks and Caicos Islands, United States of America, United States Minor Outlying Islands, US Virgin Islands
Dông	Vietnam
Drachma	Greece
Drachmae	Greece
Drachmas	Greece
Dram	Armenia
Escudo	Cape Verde, Portugal
Euro	Austria, Belgium, Finland, France, Germany, Greece, Ireland (Republic of), Italy, Luxembourg, Netherlands, Portugal, Spain. Also Andorra, Monaco, Holy See, San Marino and various French dependencies.
Eyrir	Iceland
Fen	China
Fillér	Hungary
Fils	Bahrain, Iraq, Jordan, Kuwait, United Arab Emirates, Yemen
Forint	Hungary
Franc	Belgium, Burundi, Comoros, Congo, Djibouti, France, Guinea, Luxembourg, Madagascar, Mali, Rwanda
Franc (French)	Andorra, France, French Guiana, French Southern and Antarctic Territories, Guadeloupe, Martinique,

Currency	Country
	Mayotte, Metropolitan France, Monaco, Réunion, St Pierre and Miquelon
Franc (West African)	Niger, Senegal, West Africa
Gopik	Azerbaijan
Gourde	Haiti
Groschen	Austria
Grosz	Poland
Groszy	Poland
Guarani	Paraguay
Guilder	Aruba, Netherlands, Suriname
Halala	Saudi Arabia
Haler	Czech Republic, Slovakia
Haleru	Czech Republic, Slovakia
Halier	Slovakia
Halierov	Slovakia
Halura	Czech Republic
Hryvna	Ukraine
Hryvnya	Ukraine
Jeon	South Korea
Jun	North Korea
Khoum	Mauritania
Kina	Papua New Guinea
Kip	Laos
Kobo	Nigeria
Kopeck	Belarus, Russia, Tajikstan
Kopek	Belarus, Russia, Tajikstan
Kopiyka	Ukraine
Koruna	Czech Republic, Slovakia
Krona	Sweden
Króna	Iceland
Krone (Danish)	Denmark, Faroe Islands, Greenland
Krone (Norwegian)	Antarctica, Bouvet Island, Norway, Svalbard and Jan Mayen Islands
Kronen	Denmark, Norway
Kroner	Denmark, Norway
Kronor	Sweden
Krónur	Iceland
Kroon	Estonia
Krooni	Estonia
Kroons	Estonia
Kuna	Croatia

Currency	Country
Kune	Croatia
Kurus	Turkey
Kurush	Turkey
Kwacha	Malawi, Zambia
Kwanza	Angola
Kyat	Myanmar (Burma)
Laari	Maldives
Laree	Maldives
Lari	Georgia
Lat	Latvia
Lati	Latvia
Lats	Latvia
Lei	Moldova, Romania
Lek	Albania
Leké	Albania
Leks	Albania
Lempira	Honduras
Leone	Sierra Leone
Lepta	Greece
Lepton	Greece
Leu	Moldova, Romania
Lev	Bulgaria
Leva	Bulgaria
Levs	Bulgaria
Lilangeni	Swaziland
Lipa	Croatia
Lira	Italy, Malta, Turkey
Liras	Italy, Malta, San Marino, Turkey, Vatican City
Lire	Italy, Malta, San Marino, Turkey, Vatican City
Lisente	Lesotho
Litai	Lithuania
Litas	Lithuania
Lits	Lithuania
Litu	Lithuania
Loti	Lesotho
Louma	Armenia
Lwei	Angola
Maloti	Lesotho
Manat	Azerbaijan, Turkmenistan
Marka	Bosnia-Herzegovina
Marrka	Finland

Currency	Country
Metical	Mozambique
Millime	Tunisia
Mongo	Mongolia
Nafka	Eritrea
Naira	Nigeria
Ngultrum	Bhutan
Ngwee	Zambia
Nueve Peso	Argentina
Ore	Denmark, Norway, Sweden
Ougiya	Mauritania
Ouguiya	Mauritania
Pa'anga	Tonga
Paisa	India, Nepal, Pakistan
Paise	India, Nepal, Pakistan
Para	Macedonia, Yugoslavia
Pence	Ireland (Republic of), United Kingdom
Penni	Finland
Pennia	Finland
Pennies	Ireland (Republic of), United Kingdom
Penny	Ireland (Republic of), United Kingdom
Peseta	Spain
Pesewa	Ghana
Peso	Argentina, Chile, Columbia, Cuba, Dominican Republic, Guinea-Bissau, Mexico, Philippines, Uruguay
Pfennig	Germany
Pfennige	Germany
Pfennigs	Germany
Piastre	Egypt, Lebanon, Syria
Poisha	Bangladesh
Pound	Cyprus, Egypt, Falkland Islands, Gibraltar, Lebanon, St Helena, Sudan, Syrian Arab Republic
Pound (Sterling)	British Indian Ocean Territory, British Virgin Islands, South Georgia and the South Sandwich Islands, United Kingdom
Pul	Afghanistan
Pula	Botswana
Puli	Afghanistan
Punt	Ireland (Republic of)
Pya	Myanmar (Burma)
Qindar	Albania
Qindarka	Albania

Currency	Country
Qintar	Albania
Quetzal	Guatemala
Quetzales	Guatemala
Rand	South Africa
Renminbi	China
Rial	Iran, Oman
Riyal	Yemen
Riel	Cambodia
Ringgit	Malaysia
Riyal	Qatar, Saudi Arabia, Yemen
Rouble	Belarus, Russia, Tajikstan
Rifiyaa	Maldives
Rupee	India, Mauritius, Nepal, Pakistan, Seychelles, Sri Lanka
Rupiah	Indonesia
Santimi	Latvia
Satang	Thailand
Satangs	Thailand
Schilling	Austria
Sen	Brunei, Cambodia, Indonesia, Japan, Malaysia
Sene	Samoa
Seniti	Tonga
Sent	Estonia
Sente	Lesotho
Senti	Estonia
Shekel	Israel
Sheqel	Israel
Shilling	Kenya, Somalia, Tanzania, Uganda
Sol	Peru
Soles	Peru
Som	Kyrgyzstan, Uzbekistan
Stangs	Thailand
Stotin	Slovenia
Stotinka	Bulgaria
Stotinki	Bulgaria
Sucre	Ecuador
Sum	Uzbekistan
Sumy	Uzbekistan
Taka	Bangladesh
Tala	Samoa
Tenge	Kazakhstan, Turkmenistan
Tetri	Georgia

Currency	Country
Thebe	Botswana
Toea	Papua New Guinea
Tolar	Slovenia
Tolarji	Slovenia
Tolars	Slovenia
Tugrik	Mongolia
Tyin	Kyrgyzstan
Vatu	Vanuata
Won	North Korea, South Korea
Xu	Vietnam
Yen	Japan
Yuan	China
Zloty	Poland

Weights and Measures

2

cm
dr
ft
gr
hl
in
kg
km
lb
mg
ml
mm
oz
yd

3

amp
are
bar
bel
bit
cwt
dwt
ell
erg
lux
mho
mil
mim
nit
ohm
rad
rem
rod
ton
tun

4

acre
bale
barn
bolt
byte
cask
cord
cran
dram
dyne
foot
gill
gram
hand
hide
hour
inch
kilo
knot
line
link
mile
mole
nail
peck
phon
phot
pica
pint
pipe
pole
ream
rood

slug
span
torr
troy
volt
watt
yard

5

cable
carat
chain
crith
cubit
curie
cusec
cycle
debye
farad
fermi
gauge
gauss
grain
henry
hertz
joule
litre
lumen
litre
minim
neper
ounce
perch
point
poise
pound
quart
quire
stade
stere
stilb
stoke
stone

tesla
therm
toise
tonne
weber

6

ampere
barrel
bushel
candle
cental
degree
denier
drachm
fathom
firkin
gallon
gramme
kelvin
league
megohm
micron
minute
newton
parsec
pascal
radian
reamur
second
stokes

7

calorie
candela
centner
coulomb
decibel
diopter
faraday
furlong
gilbert
hectare

kilobar
kiloton
lambert
maxwell
megaton
oersted
poundal
quarter
quintal
rontgen
scruple
seimens

8

angstrom
chaldron
hogshead
kilogram
kilowatt
quadrant
megawatt
microohm
watt-hour

9

board-foot
centigram
cubic foot
cubic inch
cubic yard
decalitre
decametre
decilitre
decimetre
foot-pound
hectogram
kilocycle
kilohertz
kilolitre
kilometre
light-year
megacycle
megafarad

megahertz
metric ton
microgram
microwatt
milligram
nanometre
scantling
steradian

10

barleycorn
centilitre
centimetre
cubic metre
decagramme
decigramme
fluid ounce
hectolitre
horsepower
kilogramme
microfarad
millilitre
millimetre
nanosecond
pennyweight
rutherford
square inch
square mile
square yard

13

hundredweight

15

square kilometre

16

square centimetre

Paper Measures

4

bale
copy
demy
post
pott
ream

5

atlas
brief
crown
draft
quire
royal

6

bag cap
bundle
casing
medium

7

emperor
kent cap

8

elephant
foolscap
haven cap
imperial

9

cartridge
colombier
large post
music demy

10

double demy
double post
grand eagle
super royal

11

antiquarian
imperial cap
pinched post

14

double elephant

15

double large post

Medicine and
Health

Medical Fields and Specialities

7

anatomy
myology
otology
urology

8

cytology
eugenics
nosology
oncology
serology

9

aetiology
andrology
audiology
histology
necrology
neurology
orthotics
osteology
pathology
pleoptics
radiology
rhinology

10

cardiology
embryology
geriatrics
immunology
morphology
nephrology
obstetrics
orthoptics
proctology
psychology

semeiology
teratology

11

dermatology
gerontology
gynaecology
haematology
laryngology
logopaedics
paediatrics
radiography
stomatology

12

cytogenetics
ephebiatrics
epidemiology
orthopaedics
pharmacology
radiobiology
rheumatology
syndesmology
therapeutics
traumatology

13

endocrinology
ophthalmology
psychometrics

14

otolaryngology
symptomatology

15

dermatoglyphics
neurophysiology
psychopathology

16

gastro-enterology
psycho-geriatrics

psycho-physiology

17+

cognitive psychology
interventional radiology
nuclear cardiology
otorhino-laryngology
psycho-linguistics
psycho-pharmacology

Complementary/Alternative Therapies

acupuncture
aromatherapy
art therapy
aversion therapy
balneotherapy
behaviour therapy
chiropractic
cognitive therapy
colour therapy
confrontation therapy
crystal therapy
drama therapy
electroconvulsive therapy
electroshock therapy
electrotherapy
family therapy
Gerson cure
Gestalt therapy
group therapy
homeopathy
humanistic therapy
hydrotherapy
hypnotherapy
insulin shock therapy
mechanotherapy
megavitamin therapy
Metrazol shock therapy

music therapy
narcotherapy
naturopathy
occupational therapy
osteopathy
play therapy
primal therapy
psychotherapy
rational-emotive
therapy
recreational therapy
reflexology
regression therapy
relaxation therapy
release therapy
Rogerian therapy
sex therapy
Shiatsu
shock therapy
sleep therapy
sound therapy

Bones

3

rib

4

ulna
5
anvil
costa
femur
ilium
incus
pubis
skull
spine
talus
tibia
vomer

6

carpal
carpus
coccyx
cuboid
fibula
hallux
hammer
pelvis
rachis
radius
sacrum
stapes
tarsal
tarsus

7

cranium
hipbone
humerus
ischium
jawbone
kneecap
kneepan
malleus
mastoid
maxilla
patella
phalanx
scapula
sternum
stirrup

8

backbone
clavicle
heel bone
mandible
scaphoid
shinbone
sphenoid
vertebra

9

anklebone
calcancus
cheekbone
funny bone
hyoid bone
maxillary
nasal bone
phalanges
thighbone
wristbone

10

astragalus
breastbone
cannon bone
collarbone
haunch bone
metacarpal
metacarpus
metatarsal
metatarsus

11

ethmoid bone
floating rib
frontal bone

12

parietal bone
spinal column
temporal bone

13

occipital bone
sesamoid bones
shoulder blade
zygomatic bone

14.

innominate bone
vertebral column

Major Arteries

aorta
brachial
carotid
femoral
hepatic
iliac
innominate
mesenteric
pulmonary
radial
renal
subclavian
thoracic
tibial
ulnar

Major Veins

basilic
brachial
cephalic
femoral
hepatic
hepatic portal
iliac
inferior vena cava
jugular
pulmonary
renal
saphenous
subclavian
superior vena cava
suprarenal
tibial

Muscles

4
psoas

5
teres

6
biceps
rectus
soleus
vastus

7
deltoid
gluteus
iliacus
triceps
anconeus
masseter
opponens
pectoral
peroneus
platysma
postural
rhomboid
scalenus
serratus
skeletal
tibialis

9
depressor
iliopsoas
mylohyoid
obturator
popliteus
quadratus
sartorius
sphincter
supinator

trapezius
voluntary

10
brachialis
buccinator
epicranius
hyoglossus
quadriceps
stylohyoid
temporalis

11
orbicularis
sternohyoid

12
styloglossus

13
gastrocnemius
sternomastoid

19
sternocleidomastoid

The Ear

anvil
auditory nerve
basilar membrane
cochlea
eardrum
Eustachian tube
fenestra ovalis
fenestra rotunda
hammer
incus
inner ear
labyrinth
malleus
membrane of Reissner

middle ear
organ of corti
ossicles
oval window
pinna
receptor cells
round window
saccule
scala media
scala tympani
scala vestibuli
semicircular canal
stapes
stirrup
tectorial membrane
tunnel of corti
tympanic membrane
utricle
vestibular nerve

The Eye

aqueous humour
blind spot
choroid
ciliary body
cone
conjunctiva
cornea
eyelash
fovea
hyaloid canal
iris
lacrimal gland
lens
meibomian gland
optic nerve
pupil
retina
rod
sclera
vitreous humour

yellow spot

Glands

5
liver
sweat

6
buccal
pineal
tarsal
thymus

7
adrenal
Cowper's
gastric
mammary
parotid
thyroid

8
Brunner's
ductless
exocrine
pancreas
prostate
salivary

9
endocrine
meibomian
pituitary
preputial
sebaceous

10
Bartholin's
sublingual
suprarenal

vestibular

11
Lieberkuhn's
parathyroid

12
submaxillary

13
bulbourethral
submandibular

Psychology Terms

2
id
IQ

3
ADD
DSM
ECT
ego
PVS
REM

4
amok
fear
koro
mind
pica
PTSD
SADS
sane
skew

5
anima

singe
fugue
furor
habit
imago
latah
mania

6

abulia
affect
animus
anomia
autism
censor
deja vu
engram
eonism
fading
libido
mencap
mutism
phobia
psyche
sadism
schism
sodomy
stress
trance

7

amentia
amnesia
anxiety
arousal
bonding
bulimia
complex
couvade
dereism
ecstasy
eidetic
elation

emotion
empathy
fantasy
imagery
insight
leresis
operant
paradox
psychic
shaping
T-group
windigo
zoopsia

8

analysis
anorexia
aphrenia
asthenic
ataraxia
avoidant
bisexual
blocking
chaining
conation
conflict
delusion
dementia
dopamine
dysbulia
dyslogia
euphoria
exposure
Freudian
frottage
genogram
hebetude
hysteria
ideation
illusion
insanity
instinct
lobotomy

neurosis
oneirism
paranoia
paranoid
psellism
reactive
superego

9

addiction
aerophagy
agromania
akathisia
analysand
anhedonia
archetype
asyndesis
autoscopy
baby blues
catalepsy
catatonia
cocainism
cognition
dysphemia
dyssocial
echolalia
eroticism
extrovert
fetishism
flashback
frigidity
geophagia
hypobulia
hypomania
ideomotor
imitation
implosion
introvert
lallation
leucotomy
masochism
mental age
modelling

monomania
neologism
obsession
obsessive
palilalia
precocity
prompting
psychosis
pyromania
sculpting
splitting
surrogate
symbolism
voyeurism
zoophobia

10

abreaction
alienation
anankastic
apotreptic
attachment
bell and pad
borderline
child abuse
citalopram
cluttering
compulsion
conversion
coprolalia
dependence
depression
dipsomania
divagation
dromomania
echopraxia
erotomania
exaltation
extinction
folie a deux
Gestaltism
handedness
hypnagogic

hypothymia
hysterical
imprinting
lesbianism
logorrhoea
monophobia
narcissism
necromania
negativism
olanzapine
paederasty
paramnesia
pareidolia
paroxetine
perception
pithiatism
polyphagia
projection
psychiatry
psychology
psychopath
regression
repression
rumination
Samaritans
satyriasis
sertindole
sertraline
stammering
sterotypy
stuttering
suggestion -
withdrawal
xenophobia
zoophilism

11

agoraphobia
alexithymia
ambivalence
biofeedback
counselling
cyclothymia

double-bind
dyspareunia
echokinesis
ganser state
glossolalia
hebephrenia
hyperpraxia
hypnopompic
idiot savant
kleptomania
lycanthropy
megalomania
melancholia
neuroticism
nyctophilia
nyctophobia
nyctophonia
nymphomania
orientation
paedophilia
paliphrasia
paragraphia
paraphrenia
parasuicide
personality
psychodrama
psychogenic
retardation
retrography
risperidone
role playing
SAD syndrome
schizotypal
sexual abuse
sublimation
thalamotomy
unconscious

12

behaviourism
cancer phobia
cingulectomy
conditioning

displacement
dissociation
extraversion
extroversion
Feingold diet
flagellation
group therapy
halfway house
hypergraphia
hyperkinesia
hypochondria
intraversion
introjection
introversion
necrophilism
neurasthenia
onomatomania
palingraphia
phaneromania
preparedness
pseudoplegia
psychiatrist
psychologist
psychoticism
somnambulism
subconscious
substitution
time sampling
transference
transvestism

13

antipsychotic
confabulation
cross-dressing
derealization
event sampling
exhibitionism
family therapy
hallucination
homosexuality
mental illness
normalization

panic disorder
perseveration
pharmacomania
psychokinesis
psychometrics
psychosomatic
psychosurgery
psychotherapy
reinforcement
Rorschach test
schizophrenia
sleep-walking
somniloquence
twilight state
verbigeration

14

autosuggestion
claustrophobia
disorientation
drug dependence
effort syndrome
encounter group
identification
mental handicap
noctambulation
Oedipus complex
onomatopoiesis
parapsychology
projective test
psychoanalysis
psychoneurosis
Rett's syndrome
security object
senile dementia
transsexualism
Wechsler scales

15

anorexia nervosa
aversion therapy
bipolar disorder
Capgras' syndrome

conduct disorder
dysmorphophobia
electronarcosis
free association
Heller's syndrome
heterosexuality
neuropsychiatry
pseudomutuality
psychopathology
rationalization
retention deficit
sexual deviation
thought stopping

16

behaviour therapy
Briquet's syndrome
cognitive therapy
core-and-cluster
defence mechanism
expressed emotion
fragile-X syndrome
globus hystericus
intelligence test
locked-in syndrome
mental deficiency
Mental Health Acts
mental impairment
nervous breakdown
overcompensation
psychogeriatrics
psychophysiology
special hospitals
trichotillomania

17

affective disorder
Asperger's syndrome
belle indifference
circumstantiality
depersonalisation
dysmnesic syndrome
dysthymic syndrome

flexibilitas cerea
mental retardation
psycholinguistics
reaction formation
relaxation therapy
separation anxiety
Tourette's syndrome

18

association of ideas
attachment disorder
conversion disorder
dopamine hypothesis
graded self-exposure

inferiority complex
knights-move thought
Korsakoff's syndrome
learning disability
response prevention
sensory deprivation

Phobias

Phobia	Subject	Phobia	Subject
acarophobia	itching	atelophobia	imperfection
acarophobia	mites	atephobia	ruin
acerbophobia	sourness	aulophobia	flutes
acerophobia	sourness	aurophobia	gold
achluophobia	darkness	autophobia	loneliness
acousticophobia	sound	bacillophobia	microbes
acrophobia	high places	bacteriophobia	bacteria
acrophobia	sharpness	ballistophobia	bullets
aerophobia	draughts	barophobia	gravity
agoraphobia	crowds	bathophobia	depth
agoraphobia	open places	batophobia	high buildings
agyrophobia	streets (crossing)	batophobia	high places
ailurophobia	cats	batrachophobia	reptiles
algophobia	pain	belonephobia	needles
altophobia	high places	blennophobia	slime
amathophobia	dust	bromidrosiphobia	body odour
anaemophobia	anaemia	brontophobia	thunder
ancraophobia	wind	cancerophobia	cancer
androphobia	men	cancerphobia	cancer
anginophobia	narrowness	carcinophobia	cancer
Anglophobia	English	cardiophobia	heart disease
anthophobia	flowers	chaetophobia	hair
anthropophobia	people	cheimaphobia	cold
antlophobia	floods	cheimatophobia	cold
apeirophobia	infinity	chionophobia	snow
apiphobia	bees	chloerophobia	cholera
arachnephobia	spiders	chrometophobia	money
asthenophobia	weakness	chromophobia	colour
astraphobia	lightning	chronophobia	time (duration)
astrapophobia	lightning	cibophobia	food

Phobia	Subject	Phobia	Subject
claustrophobia	enclosed places	Germanophobia	Germans
clinophobia	bed (going to bed)	geumatophobia	taste
		glossophobia	speech
cnidophobia	insect stings	graphophobia	writing
coitophobia	coitus	gynephobia	women
cometophobia	comets	hadephobia	hell
coprophobia	faeces	hagiophobia	saints
coprostasophobia	constipation	hamartophobia	sin
cremnophobia	precipices	haphophobia	touch
cryophobia	ice, frost	haptophobia	touch
crystallophobia	crystals	harpaxophobia	robbers
cymophobia	waves	hedonophobia	pleasure
cynophobia	dogs	heliophobia	sun
demonophobia	demons	helminthophobia	worms
demophobia	crowds	hemaphobia	blood
dermapathophobia	skin disease	hematophobia	blood
dermatosiophobia	sign	hemophobia	blood
diabetophobia	diabetes	herpetophobia	reptiles
dikephobia	justice	hierophobia	priests
doraphobia	fur	hippophobia	horses
dromophobia	motion	hodophobia	travel
ecclesiophobia	church	homichlophobia	fog
ecophobia	home	hormephobia	shock
eisoptrophobia	mirrors	hydrophobia	water
electrophobia	electricity	hydrophobophobia	rabies
eleutherophobia	freedom	hygrophobia	dampness
emetophobia	vomiting	hypegiaphobia	responsibility
enetophobia	pins	hypnophobia	sleep
entomophobia	insects	hypsophobia	high places
eosophobia	dawn	ichthyophobia	fish
ergophobia	work	ideophobia	ideas
ermitophobia	loneliness	Japanophobia	Japanese
erotophobla	sex	Judeophobia	Jews
erythrophobia	blushing	kakorraphiaphobia	failure
febriphobia	fever	katagelophobia	ridicule
Francophobia	French	kenophobia	void
Gallophobia	French	keraunophobia	thunder
gametophobia	marriage	kinetophobia	motion
genophobia	sex	kleptophobia	stealing
gephyrophobia	bridges (crossing)	koniophobia	dust
		kopophobia	fatigue

Phobia	Subject	Phobia	Subject
laliophobia	speech	parasitophobia	parasites
lalophobia	speech	parthenophobia	young girls
limnophobia	lakes	pathophobia	disease
linonophobia	string	patroiophobia	heredity
logophobia	words	peccatiphobia	sin
lyssophobia	insanity	pediculophobia	lice
maniphobia	insanity	peniaphobia	poverty
mastigophobia	beating	phagophobia	swallowing
mechanophobia	machinery	pharmacophobia	drugs
meningitophobia	meningitis	phasmophobia	ghosts
metallophobia	metal	philosophobia	philosophy
microbiophobia	microbes	phobophobia	fear
microphobia	small things	phonophobia	speech
monophobia	loneliness	photophobia	light
musicophobia	music	phronemophobia	thinking
musophobia	mice	phthisiophobia	tuberculosis
mysophobia	dirt	pneumatophobia	spirits
myxophobia	slime	pnigerophobia	smothering
necrophobia	corpses	pogonophobia	beards
Negrophobia	Negroes	poinephobia	punishment
neophobia	new things	politicophobia	politics
nephophobia	clouds	potamophobia	rivers
nephophobia	disease	potophobia	drink
nyctophobia	night	pteronophobia	feathers
ochlophobia	mobs	pyrophobia	fire
ochophobia	vehicles	rectophobia	rectum
odontophobia	teeth	rhabdophobia	magic
oecophobia	home	Russophobia	Russians
oikophobia	home	rypophobia	soiling
olfactophobia	smell	Satanophobia	Satan
ommetaphobia	eyes	scabiophobia	scabies
onomatophobia	words	sciophobia	shadows
ophiciophobia	snakes	scotophobia	darkness
ophiophobia	snakes	siderophobia	stars
ophresiophobia	smell	sinophobia	Chinese
ornithophobia	birds	sitophobia	food
osmophobia	smell	snakephobia	snakes
paedophobia	children	spermatophobia	germs
panphobia	everything	spermophobia	germs
pantophobia	everything	stasophobia	standing
papaphobia	Pope	stygiophobia	Hell

Phobia	Subject	Phobia	Subject
symmetrophobia	symmetry	toxophobia	poison
syphilophobia	syphilis	traumatophobia	injury
tachophobia	speed	tremophobia	trembling
telephonophobia	telephone	trichopathophobia	hair disease
teratrophobia	monsters	trichophobia	hair
Teutonophobia	Germans	tricinophobia	trichinosis
thaasophobia	idleness	triskaidekaphobia	thirteen
thalassophobia	sea	trypanophobia	inoculation
thanatophobia	death	tuberculophobia	tuberculosis
theophobia	God	tyrannophobia	tyrants
thermophobia	heat	uranophobia	Heaven
thixophobia	touch	urophobia	urine
tocophobia	childbirth	vaccinophobia	inoculation
tonitrophobia	thunder	venerophobia	venereal disease
topophobia	places	vermiphobia	worms
toxicophobia	poison	xenophobia	foreigners
toxiphobia	poison	zelophobia	jealousy

Surgical Operations

7

myotomy – muscle
lobotomy – nerve fibres from frontal
lobe of the brain

8

myectomy – muscle
tenotomy – tendon
vagotomy – vagus nerve
vasotomy – sperm duct

9

amniotomy – amniotic membranes
colectomy – colon
colostomy – colon
colpotomy – vagina
cordotomy – part of spinal cord
cystotomy – bladder
goniotomy – duct in eye
ileectomy – ileum

ileostomy – ileum
iridotomy – iris
leucotomy – nerve fibres in brain
lithotomy – kidney stone
lobectomy – lobe of an organ
myoplasty – muscle
neurotomy – nerve
ostectomy – bone
osteotomy – bone
otoplasty – ear
pubiotomy – pubic bone
pyelotomy – pelvis of kidney
rhizotomy – nerve roots
thyrotomy – thyroid gland
topectomy – part of brain
valvotomy – heart valve
vasectomy – sperm duct

10

antrectomy – part of stomach

antrostomy – bone cavity
apicectomy – root of tooth
arthrotomy – joint capsule
caecostomy – caecum
cordectomy - vocal cord
craniotomy – skull
cystectomy – bladder
cystostomy – bladder
embryotomy – foetus
enterotomy – intestine
episiotomy – vaginal opening
gastrotomy – stomach
hymenotomy – hymen
iridectomy – iris
jejunotomy – jejunum
keratotomy – cornea
laparotomy – abdomen
lumpectomy – breast tumour
mastectomy – breast
myomectomy – fibroids
nephrotomy – kidney
neurectomy – nerve
orbitotomy – bone around eye
ovariotomy – ovary
phlebotomy – vein
pleurotomy – pleural membrane
proctotomy – rectum or anus
rachiotomy – backbone
sclerotomy – white of eye
scrototomy – scrotum
sternotomy – breastbone
tarsectomy – ankle bone or eyelid
tissue
tenoplasty – tendon
thymectomy – thymus gland
uvulectomy – uvula
varicotomy – varicose vein
vitrextomy – vitreous humour
vulvectomy – vuvla

II

angioplasty – blood vessel
arteriotomy – artery

arthrectomy – joint
capsuloctomy – lens capsule of eye
colpoplasty – bladder
embolectomy – embolus, blood clot
enterectomy – intestine
enterostomy – small intestine
fraenectomy – tissue beneath tongue
gastrectomy – stomach
gastrostomy – stomach
genioplasty – chin
glossectomy – tongue
helcoplasty – skin ulcers
hepatectomy – liver
hysterectomy – womb
incudectomy – middle ear osside
jejunectomy – jejunum
jejunostomy – jejunum
keratectomy – cornea
labioplasty – lips
largynotomy – larynx
mammoplasty – breast
myringotomy – eardrum
nephrectomy – kidney
nephrostomy – kidney
omentectomy – peritoneum of
stomach
orchidotomy – testis
ovariectomy – ovary
papillotomy – part of bile duct
phlebectomy – vein
pleurectomy – pleural membrane
polypectomy – polyp
proctectomy – rectum
pyeloplasty – pelvis of kidney
pylorectomy – part of stomach
rhinoplasty – nose
sclerectomy – white of eye
splenectomy – spleen
synovectomy – membrane around
joint
tarsoplasty – eyelid
thalamotomy – part of brain
thoracotomy – chest cavity

tracheotomy – windpipe
tympanotomy – eardrum
ureterotomy – ureter
urethrotomy – urethra
valvulotomy – heart valve
varicectomy – varicose veins
vesicostomy – bladder

12

arteriectomy – artery
arthroplasty – joint
cheiloplasty - lips
cingulectomy – part of brain
duodenostomy – duodenum
gastroplasty – stomach
gingivectomy – gum tissue
hernioplasty – hernia
hysterectomy – womb
keratoplasty – cornea
laryngectomy – larynx
mastoidotomy – mastoid bone
meniscectomy – knee cartilage
oophorectomy – ovary
orchidectomy – testis
palatoplasty – cleft palate
pallidectomy – part of brain
phalloplasty – penis
pyloroplasty – stomach outlet
stapedectomy – third ear ossicle
thoracectomy – rib
thrombectomy – blood clot
tonsillotomy – tonsil
tracheostomy – wind pipe
turbinectomy – bone in nose
ureterectomy – ureter
ureterostomy – ureter
urethrostomy – urethra
vaginoplasty – vagina

13

adenoidectomy – adenoids
arterioplasty – artery
cardiomyotomy – stomach opening
dermatoplasty – skin
hemicolectomy – part of colon
hepaticostomy – liver
ileocolostomy – ileum and colon
mastoidectomy – mastoid
myringoplasty – eardrum
neuronoplasty – nerves
oesophagotomy – gullet
ophthalmotomy – eye
pancreatotemy – pancreas
perineoplasty – vaginal opening
phalangectomy – finger or toe bones
pharyngectomy – pharynx
phrenicectomy – phrenic nerve
pneumonectomy – lung
prostatectomy – prostate gland
pyloromyotomy – stomach outlet
salpingectomy – fallopian tube
salpingostomy – fallopian tube
sigmoidectomy – part of colon
staphylectomy – uvula
sympathectomy – sympathetic nerve
symphysiotomy – front of pelvis
thoracoplasty – chest cavity
thyroidectomy – thyroid gland
tonsillectomy – tonsils
trabeculotomy – duct in eye
myringotomy, tympanology –
eardrum
tympanoplasty – eardrum
ureteroplasty – ureter
urethroplasty – urethra
vasovasectomy – rejoining of severed
sperm duct
vesiculectomy – seminal vesicle

Military

Ranks, terms and titles (UK and US)

(RAF)

2 - 4
A.C.1
A.C.2
F.O.
L.A.C.
W.A.A.F.

5
pilot

6
airman
fitter
rigger

7
aviator

8
armourer
corporal
mechanic
observer
sergeant

9
air gunner
bomb aimer
drum-major

navigator

10
air marshal
apprentice
balloonist
nose gunner
rear gunner
tail gunner

11
aircraftman
belly gunner
second pilot

12
air commodore
group captain
pilot officer

13
flying officer
wing commander

14
air vice marshal
flight engineer
flight mechanic
flight sergeant
squadron leader
warrant officer

15
air chief marshal

16
flight lieutenant

(USAF)

5
major

7
captain
colonel
general
private

10
bombardier

12
major general

13
sergeant major
staff sergeant

14
master sergeant

15
first lieutenant

16
second lieutenant

Battles

2
Re, Ile de (1627, Anglo-French Wars)

3

Acs (1849, Hungarian Rising)
Aix, Ile D' (1758, Seven Years' War)
Dee, Brig of (1639, Bishops' War)
Goa (1511, 1570, Portuguese Conquest)

Hue (1968, Vietnam War)
Ulm (1805, Napoleonic Wars)

4

Acre (1189-1191, Third Crusade
1291, Crusader-Turkish Wars; 1799,
French Revolutionary Wars; 1840,
Egyptian Revolt)
Agra (1803, Second British-Maratha
War; 1857, Indian Mutiny)
Alma (1854, Crimea War)
Aong (1857, Indian Mutiny)
Aras (1775, First British-Maratha
War)
Avus (198 BC, Second Macedonian
War)
Baza (1489, Spanish-Muslim Wars)
Bedr (623, Islamic Wars)
Bega (1696, Ottoman Wars)
Cuba (1953, Castro Revolt)
Deeg (1780, First British-Maratha
War; 1804, Second British-Maratha
War)
Gaza (332 BC, Alexander's Asiatic
Campaigns; 312 BC, Wars of
Alexander's Successors; 1917, World
War I)
Gelt, The (1570, Anglo-Scottish Wars)
Guam (1944, World War II)
Jena (1806, Napoleonic Wars)
Kars (1855, Crimean War)
Kiev (1941, World War II)
Kulm (1813, Napoleonic Wars)
Laon (1814, Napoleonic Wars)
Leck, The (1632, Thirty Years' War)
Lens (1648, Thirty Years' War)
Lodz (1914, World War I)
Main, The (9 BC, Germanic War)
Maya, Colde 91813, Peninsular War)
Metz (1870, Franco-Prussian War)
Neon (354 BC Sacred War)
Nile (1798, French Revolutionary
Wars)

Nive (1813, Peninsular War)
Novi (1799, French Revolutionary
Wars)
Onao (1857, Indian Mutiny)
Oran (1509, Spanish Invasion of
Morocco; 1940, World War II)
Orel (1943, World War II)
Raab (1809, Napoleonic Wars)
Rome (387 BC, First Invasion of the
Gauls; 408, War of the Western
Roman Empire; 472, Ricimer's
Rebellion; 537, 546 Wars of the
Byzantine Empire; 1082, Norman
Seizure; 1527, Wars of Charles V;
1849, Italian Wars of Independence)
Scio (1769, Ottoman Wars)
Sohr (1745, War of the Austrian
Succession)
St Lo (1944, World War II)
Toba (1868, Japanese Revolution)
Troy (1100 BC)
Truk (1944, World War II)
Veii (405 BC, Rise of Rome)
Zela (67 BC, Third Mithridatic War;
47 BC, Wars of the First Triumvirate)

5

Accra (1824, 1825, First British-
Ashanti War)
Aduwa (1896, Italian Invasion of
Ethiopia)
Alamo, Storming of the (1836, Texan
Rising)
Allia, The (390 BC, The First Invasion
of the Gauls)
Alsen (1864, Schleswig-Holstein War)
Anzio (1944, World War II)
Argos (195 BC, Roman Invasion of
Greece)
Arius (214 BC, The War of the
Hellenistic Monarchies)
Arrah (1857, Indian Mutiny)
Arras (1654, Wars of Louis XIV;

1917, World War I)
A Shau (1966, Vietnam War)
Auray (1364, Hundred Years' War)
Bahur (1752, Seven Years' War)
Banda (1858, Indian Mutiny)
Bands, The (961, Danish Invasion of Scotland)
Berea (1852, Kaffir Wars)
Betwa, The (1858, Indian Mutiny)
Boyne, The (1690, War of the Grand Alliance)
Brest (1512, War of the Holy League)
Brill (1572, Netherlands War of Independence)
Burma (1942, 1943, World War II)
Buxar (1764, British Conquest of Bengal)
Cadiz (1587, Anglo-Spanish War)
Cairo (1517, Ottoman Wars)
Carpi (1701, War of the Spanish Succession)
Cesme (1770, Ottoman Wars)
Crecy (1346, Hundred Years' War)
Crete (1941 (World War II)
Dak To (1967, Vietnam War)
Delhi (1297, First Tater Invasion of India; 1398, Second Tater Invasion; 1803, 1804, Second British-Maratha War; 1857, Indian Mutiny)
Douai (1710, War of the Spanish Succession)
Douro (1809, Peninsular War)
Dover (1652, Anglo-Dutch Wars)
Downs, The (1666, Anglo-Dutch Wars)
Elena (1877, Russo-Turkish War)
El Teb (1884, British-Sudan Campaigns)
Emesa (272, Wars of the Roman Empire)
Engen (1800, French Revolutionary Wars)
Eylau (1807, Napoleonic Wars)

Genoa (1746, Patriotic Rising; 1795, 1800, French Revolutionary Wars)
Goits (1848, Italian Wars of Independence)
Gubat (1885, British Sudan Campaigns)
Hanau (1813, Napoleonic Wars)
Hippo (430, Wars of the Western Roman Empire)
Imola (1797, French Revolutionary Wars)
Issus (333 BC, Alexander's Asiatic Campaigns; 1488, Ottoman Wars)
Jassy (1620, Ottoman Wars)
Kagul (1770, Ottoman Wars)
Kalpi (1858, Indian Mutiny)
Karee (190, Second Boer War)
Kazan (1774, Cossack Rising)
Kolin (1757, Seven Years' War)
Kotah (1858, Indian Mutiny)
Lagos (War of the Grand Alliance)
La Paz (1865, Bolivian Civil War)
Largs (1263, Norse Invasion of Scotland)
Lewes (1264, Barons' War)
Leyte (1944, World War II)
Liege (1914, World War II)
Ligny (1815, Napoleonic Wars)
Lille (1708, War of the Spanish Succession)
Lissa (1866, Seven Weeks' War)
Luzon (1945, World War II)
Lyons (197, Civil Wars of the Roman Empire)
Maida (1806, Napoleonic Wars)
Malta (1565, Ottoman Wars; 1798, French Revolutionary Wars; 1942, World War II)
Marne (1914, 1918, World War I)
Maxen (1759, Seven Years' War)
Mudki (1845, First British-Sikh War)
Munda (45 BC, Civil War of Caesar and Pompey)

Mursa (351, Civil Wars of the Roman Empire)

Mylex (36 BC, Wars of the Second Triumvirate)

Namur (1914, World War I)

Paris (1814, Napoleonic Wars; 1870, Franco-Prussian War)

Patay (1429, Hundred Years' War)

Podol (1866, Seven Weeks' War)

Pruth, The (1770, Ottoman Wars)

Ramla (1177, Crusader-Turkish Wars)

Redan, The Great (1855, Crimean War)

Reims (1814, Napoleonic Wars)

Rouen (1418, Hundred Years' War)

Sedan (1870, Franco-Prussian War)

Selby (1644, English Civil War)

Seoul (1950, Korean War)

Sluys (1340, Hundred Years' War)

Somme (1916, 1918, World War I)

Spira (1703, War of the Spanish Succession)

Spurs (1302, Flemish War; 1513, Anglo-French Wars)

Stoke (1487, Lambert Simnel's Rebellion)

Tamai (1884, British Sudan Campaigns)

Texel (1653, Anglo-Dutch Wars)

Tunis (255 BC, First Punic War; 1270, Eighth Crusade)

Turin (312, Civil Wars of the Roman Empire; 1706, War of the Spanish Succession)

Utica (49 BC, Civil War of Caesar and Pompey; 694, Muslim Conquest of Africa)

Valmy (1792, French Revolutionary Wars)

Varna (1444, Anti-Turkish Crusade; 1828, Ottoman Wars)

Varus, Defeat of (AD 9, Wars of the Roman Empire)

Vasaq (1442, Ottoman Wars)

Wavre (1815, Napoleonic Wars)

Worth (1870, Franco-Prussian War)

Ypres (1914, 1915, 1917, World War I)

Zenta (1679, Ottoman Wars)

Znaim (1809, Napoleonic Wars)

6

Aachen (1944, World War II)

Abukir (1799, 1801, French Revolutionary Wars)

Abu Kru (1885, British Sudan Campaigns)

Actium (31 BC, Wars of the Second Triumvirate)

Aleppo (638, Muslim Invasion of Syria; 1400, Tatar Invasion of Syria; 1516, Ottoman Wars)

Alford (1645, English Civil War)

Aliwal (1846, First British-Sikh War)

Amiens (1870, Franco-Prussian War)

Angora (1402 Tatar Invasion of Asia Minor)

Arbela (331 BC, Alexander's Asiatic Campaigns)

Arcola (1796, French Revolutionary Wars)

Argaon (1803, Second British-Maratha War)

Arklow (1798, Irish Rebellion)

Arnhem (1944, World War II)

Arsouf (1191, Third Crusade)

Artois (1915, World War I)

Ashtee (1818, Third British-Maratha War)

Asiago (1916, World War I)

Aspern (1809, Napoleonic Wars)

Assaye (1803, Second British-Maratha War)

Atbara (1898, British Sudan Campaigns)

Azores (1591, Anglo-Spanish War)

Bardia (1941, World War II)

Barnet (1471, War of the Roses)

Basing (871, Danish Invasion of Britain)

Baylen (1808, Peninsular War)

Beauge (1421, Hundred Years' War)

Bender (1768, Ottoman Wars)

Bergen (1759, Seven Years' War)

Beylan (1831, Egyptian Revolt)

Bilbao (1937, Spanish Civil War)

Busaco (1810, Peninsular War)

Calais (1346, Hundred Years' War; 1558, Anglo-French Wars)

Camden (1780, American Revolutionary War)

Campen (1759, Seven Years' War)

Chanda (1818, Third British-Maratha War)

Chiari (1701, War of the Spanish Succession)

Chizai (1372, Hundred Years' War)

Danzig (1627, Thirty Years' War; 1807, 1813, Napoleonic Wars)

Dargai (1897, British Northwest Frontier Campaign)

Delphi (355 BC, Sacred War)

Denain (1712, War of the Spanish Succession)

Dessau (1626, Thirty Years' War)

Dieppe (1942, World War II)

Djerba (1560, Ottoman Wars)

Dollar (875, Danish Invasions of Scotland)

Dunbar (1296, 1339, Wars of Scottish Independence; 1650, Cromwell's Scottish Campaign)

Dundee (1899, Second Boer War)

Duppel (1864, Schleswig-Holstein War)

Erbach (1800, French Revolutionary Wars)

Ferkeh (1896, British Sudan Campaigns)

Gazala (1942, World War II)

Gebora (1811, Peninsular War)

Gerona (1809, Peninsular War)

Ghazni (1839, First British-Afghan War)

Gisors (1197, Anglo-French Wars)

Grozka (1739, Ottoman Wars)

Hallue (1870, Franco-Prussian War)

Harlaw (1411, Scottish Civil Wars)

Hashin (1885, British Sudan Campaigns)

Havana (1748, War of the Austrian Succession; 1762, Seven Years' War)

Hexham (1464, War of the Roses)

Hochst (1622, Thirty Years' War)

Inchon (1950, Korean War)

Ingogo (1881, First Boer War)

Ismail (1790, Ottoman Wars)

Isonzo (1915, World War II)

Jersey (1550, Anglo-French Wars)

Jhansi (1857, Indian Mutiny)

Khelat (1839, First British-Afghan War)

Kirkee (1817, Third British-Maratha War)

Kokein (1824, First Burma War)

Kotzin (1622, 1673, Ottoman Wars)

Kronia (1738, Ottoman Wars)

Landau (1702, War of the Spanish Succession)

Landen (1693, War of the Grand Alliance)

Lawari (1803, Second British-Maratha War)

Le Mans (1871, Franco-Prussian War)

Lerida (1642, 1647, Thirty Years' War)

Lonato (1796, French Revolutionary Wars)

Lutter (1626, Thirty Years' War)

Lutzen (1632, Thirty Years' War, 1813, Napoleonic Wars)

Madras (1746, War of the Austrian Succession; 1758, Seven Years' War)

Madrid (1936, Spanish Civil War)

Maidan (1842, First British-Afghan War)

Majuba (1881, First Boer War)

Malaga (1487, Spanish-Muslim Wars; 1704, War of the Spanish Succession)

Malaya (1941, World War II)

Maldon (991, Danish Invasions of Britain)

Manila (1898, Spanish-American War)

Mantua (1797, French Revolutionary Wars)

Margus (285, Civil Wars of the Roman Empire)

Medola (1796, French Revolutionary Wars)

Merton (Danish Invasion of Britain)

Mexico (1520, Conquest of Mexico)

Minden (1759, Seven Years War)

Mohacz (1526, 1687, Ottoman Wars)

Morawa (1443, Ottoman Wars)

Moscow (1941, World War II)

Mukden (1905, Russo-Japanese War; 1948, Chinese Civil War)

Multan (1848, Second British-Sikh War)

Mutina (43 BC Roman Civil Wars)

Mytton (1319, Wars of Scottish Independence)

Nachod (1866, Seven Weeks' War)

Najara (1367, Hundred Years' War)

Naseby (1645, English Civil War)

Nicaea (1097, First Crusade)

Norway (1940 (World War II)

Ockley (851, Danish Invasions of Britain)

Olmutz (1758, Seven Years' War)

Oporto (1809, Peninsular War)

Orthez (1814, Peninsular War)

Ostend (1601, Netherlands War of Independence)

Oswego (1756, Seven Years' War)

Otumba (1520, Spanish Conquest of Mexico)

Peking (1214, Tatar Invasion of China)

Plei Me (1965, Vietnam War)

Plevna (1877, Russo-Turkish War)

Poland (1939, World War II)

Ponani (1780, First British-Mysore War)

Prague (1620, Thirty Years' War; 1757, Seven Years' War)

Quebec (1759, 1760, Seven Years War)

Rabaul (1943, World War II)

Raphia (217 BC, War of the Hellenistic Monarchies)

Raszyn (1809 Napoleonic Wars)

Rhodes (1480, Ottoman Wars)

Rivoli (1797, French Revolutionary Wars)

Rocroi (1643, Thirty Years' War)

Rolica (1808, Peninsular War)

Rumani (1915, World War I)

Sacile (1809, Napoleonic Wars)

Sadowa (1866, Seven Weeks War)

Saigon (1968, Vietnam War)

Saints, The (1782, American Revolutionary War)

Sangro (1943, World war II)

Shiloh (1862, American Civil War)

Sicily (1943, World War II)

Sinope (1852, Crimean War)

Sorata (1780, Inca Rising)

Ste Foy (1760, Seven Years' War)

St Kits (1667, Anglo-Dutch Wars)

Tauris (47 BC, Civil War of Caesar and Pompey)

Thurii (282 BC, Roman Civil Wars)

Tobruk (1941, 1942, World War II)

Tofrek (1885, British Sudan Campaigns)

Torgau (1760, Seven Years' War)

Toulon (1707, War of the Spanish Succession; 1744, War of the Austrian Succession; 1793, French

Revolutionary Wars)

Towton (1461, War of the Roses)

Tsinan (1948, Chinese Civil War)

Tudela (1808, Peninsular War)

Ulundi (1879, Zulu-British War)

Ushant (1794, French Revolutionary Wars)

Venice (1846, Italian Wars of Independence)

Verdun (1916, World War I)

Verona (312, Civil Wars of the Roman Empire)

Vienna (1529, 1683, Ottoman Wars)

Wagram (1809, Napoleonic Wars)

Warsaw (1831, Second Polish Rising; 1914, World War I; 1918, Russo-Polish War; 1939, 1944, World War II)

Werben (1631, Thirty Years' War)

Wiazma (1812, Napoleonic Wars)

Zurich (1799, French Revolutionary Wars)

7

Abraham, Plains of (1759, Seven Years' War)

Abu Klea (1885, British Sudan Campaigns)

Albuera (1811, Peninsular War)

Algiers (1775, Spanish-Algerian War; 1816, Bombardment of)

Aligarh (1803, First British-Maratha War)

Alkmaar (1573, Netherlands War of Independence; 1799, French Revolutionary Wars)

Almorah (1815, British-Gurkha War)

Alnwick (1093, Anglo-Scottish Wars)

Amoaful (1874, Second British Ashanti War)

Antioch (1097, First Crusade)

Antwerp (1576, Netherlands War of Independence; 1832, Liberation of

Belgium; 1914, World War I)

Arikera (1791, Second British-Mysore War)

Ascalon (1099, First Crusade)

Ashdown (871, Danish Invasion of Britain)

Athenry (1316, Conquest of Ireland)

Aughrim (1691, War of the English Succession)

Baghdad (1401, Mongol Invasion of Mesopotamia)

Balkans (1940, 1944, World War II)

Barossa (1811, Peninsular War)

Bassano (1796, French Revolutionary Wars)

Bassein (1780, First British-Maratha War)

Batavia (1811, Napoleonic Wars)

Bautzen (1813, Napoleonic Wars)

Belmont (1899, Second Boer War)

Benburb (1646, Great Irish Rebellion)

Bethune (1707, War of the Spanish Succession)

Biberac (1796, French Revolutionary Wars)

Bourbon (1810, Napoleonic Wars)

Breslau (1757, Seven Years' War)

Brienne (1814, Napoleonic Wars)

Bull Run (1861, 1862, American Civil War)

Cadsand (1357, Hundred Years' War)

Calafat (1854, Crimean War)

Calicut (1790 Second British-Mysore War)

Carigat (1791, Second British-Mysore War)

Cassino (1944, World War II)

Chetate (1854, Crimean War)

Colenso (1899, Second Boer War)

Colombo (1796, French Revolutionary Wars)

Corinth (394 BC, Corinthian War,

1862, American Civil War)
Coronel (1914, World War I)
Corumba (1877, Paraguayan War)
Corunna (1809, Peninsular War)
Craonne (1814, Napoleonic Wars)
Cravant (1423, Hundred Years' War)
Crefeld (1758, Seven Years' War)
Crotoye (1347, Hundred Years' War)
Curicta (49 BC, Civil War of Caesar and Pompey)
Deorham (577, Wessex against the Welsh)
Dodowah (1826, First British-Ashanti War)
Dresden (1813, Napoleonic Wars)
Dundalk (1318, Scottish Invasion of Ireland)
Dunkeld (1689, Jacobite Rising)
Dunkirk (1940, World War II)
Dupplin (1332, Baliol's Rising)
Eckmuhl (1809, Napoleonic Wars)
Elk Horn (1862, American Civil War)
Essling (1809, Napoleonic Wars)
Evesham (1265, Baron's War)
Falkirk (1298, Wars of Scottish Independence, 1746, The Forty-five Rebellion)
Ferrara (1815, Napoleon's Hundred Days)
Fleurus (1622, Thirty Years' War; 1690, War of the Grand Alliance; 1794, French Revolutionary Wars)
Flodden (1513, Anglo-Scottish Wars)
Franlin (1864, American Civil War)
Fulford (1066, Norse Invasion of England)
Galicia (1914, World War I)
Gate Pah (1864, Maori-British War)
Gherain (1763, British Conquest of Bengal)
Ghoaine (1842, First British-Afghan War)
Goraria (1857, Indian Mutiny)

Gorlice (1915, World War I)
Graspan (1899, Second Boer War)
Grenada (1779, American Revolutionary War; 1983, American Invasion)
Gujerat (1849, Second British-Sikh War)
Gwalior (1780, First British-Maratha War; 1858, Indian Mutiny)
Haarlem (1572, Netherlands War of Independence)
Haslach (1805, Napoleonic Wars)
Hooghly, The (1759, Anglo-Dutch Wars in India)
Iwo-Jima (1945, World War II)
Jamaica (1655, Anglo-Spanish Wars)
Java Sea (1942, World War II)
Jitgurh (1815, British Gurkha War)
Jutland (1916, World War I)
Kalunga (1814, British Gurkha War)
Kambula (1879, Zulu War)
Kashgal (1883, British Sudan Campaigns)
Kharkov (1942, 1943, World War I)
Khe Sanh (1968, Vietnam War)
Kilsyth (1645, English Civil War)
Kineyri (1848, Second British-Sikh War)
Kinloss (1009, Danish Invasion of Scotland)
Kinsale (1601, O'Neill's Rebellion)
Krasnoi (1812, Napoleonic Wars)
La Hogue (1692, War of the Grand Alliance)
L'Ecluse (1340, Hundred Years' War)
Leghorn (1653, Anglo-Dutch Wars)
Leipzig (1631, Thirty Years' War; 1813, Napoleonic Wars)
Leuthen (1757, Seven Years' War)
Lincoln, Fair of (1217, First Baron's War)
Lindley (1900, Second Boer War)
Locninh (1967, Vietnam War)

Lucknow (1857, Indian Mutiny)

Maiwand (1880, Second British-Afghan War)

Malakov (1855, Crimean War)

Mansura (1250, Seventh Crusade)

Marengo (1800, French Revolutionary Wars)

Margate (1387, Hundred Years' War)

Marosch, The (101, Roman Empire Wars)

Matapan, Cape (1941, World War II)

Memphis (1862, American Civil War)

Methven (1306, Wars of Scottish Independence)

Minorca (1756, Seven Years' War; 1762, American Revolutionary War)

Mogilev (1812, Napoleonic Wars)

Moskowa (1812, Napoleonic Wars)

Nam Dong (1964, Vietnam War)

Nanking (1949, Chinese Civil War)

Neuwied (1797, French Revolutionary Wars)

Newburn (1640, Anglo-Scottish Wars)

Newbury (1643, 1644, English Civil War)

New Ross (1798, Irish Rebellion)

Niagara (1759, Seven Years' War)

Nivelle (1813, Peninsular War

Okinawa (1945 World War II)

Ooscata (1768, First British-Mysore War)

Opequan (1864, English Civil War)

Orleans (1428, Hundred Years' War)

Parkany (1663, Ottoman Wars)

Plassey (1757, Seven Years' War)

Polotsk (1812, Napoleonic Wars)

Preston (1648, English Civil War; 1715, The Fifteen Rebellion)

Pultusk (1806, Napoleonic Wars)

Rastadt (1796, French Revolutionary Wars)

Reading (871, Danish Invasions of Britain)

Rio Seco (1808, Peninsular War)

Rumania (1916, World War I)

Ruspina (46 BC, Civil War of Caesar and Pompey)

Sabugal (1811, Peninsular War)

Sagunto (1811, Peninsular War)

Salerno (1943, World War II)

San Juan (1898, Spanish-American War)

Scutari (1474, Ottoman Wars)

Sealion, Operation (1940, World War II)

Senekal (1900, Second Boer War)

Sharqat (1918, World War II)

Sinuiju (1951, Korean War)

Skalitz (1866, Seven Weeks' War)

Sobraon (1846, First British-Sikh War)

St Denis (1567, French Religious Wars; 1837, French-Canadian Rising)

St Lucia (1794, French Revolutionary Wars)

Surinam (1804, Napoleonic Wars)

Talneer (1818, Third British-Maratha War)

Tanjore (1758, Seven Years' War; 1773, First British-Mysore War)

Taranto (1940 World War II)

Thapsus (46 BC, Civil War of Caesar and Pompey)

Trebbia (1799, French Revolutionary Wars)

Tripoli (643, Muslim Conquest of Africa)

Tunisia (1942, World War II)

Ukraine (1943, World War II)

Vimeiro (1808, Peninsular War)

Vinaroz (1938, Spanish Civil War)

Vitoria (1813, Peninsular War)

Warburg (1760, Seven Years' War)

Wargaom (1779, First British-Maratha War)

Wepener (1900, Second Boer War)
Wimpfen (1622, Thirty Years' War)
Winkovo (1812, Napoleonic Wars)

8

Aberdeen (1644, English Civil War)
Abu Hamed (1897, British Sudan Campaigns)
Acapulco (1855, Mexican Liberal Rising)
Alicante (1706, War of the Spanish Succession)
Amalinde (1818, Kaffir Wars)
Antietam (1862 (American Civil War)
Asirghar (1819, Third British-Maratha War)
Assundun (1016, Danish Invasions of Britain)
Atlantic (1917, World War I)
Auldearn (1645, English Civil War)
Azimghur (1858, Indian Mutiny)
Bagradas (49 BC, Wars of the First Triumvirate)
Bastogne (1944, World War II)
Beda Fomm (1941, World War II)
Belgrade (1456, 1717, 1789, Ottoman Wars)
Berezina (1812, Napoleonic Wars)
Beymaroo (1841, First British-Afghan War)
Bismarck (1941, World War II)
Blenheim (1704, War of the Spanish Succession)
Blueberg (1806, Napoleonic Wars)
Borodino (1812, Napoleonic Wars)
Boulogne (1544, Anglo-French Wars)
Bouvines (1214, Anglo-French Wars)
Brooklyn (1776, American Revolutionary War)
Calcutta (1756, Seven Years' War)
Caldiero (1796, French Revolutionary Wars; 1805, Napoleonic Wars)
Carlisle (1745, The Forty-five Rebellion)
Carrical (1758, Seven Years' War)
Carthage (533, Byzantine Empire Wars)
Castella (1813, Peninsular War)
Cawnpore (1857, Indian Mutiny)
Cheriton (1644, English Civil War)
Clontarf (1014, Norse Invasion of Ireland)
Cocherel (1364, Hundred Years' War)
Coral Sea (1942, World War II)
Culloden (1746, The Forty-five Rebellion)
Czarnovo (1806, Napoleonic Wars)
Damascus (1918 World War I)
Dominica (1782, American Revolutionary War)
Drogheda (1641, Great Irish Rebellion; 1649, Cromwell's Campaign in Ireland)
Drumclog (1679, Covenanters' Rising)
Edgehill (1642, English Civil War)
Espinosa (1808, Peninsular War)
Ethandun (878, Danish Invasions of Britain)
Fair Oaks (1862, American Civil War)
Flanders (1940, World War II)
Florence (406, Wars of the Western Roman Empire)
Flushing (1809, Napoleonic Wars)
Formigny (1450, Hundred Years' War)
Freiburg (1644, Thirty Years' War)
Freteval (1194, Anglo-French Wars)
Gaulauli (1858, Indian Mutiny)
Gitschin (1866, Seven Weeks' War)
Goodwins, The (1666, Anglo-Dutch Wars)
Graf Spee (1939, World War II)
Gunzburg (1805, Napoleonic Wars)
Hastings (1066, Norman Conquest)
Heraclea (280 BC, Pyrrhus' Invasion of Italy; 313 Roman Civil Wars)

Herrings, The (1429, Hundred Years' War)

Hong Kong (1941, World War II)

Inkerman (1854, Crimean War)

Jemappes (1792, French Revolutionary Wars)

Kandahar (1648, Perso-Afghan Wars; 1834, Afghan Tribal Wars; 1880, Second British –Afghan War)

Katzbach (1813, Napoleonic Wars)

Khartoum (1884, British Sudan Campaigns)

Kirbekan (1885, British Sudan Campaigns)

Korygaom (1818, Third British-Maratha War)

Kumanovo (1912, First Balkan War)

Langport (1645, English Civil War)

Langside (1568, Scottish Civil Wars)

Le Cateau (1914m World War I)

Leitskau (1813, Napoleonic Wars)

Liegnitz (1760, Seven Years' War)

Lobositz (1756, Seven Years' War)

Luncarty (980, Danish Invasion of Scotland)

Lys River (1918, World War I)

Mafeking (1899, Second Boer War)

Mahidpur (1817, Third British-Maratha War)

Marathon (490 BC, Persian-Greek Wars)

Medillin (1809, Peninsular War)

Medenine (1943, World War II)

Messines (1917, World War I)

Montreal (1760, Seven Years' War)

Mortlack (1010, Danish Invasions of Scotland)

Mortmant (1814, Napoleonic Wars)

Moskirch (1800, French Revolutionary Wars)

Mouscron (1794, French Revolutionary Wars)

Muhlberg (1547, German Reformation Wars)

Musa Bagh (1858, Indian Mutiny)

Navarino (1827, Greek War of Independence)

Omdurman (1898, British Sudan Campaigns)

Onessant (1778, American Revolutionary War)

Ostrowno (1812, Napoleonic Wars)

Overlord, Operation (1944, World War II)

Palo Alto (1846, American-Mexican War)

Pea Ridge (1862, American Civil War)

Peshawar (1001, Afghan Invasion of India)

Philippi (42 BC, Roman Civil Wars)

Poitiers (507, Gothic Invasion of France; 1356, Hundred Years' War)

Portland (1653, Anglo-Dutch Wars)

Pyramids (1798, French Revolutionary Wars)

Pyrenees (1813, Peninsular War)

Richmond (1862, American Civil War)

Rossbach (1757, Seven Years' War)

Roveredo (1796, French Revolutionary Wars)

Saalfeld (1806, Napoleonic Wars)

Sapienza (1490, Ottoman Wars)

Saratoga (1777, American Revolutionary War)

Sholapur (1818, Third British-Maratha War)

Sidassir (1799, Third British-Mysore War)

Silistra (1854, Crimean War)

Smolensk (1708, Great Northern War; 1812, Napoleonic Wars; 1941, World War II)

Sorauren (1813, Peninsular War)

Spion Kop (1900, Second Boer War)

St Albans (1455, 1461, Wars of the

Roses)
Standard, The (1138 Anglo-Scottish Wars)
Ste Croix (1807, Napoleonic Wars)
St George (1500, Ottoman Wars)
St Mihiel (1918, World War I)
Stockach (1799, French Revolutionary Wars)
St Privat (1870, Franco-Prussian War)
Stratton (1643, English Civil War)
St Thomas (1807, Napoleonic Wars)
Talavera (1809, Peninsular War)
Thetford (870, Danish Invasions of England)
Tiberias (1187, Crusader-Saracen Wars)
Toulouse (1814, Napoleonic Wars)
Trinidad (1797, French Revolutionary Wars)
Tsingtao (1914, World War I)
Valletta (1798, French Revolutionary Wars)
Valutino (1812, Napoleonic Wars)
Verneuil (1424, Hundred Years' War)
Villiers (1870, Franco-Prussian War)
Waterloo (1815, Napoleonic Wars)
Wiesloch (1622, Thirty Years' War)
Yorktown (1781, American Revolutionary War; 1862, American Civil War)
Zorndorf (1758, Seven Years' War)

9

Abensberg (1809, Napoleonic Wars)
Agincourt (1415, Hundred Years' War)
Ahmadabad (1780, First British-Maratha War)
Ahmed Khel (1880, Second British Afghan War)
Aiguillon (1347, Hundred Years' War)
Alcantara (1580, Spanish Conquest of Portugal; 1706, War of the Spanish

Succession)
Alresford (1644, English Civil War)
Altendorf (1632, Thirty Years' War)
Amstetten (1805, Napoleonic Wars)
Angostura (1847, American Mexican War; 1868, Paraguayan War)
Askultsik (1828 Ottoman Wars)
Auerstadt (1806, Napoleonic Wars)
Aylesford (456, Jutish Invasion of Britain)
Balaclava (1854, Crimean War)
Ballymore (1798, Irish Rebellion)
Bangalore (1791, Second British-Mysore War)
Barcelona (1705 War of the Spanish Succession; 1938, Spanish Civil War)
Bergfried (1807, Napoleonic Wars)
Bhurtpore (1805, Second British-Maratha War; 1827, Second Siege of)
Bluff Cove (1982, Falkland Islands)
Bois-le-Duc (1794, French Revolutionary Wars)
Borghetto (1796, French Revolutionary Wars)
Brentford (1642, English Civil War)
Brig of Dee (1639, Bishop's Wars)
Bucharest (1771, Ottoman Wars)
Burns Hill (1847, Kaffir Wars)
Byzantium (318 BC, Wars of Alexander's Successors; 323 Civil Wars of the Roman Empire)
Cape Henry (1781, American Revolutionary War)
Caporetto (1917, World War I)
Casilinum (554, Byzantine Empire Wars)
Castillon (1453, Hundred Years' War)
Champagne (1915 World War I)
Charasiab (1879, Second British-Afghan War)
Crosskeys (1862, American Civil War)
Cuddalore (1783, American

Revolutionary War)

Dennewitz (1813, Napoleonic Wars)

Dorylaeum (1097, First Crusade)

Dunsinane (1054, Anglo-Scottish Wars)

Ebro River (1938, Spanish Civil War)

Edersberg (1809, Napoleonic Wars)

Edgeworth (1469, War of the Roses)

El Alamein (1942, World War II)

Elchingen (1805, Napoleonic Wars)

Ellandune (825, Wessex versus Mercia)

Empingham (1470, War of the Roses)

Five Forks (American Civil War)

Friedland (1807, Napoleonic Wars)

Frontiers, Battle of the (1914, World War I)

Gallipoli (1915, World War I)

Gibraltar (1704, War of the Spanish Succession; 1779, American Revolutionary War)

Gladsmuir (The Forty-five Rebellion)

Glen Fruin (1604, Scottish Civil Wars)

Glenlivet (1594, Huntly's Rebellion)

Grampians, The (Roman Invasion of Scotland)

Guinegate (1513, Anglo-French Wars)

Gumbinnen (1914, World War I)

Heilsberg (1807, Napoleonic Wars)

Hochkirch (1758, Seven Years' War)

Hochstadt (1800, French Revolutionary Wars)

Jerusalem (70 AD, Jewish Wars of Roman Empire; 637, Muslim Invasion of Syria; 1099, First Crusade; 1187, Crusader-Turkish Wars; 1917, World War I; 1948, Israeli-Arab Wars)

Jugdulluk (1842, First British-Afghan War)

Kassassin (1882, Egyptian Revolt)

Kimberley (1899, Second Boer War)

Kissingen (1866, Seven Weeks' War)

Ladysmith (1899, Second Boer War)

Lang's Neck (1881, First Boer War)

Lansdowne (1643, English Civil War)

Leningrad (1944, World War II)

Lexington (1775, American Revolutionary War; 1861, American Civil War)

Leyte Gulf (1944, World War II)

Lowenberg (1813, Napoleonic Wars)

Magdeburg (1631, Thirty Years' War)

Malavilly (1799, Third British-Mysore War)

Mangalore (1783, First British-Mysore War)

Mansfield (1864, American Civil War)

Maria Zell (1805, Napoleonic Wars)

Marsaglia (1693, War of the Grand Alliance)

Millesimo (1796, French Revolutionary Wars)

Mohrungen (1807, Napoleonic Wars)

Montereau (1814, Napoleonic Wars)

Monterrey, 1846, American-Mexican War)

Mukwanpur (1816, British-Gurkha War)

Nashville (1863, American Civil War)

Naulochus (36 BC, Wars of the Second Triumvirate)

Navarrete (1367, Hundred Years' War)

Negapatam (1746, War of the Austrian Succession; 1781, Second British-Mysore War; 1782, American Revolutionary War)

New Guinea (1942, World War II)

New Market (1864, American Civil War)

Nicopolis (1396, Ottoman Wars; 1877, Russo-Turkish War)

Nujufghur (1857, Indian Mutiny)

Ocean Pond (1864, American Civil War)

Oltenitza (1853, Crimean War)

Otterburn (1388, Wars of the Scottish Independence)

Oudenarde (1708, War of the Spanish Succession)

Pharsalus (48 BC, Civil War of Caesar and Pompey; 1897, Greco-Turkish Wars)

Pollicore (1781, First British-Mysore War)

Porto Novo (1781, First British-Mysore War)

Primolano (1796, French Revolutionary Wars)

Princeton (1777, American Revolutionary War)

Ramillies (1706, War of the Spanish Succession)

Ramnugger (1849, Second British-Sikh War)

Rathmines (1649, Cromwell's Campaign in Ireland)

Rhineland, The (1945, World War II)

Roseburgh (1460, Anglo-Scottish Wars)

Sadulapur (1848, Second British-Sikh War)

Salamanca (1812, Peninsular War; 1858, Mexican Liberal Rising)

Santander (1937 Spanish Civil War)

Saragossa (1700, War of the Spanish Succession; 1808, Peninsular War)

Sedgemoor (1685, Monmouth's Rebellion

Sevenoaks (1450. Cade's Rebellion)

Sheerness (1667, Anglo-Dutch Wars)

Sherstone (1016, Danish Invasion of England)

Sholingur (1781, First British-Mysore War)

Singapore (1942, World War II)

Sitabaldi (1817, Third British-Maratha War)

Southwark (1450, Cade's Rebellion)

Stadtlohn (1623, Thirty Years' War)

Staffarda (1690, War of the Grand Alliance)

Stormberg (1899, Second Boer War)

St Quentin (1557, Franco-Spanish Wars; 1871, Franco-Prussian War)

Stralsund (1628, Thirty Years' War; 1715, Great Northern War)

Suddasain (1848, Second British-Sikh War)

Tarragona (1811, Peninsular War)

Tchernaya (1855, Crimean War)

Tolentino (1815, Napoleonic Wars)

Tou Morong (1966, Vietnam War)

Tourcoing (1794, French Revolutionary Wars)

Trafalgar (1805, Napoleonic Wars)

Trautenau (1866, Seven Weeks' War)

Trebizond (1461, Ottoman Wars)

Trinkitat (1884, British Sudan Campaigns)

Vaalkranz (1900, Second Boer War)

Vauchamps (1814, Napoleonic Wars)

Vicksburg (1862, American Civil War)

Vimy Ridge (1917, World War I)

Wakefield (1460, War of the Roses)

Wandiwash (1760, Seven Years' War; 1780, First British-Mysore War)

Worcester (1651, English Civil War)

Wurtzburg (1796, French Revolutionary Wars)

10

Adrianople (1205, Fourth Crusade; 1913, First Balkan War)

Alexandria (642, Muslim Invasion of Egypt; 1801, British Invasion of Egypt; 1881, Egyptian Revolt)

Ancrum Moor (1545, Anglo-Scottish Wars)

Artois-Loos (1915, World War I)

Austerlitz (1805, Napoleonic Wars)

Ball's Bluff (1861, American Civil War)

Beachy Head (1690, War of the Grand Alliance)

Beausejour (1755, Seven Years' War)

Bennington (1777, American Revolutionary War)

Blackwater (1598, O'Neill's Rebellion)

Blore Heath (1459, War of the Roses)

Brandywine (1777, American Revolutionary War)

Brunanburh (937, Danish Invasion)

Buena Vista (1846, American-Mexican War)

Camperdown (1797, French Revolutionary Wars)

Cedar Creek (1864, American Civil War)

Charleston (1863, American Civil War)

Chevy Chase (1388, Wars of Scottish Independence)

Chippenham (878, Danish Invasions of Britain)

Copenhagen (1801, French Revolutionary Wars; 1807, Napoleonic Wars)

Dalmanutha (1900, Second Boer War)

Dogger Bank (1781, American Revolutionary War; 1915, World War I)

Dunganhill (1647, Great Irish Rebellion)

Dyrrachium (48 BC, Civil war of Caesar and Pompey)

Englefield (871, Danish Invasion of Britain)

Ferozeshah (1845, First British-Sikh War)

Fethanleag (584, Saxon Conquests)

Futteypore (1857, Indian Mutiny)

Gaines' Mill (1862, American Civil War)

Germantown (1777, American Revolutionary War)

Gettysburg (1863, American Civil War)

Glen Malone (1580, Colonisation of Ireland)

Gorodeczno (1812, Napoleonic Wars)

Gothic Line (1944, World War II)

Grant's Hill (1758, Seven Years' War)

Gravelines (1558, Franco-Spanish Wars)

Gravelotte (1870, Franco-Prussian War)

Guadeloupe (1794, French Revolutionary Wars)

Habbaniyah (1941, World War II)

Hastenbeck (1757, Seven Years' War)

Heathfield (633, Mercia against Northumbria)

Heligoland (1807, Napoleonic Wars)

Heliopolis (1800, French Revolutionary Wars)

Hellespont (323, War of the Two Empires)

Hollabrunn (1805, Napoleonic Wars)

Inverlochy (1645, English Civil War)

Jellalabad (1842, First British-Afghan War)

Khojah Pass (1842, First British-Afghan War)

Koniggratz (1866, Seven Weeks' War)

Kornspruit (1900, Second Boer War)

Kunersdorf (1759, Seven Years' War)

Kut-el-Amara (1915, World War I)

La Favorita (1797, French Revolutionary Wars)

Lake George (1755, Seven Years' War)

La Rochelle (1372, Hundred Years'

War; 1627, French Religious Wars)
La Rothiere (1814, Napoleonic Wars)
Loudon Hill (1307, Wars of Scottish
Independence)
Louisbourg (1745, War of the
Austrian Succession; 1758, Seven
Years' War)
Luleburgaz (1912, Balkan Wars)
Lundy's Lane (1814, War of 1812)
Maastricht (1579, Netherlands War
of Independence)
Maharajpur (1843, Gwalior
Campaign; 1857, Indian Mutiny)
Mareth Line (1943, World War II)
Mariendahl (1645, Thirty Years' War)
Martinique (1794, French
Revolutionary Wars; 1809,
Napoleonic Wars)
Maserfield (642, Northumbria against
Mercia)
Michelberg (1805, Napoleonic Wars)
Montebello (1800, French
Revolutionary Wars; 1859, Italian
Wars of Independence)
Montenotte (1796, French
Revolutionary Wars)
Montevideo (1807, Napoleonic Wars;
1843, 1851, 1863, Uruguayan Civil
War)
Montfaucon (886, Norman Conquest
of France)
Montmirail (1814, Napoleonic Wars)
Mount Tabor (1799, French
Revolutionary Wars)
Naroch Lake (1916, World War I)
Neerwinden (1693, War of the
Grand Alliance; 1793, French
Revolutionary Wars)
New Orleans (1814, War of 1812;
1862, American Civil War)
Nordlingen (1634, 1645 Thirty Years'
War)
Ostrolenka (1853, Crimean War)

Paardeberg (1900, Second Boer War)
Pandu Naddi (1857, Indian Mutiny)
Pen Selwood (1016, Danish Invasion
of Britain)
Perembacum 1780, First British-
Mysore War)
Perryville (1862, American Civil War)
Persepolis (316 BC, Wars of
Alexander's Successors)
Petersburg (1864, American Civil
War)
Piave River (1918 (World War I)
Pont Valain (1370, Hundred Years'
War)
Port Arthur (1894, Sino-Japanese
War; 1904, Russo-Japanese War)
Port Hudson (1863, American Civil
War)
Quatre Bras (1815, Napoleonic
Wars)
Rakersberg (1416, Ottoman Wars)
Ruhr Pocket (1945, World War II)
Sanna's Post (1900, Second Boer
War)
Santa Lucia (1842, Rio Grande Rising)
Savandroog (1791, Second British-
Mysore War)
Seine Mouth (1416, Hundred Years'
War)
Sevastopol (1854, Crimean War)
Seven Pines (1862, American Civil
War)
Shrewsbury (1403, Percy's Rebellion)
Shropshire (AD 50, Roman Conquest
of Britain)
Sidi Rezegh (1941, World War II)
Solway Moss (1542, Anglo-Scottish
Wars)
Stalingrad (1942, World War II)
Steenkerke (1692, War of the Grand
Alliance)
Stillwater (1777, American
Revolutionary War)

Stone River (1862, American Civil War)

Talana Hill (1899, Second Boer War)

Tannenberg (1914, World War I)

Tel-el-Kebir (1882, Egyptian Revolt)

Tettenhall (910, Danish Invasions of England)

Tewkesbury (1471, War of the Roses)

Tippermuir (1644, English Civil War)

Travancore (1789 Second British-Mysore War)

Wartemberg (1813, Napoleonic Wars)

Wattignies (1793, French Revolutionary Wars)

Wilderness, The (1864, American Civil War)

Winchester (1863, American Civil War)

11

Alam el Halfa (1942, World War II)

Alessandria (1799, French Revolutionary Wars)

An Lao Valley (1966, Vietnam War)

Bannockburn (1314, Wars of Scottish Independence)

Belleau Wood (1918, World War I)

Bismarck Sea (1943, World War II)

Blanquefort (1450, Hundred Years' War)

Bramham Moor (1408, Northumberland's Rebellion)

Breitenfeld (1642, Thirty Years' War)

Brenneville (1199, Anglo-French Wars)

Buenos Aires (1806, 1807, Napoleonic Wars; 1874, Mitre's Rebellion)

Bunker's Hill (1775, American Revolutionary War)

Camelodunum (43, Roman Invasion of Britain)

Carbiesdale (1650, English Civil War)

Carenage Bay (1778, American Revolutionary War)

Castiglione (1706, War of the Spanish Succession; 1796, French Revolutionary Wars)

Champaubert (1814, Napoleonic Wars)

Chattanooga (1863, American Civil War)

Chickamauga (1863, American Civil War)

Chilianwala (1849, Second British-Sikh War)

Chrysopolis (324, War of the Two Empires)

Coldharbour (1864, American Civil War)

Diamond Hill (1900, Second Boer War)

Dingaan's Day (1838, Afrikaner-Zulu War)

Driefontein (1900, Second Boer War)

Durrentstein (1805, Napoleonic Wars)

Elands River (1900, Second Boer War)

Farrukhabad (1804, Second British-Maratha War)

Ferrybridge (1461, War of the Roses)

Fisher's Hill (1864, American Civil War)

Fort St David. (1758, Seven Years' War)

Gibbel Rutts (1798, Irish Rebellion)

Gross-Beeren (1813, Napoleonic Wars)

Guadalajara (1937, Spanish Civil War)

Guadalcanal (1942, World War II)

Hadrianople (323, War of the Two Empires; 378, Second Gothic Invasion of the East)

Halidon Hill (1333, Wars of Scottish Independence)

Heavenfield (Northumbria against the British)

Hohenlinden (1800, French Revolutionary Wars)

Hondschoote (1793, French Revolutionary Wars)

Ile de France (1810, French Revolutionary Wars)

Isandhlwana (1879, Zulu-British War)

Langensalza (1866, Seven Weeks' War)

Londonderry (1689, War of the Grand Alliance)

Lostwithiel (1644, English Civil War)

Malvern Hill (1862, American Civil War)

Marston Moor (1644, English Civil War)

Masulipatam (1759, Seven Years' War)

Mersa Matruh (1942, World War II)

Mill Springs (1862, American Civil War)

Modder River 1899, Second Boer War)

Monte Lezino (1796, French Revolutionary Wars)

Montmorenci (1759, Seven Years' War)

Morshedabad (1763, British Conquest of Bengal)

Noisseville (1870, Franco-Prussian War)

Northampton (1460, War of the Roses)

Pearl Harbor (1941, World War II)

Peiwar Kotal (1878, Second British-Afghan War)

Philiphaugh (1645, English Civil War)

Pieter's Hill (1900, Second Boer War)

Pondicherry (1748, War of the Austrian Succession; 1760 Seven

Years' War; 1778, 1783, American Revolutionary War)

Prestonpans (1745, The Forty-five Rebellion)

Quiberon Bay (1759, Seven Years' War)

Rajahmundry (1758, Seven Years' War)

Reddersberg (1900, Second Boer War)

Rheinfelden (1638, Thirty Years' War)

Rietfontein (1899, Second Boer War)

Rorke's Drift (1879, Zulu-British War)

Rowton Heath (1645, English Civil War)

Saldanha Bay (1796, French Revolutionary Wars)

San Giovanni (1799, French Revolutionary Wars)

Sauchie Burn (1488, Rebellion of the Scottish Barons)

Sheriffmuir (1715, The Fifteen Rebellion)

Sidi Barrani (1940, World War II)

Taillebourg (1242 , Anglo-French Wars)

Tarawa-Makin (1943, World War II)

Tel-el-Mahuta (1882, Egyptian Revolt)

Tellicherry (1780, First British-Mysore War)

Teuttlingen (1643 (Thirty Years' War)

Ticonderoga (1758, Seven Years' War; 1777, American Revolutionary War)

Trincomalee (1759, Seven Years' War; 1767, First British-Mysore War; 1782, American Revolutionary War)

Vinegar Hill (1798, Irish Rebellion)

Waltersdorf (1807, Napoleonic Wars)

Wednesfield (911, Danish Invasions of England)

Weissenburg (1870 Franco-Prussian

War)

White Russia (1943, World War II)

12

Adwalton Moor (1643, English Civil War)

Algeciras Bay (1801, French Revolutionary Wars)

Arcis-Sur-Aube (1814, Napoleonic Wars)

Atherton Moor (1643, English Civil War)

Banda Islands (1796, French Revolutionary Wars)

Bergen-Op-Zoom (1747, War of the Austrian Succession; 1799, French Revolutionary Wars)

Bloemfontein (1900, Second Boer War)

Braddock Down (1643, English Civil War)

Chickahominy (1864, American Civil War)

Elandslaagte (1899, Second Boer War)

Eutaw Springs (1781, American Revolutionary War)

Fort Donelson (1862, American Civil War)

Hampton Roads (1862, American Civil War)

Harper's Ferry (1862, American Civil War)

Hedgeley Moor (1464, War of the Roses)

Hengestesdun (837, Danish Invasions of Britain)

Homildon Hill (1402, Anglo-Scottish Wars)

Kirch-Denkern (1761, Seven Years' War)

Konigswartha (1813, Napoleonic Wars)

Kursk Salient (1943, World War II)

Lynn Haven Bay (1781, American Revolutionary War)

Midway Island (1942, World War II)

Munchengratz (1866, Seven Weeks' War)

Murfreesboro (1862, American Civil War)

Nechtan's Mere (685, Northumbrian Invasion of Scotland)

Oondwa Nullah (1763, British Conquest of Bengal)

Penobscot Bay (1779, American Revolutionary War)

Peterwardein (1716, Ottoman Wars)

Pinkie Cleugh (1547, Anglo-Scottish Wars)

Port Republic (1862, American Civil War)

Prairie Grove (1862, American Civil War)

Rich Mountain (1861, American Civil War)

Roncesvalles (1813, Peninsular War)

Roundway Down (1643, English Civil War)

Rullion Green (1666, Covenanters' Rising)

San Sebastian (1813, Peninsular War; 1836, First Carlist War)

Secunderbagh (1857, Indian Mutiny)

Seringapatam (1792, Second British-Mysore War; 1799, Third British-Mysore War)

Southwold Bay (1672, Anglo-Dutch Wars)

Spotsylvania (1864, American Civil War)

Tet Offensive, The (1968, Vietnam War)

Williamsburg (1862, American Civil War)

Wilson's Creek (1861, American Civil

War)

Wrotham Heath (1554, Wyatt's Insurrection)

13

Aix-la-Chapelle (1795, French Revolutionary Wars)

Baduli-Ki-Serai (1857, Indian Mutiny)

Belle-Ile-en-Mer (1759, 1761, Seven Years' War; 1795, French Revolutionary Wars)

Boroughbridge (1322, Rebellion of the Marches)

Bosworth Field (1485, War of the Roses)

Cape St Vincent (1797, French Revolutionary Wars)

Cedar Mountain (1862, American Civil War)

Chandernagore (1757, Seven Years' War)

Ciudad Rodrigo (1812, Peninsular War)

Falkland Isles (1914, World War I; 1982, Falklands War)

Farquhar's Farm (1899, Second Boer War)

Fort Frontenac (1758, Seven Years' War)

Frankenhausen (1525, Peasant's War)

Glenmarreston (683, Angles' Invasion of Britain)

Horns of Hattin (1187, Crusader-Saracen Wars)

Inverkeithing (1317, Anglo-Scottish Wars)

Kasserine Pass (1943, World War II)

Killiecrankie (1689, Jacobite Rebellion)

Little Big Horn (1876, Sioux Rising)

Magersfontein (1899, Second Boer War)

Masurian Lake (1914, 1915 World War I)

Molinos del Ray (1808, Peninsular War)

Mount Seleucus (353 Civil Wars of the Roman Empire)

Neville's Cross (1346, Anglo-Scottish Wars)

Newtown Butler (1689, War of the Grand Alliance)

Northallerton (1138, Anglo-Scottish Wars)

North Foreland (1666, Anglo-Dutch Wars)

Passchendaele (1917, World War I)

Peleliu-Anguar (1944, World War II)

Philippine Sea (1944, World War II)

Porto Praia Bay (1781, American Revolutionary War)

Roanoke Island (1862, American Civil War)

South Mountain (1862, American Civil War)

Spanish Armada (1588, Anglo-Spanish War)

Sudley Springs (1862, American Civil War)

White Oak Swamp (1862, American Civil War)

Youghioghenny (1754, Seven Years' War)

Zusmarshausen (1647, Thirty Years' War)

Berwick-on Tweed (1296 (Wars of Scottish Independence)

Bothwell Bridge (1679, Covenanters' Rising)

Bristoe Station (1863, American Civil War)

Cape Finisterre (1747, War of the Austrian Succession; 1805, Napoleonic Wars)

Chalgrove Field (1643, English Civil War)

Chateau-Thierry (1814, Napoleonic Wars)

Constantinople (668, Muslim Invasion of Europe; 1203-4, Fourth Crusade; 1261, Reconquest by Byzantines; 1422, Ottoman Invasion of Europe: 1453, Turkish Conquest)

Cropredy Bridge (1644, English Civil War)

Drummossie Moor (1746, The Forty-five Rebellion)

Fredericksburg (1862, American Civil War)

Fuentes de Onoro (1811, Peninsular War)

Kovel-Stanislav (1916, World War I)

Le Belle Famille (1759, Seven Years' War)

Loosecoat Field (1470, War of the Roses)

Mariana Islands (1944, World War II)

Mortimer's Cross (1461, War of the Roses)

Nicholson's Neck (1899, Second Boer War)

Peach Tree Creek (1864, American Civil War)

Pusan Perimeter (1950, Korean War)

Rouvray-St-Denis (1429, Hundred Years' War)

Santiago de Cuba (1898, Spanish-American War)

Savage's Station (1862, American Civil War)

Secessionville (1862, American Civil War)

Sinai Peninsula (1956, Israeli-Arab War)

Solomon Islands (1942, World War II)

Stamford Bridge (1066, Norse Invasion of Britain; 1453, War of the Roses)

Stirling Bridge (1297, Wars of Scottish Independence)

Vittorio Veneto (1918, World War I)

15

Aleutian Islands (1943, World War II)

Amatola Mountain (1846, Kaffir Wars)

Appomattox River (1865, American Civil War)

Battle of Britain (1940, World War II)

Beaver's Dam Creek (1862, American Civil War)

Frankfurt-on-Oder (1631, Thirty Years' War)

Gross-Jagersdorf (1757, Seven Years' War)

Heligoland Bight (1914, World War I)

Khoord Kabul Pass (1842 (First British-Afghan War)

Maloyaroslavets (1812, Napoleonic Wars)

Missionary Ridge (1863, American Civil War)

Plains of Abraham (1759, Seven Years' War)

Seven Day's Battle (1862, American Civil War)

Spanish Galleons (1702, War of the Spanish Succession)

16

Bataan-Corregidor (1941, World War II)

Bronkhorst Spruit (1880, First Boer War)

Cambrai-St Quentin (1918, World War I)

Chancellorsville (1863, American Civil War)

Fort William Henry (1757, Seven Years' War)

Kinnesaw Mountain (1864, American Civil War)

Monongahela River (1755, Seven Years' War)

Salum-Halfaya Pass (1941, World War II)

17

Burlington Heights (1813, War of 1812)

Dodecanese Islands (1943, World War II)

Gustav-Cassino Line (1943, World War II)

Inhlobane Mountain (1879, Zulu War)

Kwajalein-Eniwetok (1944, World War II)

La Fere Champenoise (1814, Napoleonic Wars)

Pittsburgh Landing (1862, American Civil War)

Poland-East Prussia (1944, World War II)

Van Tuong Peninsular (1965 Vietnam War)

18

Guilford Courthouse (1781, American Revolutionary War)

Meuse-Argonne Forest (1918, World War I)

19

Chu Pong-ia Drang River (1965, Vietnam War)

'Glorious First of June' (1794, French Revolutionary Wars)

20+

Rhine and the Ruhr Pocket, The (1945, World War II)

Shannon and Chesapeake (1813, War of 1812)

Thirty-Eighth Parallel (1951, Korean War)

Decorations and Medals

Decoration/	MedalAbbreviation
Air Force Cross	AFC
Air Force Medal	AFM
Albert Medal	AM
Conspicuous Gallantry Medal	CGM
Distinguished Flying Cross	DFC
Distinguished Flying Medal	DFM
Distinguished Service Cross	DSC
Distinguished Service Medal	DSM
George Cross	GC
George Medal	GM
Medal for Distinguished Conduct in the Field	DCM
Military Cross	MC
Military Medal	MM
The Distinguished Service Order	DSO
Victoria Cross	VC

Military Names and Titles (Worldwide)

2

C.O.
G.I.
O.C.

3

A.D.C.
A.T.S.
C.S.M.
N.C.O.
R.S.M.
R.T.O.
S.A.S.

4

goum
koul
lewa
naik
para
peon

5

cadet
fifer
Jager
major
miner
piper
poilu
pongo
scout
sepoy
sowar
spahi
Tommy
Uhlan

6

archer
askari
batman
bomber
bowman
bugler
cornet
driver
ensign
gunner
Gurkha
hetman
hussar
lancer
marine
ranger
ranker
sapper
sutler
yeoman
Zouave

7

ancient
Arnaout
captain
colonel
Cossack
dragoon
drummer
estafet
farrier
general
hobbler
hoplite
janizar
jemadar
lancers
marines
marshal
militia
officer
orderly
pikeman
pioneer
private
recruit
redcoat
regular
reserve
saddler
samurai
sappers
soldier
subadar
trooper
vedette
veteran
warrior

8

adjutant
armourer
bandsman
cavalier
chasseur
commando
corporal
daffadar
decurion
deserter
doughboy
dragoons
fencible
fugelman
fusilier
havildar
infantry
janizary
Landwehr
marksman
messmate
muleteer
mutineer
partisan

rifleman
risaldar
sentinal
sergeant
spearman
turncoat
waterman

9

beefeater
berserker
brigadier
cannoneer
cannonier
centurion
combatant
commander
conductor
conscript
drum-major
estafette
field rank
fife-major
fort-major
grenadier
guardsman
guerrilla
Home Guard
irregular
Janissary
lance-naik
lifeguard
man-at-arms
musketeer
paymaster
pensioner
pipe-major
signaller
subaltern
tactician
town-major
trumpeter
tradesman

vexillary
voltigeur
volunteer

10

aide-de-camp
bandmaster
bombardier
campaigner
carabineer
cavalryman
commandant
cuirassier
drummer-boy
file-leader
footguards
halberdier
instructor
Lansquenet
lieutenant
Life Guards
militiaman
other ranks
paratroops
roughrider
strategist

11

arquebusier
artillerist
auxiliaries
bashi-bazook
bersaglieri
crack troops
crossbowman
gendarmerie
horse guards
infantryman
Landsknecht
moss-trooper
rangefinder
top sergeant
Tommy Atkins

12

armour-bearer
artilleryman
brigade-major
camp-follower
ensign-bearer
field marshal
field officer
horse soldier
jemadar-major
major-general
master gunner
officer cadet
P.T. instructor
Royal Marines
Royal Signals
staff officer
storm-trooper
subadar-major
sub-conductor
territorials

13

army commander
barrack master
brevet-colonel
bugle-corporal
color-sergeant
corporal-major
dispatch-rider
drill sergeant
first sergeant
generalissimo
lance-corporal
lance-daffadar
lance-sergeant
lifeguardsman
light infantry
machine-gunner
marine officer
mounted rifles
prisoner of war
quartermaster

risaldar major
sergeant major
staff-sergeant

14

citizen-soldier
colonel-in-chief
colour-havildar
colour-sergeant
liaison officer
master sergeant
medical officer
military police
orderly officer
provost-marshal
Royal Artillery
Royal Engineers
Royal Tank Corps
second corporal
signals officer
standard bearer
warrant officer

15

adjutant-general
corporal-of-horse
first lieutenant
gentleman-at-arms
honorary colonel
household troops
mounted infantry
orderly corporal
orderly sergeant
ordnance officer
provost sergeant

Military Terms and
Fortifications

3

aim

arm
dun
foe
gas
gun
hut
jam
kit
lay
man
map
out
pah
sap
van
war

4

ally
ammo
anfo
arms
army
A.W.O.L.
band
base
bawn
belt
berm
blip
camp
defy
draw
duck
duel
fife
file
fire
flag
flak
foot
form
fort

foss
halt
host
jeep
kern
levy
line
loot
mess
mine
moat
N.A.T.O.
O.C.T.U.
park
P.I.A.T.
plan
post
P.O.W.
push
raid
ramp
rank
raze
rear
rout
ruse
sack
shot
slay
slug
spot
spur
star
take
tank
tent
tilt
trap
turn
unit
ward
wing
zero

5

abort
agent
alarm
alert
annex
A.N.Z.A.C.
armed
armor
array
baton
beret
berme
beset
booty
boyau
busby
butts
cadre
cavin
cells
clean
corps
decoy
depot
depth
ditch
dogra
draft
drawn
dress
drill
enemy
enrol
equip
feint
field
fight
flank
flare
foray
fosse
fours

front
gazon
gorge
guard
guide
gurry
herse
horse
khaki
lance
lines
march
medal
melee
mount
mufti
onset
order
party
peace
pivot
poilu
pouch
prime
radar
rally
range
ranks
redan
relay
repel
rifle
round
route
royal
sally
salvo
scale
scarp
S.E.A.T.O.
seize
S.H.E.A.F.
shako

shell
shift
shock
shoot
siege
snipe
sonar
sonic
spoil
squad
staff
stand
storm
strap
talus
T.E.W.T.S.
track
troop
truce
unarm
veil
wheel
wound
yield

6

abates
backpack
action
affray
allies
ambush
archer
armour
assail
attack
bailey
banner
barbed
battle
beaten
billet
blinds

blow up	escort	picket
bonnet	Fabians	plonge
bouclé	fanon	pompom
brevet	firing	pompon
bunker	fleche	primer
cartel	foeman	pursue
castle	forted	raider
centre	fraises	ransom
charge	gabion	rapine
clays	glacis	rappel
cohort	guards	ration
colour	guides	ravage
column	guiding	rebuff
combat	haw haw	recall
convoy	helmet	recoil
cordon	hurter	reduce
corral	impact	relais
curfew	inroad	relief
dagger	invade	report
debris	invest	resist
decamp	inwall	retake
defeat	kitbag	retire
defend	legion	review
definer	limber	riddle
defile	marker	rideau
deploy	merlon	roster
desert	mining	saddle
detach	mobile	salute
detail	muster	sconce
disarm	mutiny	sensor
donjon	number	signal
double	obsess	sketch
dugout	occupy	sortie
embark	oppose	square
embody	orders	stores
encamp	orgues	strife
engage	outfit	strike
enlist	parade	stripe
enmity	parlay	stroke
ensign	parole	subdue
epaulet	patrol	submit
escape	pennon	supply
escarp	permit	target

tattoo
tenail
thrust
trench
trophy
umpire
vallum
valour
victor
volley
walled
warcry
zareba
zigzag

7

abattis
advance
aid-post
air-raid
airlift
archery
armoury
arsenal
assault
baggage
barrack
barrage
basenet
bastion
battery
battled
besiege
bivouac
bombard
brigade
bulwark
caltrop
canteen
carbine
caserne
cavalry
chamade

charger
chevron
citadel
cold war
colours
command
company
conquer
counter
coupure
crusade
curtain
debouch
defence
defiant
degrade
destroy
détente
detrain
disband
dismiss
dispart
drawn up
draw off
dungeon
echelon
ecoutes
enguard
enomoty
entrain
envelop
environ
epaulet
fallout
fanfare
fascine
fatigue
flanker
fortify
fortlet
forward
fourgon
foxhole

fraised
gallery
geurite
gunfire
gunnery
gun-shot
half-pay
harness
holster
hostage
hostile
hutment
jamming
Kremlin
landing
leaguer
liaison
looting
lunette
madrier
maniple
marquee
martial
megaton
moineau
mounted
neutral
nuclear
on guard
outpost
outwing
outwork
overawe
overrun
parados
parapet
pennant
phalanx
pillbox
pitfall
platoon
plongee
postern

priming
protect
provost
prowess
pursuit
quarter
rampart
rations
ravelin
redoubt
refugee
regular
remblai
remount
repulse
reserve
retaken
retreat
reverse
Riot Act
salient
sand-bag
section
service
sniping
spurred
stand0by
subvert
support
tactics
tambour
tenable
tilting
trailer
triumph
unarmed
uncased
uniform
valiant
van-foss
venture
victory
ward off

warfare
wargame
war-hoop
warlike
warpath
warsong
warworn
wheeler
windage
wounded

8

accoutre
advanced
airborne
air force
alarm gun
alliance
armament
armature
armorial
arms race
Army list
baldrick
barbette
barbican
barracks
bartizan
bawdrick
bearskin
billeted
blockade
bull's eye
camisade
camisado
campaign
casemate
casualty
chivalry
civil war
collapse
conquest
cornetcy

crusader
decimate
decisive
defended
defender
defiance
demi-lune
demolish
despatch
detonate
disarray
disenrol
dismount
dispatch
distance
division
doubling
drumhead
duelling
earth-bag
embattle
embodied
enceinte
enfilade
ensigncy
entrench
equipage
escalade
escouade
estacade
eyes left
fastness
field day
fighting
flagpost
flanking
footband
fortress
fourneau
furlough
garrison
gauntlet
gendarme

gonfalon	paradrop	squadron
guerilla	passport	stampede
half-moon	password	standard
hang-fire	pavilion	star-foot
hedgehog	pay corps	stockade
herisson	petronel	stoppage
hillfort	pipe-clay	storming
horn-work	prisoner	straddle
intrench	punitive	strategy
invasion	quarters	strength
knapsack	railhead	struggle
last post	ramparts	supplied
lay siege	rear line	support
lay waste	rear rank	surprise
limber up	rearward	surround
lodgement	recharge	sword arm
loophole	re-embark	tactical
magazine	re-embody	tenaille
majority	regiment	time-fuse
Mameluke	remounts	tortoise
mantelet	reprisal	training
marching	resalute	transfer
mark time	retirade	traverse
materiel	retrench	trooping (the colour)
mess bill	reveille	unallied
militant	ricochet	unbeaten
military	rifle-pit	unlimber
mobilize	roll-call	uprising
movement	sabotage	valorous
muniment	saboteur	vanguard
musketry	saluting	vanquish
mutinous	scout-car	vexillar
on parade	security	victuals
on parole	sentry-go	vigilant
opponent	service (the)	vincible
ordnance	shabrack	warfarer
orillion	shelling	warhorse
outflank	shooting	warpaint
outguard	shot-belt	war-plume
outlying	siege-war	war-whoop
overcome	skirmish	watch-box
overkill	soldiery	wheeling
palisade	spotting	yeomanry

zero hour

9

aggressor
alarm post
ambuscade
ambuscado
armistice
armouries
army corps
artillery
assailant
atomic war
attrition
ballastic
bandolier
banquette
barricade
barricado
battalion
batteries
battle0cry
beachhead
beleaguer
bellicose
billeting
bodyguard
bombproof
bugle call
bulldozer
cannonade
caponiere
captaincy
cashiered
cavalcade
ceasefire
challenge
chevalier
colonelcy
combatant
comitadji
conqueror
covert-way

crossfire
crown work
crow's foot
defection
defensive
defiatory
demi-gorge
desertion
devastate
discharge
disembody
disengage
dismantle
earthwork
elevation
embattled
embrasure
encompass
encounter
enfiladed
enrolment
epaulette
equipment
espionage
esplanade
eyes front
eyes right
fencibles
field rank
fire-drill
flagstaff
forage-cap
form fours
fortalice
fortifier
fortilage
fusillade
gabionade
gas attack
gladiator
guardroom
guerrilla
haversack

heliostat
hersillon
homograph
hostility
housewife
incursion
interdict
invalided
irregular
land force
Landsturm
legionary
lifeguard
logistics
loopholed
Luftwaffe
majorship
manoeuvre
mechanist
mercenary
militancy
musketoon
Mutiny Act
objective
offensive
officiate
onsetting
onslaught
operation
overpower
overshoot
overthrow
overwhelm
packdrill
pack train
palladium
parachute
predictor
pregnable
pressgang
projector
promotion
protector

promotion
protector
provender
rearguard
rebellion
reconquer
red ensign
re-enforce
refortify
reinforce
rencontre
reprimand
revetment
revictual
safeguard
sally-port
scrimmage
semaphore
sentry-box
sham-fight
slaughter
slope arms
slow-march
stack arms
stand-fast
standfire
stand-firm
stratagem
strategic
subaltern
subjugate
surrender
sword-knot
taskforce
tenaillon
terrorist
train-band
transport
treachery
tricolour
unabridged
undaunted
undrilled

unguarded
unhostile
uniformed
unopposed
unordered
unscathed
unsheathe
unstormed
unwarlike
unwounded
vigilance
war office
watchword
Wehrmacht
white flag
withstand
zigzagged

10

action left
aggressive
air-defence
ammunition
annexation
annihilate
arbalister
armipotent
arriere-ban
attackable
battlement
blitzkrieg
blockhouse
breastwork
brevet rank
bridgehead
camel corps
camouflage
cantonment
capitulate
ceremonial
challenger
color guard
commandeer

commissary
commission
contraband
crenulated
dead ground
decampment
defendable
defensible
defilading
demobilize
demolition
deployment
desolating
desolation
despatches
detachment
detonation
direct fire
dismounted
dispatches
divisional
dragonnade
drawbridge
embodiment
encampment
enfilading
engagement
engarrison
enlistment
epaulement
epauletted
escalation
escarpment
expedition
fieldworks
flying camp
garrisoned
glasshouse
ground fire
guardhouse
hand-to-hand
heliograph
indecisive

Indian file
inspection
investment
invincible
leadership
light-armed
light horse
limited war
line of fire
manoeuvres
map-reading
martial law
militarism
musketeers
muster book
muster roll
night-watch
no man's land
nuclear war
occupation
odd-numbers
operations
opposition
outgeneral
over the top
patrolling
point blank
portcullis
presidiary
prison camp
projectile
protection
provision
quartering
quick-march
raking fire
reconquest
recruiting
re-entering
regimental
rencounter
rendezvous
reorganize

reparation
resistance
respirator
retirement
revolution
rifle range
route march
sabretache
sentry beat
sentry duty
sentry post
shell-proof
siege-train
signal-fire
signalling
skirmisher
slit trench
soldiering
squad drill
state of war
sticky bomb
stronghold
subjection
subsection
submission
submissive
subversion
surrounded
sword-fight
table money
terreplein
tirailleur
trajectory
triumphant
undecisive
undefended
unequipped
unlimbered
unmolested
unsheathed
vanquisher
victorious
volunteers

vulnerable
war-council
watchtower

11

action front
action right
aides-de-camp
assaultable
barackroom
battle-array
battledress
battlefield
battle-royal
belligerent
besiegement
bombardment
bridge-train
bulletproof
button-stick
castellated
colour party
conquerable
co-operation
countermine
defenceless
demi-bastion
devastation
disarmament
disbandment
disgarrison
double-march
drawn swords
dress parade
embarkation
emplacement
envelopment
even numbers
fatigue duty
firing squad
foot-soldier
forced march
folorn hope

form two deep
fortifiable
generalship
germ warfare
guerilla war
impregnable
indefensive
machicoulis
mobile force
orderly room
penetration
postern gate
present arms
protagonist
range-finder
rank-and-file
reconnoitre
recruitment
redoubtable
review order
royal salute
running-fire
safe conduct
searchlight
shock-troop
skirmishing
smokescreen
stand-to-arms
supply depot
trous-de-loup
trumpet call
unconquered
unfortified
unprotected
unsoldierly
unsupported
vincibility
war memorial

13

accoutrements
advanced guard
carrier pigeon

cheval-de-frise
circumvallate
co-belligerent
column-of-route
counterattack
counter-parole
counterstoke
disembodiment
encompassment
fatigue parade
field equipage
field of battle
fighting force
flying colour
fortification
guards' brigade
interior lines
invincibility
lorry workshop
machicolation
martello tower
mass formation
mounted police
mushroom cloud
order of battle
ordnance depot
pontoon-bridge
radiolocation
rallying point
re-embarkation
re-enforcement
regular troops
reinforcement
sapper officer
shoulder-strap
splinter-proof
squadron drill
storming-party
strategically
swordsmanship
trench warfare
unarmed combat
unconquerable

unsoldierlike
unsurrendered
urban guerilla
Victoria Cross
vitrified fort
war department

14

ammunition dump
auxiliary force
blockade-runner
castrametation
chevaux-de-frise
demobilization
field allowance
general reserve
mechanized army
military school
miniature-range
medical officer
musketry course
musketry school
nuclear warfare
Pyrrhic victory
reconnaissance
reinforcements
reorganisation
standing orders
supreme command
trooping-season
unvanquishable
urban guerrilla
volunteer force
winter quarters

15

auxiliary forces
casualty station
circumvallation
clearing station
contravallation
counter-approach
discharge papers

dressing-station
flying artillery
guerilla warfare
intrenching tool
invulnerability
married quarters
military academy
military college
military funeral
military railway
non-commissioned
observation post
operation orders
submarine-mining
substantive rank
turning movement

British and U.S. Naval,
Fleet Air Arm,
Merchant Navy and
Merchant Marine
Ranks and Titles

4

cook
Easy
mate
wren

5

bosun
cadet
diver
middy
pilot

6

cooper
ensign
lascar
marine

master
purser
rating
reefer
seaman
snotty
stoker
topman
writer
yeoman

7

admiral
armorer
artisan
captain
deckboy
fireman
greaser
jack-tar
look-out
messman
recruit
shipman
sideboy
skipper
steward
surgeon
trimmer
wireman

8

armourer
cabinboy
chaplain
coxswain
engineer
flag rank
gun-layer
helmsman
leadsman
messmate
motorman

ship's boy
winchman

9

air-fitter
artificer
boatswain
commander
commodore
cook's mate
donkeyman
engineman
navigator
paymaster
powder-boy
ropemaker
sailmaker
ship's cook
signalman
tugmaster

10

able seaman
apprentice
coastguard
gun captain
instructor
lieutenant
midshipman
range-taker
shipmaster
ship's baker
shipwright
torpedoman
wardmaster

11

air mechanic
branch pilot
chief stoker
electrician
extra master
flag captain

flag officer
foremastman
gunner's mate
leading wren
master's mate
mechanician
port admiral
port officer
post captain
rating pilot
rear-admiral
vice-admiral
watchkeeper

12

boy artificer
cabin steward
chief officer
chief skipper
chief skipper
chief steward
first officer
master-at-arms
master gunner
officers' cook
petty officer
photographer
powder monkey
P.T. instructor
schoolmaster
seaman-bugler
seaman-gunner
second master
senior purser
ship's butcher
ship's caulker
ship's surgeon
supply rating
telegraphist
third officer

13

armourer's mate

captain's clerk
chief armourer
chief engineer
fourth officer
harbourmaster
leading seaman
leading stoker
marine officer
privateersman
quartermaster
quarter rating
radio operator
sailing master
second officer
ship's corporal
signal officer
stern-sheetman
sub-lieutenant
third engineer
torpedo-gunner

14 and 15

boarding officer
boatswain's mate
first lieutenant
flag-lieutenant
fourth engineer
half-pay officer
leading steward
liuet.-commander
officer's steward
ordinary seaman
rating observer
sailmaker's mate
second engineer
ship's carpenter
torpedo coxswain
warrant officer

U.K. Forces Titles

Royal Air Force

Marshall of the Royal
Air Force
Air Chief Marshal
Air Marshal
Air Vice-Marshal
Air Commodore
Group Captain
Wing Commander
Squadron Leader
Flight Lieutenant
Flying Officer
Pilot Officer
Master Air Loadmaster
Master Air Electronic
Operator
Master Engineer
Master Navigator
Master Signaller
Master Pilot
Warrant Officer
Chief Technician
Flight Sergeant
Sergeant
Corporal
Junior Technician
Senior Aircraftman
Leading Aircraftman
Aircraftman 1st Class
Aircraftman 2nd Class

Army

Field Marshal
General
Lieutenant-General
Major-General
Brigadier
Colonel
Lieutenant-Colonel
Major

Captain
Lieutenant
Second-Lieutenant
Sergeant-Major
Quartermaster-
Sergeant
Sergeant
Corporal
Lance-Corporal
Bombardier
Private

Royal Navy

Admiral of the Fleet
Admiral
Vice-Admiral
Rear-Admiral
Commodore
Captain
Commander
Lieutenant-Commander
Lieutenant
Sub-Lieutenant
Chief Petty Officer
Petty Officer
Leading Seaman
Able Seaman
Ordinary Seaman
Junior Seaman

Weapons And Armour

2

NU
V1
V2

3

ABM
arm

axe
bow
dag
dah
das
egg
gas
gun
gyn
jet
ram
TNT
wad

4

adze
ammo
arms
ball
barb
bill
bola
bolo
bolt
bomb
bren
butt
cane
club
colt
cosh
dart
dirk
epee
fang
flak
foil
gade
gaff
goad
helm
ICBM
jack

kora
kris
mace
mail
mere
meri
mine
nike
pike
shot
sten
tace
tank
tock
tuck
VTOL
whip
Z-gun

5

A-bomb
aegis
ancus
ankus
anlas
armet
armor
arrow
aswar
baton
bidag
bilbo
birch
bolas
boson
brand
buffe
clean
crest
culet
curat
estoc
flail

fusee
fusil
gipon
grape
gupti
H-bomb
hobit
imber
jupel
jupon
keris
khora
kilig
kilij
knife
knout
kukri
kylie
lames
lance
latch
lasso
lathi
Luger
Maxim
panga
pilum
poker
pouch
prodd
rifle
royal
sabre
saker
salet
salvo
shaft
shell
skean
skene
sling
spear
staff

stake
stave
stick
sword
tabard
tachi
targe
tasse
tawse
visor
vizor
waddy

6

ack-ack
air-gun
ailetes
amukta
anlace
armlet
armour
barkal
barong
barrel
basnet
baston
bhanju
bodkin
Bofors
bonnet
bracer
bridle
brugne
buffer
bullet
calote
camail
cannon
carcas
carrel
casque
cassis
celate

cemtex
crenel
crinet
cruise
cudgel
cuello
cuisse
dagger
daisho
dragon
dualin
dum-dum
dusack
espada
Exocet
feltre
glaive
gorget
gusset
hanger
hanjar
heaume
helmet
homing
jezail
katana
kerrie
khanda
kikuki
kodogu
kreese
lariat
lassoo
lorica
mascle
mailed
massue
mauser
mazule
mesail
minnie
morian
morion

mortar
musket
muzzle
napalm
parang
petard
pistol
pom-pom
popgun
powder
primer
qillij
quarry
quiver
ramrod
rapier
recoil
rocket
salade
sallet
saturn
scutum
scythe
semtex
shield
sickle
sparth
sparke
stylet
sumpit
swivel
tabard
talwar
target
tonite
tuille
tulwar
umbril
VGO gun
waster
weapon
Webley
zipgun

7

ailetes
anelace
arblast
assagai
assegai
ataghan
awl-pike
bacinet
balasan
baldric
balista
barbute
bar-shot
basinet
baslard
bayonet
bazooka
belfrey
biliong
bombard
bourdon
brasset
Bren gun
buckler
bundook
caestus
carbine
calibre
caliver
caltrap
caraben
chakram
chalcos
chauces
chopper
cordite
corslet
couteau
crupper
cuirass
cuisses
culeset

currier
curtana
curtein
cutlass
djerrid
dualine
dudgeon
dussack
ejector
elf-bolt
espadon
fauchon
fendace
firearm
fire-pot
frontal
gantlet
gas mask
Gatling
gauchet
gouchet
greaves
grenade
gunshot
hackbut
halberd
halbert
handgun
handjar
harpoon
hatchet
hauberk
hoguine
holster
javelin
kastane
kindjal
langrel
laniers
longbow
long tom
lyddite
machete

megaton
missile
morglay
mursail
murrion
musquet
nuclear
oil-bomb
panache
panoply
placard
poitrel
polaris
priming
pole-axe
poniard
puldron
punt gun
quarrel
rabinet
roundel
shashqa
shinken
shotgun
side-arm
sjambok
Skybolt
Spandau
sparthe
Sten gun
surcoat
teargas
tocemma
torpedo
trident
trisula
twibill
vamplet
ventail
visiere
warhead
wind-gun

8

aerodart
allecret
amusette
arbalete
arbalist
armalite
arquebus
atom bomb
attaghan
axe-knife
balister
ballista
bardings
bascinet
baselard
basilard
basilisk
baudrick
birdbolt
blowpipe
bludgeon
brassard
brassart
brayette
broad-axe
Browning
buff coat
burganet
burginot
burgonet
cabasset
calthorp
canister
carabine
case-shot
catapult
cavalier
chacheka
chamfron
champons
charfron
chauches

chausses
cladibas
claymore
cod piece
colleret
colletin
corselet
criniere
crossbow
culettes
culverin
damaskin
deringer
destrier
dynamite
eel-spear
elf-arrow
enforcer
falchion
falconet
fauchard
field-gun
firearms
fire-ball
firelock
fireship
fougasse
gadlings
gauntlet
gavelock
gunsight
hackbutt
hail shot
halecret
half-pike
hand-pike
haquebut
howitzer
jambeaux
jazerant
langrage
Lewis gun
linstock

magazine
mangonel
mantelet
Maxim gun
munition
navel gun
oerlikon
ordnance
palstaff
paravane
partisan
paterero
pauldron
pectoral
pederero
petronel
pistolet
plastron
poignard
port-fire
pyroxyle
querquer
repeater
revolver
ricochet
ringmail
sabatons
scabbard
scimitar
scorpion
shamshir
shrapnel
siege-gun
skeandhu
solarets
solerets
spadroon
spontoon
springal
steam-gun
stiletto
stinkpot
stonebow

sumpitan
testiere
Thompson
tomahawk
Tommy gun
umbriere
vambrace
vamplate
whin-yard
whitearm
yataghan

9

angel-shot
arquebuse
arrowhead
artillery
automatic
aventaile
backpiece
badelaire
bainbergs
ballistic
bandeleer
bandolier
bannerole
bastinado
battleaxe
beinbergs
Big Bertha
blackjack
Blue Water
boar-spear
Bofors gun
bomb-chest
bombshell
boomerang
brandiron
Brown Bess
brownbill
carronade
cartouche
cartridge

chain-mail
chain-shot
champfron
chassepot
chaussons
columbiad
defoliant
demi-lance
derringer
deterrent
detonator
doodle-bug
epaulette
equaliser
equalizer
espringal
face-guard
falcastra
fish-spear
flagellum
flamberge
flintlock
garde-bras
gelignite
grapeshot
guncotton
gunpowder
habergeon
half-track
hand-staff
harquebus
hausse-col
headpiece
heavy tank
heelpiece
jack boots
knobstick
light tank
matchlock
Mazzuelle
Mills bomb
munitions
musketoon

needle-gun
poison gas
pourpoint
quaker-gun
rerebrace
sabatynes
sarbacane
shillalah
slow-match
slung-shot
smallarms
smallbore
smoke-bomb
spring-gun
starshell
stinkbomb
sword-cane
teeth arms
troop ship
truncheon
turret gun
vantbrace
vant-brass
ward staff
welsh-hook
xyloidine
zumbooruk

10

ammunition
arcubalist
artillator
aventaille
banded mail
banderolle
barrel helm
battery gun
blind shell
Blue Streak
bowie-knife
brandestoc
brichettes
brigandine

broad arrow
broadsword
burrel-shot
cannonball
cannon-shot
cataphract
coat armour
coat of mail
croissants
cross-arrow
demi-cannon
ecrevisses
emboitment
field-piece
fire-barrel
flanchards
Gatling gun
grainstaff
harquebuse
knobkerrie
lambrequin
Lee-Enfield
machine-gun
medium tank
Minie rifle
mustard-gas
paixhan-gun
pea-shooter
powder horn
projectile
pyroxyline
recoilless
safety-fuse
sidewinder
six-shooter
skeneoccle
snickersee
sticky bomb
sword-stick
touchpaper
Winchester

11

anti-tank gun
armoured car
basket sword
blunderbuss
bow and arrow
breastplate
breaststrap
brigandyron
brigantayle
chapel de fer
contact-mine
cruiser tank
Dahlgren gun
depth-charge
espallieres
grande-garde
gun carriage
gun-howitzer
hand-grenade
harping iron
Jacob's staff
Khyber knife
Lochaber axe
misericorde
morgenstern
morning-star
mountain-gun
neutron bomb
plate armour
powder chest
powder flask
safety-catch
scale-armour
Snider rifle
stern-chaser
Thompson gun

12

Armstrong gun
battering ram
boarding pike
bombing plane
breech loader

bridle cutter
cartridge-box
conventional
cross-bar-shot
demi-culverin
double-charge
fire carriage
flame-thrower
fowling-piece
hydrogen bomb
Lancaster fun
landing craft
Mills grenade
mitrailleuse
muzzle-loader
quarterstaff
rocket-mortar
spigot mortar
Stokes mortar
sword-bayonet
tracer bullet
trench mortar
wheel-lock dag

13

aerial torpedo
arming doublet
armor-piercing
ball-cartridge
brass knuckles
cartridge case
cat-o'nine-tails
Damocles sword
duelling sword
guided missile
high-explosive
knuckleduster
life preserver
percussion cap
poisoned arrow
scalping-knife
shrapnel shell
submachine-gun
submarine mine
thermonuclear
throwing knife
two-edged sword

14

armour-piercing
blank cartridge
Brennan torpedo
flame-projector
incendiary bomb
miniature rifle
nitro-glycerine
nuclear weapons
powder-magazine
rocket launcher
sawn off shotgun
small-bore rifle

15+

anti-aircraft gun
ballistic missile
double-barrelled
shotgun
heat-seeking missile
imbricate armour
lachrymatory gas

Names

(Including abbreviations, nicknames, and some common foreign names.)

Boys

3

Abe
Alf
Ali
Ben
Bob
Boy
Col
Dai
Dan
Don
Eli
Ely
Gus
Guy
Hal
Hay
Hew
Ian
Ira
Ivo
Jay
Jem
Jim
Job
Joe
Jon
Jos
Ken
Kid
Len
Leo
Mac
Mat
Max
Ned
Nye
Pat
Pip
Ray

Rea
Reg
Rex
Rod
Ron
Roy
Sam
Sid
Tam
Ted
Tim
Tom
Vic

4

Abel
Adam
Alan
Alec
Algy
Ally
Amos
Andy
Axel
Bald
Bart
Beau
Bede
Bell
Bert
Bill
Boyd
Buck
Bury
Cain
Carl
Gary
Cass
Ciro
Dick
Dirk
Dion
Duff

Duke
Earl
Eddy
Eden
Emil
Eric
Esau
Esra
Euan
Evan
Ewen
Eyre
Ezra
Fitz
Fred
Gary
Gene
Glen
Glyn
Gwyn
Hans
Hope
Hugh
Hugo
Hume
Hyam
Iain
Ifor
Ikey
Iohn
Ivan
Ivor
Jack
Jake
Jean
Jess
Jock
Joel
Joey
John
Josh
Juan
Jude

Karl	Toby	Bruce
Keir	Tony	Bryan
Kemp	Vane	Bunny
Kent	Vere	Cairn
King	Walt	Caius
Leon	Will	Carew
Loel	Winn	Carol
Luke	Wynn	Cecil
Lyle	Yule	Clare
Lynd		Claud
Lyon	**5**	Clive
Marc	Aaron	Clyde
Mark	Abdul	Colet
Matt	Abner	Colin
Mick	Abram	Conan
Mike	Alban	Cosmo
Muir	Algie	Cyril
Neil	Allan	Cyrus
Nero	Aldred	Dacre
Nick	Alroy	Damon
Noah	Alves	Darcy
Noel	Alwin	D'arcy
Olaf	Aiwyn	David
Orme	Amand	Davie
Otho	André	Denis
Otis	Angus	Denny
Otto	Anson	Denys
Owen	Anton	Derby
Page	Archy	Derek
Paul	Arden	Dicky
Penn	Athol	Drake
Pery	Aubyn	Earle
Pete	Aymar	Eddie
Phil	Barry	Edgar
René	Barty	Edwin
Rhys	Basil	Edwyn
Rory	Berty	Eldon
Ross	Bevis	Ellis
Saul	Billy	Eliot
Sean	Bobby	Emery
Seth	Booth	Emile
Stan	Boris	Enoch
Theo	Brian	Ernie

Ernst	Johan	Remus
Evans	Jonah	Renée
Ewart	Jonas	Rider
Felix	Jules	Robin
Franc	Keith	Roger
Frank	Kenny	Rolfe
Franz	Kevin	Rollo
Filth	Larry	Romeo
Fritz	Leigh	Rowan
Fulke	Lewin	Royce
Garry	Lewis	Rufus
Garth	Lisle	Rumer
Gavin	Lloyd	Ryder
Geoff	Louis	Sandy
Giles	Luigi	Saxon
Glynn	Lyall	Scott
Govan	Major	Serge
Grant	Manly	Shane
Guido	Mayor	Silas
Harry	Meyer	Simon
Haydn	Micky	Speed
Hebel	Miles	Starr
Henri	Monty	Steve
Henry	Moses	Storm
Heron	Myles	Tabor
Hiram	Neil	Taffy
Hyman	Nigel	Teddy
Hymie	Oscar	Terry
Iltyd	Osman	Titus
Inigo	Oswyn	Tommy
Innes	Paddy	Trant
Isaac	Paget	Tubby
Jabez	Paton	Tudor
Jacky	Pedro	Ulick
Jacob	Pelan	Usher
Jaime	Percy	Wally
James	Perry	Willy
Jamie	Peter	Wolfe
Jason	Piers	Wyatt
Jemmy	Punch	Wylie
Jerry	Ralph	Wynne
Jesse	Ramon	Wyvil
Jimmy	Raoul	Yorke

6

Adolph	Dallas	Giulio
Adrian	Damian	Godwin
Aeneas	Daniel	Gonvil
Albert	Delves	Gordon
Albion	Declan	Graeme
Alexis	Demian	Graham
Alfred	Dennis	Gregan
Alston	Dermot	Gregor
Andrew	Derric	Gunner
Angelo	Dickie	Gunter
Anselm	Donald	Gustav
Antony	Dougal	Gwilym
Archer	Dryden	Hallam
Archie	Dudley	Hamish
Armand	Dugald	Hamlet
Arnold	Duggie	Hamlyn
Arthur	Duncan	Harold
Aubrey	Dundas	Harris
August	Dunlop	Hayden
Austin	Edmond	Haydon
Aylmer	Edmund	Hector
Aylwin	Eduard	Hedley
Balbus	Edward	Henryk
Barney	Egbert	Herman
Bennie	Eldred	Hervey
Bertie	Elliot	Hilary
Braham	Ernest	Hilton
Brodie	Erroll	Hobart
Brutus	Ervine	Holman
Bryden	Esmond	Horace
Bulwer	Eugene	Howard
Caesar	Evelyn	Howell
Calvin	Fabian	Hubert
Carlos	Fergus	Hylton
Caspar	Forbes	Ignace
Cedric	Freddy	Irvine
Cicero	Garnet	Israel
Claude	Gasper	Jackey
Conrad	Gaston	Jackie
Conway	George	Jacomb
Crusoe	Gerald	Japhet
Curran	Gerard	Jasper
	Gideon	Jeremy

Jerome	Nevill	Simons
Jervis	Ninian	Sinbad
Johann	Norman	Square
Johnny	Norris	Squire
Joseph	Norton	Steven
Joshua	Nowell	St John
Josiah	Oliver	Stuart
Julian	Osbert	Sydney
Julien	Osmond	Thomas
Julius	Oswald	Tobias
Justin	Pelham	Trefor
Kersey	Philip	Trevor
Kirwan	Pierre	Verney
Laddie	Powell	Vernon
Lawley	Prince	Victor
Leslie	Rafael	Vivian
Lionel	Ramsay	Vyvyan
Loftus	Randle	Wallis
Lucien	Raphel	Walter
	Rayner	Warren
Ludwig	Reggie	Watkin
Luther	Rendle	Wesley
Magnus	Reuben	Willem
Marcel	Rhodes	Willie
Marcus	Robbie	Wolsey
Marten	Robert	Xavier
Martin	Roddie	Yehudi
Mauris	Rodger	
Melvin	Roland	**7**
Merlin	Ronald	Abraham
Mervyn	Rowley	Aladdin
Mickie	Rowlie	Alfonso
Milton	Royden	Alister
Montie	Rudolf	Almeric
Moritz	Rupert	Alsager
Morris	Samson	Amadeus
Morvyn	Samuel	Ambrose
Mostyn	Sefton	Anatole
Murray	Selwyn	Andries
Napier	Seumas	Aneurin
Nathan	Shafto	Anthony
Nelson	Sidney	Antoine
Nevile	Simeon	Antonio

Artemus	Frankie	Lucifer
Auguste	Freddie	Ludovic
Baldwin	Gabriel	Malcolm
Balfour	Gaspard	Matthew
Barclay	Geoffry	Maurice
Barnaby	Geraint	Maxwell
Barnard	Gervais	Maynard
Beaufoi	Gervase	Merrick
Bernard	Gilbert	Michael
Bertram	Gilmour	Montagu
Burnard	Gladwyn	Neville
Calvert	Gloster	Nicolas
Cameron	Godfrey	Orlando
Carlyon	Goronwy	Orpheus
Charles	Grahame	Orville
Charley	Gregory	Osborne
Chester	Gunther	Padraic
Clayton	Gustave	Paladin
Clement	Hadrian	Patrick
Clinton	Herbert	Perseus
Compton	Hermann	Phineas
Connell	Hewlett	Pierrot
Crispin	Hilaire	Quentin
Cyprian	Hildred	Quintin
Dalziel	Horatio	Randall
Denison	Humbert	Ranulph
Derrick	Humphry	Raphael
Desmond	Ibrahim	Raymond
Dillwyn	Isidore	Raymund
Dominic	Jackson	Redvers
Donovan	Jacques	Reynard
Douglas	Jeffrey	Richard
Edouard	Jocelyn	Roderic
Emanuel	Justice	Rudolph
Emilius	Kenneth	Romulus
Ephraim	Lachlan	Rowland
Etienne	Lambert	Rudolph
Eustace	Lennard	Rudyard
Everard	Leonard	Russell
Faraday	Leopold	Sergius
Fielder	Lindsay	Seymour
FitzRoy	Lindsey	Sheldon
Francis	Lorimer	Sigmund

Solomon
Spencer
Spenser
Stanley
St. Aubyn
St. Clair
Stephen
Steuart
Stewart
St. Leger
Terence
Tertius
Timothy
Ughtred
Ulysses
Umberto
Vaughan
Vincent
Wallace
Warwick
Westley
Wilfred
Wilfrid
Wilhelm
William
Winston
Wyndham
Zachary
Zebedee

8

Achilles
Adolphus
Alasdair
Alastair
Algernon
Alisdair
Alistair
Aloysius
Alphonse
Alphonso
Annesley
Antonius

Aristide
Augustus
Aurelius
Barnabas
Bartlemy
Beaumont
Bedivere
Benjamin
Bernardi
Bertrand
Campbell
Carleton
Champion
Clarence
Clemence
Clements
Clifford
Crauford
Crawford
Cuthbert
Diarmaid
Dominick
Ebenezer
Emmanuel
Ethelred
FitzHugh
Florizel
François
Franklin
Frederic
Geoffrey
Geoffroy
Giovanni
Guiseppe
Greville
Gustavus
Hamilton
Harcourt
Harrison
Havelock
Herbrand
Hereward
Hezekiah

Horatius
Humphrey
Ignatius
Immanuel
Ironside
Jeremiah
Jonathan
Joscelyn
Josephus
Kingsley
Lancelot
Laurence
Lawrance
Lawrence
Leonhard
Leonidas
Llewelyn
Llywelyn
Maitland
Marshall
Meredith
Montague
Mortimer
Nicholas
Octavius
Oliphant
Oughtred
Paulinus
Perceval
Percival
Peregrin
Peterkin
Philemon
Randolph
Randulph
Reginald
Robinson
Roderick
Ruaraidh
Sandford
Secundus
Septimus
Sherlock

Siegmund
Sinclair
Spensley
Stafford
St. George
Sylvanus
Thaddeus
Theobald
Theodore
Trelawny
Vladimar
Vladimir
Wolseley

9

Abernethy
Abimeleck
Alaistair
Alexander
Alphonsus
Arbuthnot
Archibald
Aristotle
Armstrong
Athelstan
Augustine
Bartimeus
Beauchamp
Christian
Constable
Cornelius
Courtenay
Courteney
Creighton
Demetrius
Dionysius
Ethelbert
Ferdinand
Fortescue
Francisco
Frederick
Gascoigne
Glanville

Granville
Hazledine
Honoratus
Josceline
Llewellyn
Mackenzie
Marmaduke
Nathaniel
Peregrine
Rodriguez
Rupprecht
Sackville
Salvatore
Sebastian
Siegfried
Sigismund
Stanislas
Sylvester
Thaddaeus
Theodoric
Valentine
Valentino
Wilbraham
Zachariah
Zechariah

Girls

3

Ada
Ame
Amy
Ann
Ave
Bee
Dot
Eda
Ena
Eva
Eve
Fay

Flo
Gay
Heë
Ida
Ina
Isa
Ivy
Iza
Jen
Joy
Kay
Kit
Liz
Lot
Mai
May
Meg
Nan
Pam
Pat
Peg
Pen
Ray
Rio
Sue
Una
Val
Viv
Yda
Zia
Zoë

4

Aase
Aimé
Alba
Alma
Alys
Anna
Anne
Anny
Avis
Baba

Babs	Irma	Neva
Bebe	Isla	Niki
Bess	Isma	Nina
Beth	Ivey	Nino
Caré	Jane	Nita
Cely	Jean	Nora
Clea	Jess	Olga
Cleo	Jill	Oona
Cora	Joan	Pola
Dawn	Judy	Puss
Dido	June	Rena
Dada	Kate	Rita
Dora	Katy	Rosa
Edie	Kaye	Rose
Edna	Lacy	Rosy
Ella	Lala	Ruby
Elma	Leah	Ruth
Elsa	Lena	Sara
Else	Lila	Sari
Emma	Lily	Sita
Emmy	Lina	Suky
Enid	Lisa	Susy
Erin	Lita	Syme
Erna	Liza	Tess
Esmé	Lois	Tina
Etta	Lola	Vera
Etty	Lucy	Vida
Evie	Lulu	Vita
Fifi	Lynn	Viva
Gaby	Maie	Zara
Gage	Mana	Zena
Gail	Mary	Zita
Gene	Maud	
Gala	Meta	**5**
Gwen	Mimi	Abbie
Gwyn	Mina	Adela
Hebe	Mall	Adele
Hope	Mona	Aggie
Ilse	Muff	Agnes
Inez	Muir	Ailsa
Inge	Myra	Aimée
Ioné	Nell	Alice
Iris	Nena	Aline

Altha	Dinah	Hetty
Angel	Dodie	Hilda
Anita	Dolly	Honor
Annie	Donie	Hulda
April	Donna	Hylda
Arbel	Dorah	Idina
Ariel	Doris	Ilona
Avice	Dreda	Innes
Avril	Dulce	Irene
Barbi	Edith	Isold
Becky	Effie	Janet
Bella	Eilsa	Janey
Belle	Elena	Janie
Berta	Elfie	Janny
Beryl	Elise	Jayne
Bessy	Eliza	Jenny
Betty	Ellen	Jessy
Biddy	Ellie	Joann
Bobby	Elsie	Joyce
Budie	Emily	Julia
Buena	Emmie	Julie
Bunny	Erica	Karen
Bunty	Essie	Karin
Carol	Ethel	Katey
Carré	Ettie	Katie
Caryl	Faith	Kitty
Cathy	Fanny	Laila
Cecil	Filia	Laura
Celia	Fiona	Lelia
Chloe	Fleur	Letty
Circe	Flora	Lilia
Cissy	Freda	Lilly
Clair	Gemma	tizzy
Clara	Gerty	Lorna
Clare	Gipsy	Lotte
Coral	Grace	Lotty
Daisy	Greer	Lucia
Della	Greta	Lucie
Della	Gussy	Lydia
Denes	Hazel	Lynne
Diana	Hedda	Mabel
Diane	Helen	Madge
Dilys	Henny	Maeve

Magda	Penny	Althea
Maggy	Phebe	Amabel
Mamie	Pippa	Amanda
Manie	Pixie	Amelia
Manon	Polly	Amelie
Marge	Poppy	Anabel
Maria	Queen	Angela
Marie	Renée	Anthea
Matty	Rhoda	Armyne
Maude	Rhona	Astrid
Mavis	Robin	Audrey
Megan	Rosie	Aurora
Mercy	Sadie	Averil
Merry	Sally	Babbie
Milly	Sarah	Beatie
Minna	Sonia	Benita
Mitzi	Susan	Bertha
Moira	Susie	Bessie
Molly	Sybil	Bettie
Morag	Tania	Bibbie
Moyra	Tanya	Biddie
Myrle	Tanis	Billie
Nancy	Thora	Binnie
Nanny	Trudy	Birdie
Naomi	Unity	Blanch
Nelly	Valda	Blonde
Nerys	Venis	Bobbie
Nessa	Venus	Brenda
Nesta	Vesta	Brigid
Netta	Vicki	Candis
Ninie	Viola	Carmen
Ninny	Vivie	Carrie
Niobe	Wanda	Cecile
Norah	Wendy	Cecily
Norma	Zelda	Celina
Olive	Zelia	Cherry
Oriel		Cicely
Pansy	**6**	Cissie
Patsy	Agatha	Claire
Patty	Aileen	Connie
Paula	Alicia	Dagmar
Pearl	Alison	Daphne
Peggy	Almond	Davina

Debbie	Imogen	Marian
Denise	Ingrid	Marion
Dorcas	Ioanna	Marnie
Doreen	Isabel	Martha
Dorice	Ishbel	Marthe
Dulcie	Isobel	Mattie
Editha	Isolde	Maxine
Edwina	Jackie	Melita
Edythe	Janice	Mercia
Egeria	Jeanie	Meriel
Eileen	Jeanne	Mignon
Elaine	Jemima	Millie
Elinor	Jennie	Mimosa
Emilie	Jessie	Minnie
Esther	Joanna	Miriam
Eunice	Joanne	Mollie
Evelyn	Judith	Monica
Fannie	Juliet	Moulie
Fatima	Kirsty	Muriel
Felice	Lalage	Murtle
Galena	Lallie	Myrtle
Gerrie	Lassie	Nadine
Gertie	Leonie	Nancie
Gladys	Lesley	Nancye
Glenda	Leslie	Nellie
Gloria	Lettie	Nelsie
Glynne	Levina	Nessie
Godiva	Lilian	Nettle
Gracie	Lilias	Nicola
Gretel	Lillah	Nicole
Gussie	Lillie	Noreen
Gwenda	Lizzie	Odette
Gwynne	Lorina	Olivia
Hattie	Lottie	Paddie
Hannah	Louisa	Pamela
Helena	Louise	Parnel
Helene	Lucile	Pattie
Hester	Maggie	Pegeen
Hilary	Maidie	Peggie
Honora	Maimie	Pernel
Honour	Maisie	Persis
Ileana	Marcia	Petula
Imelda	Margot	Phoebe

Pinkie
Poppet
Poppie
Popsie
Portia
Psyche
Rachel
Ramona
Regina
Renira
Richie
Robina
Rosina
Rowena
Roxana
Sabina
Sabine
Salome
Sandra
Sappho
Selina
Seonad
Serena
Sharon
Sheena
Sheila
Simone
Sophia
Sophie
Stella
Sybell
Sylvia
Tamsin
Teresa
Tertia
Tessie
Thalia
Thelma
Tootie
Trixie
Ulrica
Ursula
Verity

Verona
Violet
Vivian
Vivien
Vyvyen
Willow
Winnie
Yvette
Yvonne

7

Abigail
Adeline
Alberta
Alethea
Alfrida
Ameline
Annabel
Annette
Anstice
Antonia
Antonie
Ariadne
Athenia
Augusta
Aurelia
Babette
Barbara
Barbary
Beatrix
Belinda
Bettina
Billy Jo
Blanche
Blodwen
Blossom
Bridget
Camilla
Cecilia
Cherrie
Glance
Claudia
Colette

Colleen
Coralie
Cynthia
Damaris
Darling
Deborah
Deirdre
Delysia
Diamond
Dolores
Dorinda
Dorothe
Dorothy
Dorrice
Dulcima
Eleanor
Elfreda
Elfrida
Ellenor
Ellinor
Elspeth
Emerald
Emiline
Estelle
Etienne
Eudoxia
Eugenia
Eugenie
Evaline
Eveline
Fayette
Felicia
Fenella
Feodora
Florrie
Flossie
Frances
Georgia
Gertrud
Gillian
Gwennie
Gwenyth
Gwladys

Gwyneth	Ninette	Amabelle
Gwynnie	Octavia	Angelica
Harriet	Ophelia	Angelina
Heather	Ottilie	Angeline
Hellena	Palmyra	Angharad
Horatia	Pandora	Arabella
Hypatia	Paulina	Araminta
Janette	Pauline	Atalanta
Janitha	Perdita	Beatrice
Jessamy	Phillis	Berenice
Jessica	Phyllis	Carlotta
Jocelyn	Queenie	Carolina
Johanna	Rebecca	Caroline
Juliana	Rhodena	Cathleen
Lavinia	Ricarda	Catriona
Leoline	Roberta	Christie
Leonora	Rosalie	Chrystal
Letitia	Rosella	Clemency
Lettice	Rosetta	Clotilde
Lettuce	Rosette	Consuelo
Lillian	Sidonia	Cordelia
Lillias	Susanna	Cornelia
Lisbeth	Susanne	Dorothea
Lucilla	Suzanne	Dorothie
Lucille	Suzette	Drusilla
Mabelle	Sybilla	Dulcinia
Margery	Tabitha	Eleanora
Marjery	Tatiana	Eleanore
Marjory	Theresa	Elfriede
Martina	Therese	Ellaline
Matilda	Titiana	Emmeline
Maureen	Tootles	Euphemia
Melanie	Valerie	Evelinda
Melissa	Valetta	Everalda
Michéle	Vanessa	Felicity
Mildred	Venetia	Filomena
Minerva	Winsome	Florence
Miralda	Yolande	Francine
Miranda		Georgina
Myfanwy	*8*	Germaine
Natalie	Adelaide	Gertrude
Natasha	Adrienne	Gretchen
Nigella	Albertha	Grizelda

Grizelle
Harriett
Hermione
Hortense
Isabella
Jeanette
Jennifer
Jeromina
Julianna
Julietta
Juliette
Katharin
Kathleen
Laburnum
Laetitia
Lavender
Lorraine
Lucretia
Madeline
Magdalen
Marcella
Marcelle
Margaret
Marianne
Mariette
Marigold
Marjorie
Michelle
Mireille
Morwenna
Murielle
Nathanie
Nathalie
Patience
Patricia
Penelope
Petronel
Philippa
Primrose
Prudence
Prunella
Raymonde

Rebeccah
Reinagle
Reinelde
Rosalind
Rosamond
Rosamund
Rosemary
Samantha
Sapphire
Seabelle
Sheelagh
Susannah
Tallulah
Theodora
Veronica
Victoria
Violetta
Virginia
Vivienne
Vourneen
Winifred

9

Albertine
Alexandra
Ambrosine
Anastasia
Annabelle
Britannia
Cassandra
Catherine
Celestine
Charlotte
Christian
Christina
Christine
Cleopatra
Clothilde
Columbine
Constance
Corisande

Desdemona
Eglantine
Elisabeth
Elizabeth
Ermengard
Ernestine
Esmeralda
Esperance
Francisca
Frederica
Gabrielle
Georgiana
Geraldine
Guglielma
Guinivere
Gwendolen
Harriette
Henrietta
Henriette
Hortensia
Hyacinthe
Iphigenia
Josephine
Kathailin
Katharine
Katherine
Madeleine
Magdalena
Magdalene
Margarita
Melisande
Millicent
Philomena
Pierrette
Priscilla
Rosabelle
Stephanie
Theodosia
Thomasina
Valentine
Winefride

Nationalities,
Languages
and Peoples

Peoples and languages

African tribes

3

Ewe
Fon
Ibo
Ijo
Iru
Suk
Tiv
Vai
Yao

4

Agni
Baga
Bena
Bete
Bini
Bisa
Bubi
Fang
Fula
Guro
Haya
Hehe
Hima
Hutu
Lala
Lozi
Mali
Meru
Nama
Nupe
Nyao
Teso
Yako
Zulu

5

Afars

Anuak
Bamum
Bantu
Bassa
Baule
Bemba
Chewa
Chopi
Dinka
Dogon
Galla
Ganda
Gissi
Grebo
Hausa
Iraqu
Kamba
Lulua
Lunda
Masai
Mende
Mossi
Nandi
Ngoni
Nguni
Nguru
Pygmy
Riffs
Rundi
Shona
Sotho
Swazi
Tonga
Tussi
Tutsi
Venda
Xhosa

6

Angoni
Bakota
Balega
Basuto

Bateke
Bayaka
Chagga
Fulani
Herero
Ibibio
Kikuyu
Kpwesi
Lumbwa
Luvale
Murozi
Ngwato
Rolong
Sambaa
Senufo
Somali
Sukuma
Thonga
Tlokwa
Tsonga
Tswana
Tuareg
Veddah
Warega
Yoruba

7

Ashanti
Baganda
Bakweii
Bambara
Bangala
Bapende
Barotse
Barundi
Basonge
Batonka
Batutsi
Berbers
Bunduka
Bushmen
Dagomba
Griquas

Mashona
Namaqua
Nilotes
Samburu
Shillak
Songhai
Turkana
Watutsi

8

Bergdama
Bushongo
Kipsigis
Mamprusi
Mandingo
Matabele
Tallensi

9

Kgalagedi

10

Bathiaping
Hottentots
Karamojong

11

Bangarwanda

12

Lunda-Bajokwe

American Indian Peoples

3 and 4

Cree
Crow
Fox
Hopi
Hupa

Iowa
Maya
Moki
Pima
Sauk
Ute
Yuma
Zuni

5

Aztec
Blood
Caddo
Campa
Creek
Haida
Huron
Incas
Kansa
Kiowa
Lipan
Miami
Moqui
Nahua
Omaha
Osage
Sioux
Teton
Wappo
Yaqui
Yuchi
Yunca

6

Abnaki
Apache
Aymara
Aztecs
Biloxi
Caribs
Cayuga
Cocopa
Dakota

Dogrib
Kichai
Mandan
Micmac
Mixtec
Mohave
Mohawk
Navaho
Nootka
Ojibwa
Oneida
Ostiak
Ottawa
Paiute
Pawnee
Pequot
Pericu
Piegan
Pueblo
Quakaw
Salish
Santee
Sarcee
Seneca
Toltec
Warrau

7

Abenaki
Amerind
Arapaho
Araucan
Arikara
Catawba
Chilcal
Chinook
Choctaw
Hidatsa
Mapuche
Mohegan
Mohican
Natchez
Ojibway

Orejone
Quechua
Serrano
Shawnee
Stonies
Tlingit
Tonkawa
Wichita
Wyandot

8

Aguaruna
Cherokee
Cheyenne
Comanche
Delaware
Illinois
Iroquois
Kickapoo
Kootenay
Kwakiutl
Menomini
Muskogee
Nez Perce
Onondaga
Powhatan
Quichuan
Seminole
Shoshoni
Shushwap

9

Algonkian
Algonquin
Apalachee
Ashochimi
Blackfeet
Chickasaw
Chipewyan
Chippeway
Flatheads
Karankawa
Menominee

Penobscot
Tuscarora
Winnebago

10

Araucanian
Assiniboin
Athabascan
Bella Coola
Leni-Lenape
Minnetaree
Montagnais
Shoshonean

11

Narraganset
Root-diggers
Susquehanna

12

Pasamaquoddy

Languages,
Nationalities and
Races

2

Ga
Wa
Wu

3

Edo
Ewe
Fon
Fur
Gur
Hun
Ibo
Ido

Ila
Jew
Kru
Kui
Kwa
Lao
Luo
Mon
Shi
Tiv
Twi
Vai
Yao

4

Akan
Ambo
Arab
Avar
Bali
Beja
Bini
Bodo
Boer
Celt
Chad
Copt
Dane
Efik
Erse
Fang
Finn
Garo
Gaul
Ge'ez
Gogo
Gond
Grig
Igbo
Kelt
Kurd
Lala
Lapp

Lari	Batak	Khmer
Lett	Bemba	Kissi
Loma	Benga	Kongo
Lozi	Berta	Lamba
Luba	Bhili	Lango
Mano	Bulom	Latin
Manx	Bussi	Lenge
Moor	Carib	Lomwe
Moxu	Chaga	Malay
Naga	Chopi	Mande
Nuba	Croat	Maori
Nuer	Cuban	Masai
Nupe	Cymry	Mossi
Pali	Czech	Munda
Pedi	Dayak	Nandi
Pict	Dinka	Naron
Pole	Doric	Negro
Russ	Dutch	Ngala
Scot	Dyold	Nguni
Sena	Dyula	Nkore
Serb	Fante	Norse
Shan	Frank	Nyong
Sikh	Galla	Nyoro
Slav	Ganda	Oriya
Sobo	Gbari	Oscan
Susu	Gipsy	Punic
Teso	Gondi	Roman
Thai	Greek	Ronga
Tswa	Gypsy	Rundi
Turk	Hadza	Sango
Urdu	Hausa	Saudi
Wend	Hindi	Saxon
Zend	Idoma	Scots
Zulu	Indic	Shilh
	Ionic	Shona
5	Iraqi	Sinic
Acoli	Irish	Sotho
Aleut	Kadai	Swazi
Aryan	Kafir	Swede
Asian	Kamla	Swiss
Attic	Karen	Tamil
Bantu	Kazak	Temne
Bassa	Khasi	Tigre

Tonga
Uzbeg
Venda
Welsh
Wolof
Xhosa
Yupik
Zande

6

Acholi
Aeolic
Afghan
Altaic
Arabic
Arawak
Argive
Aymara
Baltic
Baoule
Basque
Berber
Bokmal
Brahui
Breton
Briton
Bulgar
Celtic
Chokwe
Coptic
Creole
Cymric
Danish
Dorian
Eskimo
Fijian
French
Fulani
Gaelic
Gallic
Gascon
German
Gothic

Hebrew
Herero
Ibibio
Indian
Inupik
Ionian
Italic
Jewess
Jewish
Judaic
Kabyle
Kaffir
Kanuri
Kikuyu
Korean
Kpelle
Kpessi
Kurukh
Libyan
Luvale
Manchu
Mongol
Navaho
Ndonga
Nepali
Ngbaka
Ngombe
Norman
Nsenga
Nubian
Nyanja
Ostman
Papuan
Parian
Parsee
Patois
Polish
Pushto
Pushtu
Rajput
Romaic
Romany
Rwanda

Ryukyu
Sabine
Samoan
Serere
Sindhi
Slavic
Slovak
Somali
Soviet
Sukuma
Syriac
Syrian
Telegu
Teuton
Theban
Thonga
Tongan
Trojan
Tsonga
Tswana
Tuareg
Tungus
Turkic
Tuscan
Viking
Votyak
Yankee
Yemeni
Yoruba
Zenaga

7

Acadian
African
Amharic
Angolan
Arabian
Aramaic
Aramean
Armoric
Asiatic
Avestan
Bagirmi

Balanta	Laotien	Siamese
Balochi	Lappish	Slovene
Bambara	Latvian	Songhai
Bedouin	Lingala	Spanish
Belgian	Lombard	Spartan
Bengali	Lugbara	Swahili
Bisayan	Maduran	Swedish
British	Malinke	Tagalog
Burmese	Maltese	Tibetan
Bushmen	Mandyak	Tigrina
Catalan	Manxman	Turkish
Chechen	Marathi	Ugandan
Chilean	Mexican	Umbrian
Chinese	Moorish	Umbundu
Cornish	Mordvin	Venetic
Cypriot	Morisco	Walloon
Dagomba	Mozareb	Yiddish
Dalicad	Mulatto	Zairese
Dialect	Nahuatl	Zambian
English	Nauruan	
Finnish	Ndebele	**8**
Fleming	Negress	Abderite
Flemish	Ngbandi	Akkadian
Frisian	Nilotic	Albanian
Gambian	Nynorsk	Algerian
Gaulish	Ottoman	American
Guarani	Pahlavi	Andorran
Haitian	Palaung	Antiguan
Hamitic	Persian	Armenian
Hebraic	Prakrit	Assamese
Hessian	Punjabi	Assyrian
Hittite	Quechua	Austrian
Iberian	Romance	Balinese
Ilocano	Romansh	Bavarian
Iranian	Russian	Bermudan
Israeli	Rwandan	Bohemian
Italian	Samiote	Bolivian
Karanga	Samoyed	Cambrian
Khoisan	Sandawe	Canadian
Kirghiz	Santali	Chaldaic
Kurdish	Semitic	Chaldean
Kuwaiti	Serbian	Chamorro
Laotian	Shilluk	Cherokee

Corsican
Cushitic
Cyrenaic
Delphian
Dutchman
Egyptian
Estonian
Ethiopic
Etruscan
Eurasian
Frankish
Gallican
Georgian
Germanic
Ghanaian
Gujarati
Gujariti
Guyanese
Hawaiian
Hellenic
Helvetic
Honduran
Illyrian
Irishman
Japanese
Javanese
Kashmiri
Kimbundu
Kingwana
Kuki-Chin
Kukuruku
Kwanyama
Lebanese
Liberian
Makassar
Malagasy
Malawian
Mandarin
Mandingo
Mandinka
Memphian
Moroccan
Moru-Madi

Negritos
Nepalese
Nigerian
Nuba-Fula
Nyamwesi
Octoroon
Old Norse
Old Saxon
Parthian
Pelasgic
Peruvian
Phrygian
Prussian
Romanian
Romansch
Rumanian
Sanskrit
Scotsman
Scottish
Sicilian
Slavonic
Spaniard
Sudanese
Sumerian
Teutonic
Tunisian
Turanian
Turkomen
Vandalic
Visigoth
Welshman

9

Abkhasian
Afrikaans
Afrikaner
Anatolian
Armorican
Barbadian
Bengalese
Brazilian
Bulgarian
Byzantian

Byzantine
Cambodian
Cantonese
Caucasian
Ceylonese
Chari-Nile
Cheremiss
Cimmerian
Colombian
Congolese
Dravidian
Esperanto
Esquimaux
Ethiopian
Frenchman
Hanseatic
Hibernian
Hottentot
Hungarian
Icelander
Icelandic
Israelite
Jordanian
Kabardian
Kannarese
Low German
Malayalam
Malaysian
Mauritian
Mongolian
Negrillos
Nepaulese
Norwegian
Ostrogoth
Pakistani
Provencal
Red Indian
Rhodesian
Roumanian
Samaritan
Sardinian
Sere Mundu
Sinhalese

Sri Lankan
Sundanese
Taiwanese
Tanzanian
Tocharian
Ukrainian
Ulotrichi
Uruguayan

10

Abyssinian
Afrikander
Algonquian
Anglo-Saxon
Australian
Autochthon
Babylonian
Circassian
Costa Rican
Ecuadorian
Englishman
Finno-Ugric
Florentine
Guatemalan
High German
Hindustani
Indonesian
Israelitic
Lithuanian
Melanesian
Mingrelian
Monegasque
Neapolitan
Nicaraguan
Nicobarese
Niger-Congo
Panamanian
Paraguayan
Patagonian
Philippine
Philistine
Phoenician
Polynesian

Pomeranian
Portuguese
Rajasthani
Senegalese
Serbo-Croat
Singhalese
Venezuelan
Vernacular
Vietnamese

11

Afro-Asiatic
Argentinian
Azerbaijani
Bangladeshi
Greenlander
Indo-Hittite
Indo-Iranian
Mauretanian
Palestinian
Scots Gaelic
Sino-Tibetan
Trinidadian

12

Basic English
Byelorussian
Indo-European
King's English
Moru-Mangbetu
mother tongue
New Zealander
Plattdeutsch
Scandinavian
Tibeto-Burman

13

Pidgin English
Queen's English
Rhaeto-Romanic
Serbo-Croatian

People

(This list is anything to do with people, including what a person might be called (i.e. man, son, chum, bride, idiot etc), be or do as opposed to an official title as in Official Positions and Religious Titles section)

2 and 3

A.B.
ace
ass
B.A
boy
B.Sc.
cad
cit
dab
dad
D.D.
deb
dux
elf
fag
fan
fop
fub
G.I.
gun
guy
hag
ham
imp
kid
kin
lad
lob
M.A

ma	bevy	hick
man	bird'	hobo
me	blue	host
men	boor	idol
mob	bore	jack
M.P.	boss	jade
Mr.	brat	jill
Mrs.	buck	jilt
mug	bull	jury
mum	chap	kith
N.C.O.	chum	lass
nun	clan	liar
oaf	colt	loon
pa	cove	lout
pal	crew	lush
pet	dame	magi
Ph.D.	dear	maid
pig	demy	male
rat	doer	mama
rip	doll	mate
R.S.M.	dolt	mess
she	doxy	mime
sir	drip	minx
spy	duck	miss
son	dude	mite
sot	dupe	mome
tar us	feed	monk
wag	folk	muff
we	fool	mute
wit	funk	mutt
ye	gaby	nizy
yob	gang	ogre
you	gawk	papa
	girl	peer
4	goer	peon
ally	goth	pimp
aunt	grub	prig
babe	gull	rake
baby	haji	roué
band	heel	runt
bard	heir	sage
bear	herd	salt
beau	hero	sect

seer	bairn	dozer
self	beast	droll
sept	being	drone
serf	belle	dummy
shot	bigot	dunce
silk	biter	duper
sire	black	dwarf
slut	blade	eater
snob	blood	enemy
soak	booby	exile
star	bride	extra
swot	broad	fakir
tart	brute	felon
team	bully	fence
them	cadet	fiend
thug	carle	fifer
tike	cheat	filer
toff	child	firer
tony	choir	flier
tool	chuff	flirt
tory	chump	flock
twin	churl	fogey
tyke	dare	fraud
tyro	clown	freak
user	co-aid	freer
vamp	couch	gamin
waif	crank	gaper
ward	crone	gazer
whig	crony	genii
wife	crook	ghost
wino	crowd	giant
yogi	cynic	giber
zany	dandy	gipsy
	darky	giver
5	decoy	goose
adept	deist	grass
adult	devil	groom
aider	dicer	guest
airer	diver	guide
alien	do-all	hater
angel	donce	heavy
argus	donor	hewer
aunty	doter	hider

hiker	ogler	scold
hodge	owner	scout
hunks	pacer	screw
hussy	pagan	shark
idiot	party	shrew
idler	pater	sider
in-law	patsy	silly
issue	payee	siren
jingo	payer	sizar
joker	peach	skier
Judas	pigmy	snail
juror	piler	sneak
knave	pin-up	sorry
lazar	piper	sower
leper	porer	spark
limey	poser	sport
local	posse	squab
locum	proxy	squaw
loser	prude	staff
lover	pryer	stoic
madam	puker	stray
maker	punch	sumph
mamma	pupil	swain
mater	puppy	swell
mimic	pygmy	taker
minim	quack	tenor
minor	queen	thief
miser	queer	toady
moron	racer	tommy
mouse	raker	toper
mover	raver	toyer
mower	rebel	tramp
mummy	rider	trier
muser	rival	troop
namer	rogue	trull
nanny	rough	trump
Negro	rover	twins
niece	rower	uncle
ninny	sahib	urger
noddy	saint	vexer
nomad	saver	vixen
nymph	scamp	voter
odist	scion	wader

wench	bilker	dipper
whore	blacks	dodger
whoso	blonde	doodle
widow	bomber	dotard
wight	boozer	double
wiper	bowler	dragon
witch	buster	drawee
women	cadger	drawer
wooer	caller	drazel
yahoo	camper	driver
yobbo	captor	drudge
yokel	carper	dry-bob
youth	carver	ducker
	casual	duffer
6	chaser	dyvour
abaser	client	earwig
abider	clique	egoist
abuser	co-ally	elator
admass	coaxer	envier
adored	codder	eraser
adorer	codger	escort
agnate	co-heir	eunuch
albino	coolie	expert
allies	copier	fabler
alumna	co-star	faggot
amazon	cottar	family
ambler	cotter	fanner
angler	cousin	father
apache	coward	fawner
auntie	craven	feeler
au pair	creole	fellow
backer	cretin	female
bandit	cueist	fencer
barfly	damsel	Fenian
batman	dancer	fiancé
bayard	darner	fibber
beater	dauber	filler
beauty	debtor	finder
beldam	defier	foeman
better	delver	foiler
bettor	denier	forcer
bibber	deputy	friend
bidder	digger	gadder

gaffer	hopper	leaser
gagger	howler	leaver
gainer	hoyden	lecher
gammer	huffer	legist
gasbag	humbug	lender
genius	hummer	lessee
gentry	hunter	lessor
getter	hurler	letter
geezer	hussar	lifter
giglot	hymner	limner
gigman	iceman	lisper
gigolo	infant	lister
gillie	inmate	loafer
glider	ironer	lobber
godson	jeerer	lodger
golfer	jerker	looker
gossip	jester	loonie
granny	Jesuit	looter
grazer	jet set	lubber
griper	jilter	lurker
grouch	jogger	lyrist
grower	jolter	madcap
guiser	jumper	madman
guller	junior	maiden
gulper	junker	maniac
gunman	junkie	marine
gunner	keeper	marker
gusher	kicker	maroon
halter	kidder	marrer
harlot	killer	martyr
healer	kisser	masher
hearer	knower	masker
heater	lacker	master
heaver	lagger	matron
hector	lancer	medium
hedger	lander	melter
helper	lapper	member
hermit	lasher	menial
hinter	lassie	mentor
hippie	layman	mestee
hoaxer	leader	midget
holder	league	minion
hooter	leaper	misses

missis	patron	rabble
missus	pauper	racist
mister	pawnee	racker
mocker	pawner	ragtag
modist	paynim	raider
mohawk	pecker	railer
mohock	pedant	rammer
moiler	pedlar	ranter
monkey	peeler	rapist
mooter	peeper	rascal
moppet	pelter	rating
mortal	penman	reader
mother	penpal	reaper
mugger	person	relict
mulier	piecer	relier
mummer	pigeon	rhymer
myself	pinner	rifter
nagger	placer	ringer
nation	player	rinker
native	poller	rinser
needer	Pommie	rioter
nephew	poseur	ripper
nipper	poster	risker
nitwit	pourer	roamer
nobody	pouter	roarer
nodder	prater	rocker
noodle	prayer	Romany
novice	preyer	rookie
nudist	proser	rotter
ogress	prover	rouser
old boy	public	rubber
old man	puffer	ruiner
opener	puller	runner
oracle	pumper	rusher
orator	pundit	rustic
orphan	punter	sadist
outlaw	puppet	sailor
pandit	purger	santon
panter	purist	savage
papist	pusher	savant
parent	quaker	scaler
pariah	quoter	scorer
parter	rabbit	scouse

scrimp
second
seeker
seizer
selves
sender
senior
sentry
shadow
shaker
shaman
sharer
shaver
sheila
shover
shower
shrimp
sigher
sinner
sipper
sister
sitter
skater
slayer
slicer
slider
sloven
smiler
smiter
smoker
snarer
sniper
snorer
snudge
soaker
solver
sparer
spouse
squire
square
stager
starer
stayer

stoner
stooge
stroke
sucker
suitor
surety
tacker
talker
tartar
tasker
taster
tatler
tearer
teaser
teller
tenant
Teuton
theist
thrall
throng
tilter
toiler
tomboy
tooter
tosser
truant
tutrix
tyrant
umpire
undoer
uniter
urchin
vamper
vandal
vanner
varlet
vendee
vendor
vestal
viator
victim
victor
viewer

Viking
virago
virgin
votary
voyeur
wafter
walker
wanton
warmer
warner
washer
waster
wearer
weeder
weeper
wet-bob
whiner
wincer
winder
winker
winner
wisher
wizard
wittol
worker
worthy
wretch
writer
yapper
yeoman
yonker
zealot
zombie

7

abactor
abetter
abettor
acceder
accuser
adapter
admirer
adviser

agamist	cackler	cripple
aircrew	caitiff	croaker
also-ran	captain	crooner
alumnus	captive	crusher
amateur	casuist	cry baby
amorosa	caveman	cuckold
amoroso	changer	culprit
anybody	chanter	curioso
ascetic	Charlie	cyclist
assizer	charmer	dabbler
assumer	cheater	dabster
atheist	checker	dallier
athlete	Chindit	damosel
avenger	citizen	dangler
averter	clapper	darling
babbler	cleaver	dastard
ballboy	climber	dawdler
bastard	clipper	daysman
batsman	clubman	debaser
beatnik	cockney	debater
bedmate	cognate	defacer
bedouin	colleen	defamer
beldame	colonel	defiler
beloved	combine	defunct
best man	commons	delator
bigshot	company	deluder
blabber	compere	denizen
blender	comrade	derider
boarder	consort	desirer
boaster	convert	devisee
boggler	convict	deviser
bookman	copycat	devisor
bouncer	co-rival	devotee
bounder	Cossack	diarist
breeder	coterie	dibbler
brother	counter	diehard
bucolic	courser	dilator
buffoon	courter	divider
bumpkin	coxcomb	diviner
bungler	crawler	dizzard
burgher	creator	doubter
bushman	creeper	dowager
bustler	cringer	dragoon

dreader	fancier	gownman
dreamer	fantast	grandam
drifter	fascist	grandma
driller	fathead	grantee
drinker	faulter	granter
droller	favorer	grantor
drowner	feaster	grasper
drubber	feoffee	griffin
dualist	feoffor	groupie
dueller	fiancée	grouser
dullard	fiddler	growler
dweller	fielder	grown-up
edifier	filcher	grubber
egghead	flapper	grudger
egotist	flasher	grunter
ejector	fleecer	guesser
elector	floater	guildry
elegist	flouter	guzzler
elogist	foister	gymnast
elohist	fondler	habitué
empiric	fopling	haggler
emptier	forager	half-wit
enactor	founder	handler
endower	freeman	has-been
endurer	freezer	hatcher
engager	frisker	haunter
enjoyer	frowner	heathen
enticer	frumper	heckler
entrant	fuddler	heiress
epicure	fumbler	hell-hag
erecter	gabbler	hellier
eremite	gallant	heretic
escapee	gambler	heroine
escaper	garbler	hipster
exactor	general	hoarder
exalter	gentile	hobbler
exciter	giggler	homager
exegete	glutton	hoodlum
exposer	gobbler	hostage
failure	goodman	hostess
fair sex	gormand	hothead
fall-guy	gossoon	huddler
fanatic	gourmet	humbler

hurrier	laggard	nettler
husband	landman	nibbler
hustler	laugher	niggard
hymnist	leaguer	niggler
imagist	learner	nithing
imbiber	legatee	nominee
impeder	liberal	oarsman
imposer	limiter	obilgee
imputer	loather	obliger
inciter	lobcock	obligor
inducer	lookout	oddball
infidel	lorette	offerer
infuser	lounger	old fogy
ingrate	lowbrow	old girl
inhaler	lunatic	old maid
injurer	lurcher	old salt
insured	magnate	oppidan
insurer	mangler	opposer
invader	manikin	orderer
invalid	mankind	outcast
inviter	marcher	Oxonian
invoker	marplot	paddler
jackass	meddler	papoose
jack-tar	menacer	paragon
jacobin	mestino	partner
jangler	mestizo	parvenu
Jezebel	milksop	patcher
Joe Soap	mingler	patient
jostler	minikin	patriot
juggler	misdoer	Paul Pry
jumbler	mobster	peasant
juryman	modiste	peruser
juvenal	monitor	pervert
Kantist	moulder	piercer
killjoy	mounter	pilgrim
kindler	mourner	pincher
kindred	mouther	pioneer
kingpin	mudlark	plaiter
kinsman	mugwump	planner
kneeler	mulatto	playboy
knocker	mumbler	pleadee
knoller	Negress	pleader
know-all	Negrita	pleaser

plenist	regular	service
plodder	relater	settler
plotter	remover	shammer
plucker	renewer	sharker
plumper	repiner	sharper
plunger	replier	shedder
pounder	rescuer	shifter
praiser	reserve	shooter
pranker	retaker	shopper
presser	retinue	shouter
pricker	reverer	show-off
pinker	reviver	shutter
private	rhymist	shyster
prodigy	riddler	sibling
progeny	roadhog	skimmer
protégé	royalty	skipper
prowler	ruffian	skulker
puncher	ruffler	slacker
punster	rumbler	slammer
puritan	runaway	slasher
pursuer	rustler	sleeper
puzzler	saluter	slinger
quaffer	sandman	slipper
queller	saviour	slitter
querent	scalder	smasher
querist	scalper	snapper
quieter	sceptic	snarler
quitter	schemer	sniffer
radical	scholar	snipper
rambler	scoffer	snoozer
ravener	scolder	snorter
reacher	scooper	snuffer
realist	scorner	society
rebuker	scraper	soloist
reciter	scraple	someone
recluse	scrooge	soother
redhead	scroyle	sophist
redskin	sculler	soprano
reducer	seceder	spaniel
referee	sectary	spanker
refugee	securer	spanner
refuser	seducer	speaker
refuter	seminar	speeder

speller	swearer	upstart
spender	sweater	usurper
spiller	sweeper	utopian
spitter	swiller	utterer
spoiler	swimmer	vacuist
sponger	swinger	vagrant
sponsor	tarrier	vampire
sporter	tattler	vaulter
spotter	taunter	vaunter
spouter	templar	veteran
sprayer	tempter	villain
spurner	text-man	villein
spurrer	thinker	visitor
stabber	thriver	vouchee
stand-by	thrower	voucher
stand-in	thumper	voyager
starlet	tickler	vulture
starter	tippler	waddler
stealer	toaster	wagerer
stentor	toddler	wakener
stepson	tomfool	waltzer
sticker	toppler	want-wit
stiller	tosspot	warbler
stinger	tourist	warlock
stinker	trainee	wastrel
stinter	trainer	watcher
stirrer	traitor	waterer
stooper	treader	waverer
stopper	treater	weigher
strayer	tricker	welcher
striker	trifler	wencher
striver	tripper	whipper
stroker	trollop	whisker
student	trooper	widower
studier	tropist	wielder
stumper	trouper	windbag
stylist	trudger	wise guy
subduer	trustee	witling
subject	truster	witness
suicide	tumbler	wolf cub
suspect	twirler	worrier
swagman	twister	wounder
swinger	twitter	wrapper

wrecker
wrester
wringer
yielder
younker
Zionist

8

abdicant
abductor
absentee
academic
accepter
achiever
adherent
adjutant
adulator
advocate
aesthete
agitator
agnostic
alarmist
allottee
allotter
alter ego
altruist
ancestor
ancestry
anchoret
antihero
antipope
apostate
appellee
appellor
approver
arranger
aspirant
assassin
assembly
assertor
assignee
assignor
assuager

attacker
attestor
audience
aularian
awakener
bachelor
balancer
bankrupt
banterer
baritone
barrator
beadsman
beginner
beguiler
believer
bellower
benedict
bestower
betrayer
bigamist
big noise
blackleg
blazoner
blighter
bluecoat
bohemian
bookworm
borderer
borrower
boy scout
braggart
brethren
brunette
busybody
cabalist
caballer
callgirl
canaille
cannibal
canoeist
carouser
castaway
catamite

Catholic
caviller
celibate
cenobite
champion
chaperon
children
chiliast
chuckler
cicerone
cicisbeo
civilian
claimant
clansman
classman
clincher
clodpoll
cognizee
cognizor
colonial
colonist
combiner
commando
commoner
commuter
complier
computer
consumer
convener
conveyer
coquette
corporal
co-surety
cottager
courtier
co-worker
crackpot
creditor
criminal
customer
crusader
dalesman
daughter

deadhead
deaf-mute
debutant
deceased
deceiver
defector
defender
deferrer
democrat
demoniac
departer
deponent
depraver
depriver
derelict
deserter
deserver
despiser
detainee
detainer
detector
devourer
diffuser
digester
diner-out
dirty dog
disciple
disponee
disponer
disposer
disputer
ditheist
diverter
divorcee
divorcer
divulger
do-gooder
dogsbody
drencher
dribbler
drunkard
duellist
duettist

dullard
effector
elegiast
elevator
embracer
emigrant
emulator
enchanter
encloser
enforcer
enhancer
enjoiner
enlarger
enricher
enslaver
ensnarer
ephesian
erastian
eschewer
espouser
esteemer
eulogist
euphuist
Eurasian
everyman
everyone
evildoer
evocator
examinee
examiner
exceeder
exceptor
executor
expiator
expirant
exploder
explorer
exponent
extender
extoller
fanfaron
fatalist
favourer

feminist
ferreter
figurant
finalist
finisher
flaunter
flincher
folk-hero
follower
fomenter
fondling
foregoer
foreseer
forgiver
fourling
franklin
freedman
freshman
fribbler
frizzler
front man
fugitive
fusilier
futurist
gadabout
galloper
gamester
gaolbird
garroter
gatherer
genearch
geometer
getter-on
giantess
godchild
goodwife
gourmand
gownsman
graduate
grandson
grisette
grumbler
habitant

hanger-on	inductee	legalist
harasser	inductor	levanter
hardener	indulger	leveller
harridan	infecter	libellee
harrower	inferior	libeller
hastener	inflamer	liegeman
hazarder	informer	linesman
hectorer	initiate	lingerer
hedonist	innocent	linguist
helpmate	inquirer	listener
helpmeet	insister	literate
highbrow	insnarer	literati
hijacker	inspirer	litigant
hinderer	insulter	livewire
homicide	intended	logician
honourer	intender	loiterer
hooligan	intimate	looker-on
horseman	intruder	loyalist
huckster	investor	luminary
Huguenot	islander	lunarian
humanist	jabberer	lutanist
humorist	jackaroo	luxurist
humpback	Jacobite	lyricist
idealist	jailbird	macaroni
idolater	Jehovist	malapert
idolizer	jingoist	malaprop
idyllist	John Bull	maligner
imaginer	Jonathan	mandarin
imbecile	joy-rider	man-hater
imitator	Judaizer	mannikin
immortal	juvenile	marauder
impairer	kinsfolk	marksman
imparter	lady-love	martinet
impeller	lame duck	may-queen
implorer	lamenter	medalist
impostor	landsman	mediator
improver	landsmen	merryman
impugner	latinist	mesmeree
inceptor	launcher	messmate
incloser	layabout	mimicker
indictee	lay-clerk	mislayer
indicter	layer-out	mistress
indigene	laywoman	modalist

modifier	oratress	prize-man
molester	outliver	prodigal
monodist	outsider	producer
monsieur	pacifier	profaner
moon-calf	pacifist	promisee
moonling	paleface	promiser
moralist	palterer	promoter
Moravian	pamperer	proposer
motorist	panderer	protégée
murderer	Papalist	provoker
murmurer	paramour	punisher
mutineer	parasite	purifier
mutterer	parcener	Puseyite
namesake	pardoner	quadroon
narrator	parodist	quaverer
narrower	partaker	quencher
naturist	partisan	quibbler
neophyte	passer-by	quidnunc
nepotist	patentee	quietist
neurotic	pelagian	Quisling
new broom	penitent	rakehell
newcomer	perjurer	ransomer
nihilist	pesterer	ratifier
nuisance	pharisee	ravisher
numberer	picaroon	reasoner
numskull	pilferer	rebutter
nursling	pillager	recaptor
objector	plagiary	receiver
obscurer	playgoer	reckoner
observer	playmate	recliner
obtainer	plebeian	recoiler
obtruder	poisoner	recorder
occupant	polluter	recreant
occupier	poltroon	redeemer
offender	ponderer	reformer
old-timer	popinjay	refunder
old woman	populace	regicide
onlooker	prattler	rejecter
operator	preparer	rejoicer
opificer	presager	relapser
opponent	presbyte	relation
oppugner	presumer	releasee
optimist	prisoner	releaser

reliever	sciolist	sprinter
remarker	scorcher	squaller
reminder	scourger	squasher
remitter	scrawler	squatter
renderer	scuffler	squeaker
renegade	seafarer	squealer
repealer	searcher	squeezer
repeater	seconder	squinter
repeller	selector	squireen
reporter	sentinel	squirter
reprover	sergeant	stancher
repulser	shortner	stickler
reseizer	shrieker	stinkard
resenter	shrimper	stitcher
reserver	shrinker	stowaway
resident	shuffler	stranger
resigner	sidekick	stripper
resister	sidesman	stroller
resolver	simoniac	strutter
resorter	simperer	stumbler
restorer	skeleton	suborner
retarder	sketcher	suckling
retorter	slattern	sufferer
returner	slugabed	superior
revealer	sluggard	superman
reveller	slyboots	supposer
revenger	small fry	surmiser
revolter	snatcher	survivor
rewarder	snuffler	sybarite
riffraff	sodomite	tacksman
rifleman	softener	talesman
rigorist	softling	tartuffe
rodomont	solecist	taxpayer
romancer	solitary	teddy boy
Romanist	somebody	teenager
romantic	songster	telltale
rotarian	son-in-law	tenantry
royalist	sorcerer	testator
runagate	spinster	theorist
ruralist	spitfire	thrasher
saboteur	splitter	threader
satanist	spreader	thruster
saucebox	springer	thurifer

thwarter	whitener	automaton
tightwad	whizz-kid	bacchanal
top brass	wiseacre	backbiter
torturer	wonderer	banqueter
townsman	wrangler	barbarian
traditor	wrestler	bargainee
traducer	wriggler	bargainer
trampler	yeomanry	battleaxe
trappist	yodeller	bedfellow
trembler	yokemate	bedlamite
triplets	yourself	beggarman
truckler		bel esprit
truelove	**9**	biblicist
turncoat	abecedary	bicyclist
twaddler	aborigine	blockhead
twitcher	absconder	bluebeard
two-timer	abstainer	blunderer
underdog	academist	blusterer
unionist	accessory	bolsterer
upholder	acclaimer	bon vivant
upper ten	addressee	bourgeois
vagabond	addresser	boy friend
vanguard	admiralty	bridesman
vapourer	adulterer	brigadier
venturer	adversary	bystander
verifier	affirmant	cabin crew
vilifier	aggressor	Calvinist
villager	alcoholic	candidate
violator	analogist	canvasser
visitant	anarchist	careerist
votaress	anchoress	carnalist
votarist	anchorite	celebrity
wallower	annuitant	chain-gang
wanderer	apologist	chantress
wayfarer	appellant	character
waylayer	applauder	charlatan
waymaker	applicant	charterer
weakener	appraiser	chatterer
weanling	arch-enemy	chiseller
welcomer	assailant	Christian
Wesleyan	associate	churchman
wheedler	augmenter	clatterer
whistler	authority	clientele

coadjutor	creditrix	disturber
coalition	cricketer	disuniter
cocklaird	crookback	divinator
co-heiress	cut-throat	dogmatist
colleague	daredevil	dolly bird
collegian	dark horse	do-nothing
combatant	debauchee	driveller
comforter	debutante	dyspeptic
commander	declaimer	early bird
committee	declarant	earthling
committer	defaulter	eccentric
committor	defeatist	Edwardian
commodore	defendant	emendator
communist	defrauder	enchanter
community	deliverer	encomiast
compacter	demagogue	energizer
companion	demandant	energumen
concubine	demi-monde	enfeebler
confessor	dependant	engrosser
confidant	depositor	enlivener
conformer	depressor	entangler
Confucian	depurator	entourage
co-nominee	designate	entreater
conqueror	desperado	epicurean
conscript	despoiler	epileptic
consenter	destinist	epistoler
consignee	destroyer	evacuator
consignor	detractor	everybody
conspirer	dialector	exactress
constable	dialogist	examinant
consulter	disburser	excusator
contemner	discerner	executant
contender	discloser	executrix
continuer	disgracer	exhauster
contralto	disguiser	exhibiter
contriver	dispeller	exhibitor
converter	disperser	exploiter
co-patriot	displayer	expositor
corrector	disprover	expounder
corrupter	disputant	exquisite
covergirl	disseizor	extractor
crack shot	dissenter	extravert
creatress	dissident	extrovert

extremist	grandpapa	infringer
falsifier	grandsire	inhabiter
family man	gratifier	inheritor
favourite	great-aunt	initiator
fetishist	greenhorn	innovator
find-fault	grenadier	in-patient
fire-eater	greybeard	inscriber
first born	groomsman	insolvent
flatterer	groveller	instiller
flay-flint	guerrilla	insurgent
fleshling	guest star	intestate
forbidder	guineapig	intriguer
forebears	hall-breed	introvert
foreigner	half-caste	inveigher
forfeiter	haranguer	inveigler
forgetter	harbinger	Jansenist
formalist	harbourer	jay-walker
fortifier	harnesser	jitterbug
forwarder	hearkener	joculator
fossicker	hell-hound	joint-heir
foster-son	highflier	journeyer
foundling	hillbilly	jovialist
foundress	Hottentot	justifier
fratricide	household	kidnapper
free agent	housewife	kinswoman
freelance	hunchback	lackbrain
free-liver	hylozoist	ladies' man
freemason	hypocrite	landowner
fulfiller	ignoramus	law-monger
furtherer	immigrant	lay reader
gainsayer	immolator	lazybones
garnishee	impeacher	libellant
garnisher	impleader	liberator
garreteer	inamorata	libertine
garrotter	inamorato	lionheart
gathering	increaser	lip-reader
gentleman	incurable	liturgist
girl guide	indicator	lost sheep
Girondist	indweller	loud-mouth
go-between	inebriate	lowlander
godfather	inflicter	magnifier
godmother	informant	makepeace
Gothamite	infractor	malthorse

mammonist	offspring	postponer
mannerist	old master	postulant
masochist	oppressor	pot-hunter
matricide	organizer	practiser
meanderer	ourselves	precursor
medallist	pacemaker	predicant
mediatrix	palaverer	predictor
messieurs	panellist	preferrer
Methodist	paralytic	prelatist
metrician	paranymph	presbyope
middleman	parricide	presentee
millenary	part-owner	presenter
miscreant	passenger	preserver
mitigator	patricide	pretender
moderator	patroness	preventer
modernist	peasantry	proceeder
modulator	Pecksniff	profferer
monitress	peculator	profiteer
moonraker	pen-friend	projector
moralizer	pen-pusher	prolonger
mortgagee	pensioner	promissor
mortgagor	perceiver	promulger
mortifier	perfecter	proselyte
Mrs. Grundy	performer	prosodist
multitude	permitter	protector
muscleman	personage	protester
mutilator	personnel	protruder
mythmaker	persuader	punctuist
Narcissus	perturber	purchaser
neglecter	perverter	purloiner
neighbour	pessimist	pussyfoot
neogamist	pilgarlic	Quakeress
Neptunian	pinchfist	quickener
next of kin	pin-up girl	rabbinist
nominator	plaintiff	racketeer
nonentity	platonist	raconteur
non-smoker	plunderer	rainmaker
nourisher	plutocrat	ransacker
novitiate	plutonist	rapturist
nullifier	poetaster	ratepayer
numerator	portioner	recipient
observant	possessor	recordist
occultist	posterity	recoveree

recoverer	sermonist	stutterer
rectifier	sexualist	subaltern
redresser	shaveling	submitter
reflector	shortener	subverter
refresher	shoveller	succeeder
regulator	sightseer	successor
rehearser	simpleton	succourer
reinsurer	skin-diver	suggester
renouncer	skinflint	sundowner
renovator	skylarker	suppliant
represser	slanderer	supporter
reprobate	slobberer	surfeiter
requester	slowcoach	susceptor
respecter	slumberer	suspecter
rhymester	smatterer	suspender
ridiculer	sniveller	sustainer
ritualist	socialist	swaggerer
roisterer	socialite	swallower
Romanizer	sojourner	sweetener
roughneck	solicitor	sycophant
routinist	solitaire	symbolist
rubrician	son-of-a-gun	syncopist
ruminator	sophister	tactician
Samaritan	sophomore	Talmudist
Sassenach	spadassin	targumist
satellite	spectator	temptress
satisfier	Spinozist	termagant
Saturnist	spiritist	terminist
saunterer	spokesman	terrorist
scapegoat	sportsman	testatrix
scarecrow	sprinkler	testifier
scavenger	sputterer	theorizer
scholiast	squabbler	thickskin
schoolboy	stammerer	thunderer
scoundrel	stargazer	toad-eater
scrambler	star pupil	tormentor
scratcher	stigmatic	townsfolk
scribbler	straggler	traitress
scrutator	strangler	trapanner
sea-lawyer	stretcher	traveller
sectarian	stripling	traverser
separator	strongman	trepanner
serenader	struggler	tribesman

trickster
trigamist
tritheist
truepenny
underling
unitarian
valentine
venerator
verbalist
versifier
Victorian
vigilante
visionary
volunteer
vulcanist
warmonger
wassailer
whosoever
womanizer
womankind
womenfolk
worldling
wrongdoer
xenophobe
yachtsman
young lady
youngling
youngster

10

aboriginal
aborigines
Abraham man
absolutist
accomplice
admonisher
adulterant
adulteress
adventurer
aficionado
alcoranist
allegorist
alms people

ambidexter
ambodexter
anabaptist
ancestress
anecdotist
anglophile
anglophobe
Anglo-Saxon
antagonist
antecedent
antecessor
antecursor
antichthon
antiscians
apologizer
aristocrat
assemblage
assentient
babe-in-arms
baby-sitter
bamboozler
beautifier
bed-presser
bedswerver
Belgravian
belswagger
benefactor
Benthamite
Bethlemite
better half
big brother
blackamoor
blackguard
black sheep
blasphemer
bobbysoxer
bogtrotter
bold spirit
bootlicker
borstal boy
bridegroom
bridesmaid
bureaucrat

bushranger
campaigner
capitalist
caravanner
card-player
cavalryman
centralist
changeling
chatterbox
chauvinist
cheesecake
churchgoer
Cinderella
clodhopper
cloisterer
cloistress
coadjutant
coadjutrix
cohabitant
coloratura
commonalty
competitor
complainer
confessant
confessary
confidante
considerer
contendent
contestant
controller
co-operator
coparcener
copyholder
co-relation
councillor
counsellor
countryman
crackbrain
cringeling
criticizer
crosspatch
curmudgeon
daggle-tail

daydreamer
day-tripper
declaimant
deforciant
delinquent
demoiselle
depositary
deprecator
depredator
deputation
descendant
diatribist
dilettante
diminisher
directress
discharger
discourser
discoverer
discursist
disheritor
disparager
dispraiser
dispreader
disquieter
dissembler
distracter
distruster
divineress
divisioner
dogmatizer
dominicide
dramatizer
Drawcansir
drug addict
drug pusher
dunderpate
dunderhead
Dutch uncle
dynamitard
early riser
ear-witness
elaborator
electorate

electoress
elucidator
emboldener
empiricist
empoisoner
emulatress
encourager
encroacher
engenderer
Englishman
enigmatist
enthusiast
enumerator
enunciator
epitaphist
epitomizer
equestrian
eternalist
evangelist
exhortator
expatiator
explicator
expurgator
extenuator
extirpator
eye-witness
fabricator
factionist
fagot-voter
fashionist
federalist
fire-raiser
flagellant
flourisher
fly-by-night
footballer
footlicker
forefather
foreleader
foremother
forerunner
forswearer
fosterling

foxhunter
fraternity
freeholder
free-trader
frequenter
fuddy-duddy
fund-holder
fund-raiser
Gasconader
gastronome
gentlefolk
girl friend
glacialist
goal keeper
gold-digger
goodfellow
grandchild
grand juror
grandmamma
grandniece
grand-uncle
grass widow
great-uncle
half-sister
harmonizer
hatchet man
head hunter
heliolater
heresiarch
highjacker
highlander
hitch-hiker
human being
iconoclast
identifier
ideologist
idolatress
impenitent
impoisoner
importuner
imprisoner
incendiary
individual

inhabitant	mastermind	patronizer
inheritrix	matchmaker	peacemaker
inquisitor	merrymaker	pedestrian
insinuator	metaphrast	Peeping Tom
instigator	methuselah	pensionary
interceder	middlebrow	persecutor
interferer	militarist	persifleur
interloper	mindreader	personator
interposer	misogamist	petitioner
intervener	misogynist	phenomenon
introducer	monarchist	philistine
Ishmaelite	moneyed man	pinchpenny
jackadandy	monogamist	plagiarist
jackanapes	monologist	polo player
jobbernowl	monomaniac	polygamist
job-hunter	monopolist	polyhistor
jolterhead	monotheist	polytheist
kith and kin	mountebank	population
lady-killer	mouthpiece	positivist
land-holder	muddied oaf	pragmatist
landlubber	multiplier	preadamite
languisher	namby-pamby	procreator
lawbreaker	ne'er-do-well	profligate
left-winger	neutralist	progenitor
legitimist	nincompoop	prohibiter
liberty man	nominalist	promenader
licentiate	non-starter	pronouncer
lieutenant	notability	propagator
literalist	obstructer	prophesier
loggerhead	occasioner	propounder
lotus-eater	old soldier	proprietor
lower class	opinionist	prosecutor
Lychnobite	opium-eater	prostitute
machinator	originator	Protestant
magnetizer	orthoepist	psychopath
maiden aunt	out-patient	pulverizer
maiden lady	overrunner	pyrrhonist
malefactor	overturner	quarreller
malingerer	painstaker	questioner
manoeuvrer	pall-bearer	rabblement
man of straw	panegyrist	ragamuffin
married man	paraphrast	rascallion
marshaller	past master	Rechabites

recidivist
reclaimant
recognizer
recognitor
reconciler
reimburser
relinquent
rememberer
reproacher
reprobater
reproducer
republican
repudiator
restrainer
restricter
retributer
reverencer
revivalist
rhapsodist
ringleader
sacrificer
scrapegrace
Scaramouch
schematist
schismatic
scrutineer
secularist
sensualist
separatist
sermonizer
seventh son
shoplifter
shanghaier
sinecurist
slammerkin
smart aleck
snuff-taker
solemnizer
solicitant
solifidian
solitarian
son and heir
songstress

soothsayer
Sorbonnist
speculator
spoilsport
squanderer
starveling
stepfather
stepmother
stepsister
stimulator
stipulator
strategist
street arab
strokesman
subscriber
substitute
subtracter
sugar daddy
supplanter
supplicant
suppressor
surmounter
suscipient
sweetheart
sworn enemy
syllogizer
syncopater
syncretist
synonymist
tale-bearer
tale-teller
tantalizer
taskmaster
tea-drinker
televiewer
temporalty
temporizer
tenderfoot
tenderling
textualist
textuarist
themselves
thickskull

third party
threatener
timeserver
tramontane
transferee
transferer
transmuter
trespasser
troglodyte
troubadour
tub-thumper
tweedledee
tweedledum
tuft-hunter
unbeliever
undertaker
unemployed
upper class
upper crust
utopianist
vacillator
vanquished
vanquisher
Vaticanist
vegetarian
vindicator
voluptuary
wallflower
well-wisher
white friar
whomsoever
widow-maker
wine-bibber
wirepuller
withdrawer
withholder
woman-hater
worshipper
yoke-fellow
young blood
yourselves

11

abbreviator
abecedarian
academician
accompanier
accumulator
adventuress
animal lover
aristocracy
association
bandy-player
beauty queen
belligerent
beneficiary
Bible reader
bibliolater
bibliophile
bird's-nester
blackmailer
bloodsucker
blue-eyed boy
blunderhead
bourgeoisie
braggadocio
breadwinner
brotherhood
calumniator
catabaptist
cave-dweller
centenarian
chance-comer
cheer leader
cheese parer
chucklehead
clairvoyant
coalitioner
cognoscenti
co-inheritor
collitigant
commentator
complainant
condisciple
confamiliar
confiscator

conjecturer
connoisseur
conspirator
constituent
continuator
contributor
co-ordinator
deliberator
denominator
denunciator
depopulator
depreciator
detractress
devotionist
dilapidator
diluvialist
dipsomaniac
discipliner
discourager
dishonourer
dissentient
dissertator
distributor
disunionist
doctrinaire
domestician
double agent
draggle-tail
dram-drinker
drug peddler
eager beaver
electioneer
emancipator
embellisher
embroiderer
enchantress
encounterer
endeavourer
enlightener
enlisted man
enterpriser
entertainer
epigenesist

epistolizer
equilibrist
equivocator
establisher
euphemerist
exaggerator
exasperater
father-in-law
fault-finder
femme fatale
fifth column
fighting man
first cousin
flat dweller
flying squad
foot soldier
forestaller
foster-child
francophile
francophobe
freethinker
frothblower
fustilarian
galley slave
gallows bird
gatecrasher
gentlefolks
gentlewoman
ginger group
god-daughter
gormandizer
grandfather
grandmother
grandnephew
grandparent
gull-catcher
guttersnipe
half brother
hard drinker
harum-scarum
helping hand
high society
hobbledehoy

holder-forth
homo sapiens
hyperbolist
hypercritic
ideopraxist
imperialist
inaugurator
infantryman
inhabitress
inheritress
interceptor
intercessor
interrupter
interviewer
intimidater
joint-tenant
knucklehead
leaseholder
libertarian
lickspittle
lilliputian
litterateur
living image
Lycanthrope
manipulator
marrying-man
masquerader
materialist
matinee idol
maxim-monger
merry Andrew
metaphorist
middle class
millenarian
millionaire
misanthrope
misbeliever
misinformer
monopolizer
moonlighter
mother-in-law
mountaineer
mouth-friend

Mrs. Malaprop
name dropper
nationalist
necessarian
neutralizer
night-walker
nondescript
non-resident
nosey-parker
opportunist
owner-driver
pacificator
panic-monger
parishioner
participant
pearly queen
pedobaptist
peripatetic
perpetrator
personality
perturbator
phenomenist
philosopher
physicalist
predecessor
prize-winner
probabilist
probationer
prodigal son
proletarian
proletariat
promulgator
propitiator
prosecutrix
protagonist
protectress
protestator
Punchinello
punctualist
purgatorian
questionist
rank and file
rapscallion

rationalist
reactionary
recommender
recompenser
religionist
replenisher
reprehender
resuscitant
reversioner
right-winger
Rosicrucian
royal family
rugby player
sabbatarian
sacrilegist
sans-culotte
scaremonger
scatterling
scoutmaster
scripturist
scrutinizer
search party
shareholder
simple Simon
singularist
sister-in-law
sleepwalker
spectatress
speculatist
speech-maker
speed-skater
spendthrift
spindlelegs
stepbrother
stockholder
stonewaller
stool pigeon
storyteller
stump-orator
subordinate
suffragette
surrenderee
surrenderer

sword player
sworn friend
sympathizer
systematist
system-maker
tautologist
teetotaller
teleologist
telepathist
thanksgiver
theosophist
time-pleaser
Tommy Atkins
torch-bearer
town-dweller
traditioner
transmitter
trencherman
trend setter
undersigned
undervaluer
undesirable
Walter Mitty
war criminal
wastethrift
weathercock
wholehogger
withstander

12

abolitionist
acquaintance
advance party
antediluvian
anticourtier
appropriator
artful dodger
assassinator
awkward squad
bachelor girl
backwoodsman
barber monger
benefactress

bible-thumper
bibliomaniac
blood brother
blue stocking
bond-creditor
bottle-friend
bottle-washer
brother-in-law
bounty hunter
carpet-knight
chief mourner
church-member
coalitionist
collaborator
Colonel Blimp
commiserator
committeeman
communicator
competitress
complimenter
compossessor
conservative
consignatory
conquistador
contemplator
contemporary
controverter
convalescent
conventicular
conventioner
convivialist
co-respondent
corporealist
cosmopolitan
cousingerman
defectionist
demimondaine
demonstrator
determinator
dialectician
disciplinant
discommender
discontinuer

disenchanter
disorganiser
dispossessor
disseminator
doppelganger
double-dealer
eavesdropper
educationalist
elocutionist
encumbrancer
enfranchiser
equestrienne
exclusionist
excursionist
exhibitioner
experimenter
expostulator
exserviceman
extemporizer
extensionist
exterminator
extinguisher
featherbrain
filibusterer
firstnighter
foster father
foster mother
foster parent
foster sister
foundationer
gastronomist
gesticulator
globe-trotter
gospel-gossip
grey eminence
guest speaker
hair-splitter
headshrinker
heir-apparent
holidaymaker
humanitarian
impersonator
impoverisher

improvisator
inseparables
intellectual
intercipient
interlocutor
intermeddler
intermediary
interpolator
interrogator
investigator
irregularist
kleptomaniac
knight-errant
landed gentry
leading light
legacy-hunter
letter-writer
longshoreman
lounge lizard
mademoiselle
man-about-town
married woman
melancholist
mercurialist
mezzo soprano
misconstruer
misinformant
modest violet
morris dancer
natural child
near relation
neoplatonist
noctambulist
nonagenarian
obscurantist
octogenarian
old gentleman
pantophagist
participator
peace-breaker
penitentiary
perambulator
peregrinator

persona grata
philosophist
pillion-rider
poor relation
postdiluvian
postgraduate
pot-companion
precipitator
prevaricator
primogenitor
proprietress
proselytiser
public figure
quarter-cousin
recriminator
redemptioner
relinquisher
remonstrator
residentiary
resolutioner
resuscitator
roller-skater
rolling stone
salvationist
scatterbrain
schoolfellow
second cousin
second fiddle
sequestrator
sexagenarian
significator
single person
sister-german
sole occupant
somnambulist
somniloquist
spiritualist
spirit-rapper
stepdaughter
stormtrooper
straightener
street-urchin
stuffed shirt

sub-committee
sublapsarian
subpurchaser
Sunday driver
swashbuckler
sworn enemies
systematizer
system-monger
tennis player
testificator
theologaster
transgressor
transmigrant
transvestite
troublemaker
truce-breaker
truncheoneer
ugly customer
ugly duckling
ultramontane
undermanager
unemployable
universalist
velocipedist
versificator
village idiot
way passenger
wicket keeper
wool gatherer
working class

13
_____

adminiculator
administrator
anagrammatist
Anglo-American
Anglo-Catholic
annexationist
anthropophagi
antisocialist
apothegmatist
bibliophilist
blood relation

brother-german
bureaucratist
castle-builder
chamber-fellow
comprovincial
conceptualist
concessionist
conspiratress
conventionist
co-religionist
correspondent
daughter-in-law
deck passenger
deuterogamist
devotionalist
discriminator
distinguisher
exhibitionist
experimentist
fashion-monger
first offender
foot passenger
fortune-hunter
foster brother
fresh-air fiend
grand-daughter
hard bargainer
high churchman
hypochondriac
immaterialist
irreligionist
Job's comforter
laughing stock
life-annuitant
machiavellian
millennialist
miracle-monger
miracle-worker
misanthropist
mischief-maker
multiplicator
necessitarian
nonconformist

paterfamilias
perfectionist
philhellenist
philosophizer
predestinator
protectionist
proverbialist
reprobationer
revolutionary
sophisticator
speed merchant
spindleshanks
spiritualizer
state criminal
state prisoner
strike-breaker
tranquilliser
transmigrator
undergraduate
understrapper

14

antiaristocrat
armchair critic
billiard-player
corpuscularian
destructionist
disciplinarian
disenchantress
foster daughter
galactophagist
good-for-nothing
grammaticaster
ichthyophagist
improvisatrice
indifferentist
latitudinarian
ministerialist
misinterpreter
obstructionist
paragrammatist
philanthropist
procrastinator

prognosticator
progressionist
prohibitionist
promise-breaker
psilanthropist
quadragenarian
quodlibetarian
requisitionist
restorationist
sabbath-breaker
sacramentarian
sensationalist
sentimentalist
septuagenarian
skittles-player
squandermaniac
stamp-collector
superior person
tatterdemalion
trencher-friend
ultramontanist
undergraduette
valetudinarian
waifs-and-strays
weather prophet
whippersnapper

15

antitrinitarian
autograph hunter
circumnavigator
constitutionist
conversationist
emancipationist
experimentalist
heir-presumptive
insurrectionary
insurrectionist
intellectualist
supernaturalist
Tom, Dick and Harry

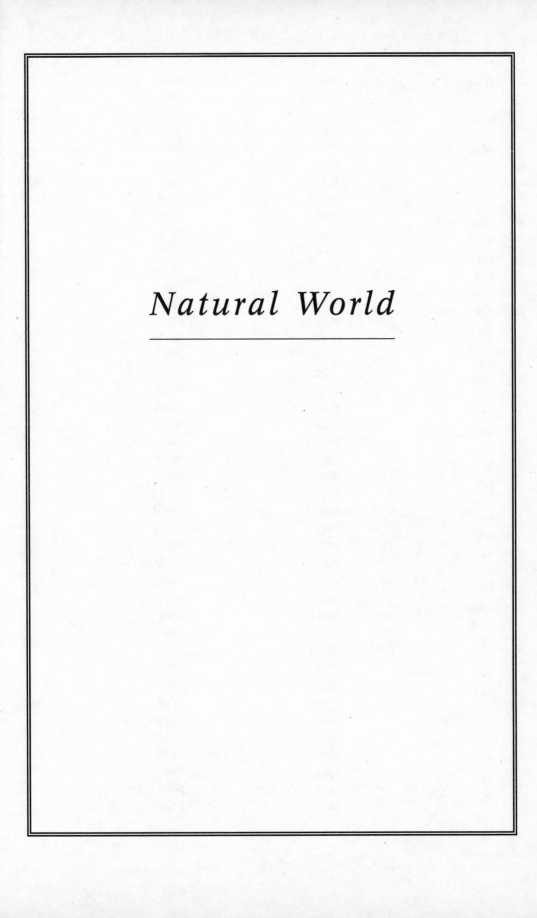

Natural World

Living Creature

Animals

2 and 3

ai
ape
ass
bat
bok
cat
cob
cow
cub
cur
dam
doe
dog
dso
dzo
elk
ewe
fox
gib
gnu
goa
hog
kid
kob
ky
man
mog
nag
orc
ox
pad
pig
ram
rat
Rex
roe
sai

seg
sow
tat
teg
fit
tod
tup
ure
wat
yak
zho
zo

4

alce
anoa
Arab
atoc
atok
axis
baln
barb
bear
boar
buck
bull
cain
calf
cavy
colt
cony
coon
dant
dauw
deer
dieb
dogy
dood
douc
euro
eyra
fawn
foal

gaur
girl
goat
gyal
hack
hare
hart
hind
ibex
jade
joey
jomo
kine
koba
kudu
lamb
lion
lynx
maid
mara
mare
mice
mico
mink
moco
mohr
moke
mole
mule
mona
musk
napu
neat
nout
nowt
oont
oryx
oxen
paca
paco
pala
pard
peba

pika	aguti	gayal
poka	alces	genet
pony	ammon	goral
prad	ariel	grice
pudu	arnee	grise
puma	baloo	gyall
quey	beast	harpy
rane	bhyle	hinny
reem	bidet	horse
roan	biped	hound
runt	bison	hutia
rusa	bitch	hyena
said	bongo	hyrax
saki	brach	indri
seal	brock	inuus
seeg	bruin	izard
shou	bunny	jocko
skug	burro	jumbo
sore	camel	kaama
stag	caple	kalan
stot	capra	kevel
stud	capul	kiang
suni	chiru	koala
tahr	civet	kulan
tait	coati	kyloe
tegg	coney	lemur
tehr	coypu	liger
titi	crone	llama
topi	cuddy	loris
unau	daman	magot
urus	dhole	major
urva	dingo	manis
vari	dipus	manul
vole	dogie	maral
wolf	drill	meles
yale	dsomo	mhorr
zati	eland	moose
zebu	equus	morse
zobo	fauna	mount
zuna	fells	mouse
	filly	nagor
5	fitch	nandu
addax	fossa	nyala

okapi	tabby	bawson
oribi	talpa	bayard
otary	tapir	beagle
otter	tatou	beaver
ounce	taxel	beeves
panda	tayra	bobcat
pekan	tiger	boomer
phoca	tigon	bovine
pinto	tucan	bronco
pongo	urial	brumby
potto	urson	burhel
poyou	ursus	cabrie
punch	vison	cabrit
puppy	vixen	castor
quoll	waler	catalo
ranny	whale	cattle
rasse	whelp	cayman
ratel	yapok	cayuse
royal	zebra	cervus
sable	zerda	chacma
saiga	zibet	chetah
sajou	zizel	chital
sasin	zoril	coaita
screw	zorra	cocker
serow	zorro	colugo
sheep		cosset
shoat	**6**	cougar
shott	agouti	coyote
shrew	aliped	craber
simia	alpaca	cuscus
skunk	angola	dassie
sloth	angora	desman
sorel	aoudad	dickey
sorex	argali	dik-dik
spade	aswail	dobbin
spado	auroch	dogape
spitz	aye-aye	dog fox
staig	baboon	donkey
steed	badger	dragon
steer	bandar	dugong
stirk	bandog	duiker
stoat	barrow	dzeren
swine	bawsin	dzeron

entire	kitten	quagga
ermine	koodoo	quokka
farrow	kyloes	rabbit
fennec	langur	racoon
ferret	lapdog	red fox
fisher	lechwe	reebok
foussa	lionel	renard
fox bat	malkin	rhebok
galago	malmag	rhesus
garran	mammal	ridgil
garron	margay	roarer
gavial	marmot	rodent
gelada	marten	ronion
gerbil	mataco	rouncy
gibbon	mawkin	sagoin
ginnet	merino	saguin
gopher	messin	sambar
goslet	monkey	sambur
grison	morkin	sarlac
grivet	musk ox	sarlyk
guemal	musmon	sea-ape
guenon	mustac	sea cow
hacker	nahoor	serval
halfer	nilgai	setter
hangul	nilgau	shammy
heifer	numbat	sheass
hircus	nutria	shelty
hogget	ocelot	sifaka
howler	olingo	sorrel
hyaena	onager	sphinx
hybrid	oorial	sponge
impala	ourebi	suslik
inyala	ovibos	taguan
jackal	padnag	tajacu
jaguar	pallah	talbot
jennet	panter	taurec
jerboa	poodle	tapeti
Jersey	porker	tarand
jument	possum	tarpan
kalong	pownie	taurec
kelpie	pugdog	taurus
keltie	pygarg	teledu
kennet	python	tenrec

thamin
theave
tomcat
tupala
tusker
urchin
vermin
vervet
vicuna
walrus
wapiti
warine
weanel
weasel
weeper
wether
wisent
wivern
wombat
wow-wow
wyvern
yapock

7

acouchi
acouchy
ant-bear
assapan
aurochs
banting
banteng
bearcat
bettong
bighorn
blesbok
blue cat
blue fox
bonasus
boshbop
Bovidae
brawner
brocket
broncho

bubalis
buffalo
bulchin
bulldog
bullock
burmese
bushcat
bush pig
cane rat
caracal
caribou
cattalo
cervine
cetacea
chamois
charger
cheetah
cheslip
cheviot
chikari
chimera
chincha
clumber
colobus
courser
dasypod
dasypus
dasyure
dinmont
dolphin
draft-ox
eanling
Echidna
echimyd
echinus
epizoan
epizoon
ermelin
felidae
fatling
finback
fitchet
fitchew

foumart
fur seal
galla ox
gazelle
gelding
gemsbok
genette
gerenuk
giraffe
glutton
gorilla
grampus
griffin
griffon
grizzly
guanaco
gymnure
hackney
halfape
hamster
harrier
huanaco
hystrix
jacchus
jackass
jumbuck
karagan
keitloa
kidling
klipdas
lagomys
lambkin
lemming
leopard
leveret
libbard
linsang
lioness
lurcher
macacus
macaque
madoqua
mammoth

manatee	primate	terrier
mangaby	procyon	testudo
Manx cat	pterope	thiller
maracan	raccoon	tigress
marikin	red deer	toxodon
mariput	reed rat	trotter
markhor	rietbok	twinter
marmose	rock doe	unicorn
megamys	roe buck	urocyon
meerkat	roe deer	urodele
minever	rorqual	vampire
miniver	sagouin	vansire
mole-rat	saimiri	vicuana
mongrel	sambhur	viverra
monture	sapajou	voengra
moon rat	sapling	wallaby
morling	sassaby	wart-hog
mormops	sciurus	wheeler
moschus	scorpio	wild ass
mouflon	sea-bear	wild cat
muglamb	sea-calf	wild dog
muntjak	sea-lion	wistiti
musiman	serpent	wolf-dog
muskrat	sheltie	zamouse
mustang	siamang	zorille
mustela	Siamese	zorilla
mycetes	silenus	
mycetis	soliped	**8**
mylodon	sondeli	aardvark
narwhal	sounder	aardwolf
nasalis	souslik	anteater
noctule	spaniel	antelope
nylghau	spanker	axis deer
opossum	spitter	babirusa
pack rat	stembok	Bactrian
palfrey	sumpter	bathorse
panther	sunbear	behemoth
pardale	tadpole	black fox
peccary	tamanoa	black rat
polecat	tamarin	bontebok
potoroo	tamarou	brant fox
prancer	tarsier	brown rat
pricket	tatouay	bull-calf

bushbaby	hylobate	sea-otter
bushbuck	indigene	serotine
cachalot	Irish elk	sewelled
cacholot	kangaroo	sewer-rat
capuchin	kinkajou	shorling
capucine	kiwikiwi	sika deer
capybara	kolinsky	sirenian
carcajou	lamantin	springer
cariacou	lamentin	squirrel
cavebear	landrace	staggard
cavicorn	macropus	stallion
chimaera	mammalia	steambok
chipmuck	mandrill	stinkard
chipmunk	mangabey	suilline
civet-cat	mantiger	suricate
coachdog	marmoset	surmulot
colocola	mastodon	tabby-cat
cotswold	meriones	talapoin
creodont	maverick	tamandua
cricetus	milch-cow	teguexin
cunjevoi	mongoose	terrapin
demi-wolf	moufflon	tetrapod
dinosaur	musk deer	tiger cat
dormouse	musquash	tortoise
duckbill	noctilio	treefrog
duckmole	ouistiti	twinling
earthhog	packmule	ungulata
Echippus	palebuck	viscacha
elephant	pangolin	wallaroo
entellus	physeter	wanderoo
filander	platypus	war-horse
foxhound	polliwig	warrigal
fruit bat	pollywog	water-hog
galloway	polo pony	water-rat
gin-horse	porkling	weanling
grysbock	porpoise	wild boar
Guernsey	red panda	wild goat
hairseal	reedbuck	yeanling
hartbeer	reindeer	yearling
hedgehog	riverhog	
hedgepig	Rodentia	*9*
hoggerel	ruminant	adelopode
hog steer	schimmel	alligator

amphioxus
amphipoda
Angola cat
annellata
anthobian
arctic fox
armadillo
babacoote
babyrussa
bandicoot
barbastel
batrachia
bay-duiker
bezantler
binturong
black bear
black buck
blue whale
brood-mare
brown bear
buckhound
canpagnol
carnivore
carpincho
cart-horse
catamount
chameleon
chickadee
chickaree
coalmouse
colemouse
commensal
dachshund
deermouse
delundung
desert rat
dicotyles
didelphys
dinoceras
draught-ox
dray-horse
dromedary
dziggetai

eared seal
flying fox
glyptodon
golden cat
greyhound
grimalkin
ground-hog
gruntling
guinea pig
hamadryas
honey-bear
ichneumon
lagomorph
leviathan
livestock
malt-horse
marsupial
megalonyx
monoceros
monotreme
mousedeer
orang-utan
pachyderm
pack-horse
pademelon
padymelon
palm civet
pampas cat
percheron
petaurist
phalanger
pipistrel
polar bear
porcupine
post-horse
predacean
prong-buck
prong-horn
prosimian
quadruman
quadruped
racehorse
razorbuck

rearmouse
reermouse
reremouse
retriever
rosmarine
shearling
shoreling
shorthorn
shrew-mole
silver fox
sitatunga
sloth bear
solenodon
southdown
spatangus
springbok
steerling
steinbock
stonebuck
stud-horse
tchneuman
thylacine
todlowrie
tragelaph
tree hyrax
tree shrew
trematode
trematoid
waterbuck
watermole
watervole
white bear
wild horse
wolverene
wolverine
woodchuck
woodshock
youngling
zoophagon

10
_____

amorphozoa
amphibials

angora goat
angwantibo
animalcule
anthropoid
articulata
babiroussa
barasingha
Barbary ape
birch mouse
bloodhound
bottlenose
buckjumper
cacomistle
camelopard
cardophagi
catarrhine
chevrotain
chimpanzee
chinchilla
chiroptera
chittagong
chousingha
clydesdale
coach-horse
coatimondi
cockatrice
cottontail
dachshound
Diphyodont
dolichotis
draft-horse
fallow deer
fieldmouse
fistulidae
giant panda
golden mole
halmaturus
hartebeest
hippogriff
hippogryff
honey mouse
hooded seal
housemouse

human-being
jaguarundi
Kodiak bear
Malay tapir
marsupials
Mona monkey
monotremes
muscardine
musk beaver
natterjack
paddymelon
Pallas's cat
pantheress
paradoxure
Persian cat
pichiciago
pilot whale
pine marten
pouched rat
prairie dog
pygmy shrew
quadricorn
quadrumana
raccoon dog
rhinoceros
right whale
river horse
rock badger
rock rabbit
ruminantia
saki monkey
scavernick
sea-leopard
sea-unicorn
shrew-mouse
sperm whale
springhaas
starveling
Thecodonts
timber wolf
vampire bat
water shrew
white whale

wildebeest

11

American elk
anoplothere
barbastelle
barking deer
black cattle
blood-sucker
branchireme
brown hyena
bullterrier
chlamyphore
digitigrade
douroucouli
entomophaga
fistulidans
flying lemur
flying mouse
fox squirrel
globigerina
grass monkey
Grevy's zebra
grizzly-bear
harbour seal
honey badger
horned-horse
insectivora
jumping deer
kangaroo rat
killer whale
leopard seal
Megatherium
mountain cat
orang-outang
patas monkey
pipistrelle
prairie wolf
Pterodactyl
rat kangaroo
red kangaroo
red squirrel
rock wallaby

sea elephant
serotine bat
sleuthhound
snow leopard
tragelaphus
vespertilio
wildebeeste
wishtonwish
woolly lemur

12

anthropoglot
Barbary sheep
Bengal monkey
catamountain
chlamyphorus
chrysochlore
draught-horse
elephant seal
ferae-naturae
flittermouse
grey squirrel
harvest mouse
hippopotamus
horseshoe bat
howler monkey
jumping mouse
klipspringer
Megalosaurus
mountain hare
mountain lion
pachydermata
Paleotherium
pocket gopher
pouched mouse
rhesus monkey
roan antelope
rock squirrel
scheltopusik
Shetland pony
Simmenthaler
snowshoe hare
spider monkey

spotted hyena
striped hyena
tree kangaroo
eater buffalo
water opossum
water spaniel
woolly monkey

13

Abyssinian cat
anthropoid ape
Anoplotherium
Australian cat
Bactrian camel
bearded lizard
carriage horse
Chapman's zebra
Cheirotherium
chinchilla cat
crabeater seal
dorcas gazelle
European bison
galeopithecus
golden hamster
hermaphrodite
humpback whale
Indian buffalo
laughing hyena
marsupial mole
mountain zebra
Parry's wallaby
polyprotodont
ring-tail coati
royal antelope
sable antelope
semnopithecus
shorthorn bull
solidungulate
spiny anteater
Tasmanian wolf
tree porcupine

14

Australian bear
bridled wallaby
Burchell's zebra
capuchin monkey
clouded leopard
crab-eating seal
dormouse-possum
flying squirrel
ground squirrel
Indian elephant
Indian pangolin
Isabelline bear
laughing hyaena
marmoset monkey
mountain beaver
New World monkey
Old World monkey
Patagonian cavy
Pere David's deer
snoeshoe rabbit
spectacled bear
squirrel monkey
Tasmanian devil

15+

African elephant
American buffalo
Barber Leicester
Bennett's wallaby
Chinese water deer
duck-billed platypus
flying phalanger
proboscis monkey
pygmy hippopotamus
rabbit bandicoot
sabretooth tiger
scaly-tailed squirrel
Tasmanian possum
Thomson's gazelle
white rhinoceros
woolly rhinoceros
woolly spider monkey

Prehistoric Animals

8

eohippus
rutiodon
smilodon

9

iguanodon
trachodon

10

allosaurus
altispinax
barosaurus
diplodocus
dryosaurus
euparkeria
mesohippus
orthomerus
pliohippus
pteranodon
stegoceras

11

anatosaurus
anchisaurus
apatosaurus
aphaneramma
cetiosaurus
coelophysis
deinonychus
kritosaurus
mandasuchus
merychippus
monoclonius
polacanthus
pterodactyl
riojasaurus
saurolophus
scolosaurus
spinosaurus

stegosaurus
tarbosaurus
triceratops

12

ankylosaurus
brontosaurus
camptosaurus
ceratosaurus
chasmosaurus
deinocheirus
hylaeosaurus
kentrosaurus
lambeosaurus
megalosaurus
ornithomimus
ouranosaurus
plateosaurus
ticinosuchus

13

brachiosaurus
compsognathus
corythosaurus
desmatosuchus
dilophosaurus
edmontosaurus
erythrosuchus
hypselosaurus
hypsilophodon
lesothosaurus
panoplosaurus
pentaceratops
protoceratops
pterodactylus
scelidosaurus
scleromochlus
styracosaurus
tenontosaurus
tyrannosaurus

14

baluchitherium

cetiosauriscus
chasmatosaurus
euoplocephalus
massospondylus
psittacosaurus
thescelosaurus

15

parasaurolophus
procheneosaurus

16

pachyrhinosaurus
procompsognathus

17

heterodontosaurus

18

pachycephalosaurus

Birds

2 and 3

auk
cob
daw
emu
fop
fum
hen
jay
ka
kae
kea
kia
mew
moa
owl
pen

pie
poe
ree
roc
ruc
tit
tui

4

alca
anas
arco
aves
barb
baya
bird
bubo
chat
cock
coly
coot
crax
crow
dodo
dove
duck
dupe
erne
eyas
fowl
fling
gawk
gier
guan
gull
hawk
hern
huia
huma
ibis
iunx
kagu
kaka

kite
kiwi
knot
koel
kora
kuku
lark
loom
loon
lory
mina
myna
naff
nene
nias
nyas
otis
pauw
pavo
pern
pica
piet
poll
pope
pout
rail
rhea
rixy
roch
rock
rook
ruff
rukh
runt
rype
shag
skua
smee
smew
sora
sord
sore
spot

swan
taha
teal
tern
tody
wavy
wren
xema
yaup
yite
yunx
zati

5

agami
ajuru
amsel
amzel
ardea
ariel
biddy
bongo
booby
bowet
brant
bucco
capon
chick
chirm
claik
colin
crake
crane
creak
daker
didus
diver
drake
dunny
eagle
egret
eider
finch

galah	radge	whaup
ganza	raven	wonga
geese	reeve	
glede	robin	**6**
goose	rodge	aiglet
goura	sacre	aigret
grebe	saker	alcedo
gripe	sally	alcyon
harpy	sasia	ancona
heron	saury	argala
hobby	scape	avocet
jager	scarf	avoset
junco	scaup	bantam
larus	scops	barbet
lowan	scray	bonxie
lyrie	senex	bowess
macaw	serin	brolga
madge	shama	buffel
maneh	sitta	bulbul
mavis	skite	cagmag
merle	stilt	canary
minah	snipe	chewet
miner	solan	chough
monal	soree	chukar
murre	spink	citril
mynah	squab	condor
nandu	stare	corbie
noddy	stilt	corvus
ornis	stint	coucal
ortyx	stork	cuckoo
ousel	strix	culver
ouzel	swift	curlew
owlet	tarin	cushat
pewet	terek	cygnet
pewit	topau	cygnus
picus	topet	darter
pipit	twite	dipper
pitta	umbre	drongo
poaka	urubu	ducker
poult	veery	dunlin
prion	virgo	eaglet
purre	wader	einack
quail	wagel	elanet

falcon	mot-mot	sicsac
fulmar	musket	simurg
galeen	nandow	siskin
gambet	nestor	smeath
gander	oriole	strich
gannet	osprey	strick
garrot	oxbird	sultan
gentoo	parrot	takahe
godurt	paster	tarsel
godwit	pavone	tercel
gooney	peahen	thrush
gorhen	pecker	tirwit
goslet	peewit	tomtit
grakle	perms	toucan
grouse	petrel	towhee
hacket	pigeon	tringa
hagden	plover	trogon
hammer	poulet	turaco
hareld	pouter	turbit
hoazin	powter	Turdus
hoopoe	puffin	turkey
hoopoo	pullet	turner
howlet	pygarg	turtle
jabiru	queest	waggel
jacana	quelea	weaver
jaeger	racama	whidah
jerkin	ratite	whydah
kakapo	redcap	wigeon
kiddow	reeler	willet
lanner	roberd	witwal
leipoa	roller	woosel
linnet	rotche	yaffle
loriot	ruddoc	ynambu
magpie	runner	zivola
marrot	scamel	zoozoo
martin	scobby	
menura	scoter	**7**
merlin	sea-bar	
merops	sea-cob	antbird
merula	sea-mew	apteryx
missel	sea-pie	attagas
monaul	shrike	attagen
mopoke	shrite	awl-bird
		babbler

barn owl	fantail	lavrock
bee-bird	fen duck	Leghorn
bittern	fern owl	lentner
blue-cap	fig-bird	lich-owl
bluetit	fin-foot	limpkin
buceros	fish owl	lorilet
bull-bat	flusher	mallard
bummalo	gadwall	manakin
bunting	gavilan	manikin
buphaga	gobbler	marabou
bustard	gorcock	maracan
buzzard	gorcrow	martlet
cackler	goshawk	megamys
caponet	gosling	migrant
cariama	grackle	minivet
carvist	grallae	modwall
cat-bird	greyhen	moorhen
cheeper	greylag	motacil
chewink	griffin	moth-owl
chicken	haggard	mudlark
ciconia	halcyon	muggent
coaltit	harfang	oilbird
cobswan	harrier	ortolan
colibri	hawk owl	oscines
columba	hen-harm	ostrich
corella	hickway	oven-tit
cotinga	hoatzin	pandion
courlan	horn owl	partlet
courser	ice-bird	peacock
cow-bird	impeyan	peafowl
creeper	jacamar	pelican
cropper	jackass	penguin
Cuculus	jackdaw	percher
dorhawk	jacksaw	peterel
dorking	jacobin	phaeton
dottrel	jashawk	phoenix
doucher	jedcock	pinnock
dovekie	kamichi	pintado
dovelet	kestrel	pintail
dum-bird	killdee	pochard
dunnock	kinglet	poe-bird
egg-bird	lagopus	poultry
emu-wren	lapwing	puttock

quabird
quetzel
raddock
rantock
redhead
redpoll
redwing
robinet
rooster
rosella
rotchie
ruddock
sakeret
sawbill
scammel
scooper
sea-crow
sea-duck
sea-fowl
seagull
sea-hawk
senegal
seriema
serinus
shirley
simargh
sirgang
skimmer
skylark
snow-owl
spadger
sparrow
squacco
staniel
stannel
stanyel
stumpie
sturnus
sunbird
swallow
swimmer
tadorna
tanager

tarrock
tattler
tiercel
tinamou
tinamus
titlark
titling
titmice
touraco
tree tit
trochil
tumbler
turakoo
vulture
vulturn
wagtail
wapacut
warbler
waxbill
waxwing
weebill
whooper
widgeon
wimbrel
witlock
witwall
wood owl
wrybill
wryneck
yeldrin

8

aasvogel
accentor
adjutant
aigrette
alcatras
amadavat
arapunga
avadavit
barnacle
bateleur
beam-bird

becafico
bee-eater
bell-bird
blackcap
bluebird
blue-wren
boat-bill
boat-tail
bobolink
bob-white
bockelet
bockeret
brancher
brevipen
bush chat
bush lark
calandra
calangay
caneroma
caracara
cardinal
cargoose
cheewink
clot-bird
cockatoo
cockerel
coquimbo
corn bird
curassow
cursores
cutwater
dabchick
daker-hen
dandy-hen
didapper
dinornis
dipchick
dorr-hawk
dotterel
duck-hawk
duckling
dun-diver
eagle-owl

estridge
fauvette
fig-eater
finnikin
firetail
fish-hawk
flamingo
gairfow
gamebird
gamecock
gang-gang
garefowl
garganey
great tit
greenlet
grey teal
grosbeak
guachero
hackbolt
hamburgh
hawfinch
hazel-hen
hemipode
hernshaw
hickwall
hornbill
hula-bird
keskidee
killdeer
kingbird
landrail
langshan
lanneret
laverock
lorikeet
love-bird
lyrebird
mandarin
mannikin
marabout
marsh fit
megapode
mina bird

mire crow
mire drum
moorcock
moorfowl
moorgame
morillon
musk duck
mute swan
mynabird
nestling
nightjar
notornis
nuthatch
oldsquaw
paitrick
parakeet
paroquet
peachick
petchary
percolin
pheasant
plungeon
podargus
popinjay
prunella
puff-bird
pygmy owl
redshank
redstart
ricebird
rifleman
ring dove
ring-tail
rock dove
sagecock
sandpeep
scops owl
screamer
scrub-fit
sea-eagle
shelduck
shoebill
shoveler

sittella
skuagull
snowbird
snowy owl
songbird
songlark
songster
starling
struthio
swamphen
swiftlet
tanagers
tantalus
tawny owl
terntero
thrasher
thresher
throstle
titmouse
tomnoddy
tragopan
tuke-nose
umbrette
waterhen
wheatear
whimbrel
whinchat
whip-bird
whistler
white-ear
white-eye
wildfowl
woodchat
woodcock
wood duck
woodlark
xanthura
yeldring
yeldrock
yoldring
zopilote

9

aepyornis
accipiter
albatross
andorinha
ant-thrush
autophagi
bald eagle
baltimore
bean goose
beccafico
beefeater
bell-minah
bergander
birgander
blackbird
black cock
black duck
black swan
blacktail
black tern
blue crane
bottletit
bower-bird
brambling
broadbill
brown hawk
bullfinch
buzzardet
campanero
cassowary
cereopsis
chaffinch
chatterer
chevalier
chickling
church owl
cockatiel
columbine
cormorant
corncrake
crossbill
currawong

dandy-cock
deinornis
dowitcher
eagle-hawk
eider duck
field-duck
fieldfare
field wren
fig parrot
figpecker
firecrest
francolin
French pie
friar-bird
fringilla
frogmouth
gallinazo
gallinule
gerfalcon
gier-eagle
glaucopis
goldcrest
golden-eye
goldfinch
goldspink
goosander
grassbird
grass wren
great skua
grenadier
grey heron
grossbeak
guillemot
guinea-hen
gyrfalcon
hammerkop
heathbird
heathcock
heronshaw
hill mynah
horned owl
Jenny-wren
jerfalcon

kittiwake
lint-white
little owl
log-runner
lorrikeet
macartney
mallemuck
mango bird
marshbird
merganser
merulidan
miresnipe
mollymauk
mousebird
mouse-hawk
mud-sucker
muscicapa
natatores
night hawk
ossifrage
paradisea
paraquito
pardalote
parrakeet
parroquet
partridge
passerine
peregrine
phalarope
pied-goose
pinefinch
ptarmigan
quachilto
razorbill
redbreast
red grouse
rhynchops
rifle-bird
ring-ousel
rosefinch
rossignol
salangale
sandpiper

scratcher
scrub-bird
scrub-fowl
scrub-wren
seaparrot
shearbill
sheldrake
shitepoke
shoveller
shrike-tit
silver-eye
skunk-bird
snake-bird
snow goose
sooty tern
soareagle
sore eagle
spinebill
spoonbill
stick-bird
stilt-bird
stock-dove
stonechat
stone-hawk
storm-bird
strigidae
swamp-hawk
swine-pipe
talegalla
tetraonid
thickhead
thornbill
tiercelet
trochilus
trumpeter
turnstone
waterbird
waterfowl
water-rail
wedgebill
wheat-bird
whiteface
whitetail

widow-bird
wild goose
willow tit
windhover
woodspite
wyandotte

10

aberdevine
ant-catcher
Arctic skua
Arctic tern
bearded tit
bell-magpie
bird of prey
blight-bird
blue-bonnet
blue-breast
blue-throat
boobook owl
brent goose
budgerigar
budgerygah
burrow-duck
butter-bird
butterbump
canary bird
canvas-back
chiffchaff
coddy-moddy
cow-bunting
crested tit
crow-shrike
demoiselle
didunculus
dishwasher
diving duck
dollar bird
dusky minah
dusky robin
ember goose
eurylaimus
eyas-musket

fallochat
fledgeling
flycatcher
fratercula
goatmilker
goatsucker
goldhammer
gooneybird
grassfinch
greenfinch
greenshank
grey falcon
grey parrot
grey plover
ground dove
ground lark
ground robin
guinea-fowl
gymnocitta
hammerhead
harpy eagle
hen-harrier
honeyeater
honey-guide
hooded crow
jungle-fowl
kingfisher
king parrot
kookaburra
love-parrot
magpie-lark
mallee-fowl
maned-goose
meadow-lark
mutton-bird
night heron
night raven
noisy-minah
nutcracker
parson-bird
peewee-lark
petty-chaps
prairie hen

pratincole
ramphastos
regent-bird
rock parrot
rock pigeon
sacred ibis
saddleback
sage grouse
salpinctes
sanderling
sandgrouse
sandmartin
sassorolla
screech-owl
sea-swallow
shearwater
sheath bill
silver-gull
solan goose
song shrike
song thrush
summer-duck
sun bittern
tailor-bird
talegallus
tanagridae
tit-warbler
tree-runner
tropic-bird
turkey-cock
turtle dove
water-ousel
wattle-bird
weasel-coat
weaver-bird
whidah-bird
white brant
white egret
white stork
whydah-bird
willow wren
wonga-wonga
woodgrouse

woodpecker
wood-pigeon
wood-shrike
yaffingale
yellow-bird
yellowlegs
zebra finch

I I

apostle-bird
banded stilt
barn swallow
black falcon
black grouse
black martin
bonebreaker
bristle-bird
brush-turkey
bush-creeper
butcher-bird
button quail
Canada goose
carrion crow
cattle egret
chanticleer
cochinchina
cock-sparrow
conirostres
corn bunting
diamondbird
Dorking fowl
dragoon-bird
fairy martin
fallow finch
flock pigeon
frigate-bird
fruit-pigeon
gallows-bird
gnat-catcher
gnat-snapper
golden eagle
grallatores
grey wagtail

harrier-hawk
herring gull
hooded robin
house martin
humming-bird
insectivora
kestrel-hawk
king penguin
king vulture
lammergeier
laughing owl
leatherhead
leptodactyl
lily-trotter
magpie-goose
meadow-pipit
mocking-bird
mulga parrot
Muscovy duck
nightingale
Pacific gull
plain-turkey
powerful-fowl
procellaria
pterodactyl
punchinello
quail-thrush
querguedule
rainbow-bird
reed bunting
reed sparrow
reed warbler
rhamphastos
rock warbler
scarlet ibis
scissor-bill
sea-pheasant
shell-parrot
shrike-robin
singing-bird
snow-bunting
snow-ortolan
soldier-bird

song sparrow
sparrowhawk
stone curlew
stone plover
storm petrel
tree-creeper
tree sparrow
tree swallow
wall-creeper
weaverfinch
whitethroat
whooper swan
wood creeper
wood-swallow
wood warbler
wren babbler
yellow robin

12

Adele penguin
adjutant bird
bronze pigeon
burrowing-owl
capercaillie
capercailzie
cardinal-bird
collared dove
crested grebe
cuckoo-shrike
curvirostral
dabbling duck
dentirostres
falcon-gentle
fairy penguin
fissirostres
flower pecker
golden oriole
golden plover
grass warbler
greylag goose
ground thrush
harvestgoose
hedge sparrow

honey-buzzard
honey-creeper
house sparrow
lanner falcon
Mandarin duck
marsh harrier
marsh warbler
missel-thrush
mistel-thrush
mourning-dove
musophagidae
nutmeg-pigeon
painted quail
pallid-cuckoo
peaceful dove
perching duck
pink cockatoo
razor-grinder
red-head finch
sage-thrasher
sedge warbler
serpent eater
shoveler duck
shrike-thrush
standard wing
stone-chatter
stone's-mickle
stormy petrel
stubble-goose
stubble-quail
swamp-harrier
tachydromian
tenuirosters
tiger-bittern
turbit-pigeon
turner-pigeon
umbrella bird
water-wagtail
wattle turkey
whip-poor-will
white goshawk
yellowhammer

13

adjutant stork
American eagle
Baltimore bird
barnacle goose
black cockatoo
carrier pigeon
coachwhip-bird
crested pigeon
crocodile bird
elephant birds
fairy bluebird
fantail pigeon
harlequin duck
Hawaiian goose
long-tailed tit
mistletoe-bird
musk parrakeet
owlet-nightjar
oystercatcher
passerine bird
plain-wanderer
recurviroster
red-waffle bird
rosella parrot
secretary bird
shining parrot
spider-catcher
stink-pheasant
swallow-shrike
tumbler-pigeon
turkey-buzzard
turkey vulture
whistling duck
white cockatoo
whooping crane
willow warbler
yellow bunting
yellow wagtail

14

babbling thrush
bearded vulture

bird of paradise
canvas-back duck
Darwin's finches
diamond sparrow
double-bar finch
Emperor penguin
golden pheasant
griffon vulture
horned screamer
king-lory parrot
Manx shearwater
mountain thrush
nankeen kestrel
owlet frog-mouth
plains wanderer
prairie-chicken
rhinoceros-bird
robin-redbreast
silver pheasant
spotted harrier
tawny frogmouth
welcome swallow
whistling eagle

15+

Baltimore oriole (15)
great crested grebe (17)
ivory-billed woodpecker (21)
laughing jackass (15)
passenger pigeon (15)
peregrine falcon (15)
Philippine eagle (15)
tyrant fly-catcher (16)

Adjectives

Bird	Adjective
bird	avian
crow	corvine
dove	columbine

eagle	aquiline
fowl	gallinaceous
parrot	psittacine
songbird	oscine
sparrow	paserine
swallow	hirundine
thrush	turdine

Cats

3

Rex

4

Manx

5

cream
smoke
tabby

6

birman
havana

7

Burmese
Persian
red self
Siamese
spotted
Turkish

8

Devon Rex
red tabby

9

blue cream

10

Abyssinian
brown tabby
chinchilla
Cornish Rex

11

blue Burmese
British blue
colourpoint
Russian blue
silver tabby

12

brown Burmese

13

chestnut brown
red Abyssinian
tortoiseshell

14

long haired blue
tortie and white

15

red-point Siamese

18+

blue-pointed Siamese (18)
chocolate-pointed Siamese (20)
lilac-pointed Siamese (19)
seal-pointed Siamese (18)
tabby-pointed Siamese (19)
tortie-point Siamese (18)

Dogs

3 and 4

chow
cur
lyam
lym
minx
peke
pom
pug
puli
pup
rach
rug
skye
tike
tyke

5

bitch
boxer
brach
cairn
corgi
dhole
dingo
hound
husky
laika
pi-dog
pooch
puppy
spitz
whelp

6

afghan
bandog
barbet
basset

beagle
borzoi
bow-wow
briard
canine
cocker
collie
Eskimo
gun-dog
jowler
kelpie
lap-dog
limmer
pariah
poodle
pug-dog
pye-dog
pyrame
ranger
ratter
saluki
setter
shough
talbot
toy dog

7

basenji
beardie
bird-dog
bulldog
clumber
deer-dog
dry-foot
griffon
harrier
lion-dog
lowchen
lurcher
Maltese
mastiff
mongrel
pointer

samoyed
sheltie
shih tzu
spaniel
starter
tarrier
terrier
tumbler
whippet
wolf-dog

8

Airedale
Alsatian
Blenheim
chow-chow
coach-dog
demi-wolf
Derby dog
Doberman
elkhound
field-dog
foxhound
hound-dog
house dog
keeshond
Labrador
malemute
papillon
Pekinese
St. Hubert
samoyede
sealyham
sheepdog
spitz dog
springer
turnspit
watchdog
water-dog

9

badger dog
boarhound

buckhound
chihuahua
dachshund
Dalmatian
deerhound
Eskimo dog
Great Dane
greyhound
harehound
Kerry blue
lhasa apso
limehound
Llewellyn
Molossian
Pekingese
police dog
red setter
retriever
St. Bernard
Schnauzer
staghound
wolfhound
yellow dog

10

Bedlington
bloodhound
Clydesdale
dachshound
elterwater
fox terrier
Iceland dog
Maltese dog
otter hound
Pomeranian
prairie dog
Rottweiler
schipperke
weimaraner
weimeraner
Welsh corgi
Welsh hound

11

Afghan hound
basset hound
Bruxelloise
bull mastiff
bull terrier
carriage dog
ibizan hound
Irish setter
Kerry beagle
King Charles
Skye terrier
wishtarwish

12

Belvoir hound
Cairn terrier
Dandy Dinmont
Finnish spitz
gazelle hound
German collie
Gordon setter
Irish spaniel
Irish terrier
Japanese chin
Newfoundland
Pharaoh hound
Saint Bernard
Saintongeois
shepherd's dog
silky terrier
water spaniel
Welsh terrier

13

affenpinscher
Alpine spaniel
border terrier
Boston terrier
cocker spaniel
Dandie Dinmont
English setter
French bulldog

Hungarian puli
Scotch terrier
southern hound
Sussex spaniel

14

clumber spaniel
German shepherd
Irish wolfhound
Norfolk spaniel
Tibetan mastiff

15

Aberdeen terrier
Airedale terrier
Alaskan Malamute
American pitbull
blue Gascon hound
Brussels griffon
Cuban bloodhound
Egyptian bassett
English springer
golden retriever
Highland terrier
Hungarian vizsla
Japanese spaniel
Lakeland terrier
Norfolk springer
Porcelaine hound
Pyrenean mastiff
Scottish terrier
Sealyham terrier
Siberian wolf-dog
springer spaniel
Thibetan mastiff

16

Kerry blue terrier
Pyrenean mountain
Shetland sheepdog
Yorkshire terrier

17

Belington terrier
Doberman pinscher
labrador retriever

18

Jack Russell terrier
King Charles spaniel
large munsterlander
old English sheepdog
Rhodesian ridgeback

20+

Dandie Dinmont terrier
Staffordshire bull
terrier
West Highland white
terrier
wirehaired pointing
griffon

Fish, Fossils, Marine Life and Shells

Fish, shellfish etc

2 and 3

bib
cod
dab
dar
eel
eft
fin
gar
ged
hag
id

ide
lob
lox
ray
roe
sar
sei
tai
tau

4

amia
bass
blay
bley
bret
brit
burt
cale
carp
chad
char
chub
chum
clam
coho
crab
cusk
dace
dare
dart
dorn
dory
elva
esox
fash
file
goby
grig
hake
huck
huso
jack

kelt
keta
ling
lipp
lomp
luce
mako
masu
moki
mort
newt
opah
orca
orfe
parr
peal
pike
pope
pout
quab
raun
rudd
ruff
sapo
scad
scar
scup
shad
snig
sole
tope
tuna
tusk
woof
zant

5

ablen
ablet
allis
angel
apode
banny

beroe
binny
blain
bleak
bleck
bogue
boops
bream
brill
charr
cisco
cobia
cohoe
cuddy
cudle
danio
doree
dorse
elops
elver
fleck
fusus
gadus
gibel
grunt
gummy
guppy
hilsa
julis
laker
loach
loche
maray
minim
molly
moray
morse
mugil
muray
murry
mysis
myxon
nacre

nurse
perai
perca
perch
phoca
piper
pogge
porgy
poulp
powan
prawn
reeve
roach
roker
ruffe
saith
salmo
sargo
saury
scrod
scurf
sepia
sewin
shark
skate
smelt
smolt
smout
smowt
snook
solen
sprag
sprat
sprod
squid
sudak
sweep
tench
tetra
toado
togue
torsk
troll

trout
tunny
twait
umber
whelk
whiff
witch

6

alburn
alevin
allice
anabas
angler
barbel
beakie
belone
beluga
blenny
blower
bonito
bounce
bowfin
braise
buckie
burbot
caplin
caranx
cepola
cheven
chevin
clupea
cockle
comber
conger
conner
cultch
cuttle
dagoba
dentex
diodon
doctor
Dorado

dugong
dun-cow
ellops
espada
finnan
gadoid
ganoid
gardon
ginkin
goramy
grilse
groper
gunnel
gurami
gurnet
hermit
hilsah
hussar
isopod
jerkin
keltie
kipper
launce
maigre
margot
marlin
meagre
medusa
megrim
milter
minnow
morgay
mud-eel
mullet
mussel
narwal
nereid
otaria
oyster
partan
pholas
plaice
pollan

porgie
poulpe
puffer
puller
quahog
redcap
red-cod
red-eye
remora
robalo
rochet
romero
roughy
ruffin
runner
sabalo
sadina
saithe
salmon
samlet
sander
sardel
sargus
sauger
saurel
saynay
scampi
scarus
scurff
sea-ape
sea-bat
sea-cat
sea-cow
sea-dog
sea-eel
sea-egg
sea-fox
sea-hog
sea-owl
sea-pad
sea-pig
sephen
shanny

shiner
shrimp
snacol
soosoo
sparid
sucker
tailor
tarpon
tarpum
tautog
tawtog
teredo
tiburo
tomcord
trygon
turbit
turbot
twaite
ulican
urchin
vendis
wapper
weever
whaler
winkle
wirrah
wrasse
zander
zeidae
zingel

7

abalone
acaleph
actinia
ale-wife
anchovy
asterid
batfish
bergylt
bloater
blue-cap
blue-eye

bocking	grampus	osseter
bonetta	grouper	pandore
box-fish	grundel	pegasus
brassie	grunter	pen-fish
bubbler	gudgeon	piddock
bummalo	gurnard	pig-fish
calamar	gwiniad	piranha
capelin	gwyniad	pointer
cat-fish	haddock	pollack
catodon	hagbolt	pollard
cetacea	hagfish	pollock
chimera	haireel	polypus
cichlid	halibut	pomfret
cidaris	herling	pompano
cod-fish	herring	quinnet
codling	hogfish	ratfish
copepod	homelyn	rat-tail
cow-fish	houting	red-fish
crabite	icefish	reef-eel
croaker	jewfish	ripsack
crucian	keeling	rock-cod
crusien	lampern	ronchil
cyprine	lamprey	ronquil
dog-fish	latchet	rorqual
dolphin	lobster	rotifer
drummer	long-tom	sand-eel
dun-fish	mahseer	sardine
echinus	manatee	sawfish
eel-fare	manchet	scallop
eel-pout	merling	schelly
escolar	monodon	scomber
fiddler	moon-eye	sculpin
fin-back	morwong	sea-bass
fin-fish	mud-fish	sea-bear
finnock	muraena	sea-calf
garfish	murexes	sea-fish
garpike	murices	sea-hare
garvock	narwhal	sea-lion
girrock	nautili	sea-pike
gladius	oar-fish	sea-slug
goldney	octopod	sea-wolf
gourami	octopus	shadine
gournet	old-wife	sillock

silurus
skegger
smerlin
snapper
sock-eye
spawner
sphyrna
squalus
sterlet
stripey
sun-fish
teleost
thwaite
top-knot
torgoch
torpedo
tub-fish
ulichon
umbrine
vendace
whiting
worm-eel
xippias

8

acalepha
albacore
albicore
ammodyte
anableps
anguilla
arapaima
arapunga
argonaut
asterias
band-fish
barnacle
bill fish
blue fish
boarfish
brisling
brotulid
buckling

bullhead
cachalot
cackerel
calamory
cave fish
cetacean
characin
chimaera
coalfish
corkwing
corystes
crawfish
crayfish
dapedium
dapedius
dealfish
devil ray
dragonet
drum-fish
eagle-ray
earshell
errantes
eulachon
exocetus
file-fish
fin-scale
fire-fish
flagtail
flatfish
flathead
flounder
forktail
fox-shark
frog-fish
gillaroo
gilt-head
glass-eel
goatfish
goldfish
graining
grayling
green eel
grub-fish

gymnotus
hair-tail
halicore
hand-fish
horn-beak
horn-fish
jentling
John Dory
jugulars
kelp-fish
king crab
king-fish
lady-fish
lancelet
land crab
lump-fish
lung-fish
mackerel
malarmat
manta ray
melanure
menhaden
monkfish
moon-fish
moray eel
mormyrus
nannygai
numbfish
ophidion
pennydog
phinnock
physalia
physeter
pickerel
pigmy-eel
pilchard
pipe-fish
piraruck
polyneme
Poor John
porpoise
raft-fish
redbelly

red perch
rhizopod
rock-bass
rock-cale
rock-fish
rockling
roncador
sail-fish
salt-fish
sand-fish
sardelle
saw-shark
scopelus
sea-acorn
sea-bream
sea-devil
sea-horse
sea-lemon
sea-louse
sea-perch
sea robin
sea snipe
shore-eel
siskiwit
skipjack
snake-eel
sparling
spelding
speldrin
speldron
spirling
springer
spurting
starfish
sting-ray
sturgeon
swamp eel
sun-bream
surf-fish
tarwhine
teraglin
testacea
thornbut

thrasher
thresher
toad-fish
trevally
troutlet
tusk-fish
ribbon-fish
water-fox
weed-fish
wolf-fish
zoophyte

9

acalephae
acipenser
angel-fish
Argentine
ascidians
asteroida
barracuda
blackfish
black sole
blue nurse
blue shark
blue sprat
bony bream
brandling
bulltrout
bummaloti
calamarys
ceratodus
chaetodon
cling-fish
cole-perch
conger eel
coral fish
coryphene
cover-clip
crampfish
crustacea
devil fish
dimyarian
dolphinet

echinidan
engraulis
finny-scad
fire-flair
fish-louse
fish-royal
fortesque
frost-fish
glass fish
globe-fish
goldsinny
golomynka
goose fish
grenadier
grey nurse
hard-belly
hardyhead
hippodame
houndfish
hybodonts
jaculator
jellyfish
John Dorée
jollytail
killifish
kingstone
lampshell
latimeria
lemon sole
murray cod
mango fish
menominee
murray cod
ostracian
pilot fish
placoderm
porbeagle
pyllopodo
razor fish
red mullet
red salmon
river crab
roundhead

sand-lance
saury-pike
schnapper
sea-mullet
sea-needle
sea-nettle
sea-spirit
sea-urchin
sheat-fish
silver-eel
spear-fish
stargazer
stingaree
sting-fish
stink-fish
stockfish
stomapoda
stone bass
stonefish
suctorian
surmullet
sweetlips
swordfish
sword tail
thorn-back
threadfin
tiffenbat
tigerfish
tittlebat
troutling
trumpeter
trunk fish
tunny fish
whitebait
whitefish
wobbegong
wreck fish
zebra fish

10

acornshell
amblyopsis
amphytrite

angel-shark
angler fish
archerfish
banstickle
barracoota
barracouta
basket fish
black bream
black whale
blind shark
blue groper
blue puller
Bombay duck
bottle-fish
bottle-nose
brown trout
butterfish
canolefish
cestracion
clouded eel
clypeaster
cock-paddle
coelacanth
cornet fish
cowanyoung
ctenoidans
cuttlefish
damsel fish
demoiselle
dragon-fish
echinoderm
fiddle-fish
fingerling
fistularia
flute-mouth
flying fish
ganoidians
garter fish
ghost-shark
giant toado
goblin-fish
great skate
grey mullet

groundling
guitar fish
hammerfish
hammerhead
hermit crab
holothuria
horseleech
knight-fish
loggerhead
lumpsucker
maskanonge
maskinonge
mirror dory
morris pike
Moses perch
mudskipper
needle fish
nurse shark
paddlefish
parrot-fish
pearl perch
periwinkle
pink salmon
pigmy perch
placodermi
purplefish
pycnodonts
rapier fish
red gurnard
red morwong
red rockcod
ribbon fish
ribbon worm
robbercrab
rudder-fish
Samsonfish
sand-hopper
sand-mullet
sandy sprat
scopelidae
sea-garfish
sea-leopard
sea poacher

sea-unicorn
shield fern
silver dory
silverfish
silverside
square-tail
squeteague
sturionian
sucker-fish
tailor-fish
tassel-fish
tiger shark
tongue-sole
triple-tail
turret-fish
velvet-fish
weaver-fish
whale-shark
white shark
yellow-tail
zebra shark

11

balance-fish
banded toado
bellows-fish
black-angler
blue-pointer
bridled goby
brineshrimp
brown-groper
brown-puller
calling-crab
carpet-shark
carp-gudgeon
chanda perch
chondrostei
common skate
common toado
crested goby
cycloidians
electric eel
electric ray

finner-whale
five-fingers
flying squid
goblin shark
golden perch
green turtle
gurnet perch
hatchetfish
herring-cale
hippocampus
holothurian
jackass-fish
javelin-fish
Jumping-Joey
kingsnapper
lantern fish
leatherskin
leopard-fish
lepidosiren
little tunny
man-o'-war fish
Moorish idol
orange perch
papersailor
peacock-fish
peacock-sole
pearl mussel
pearl oyster
pennant-fish
prickleback
pterichthys
rainbow-fish
red bullseye
red fire-fish
rock-whiting
salmon-trout
sand-whiting
school-shark
scleroderms
sea-cucumber
sea-elephant
sea-hedgehog
sea-scorpion

serpentfish
silver-belly
silver perch
silver toado
smooth toado
soldier-crab
soldier-fish
starry toado
stickleback
stonelifter
suckingfish
surgeon-fish
swallow-fish
tallegalane
triggerfish
trumpet-fish
wheelanimal
whistle-fish
wolf-herring

12

basking shark
black drummer
black rock-cod
blue trevally
coachwhip ray
cucumber-fish
dipterygians
dusky morwong
fan-tailed ray
fatherlasher
fighting-fish
forehead-fish
gargoyle-fish
giant herring
gray tusk-fish
oyster-blenny
painted saury
piked dog-fish
plectognathi
Plesiosaurus
rainbow-trout
rat-tailed ray

river garfish
rock flathead
scarlet bream
seaporcupine
sentinel crab
silver mullet
smooth angler
Stout Long-Tom

13

allports perch
banded-pigfish
barred-garfish
Barred Long-Tom
black king-fish
black-trevally
branchiostoma
climbing perch
dactylopterus
dusky flathead
entomostracan
findon-haddock
finnan-haddock
flying gurnard
giant boar-fish
horse-mackerel
leafy seahorse
leatherjacket
long-finned eel
magpie-morwong
marbled angler
mountain-trout
ox-eyed herring
paper nautilus
porcupine-fish
Red-Indian fish
salmon catfish
salt-water fish
sandpaper-fish
scarlet angler
Sergeant Baker
silver batfish
silver drummer

snub-nosed dart
southern tunny
spiny flathead
spiny seahorse
striped angler
thresher-shark
tiger-flathead

14

banded sea-perch
black stingaree
branchiostegan
brown-sweetlips
butterfly-bream
enaliosaurians
estuary cat-fish
Greenland-shark
Greenland-whale
king barracouta
king parrot-fish
little numbfish
Macquarie perch
many-banded sole
marine annelida
one-finned shark
painted gurnard
purple sea-perch
red gurnet-perch
river blackfish
short-finned eel
shovel-nosed ray
Slender Long-Tom
smooth flathead
spotted whiting
striped catfish
striped gudgeon
striped sea-pike
white horse-fish

15

acanthopterygii
Australian perch
Australian smelt

beaked coral-fish
bottle-nose shark
common stingaree
crusted flounder
crusted weed-fish
edriophthalmata
frigate mackerel
hairback herring
little cling-fish
little conger eel
long-finned perch
marbled flathead
painted dragonet
short sucker-fish
small-headed sole
smooth stingaree
spangled grunter
Spanish mackerel
spotted cat-shark
spotted eagle-ray
spotted pipe-fish
white-spotted ray

Fossils, shells, etc.

(f.s.) = fossil shell (s.) = shell

4 and 5

amber
auger
baler
chama (s)
chank (s)
conch (s)
cone (s)
donax (s)
drill (s)
galea

gaper (s)
murex (s)
nacre
ormer
peuce
razor (s)
snail (s)
tooth (s)
tulip (s)
Venus (s)
whelk (s)

6

bonnet (s)
buckle (s.)
chiton (s)
cockle (s.)
cowrie
crinoid
fornix (s)
helmet (s)
jingle (s)
limpet (s)
macoma (s)
matrix
mussel (s)
natica
nerite
Ogygia
olenus
oyster (s)
quahog (s)
seaear
tellin (s)
triton (s)
trivea (s)
turban (s.)
volute (s)
winkle (s.)

7

abalone (s.)
artemis (s)

astarte (s)
Babylon
crabite
crinoid
discoid (s)
fungite
muscite
neptune (s)
ovulite
piddock (s)
scallop (s)
sundial
zoolite

8

ammonite (f.s.)
argonaut (s)
ark shell (s)
balanite
buccinum (s)
capstone
ceratite
choanite
cololite
conchite (f.s.)
dendrite
dog whelk (s)
ear shell (s)
echinite
epiornis
escallop (s)
favosite
fig shell (s)
galerite
janthina (s)
mangelia (s)
muricite
mytilite
nautilus (s.)
penshell (s)
phyllite
ram's horn (f.s.)
retinite

scaphite (f.s)
seashell
sea snail
solenite (f.s.)
strombus (s)
testacel (s)
topshell (s)
trochite
tunshell (s)
volulite (f.s.)
volutite (f.s.)

9

aepiornis
alasmodon (s)
alcyonite
belemnite
buccinite (f.s.)
cancerite
carpolite
clam shell (s.)
comb shell (s.)
cone shell (s.)
Conularia
copralite
corallite
crow stone
dicynodon
encrinite
fan mussel (s.)
file shell (s.)
foot shell (s.)
frog shell (s.)
giant clam (s.)
harp shell (s.)
hippurite
horn shell (s.)
lima shell (s.)
lithocarp
lithophyl
marsupite
miliolite (f.s.)
moon shell (s.)

moon snail
muscalite (f.s.)
nautilite
nummulite
ostracite (f.s.)
palmacite
patellite (f.s.)
polymorphe (s.)
reliquiae
rock-borer (s.)
serpulite (f.s.)
slip shell (s.)
star shell (s.)
stone lily
strombite (f.s.)
tellinite (f.s.)
trilobite
turbinite (f.s.)
turrilite (f.s.)
tusk shell (s.)

10

agate shell
batrachite
canoe shell (s.)
confervite
dendrolite
entomolite
entrochite
euomphalus (f.s.)
gyrogonite
odontolite
palmacites
periwinkle (s.)
razor shell (s.)
screw shell (s.)
snake stone (f.s.)
tiger shell (s.)
tubiporite
ulodendron
wentletrap (s.)
wing oyster (s.)
xanthidium

11

asterialite
asterolepis
basket shell (s.)
carpet shell (s.)
cetotolites
cheirolepis
dinotherium
fairy stones
finger shell (s.)
finger stone
furrowshell (s.)
gongiatites (f.s.)
helmet shell (s.)
ichthyolite
madreporite
margin shell
milleporite
mohair shell (s.)
needle shell (s.)
needle whelk (s)
ornitholite
oyster drill (s.)
rhyncholite
sting winkle (s.)
strobolites
sunset shell (s.)
tiger cowrie (s.)
trough shell (s.)
turtle shell (s.)

12

amphibiolite
brocade shell (s.)
Chinama's hat (s.)
cornu-ammonis (f.s.)
deinotherium
figured stone
holoptychis
Hungarian cap (s.)
lantern shell (s.)
macrotherium

megalichthys
pandora shell (s.)
pelican's foot (s.)
pentacrinite
saddle oyster (s.)
serpentstone
slipper shell (s.)
spindle shell (s.)
sundial shell (s.)
trumpet shell (s)
zamiostrobus

13 and 14

bothrodendron (13)
carboniferous (13)
conchyliaceous (f.s.)
(14)
dolichosaurus (13)
lepidodendron (13)
lithoglyphite (13)
nacreous shells (s.) (14)
necklace shell (s.) (13)
palaeontology (13)
porphyry shell (s.) (13)
staircase shell (s.) (14)
syringodendron (14)
woodcock shell (s.)
(13)

Marine growths, algae, mosses etc.

4 - 6

algae (5)
astrea (6)
coral (5)
dulse (5)
fungia (6)

kelp (4)
laver (5)
limpet (6)
mussel (6)
naiads (6)
polyp (5)
sponge (6)
tang (4)
tangle (6)
varec (5)
ware (4)
wrack (5)

7 and 8

actinia (7)
agar agar (8
alcyonic (8)
astraea (7)
badioga (7)
barnacle (8)
blubber (7)
calycle (7)
eschara (7)
fungite (7)
gulf weed (8)
polypary (8)
polypus (7)
porifera (8)
red algae (8)
red coral (8)
sea moss (7)
seaweed (7
seawrack (8
tubipore (8
zoophyte (8)

9

alcyoneae
alcyonite
bathybius
blue algae
ecardines
Irish moss

madrepore
millepore
nullipore
pink coral
sea nettle
zoophytes

10 and over

abrotanoid (10
acorn barnacle (13)
alva marina (10)
animal flower (12)
bladder kelp (11)
bladderwrack (12)
brown algae (10
coral zoophytes (14)
goose barnacle (13)
lithodendron (12
lithogenous (11)
lithophyte (10)
marine plants (12)
milliporite (11)
sea anemone (10)
tubiporite (10)
ulotrichales (12
utricularia (11)

Molluscs and seashells

3 - 5

bulla
chank
clam
clio
ensis
fusus
gaper
harp
helix

murex
mya
sepia
slug
snail
solen
spat
squid
sun
tulip
unio
venus
whelk

6

buckie
chiton
cockle
cuttle
dodman
dollum
isopod
limpet
loligo
mantle
mussel
naiads
nerite
nutmeg
ostrea
oyster
pecten
quahog
sea ear
teredo
triton
voluta
winkle

7

acerans
actaeon
aplysia

ascidia
balanus
bivalve
diceras
eschera
etheria
glaucus
junonia
mollusc
mytilus
nauplii
octopod
octopus
patella
paddock
polio
purport
quahog
scallop
scallop
sea hare
spiral
spindly
sundial
toccata
tellina
toheroa

8

anodonta
argonaut
blue-nose
buccinum
decapoda
dye murex
lion's paw
Limnaeid
mollusca
nautilus
noble pen
ostracea
pagurian
pedireme

pheasant
sea lemon
spirifer
strombus
teredine
tridacna
tunicary
Turk's cup

9

acephalan
angel wing
bat volute
bursa frog
clausilia
dentalium
dolabella
ecardines
gastropod
giant clam
hodmandod
lithodome
ostracian
pink conch
pondsnail
pteropods
rota murex
scaphopod
shellfish
spiny vase
telescope
tent olive
wedge clam

10

amphineura
amphitrite
blue mussel
brachiopod
cameo helmt
cephalopod
coat-of-mail
conchifera

crown conch
cuttlefish
date-mussel
delphinula
drupe snail
eyed cowrie
haliotidae
heteropoda
papery rapa
periwinkle
qhahog clam
razorshell
scaled worm
stone borer
stone eater
winged frog

11

bear paw clam
clione snail
dragon shell
fasciolaria
frons oyster
gasteropoda
green turban
heart cockle
music volute
onyx slipper
ostrich foot
paper bubble
pearl oyster
river oyster
sacred chank
siphonifers
terebratula
textile cone
tiger cowrie
trachelipod

12

amoria volute
Atlantic cone
boring mussel

Florida miter
gaudy asaphis
golden cowrie
golden tellin
lima file clam
money cowries
Pacific auger
partridge tun
pelican's foot
Scotch bonnet
spindleshell
spiked limpet
spindle tibia

13

angular volute
Babylon turrid
bleeding tooth
cardinal miter
commercial top
costate cockle
entomostomata
fighting conch
geography cone
jackknife clam
Japanese cones
lamellibranch
paper nautilus
prickly helmet
ridges abalone
spiral Babylon
sunrise tellin
turkey wing ark
Venus comb clam

14

channeled whelk

distaff spindle
elegant fimbria
Episcopal miter
imperial volute
Indonesian clam
leucodon cowrie
Lewis' moon snail
lightening whelk
Panamanian cone
Philippine cone
Polynesian cone
tapestry turban
triton's trumpet
Venus comb murex

15

bittersweet clam
bull-mouth helmet
cyclobranchiata
Japanese carrier
New England whelk
Panamanian auger
pilgrim's scallop
sunburst carrier
tectibranchiata
turritella snail
watering pot clam
West Indian chank
West African cone

16

Asian moon scallop
Atlantic surf clam
donkey ear abalone
edible bay scallop
frilled dogwinkle
glory-of-India cone

orange-mouth olive
pagoda periwinkle
perplicate volute
pink-mouthed murex
roostertail conch
wedding cake Venus

17

Australian trumpet
chambered nautilus
Florida horse conch
Pacific wing oyster
Santa Cruz latiaxis
violet spider conch

18

Atlantic deer cowrie
giant knobbed cerith
glory-of-the-seas cone
great keyhole limpet
Pacific grinning tun
precious wentle-trap
white spotted margin

19

Tankerville's ancilla

20+

arthritic spider conch
Atlantic thorny oyster
colourful Atlantic moon
elephant's snout volute
imbricate cup-and-
saucer
miraculous thatcheria

Gender, Collective Terms etc

Animals and Gender

Animal	Male	Female
antelope	buck	doe
ass	jackass	jennyass
badger	boar	sow
bear	boar	sow
bobcat	tom	lioness
buffalo	bull	cow
camel	bull	cow
caribou	stag	doe
cat	tom	queen
cattle	bull	cow
chicken	cock	hen
cougar	tom	lioness
coyote	dog	bitch
deer	stag	doe
dog	dog	bitch
donkey	jackass	jennyass
duck	drake	duck
eland	bull	cow
elephant	bull	cow
ferret	jack	jill
fish	cock	hen
fox	fox	vixen
giraffe	bull	cow
goat	billygoat	nannygoat
goose	gander	goose
hare	buck	doe
hartebeast	bull	cow
horse	stallion	mare
impala	ram	ewe
jackrabbit	buck	doe
kangaroo	buck	doe
leopard	leopard	leopardess
lion	lion	lioness
moose	bull	cow
ox	bullock	cow
peacock	peacock	peahen
pheasant	cock	hen

Animal	Male	Female
pig	boar	sow
rhinoceros	bull	cow
roedeer	roebuck	doedeer
seal	bull	cow
sheep	ram	ewe
swan	cob	pen
tiger	tiger	tigress
walrus	bull	cow
weasel	boar	cow
whale	bull	cow
wolf	dog	bitch
zebra	stallion	mare

Adjectives

Creature	Adjective	Creature	Adjective
bear	ursine	hircinegoose	anserine
bee	apian	hare	leporine
bull	taurine	horse	equine
cat	feline	lion	leoline
chipmunk	sciurine	lizard	saurian
civet	viverrine	lobster	crustacean or
cow	bovine		crustaceous
crab	crustacean	mongoose	viverrine
	or crustaceous	monkey	simian
deer	cervid or cervine	mouse	murine
dog	canine	pig	porcine
dolphin	cetacean or	porpoise	cetacean or
	cetaceous		cetaceous
donkey	asinine	rat	murine
eel	anguilliform	seal	otarid; phocine
elephant	elephantine	sea lion	otarid
ferret	musteline	shrimp	crustacean or
fish	piscine		crustaceous
fowl	gallinaceous	skunk	musteline
fox	vulpine	snake	anguine; colubrine;
frog	batrachian		ophidian;
goat	caprine;		serpentine

Creature	Adjective
spider	arachnoid
squirrel	sciurine
terrapin	chelonian
toad	batrachian
tortoise	chelonian
turtle	chelonian
viper	viperine or viperous
weasel	musteline
whale	cetacean or cetaceous
wolf	lupine
worm	vermiform

Animals and their Young

Animal	Young
antelope	kid
badger	cub
bear	cub
beaver	kitten
bobcat	kitten
buffalo	calf
camel	calf
caribou	fawn
cat	kitten
cattle	calf
chicken	chick
cougar	kitten
coyote	puppy
deer	fawn
dog	puppy
duck	duckling
eland	calf
elephant	calf
elk	calf
fish	fry
frog	tadpole
fox	cub

Animal	Young
giraffe	calf
goat	kid
goose	gosling
hare	leveret
hartebeast	calf
hawk	chick
horse	foal
jackrabbit	kitten
kangaroo	joey
leopard	cub
lion	cub
monkey	infant
ox	stot
pheasant	chick
pig	piglet
rhinoceros	calf
roedeer	kid
seal	calf
sheep	lamb
skunk	kitten
swan	cygnet
tiger	cub
toad	tadpole
walrus	cub
weasel	kit
whale	calf
wolf	cub
zebra	foal

Collective Terms

Animal	Collective Terms
antelope	herd
ape	shrewdness
ass	drove
badger	cete
bear	sleuth
beaver	colony
bloodhound	sute

Animal	Collective Terms	Animal	Collective Terms
boar	sounder	hawk	cast
buffalo	herd	horse	herd
camel	train	impala	couple
caribou	herd	jackrabbit	husk
cat	cluster	kangaroo	troop
cattle	herd	kine	drove
chamois	herd	leopard	leap
chicken	flock	lion	pride
chough	chattering	mole	labour
colt	rag	monkey	troop
coot	fleet	moose	herd
coyote	pack	mouse	nest
deer	herd	ox	team
dog	pack	peacock	pride
donkey	drove	pheasant	brood
duck	paddling	pig	trip
eland	herd	rhinoceros	crash
elephant	herd	roedeer	bevy
elk	gang	rook	building
ferret	business	seal	pod
fish	school	sheep	flock
fox	troop	snake	knot
gelding	brace	toad	nest
giraffe	herd	walrus	pod
goat	flock	weasel	pack
goose	gaggle	whale	school
hare	huske	wolf	pack
hartebeast	herd	zebra	herd

Insects, Butterflies and Moths

3

ant
bee
bot
bug
cob
dor
fly
tau

4

flea
gnat
grub
lice
mite
pupa
slug
tick
wasp

5

zimb

aphid
borer
brize
comma
drone
emmet
fluke
imago
larva

louse
midge
ox-fly
pulex

termes
thrips
weevil
woubit

tin-worm
wasp-fly
wood-ant

6

acarid
acarus
ash-fly
bedbug
beetle
blatta
bot fly
burnet
capsid
chafer
chigoe
cicada
cimbex
cocoon
crabro
cynips
dayfly
dog-fly
dorfly
earwig
eupoda
evania
gad fly
hop-fly
hornet
locust
looper
maggot
mantis
mayfly
midget
motuca
mygale
sawfly
scarab
sow-bug
squill

7

acerans
antenna
ant-hill
antlion
aphids
army ant
bean fly
bee moth
blowfly
boat fly
bruchus
bull-bee
bull fly
carabus
cricket
cutworm
deer-fly
diopsis
diptera
duck-ant
fig gnat
fire ant
firefly
hexapod
hine-bee
horn-bug
hornfly
katydid
lobworm
lugworm
microbe
protura
sandfly
sawback
shad fly
stylops
termite

8

adder-fly
alderfly
antennae
arachnid
army worm
black ant
blackfly
bookworm
calandra
case-worm
cranefly
dog-louse
drake-fly
firebrat
flatworm
fruit fly
gall gnat
gall wasp
glow worm
greenfly
honey ant
honeybee
horntail
horse fly
housefly
hoverfly
lacewing
ladybird
mason bee
mealworm
mealybug
milliped
mosquito
multiped
night-fly
nocturna
parasite
phasmida

plant bug
queen ant
queen bee
sand flea
sheep ked
silkworm
shipworm
snakefly
stink bug
stonefly
tapeworm
tung-tung
water bug
white ant
white fly
wireworm
woodlice
wood-mite
woodwasp
woodworm

9

Amazon ant
anopheles
aphid pest
bloodworm
booklouse
breezefly
bumblebee
burrel fly
buzzardet
caddis fly
canker-fly
centipede
cheesfly
chrysalis
chinch bug
churrworm
cochineal
cockroach
coffeebug
corn borer
crab-louse

damselfly
dobsonfly
dor beetle
dragonfly
driver ant
dumbledor
earthworm
flying ant
forest-fly
gall midge
ground bug
hornet fly
humble bee
ichneumon
lac insect
longicorn
membracid
millipede
oil beetle
orange-bug
orange-tip
plant-lice
rug-weevil
robber fly
screwworm
sheep tick
shield bug
squash-bug
sugar-mite
tree-louse
tsetse fly
tumblebug
turnip-fly
warble fly
water flea
wax insect
whirligig
whirlygig
wood louse
worker ant
worker bee

10

bark beetle
blue bottle
boll weevil
cankerworm
cockchafer
coleoptera
corn beetle
digger wasp
drosophila
dung beetle
fan-cricket
flea beetle
froghoppe
harvest bug
hessian fly
jigger flea
June beetle
leaf beetle
leaf hopper
leaf insect
phylloxera
pine-weevil
plant-louse
pond skater
potter wasp
rove beetle
sand-hopper
silverfish
Spanish fly
spider wasp
spittlebug
springtail
stag beetle
treehopper
turnipflea
webspinner
wheat midge
woolly bear

11

assassin bug
auger beetle

backswimmer
balm cricket
black beetle
bristletail
buffalo gnat
bush cricket
cantharidin
caterpillar
click beetle
flour weevil
grain beetle
grasshopper
green-bottle
mole cricket
plant hopper
scale insect
scorpion fly
sponge-flies
stick insect
tiger beetle
timber borer
water beetle
water-skater
wood-fretter

12

cactoblastis
carpenter ant
carpenter bee
carpet beetle
diving beetle
flower-beetle
ground beetle
Hercules moth
milk-white ant
nightcrawler
pinhole-borer
scarab beetle
sexton beetle
spring beetle
spruce sawfly
water boatman
water strider

13

blister beetle
burying beetle
carpenter's bee
cotton stainer
daddy longlegs
diamond beetle
elm bark beetle
fig-leaf beetle
giant water bug
goliath beetle
jumping-spider
leafcutter ant
leafcutter bee
lime-tree borer
mangold beetle
praying mantis
shot-hole borer
slender-weevil
soldier beetle
water scorpion

14+

ambrosia beetle
bombardier beetle
cabbage root fly
Colorado beetle
cuckoo-spit insect
darkling beetle
death-watch beetle
devil's coach house
fig-branch borer
furniture beetle
Hercules beetle
ironbark saw-fly
serricorn beetle
slave-making ant
tortoise beetle

Butterflies

3 and 4

owl
blue
leaf
monk

5

argus
brown
dryad
friar
heath
joker
nymph
satyr
snout
white
zebra

6

acraea
Apollo
copper
diadem
glider
hermit
morpho

7

admiral
festoon
leopard
monarch
ringlet
skipper
sulphur

8

birdwing

black eye
black-tip
cardinal
charaxes
cymothoe
grayling
milkweed

9

atlas blue
bath white
brimstone
Cleopatra
commodore
golden tip
hackberry
metalmark
orange tip
swordtail
wall brown
wood white

10

Adonis blue
Arctic blue
Arran brown
black satyr
bush beauty
crimson tip
fritillary
gatekeeper
grass jewel
hairstreak
large white
plain tiger
red admiral
silver-line
small white

11

Amanda's blue
forest queen
grass yellow

meadow brown
painted lady
Parnassians
swallowtail

12

dotted border
map butterfly
marbled white
speckled wood
white admiral

13

clouded yellow
chalk hill blue
pearl crescent
purple emperor
tortoiseshell
woodland brown

14

African migrant
comma butterfly
lemon traveller
mountain beauty
painted empress

15+

Camberwell beauty
great sooty satyr
mother-of-pearl blue
nettle-tree butterfly
peacock butterfly
two-tailed pasha

Moths

2 and 3

IO
owl

4

goat
hawk
puss

5

atlas
eggar
fairy
ghost
gypsy
owlet
regal
swift
tiger
yucca

6

burnet
calico
ermine
lappet

7

bagworm
clothes
Emperor
flannel
pyralid
tussock
uranias

8

cinnabar
forester
silkworm

9

ailanthus
brahmaeid
carpenter
clearwing

geometrid
salt marsh
Saturnid
underwing

10

black witch
leaf roller

11

hummingbird
olethreutid
pyromorphid

13

blinded sphinx
giant silkworm

14

death's head hawk
Pandora's sphinx

Reptiles and amphibians

3 - 5

aboma
adder
agama
anole
anura
apod
asp
aspic
boa
born
cobra
draco
eft
elaps
emys

evet
frog
gecko
guana
hydra
jiboa
kaa
krait
kufi
mamba
naga
naia
newt
olm
pama
pipa
rana
seps
siren
skink
snake
toad
tokay
varan
viper
waral
worm

6

agamid
anolis
caiman
cayman
daboia
dipsas
dragon
gavial
hassar
hydrus
iguana
karait
lizard
moloch

mugger
python
Sauria
taipan
triton
turtle
uraeus
vipera
worral
worrel
zaltys

7

axolotl
chelone
coluber
gharial
ghavial
hicatee
labarri
lacerta
langaha
monitor
ophidia
paddock
rattler
reptile
saurian
scincus
serpent
snapper
tadpole
testudo
tuatara
urodela
varanus
zonurus

8

acontias
amphibia
anaconda
asp viper

basilisk
bullfrog
cat snake
cerastes
chelonia
Congo eel
dinosaur
dragonet
fox snake
hatteria
hiccatee
horn toad
jararaca
keelback
lachesis
matamata
menopome
moccasin
pit viper
platanna
rat snake
red snake
ringhals
sand fish
sand toad
sea snake
slow-worm
terrapin
tortoise
tree frog
typhlops

9

alligator
batrachia
blind-worm
blue krait
boomslang
box turtle
caecilian
chameleon
chelonian
corn snake

crocodile
dart snake
eyed skink
galliwasp
giant frog
giant toad
green toad
hairy frog
hamadryad
horned asp
king cobra
king snake
marsh frog
Ophidians
pine snake
Pterosaur
puff adder
ring snake
terrapeen
tree snake
vine snake
wart snake
water newt
whip snake
white snake
wolf snake

10

amphibians
black mamba
black snake
bushmaster
chuckwalla
clawed frog
cockatrice
copperhead
coral snake
Cotylosaur
dabb lizard
death adder
dendrophis
Diplodocus
edible frog

eyed lizard
false viper
fer-de-lance
glass snake
grass snake
green mamba
green racer
green snake
hellbender
homorelaps
horned frog
horned toad
Mosasaurus
natterjack
night adder
Plesiosaur
pond tutrle
river snake
rock python
salamander
sand lizard
sea serpent
sidewinder
smooth newt
tic polonga
tiger snake
wall lizard
water pilot
water snake
worm lizard

11

amphisbaena
banded krait
black cayman
carpet viper
constrictor
cottonmouth
crested newt
diamondback
flying snake
Gaboon viper
gartersnake

gila monster
Goliath frog
green lizard
green turtle
horned viper
Ichthyosaur
Indian cobra
lace monitor
leopard frog
midwife toad
Ophiosaurus
Pterodactyl
rattlesnake
royal python
smooth snake
Stegosaurus
Surinam toad
thorn lizard
thorny devil
Triceratops
water lizard
water python

12

Brontosaurus
chained snake
chicken snake
flying lizard
green tree boa
herpetofauna
horned iguana
horned lizard
Hylaesaurus
Komodo dragon
leopard snake
pond tortoise

13 and over

aquatic lizard (13)
bearded lizard (13)
boa constrictor (14)
brown tree snake (14)
coach-whip snake (14)

cobra de capello (14)
Dolichosaurus (13)
egg-eating snakes (15)
fire salamander (14)
four-lined snake (14)
frilled lizard (13)
giant tortoise (13)
golden tree frog (14)
golden tree snake (15)
green pit viper (13)
green tree frog (13)
hawksbill turtle (14)
Himalayan viper (14)
horn-nosed viper (14)
Ichthyosaurus (13)
leatherback turtle (17)
long-nosed viper (14)
Nile crocodile (13)
mangrove snake (13)
monitor lizard (13)
painted terrapin (15)
rat-tailed snake (14)
Russell's viper (13)
saw-scaled viper (14)
schaapsticker (13)
snake-eyed skink (14)
snapping turtle (14)
soft-shelled turtle (17)
spade-foot toad (13)
spotted lizard (13)
Tyrannosaurus (13)
water moccasin (13)

Specific Animal Breeds

Horses and Ponies

3

cob
don

4

Arab
barb
fell
polo
russ

5

dales
fjord
hucul
konik
lokai
orlov
pinto
shire
tersk
timor
Welsh

6

albino
basuto
Exmoor
merens
morgan
tarpan
viatka

7

Caspian
comtois
criollo
furiosa
hackney
Jutland
llanero
mustang
noriker
quarter
sorraia

8

budeonny
camargue
Dartmoor
galiceno
Highland
Holstein
kabardin
karabair
karabakh
lusitano
palomino
Shetland

9

akhal-teke
alter-real
appaloosa
connemara
falabella
haflinger
knabstrup
New Forest
Oldenburg
percheron
schleswig

10

anadalusian
avelignese
Clydesdale
gelderland
Hanoverian
Irish draft
lipizzaner

11+

Cleveland bay (12)
novokirghiz (11)
Suffolk punch (12)
Tennessee walking (16)
thoroughbred (12)

Welsh mountain (13)

Points of a horse

cannon bone
cheek
chest
chestnut
chin groove
coffin bone
coronet
crest
croup
dock
elbow
ergot
feathers
fetlock
fetlock joint
flank
forearm
forelock
frog
gaskin
gullet
heel
hind quarters
hock
hook
knee
loin
mane
navicular bone
pastern
pedal bone
point of hip
point of shoulder
poll
ribs
shank
sheath
shoulder

splint bone
stifle
tail
tendon
windpipe
withers

Cattle

3

gir

5

Devon
Kerry
luing

6

Dexter
Jersey
Sussex

7

beefalo
brangus

8

Ayrshire
Friesian
Galloway
Guernsey
Hereford
Highland
limousin

9

charolais
shorthorn
Simmental

10

brown Swiss
Lincoln red
Murray grey
Welsh black

11

Jamaica hope
marchigiana

13

Aberdeen Angus
droughtmaster
Texas longhorn

Pigs

5

duroc
Welsh

8

pietrain
Tamworth

9

Berkshire
Hampshire

10

large white

15

Swedish landrace

17

British saddleback
Gloucester old spot

Sheep

4

lonk
mule
soay

5

cardy
chios
jacob
lleyn
morfe
texel

6

awassi
masham
minero
Romney

7

Cheviot
gotland
karakul
lacaune
Suffolk

8

herdwick
longmynd
polwarth
Portland
Shetland

9

Hebridean
longwools
oldenberg
rough fell
Swaledale
teeswater

10

corriedale
Dorset horn
Exmoor horn
poll Dorset

11

Manx loghtan
Wensleydale

13

Welsh mountain
Wiltshire horn

15

Fries Melkschaap

17

Scottish blackface

18

whitefaced woodland

Poultry

4

buff (goose)

5

maran (chicken)
pearl (guinea fowl)
pekin (duck)
roman (goose
Rouen (duck)
white (guinea fowl)

6

ancona (chicken)
Cayuga (duck)
embden (goose)

silkie (chicken)

7

African (goose)
Chinese (goose)
crested (duck)
Dorking (chicken)
leghorn (chicken)
Muscovy (duck)
pilgrim (goose)

8

lavender (guinea fowl)
Toulouse (goose)

9

Aylesbury (duck)
welsummer (chicken)

10

barnvelder (chicken)
beltsville (turkey)
bourbon red (turkey)
Indian game (chicken)
ross ranger (chicken)
Sebastopol (goose)

11

cuckoo maran (chicken)
light Sussex (chicken)

12

black Norfolk (turkey)
Indian runner (duck)
Narragansett (turkey)
Plymouth rock
(chicken)
white Holland (turkey)

13

buff Orpington (duck)
khaki Campbell (duck)
mammoth bronze

(turkey)
white Austrian (turkey)

14

black east indie (duck)
Rhode Island red
(chicken)
Welsh harlequin (duck)
white Wyandotte
(chicken)

15

Cambridge bronze
(turkey)

Cereals, grain etc.

3 and 4

bere
bigg
bran
corn
dari
dohi
dura
far
gram
malt
meal
oats
oca
poar
rice
rye
sago
tef
teff
zea

5

bajra
bajri
brank
durra
durum
emmer
ervum
fundi
grain
grama
grist
grout
maize
mummy
paddy
panic
pulse
rivet
spelt
straw
typha
wheat

6

barley
casava
darnel
dhurra
farina
groats
hominy
mealie
meslin
millet
muesli
nocake
raggee
shorts

7

corncob
rokeage

sorghum
tapioca
zea mays

8

espiotte
mangcorn
seed corn
semolina

9

arrowroot
buckwheat
garavance
middlings
pearl rice
pot barley
seed grain
sweet corn

10

barleycorn
barleymeal
Guinea corn
Indian corn

11

pearl barley
pearl millet
spring wheat
summer wheat
turkey wheat
winter barley
winter wheat

12

German millet
Indian millet
mountain rice
Scotch barley

Flowers

3 and 4

aloe
arum
balm
flag
geum
iris
ixia
lei
lily
lote
may
musk
pink
rabi
rose
sego
weld
whin
wold

5

agave
aspic
aster
avens
blite
briar
broom
canna
daisy
erica
faham
flora
gilia
gorse
gowan
henna
linum
lotus

lupin
orris
ox-eye
oxlip
padma
pagle
pansy
peony
petal
phlox
poker
poppy
sepal
stock
tansy
thyme
tulip
viola
yucca
yulan

6

acacia
acaena
acorus
alisma
alpine
alsike
arnica
azalea
balsam
bellis
bennet
borage
cactus
camass
cistus
clover
coleus
cosmea
cosmos
crants
crocus

dahlia
datura
fennel
iberis
kochia
lupine
madder
mallow
malope
mimosa
myrtle
nerine
nuphar
opulus
orchid
orchis
oxalis
paeony
paigle
reseda
rocket
rosula
salvia
scilla
sesame
silene
sundew
thrift
torana
tulipa
violet
wattle
zinnia

7

aconite
alonsoa
aloysia
alyssum
anchusa
anemone
begonia
blawort

blewert
blossom
bouquet
bugloss
campion
candock
catmint
chaplet
chelone
chicory
clarkia
cowslip
cup rose
cytisus
day lily
deutzia
dittany
dog rose
festoon
freesia
fuchsia
gazania
genista
gentian
gerbera
godetia
heather
honesty
hyacine
jacinth
jasmine
jessamy
jonquil
kingcup
lantana
linaria
lobelia
lupinus
marybud
may-lily
melissa
milfoil
mimulus

nelumbo
nemesia
nigella
nosegay
opuntia
papaver
petunia
picotee
primula
rambler
rampion
sea-pink
seringa
spiraea
statice
succory
syringa
tagetes
tea rose
thistle
tritoma
ursinia
verbena
vervain
witloof

8

abutilon
acanthus
achillia
ageratum
amaranth
angelica
arum lily
asphodel
aubretia
auricula
bartonia
bearsear
bedstraw
bignonia
bluebell
buddleia

calamint
camellia
capsicum
catchfly
cattleya
clematis
cockspur
cyclamen
daffodil
dianthus
dicentra
dropwort
erigeron
feverfew
foxglove
gardenia
geranium
gillyvor
girasole
gladiola
gladiole
glaucium
gloriosa
gloxinia
harebell
haresear
helenium
hepatica
hibiscus
hottonia
hyacinth
japonica
laburnum
larkspur
lavatera
lavender
lent-lily
magnolia
marigold
martagon
moss rose
musk rose
myosotis

nenuphar
noisette
nymphaea
oleander
phacetia
phormium
plumbago
pond lily
primrose
rock-rose
scabious
skull-cap
snowdrop
stapelia
starwort
sweetpea
tigridia
toad-flax
tuberose
turnsole
valerian
veronica
viscaria
wild rose
wisteria
woodbind
woodbine
xanthium

9

Aaron's-rod
achimines
amaryllis
anagallis
aquilegia
buttercup
calendula
campanula
candytuft
carnation
carthamus
celandine
cherry pie

China rose
cineraria
clove pink
cockscomb
colt's foot
columbine
composite
coreopsis
corn-poppy
dandelion
digitalis
dog violet
dove's foot
edelweiss
eglantine
forsythia
gessamine
gladiolus
golden rod
hellebore
hollyhock
hydrangea
jessamine
kniphofia
lotus lily
mayflower
meadowrne
monkshood
moon daisy
narcissus
nemophila
oenothera
pimpernel
polygonum
pyrethrum
remontant
rudbeckia
saxifrage
speedwell
spikenard
sunflower
tiger lily
twayblade

verbascum
water flag
waterlily
wolf's-bane

10

agapanthus
amaranthus
aspidistra
belladonna
bell flower
caffre lilly
calliopsis
China aster
chionodoxa
cinquefoil
coquelicot
cornflower
corn violet
crane's-bill
crow flower
damask rose
delphinium
Easter lily
fritillary
gaillardia
gelder rose
goatsbeard
golden drop
gypsophila
heart's-ease
helianthus
heliophila
heliotrope
immortelle
lady's-mock
limnanthes
marguerite
mayblossom
mignonette
nasturtium
nightshade
orange lily

ox-eye-daisy
penny-royal
pentstemon
periwinkle
poinsettia
polianthus
potentilla
ranunculus
snapdragon
sweet briar
thalictrum
wallflower
white poppy
wind flower

11

antirrhinum
blood flower
cabbage rose
calandrinia
calceolaria
cheiranthus
convallaria
convolvulus
cotoneaster
everlasting
featherstar
fig marigold
forget-me-not
gillyflower
globeflower
greendragon
guelder rose
helichrysum
honey-flower
honeysuckle
kidney-vetch
lady's mantle
London pride
loosestrife
love-in-a-mist
meadowsweet
Nancy pretty

pelargonium
pepper elder
poppy mallow
ragged robin
rambler rose
red-hot poker
schizanthus
sea lavender
spear flower
sweet rocket
sweet sultan
tiger flower
wild flowers
wood anemone
xeranthemum

12

apple blossom
autumn crocus
boraginaceae
bougainvilia
cuckoo-flower
heather bells
horn-of-plenty
Iceland poppy
Jacob's ladder
lady's slipper
none-so-pretty
old man's-beard
orange flower
pasque flower
pheasant's ego
rhododendron
salpiglossis
shirley poppy
snow in summer
Solomon's seal
sweet william
tradescantia
virgin's bower

13

alpine flowers

blanket flower
bleeding heart
bougainvillea
Bristol flower
cherry blossom
Christmas rose
chrysanthemum
creeping jenny
crown imperial
eschscholtzia
grape-hyacinth
huntsman's horn
orange blossom
passion flower
sweet calabash
traveller's joy
trumpet flower
water hyacinth

14
Canterbury bell
cardinal flower
lords and ladies
love-in-idleness
shepherd's purse

15
Christmas flower
lily of the valley
Michaelmas daisy
star of Bethlehem

Ferns

4
tree

5
royal

7
bracken
osmunda

8
lady fern
polypody
staghorn

9
bird's nest

10
cliffbrake
dryopteris
maidenhair
spleenwort

11
hart's tongue

Fruit

3 and 4
akee
bito
Cox
crab
date
fig
gage
gean
haw
hep
hip
kaki
kiwi
lime
mare

mast
musa
nut
ogen
pear
pepo
plum
pome
rasp
skeg
sloe
ugli
uva

5
abhal
agava
agave
akena
anana
apple
arnot
betel
cubeb
drupe
eleot
grape
grout
guava
lemon
lichi
mango
melon
merry
morel
morus
naras
olive
papaw
peach
pecan
prune
regma

ribes
rubus
whort
whurt

6

achene
almond
ananas
banana
beurré
biffin
cedrat
cherry
citron
citrus
cobnut
colmar
damson
drupel
durian
egriot
elk nut
ginger
groser
lichee
longan
loquat
lychee
mammee
medlar
muscat
narras
nelies
nutmeg
orange
papaya
pawpaw
peanut
pignut
pippin
pomelo
punica

quince
raisin
rennet
russet
samara
walnut
zapote

7

apricot
avocado
bilimbi
buckeye
bullace
capulin
cassava
catawba
cedrate
cheston
coconut
codling
corinth
costard
currant
deal-nut
dessert
dog-wood
etaerio
filbert
genipap
golding
hautboy
hog-plum
karatas
kumquat
litchee
mahaleb
malmsey
mayduke
mineola
morello
naartje
pompion

pumpkin
quashey
rhubarb
rizzart
rosehip
satsuma
soursop
sultana
tangelo
wilding
winesap

8

allspice
bayberry
beechnut
bergamot
betelnut
bilberry
breadnut
buckmast
burgamot
calabash
cat's-head
chestnut
citrange
coquilla
cream-nut
date-plum
dogberry
earthnut
earthpea
fenberry
fig-apple
fox grape
hastings
hazelnut
honeydew
ivory nut
japonica
jonathan
mandarin
may apple

minneola
mulberry
muscadel
muscatel
musk pear
oleaster
pearmain
plantain
prunello
quandong
queening
rambutan
shaddock
spondias
sweeting
tamarind
Valencia
whitsour
windfall

9

alkekengi
apple-john
aubergine
beechmast
blueberry
brazilnut
buck's horn
butternut
cantaloup
canteloup
carmelite
cherimoya
chokepear
corozo nut
crab-apple
cranberry
damascene
drupaceae
elvas plum
greengage
groundnut
haanepoot

hindberry
king apple
love apple
melocoton
mirabelle
monkey nut
muscadine
musk-apple
musk-melon
nectarine
nonpareil
ortanique
oxycoccus
persimmon
pineapple
pistachio
rambootan
rambostan
raspberry
star apple
tamarinds
tangerine
victorine
Worcester

10

adam's apple
bird cherry
blackberry
blackheart
breadfruit
cantaloupe
charentais
clementine
clingstone
corozo nuts
cream-fruit
damask plum
dried fruit
elderberry
florentine
gooseberry
granadilla

grapefruit
Indian date
loganberry
Madeira nut
mangosteen
marking nut
melocotoon
orange musk
pome-citron
pompelmous
queen apple
redcurrant
redstreak
sorbapple
stone fruit
strawberry
waterlemon
watermelon
wild cherry
winter pear

11

anchovy pear
bitter apple
blood orange
boysenberry
candleberry
China orange
chokecherry
coquilla nut
French berry
granny smith
huckleberry
hurtleberry
Jaffa orange
leathercoat
monkey bread
myrtle berry
navel orange
pomegranate
pompelmoose
quarrington

russet apple
scuppernong
winter apple

12

bitter almond
blackcurrant
chaumontelle
Chester grape
chocolate nut
cochineal fig
cooking apple
custard apple
mammeesapote
passionfruit
pistachio nut
serviceberry
Victoria plum
white currant
whortleberry
winter cherry
winter citron

13

alligator pear
Catherine pear
morello cherry
Seville orange

14

Barbados cherry
Blenheim orange
Cape gooseberry
conference pear
mandarin orange
preserved fruit

15

golden delicious

16

cornelian cherry

Fungi

4

cepe

5

morel
yeast

6

agaric
ink cap

7

amanita
blewits
boletus
candida
truffle

8

death cap
mushroom
puffball

9

cup fungus
earthstar
fly agaric
psilocybe
rust fungi
stinkhorn
toadstool

10

bread mould
champignon

11

ascomycetes
aspergillums
chanterelle

honey fungus
penecillium
slime moulds

13

bracket fungus

14

basid-iomycetes

15

parasol mushroom

Grasses, Sedges and Rushes

3

fog
oat
rye
tef

4

bent
corn
reed
rice
rush

5

brome
durra
maize
paddy
panic
sedge
spelt
wheat

6

bamboo
barley
darnel
fescue
fiorin
melick
millet
quitch
redtop
zoysia

7

bulrush
esparto
foxtail
papyrus
sorghum
wild oat

8

cutgrass
dog's-tail
oat-grass
reed mace
ryegrass
spartina
spinifex
teosinte
wild rice
woodrush

9

bluegrass
broomcorn
cocksfoot
cordgrass
crabgrass
gama grass
hair-grass
lyme grass
reed grass
star grass

sugar cane
wire grass

10

beach grass
beard grass
bunch grass
china grass
couch grass
herd's grass
Indian corn
Indian rice
lemon grass
quack grass
spear grass
sword grass

11

canary grass
cotton grass
finger grass
marram grass
meadow grass
pampas grass
switch grass
twitch grass
vernal grass

12

Bermuda grass
bristle grass
buffalo grass
feather grass
orchard grass
quaking grass
timothy grass
tussock grass
Yorkshire fog

13

elephant grass

15

Kentucky bluegrass

17

squirrel-tail grass

Plants

3

box
cos
ers
hay
hop
ivy
nep
oat
oca
pea
pia
poa
rue
rye
seg
tea
tef
tod
yam
zea

4

aira
akee
alfa
aloe
anil
arum
balm
bean
beet

bent	race	arnut
bigg	rami	aspic
bulb	rape	aster
cane	reed	avena
coca	rhea	bhang
coco	rice	brake
coix	root	brank
cole	rusa	briar
corn	rush	broom
crab	ruta	bugle
dari	sage	cacao
dill	sago	calla
diss	sida	canna
dock	slum	cicer
doob	sloe	clary
dorn	sola	dote
ecad	spud	clove
fern	star	couch
flag	tara	cress
flax	tare	cumin
gale	taro	cycad
gama	teff	daisy
geum	thea	dicot
goss	tree	dryas
hemp	tule	durra
herb	tutu	dwale
holm	ulex	erica
ilex	vine	eruca
iris	wald	ficus
jute	weed	fitch
kail	weld	fungi
kale	whin	furze
kali	woad	glaux
kans	wold	goman
leek	wort	gorse
ling		gourd
mint	**5**	grama
moss		grass
musa	agave	grias
musk	ajuga	henna
nard	algae	holly
peat	alpia	hosta
pipi	anise	kunai
	apium	

ledum
liana
liane
lotus
loufa
lupin
madia
maize
medic
melic
morel
moril
mucor
mudar
musci
napal
olive
orach
orpin
orris
oryza
oshac
osier
oxlip
paddy
palas
palea
panic
poker
radix
reate
rheum
roosa
rubia
rubus
runch
savin
savoy
scrog
sedge
shrub
sison
solah

starr
stipa
stole
sumac
swede
tacca
tamus
tansy
thorn
thyme
trapa
tucum
urena
vetch
vicia
vinca
viola
vitis
wahoo
wapon
wheat
whort
withy
wrack
yerba
yucca
yupon
zamia

6

acorus
alisma
amomum
aninga
annual
arabis
arbute
azalea
bamboo
barley
batata
bejuco
bennet

betony
biblus
borage
bryony
burnet
cactal
cactus
caltha
cassia
catnip
cicely
cicuta
cissus
cistus
clover
cockle
conium
conyza
cosmos
cowage
croton
cynara
daphne
darnel
dodder
eddoes
elaeis
endive
eringo
eryngo
exogen
fathen
fennel
ferula
fescue
filago
fimble
form
frutex
fungus
funkia
fustet
galium

garlic
garrya
gervan
gnetum
gromil
guills
henbit
hervea
hyssop
iberis
indigo
jawari
jujube
juncus
kalmia
kiekie
kousso
lichen
locust
lolium
loofah
lupine
luzula
madder
maguey
mallow
manioc
marram
matico
milium
millet
mimosa
myrica
myrtle
nardoo
nerium
nettle
nubbin
oilnut
orache
orchid
orchis
origan

osmund
oxalis
paigle
pampas
peanut
peplis
pepper
phleum
potato
privet
protea
quinoa
quitch
radish
raggee
rattan
redtop
reseda
rocket
ruscus
sabine
savine
savory
scilla
secale
sesame
sesban
seseli
smilax
sorrel
spurge
squash
squill
stolon
styrax
sumach
sundew
teasel
teazel
thrift
tutsan
urtica
viscum

wicker
yamboo
yarrow

7

absinth
aconite
alcanna
alhenna
all-good
all-heal
althaea
aquatic
arabine
arbutus
awlwort
azarole
barilla
bartram
begonia
bistort
bogbean
bracken
bramble
bugloss
bugwort
bulbule
bulrush
burdock
bur-reed
calamus
calypso
campion
cannach
caraway
carduus
cassada
cassado
cassava
catmint
chicory
clarkia
divers

clot-bur	heather	rhubarb
columba	hemlock	robinia
comfrey	henbane	ruderal
cowbane	herbage	saffron
cowhage	honesty	saligot
cow-itch	hop-bind	salsify
cowslip	hop-bine	salsola
cow-weed	hop-vine	sanicle
creeper	humulus	sarcina
cudbear	ipomaea	saw-wort
cudweed	jasmine	sencion
cup moss	Jew's ear	senecio
cytisus	jonquil	seringa
dionaea	juniper	solanum
dittany	karatas	sonchus
dogbane	kedlack	soybean
dog's rue	lobelia	spiraea
ear-wort	lucerne	sporule
ehretia	lychnis	statice
elatine	madwort	syringa
epacris	mahonica	tagetes
esparto	matweed	talipot
eugenia	melilot	taliput
euryale	monocot	tannier
euterpe	munjeet	thistle
felwort	mustard	tobacco
festuca	nonsuch	trefoil
ficaria	opuntia	truffle
figwort	panicum	turpeth
fitweed	papyrus	uncaria
foggage	pareira	vanilla
foxtail	parella	verbena
frogbit	parelle	vervain
fumaria	parsley	vetiver
funaria	primula	waratah
genista	pumpion	wcorara
gentian	pumpkin	zalacca
gerbera	quamash	zanonia
ginseng	quassia	zedoary
gladwyn	ragwort	zizania
gunnera	rambler	
gutwort	rampion	**8**
hardock	rhatany	
		acanthus

adiantum
agrimony
air plant
amaranth
amphigen
angelica
anthemis
asphodel
banewort
barberry
barometz
bearbind
bear's ear
bellwort
berberis
berberry
bignonia
bilberry
bindweed
bogberry
bogwhort
boxthorn
brassica
bullweed
bullwort
calamint
camomile
cannabis
capsicum
carraway
cassweed
catchfly
cat's tail
centaury
cerealia
cetraria
charlock
chayroot
choyroot
cinchona
cinnamon
cleavers
clematis

clubmoss
clubrush
cocculus
cockspur
cockweed
coleseed
cornflag
cornrose
costmary
cowberry
cowgrass
cow-wheat
crithmum
crow silk
cunjevoli
damewort
danewort
dewberry
diandria
dog briar
dog grass
dog's bane
dolichos
downweed
dropwort
duckmeat
duckweed
dumb-cane
earth nut
earth-pea
echinops
eggplant
eglatere
eleusine
epiphyte
erigeron
erisimum
euonymus
feverfew
finochio
fireweed
flaxweed
fleabane

fleawort
flixweed
foalfoot
foxglove
fragaria
fumitory
fussball
galangal
garcinia
gillenia
girasole
gloxinia
glumales
glumella
glyceria
goutweed
goutwort
gratiola
gromwell
hagtaper
harebell
hare's ear
hartwort
hawkweed
hawthorn
hibiscus
hockherb
ice plant
isnardia
knapweed
lacebark
laceleaf
larkspur
lavender
lungwort
lustwort
male fern
mandrake
mangrove
marjoram
matfelon
mat grass
may bloom

mezereon
milkweed
monocarp
moonseed
moonwort
mulewort
mushroom
myosotis
nonesuch
nut grass
oenanthe
oleander
oleaster
orchanet
paspalum
peat moss
phormium
pilewort
pink root
plantlet
plantule
plumbago
polygala
pond weed
prunella
puffball
purslane
putchock
red algae
rib grass
roccella
rock-rose
rosebush
rosemary
rye grass
sainfoin
saltwort
scammony
seedling
sengreen
septfoil
shamrock
simaruba

skull-cap
smallage
soapwort
sourdock
sow bread
stapelia
starwort
strobile
sun-plant
sweetsop
tamarack
tamarisk
tara fern
tarragon
tea plant
tentwort
tickweed
toad-flax
tree-fern
tremella
triticum
tuberose
turk's cap
turmeric
turnsole
valerian
veratrum
veronica
viburnum
victoria
wait-a-bit
wall-moss
wall-wort
wartwort
water-poa
wild oats
wild rose
wind seed
wistaria
with-wine
woodbine
woodroof
woodruff

woodsage
woodwart
wormwood
wrightia
xanthium
zingiber

9

abrotanum
aerophyte
alpargata
amaryllis
ampelosis
arbor-vine
arracacha
arsesmart
artemisia
artichoke
asclepias
balsamine
basil weed
bean caper
bearberry
bent grass
bird's foot
bloodroot
bloodwort
blue algae
briar-root
brooklime
brookmint
brookweed
broomcorn
broomrape
burstwort
butterbur
candytuft
canebrake
caprifole
cardamine
cariopsis
carrageen
caryopsis

celandine	dyer's weed	lark's heel
cetrarine	eglantine	laserwort
chamomile	elaeagnus	liquorice
chaparral	equisetum	liverwort
chaya root	euphorbia	meadow rue
cherry-bay	euphrasia	milk vetch
chickweed	evergreen	mistletoe
china root	evolvulus	monk's hood
choke-weed	eyebright	moschatel
cinerama	fenugreek	mousetail
club-grass	fever root	nelumbium
coal plant	feverwort	nepenthes
cockscomb	forsythia	nicotiana
cock's head	gamagrass	patchouli
colchicum	gelanthus	pellitory
colocynth	germander	penstemon
colt's foot	glasswort	pilularia
columbine	golden cup	pimpernel
commensal	golden rod	planticle
coniferae	goose corn	poison ivy
coral wort	goosefoot	poison oak
coriander	grapewort	pyracanth
corn poppy	grasspoly	pyrethrum
corn salad	greenweed	rafflesia
cotyledon	ground ivy	red clover
cramp-bark	groundnut	red pepper
crataegus	groundsel	rocambole
crowberry	hair grass	rockcress
cuckoo bud	hellebore	rosmarine
culver key	hoarhound	safflower
cyclamine	holly fern	saintfoin
decagynia	honeywort	saxifrage
decandria	horehound	smartweed
desert rod	horsefoot	snakeroot
didynamia	horsetail	snakeweed
digitalis	hypericum	snowberry
digitaria	Indian fig	soap plant
dittander	jessamine	socotrine
dockcress	Job's tears	spearmint
doob grass	kite's foot	spearwort
duck's foot	knee holly	speedwell
duck's meat	knot grass	spikenard
dulcamara	lady's muck	spirogyra

spoonwort
stellaria
stonecrop
sugarbeet
sugar cane
sun spurge
sweet flag
sweet john
sweet root
sweet rush
sweet wood
sweet wort
taraxacum
thallogen
theobroma
thorn-bush
toadstool
tonka bean
toothwort
tormentil
trifolium
twayblade
umbilicus
villarsia
wakerobin
wall cress
waterlath
waterwort
wax myrtle
whitecrop
widow wail
wincopipe
wolf's bane
wolf's claw
wormgrass
woundwort
xanthosia

10

Adam-and-Eve
adam's apple
adder grass
agrostemma

alabastrus
alexanders
amaranthus
angiosperm
arbor vitae
asarabacca
beccabunga
belladonna
bitterwort
brome grass
brown algae
butterbush
butterweed
butterwood
butterwort
candelilla
cascarilla
cassumunar
cellulares
cinquefoil
cloudberry
corn cockle
corn rocket
cotton rose
cottonweed
couch grass
cow parsley
crake berry
crotalaria
cuckoopint
devil's club
diadelphia
dog's fennel
dog's poison
dog's tongue
dracontium
elacampane
elaeococca
entophytes
eriocaulon
eriophoron
escallonia
eupatorium

fimble-hemp
friar's cowl
fritillary
furrow weed
gaultheria
globe daisy
globularia
goatsbeard
goldenhair
goldy locks
goose grass
granadilla
grass-wrack
gymnosperm
heartsease
helianthus
hemp neetle
herb robert
herds grass
honey stalk
Indian corn
Indian reed
Indian shot
Jew's mallow
kidney-wort
king's spear
knapbottle
lycopodium
maidenhair
manila hemp
may blossom
mock orange
mock privet
muscardine
nasturtium
nightshade
nipplewort
panic grass
passiflora
pennyroyal
pentstemon
peppermint
pepperwort

periwinkle
poker plant
potentilla
pyracantha
race ginger
ranunculus
rest harrow
rhein berry
rhinanthus
rose acacia
rose mallow
salicornia
saprophyte
sarracenia
setterwort
shave grass
silver weed
sneezewort
sow thistle
Spanish nut
speargrass
spleenwort
stavesacre
stitchwort
stonebreak
stork's bill
sweet briar
sweet brier
swine bread
swinegrass
swordgrass
throatwort
tiger's foot
touch-me-not
tragacanth
tropaeolum
Venus's comb
wall pepper
water plant
way thistle
whitethorn
wild indigo
willow herb

willow weed
witch hazel
wolf's peach
wood sorrel
yellow-root
yellow-wort

11

bear's breech
bishop's weed
blackbonnet
bottle gourd
brank ursine
calceolaria
calcyanthus
canary grass
chanterelle
coffee plant
contrayerva
convolvulus
corn parsley
cotton grass
cotton plant
crest marine
cuckoo's meat
dame's violet
dog's cabbage
dog's mercury
dracunculus
dragon's head
Dragon's wort
Dutch clover
erythronium
everlasting
fescue grass
fig marigold
finger grass
fuller's weed
gentianella
giant cactus
giant fennel
greendragon
guelder rose

hart's tongue
holy thistle
honeysuckle
humble plant
Iceland moss
Indian berry
Indian cress
indigo plant
ipecacuanha
kidney vetch
latticeleaf
laurustinus
London pride
marram grass
marsh mallow
meadow-sweet
milk thistle
millet grass
moon trefoil
moving plant
myoporaceae
oyster plant
pedicedaris
pelargonium
pepper grass
poison sumac
prickly pear
red-hot poker
ribbon grass
ripple grass
scurvy grass
sempervivum
serpentaria
snail clover
snail flower
sparrow wort
spergularia
stagger bush
star thistle
sulphur-wort
swallow-wort
sweet cicely
sweet cistus

sweet potato
swine's cress
thorough wax
tinkar's root
tonquin bean
tussac grass
twitch grass
viper's grass
water radish
water violet
welwitschia
white clover
white darnel
winter berry
winter bloom
winter cress
wintergreen
wood anemone
xanthoxylum
zygophyllum

12

adderstongue
adderstoupie
aerial plants
bladderwrack
buffalo grass
Christ's thorn
coloquintida
compass plant
corn marigold
cow s lungwort
custard apple
deadly carrot
dragon's blood
echinocactus
erythroxylon
feather grass
fennel flower
fool's parsley
German millet
globe thistle
hempagrimony

hound's tongue
Indian millet
Indian turnip
mangel wurzel
marsileaceae
melon thistle
palma christi
pickerel weed
pitcher plant
quaking grass
reindeer moss
rhododendron
sarsaparilla
snail trefoil
Solomon's seal
southern wood
Spanish broom
Spanish grass
sparrow-grass
spear thistle
strangleweed
swine thistle
telentospore
timothy grass
tobacco plant
torch thistle
Venus flytrap
Venus's sumack
vinegar plant
virgin's bower
water parsnip
water pitcher
water soldier
white campion
whitlow grass
whortleberry
wild williams
winter cherry
xanthorrhiza
yellow rattle

13

chrysanthemum

crown imperial
dog's-tail grass
elephant grass
elephant's foot
eschscholtzia
flowering fern
flowering rush
globe amaranth
golden thistle
Indian tobacco
meadow saffron
raspberry bush
Scotch thistle
spike lavender
summer cypress
sweet marjoram
traveller's joy
Venus's fly trap
vervain mallow
viper's bugloss
wall pennywort
water calamint
water crowfoot
water hyacinth
wayfaring tree

14

blackberry bush
blue couch grass
carline thistle
distaff thistle
fuller's thistle
giant groundsel
golden lungwort
golden mouse-ear
gooseberry bush
lords and ladies
mountain sorrel
prince's feather
sensitive plant
shepherd's pouch
shepherd's purse
shepherd's staff

snake's-head iris
Spanish bayonet
starch hyacinth
treacle mustard
wood nightshade

15

golden saxifrage
Italian rye grass
shepherd's needle
Venus's navelwort
virginia creeper
woody nightshade

Trees, shrubs, etc.

2 and 3

asa
ash
bay
bel
bo
box
elm
fig
fir
gum
haw
hip
hop
ita
ivy
may
nut
oak
sal
sap
tea
ti

tod
yew

4

acer
akee
aloe
amla
arar
arum
atap
bael
balm
bark
bass
bead
beam
bhel
bito
bixa
bole
cork
dali
dari
date
deal
dhak
doob
holm
huon
hura
ilex
jaca
kina
kiri
lana
leaf
lime
lote
milk
mowa
nipa
ombu

palm
pear
pine
pipe
plum
pole
rata
rimu
roan
root
rose
shea
sloe
sorb
teak
teil
toon
twig
ulex
upas
vine

5

abele
Abies
acorn
afara
agave
agila
alder
almug
amber
anise
anona
apple
arbor
areca
Argan
aspen
assai
balsa
Banga
beech

belah	oaken	aralia
birch	olive	arbute
bunya	osier	arolla
butea	palas	balata
cacao	palay	balsam
carob	papaw	bamboo
cedar	peach	banana
china	pecan	banyan
clove	picea	baobab
copse	pinon	bog-oak
coral	pipal	bombax
durio	plane	bo-tree
dwarf	plank	bottle
ebony	quina	branch
elder	roble	brazil
fagus	roots	buriti
fruit	rowan	busket
glade	salal	butter
glory	salix	button
grass	sally	carapa
grove	saman	carica
guava	sapan	cashew
hazel	smoke	catkin
henna	sumac	caudex
holly	taxus	cedrat
iroko	thorn	cembra
jambu	tilia	cerris
judas	tingi	cerrus
karri	trunk	cherry
kauri	tsuga	citron
kokra	tuart	coffee
kunai	tulip	cornel
larch	ulmus	daphne
lemon	walan	deodar
lilac	yucca	elaeis
macaw	yulan	emblic
mahwa	zamia	fustet
mango		fustic
maple	**6**	gatten
mulga	abroma	ginkgo
myall	acacia	gomuti
ngaio	alerce	gomuto
nyssa	almond	illipe

jarool	sumach	corylus
jarrah	sylvan	cowtree
kittul	tallow	cypress
kumbuk	tamanu	daddock
kunari	tewart	dammara
laurel	timber	determa
lignum	titoki	dogwood
linden	tooart	dottard
locust	tupelo	duramen
macoya	veneer	elk-wood
mallee	vinery	elm tree
manuka	walnut	emblica
mastic	wampee	enterpe
medlar	wattle	fan palm
mimosa	wicken	fig tree
miriti	willow	fir cone
myrtle	yampon	fir tree
nargil		foliage
nettle	**7**	genipap
obeche	ailanto	gum tree
orange	ambatch	hemlock
papaya	amboyna	hickory
pawpaw	aniseed	hog palm
pepper	Arbutus	holm oak
pinery	ash tree	jasmine
poplar	avocado	jugians
privet	banksia	juniper
quince	bay tree	king gum
redbud	blossom	kumquat
red fir	blue gum	lentisk
red gum	boxwood	logwood
ricker	bubinga	lumbang
rubber	buckeye	madrono
sallal	bursera	margosa
sallow	cabbage	mastich
sapota	camphor	moriche
sappan	cam-wood	moringa
saxaul	canella	nut pine
she-oak	catalpa	oakling
sissoo	champac	oak tree
sorrel	coconut	oil palm
souari	conifer	orchard
spruce	coquito	platane

pollard
quercus
quillai
red pine
redwood
saksaul
sandbox
sanders
sapling
sapwood
Sequoia
seringa
service
shallon
shittah
shittim
silk oak
snow-gum
sour-sop
spindle
sundari
tanghin
teatree
varnish
wallaba
wax palm
wax tree
wych-elm

8

agalloch
agalwood
alburnum
algaroba
allspice
arbuscle
ash grove
bass wood
beam tree
beachnut
benjamin
black gum
box elder

bud-scale
calabash
castanea
chestnut
cinchona
coco-palm
coco-tree
cork tree
coolabah
crab-tree
date palm
date plum
doom-palm
eucalypt
fraxinus
gardenia
giant gum
Groogroo
guaiacum
hardbeam
hawthorn
holly-oak
hornbeam
ironbark
ironwood
jack tree
jack wood
kingwood
laburnum
lacebark
lima wood
long jack
magnolia
mahogany
mangrove
manna-ash
mezereon
milk tree
mulberry
musk wood
mustaiba
oiticica
oleaster

palmetto
palm tree
pandanus
pear tree
pichurim
pinaster
pine cone
pine tree
pistacia
pockwood
quillaia
raintree
red cedar
red maple
rosemary
rosewood
royal oak
sago palm
sandarac
sapindus
scrub-oak
searwood
seedling
silky oak
sugar gum
swamp oak
sweet-bay
sweet gum
sycamore
tamarind
tamarisk
taxodium
toon-wood
tungtree
white ash
white fir
white gum
white oak
wistaria
witch-elm

9

adansonia

ailanthus
algarroba
aloes wood
alpine fir
angophora
araucaria
balsam fir
blackwood
brown pine
buckthorn
butternut
calambour
caliatour
caliature
china tree
chincapin
courbaril
crab apple
Cupressus
deciduous
erythrine
evergreen
forest oak
fruit tree
grapevine
greenwood
ground ash
ground oak
hackberry
ivory palm
jacaranda
Judas tree
kokrawood
lance wood
lentiscus
maracauba
mustahiba
paper bark
persimmon
pistachio
plane tree
quickbeam
rowan tree

sandarach
sapan wood
sapodilla
saskatoon
sassafras
satinwood
Scotch elm
Scotch fir
screw-pine
scrogbush
shade tree
shell-bark
silver fir
sloethorn
snake-wood
sour-gourd
spicewood
stone pine
suradanni
terebinth
thorn tree
tigerwood
toothache
touch-wood
tulip tree
whitebeam
white pine
whitewood
woodlayer
yacca wood
zebra wood

10

agollochum
almond tree
artocarpus
balaustine
blackthorn
blue spruce
brazilwood
breadfruit
bunji-bunji
bunya-bunya

burra-murra
butter tree
coastal-tea
coccomilia
coniferous
cotton tree
cottonwood
Douglas fir
eucalyptus
fiddle wood
flindersia
flooded gum
garlic-pear
green-heart
hackmatack
holly berry
Indian date
japati palm
kunai grass
letter wood
lilly-pilly
manchineel
mangosteen
orange-ball
orange wood
palisander
paper birch
pine needle
prickly ash
quercitron
redsanders
sandalwood
sand-cherry
sand-myrtle
Scotch pine
silk-cotton
silver-bell
sneeze-wood
Spanish fir
strawberry
sugar-maple
swamp maple
tall wattle

thyme wood
weeping ash
white cedar
white thorn
wild cherry
witch hazel
woolly butt
yellow-wood

11

Algerian fir
bean trefoil
black walnut
black wattle
black willow
bottle-brush
cedar wattle
chrysobalan
coconut palm
cootamundra
copper beech
cypress pine
elaeocarpus
eriodendron
golden chain
golden mohur
hoary poplar
honey locust
Japan laurel
leper-wattle
lignum vitae
mountain ash
pandanaceae
phoenix-palm
pomegranate
quicken tree
red-iron bark
red mahogany
sideroxylon
silver birch
stringybark
white poplar
white spruce

white willow

12

almond willow
benjamin-tree
betel-nut palm
caryophyllus
crow's-foot elm
cucumber tree
custard apple
flowering ash
golden waffle
horse-chestnut
monkey-puzzle
Norway spruce
silver-waffle
Spanish cedar
tree of heaven
umbrella palm
virgin's-bower
weeping birch
welllngtonia
white cypress
winter cherry
xylobalsamum

13

bird's-eye maple
campeachy wood
Christmas tree
cornus florida
dog-wood waffle
horse-chestnut
Japanese cedar
partridge wood
toxicodendron
weeping willow

14

Cedar of Lebanon
galactodendron
sunshine wattle

15

Spanish chestnut
trembling poplar

Vegetables

3 and 4

bean
beet
cole
corn
faba
kale
leek
lima
neep
oca
okra
pea(s)
sage
soy(a)
spud
urd
yam

5

caper
chard
chick
chili
chive
cibol
colza
cress
fitch
gourd
maize
navew
onion
orach

pease
pulse
savoy
swede

6

carrot
celery
daucus
endive
fennel
garlic
girkin
greens
lentil
marrow
murphy
nettle
orache
porret
potato
pratie
radish
sprout
squash
tomato
turnip

7

batatas
cabbage
cardoon
chicory
frijole
gherkin
haricot
hotspur
lactuca
lettuce
mustard
parsley
parsnip
pea bean

peppers
pimento
pompion
pumpkin
salsify
seakale
shallot
skirret
spinach
sprouts
zanonia

8

allspice
beetrave
beetroot
borecole
broccoli
capsicum
celeriac
chickpea
colewort
cucumber
eggplant
eschalot
hastings
kohlrabi
lima bean
mirepoix
mushroom
plantain
scallion
smallage
soyabean
tickbean
zucchini

9

artichoke
asparagus
aubergine
broad bean
calabrese

courgette
curly kale
dandelion
green peas
horsebean
mangetout
marrowfat
red pepper
split peas
sweetcorn
turban-top
turnip top

10

adzuki bean
beet radish
cos lettuce
cow parsnip
French bean
kidney bean
King Edward
red cabbage
runner bean
scorzonera
turnip tops
watercress
Welsh onion

11

cauliflower
French beans
green pepper
haricot bean
horseradish
ratatouille
scarlet bean
spinach beet
sweet potato
water radish
water rocket

12

bamboo shoots

chat potatoes
corn on the cob
giant shallot
savoy cabbage
Spanish onion
spring onions
spring greens
white cabbage

13

horse cucumber
ladies' fingers
marrowfat peas
scarlet runner
spring cabbage
tankard turnip

14

globe artichoke
purple broccoli

15

broccoli sprouts
Brussels sprouts
vegetable marrow

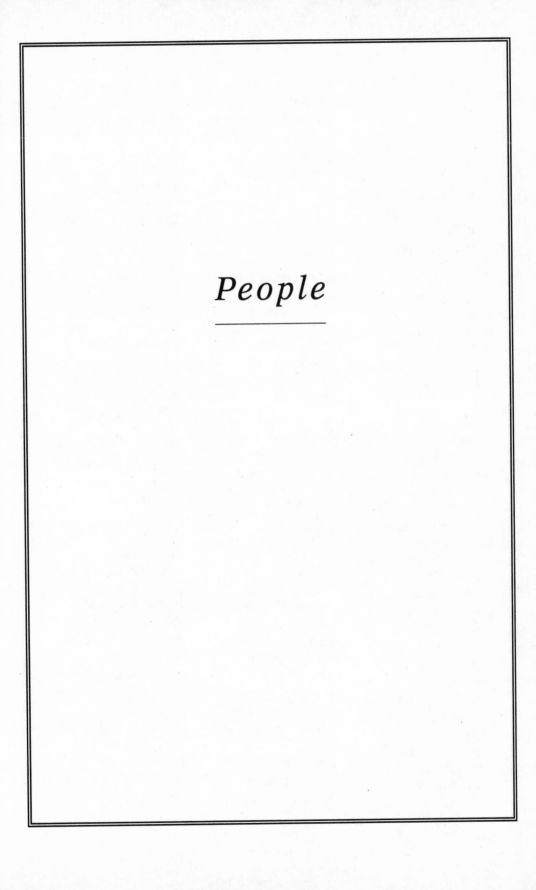

People

Adventurers, Explorers and Pioneers

4

Byrd, Richard E
Cano, Juan Sebastian del
Cook, Captain James
Dias, Bartolomeu
Eyre, Edward John
Gama, Vasco da
Hume, Hamilton
Hunt, John, Baron
Kidd, William
Park, Mungo
Polo, Marco
Ross, Sir James Clark
Soto, Hernando de

5

Baker, Sir Samuel White
Barth, Heinrich
Boone, Daniel
Bruce, James
Burke, Robert O'Hara
Cabot, John (Giovanni Caboto)
Davis, John (or J Davys)
Fuchs, Sir Vivian
Laird, Macgregor
Oates, Lawrence Edward Grace
Onate, Juan de
Parry, Sir William Edward
Peary, Robert Edwin
Scott, Robert Falcon
Smith, Dick
Speke, John Hanning
Sturt, Charles
Teach, Edward

6

Alcock, Sir John
Baffin, William
Balboa, Vasco Nunez de
Bering, Vitus Jonassen
Brazza, Pierre Paul Francois Camille Savorgnan de
Brook, Sir James
Burton, Sir Richard
Cabral, Pedro Alvares
Carson, Kit (Christopher Carson)
Cortes, Hernan
Hudson, Henry
Morgan, Sir Henry
Nansen, Fridtjof
Nobile, Umberto
Stuart, John McDouall
Tasman, Abel Janszoon

7

Barents, Willem
Bleriot, Louis
Branson, Richard
Carpini, Giovanni da Pian del
Cartier, Jacques
Cordoba, Francisco Fernando de
Covilha, Pero da
Dampier, William
Earhart, Amelia
Fiennes, Sir Ranulph
Fremont, John C
Gilbert, Sir Humphrey
Hawkins, Sir John
Hillary, Sir Edmund
Hinkler, Herbert John Lewis
La Salle, Robert Cavelier, Sieur de
McClure, Sir Robert

John Le Mesurier
Pizarro, Francisco
Pytheas
Raleigh, Sir Walter
Selkirk, Alexander
Stanley, Sir Henry Morton
Wilkins, Sir George Hubert
Wrangel, Ferdinand Petrovich, Baron von

8

Amundsen, Roald
Columbus, Christopher
Cousteau, Jacques Yves
Flinders, Matthew
Franklin, Sir John
Magellan, Ferdinand
Marchand, Jean Baptiste
Vespucci, Amerigo

9

Blanchard, Jean Pierre
Champlain, Samuel de
Frobisher, Sir Martin
Heyerdahl, Thor
Iberville, Pierre Le Moyne Sieur d'
Leichardt, Ludwig
Lindbergh, Charles A
Marquette, Jacques
Pausanias
Rasmussen, Knud Johan
Vancouver, George
Velasquez, Diego

10

Barbarossa (Khayr ad-Din)
Eric the Red
Shackleton, Sir Ernest

11

Ibn Battutah
La Condamine, Charles
Marie de
Livingstone, David
Ponce de Leon, Juan

12

Bougainville, Louis
Antoine de
Leif Eriksson
Nordenskjold, Nils
Adolf Erik, Baron

14

Bellinghausen, Fabian
Gottlieb, Baron von
Dumont D'Urville, Jules
Sebastian Cesar

17

Henry the Navigator

Artists, Sculptors,
Designers and
Architects

3

Arp, Jean
Dou, Gerrit
Fry, Roger
Lin, Maya
Low, Sir David

4

Adam, Robert
Capp, Al (Alfred Caplin)
Cuyp, Aelbert Jacobsz

Dadd, Richard
Dali, Salvador
Dior, Christian
Dore, Gustave
Dufy, Raoul
Erte (Romain de Tirtoff)
Etty, William
Gabo, Naum (Naum
Neemia Pevsner)
Goes, Hugo van der
Goya, Francesco de
Gris, Juan (Jose
Victoriano Gonzalez)
Gros, Antoine Jean
Baron
Hals, Frans
Hill, David Octavius
Hunt, William Holman
John, Augustus
Kahn, Louis Isadore
Kent, William
Klee, Paul
Lamb, Henry
Lely, Sir Peter (Pieter
van der Faes)
Loos, Adolph
Maes, Nicolas (or
Nicolas Mass)
Marc, Franz
Miro, Joan
Nash, John
Nash, Paul
Neer, Aert van der
Opie, John
Reni, Guido
Rosa, Salvator
Shaw, Norman
Ward, Sir Leslie
West, Benjamin
Wood, Christopher
Wood, John, of Bath
Wren, Sir Christopher
Zorn, Anders

5

Aalto, Alvar
Atget, Eugene
Bacon, Francis
Bacon, John
Bakst, Leon
Balla, Giacomo
Barry, Sir Charles
Blake, Peter
Bosch, Hieronymus
Bouts, Dierick
Brown, Capability
(Lancelot Brown)
Brown, Ford Madox
Burra, Edward
Campi, Giulio
Corot, Jean Baptiste
Camille
Crane, Walter
Crome, John
Dagly, Gerhard
Danby, Francis
Dance, George
David, Gerard
David, Jacques Louis
Degas, Edgar
Denis, Maurice
Durer, Albrecht
Ensor, James Sydney,
Baron
Ernst, Max
Foley, John Henry
Freud, Lucian
Gaddi, Taddeo
Gibbs, James
Giles, Carl Ronald
Gorky, Arshile
(Vosdanig Adoian)
Goyen, Jan Josephszoon
van
Grant, Duncan James
Corrowr
Grosz, George

Hirst, Damien
Homer, Winslow
Hooch, Pieter de
Horta, Victor
Johns, Jasper
Jones, Inigo
Keene, Charles Samuel
Klimt, Gustav
Klint, Kaare
Leach, Bernard
Leech, John
Leger, Fernand
Le Vau, Louis
Lippi, Fra Filippo
Lotto, Lorenzo
Lowry, L.S.
Macke, August
Manet, Edouard
Mengs, Anton Raphael
Metsu, Gabriel
Monet, Claude
Moore, Henry
Moses, Grandma (Anna
Mary Robertson M.)
Munch, Edvard
Myron
Nadar (Gaspard Felix
Tournachon)
Nervi, Pier Luigi
Nolan, Sir Sidney
Nolde, Emil (Emil
Hansen)
Oudry, Jean-Baptiste
Phyfe, Duncan (or Fife)
Piper, John
Pugin, Augustus Welby
Northmore
Quant, Mary
Redon, Odilon
Ricci, Sebastiano
Riley, Bridget Louise
Rodin, Auguste
Scott, Sir George

Gilbert
Shahn, Ben
Soane, Sir John
Steen, Jan
Stoss, Veit
Tobey, Mark
Vicky (Victor Weisz)
Watts, George
Frederick
Wyatt, James

6

Albers, Josef
Archer, Thomas
Beaton, Sir Cecil
Behzad
Benton, Thomas Hart
Bewick, Thomas
Boudin, Eugene
Boulle, Andre Charles
(or Buhl)
Brandt, Bill
Braque, Georges
Bratby, John
Breuer, Marcel Lajos
Buffet, Bernard
Butler, Reg Cotterell
Calder, Alexander
Callot, Jacques
Canova, Antonio
Cardin, Pierre
Casson, Sir Hugh
Chanel, Coco
Clouet, Jean
Cooper, Samuel
Cosway, Richard
Cotman, John Sell
Derain, Andre
De Wint, Peter
Eakins, Thomas
Floris, Cornelis
Floris, Frans
Foster, Sir Norman

Fuller, Richard
Buckminster
Fuseli, Henry (Johann
Heinrich Fussli)
Gerard, Francois, Baron
Giotto (Giotto di
Bondone)
Girtin, Thomas
Greuze, Jean-Baptiste
Guardi, Francesco
Hollar, Wenceslaus
Houdon, Jean Antoine
Ingres, Jean-August-
Dominique
Isabey, Jean-Baptiste
Jochho
Knight, Dame Laura
Lasdun, Sir Denys
La Tour, Maurice-
Quinten de
Le Brun, Charles
Le Nain, Antoine
Le Nain, Louis
Le Nain, Mathieu
Lescot, Pierre
Longhi, Pietro (Pietro
Falca)
Lurcat, Jean
Marini, Marino
Martin, John
Massys, Quentin (or
Matsys, Messys, Metsys)
Millet, Jean Francois
Moreau, Gustave
Moroni, Giovanni
Battista
Morris, William
Oliver, Isaac
Orozco, Jose
Ostade, Adrian van
Palmer, Samuel
Paxton, Sir Joseph
Pisano, Andrea (Andrea

de Pontedera)
Pisano, Nicola
Renoir, Pierre Auguste
Ribera, Jose de (or
Jusepe Ribera)
Rivera, Diego
Romney, George
Rothko, Mark (Marcus
Rothkovitch)
Rubens, Peter Paul
Scarfe, Gerald
Searle, Ronald William
Fordham
Sesshu (Sesshu Toyo)
Seurat, Georges
Signac, Paul
Sisley, Alfred
Sluter, Claus
Spence, Sir Basil
Stubbs, George
Tanguy, Yves
Tissot, James Joseph
Titian, (Tiziano Vecellio)
Turner, Joseph Mallord
William
Vasari, Giorgio
Voysey, Charles Frances
Annesley
Warhol, Andy (Andrew
Warhola)
Weyden, Rogier van der
Wilkie, Sir David
Wilson, Richard
Wright, Frank Lloyd
Xia Gui (or Hsia Knei)
Zeuxis

7

Alberti, Leon Battista
Allston, Washington
Antenor
Apelles
Astbury, John

Barlach, Ernst
Bassano, Jacopo (Jacopo
or Giacomo da Ponte)
Behrens, Peter
Bellini, Jacopo
Bernini, Gian Lorenzo
Bonnard, Pierre
Borglum, Gutzon
Boucher, Francois
Brouwer, Adriaen
Cameron, Julia Margaret
Cassatt, Mary
Cellini, Benvenuto
Cézanne, Paul
Chagall, Marc
Chardin, Jean-Baptiste-
Simeon
Chirico, Giorgio de
Christo
Cimabue, Giovanni
Clodion (Claude
Michel)
Courbet, Gustave
Daumier, Honore
Delorme, Philibert
Delvaux, Paul
Duchamp, Marcel
El Greco (Domenikos
Theotokopoulos)
Epstein, Sir Jacob
Exekias
Faberge, Peter Carl
Flaxman, John Henry
Fontana, Domenico
Fouquet, Jean
Gauguin, Paul
Gibbons, Grinling
Gillray, James
Gozzoli, Benozzo
(Benozzo di Lese)
Gropius, Walter
Guarini, Guarino
Hassall, John

Herrera, Juan de
Hobbema, Meindert
Hockney, David
Hogarth, William
Hokusai (Katsushika
Hokusai)
Holland, Henry
Hoppner, John
Ictinus
Johnson, Cornelius
(Janssen van Ceulen)
Kneller, Sir Godfrey
Lalique, Rene
Lamerie, Paul de
L'Enfant, Pierre-Charles
Le Notre, Andre
Limburg, Pol de
Limosin, Leonard (or
Limousin)
Lochner, Stefan
Lutyens, Sir Edwin
Landseer
Maclise, Daniel
Maderna, Carlo
Maillol, Aristide
Mansart, Francois (or
Mansard)
Martini, Simone
Matisse, Henri
Memling, Hans (or
Memlinc)
Millais, Sir John Everett
Morandi, Giorgio
Morisot, Berthe
Morland, George
Murillo, Bartolome
Esteban
Neumann, Balthasar
O'Keeffe, Georgia
Orcagna, Andrea
(Andrea di Cione)
Palissy, Bernard
Pasmore, Victor

Patinir, Joachim (or
Patenier)
Pevsner, Antoine
Phidias
Picabia, Francis
Picasso, Pablo
Pollock, Jackson
Poussin, Nicolas
Prud'hon, Pierre Paul
Rackham, Arthur
Raeburn, Sir Henry
Raphael (Raffaello
Sanzio)
Redoute, Pierre, Joseph
Roberts, Tom
Rouault, Georges
Rublyov, Andrey (or
Andrey Rublev)
Sargent, John Singer
Schiele, Egon
Seghers, Hercules
Shepard, Ernest
Howard
Sickert, Walter Richard
Snowdon, Antony
Armstrong-Jones, Earl
of
Snyders, Frans
Soutine, Chaim
Spencer, Sir Stanley
Tenniel, Sir John
Tibaldi, Pellegrino
Tiepolo, Giovanni
Battista
Uccello, Paolo
Utrillo, Maurice
Van Dyck, Sir Anthony
(or Vandyke)
Van Eyck, Jan
Van Gogh, Vincent
Vermeer, Jan
Vignola, Giacomo da
Watteau, Antione

Zadkine, Ossip
Zoffany, Johann
Zuccaro, Federico
Zuccaro, Taddeo

8

Aaltonen, Waino
Ammanati,
Bartolommeo
Angelico, Fra (Guido di
Pietro)
Annigoni, Pietro
Antelami, Benedetto
Beckmann, Max
Boccioni, Umberto
Bramante, Donato
Brancusi, Constantin
Bronzino, Il (Agnolo di
Cosimo)
Carracci, Annibale
Castagno, Andrea del
(Andrea di Bartolo de
Simone)
Chambers, Sir William
Cressent, Charles
Crivelli, Carlo
Daubigny, Charles-
Francois
Delaunay, Robert
Drysdale, Sir Russell
Dubuffet, Jean
Filarete (Antonio
Averlino)
Frampton, Sir George
James
Ghiberti, Lorenzo
Giordano, Luca
(nickname Luca Fa
Presto)
Gossaert, Jan
Guercino (Giovanni
Francesco Barbieri)
Hepworth (Dame

Barbara
Hilliard, Nicholas
Jacobsen, Arne
Jongkind, Johan
Barthold
Jordaens, Jakob
Kirchner, Ernst Ludwig
Landseer, Sir Edwin
Henry
Lawrence, Sir Thomas
Lipchitz, Jacques
Lombardo, Pietro
Lysippus
Magritte, Rene
Malevich, Kazimir
Mantegna, Andrea
Masaccio (Tommaso di
Giovanni di Simone
Guidi)
Meegeren, Hans van
Mondrian, Piet (Pieter
Cornelis Mondriaan)
Mulready William
Munnings, Sir Alfred
Niemeyer, Oscar
Palladio, Andrea
Piranesi, Giambattista
Pissarro, Camille
Pontormo, Jacopo da
(Jacopo Carrucci)
Reynolds, Sir Joshua
Robinson, William
Heath
Rousseau, Henri
Rousseau, Theodore
Ruisdael, Jacob van
Saarinen, Eero
Sassetta (Stefano di
Giovanni)
Severini, Gino
Sheraton, Thomas
Soufflot, Jacques
Germain

Sullivan, Louis Henry
Terborch, Gerard
Vanbrugh, Sir John
Vasarely, Victor
Veronese, Paolo (Paolo Caliari)
Vlaminck, Maurice de
Vuillard, Edouard
Wedgwood, Josiah
Whistler, James McNeill
Whistler, Rex
Woollett, William
Zurbaran, Francisco de

9

Altdorfer, Albrecht
Bartholdi, Frederic August
Beardsley, Aubrey Vincent
Bonington, Richard Parkes
Borromini, Francesco
Bourdelle, Emile
Canaletto (Antonio Canal)
Carpaccio, Vittore
Cavallini, Pietro
Cockerell, Charles Robert
Constable, John
Cornelius, Peter von
Correggio, (Antonio Allegri)
Courreges, Andre
De Kooning, Willem
Delacroix, Eugene
Delaroche, Paul
Donatello (Donato de Nicolo di Betti Bardi)
Fabritius, Carel
Feininger, Lyonel
Fragonard, Jean Honore

Friedrich, Caspar David
Gericault, Theodore
Giorgione
Greenaway, Kate
Greenough, Horatio
Grunewald, Matthias
Hawksmoor, Nicholas
Hiroshige, (Ando Tokitaro)
Honthorst, Gerrit von
Jawlensky, Alexey von
Kadinsky, Wassily
Kauffmann, Angelica
Kokoschka, Oskar
Lissitzky, El (Eliezer Lissitzky)
Mestrovic, Ivan
Muybridge, Eadweard (Edward James Muggeridge)
Nicholson, Ben
Nollekens, Joseph
Oldenburg, Claes
Pisanello (Antonio Pisano)
Roubillac, Louis Francois (or Louis Francois Roubiliac)
Siqueiros, David Alfaro
Stieglitz, Alfred
Thornhill, Sir James
Velazquez, Diego Rodriguez de Silva
Vitruvius (Marcus Vitruvius Pollio)
Wouwerman, Philips

10

Alma-Tadema, Sir Lawrence
Altichiero
Archipenko, Alexander
Arcimboldo, Giuseppe

Berruguete, Pedro
Botticelli, Sandro (Alessandro di Mariano Filipepi)
Burlington, Richard Boyle, 3rd Earl of
Burne-Jones, Sir Edward Coley
Caravaggio (Michelango Merisi)
Champaigne, Philippe de
Cruikshank, George
Euphronios
Giacometti, Albert
Lorenzetti, Ambrogio
Mackintosh, Charles Rennie
Meissonier, Jean-Louis-Ernest
Modigliani, Amedeo
Moholy-Nagy, Laszlo
Motherwell, Robert
Pollaiuolo, Antonio
Polyclitus
Praxiteles
Richardson, Henry Hobson
Rowlandson, Thomas
Schwitters, Kurt
Senefelder, Aloys
Signorelli, Luca
Sutherland, Graham Vivian
Tange Kenzo
Tintoretto (Jacopo Robusti)
Van de Velde, Henry
Verrocchio, Andrea del (Andrea del Cione)
Waterhouse, Alfred
Zuccarelli, Francesco

11

Abercrombie, Sir Patrick
Bartolommeo, Fra (Baccio della Porta)
Butterfield, William
Callicrates
Callimachus
Chippendale, Thomas
Chodowiecki, Daniel Nikolaus
Della Robbia, Luca
Domenichino (Domenico Zampieri)
Ghirlandaio Domenico (Domenico di Tommaso Bigordi)
Giambologna (Giovanni da Bologna or Jean de Boulogne)
Gislebertus
Hepplewhite, George
Le Corbusier (Charles-Edouard Jeanneret)
Terbrugghen, Hendrik
Thorvaldsen, Bertel (or Bertel Thorwaldsen)

12

Brunelleschi, Filippo
Fantin-Latour, Henri
Gainsborough, Thomas
Gaudi Y Cornet, Antonio
Guilio Romano (Giulio Pippi)
Lichtenstein, Roy
Luca Fa Presto (Nickname of Luca Giordano)
Palma Vecchio, Jacopo (Jacopo Negretti)

Parmigianino (Girolamo Francesco Maria Mazzola)
Pinturicchio (Bernardino di Betto)
Rauschenberg, Robert
Saint-Laurent, Yves
Sciaparelli, Elsa
Viollet-le-Duc, Eugene Emmanuel
Winterhalter, Franz Xavier

13

Lorenzo Monaco (Piero di Giovanni)
Piero di Cosimo (Piero de Lorenzo)
Williams-Ellis, Sir Clough

14

Andrea del Sarto (Andrea d'Agnolo)
Berain the Elder, Jean
Cartier-Bresson, Henri
Claude Lorraine (Claude Gellee)
Cousin the Elder, Jean
Gaudier-Brzeska, Henri
Lucas van Leyden (Lucas Hugensz or Jacobsz)
Mies van der Rohe, Ludwig

15

Cranach the Elder, Lucas (Lucas Muller)
Hardouin-Mansart, Jules
Kitagawa Utamaro
Leonardo da Vinci

Toulouse-Lautrec, Henri

16

Brueghel the Elder, Pieter (or Bruegel)
Fischer von Erlach, Johann Bernhard
Puvis de Chavannes, Pierre
Rembrandt van Rijn
Utagawa Kuniyoshi (Igusa Magosaburo)

17

Domenico Veneziano
Gentile da Fabriano (Niccolo di Giovanni di Massio)
Herrera the Younger, Francisco de
Holbein the Younger, Hans
Teniers the Younger, David

18

Antonello da Messina
Jacopo della Quercia
Leighton of Stretton, Frederic, Baron

19

Duccio di Buoninsegna
Piero Della Francesca

20

Desiderio da Settignano
Michelangelo Buonarroti
Michelozzo di Bartolommeo

Astronomers, Engineers, Scientists and Inventors

3

Dam, Carl Peter Henrik
Kay, John
Lee, Tsung-Dao
Ohm, Georg Simon
Ray, John

4

Abel, Niels Henrik
Abel, Sir Frederick
Augustus
Ader, Clement
Airy, Sir George Biddell
Baer, Karl Ernest von
Bell, Alexander Graham
Benz, Karl
Biro, Laszlo
Bohr, Niels Henrik
David
Born, Max
Bose, Sir Jagadis
Chandra
Cohn, Ferdinand Julius
Coke, Thomas William,
of Holkham, Earl of
Leicester
Cort, Henry
Davy, Sir Humphry
Eads, John Buchanan
Fust, Johann
Gold, Thomas
Gray, Asa
Hahn, Otto
Hess, Victor Francis
Howe, Elias
Koch, Robert
Land, Edwin Herbert

Laue, Max Theodor
Felix Von
Loeb, Jacques
Mach, Ernst
Mayo (Family)
Otis, Elisha Graves
Otto, Nikolaus August
Rabi, Isidor Isaac
Ryle, Sir Martin
Swan, Sir Joseph Wilson
Todd, Alexander
Robertus, Baron
Tull, Jethro
Urey, Harold Clayton
Watt, James
Yang, Chen Ning

5

Adams, John Couch
Aiken, Howard
Hathaway
Amici, Giovanni Battista
Aston, Francis William
Avery, Oswald
Theodore
Bacon, Roger
Baily, Francis
Baird, John Logie
Baker, Sir Benjamin
Banks, Sir Joseph
Bates, Henry Walter
Beebe, Charles William
Bethe, Hans Albrecht
Black, Joseph
Bloch, Felix
Bondi, Sir Hermann
Boole, George
Bosch, Carl
Bothe, Walther Wilhelm
George Franz
Bovet, Daniel
Bowen, Norman Levi
Bower, Frederick

Orpen
Boyle, Robert
Bragg, Sir William
Henry
Brahe, Tycho
Brown, Robert
Burge, Joost
Chain, Sir Ernst Boris
Creed, Frederick
Crick, Francis Harry
Compton
Curie, Marie
Curie, Pierre
Debye, Peter Joseph
Wilhelm
Diels, Otto Paul
Hermann
Dirac, Paul Adrien
Maurice
Elton, Charles
Euler, Leonhard
Evans, Oliver
Fabre, Jean Henri
Fabry, Charles
Fermi, Enrico
Frege, Gottlob
Gabor, Dennis
Galle, Johann Gottfried
Gauss, Karl Friedrich
Geber
Gibbs, Josiah Willard
Godel, Kurt
Haber, Fritz
Hardy, Godfrey Harold
Henry, Joseph
Hertz, Heinrich Rudolf
Hooke, Robert
Hoyle, Sir Fred
Jeans, Sir James
Hopwood
Joule, James Prescott
Kolbe, Hermann
Krebs, Sir Hans Adolf

Kroto, Sir Harold

Lawes, Sir John Bennet

Libby, Willard Frank

Lodge, Sir Oliver Joseph

Lyell, Sir Charles

Maxim, Sir Hiram
Stevens

Mayer, Julius Robert Von

Monge, Gaspard

Monod, Jacques-Lucien

Morse, Samuel Finley
Breese

Nobel, Alfred Sir
Andrew

Pauli, Wolfgang

Popov, Aleksandr
Stepanovich

Prout, William

Raman, Sir
Chandrasekhara
Venkata

Reber, Grote

Rhine, Joseph Banks

Rosse, William Parsons,
3rd Earl of

Segre, Emilio

Smith, Sir Keith
Macpherson

Soddy, Frederick

Stahl, Georg Ernst

Tatum, Edward Lawrie

Tesla, Nikola

Volta, Alessandro
Giuseppe Antonio
Anastasio, Count

Weber, Ernst Heinrich

White, Gilbert

Young, Thomas

6

Achard, Franz Karl

Adrian, Edgar Douglas,
1st Baron

Agnesi, Maria Gaetana

Alfven, Hannes Olof
Gosta

Ampere, Andre Marie

Appert, Nicolas

Archer, Frederick Scott

Baeyer, Adolf Von

Beadle, George Wells

Bodini, Giambattista

Bolyai, Janos

Bonnet, Charles

Bordet, Jules Jean
Baptiste Vincent

Boveri, Theodor
Heinrich

Bramah, Joseph

Briggs, Henry

Brunel, Isambard
Kingdom

Buffon, Georges Louis
Leclerc, Comte de

Bunsen, Robert
Wilhelm

Calvin, Melvin

Cantor, Georg

Carnot, Sadi

Carrel, Alexis

Carver, George
Washington

Cauchy, Augustin Louis,
Baron

Caxton, William

Cayley, Arthur

Cayley, Sir George

Cuvier, Georges, Baron

Dalton, John

Darwin, Charles Robert

De Bary, Heinrich
Anton

De Duve, Christian

Dreyer, Johan Ludvig
Emil

Du Mont, Allen Balcom

Dunlop, John Boyd

Eckert, John Presper

Edison, Thomas Alva

Enders, John Franklin

Engler, Gustav Heinrich
Adolf

Euclid

Fermat, Pierre de

Finsen, Niels Ryberg

Fokker, Anthony
Hermann Gerard

Franck, James

Frisch, Karl Von

Frisch, Otto Robert

Fulton, Robert

Galois, Evariste

Galton, Sir Francis

Geiger, Hans

Gesner, Conrad

Graham, Thomas

Halley, Edmund

Hevesy, George Charles
Von

Hooker, Sir William
Jackson

Hubble, Edwin Powell

Hutton, James

Huxley, Thomas, Henry

Jansky, Karl Guthe

Jenson, Nicolas

Joliot, Frederic

Kelvin, William,
Thomson, 1st Baron

Kepler, Johannes

Kinsey, Alfred

Landau, Lev Davidovich

Lartet, Edouard Armand
Isidore Hippolyte

Liebig, Justus, Baron Von

Lorenz, Konrad

Lovell, Sir Bernard

Lowell, Percival

Markov, Andrei

Andreevich
Martin, Archer John
Porter
Martin Pierre-Emile
McAdam, John Loudon
Mendel, Gregor Johann
Morgan, Thomas Hunt
Morley, Edward
Williams
Morris, Desmond John
Muller, Hermann Joseph
Muller, Paul Hermann
Napier, John
Nernst, Walther
Hermann
Newton, Sir Isaac
Olbers, Heinrich
Wilhelm
Pascal, Blaise
Penney, William George,
Baron
Perkin, Sir William
Henry
Perrin, Jean-Baptiste
Planck, Max Karl Ernst
Ludwig
Powell, Cecil Frank
Proust, Joseph-Louis
Ramsay, Sir William
Rennie, John
Sanger, Frederick
Savery, Thomas
Sholes, Christopher
Latham
Singer, Isaac Merrit
Sloane, Sir Hans
Stokes, Sir George
Gabriel
Struve, Otto
Sutton, Walter
Stanborough
Talbot, William Henry
Fox

Taylor, Brook
Taylor, Frederick
Winslow
Teller, Edward
Townes, Charles Hard
Vauban, Sebastian Le
Prestre
Wallis, Sir Barnes
Walton, Ernest Thomas
Sinton
Watson, James Dewey
Wiener, Norbert
Wigner, Eugene Paul
Wilson, Edmund
Beecher
Wohler, Friedrich
Wright, Orville
Yukawa, Hideki
Zeeman, Pieter

7

Agassiz, Jean Louis
Rodolphe
Alvarez, Luis Walter
Audubon, John James
Babbage, Charles
Bardeen, John
Barnard, Edward
Emerson
Bateson, William
Battani, Al-
Bergius, Friedrich
Borlaug, Norman
Braille, Louis
Brouwer, Luitzen
Egbertus Jan
Burbank, Luther
Candela, Felix
Cardano, Girolamo
Compton, Arthur Holly
Correns, Carl Erich
Coulomb, Charles
Augustin

Crookes, Sir William
Curtiss, Glenn
Daimler, Gottlieb
Daniell, John Frederic
De La Rue, Warren
De Vries, Hugo Marie
Doppler, Christian
Johann
Driesch, Hans Adolph
Eduard
Eichler, August Wilhelm
Faraday, Michael
Feynman, Richard
Phillips
Fischer, Emil Hermann
Fleming, Sir John
Ambrose
Fourier, Jean Baptiste
Joseph, Baron
Fresnel, Augustin Jean
Gagarin, Yuri
Alekseevich
Galvani, Luigi
Gilbert, William
Goddard, Robert
Hutchings
Gregory, James
Haeckel, Ernst Heinrich
Haworth, Sir Walter
Norman
Helmont, Jan Baptist
van
Hermite, Charles
Hilbert, David
Hodgkin, Alan Lloyd
Hodgkin, Dorothy Mary
Crowfoot
Hopkins, Fir Frederick
Gowland
Huggins, Sir William
Huygens, Christiaan
Jussieu (Family)
Kapitza, Peter

Leonidovich
Kendall, Edward Calvin
Kendrew, Sir John
Cowdery
Khorana, Har Gobind
Kidinnu
Kozirev, Nikolai
Aleksandrovich
Lalande, Joseph-Jerome
le Francais de
Lamarck, Jean-Baptiste
de Monet, Chevalier de
Lambert, Johann
Heinrich
Langley, Samuel
Pierpont
Laplace, Pierre Simon,
Marquis de
Lesseps, Ferdinand de
Lockyer, Sir Joseph
Norman
Lorentz, Hendrick
Antoon
Lumiere, Auguste
Lysenko, Trofim
Denisovich
Marconi, Guglielmo
Maxwell, James Clerk
Meitner, Lise
Messier, Charles
Moseley, Henry Gwyn
Jeffries
Neumann, John Von
Oersted, Hans
Christian
Onsager, Lars
Ostwald, Wilhelm
Parsons, Sir Charles
Algernon
Pasteur, Louis
Pauling, Linus Carl
Piccard (Family)
Poisson, Simeon Denis

Prandtl, Ludwig
Ptolemy (or Claudius
Ptolemaeus)
Purcell, Edward Mills
Reamur, Rene-Antoine
Ferchault de
Riemann, Georg
Friedrich Bernard
Rumford, Benjamin
Thompson, Count
Sandage, Allan Rex
Scheele, Carl Wilhelm
Schwann, Theodor
Seaborg, Glenn
Theodore
Shepard, Jr, Allan
Bartlett
Siemens, Ernst Werner
von
Simpson, George
Gaylord
Szilard, Leo
Telford, Thomas
Thenard, Louis-Jacques
Thomson, Sir Joseph
John
Tupolev, Andrei
Niklaievich
Tyndall, John
Vavilov, Nikolai
Ivanovich
Waksman, Selman
Abraham
Wallace, Alfred Russel
Wegener, Alfred Lothar
Whitney, Eli
Whittle, Sir Frank
Wilkins, Maurice Hugh
Frederick
Ziegler, Karl

8
_____

Agricola, Georgius

Anderson, Carl David
Angstrom, Anders Jonas
Avogadro, Amedeo,
Conte di Quarenga e
Ceretto
Bakewell, Robert
Bessemer, Sir Henry
Birkhoff, George Davis
Bjerknes, Vilhelm
Friman Koren
Blackett, Patrick
Maynard Stuart, Baron
Brattain, Walter Houser
Brewster, Sir David
Bridgman, Percy
Williams
Brindley, James
Bushnell, David
Calmette, Albert Leon
Charles
Chadwick, Sir James
Clausius, Rudolf Julius
Emanuel
Crompton, Samuel
Culpeper, Nicholas
Daguerre, Louis-
Jacques-Mande
Dedekind, Richard
De Forest, Lee
De Morgan, Augustus
Einstein, Albert
Ericsson, John
Foucault, Jean Bernard
Leon
Gassendi, Pierre
Gell-Mann, Murray
Guericke, Otto Von
Hamilton, Sir William
Rowan
Herschel, Sir William
Ilyushin, Sergei
Vladimirovich
Ipatieff, Vladimir

Nikolaievich

Jacquard, Joseph-Marie

Kennelly, Arthur Edwin

Klaproth, Martin
Heinrich

Koroliov, Sergei
Pavlovich

Lagrange, Joseph Louis,
Comte de

Langmuir, Irving

Lawrence, Ernest
Orlando

Legendre, Adrien Marie

Lemaitre, Georges
Edouard, Abbe

Leuckart, Karl Georg
Friedrich Rudolph

Linnaeus, Carolus (Carl
Linne)

Lipscomb, William Nunn

Lonsdale, Dame
Kathleen

Maudslay, Henry

McMillan, Edwin
Mattison

Mercator, Gerardus

Meyerhof, Otto Fritz

Millikan, Robert
Andrews

Milstein, Cesar

Mitchell, Reginald
Joseph

Mulliken, Robert
Sanderson

Newcomen, Thomas

Oliphant, Sir Mark
Laurence Elwin

Poincare, Jules Henri

Rayleigh, John William
Strutt, 3rd Baron

Rheticus

Robinson, Sir Robert

Roebling, John Augustus

Roentgen, Wilhelm
Konrad

Sabatier, Paul

Sakharov, Andrei
Dimitrievich

Shockley, William
Bradfield

Shrapnel, Henry

Sikorsky, Igor Ivan

Stirling, James

Van Allen, James Alfred

Van't Hoff, Jacobus
Henricus

Weismann, August
Friedrich Leopold

Woodward, Robert
Burns

Zernicke, Frits

Zworykin, Vladimir
Kosma

9

Abu-al-Wafa

Arkwright, Sir Richard

Armstrong, Edwin
Howard

Armstrong, William
George, Baron

Arrhenius, Svante
August

Becquerel, Henri

Bernoulli (Family)

Berthelot, Marcelin

Berzelius, Jons Jakob

Boltzmann, Ludwig
Eduard

Bronowski, Jacob

Cavendish, Henry

Chebishev, Pafnuti
Lvovich

Cherenkov, Pavel
Alekseievich

Cockcroft, Sir John

Douglas

Cornforth, Sir John

D'Alembert, Jean Le
Rond

Daubenton, Louis Jean
Marie

Davenport, Charles
Benedict

Eddington, Sir Arthur
Stanley

Endlicher, Stephan
Ladislaus

Fibonacci, Leonardo

Flamsteed, John

Gay-Lussac, Joseph
Louis

Gutenberg, Johann

Heaviside, Oliver

Helmholtz, Hermann
Ludwig Ferdinand Von

Hopkinson, John

Johannsen, Wilhelm
Ludvig

Josephson, Brian David

Kirchhoff, Gustav
Robert

Kurchatov, Igor
Vasilievich

Lankester, Sir Edwin Ray

Lavoisier, Antoine
Laurent

Lederberg, Joshua

Leverrier, Urbain Jean
Joseph

Liouville, Joseph

Macintosh, Charles

Macmillan, Kirkpatrick

Michelson, Albert
Abraham

Nicholson, William

Nirenberg, Marshall
Warren

Pelletier, Pierre Joseph

Priestley, Joseph
Remington, Eliphalet
Schleiden, Matthias Jakob
Steinmetz, Charles Proteus
Tinbergen, Nikolaas
Zsigmondy, Richard Adolph
Zuckerman, Solly, Baron

10

Archimedes
Arrowsmith, Aaron
Barkhausen, Heinrich
Berthollet, Claude Louis, Comte
Blenkinsop, John
Cannizzaro, Stanislao
Cartwright, Edmund
Copernicus
Dobzhansky, Theodosius
Fitzgerald, George Francis
Fourneyron, Benoit
Fraunhofer, Joseph Von
Hargreaves, James
Heisenberg, Werner Karl
Hipparchus
Hofmeister, Wilhelm Friedrich Benedict
Ingenhousz, Jan
Kolmogorov, Andrei Nikolaevich
Lilienthal, Otto
Lippershey, Hans
Maupertius, Pierre Louis Moreau de
Mendeleyev, Dimitrii Ivanovich
Metchnikov, Ilya Ilich

Rutherford, Ernest, 1st Baron
Sommerfield, Arnold Johannes Wilhelm
Staudinger, Hermann
Stephenson, George
Swammerdam, Jan
Torricelli, Evangelista
Tournefort, Joseph Pitton de
Trevithick, Richard
Watson-Watt, Sir Robert Alexander
Wheatstone, Sir Charles

11

Al-Khwarizmi, Muhammed Ibn Musa
Baskerville, John
Bhoskhara II
Chamberlain, Owen
Goldschmidt, Richard Benedict
Hinshelwood, Sir Cyril Norman
Joliot-Curie, Irene
Le Chatelier, Henri-Louis
Leeuwenhoek, Antonie van
Lobachevski, Nikolai Ivanovich
Montgolfier, Jacques-Etienne
Nostradamus
Oppenheimer, J Robert
Schrodinger, Erwin
Sherrington, Sir Charles
Spallanzani, Lazzaro
Tsiolkovski, Konstantin Eduardovich
Van der Waals, Johannes

Diderik

12

Ambartsumian, Victor Amazaspovich
Szent-Gyorgyi, Albert

13

Arago Francois
Chandrasekhar, Subrahmanyan
Regiomontanus

14

Galileo Galilei

15

Eudoxus of Cnidus

16

Hero of Alexandria

17

Appolonius of Perga

18

Aristarchus of Samos
Lecoq de Boisbaudran
Pappus of Alexandria

19

Dioscorides Pedanius
Kekule von Stradonitz

20+

Iophantus of Alexandria
Eratosthenes of Cyrene
Geoffroy Saint-Hilaire
Sosigenes of Alexandria

Murderers

Murderer(s): Allen, Peter and Welby, John
Year: 1964
Details: Murdered John West. They were the last two men to be hanged in Britain.

Murderer(s): Bentley, Derek and Craig, Christopher
Year: 1952
Details: Both men were convicted of the murder of PC Miles, who had been shot. Bentley was hanged, although he did not fire a shot, on the grounds that he had incited his younger partner to murder. Craig, who was too young for the death sentence, was imprisoned until 1963. The case caused considerable public disquiet and was used in the abolition-of-hanging debate. After a lengthy and sustained campaign, Bentley's conviction was found to be unsafe in 1998.

Murderer: Borden, Lizzie
Year: 1892
Details: Accused of the murder of her father and stepmother in Fall River, Massachusetts, she was acquitted. Public opinion was that she was guilty and the case brought about the poem:

Lizzie Borden took an axe
And gave her mother forty whacks.
When she saw what she had done,
She gave her father forty-one.

Murderer(s): Brady, Ian and Hindley, Myra
Year: 1966
Details: Sentenced to life imprisonment for the brutal murders of five children. They became known as the Moors Murderers because at least three of their victims were killed and buried on the Lancashire Moors. Some of the bodies were never recovered.

Murderer(s): Burke, William and Hare, William
Year: 1827 – 1828
Details: Burke and Hare, with the help of their partners, lured victims to their lodging house, murdered them and sold their bodies to an Edinburgh anatomist, Dr Knox. Burke was sentenced to death for the murders of Mary Patterson, James Wilson and Margaret Docherty; Hare was granted immunity from prosecution by offering to turn King's Evidence. They are known to have murdered at least 16 people over a nine-month period, although the exact total is unknown.

Murderer: Bush, Edwin
Year: 1961
Details: Hanged for the murder of Mrs Elsie Bratten. He was identified from an identikit portrait – the first use of the system in Britain.

Murderer: Christie. John
Year: 1943 – 1953
Details: Hanged for the murder of his wife, Ethel Christie, whose body was found under the floorboards of 10 Rillington Place, London. The bodies

of five other women were found behind the kitchen wall and buried in the garden.

Murderer: Corder, William
Year: 1827
Details: Sentenced to death for the murder of Maria Marten. Although her family had been led to believe that she was happily married and living on the Isle of Wight, her mother had a dream that she had been murdered and her body buried in the Red Barn on Corder's father's farm. Her body was found there.

Murderer: Cotton, Mary Ann
Year: 1872
Details: Hanged for the murder of her stepson Charles Cotton. She was estimated to have murdered at least 14 people who, at the time, had been diagnosed as dying of gastric fever. She was arrested following the discovery of arsenic in the body of her stepson. Following this, the bodies of her husband, baby and two stepchildren were exhumed; they were also found to have died from arsenic poisoning.

Murderer: Crippen, Dr Hawley Harvey
Year: 1910
Details: US doctor who poisoned his actress wife Cora (Belle Elmore) in London. He attempted to escape to America with his mistress Ethel LeNeve on the SS Montrose. He was recognised on board and arrested following one of the first uses of ship-to-shore radio,

Murderer: Ellis, Ruth
Year: 1955
Details: Convicted of the murder of David Blakely, she was the last woman to be hanged in Britain.

Murderer: Haigh, John
Year: 1949
Details: Hanged for the murder of Olivia Durand-Deacon, Haigh thought he could not be tried for murder because he had destroyed the body in an acid bath. However, the discovery of gallstones, bone fragments and false teeth meant that the remains could be identified.

Murderer: Halliwell, Kenneth
Year: 1967
Details: Murdered his lover, the British dramatist Joe Orton.

Murderer: Hanratty, James
Year: 1961
Details: Hanged for the murder of Michael Gregsten after a trial lasting 21 days. Much of the evidence was based on the identification of Hanratty by Valerie Storie (Gregsten's lover, who had been present at the murder). Hanratty's alibi that he had been in Rhyl at the time of the murder was disbelieved, although much controversy surrounded the verdict. The uncertainty relating to the verdict added fuel to the campaign against hanging. Recent testing of DNA discovered at the scene lead to the conviction being upheld in 2002.

Murderer: Jack the Ripper
Year: 1888
Details: Notoriously brutally

murdered at least five prostitutes in the Whitechapel area of London. There has been much discussion, debate and controversy about the identity of the murderer and his true identity remains unknown to this day.

Murderer: Kent, Constance
Year: 1860
Details: Convicted of the murder of her half-brother, Francis, she was sentenced to death, although the sentence was later commuted to life imprisonment. She was released in 1885 and moved to Australia where she trained as a nurse under the name of Ruth Kaye. She rebuilt her life and died in 1944 at the age of 100.

Murderer: Neilson, Donald
Year: 1974-1975
Details: Known as 'The Black Panther' he was sentenced to life impris-onment for the murder of four men.

Murderer: Nilsen, Denis
Year: 1979 - 1983
Details: Convicted of the murder of six men after the discovery of human remains in a manhole at the side of the property where he lived. He boasted of killing more than 15 men in total.

Murderer: Peace, Charles
Year: 1876
Details: A burglar who carried the tools of his trade in a violin case, he was hanged for the murder of James Dyson. His criminal activities were spread out over a period of 25 years, during which he became notorious.

Murderer: Robinson, John
Year: 1927
Details: Suffocated Minnie Alice Bonati. He dismembered her body and hid it in a trunk which he handed to the left-luggage office at Charing Cross Station in London.

Murderer: Smith, George (alias Oliver Love, George Rose, Henry Williams, Oliver James, John Lloyd)
Year: 1912
Details: Hanged for the murder of Bessie Mundy. The story became known as 'The Brides in the Bath Murders' when it was revealed that Smith bigamously married his victims and, in three cases, killed them in their baths. A verdict of accidental drowning was brought in at each inquest and Smith claimed the belongings or life insurance of his 'wife'.

Murderer(s): Stratton, Alfred and Albert
Year: 1905
Details: Convicted of the murders of Mr and Mrs Farrow. The case made legal history because the jury was convinced of the guilt of the two brothers following the discovery of a fingerprint at the scene which matched that of Alfred Stratton.

Murderer: Sutcliffe, Peter
Year: 1975 – 1980
Details: Sentenced to life impris-onment following the murders of 13 women. Known as the Yorkshire Ripper, Sutcliffe claimed he had a mission from God to kill prostitutes, although, in fact, several of his victims were not prostitutes.

Murderer: Turpin, Dick
Year: 1735
Details: Hanged at York for the murder of Thomas Morris, Turpin was notorious for committing highway robberies. A reward of £200 had been placed on his head.

Murderer(s): West, Frederick and Rosemary
Year: 1970 – 1994
Details: Charged with the murder of 12 young women, Frederick West committed suicide before he was brought to trial. Rosemary West was sentenced to life imprisonment for the murder of 10 young women.

Musicians, Singers and Composers

3

Bax, Sir Arnold Edward Trevor

4

Adam, Adolphe-Charles
Arne, Thomas
Augustine
Bach, Johann Sebastian
Berg, Alban
Bing, Sir Rudolf
Blow John
Boehm, Karl
Bull, John
Bush, Alan Dudley
Butt, Dames Clara
Byrd, William
Cage, John
Hess, Dame Myra
Ives, Charles
Lolo, Edouard
Lill, John
Lind, Jenny
Nono, Luigi
Orff, Carl
Part, Arvo
Wolf, Hugo
Wood, Sir Henry

5

Alkan, Charles Henri Valentin (Charles Henry Valentin Morhange)
Arrau, Claudio
Auber, Daniel Francois Esprit
Auric, Georges
Baker, Dame Janet
Berio, Luciano
Bizet, Georges (Alexandre Cesar Leopold Bizet)
Bliss, Sir Arthur Edward Drummond
Bloch, Ernest
Boehm, Theobald
Boult, Sir Adrian
Boyce, William
Bream, Julian Alexander
Brian, Havergal
Bruch, Max
Bulow, Hans Guido, Freiherr von
Davis, Sir Colin
D'Indy, Vincent
Dufay, Guillaume
Dukas, Paul
Dupre, Marcel
Elgar, Sir Edward

Evans, Sir Geraint
Falla, Manuel de
Faure, Gabriel
Field, John
Friml, Rudolph
Gigli, Beniamino
Glass, Sir Philip
Gluck, Christoph Willibald
Gobbi, Tito
Goehr, Alexander
Grieg, Edvard Hagerup
Grove, Sir George
Halle, Sir Charles
Haydn, Franz Joseph
Henze, Hans Werner
Holst, Gustav
Ibert, Jacques
Lehar, Franz
Liszt, Franz
Locke, Matthew
Lully, Jean Baptiste (Giovanni Battista Luilli)
Melba, Dame Nellie (Helen Porter Armstrong)
Moore, Gerald
Munch, Charles
Ogdon, John
Parry, Sir Hubert
Patti, Adelina (Adela

Juana Maria)
Pears, Sir Peter
Ravel, Maurice
Reger, Max
Satie, Erik
Sharp, Cecil
Solti, Sir Georg
Sousa, John Philip
Spohr, Louis (Ludwig
Spohr)
Stern, Isaac
Szell, George
Teyte, Dame Maggie
Verdi, Giuseppe
Weber, Carl Maria von
Weill, Kurt
Widor, Charles Marie

6

Arnold, Malcolm
Barber, Samuel
Bartok, Bela
Battle, Kathleen
Bishop, Sir Henry
Rowley
Boulez, Pierre
Brahms, Johannes
Bridge, Frank
Burney, Charles
Busoni, Ferruccio
Callas, Maria (Maria
Anna Kalageropoulos)
Carter, Elliott
Caruso, Enrico
Casals, Pablo (Pau
Casals)
Chopin, Frederic
(Francois)
Clarke, Jeremiah
Cortot, Alfred
Cowell, Henry
Curwen, John
Curzon, Sir Clifford

Davies, Sir Peter
Maxwell
Delius, Frederick
Dibdin, Charles
Duparc, Henri (Marie
Eugene Henri Foucques
Duparc)
Dvorak, Antonin
Enesco, Georges
(Georges Enescu)
Flotow, Friedrich von
Franck, Cesar Auguste
Galway, James
Glinka, Mikhail
Ivanovich
Gounod, Charles
Francois
Gretry, Andre Ernest
Modeste
Groves, Sir Charles
Halevy, Jacques Francois
(Fromental Elias Levy)
Handel, George
Frederick
Harris Roy
Hotter, Hans
Hummel, Johann
Nepomuk
Jochum, Eugen
Kodaly, Zoltan
Krenek, Ernst
Lassus, Ronald de
Ligeti, Gyorgy
Maazel, Lorin
Mahler, Gustav
Morley, Thomas
Mozart, Wolfgang
Amadeus
Previn, Andre (Andreas
Ludwig Priwin)
Rameau, Jean Philippe
Rattle, Sir Simon
Rubbra, Edmund

Schutz, Heinrich
Tallis, Thomas
Varese, Edgard
Wagner, Richard
Walter, Bruno (Bruno
Walter Schlesinger)
Walton, Sir William
Webern, Anton von

7

Albeniz, Isaac Manuel
Francisco
Allegri, Gregorio
Antheil, George
Babbitt, Milton
Beecham, Sir Thomas
Bellini, Vincenzo
Bennett, Richard
Rodney
Bennett, Sir William
Berlioz, Hector
Borodin, Aleksandr
Porfirevich
Brendel, Alfred
Braxton, Anthony
Britten, Benjamin, Baron
Caballe, Montserrat
Caccini, Guilio
Campion, Thomas (or
Campian)
Cavalli, Francesco
Copland, Aaron
Corelli, Arcangelo
Debussy, Claude
Delibes, Leo
Domingo, Placido
Dowland, John
Farnaby, Giles
Ferrier, Kathleen
Galuppi, Baldassare
Gibbons, Orlando
Giulini, Carlos Maria
Gorecki, Henryk

Hammond, Dame Joan
Hofmann, Joseph Casimir
Ireland, John Nicholson
Janacek, Leos
Joachim, Joseph
Karajan, Herbert von
Kubelik, Rafael
Lambert, Constant
Lehmann, Lilli
Lehmann, Lotte
Malcolm, George John
Martinu, Bohuslav
Menotti, Gian Carlo
Menuhin, Sir Yehudi
Milhaud, Darius
Monteux, Pierre
Nicolai, Otto Ehrenfried
Nielsen, Carl
Nikisch, Arthur
Nilsson, Birgit Marta
Okeghem, Jean d'
Ormandy, Eugene (Eugene Blau)
Perotin (Latin name: Perotinus Magnus)
Poulenc, Francis
Puccini, Giacomo
Purcell, Henry
Richter, Hans
Richter, Sviatoslav
Rodrigo, Joaquin
Rossini, Gioacchino Antonio
Roussel, Albert
Ruggles, Carl
Salieri, Antonio
Sargent, Sir Malcolm
Schuman, William
Smetana, Bedrich
Solomon (Solomon Cutner)

Stainer, Sir John
Stamitz, Johann (Jan Stamic)
Strauss, Richard
Thibaud, Jacques
Thomson, Virgil
Tippett, Sir Michael
Vivaldi, Antonio
Warlock, Peter (Philip Heseltine)
Weelkes, Thomas
Wellesz, Egon
Xenakis, Yannis

8

Albinoni, Tomaso
Ansermet, Ernest
Berkeley, Sir Lennox Randal Francis
Bruckner, Anton
Chabrier, Emmanuel
Chausson, Ernest
Cimarosa, Domenico
Clementi, Muzio
Couperin, Francois
Dohnanyi, Erno (Ernst von Dohnanyi)
Flagstad, Kirsten Malfrid
Gardiner, Sir John Eliot
Gershwin, George (Jacob Gershvin)
Gesualdo, Carlo, Prince of Venosa
Glazunov, Aleksandr Konstantinovich
Goossens, Sir Eugene
Grainger, Percy Aldridge
Granados, Enrique
Honegger, Arthur
Horowitz, Vladimir
Kreisler, Fritz
Maconchy, Dame Elizabeth

Marenzio, Luca
Mascagni, Pietro
Massenet, Jules
Melchior, Lauritz
Messager, Andre
Messiaen, Oliver
Milstein, Nathan
Musgrave, Thea
Oistrakh, David
Paganini, Niccolo
Philidor, Andre Danican
Respighi, Ottorino
Schnabal, Artur
Schubert, Franz
Schuller, Gunther
Schumann, Elisabeth
Schumann, Robert
Scriabin, Alexander
Sessions, Roger
Sibelius, John (Johan Julius Christian Sibelius)
Stanford, Sir Charles
Sullivan, Sir Arthur
Taverner, John
Te Kanawa, Dame Kiri
Telemann, Georg Philipp
Victoria, Tomas Luis de
Williams, John
Zabaleta, Nicanor

9

Addinsell, Richard
Ashkenazy, Vladimir
Balakirev, Mili Alekseevich
Barenboim, Daniel
Beethoven, Ludwig van
Bernstein, Leonard
Boulanger, Nadia
Buxtehude, Dietrich
Chaliapin, Feodor Ivanovich

Cherubini, Maria Luigi
Christoff, Boris
Dolmetsch, Arnold
Donizetti, Gaetano
Dunstable, John
Hindemith, Paul
Hoddinott, Alun
Klemperer, Otto
Landowska, Wanda
Mackerras, Sir Charles
Malipiero, Gian
Francesco
Meyerbeer, Giacomo
(Jacob Liebmann Beer)
Offenbach, Jacques
(Jacques Eberst)
Pavarotti, Luciano
Pergolesi, Giovanni
Scarlatti, Domenico
Stokowski, Leopold
Tortelier, Paul
Toscanini, Arturo

10

Barbirolli, Sir John
Birtwistle, Harrison
Boccherini, Luigi
Galli-Curci, Amelita
Los Angeles, Victoria de
Mengelberg, William
Monteverdi, Claudio
Mussorgski, Modest
Petrovich
Paderewski, Ignacy
Palestrina, Giovanni
Pierluigi da
Penderecki, Krzysztof
Praetorius, Michael
(Michael Schultheiss)
Rawsthorne, Alan
Rubinstein, Artur
Saint-Saens, Camille
Schoenberg, Arnold

Skalkottas, Nikos
Stradivari, Antonio
Stravinsky, Igor
Sutherland, Dame Joan
Tetrazzini, Luisa
Villa-Lobos, Heitor

11

Charpentier, Gustave
Furtwangler, Wilhelm
Humperdinck, Engelbert
Leoncavallo, Ruggiero
Leschetizky, Theodor
Lloyd-Webber, Andrew
Lloyd-Webber, Julian
Lutoslawski, Witold
Mendelssohn, Felix
(Jacob Ludwig Felix
Mendelssohn-
Bartholdy)
Rachmaninov, Sergei
Schwarzkopf, Elisabeth
Stockhausen, Karlheinz
Szymanowski, Karol
Tchaikovsky, Peter Ilich
Wolf-Ferrari, Ermanno

12

Dallapiccola, Luigi
Guido, D'Arezzo
Khachaturian, Aram Ilich
Koussevitsky, Sergei

13

Rouget de L'isle, Claude
Joseph

14

Fischer-Dieskau,
Dietrich
Jaques-Dalcroze, Emile
Josquin des Prez
Rimsky Korsakov,

Nikolai

15

Coleridge-Taylor,
Samuel
Vaughan Williams, Ralph

17

Strauss the Younger,
Johann

Philosophers

4

Ayer, Sir Alfred (Jules)
Hume, David
Kant, Immanuel
Mach, Ernst
Marx, Karl (Heinrich)
Mill, James
More, Henry
Mozi (or Motzu)
Razi, ar (or Rhazes)
Reid, Thomas
Ryle, Gilbert
Vico, Giambattista (or
Giovanni Batissta Vico)
Weil, Simone

5

Amiel, Henri Frederic
Bacon, Francis, 1st
Baron Verulam, Viscount
St Albans
Benda, Julien
Bodin, Jean
Bruno, Giordano
Buber, Martin
Burke, Edmund
Chu Xi (or Chu Hsi)
Comte, Auguste

Croce, Benedetto
Dewey, John
Fludd, Robert
Fromm, Erich
Hegel, Georg Wilhelm
Friedrich
Iqbal, Sir Mohammed
Lacan, Jacques (Marie
Emile)
Locke, John
Moore, G(eorge)
E(dward)

Plato
Quine, Willard van
Orman
Ramus, Petrus (Pierre
de la Ramee)
Renan (Joseph; Ernest)
Smith, Adam
Sorel, Georges

6

Adorno, Theodor
(Wiesengrund)
Agnesi, Maria Gaetana
Arendt, Hannah
Austin, John Langshaw
Berlin, Sir Isaiah
Carnap, Rudolf
Cousin, Victor
Fichte, Johann Gottlieb
Godwin, William
Herder, Johann
Gottfried
Herzen, Aleksandr
(Ivanovich)
Hobbes, Thomas
Kripke, Saul
Lukacs, Giorgi
Oresme, Nicole d'
Pierce, Charles Sanders
Popper, Sir Karl

Raimund
Sartre, Jean-Paul
Tagore, Rabindranath

7

Abelard, Peter
Alkindi, Abu Yusuf
Ya'qub ibn Ishaq
Aquinas, St Thomas
Arnauld, Antoine
Bentham, Jeremy
Bergson, Henri
Blondel, Maurice
Bradley, Francis
Herbert
Buridan, Jean
Charron, Pierre
Derrida, Jacques
Destutt, Antoine Louis
Claude, Comte de Tracy
Diderot, Denis
Edwards, Jonathan
Erigena, John Scotus
Gentile, Giovanni
Guarini, Guarino
Husserl, Edmund
Hypatia
Jaspers, Karl (Theodor)
Leibniz, Gottfried
Wilhelm
Mencius (Mengzi or
Mengtzu)
Mumforf, Lewis
Murdoch, Dame Iris
Proclus
Pyrrhon (or Pyrrho)
Russell, Bertrand
Arthur William, 3Rd
Earl
Sankara (or Shankara)
Schlick, Moritz
Scruton, Roger
(Vernon)

Spencer, Herbert
Spinoza, Benedict (or
Baruch de Spinoza)

8

Alfarabi, Mohammed
Ibn Tarkhan
Averroes (Ibn Rushd)
Avicenna
Berdyaev, Nikolai
Berkeley, George
Boethius, Anicius
Manlius Severinus
Brentano, Franz
Cassirer, Ernst
Epicurus
Foucault, Michel
Gassendi, Pierre
Geulincx, Arnold
Han Fei Zi
Hartmann, Eduard von
Hartmann, Nicolai
Krochmal, Nachman
Plotinus
Porphyry
Ramanuja
Roscelin
Rousseau, Jean Jacques
Sidgwick, Henry
Socrates
Soloviov, Vladimir
Sergevich
Spengler, Oswald
Strawson, Sir Peter
Frederick
Voltaire, Francois Marie
Arouet
Zhuangzi (or Chaung
Tzu)

9

Althusser, Louis
Aristotle

Bosanquet, Bernard
Cleanthes
Condillac, Etienne
Bonnet de
Condorcet, Marie Jean
Antoine de Caritat,
Marquis de
Confucius (Kong Zi or
K'ungfutzu)
Descartes, Rene
Epictetus
Feuerbach, Ludwig
Andreas
Heidegger, Martin
Helvetius, Claude
Adrien
Hutcheson, Francis
Leucippus
Lucretius (Titus
Lucretius Carus)
Nagarjuna
Nietzsche, Friedrich
Plekhanov, Georgi
Valentinovich
Pufendorf, Samuel von
Santayana, George
Schelling, Friedrich
Whitehead, A(lfred)
N(orth)

10

Anaxagoras
Anaximenes
Aristippus
Baumgarten, Alexander
Gottlieb
Campanella, Tommaso
Cumberland, Richard
Democritus
Duns Scotus, John
Empedocles
Fontenelle, Bernard le
Bovier de

Heraclitus
Ibn Gabirol, Solomon
Ibn Khaldun
Maimonides, Moses
Parmenides
Pythagoras
Swedenborg, Emanuel
Zeno of Elea

11

Bolingbroke, Henry St
John, 1st Viscount
Collingwood, R(obin
G(eorge)
Judah Halevi (or
Halevy)
Kierkegaard, Soren
Malebranche, Nicolas
Mendelssohn, Moses
Montesquieu, Charles
Louis de Secondant,
Baron de
Vivekananda, Swami
Anaximander
Antisthenes

12

MerleaupONTY, Maurice
Philo Judaeus
Schopenhauer, Arthur
Theophrastus
Unamuno y Jugo, Miguel
de
Wittgenstein, Ludwig
Zeno of Citium

13

Dio Chrysostom
Ortega y Gasset, Jose

14

Albertus Magnus, St
Wollstonecraft, Mary

15

John of Salisbury
William of Ockham

16

Alexander of Hales

17

Apollonius of Tyana
Bernard of Chartres

18

Pico della Mirandola,
Giovanni, Conte

Writers, Playwrights and Poets

2

Fo, Dario

3

Eco, Umberto
Fry Christopher (C
Harris)
Gay, John
Kyd, Thomas
Paz, Octavio
Sue, Eugene (Joseph
Marie Sue)

4

Agee, James
Amis, Kingsley
Amis, Martin
Asch, Sholem
Bana
Baum, L Frank
Benn, Gottfried
Blok, Aleksandr
Aleksandrovich

Boll, Heinrich
Bolt, Robert Oxton
Bond, Edward
Buck, Pearl S.
Cary, Joyce
Cruz, Sor Juana Inez de la
Dahl, Roald
Dues, Joao de
Du Fu (or Tu Fu)
Ford, Ford Madox (Ford Hermann Hueffer)
Ford, John
Foxe, John
Galt, John
Gide, Andre
Gray, Thomas
Gunn, Thomson W
Hare, Sir David
Hart, Moss
Hill, Geoffrey
Hogg, James
Hood, Thomas
Hope, Anthony (Sir Anthony Hope Hawkins)
Hugo, Victor
Hunt, Leigh
Kivi, Alexis (Alexis Stenvall)
Lamb, Charles
Lear, Edward
Livy (Titus Livius)
Loti, Pierre (Julien Viaud)
Lyly, John
Mann, Thomas
Muir, Edwin
Nash, Ogden
Nexo, Martin Andersen
Ovid (Publius Ovidius Naso)
Owen, Wilfred

Pope, Alexander
Read, Sir Herbert
Rhys, Jean
Roth, Philip
Rowe, Nicholas
Ruiz, Juan
Sade, Donatien Alphonse Francois, Marquis de
Sa'di (Mosleh al-Din Sa'di.)
Saki (H.H. Munro)
Sand, George (Aurore Dupin, Baronne Dudevant)
Seth, Vikram
Shaw, George Bernard
Snow, C P, Baron
Tate, Allen
Tate, Nahum
Urfe, Honore d'
Vega, Lope Felix de
Wain, John
Ward, Artemus (Charles Farrar Browne)
Ward, Mrs Humphrey
Webb, Mary
West, Dame Rebecca (Cicely Isabel Fairfield)
West, Nathanael (Nathan Weinstein)
Wood, Mrs Henry
Wren, P C
Wyss, Johann Rudolph
Zola, Emile

5

Adams, Henry
Adams, Richard
Agnon, Shmuel Yosef (Samuel Josef Czaczkes)
Albee, Edward

Arany, Janos
Auden, W H
Babel, Isaac Emmanuilovich
Barth, John
Bates, H E
Behan, Brendan
Bello, Andres
Belyi, Andrei (Boris Nikolaevich Bugaev)
Bembo, Pietro
Benda, Julien
Benet, Stephen Vincent
Betti, Ugo
Bowen, Elizabeth
Brant, Sebastian
Broch, Hermann
Bunin, Ivan Alekseevich
Burns, Robert
Butor, Michel
Byatt, A S
Byron, George Gordon, Lord
Camus, Albert
Carew, Thomas
Clare, John
Colum, Padraic (Patrick Colm)
Craik, Dinah Maria Mulock
Crane, Hart
Crane, Stephen
Dario, Ruben (Felix, Garcia Sarmiento)
Defoe, Daniel
Donne, John
Doyle, Sir Arthur Conan
Doyle, Roddy
Dumas, Alexandre
Duras, Marguerite
Eliot, George (Mary Ann Evans)

Eliot, T S
Elyot, Sir Thomas
Ewald, Johannes
Friel, Brian
Frost, Robert Lee
Genet, Jean
Gogol, Nikolai Vasilievich
Gorki, Maksim (Aleksei Maksimovich Peshkov)
Gosse, Sir Edmund
Gower, John
Grass, Gunter
Green, Henry (Henry Vincent Yorke)
Hafiz, Shams al-Din Muhammad
Halle, Adam de la
Hardy, Thomas
Harte, Brett
Hasek, Jaroslav
Heine, Heinrich
Henry, O (William Sidney Porter)
Hesse, Hermann
Homer
Hooft, Pieter Corneliszoon
Ibsen, Henrik
James, Henry
James, P D
Jarry, Alfred
Jones, David
Jones, LeRoi
Joyce, James
Kakfa, Franz
Keats, John
Kemal, Namik
Kesey, Ken
Lewis, C S
Lewis, Matthew Gregory
Lewis, Sinclair

Lewis, Wyndham
Lodge, David
Lodge, Thomas
Lowry, Malcolm
Lucan (Marcus Annaeus Lucanus)
Mamet, David
Marot, Clement
Marsh, Dame Ngaio
Marti, Jose Julian
Mason, A E W
Milne, A A
Moore, Marianne
Moore, Thomas
Murry, John Middleton
Musil, Robert
Myers, F H W
Nashe, Thomas
Noyes, Alfred
Odets, Clifford
O'Hara John
Opitz, Martin
Orczy, Baroness Emmusca
Otway, Thomas
Ouida (Marie Louise de la Ramee)
Pan Gu (or P'an Ku)
Paton, Alan
Peake, Mervyn
Peele, George
Peguy, Charles
Perse, Saint-John (Alexis Saint-Leger)
Plath, Sylvia
Pound, Ezra
Powys, John Cowper
Prior, Matthew
Pulci, Luigi
Raine, Kathleen
Reade, Charles
Rilke, Rainer Maria
Rolfe, Frederick William

Sachs, Nelly
Sagan, Françoise (Françoise Quoirez)
Scott, Sir Walter
Seton, Ernest Thompson
Shute, Nevil (Nevil Shute Norway)
Simms, William Gilmore
Smart, Christopher
Smith, Stevie (Florence Margaret Smith)
Spark, Muriel
Stael, Anne Louise Germaine Necker, Madame de
Stein, Gertrude
Storm, Theodor Woldsen
Stowe, Harriet Beecher
Svevo, Italo (Ettore Schmitz)
Swift, Graham
Swift, Jonathan
Synge, John Millington
Tasso, Torquato
Tieck, Ludwig
Twain, Mark (Samuel Langhorne Clemens)
Udall, Nicholas
Varro, Marcus Terentius
Verne, Jules
Vidal, Gore
Vigny, Alfred de
Waley, Arthur
Waugh, Evelyn
Weiss, Peter
Wells H G
White, Patrick
White T H
Wilde, Oscar (O Fingal O'Flahertie Wills Wilde)
Wolfe, Charles

Wolfe, Thomas
Woolf, Virginia
Wyatt, Sir Thomas
Yeats, William Butler
Yonge, Charlotte
Zweig, Arnold
Zweig Stefan

6

Accius, Lucius
Adamov, Arthur
Alcott, Louisa May
Aldiss, Brian W
Aleman, Mateo
Algren, Nelson
Ambler, Eric
Andric, Ivo
Aragon, Louis
Ascham, Roger
Asimov, Isaac
Aubrey, John
Austen, Jane
Azorin (Jose Martinez Ruiz)
Azuela, Mariano
Balzac, Honore de
Barham, Richard Harris
Barker, George
Barnes, William
Baroja, Pio
Barres, Maurice
Barrie, Sir James
Bellay, Joachim de
Belloc, Hilaire
Bellow, Saul
Besant, Sir Walter
Bialik, Chaim Nachman
Bierce, Ambrose Gwinnett
Binyon, Laurence
Blyton, Enid
Borges, Jorge Luis
Borrow, George Henry

Brecht, Bertolt
Breton, Andre
Bridie, James (Osborne Henry Mavor)
Bronte, Anne
Bronte, Charlotte
Bronte, Emily
Brooke, Rupert
Browne, Sir Thomas
Bryant, William Cullen
Buchan, John, 1st Baron Tweedsmuir
Bunyan, John
Burger, Gottfried
Burney, Fanny (Mrs Frances Burney D'Arblay)
Butler, Samuel (Poet, 1612 – 1680)
Butler, Samuel (Novelist, 1835 – 1902)
Camoes, Luis de
Capote, Truman
Carson, Rachel Louise
Cavafy, Constantine (Constantine Kavafis)
Celine, Louis Ferdinand (Louis Ferdinand Destouches)
Cibber, Colley
Clarke, Marcus
Colman, George
Conrad, Joseph (Teodor Josef Konrad Watecz Korzeniowski)
Cooper, James Fenimore
Cowley, Abraham
Cowper, William
Crabbe, George
Cronin A J
Daniel, Samuel
Daudet, Alphonse

Davies, W H
Dekker, Thomas
Dowson, Ernest
Dryden, John
Dunbar, William
Eluard, Paul (Eugene Grindel)
Empson, Sir William
Ennius, Quintus
Evelyn, John
Fouque, Friedrich Heinrich Karl, Baron de la Mote
Fowles, John
France, Anatole (Jacques Anatole François Thibault)
Frisch, Max
Fugard, Athol
Fuller, Roy
Fuller, Thomas
George, Stefan
Gibbon, Edward
Gibran, Khalil
Goethe, Johann Wolfgang von
Graves, Robert
Greene, Graham
Hamsun, Knut
Harris, Joel Chandler
Heaney, Seamus
Hebbel, Friedrich
Heller, Joseph
Hesiod
Hilton, James
Holmes, Oliver Wendell
Horace (Quintus Horatius Flaccus)
Hudson W H
Hughes, Richard
Hughes, Ted
Hughes, Thomas
Irving, Washington

Isaacs, Jorge
Jensen, Johannes
Jonson, Ben
Kaiser, Georg
Keller, Gottfried
Kleist, Heinrich von
Laclos, Pierre
Choderlos de
Landor, Walter Savage
Lanier, Sidney
Larkin, Philip
Lawler, Ray
Le Fanu, Sheridan
Leonov, Leonid
Lesage, Alain-Rene
Lively, Penelope
London, Jack
Lowell, Amy
Lowell, James Russell
Lowell, Robert
Lu Hsun (or Chou Shu-
jen)
Machen, Arthur
Mailer, Norman
Malory, Sir Thomas
McEwan, Ian
Mercer, Davis
Millay, Edna St Vincent
Miller, Arthur
Miller, Henry
Milton, John
Molnar, Ferenc
Morgan, Charles
Morike, Eduard
Friedrich
Motion, Andrew
Munthe, Axel
Musset, Alfred de
Neruda, Pablo (Neftali
Ricardo Reyes)
Nerval, Gerard de
(Gerard Labrunie)
Nesbit, Edith

O'Brien, Flann (Brian
O'Nolan)
O'Casey, Sean
O'Neill, Eugene
Orwell, George (Eric
Blair)
Parker, Dorothy
Rothschild
Pavese, Cesare
Petofi, Sandor
Pindar
Pinero, Sir Arthur Wing
Pinter, Harold
Piozzi, Hester Lynch
Plomer, William
Porter, Katherine Anne
Porter, Peter
Potter, Beatrix
Potter, Stephen
Powell, Anthony
Proust, Marcel
Racine, Jean
Ramsey, Allan
Ransom, John Crowe
Runyon, Damon
Sapper (H C McNeile)
Sappho
Sardou, Victorien
Sartre, Jean-Paul
Savage, Richard
Sayers, Dorothy L
Sidney, Sir Philip
Silone, Ignazio (Secondo
Tranquilli)
Singer, Isaac Bashevis
Smiles, Samuel
Steele, Sir Richard
Sterne, Laurence
Stoker, Bram (Abraham
Stoker)
Storey, David
Surrey, Henry Howard,
Earl of

Symons, Arthur
Tagore, Rabindranath
Thomas, Dylan
Thomas, Edward
Toller, Ernst
Traven, B (Berick Traven
Torsvan)
Uhland, Ludwig
Undset, Sigrid
Updike, John
Valery, Paul
Villon, François
Virgil (Publius Vergilius
Maro)
Vondel, Joost van den
Waller, Edmund
Walton, Izaak
Warton, Joseph
Weldon, Pay
Werfel, Franz
Wesker, Arnold
Wilder, Thornton
Wilson, Colin
Wilson, Edmund
Wilson, Sir Angus
Wotton, Sir Henry
Wright, Judith
Wright, Richard

7

Addison, Joseph
Aelfric
Alarcon, Pedro Antonio
de
Alberti, Raphael
Alcaeus
Aldanov, Mark (Mark
Aleksandrovich Landau)
Aldrich, Thomas Bailey
Alegria, Ciro
Alfieri, Vittorio, Count
Allende, Isabel
Aneirin

Aretino, Pietro
Ariosto, Ludovico
Arrabal, Fernando
Balchin, Nigel
Baldwin, James Arthur
Barbour, John
Beckett, Samuel
Beddoes, Thomas Lovell
Bennett, Arnold
Bentley, Edmund
Clerihew
Bergman, Hjalmar
Blunden, Edmund
Charles
Boiardo, Matteo Maria,
Conte di Scandiano
Boileau (-Despreaux),
Nicolas
Boswell, James
Bo Zhu Yi (or Po Chu-
i)
Bradley, Andrew Cecil
Bridges, Robert
Seymour
Buchner, Georg
Burgess, Anthony (John
Burgess Wilson)
Burnett, Frances Eliza
Hodgson
Ceadmon
Cao Chan (or Zao
Zhan)
Carossa, Hans
Carroll, Lewis (Charles
Lutwidge Dodgson)
Chapman, George
Chaucher, Geoffrey
Chekov, Anton
Pavlovich
Chenier, Andre de
Chu Yuan
Claudel, Paul
Cleland, John

Cocteau, Jean
Coetzee, J M
Colette (Sidonie-
Gabrielle Colette)
Collins, William
Collins, William Wilkie
Corelli, Marie
Crashaw, Richard
Creeley, Robert
Da Ponte, Lorenzo
Deledda, Grazia
Dickens, Charles
Dinesen, Isak (Karen
Blixen Baroness Blixen-
Finecke)
Douglas, Gavin
Douglas, Norman
Drabble, Margaret
Drayton, Michael
Dreiser, Theodore
Duhamel, Georges
Dunsany, Edward John
Moreton Drax Plunkett,
18th Baron
Durrell, Lawrence
George
Emerson, Ralph Waldo
Ercilla, Alonso de
Eupolis
Ferrier, Susan
Edmonstone
Feydeau, Georges
Firbank, Ronald
Flecker, James Elroy
Fleming, Ian
Fleming, Paul
Fontane, Theodor
Forster, E M
Foscolo, Ugo
Freneau, Philip
Froding, Gustaf
Gaarder, Jostein
Gaskell, Elizabeth

Cleghorn
Gautier, Theophile
Gilbert, Sir William
Schwenk
Gissing, George Robert
Golding, William
Goldini, Carlo
Grahame, Kenneth
Grisham, John
Guarini, Giovanni
Battista
Haggard, Sir H Rider
Hammett, Dashiell
Hartley, L P
Hellman, Lillian
Herbert, George
Herrick, Robert
Heywood, Thomas
Holberg, Ludvig, Baron
Hopkins, Gerard
Manley
Housman, A E
Ibn Ezra, Abraham Ben
Meir
Ionesco, Eugene
Jeffers, Robinson
Jimenez, Juan Ramon
Juvenal (Decimus Junius
Juvenalis)
Kastner, Erich
Kaufman, George S
Kendall, Henry
Kerouac, Jack
Kipling, Rudyard
Klinger, Friedrich
Maximilian von
Labiche, Eugene
Lardner, Ring
Laxness, Halldor
Layamon
Leacock, Stephen
Le Carre, John (David
Cornwell)

Lessing, Doris
Lessing, Gotthold
Ephraim
Lindsay, Vachel
Lydgate, John
Machaut, Guillaume de
Malamad, Bernard
Malraux, Andre
Manzoni, Alessandro
Marlowe, Christopher
Marryat, Captain,
Frederick
Marston, John
Martial (Marcus Valerius
Martialis)
Marvell, Andrew
Masters, Edgar Lee
Maugham, W Somerset
Mauriac, Francois
Maurois, Andre (Emile
Herzog)
Merimee, Prosper
Mishima, Yukio
(Kamitake Hiraoka)
Mistral, Frederic
Mistral, Gabriela (Lucila
Godoy Alcayaga)
Moliere (Jean-Baptiste
Poquelin)
Montagu, Lady Mary
Wortley
Montale, Eugenio
Moravia, Alberto
(Alberto Pincherle)
Murdoch, Dame Iris
Nabokov, Vladimir
Naevius, Gnaeus
Naipaul, V S
Novalis (Friedrich
Leopold, Freiherr von
Hardenberg)
O'Connor, Frank
(Michael O'Donovan)

Osborne, John
Patmore, Coventry
Peacock, Thomas Love
Plautus, Titus Maccius
Prevert, Jacques
Puskhin, Aleksandr
Pynchon, Thomas
Queneau, Raymond
Ransome, Arthur
Mitchell
Regnier, Henri Francois
Joseph de
Richler, Mordecai
Rimbaud, Arthur
Rolland, Romain
Romains, Jules (Louis
Farigoule)
Ronsard, Pierre de
Rostand, Edmond
Roussel, Raymond
Rowling, J K
Rushdie, Salman
Saroyan, William
Sassoon, Siegfried
Scarron, Paul
Seferis, George
(Georgios Seferiadis)
Shaffer, Peter
Shelley, Percy Bysshe
Simenon, Georges
Simonov, Konstantin
Sitwell, Edith
Skelton, John
Southey, Robert
Soyinka, Wole
Spender, Sir Stephen
Spenser, Edmund
Stevens, Wallace
Surtees, Robert Smith
Terence (Publius
Terentius Afer)
Thespis
Thomson, James

Thurber, James
Tolkien J R R
Tolstoy, Leo, Count
Travers, Ben
Tutuola, Amos
Van Duyn, Mona
Vaughan, Henry
Vicente, Gil
Wallace, Edgar
Walpole, Sir Hugh
Webster, John
Wharton, Edith
Whitman, Walt
Wieland, Christoph
Martin
Yesenin, Sergei

8

Abu Nuwas
Anacreon
Anchieta, Jose de
Andersen, Hans
Christian
Anderson, Sherwood
Apuleius, Lucius
Asturias, Miguel Angel
Bandeira, Manuel
Carneiro de Sousa
Banville, Theodore
Faullain
Barbusse, Henri
Beaumont, Francis
Beauvoir, Simone de
Beckford, William
Beerbohm, Sir Max
Belinsky, Vissarion
Benchley, Robert
Charles
Beranger, Pierre Jean de
Bernanos, Georges
Betjeman, Sir John
Bjornson, Bjornstjerne
Bradbury, Ray

Brentano, Clemens
Brookner, Anita
Browning, Robert
Campbell, Thomas
Carducci, Giosue
Castilho, Antonio
Feliciano de
Catullus, Valerius
Chandler, Raymond
Chartier, Alain
Christie, Dame Agatha
Claudian
Congreve, William
Constant, Benjamin
Crompton, Richmal
(Richmal Crompton
Lamburn)
Cummings, E E
Cynewulf
Davenant, Sir William
Cay Lewis, C
De la Mare, Walter
Donleavy, J P
Etherege, Sir George
Farquhar, George
Faulkner, William
Fielding, Henry
Firdausi (Abul Qasim
Mansur)
Flaubert, Gustave
Fletcher, John
Forester, C S
Ginsberg Allen
Goncourt, Edmond de
Henryson, Robert
Hochhuth, Rolf
Huysmans, Joris Karl
Jean Paul (Johann Paul
Friedrich Richter)
Kalidasa
Keneally, Thomas
Kingsley, Charles
Koestler, Arthur

Kotzebue, August von
Laforgue, Jules
Lagerlof, Selma
Ottiliana Lovisa
Langland, William
Las Cases, Emmanuel,
Comte de
Lawrence D H
Leopardi, Giacomo
Lockhart, John Gibson
Longinus
Lovelace, Richard
Macaulay, Dame Rose
Macleish, Archibald
Macneice, Louis
Malherbe, Francois de
Mallarme, Stephane
Marivaux, Pierre Carlet
de Chamblain de
Marquand, J P
McCarthy, Mary
Melville, Herman
Menander
Meredith, George
Michelet, Jules
Mitchell, Margaret
Morrison, Toni
Nekrasov, Nikolai
Alekseevich
Nicolson, Sir Harold
Ondaatje, Michael
Palgrave, Francis Turner
Perelman, S J
Perrault, Charles
Petrarch (Francesco
Petrarca)
Phaedrus
Philemon
Plutarch
Rabelais, Francois
Radiguet, Raymond
Rattigan, Sir Terence
Remarque, Erich Maria

Richards, Frank
(Charles Hamilton)
Runeberg, Johan Ludvig
Salinger, J D
Sandburg, Carl
Saramago, Jose
Sarraute, Nathalie
Scaliger, Julius Caesar
Schiller, Friedrich
Shadwell, Thomas
Sillitoe, Alan
Sinclair, Upton
Smollett, Tobias
Spillane, Mickey (Frank
Morrison Spillane)
Stendhal (Henri Beyle)
Stoppard, Sir Tom
Suckling, Sir John
Su Dong Po (Su Tung-
p'o)
Taliesin
Tennyson, Lord Alfred
Thompson, Francis
Tibullus, Albius
Tourneur, Cyril
Traherne, Thomas
Trilling, Lionel
Trollope, Anthony
Tulsidas
Turgenev, Ivan
Verlaine, Paul
Voltaire (Francois-Marie
Arouet)
Vonnegut, Kurt
Wedekind, Frank
Whittier, John
Greenleaf
Williams, Tennessee
Williams, William
Carlos
Zamyatin, Yevgenii
Ivanovich

9

Aeschylus
Ainsworth, W Harrison
Akhmatova, Anna (Anna Andreevna Gorenko)
Aldington, Richard
Allingham, Margery
Arbuthnot, John
Ayckbourn, Alan
Blackmore R D
Blackwood, Algernon Henry
Boccaccio, Giovanni
Burroughs, Edgar Rice
Burroughs, William
Cervantes, Miguel de
Charteris, Leslie (Leslie Charles Bowyer Yin)
Charles, Churchill
Coleridge, Samuel Taylor
Corneille, Pierre
D'Annunzio, Gabriele
De La Roche, Mazo
De Quincey, Thomas
Dickinson, Emily
Doolittle, Hilda
Dos Passos, John
Du Maurier, George
Du Maurier, Daphne
Eckermann, Johann Peter
Edgeworth, Maria
Ehrenberg, Iliya Grigorievich
Euripides
Froissart, Jean
Giraudoux, Jean
Goldsmith, Oliver
Goncharov, Ivan Aleksandrovich
Gottsched, Johann Christoph
Greenwood, Walter
Hauptmann, Gehart
Hawthorne, Nathaniel
Hemingway, Ernest
Highsmith, Patricia
Holderlin, Friedrich
Isherwood, Christopher
Jeffries, Richard
Klopstock, Friedrich Gottlieb
La Bruyere, Jean de
La Fayette, Mme de (Marie Madeleine, Comtesse de La Fayette)
LaMartine, Alphonse de
Lampedusa, Guiseppe Tomasi di
Lermontov, Mikhail
Linklater, Eric
Llewellyn, Richard (R D V L Lloyd)
Lomonosov, Mikhail Vasilievich
Lovecraft, H P
Lucretius (Titus Lucretius Carus)
Mackenzie, Sir Compton
Malaparte, Curzio (Kurt Erich Suckert)
Mansfield, Katherine (Kathleen Mansfield Beauchamp)
Marinetti, Filippo Tommaso
Martineau, Harriet
Masefield, John
Massinger, Philip
McCullers, Carson
Middleton, Thomas
Monsarrat, Nicholas (John Turney)
Montaigne, Michel de
Mutanabbi, Abu At-Tayyib Ahmad Ibn Husayn al-
O'Flaherty, Liam
Parkinson, Northcote
Pasternak, Boris
Poliziano (or Politian)
Pritchett, V S
Radcliffe, Ann
Rochester, John Wilmot, 2nd Earl of
Sackville, Thomas, 1st Earl of Dorset
Schreiner, Olive
Shenstone, William
Sholokhov, Mikhail
Sophocles
Steinbeck, John
Stevenson, Robert Louis
Sturluson, Snorri
Swinburne, Algernon Charles
Thackeray, William Makepeace
Tsvetaeva, Marina
Ungaretti, Guiseppe
Verhaeren, Emile
Vittorini, Elio
Wergeland, Henrik Arnold
Wodehouse, Sir P G
Wycherley, William

10

Bainbridge, Beryl
Baudelaire, Charles
Bilberdijk, Willem
Cavalcanti, Guide
Chatterjee, Bankim Chandra
Chatterton, Thomas
Chesterton, G K

Conscience, Hendrik
Dazai Osamu
(Tsushima Shuji)
Dio Cassius
Drinkwater, John
Durrenmatt, Friedrich
Fitzgerald, Edward
Fitzgerald, F Scott
Galsworthy. John
Jean de Meun
Khlebnikov, Velimir
(Victor Khlebnikov)
La Fontaine, Jean de
Lagerkvist, Par
Longfellow, Henry
Macdiarmid, Hugh
(Christopher Murray
Grieve)
Mandelstam, Osip
Maupassant, Guy de
McGonagall, William
Mickiewicz, Adam
Ostrovskii, Aleksandr
Nikolaevich
Pirandello, Luigi
Propertius, Sextus
Richardson, Henry
Handel (Ethel Florence
Richardson)
Richardson, Samuel
Rutherford, Mark
(William Hale White)
Schnitzler, Arthur
Strindberg, August
Tannhauser
Theocritus
van der Post, Sir
Laurens
Williamson, Henry
Wordsworth, William
Xenophanes

11

Anzengruber, Ludwig
Apollinaire, Guillaume
(Wilhelm de
Kostrowitzky)
Archilochus
Bacchylides
Blessington, Marguerite,
Countess of
Callimachus
Castiglione, Baldassare
Dostoievski, Fedor
Mikhailovich
Eichendorff, Josef,
Freiherr von
Garcia Lorca, Federico
Grillparzer, Franz
Kazantzakis, Nikos
Lautreamont, Comte de
(Isidor Ducasse)
Maeterlinck, Maurice
Matsuo, Basho (Matsuo
Munefusa)
Mayakovskii, Vladimir
Montherlant, Henry de
Omar Khyyam
Perez Galdos, Benito
Shakespeare, William
Sienkiewicz, Henryk
Stiernhielm, George
Olofson
Yevtushenko, Yevgenii

12

Aristophanes
Beaumarchais, Pierre-
Augustin Caron de
Blasco Ibanez, Vicente
Ferlinghetti, Lawrence
Feuchtwanger, Lion
Hofmannsthal, Hugo
von
Lopez de Ayala, Pero

Martin du Gard, Roger
Matthew Paris
Robbe-Grillet, Alain
Saint-Exupery, Antoine
de
Solzhenitsyn, Aleksandr
Voznesenkii, Andrei

13

Bertran de Born
Castelo Branco
Chateaubriand, Vicomte
de
Csokonai Vitez, Mihaly
Garcia Marquez, Gabriel
Harishchandra
Marie de France
Tirso de Molina
(Gabriel Tellez)
Zeami Motokiyo

14

Brillat-Savarin, Anthelme
Compton-Burnett,
Dame Ivy
Dafydd Ap Gwilym
Dante Alighieri
Droste-Hulshoff,
Annette von
Gongora y Argote, Luis
de
Grimmelshausen, Hans
Jacob Christoph von
Jacopone da Todi
Leconte de Lisle,
Charles Marie Rene
Oehlenschlager, Adam
Prevost D'Exiles,
Antione Francois, Abbe
Sully-Prudhomme, Rene
Francois Armand
Wollstonecraft, Mary
Zorrilla y Moral, Jose

15

Alarcon y Mendoza,
Juan Ruiz de
Diodorus, Siculus
Pliny the Younger
(Gaius Plinius Caecilius
Secundus)

16

Chretien de Troyes
Cyrano de Bergerac,
Savinien
Kawabata Yasunari
Petronius Arbiter

17

Calderon de la Barca,

Pedro
Guillaume de Lorris
Tanizaki Jun-Ichiro

18

Apollonius of Rhodes
Kakinomoto Hitomaro
Thomas of Erceldoune

19

Benoit de Sainte-Maure
Chikamatsu
Monzaemon (Sugimori
Nobumori)
Villiers de L'Isle-Adam
(Philippe Auguste,
Comte de)

20+

Bernardin de Saint-
Pierre, Jacques Henri
Dionysus of
Halicarnassus
Drummond of
Hawthornden, William
Echegaray y Eizaguirre,
Jose
Gottfried von
Strassburg
Walther von der
Vogelweide
Wolfram von
Eschenbach

Prime Ministers of Great Britain from 1721

Name	Term	Party
Robert Walpole	1721 – 1742	Whig
Spencer Compton, Earl of Wilmington	1742 – 1743	Whig
Henry Pelham	1743 – 1754	Whig
Thomas Pelham-Holles, Duke of Newcastle	1754 – 1756	Whig
William Cavendish, Duke of Devonshire	1756 – 1757	Whig
Thomas Pelham-Holles, Duke of Newcastle	1757 – 1762	Whig
John Stuart, Earl of Bute	1762 – 1763	Tory
George Grenville	1763 – 1765	Whig
Charles Watson-Wentworth, Marquis of Rockingham	1765 – 1766	Whig
William Pitt, Earl of Chatham	1766 – 1768	Whig
Augustus Henry Fitzroy, Duke of Grafton	1768 – 1770	Whig
Lord Frederick North	1770 – 1782	Tory
Charles Watson-Wentworth, Marquis of Rockingham	1782	Whig
William Petty, Earl of Shelburne	1782 – 1783	Whig
William Henry Cavendish Bentinck, Duke of Portland	1783	coalition
William Pitt (son of Earl of Chatham)	1783 – 1801	Tory
Henry Addington	1801 – 1804	Tory

Name	Term	Party
William Pitt	1804 – 1806	Tory
William Wyndham Grenville, Baron Grenville	1806 – 1807	Whig
William Bentinck, Duke of Portland	1807 – 1809	Tory
Spencer Perceval	1809 – 1812	Tory
Robert Banks Jenkinson, Earl of Liverpool	1812 – 1827	Tory
George Canning	1827	Tory
Frederick John Robinson, Viscount Goderich	1827 – 1828	Tory
Arthur Wellesley, Duke of Wellington	1828 – 1830	Tory
Charles Grey, Earl Grey	1830 – 1834	Whig
William Lamb, Viscount Melbourne	1834	Whig
Robert Peel	1834 – 1835	Cons ervative
William Lamb, Viscount Melbourne	1835 – 1841	Whig
Robert Peel	1841 – 1846	Conservative
John Russell	1846 – 1852	Whig
Edward George Geoffrey Smith Stanley, Earl of Derby	1852	Conservative
George Hamilton Gordon, Earl of Aberdeen	1852 – 1855	coalition
Henry John Temple, Viscount Palmerston	1855 – 1858	Liberal
Edward Stanley, Earl of Derby	1858 – 1859	Conservative
Henry Temple, Viscount Palmerston	1859 – 1865	Liberal
John Russell, Earl Russell	1865 – 1866	Liberal
Edward Stanley, Earl of Derby	1866 – 1868	Conservative
Benjamin Disraeli	1868	Conservative
William Ewart Gladstone	1868 – 1874	Liberal
Benjamin Disraeli, Earl of Beaconsfield	1874 - 1880	Conservative
William Ewart Gladstone	1880 – 1885	Liberal
Robert Gascoyne-Cecil, Marquis of Salisbury	1885 – 1886	Conservative
William Ewart Gladstone	1886	Liberal
Robert Gascoyne-Cecil, Marquis of Salisbury	1886 – 1892	Conservative
William Ewart Gladstone	1892 – 1894	Liberal
Archibald Philip Primrose, Earl of Rosebery	1894 – 1895	Liberal
Robert Gascoyne-Cecil, Marquis of Salisbury	1895 – 1902	Conservative
Arthur James Balfour	1902 – 1905	Conservative
Henry Campbell Bannerman	1905 – 1908	Liberal
Herbert Henry Asquith	1908 – 1916	Liberal
David Lloyd George	1916 – 1922	coalition
Andrew Bonar Law	1922 – 1923	Conservative
Stanley Baldwin	1923 – 1924	Conservative
James Ramsey Macdonald	1924	Liberal
Stanley Baldwin	1924 – 1929	Conservative
James Ramsey Macdonald	1929 – 1935	coalition

Name	Term	Party
Stanley Baldwin	1935 – 1937	coalition
Neville Chamberlain	1937 – 1940	coalition
Winston Churchill	1940 – 1945	coalition
Clement Richard Attlee	1945 – 1951	Labour
Winston Churchill	1951 – 1955	Conservative
Antony Eden	1955 – 1957	Conservative
Harold Macmillan	1957 – 1963	Conservative
Alec Douglas-Home	1963 – 1964	Conservative
Harold Wilson	1964 – 1970	Labour
Edward Heath	1970 – 1974	Conservative
Harold Wilson	1974 – 1976	Labour
James Callaghan	1976 – 1979	Labour
Margaret Thatcher	1979 – 1990	Conservative
John Major	1990 – 1997	Conservative
Tony Blair	1997 -	Labour

Presidents of the United States of America

Name	Term
George Washington	1789 – 1797
John Adams	1797 – 1801
Thomas Jefferson	1801 – 1809
James Madison	1809 – 1817
James Monroe	1817 – 1825
John Quincy Adams	1825 – 1829
Andrew Jackson	1829 – 1837
Martin Van Buren	1837 – 1841
William Henry Harrison	1841
John Tyler	1841 – 1845
James Knox Polk	1845 – 1849
Zachary Taylor	1845 – 1850
Millard Fillmore	1850 – 1853
Franklin Pearce	1853 – 1857
James Buchanan	1857 – 1861
Abraham Lincoln	1861 – 1865
Andrew Johnson	1865 – 1869
Ulysses Simpson Grant	1869 – 1877
Rutherford Birchard Hayes	1877 – 1881

Name	Term
James Abram Garfield	1881
Chester Alan Arthur	1881 – 1885
Grover Cleveland	1885 – 1889
Benjamin Harrison	1889 – 1893
Grover Cleveland	1893 – 1897
William McKinley	1897 – 1901
Theodore Roosevelt	1901 – 1909
William Howard Taft	1909 – 1913
Woodrow Wilson	1913 – 1921
Warren Gamaliel Harding	1921 – 1923
Calvin Coolidge	1923 – 1929
Herbert Clark Hoover	1929 - 1933
Franklin Delano Roosevelt	1933 – 1945
Harry S, Truman	1945 – 1953
Dwight David Eisenhower	1953 – 1961
John Fitzgerald Kennedy	1961 – 1963
Lyndon Baines Johnson	1963 – 1969
Richard Milhous Nixon	1969 – 1974
Gerald Rudolph Ford	1974 – 1977
James Earl Carter	1977 – 1981
Ronald Wilson Reagan	1981 – 1989
George Herbert Walker Bush	1989 – 1993
William Jefferson Clinton	1993 – 2001
George W Bush	2001 –

Rulers of England

Note: * = joint ruler

Kings of Kent

Hengest	c. 455 – 488
Geric (surnamed Oisc)	488 - ?512
Octa	?512 - ?
Eormenric	560
Ethelbert I	560 – 616
Eadbald	616 – 640
Earconbert	640 – 664
Egbert I	664 – 673
*Hlothere	673 – 685
*Eadric	685 – 686
*Suaebhard	676 – 692
*Oswini	?688 - ?690
*Wihtred	690 – 725
*Ethelbert II	725 – 762
*Eadbert	?725 - ?762
*Alric	c. 750s
*Eardwulf	747 – 762
*Sigered	?762
*Eanmund	c. 759 – 765
*Heaberht	764 – 765
Egbert II	c. 765 – 780
Ealhmund	784 – 786
Eadbert (Praen)	796 – 798
Eadwald	?798 or 807

Cuthred	798 – 807	Egbert I	867 – 973
Baldred	? – 825	Ricsig	873 – 876
		Egbert II	876 - ?878

Kings of Deira

Aelli	c 560 – 590
Edwin	?590 – 592
Ethelfrith	592 – 616
Edwin	616 – 632
Osric	632 – 633
Oswald (St.)	633 – 641
Oswine	644 – 651
Ethelwald	651 – 654

Kings of Northumbria

Elthelfrith	592 – 616
Edwin	616 – 632
Oswald (St.)	633 – 641
Oswiu	654 – 670
Egfrith	670 – 685
Aldfrith	685 – 704
Osred I	704 – 716
Coenred	716 – 718
Osric	718 – 729
Ceolwulf	729 – 737
Eadbert	737 – 758
Oswulf	c. 758
Ethelwald Moll	758 – 765
Alchred	765 – 774
Ethelred I	774 – 778
Elfwald I	778 – 788
Osred II	788 – 790
Ethelred I	790 – 796
Osbald	796
Eardwulf	796 – 806
Elfwald II	806 – 808
Eardwulf	?808
Eanred	808 – 840
Ethelred II	840 – 844
Redwulf	844
Ethelred II	844 – 849
Osbert	849 – 862
Aelle	862 – 867

Kings of Mercia

Cearl	c. 600
Penda	632 – 654
Wulfhere	657 – 674
Ethelred	674 – 704
Coenred	704 – 709
Ceolred	709 – 716
Ethelbald	716 - ?757
Beornred	757
Offa	757 – 796
Egfrith	796
Coenwulf	796 - ?821
Ceolwulf I	821 – 823
Beornwulf	823 – 825
Ludecan	825 – 827
Wiglaf	827 – 840
Beorhtwulf	840 – 852
Burgred	852 – 874
Ceolwulf II	874 - ?883

Kings of the West Saxons

Cerdic	519 – 534
Cynric	534 – 560
Ceawlin	560 – 591
Coel	591 – 597
Ceolwulf	597 – 611
Cynegils	611 – 643
Cenwalh	643 – 672
Seaxburh (Queen)	?672 - ?674
Aescwine	674 – 676
Centwine	676 – 685
Caedwalla	685 – 688
Ini	688 – 726
Aethelheard	726 - ?740
Cuthred	740 – 756
Sigeberht	756 – 757
Cynewulf	757 – 786
Beorhtric	786 – 802

Egbert	802 – 839	Edward IV	1461 – 1483
Ethelwulf	839 – 855	Edward V	1483
Ethelbald	855 – 860	Richard III	1483 – 1485
Ethelbert	860 – 866	Henry VII	1485 – 1509
Ethelred	866 – 871	Henry VIII	1509 – 1547
Alfred	870 – 899	Edward VI	1547 – 1553
Edward the Elder	899 – 925	Jane (Lady Jane Grey)	1553
Athelstan	925 – 939	Mary	1553 – 1558
Edmund	939 – 946	*Philip	1554 – 1558
Edred	946 – 955	Elizabeth I	1558 – 1603
		James I	1603 – 1625
		Charles I	1625 – 1649
Rulers of England		The Commonwealth	1649 – 1660
Edwy	955 – 959	[Oliver Cromwell	1653 – 1658
Edgar	959 – 975	Richard Cromwell	1658 – 1659]
Edward the Martyr	975 – 979	Charles II	1660 – 1685
Ethelred	979 – 1013	James II	1685 – 1688
Swegn Forkbeard	1013 – 1014	William and Mary	1689 – 1694
Ethelred	1014 – 1016	William II	1695 – 1702
Edmund Ironside	1016	Anne	1702 – 1714
Canute	1016 – 1035	George I	1714 – 1727
Harold Harefoot	1035 – 1040	George II	1727 – 1760
Hartacnut	1040 – 1042	George III	1760 – 1820
Edward the Confessor	1042 – 1066	George IV	1820 – 1830
Harold Godwinson	1066	William IV	1830 – 1837
Edgar Etheling	1066	Victoria	1837 – 1901
(The Conqueror)		Edward VII	1901 – 1910
William I	(1066 – 1087	George V	1910 – 1936
William II (Rufus)	1087 – 1100	Edward VIII	1936
Henry I	1100- -1135	(Duke of Windsor)	
Stephen	1135 – 1154	George VI	1936 – 1952
Henry II	1154 – 1189	Elizabeth II	1952
Richard I	1189 – 1199		
John	1199 – 1216		
Henry III	1216 – 1272	*Scottish Rulers*	
Edward I	1272 – 1307	Kenneth I (MacAlpin)	843 – 858
Edward II	1307 – 1327	Donald I	858 – 862
Edward III	1327 – 1377	Constantine I	862 – 877
Richard II	1377 – 1399	Aedh	877 – 878
Henry IV	1399 – 1413	Girac	878 – 889
Henry V	1413 – 1422	Eocha	878 – 889
Henry VI	1422 – 1461;	Donald II	889 – 900
	1470 – 1471	Constantine II	900 – 943

Malcolm I	943 – 954
Indulphus	954 – 962
Duff	962 – 966
Colin	966 – 971
Kenneth II	971 – 995
Constantine III	995 – 997
Kenneth III	997 – 1005
Malcolm II	1005 – 1034
Duncan I	1034 – 1040
Macbeth	1040 – 1057
Malcolm III	1058 – 1093
Donald III (Bane)	1093 – 1094; 1094 – 1097
Duncan II	1094
Edgar	1097 – 1107
Alexander I	1107 – 1124
David I	1124 – 1153
Malcolm IV	1153 – 1165
William the Lion	1165 – 1214
Alexander II	1214 – 1249
Alexander III	1249 – 1286
Margaret, Maid of Norway	1286 – 1290
John Balliol	1292 – 1296
Robert I (Bruce)	1306 – 1329
David II	1329 – 1371
Robert II	1371 – 1390
Robert III	1390 – 1406
James I	1406 – 1437
James II	1437 – 1460
James III	1460 – 1488
James IV	1488 – 1513
James V	1513 – 1542
Mary Stuart, Queen of Scots	1542 – 1567
James VI of Scotland	1567 – 1625

Roman Rulers

Note:
* = Emperors of the Western Roman Empire only

** = Emperors of the Eastern Roman Empire (at Constantinople) before the fall of Rome (476). For Eastern emperors after 476, see Byzantine Rulers

Name	Date of Office
(Usurpers in italics)	
Augustus	27 BC – AD 14
Tiberius	14 – 37
Caligula	37 – 41
Claudius	41 – 54
Nero	54 – 68
Galba	68 – 69
Otho	69
Vitellius	69
Vespasian	69 – 79
Titus	79 – 81
Domitian	81 – 96
Nerva	96 – 98
Trajan	98 – 117
Hadrian	117 – 138
Antoninus Pius	138 – 161
Marcus Aurelius	161 – 180
Lucius Verus	161 – 169
Commodus	180 – 192
Pertinax	193
Didus Julianus	193
Niger	193
Septimus Severus	193 – 311
Caracalla	211 – 217
Geta	209 – 212
Macrinus	217 – 218
Elagabalus	218 – 222

Name	Date of Office	Name	Date of Office
Alexander Severus	222 – 235	Constantine I (The Great)	312 – 337
Maximin I	235 – 238		
Gordian I	238	Constantine II	337 – 340
Gordian II	238	Constans	337 – 350
Balbinus	238	Constantius II	337 – 361
Maximus	238	Magnentius	350 – 351
Gordian III	238 – 244	Julian	360 – 363
Philip	244 – 249	Jovian	363 – 364
Decius	249 – 251	*Valentinian I	364 – 375
Hostilian	251	**Valens	364 – 378
Gallus	251 – 253	**Procopius	365 – 366
Aemilian	253	*Gratian	375 – 383
Valerian	253 – 260	*Valentinian II	375 – 392
Gallienus	253 – 268	Theodosius I	379 – 395
Claudius II	268 – 269	**Arcadius	395 – 408
Quintillus	269 – 270	*Honorius	395 – 423
Aurelian	270 – 275	Constantine III	407 – 411
Tacitus	275 – 276	** Theodosius II	408 – 450
Florian	276	* Constantius III	421 – 423
Probus	276 – 282	Valentinian III	423 – 455
Carus	282 – 283	** Marcian	450 – 457
Carinus	283 – 285	*Petronius Maximus	455
Numerian	283 – 284	Avitus	455 – 456
**Diocletian abdicated	284 – 3	**Leo I	457 – 474
		*Majorian	457 – 461
*Maximian	286 – 305; 306 – 308	*Libius Severus	461 – 467
		*Anthemius	467 – 472
*Constantius I	305 – 308	*Olybrius	472 – 473
**Galerius	305 – 311	Glycerius	473
*Severus	306 – 307	*Julius Nepos	474 – 475
** Licinius	308 – 324	**Leo II	474
Maximin	310 – 313	**Zeno	474 – 491
*Maxentius	306 – 312	Romulus Augustulus	475 – 476

Byzantine Rulers

Note:
* = Latin emperors
** = Nicaean emperors

Name	Date of Office
(Usurpers in italics)	
Zeno	474 – 491
Basilicus	475 – 476
Anastasius I	491 – 518
Justin I	518 – 527
Justinian I	527 – 565
Justin II	565 – 578
Tiberius II Constantine	578 – 582
Maurice Tiberius	582 – 602
Phocas	602 – 610
Heraclius	610 – 641
Heraclius Constantine	641
Heraclonas	641
Constans II	641 – 668
Constantine IV	668 – 685
Justinian II Rhinotmetus	685 – 695; 705 – 711
Leontius	695 – 698
Tiberius III	698 – 705
Philippicus	711 – 713
Anastasius II	713 – 716
Theodosius III	716 – 717
Leo III	717 – 741
Constantine V Copronymus	741 – 775
Leo IV	775 – 780
Constantine VI	780 – 797
Irene	797 – 802
Nicephorus I	802 – 811
Stauracius	811
Michael I Rhangabe	811 – 813
Leo V	813 – 820

Name	Date of Office
Michael II Balbus	820 – 829
Theophilus	829 – 842
Michael III	842 – 867
Basil I	867 – 886
Leo VI	886 – 912
Alexander	912 – 913
Constantine VII Porphyrogenitus	913 – 959
Romanus I Lecapenus	920 – 944
Romanus II	959 – 963
Nicephorous II Phocas	963 – 969
John I Tzimisces	969 – 976
Basil II Bulgaroctonus	976 – 1025
Constantine VIII	1025 – 1028
Romanus III Argyrus	1028 – 1034
Michael IV	1034 – 1041
Michael V Calaphates	1041 – 1042
Zoe	1042 – 1056
Constantine IX Monomachus	1042 – 1055
Theodora	1055 – 1056
Michael VI Stratioticus	1056 – 1057
Isaac I Comnenus	1057 – 1059
Constantine X Ducas	1071 – 1078
Nicephorus III Botaniates	1078 – 1081
Alexius I Comnenus	1081 – 1118
John II Comnenus	1118 – 1143
Manuel I Comnenus	1143 – 1180
Alexius II Comnenus	1180 – 1183
Andronicus I Comnenus	1183 – 1185
Isaac II Angelus	1185; 1203 – 1204
Alexius III Angelus	1195 – 1203
Alexius V Ducas Murtzuphlus	1204
*Baldwin I	1204 – 1206
*Henry	1206 – 1216
*Peter	1217
*Yolande	1217 – 1219

Name	Date of Office
*Robert	1219 – 1228
*Baldwin II	1228 – 1261
*John	1231 – 1237
**Constantine (XI) Lascaris	1204 - ?1205
**Theodore I Lascaris	1205 – 1222
**John III Ducas Vatatzes	1222 – 1254
**Theodore II Lascaris	1254 – 1258
**John IV Lascaris	1258 – 1261
Michael VIII Palaeologus	1261 – 1282
Andronicus II Palaeologus	1282 – 1328
Andronicus III Palaeologus	1328 – 1341
John V Palaeologus	1341 –1376; 1379 –1390; 1390 – 1391
John VI Cantacuzenus	1347 – 1354
Andronicus IV Palaeologus	1376 – 1377
John VII Palaeologus	1390
Manuel II Palaeologus	1391 – 1425
John VIII Palaeologus	1421 – 1448
Constantine XI Palaeologus	1448 – 1453

Ancient Egyptian Rulers

Note: All dates are BC

Dynasties

Earliest dynasties

I	3200 – 3000
II	3000 – 2780

Old Kingdom

III	2780 – 2720
IV	2720 – 2560
V	2560 – 2420
VI	2420 – 2270

First Intermediate Period

VII- VIII	2270 – 2240
IX – X	2240 – 2100

Middle Kingdom

XI	2100 – 2000
XII	2000 – 1788

Second Intermediate Period

XIII – XVI	1788 – 1600
XVII	1600 – 1555

The Empire

XVIII	1555 – 1350
XIX	1350 – 1200
XX	1200 – 1090
XXI	1090 – 945
XXII	945 – c.745
XXIII	c.745 – 718
XXIV	718 – 712

Late Period

XXV	712 – 663
XXVI	663 – 525
XXVII	525 – 332
XXVIII	405 – 399
XXIX	399 – 379
XXX	379 – 341
Ptolemaic	323 – 30

Rulers

Narmer
Menes
Aha
Den
Hetepsekhemwy

Reneb		Sesostris III	1836 – 1818 BC
Nynetjer		Amenemhet III	1818 – 1770 BC
Peribsen		Amenemhet IV	1770 – 1760 BC
Khasekhem		Sebeknefru	1760 – 1756 BC
Khasekhemwy		Apopis	
Sanakhte		Kamose	
Djoser		Ahmose	c. 1539 – 1514 BC
Netjerykhet		Amenhotep I	c. 1514 – 1493 BC
Sekhemkhet		Thutmose I	1493 – c. 1479 BC
Khaba		Thutmose II	c. 1482 – 1479 BC
Huni		Thutmose III	1479 – 1426 BC
Snefru		Hatshepsut	c. 1481 – c. 1458 BC
Khufu		Amenhotep II	c. 1426 – 1400 BC
Cheops		Thutmose IV	1400 – 1390 BC
Redjedef		Amenhotep III	1390 – 1353 BC
Shepseskaf		Amenhotep IV	1353 – 1336 BC
Khafre		Akhenaton	1353 – 1336 BC
Userkaf		Smenkhkare	1335 – 1332 BC
Sahure		Tutankhaten	1352 – c. 1323 BC
Neferiakare		Tutankhamen	1352 – c. 1323 BC
Reneferef		Ay	1323 – 1319 BC
Nuserre		Horemheb	1319 – c. 1292 BC
Menkauhor		Ramses I	1292 – 1290 BC
Djedkare Izezi		Seti I	1290 – 1279 BC
Unas		Ramses II	1279 – 1213 BC
Teti		Marneptah	1213 – 1204 BC
Pepi I		Seti II	1204 – 1198 BC
Merenre		Siptah	1198 – 1193 BC
Pepi II		Tausert	1193 – 1190 BC
Ibi		Setnakht	1190 – 1187 BC
Neferkare		Ramses III	1187 – 1156 BC
Khety		Ramses IV	1156 – 1150 BC
Merikare		Ramses V	1150 – 1145 BC
Inyotef I	2081 – 2065 BC	Ramses VI	1145 – 1137 BC
Inyotef II	2065 – 2016 BC	Ramses VII	1137 – c. 1132 BC
Inyotef III	2016 – 2008 BC	Ramses VIII	c. 1132 – 1126 BC
Mentuhotep I	2008 – 1957 BC	Ramses IX	1126 – 1108 BC
Mentuhotep II	1057 – 1945 BC	Ramses X	1108 – 1104 BC
Mentuhotep III	1945 – 1938 BC	Ramses XI	1104 – c. 1075 BC
Amenemhet I	1938 – 1908 BC	Smendes	c. 1075 BC
Sesostris I	1918 – 1875 BC	Pinudjem I	
Amenemhet II	1876 – 1842 BC	Psusennes I	c. 1045 – c. 997 BC
Sesostris II	1844 – 1837 BC	Amenemope	c. 998 – c. 989 BC

Osorkon I	c. 979 – c. 973 BC	Darius II	424 – 404 BC
Psusennes II	c. 964 – 950 BC	Amyrtaeus	404 – 399 BC
Sheshonk	c. 950 - 929 BC	Achoris	939 – 380 BC
Osorkon II	c. 929 – c. 914 BC	Nepherites II	380 BC
Osorkon III	c. 888 – c. 860 BC	Nectanebo I	380 – 362 BC
Osorkon IV	c. 777 – 750 BC	Tachos	c. 365 – 360 BC
Kashta		Nectanebo II	360 – 343 BC
Shepenwepe I		Ptolemy I Soter	305 – 282 BC
Amonirdis I		Ptolemy II	285 – 246 BC
Bocchoris	c. 722 – c. 715 BC	Philadelphus	
Shabaka	c. 719 – 703 BC	Ptolemy III	246 – 222 BC
Shebitku	703 – 690 BC	Evergetes	
Taharqa	690 – 664 BC	Ptolemy IV	222 – 205 BC
Tanutamon	664 BC	Philopator	
Psamtik I	664 – 610 BC	Ptolemy V	205 – 180 BC
Psammetichus I	664 – 610 BC	Epiphanes	
Necho II	610 – 595 BC	Ptolemy VI	180 – 145 BC
Psamtik II	595 – 589 BC	Philometor	
Apries	589 – 570 BC	Ptolemy VIII	145 – 116 BC
Amasis II	570 – 526 BC	Eurgetes II	
Ahmose II	570 – 526 BC	Physcon	
Cambyses II	526 – 522 BC	Ptolemy XII Auletes	80 – 51 BC
Darius I	522 – 486 BC	Ptolemy XIII	51 – 47 BC
Artaxerxes I	465 – 424 BC	Cleopatra VII	51 – 30 BC

Religion

Belief Systems, Religions and Religious Terms

2 - 4

abbe
alb
alms
ambo
amen
apse
ara
ark
aum
ave
azan
Baal
bema
bier
bon
buji
bull
chan
cope
Copt
cowl
cure
dana
dean
Ebor
Eden
Eve
evil
ewer
fane
fast
font
God
guni
hadj
hajj
halo
hell
ho
holy
hood
host
hymn
icon
idol
I.H.S.
Imam
I.N.R.I.
jah
Jain
Jew
joss
jube
ka'ba
kama
lama
lay
Lent
mace
mass
monk
naos
nave
N. or M.
nun
obit
olah
om
pall
pew
pica
pie
pix
pome
pope
pray
pyx
rama
R.I.P.
rite
rood
rupa
sect
see
sext
sin
Siva
soma
soul
Sufi
text
tien
Toc H
Veda
veil
void
vow
wake
Xmas
yad
yang
yin
yoga
Zen
Zion

5

abbey
abbot
abdal
abyss
agati
agape
aisle
Allah
alley
altar
ambry
amice
angel
apron
Arian

banns	grace	shiva
bason	Grail	stole
beads	guild	Sudra
Bible	hades	Sunna
bigot	hafiz	sutra
bimah	Hindu	synod
bless	hylic	taboo
bodhi	image	terce
brief	imaum	Torah
bugia	Islam	totem
burse	Kaaba	tract
canon	kalpa	usher
carol	karma	vedas
cotta	Koran	vedic
chant	laity	vicar
chela	lauds	vigil
choir	laver	wafer
credo	limbo	zazen
creed	logos	
cross	manse	**6**
curia	matin	abbacy
Dagon	mitre	abbess
deity	morse	abodah
deism	myrrh	adamic
deist	niche	Advent
deity	pagan	adytum
demon	papal	agunah
devil	pasch	ahimsa
dikka	pesah	akasha
dirge	pesha	akedah
dogma	paten	anoint
double	piety	anthem
druid	pious	ashram
elder	prior	aumbry
emeth	psalm	avodah
ephod	purim	banner
exeat	rabbi	barsom
faith	relic	beadle
fakir	roshi	belfry
falda	saint	Belial
friar	Sarum	bikkhu
glory	Satan	bikshu
godly	selah	bishop

Brahma	hermit	papacy
Buddha	homily	papism
burial	housel	papist
cantor	hymnal	parish
censer	I-ching	Parsee
chapel	intone	parvis
cherub	Jesuit	parson
chohan	Jewess	pastor
chrism	Jewish	pesach
Christ	Judaic	popery
church	keblah	prayer
cierge	kismet	preach
clergy	latria	priest
cleric	lavabo	primus
corban	lector	priory
culdee	legate	proper
cruets	Levite	psalms
curacy	litany	pulpit
curate	living	purana
deacon	mantra	Quaker
decani	martyr	rector
dervis	matins	repent
devout	missal	ritual
dharma	Mormon	rochet
divine	mosaic	rosary
donary	Moslem	rubric
dossal	mosque	sacred
duchan	mullah	Saddhu
dunker	Muslim	sangha
Easter	mystic	santon
Elohim	niggun	schism
Exodus	nimbus	scribe
ferial	novice	seraph
flamen	nuncio	sermon
fleche	oblate	server
friary	octave	Shaker
gloria	oratio	shaman
Gospel	ordain	sharia
hallow	orders	Shiite
heaven	orison	Shinto
Hebrew	pagoda	shrine
Hegira	painim	shrive
heresy	palmer	sinful

sinner	Arahant	deified
solemn	ashmanu	dervise
Sofism	atheism	dervish
spirit	atheist	devilet
Sunday	aureole	dharani
sutras	badchan	diocese
suttee	baptism	diptych
Talmud	baptist	diviner
tantra	baptize	docetae
tauhid	bathing	eileton
te deum	beatify	Elohist
temple	Beghard	epistle
theism	Beguard	Essenes
trance	Beguine	eternal
triune	berakah	evangel
tunker	bigotry	exegete
verger	biretta	faculty
vestry	Brahman	fasting
virgin	Brahmin	fistula
Vishnu	calvary	frontal
votive	cassock	Galilee
Wahabi	chalice	gayatri
	chancel	gaudete
7	chancel	Gehenna
Aaronic	chantry	Genesis
Abaddon	chaplet	gentile
abelian	chapter	glorify
accidia	charity	gnostic
accidie	chazzan	goddess
acolyte	chrisom	godhead
acolyth	Cluniac	godhood
Adamite	collect	godless
advowee	complin	godlike
agrapha	confirm	godling
Alcoran	convent	godship
Alkoran	convert	gradine
alms-bag	croslet	gradual
ampulla	crosier	gremial
angelic	crozier	hassock
angelus	crusade	heathen
animism	dataria	hekdesh
apostil	deanery	heretic
apostle	decanal	hexapla

holy day
hosanna
impiety
incense
infidel
introit
Jainism
Jehovah
Judaism
Judaize
kherebu
Lady Day
Lamaism
Lateran
lectern
lection
liturgy
loculus
Lollard
low mass
madonna
maniple
mattins
messiah
mid-Lent
minaret
minster
miracle
mission
mozetta
muezzin
mystics
narthex
nirvana
nocturn
numbers
nunnery
oratory
ordinal
orphrey
Our Lady
pallium
penance

peshito
pietist
pilgrim
piscina
pontiff
popedom
prayers
prebend
prelate
prester
primacy
primate
profane
prophet
psalter
puritan
Quakery
Ramadan
rebirth
rectory
requiem
reredos
retable
retreat
Sabbath
sacring
sainted
saintly
samsara
sanctum
Saracen
satanic
saviour
sedilia
service
Shaster
Shastra
Sivaite
soutane
steeple
stipend
sub-dean
Sunnite

synodal
tallith
tantric
tempter
tonsure
trinity
tunicle
unblest
unction
unfrock
Vatican
Vedanta
vespers
Vulgate
worship
Xmas day

8

ablution
abstemii
aceldama
acephali
advowson
agnostic
agnus dei
alleluia
almighty
altarage
anathema
anchoret
Anglican
anointed
antiphon
antipope
antistes
apostasy
apostate
apparels
Arianism
Arminian
atheneum
auto da fe
ave maria

beatific	diaconal	hinayana
benifice	dies irae	holy name
benitier	diocesan	homilies
biblical	disciple	holy rood
brethren	ditheism	Holy Week
breviary	ditheist	Huguenot
Buddhism	divinity	hymn book
Buddhist	divinize	idolater
cantoris	doctrine	idolatry
capuchin	Donatism	immortal
cardinal	donatist	indevout
carmelin	doxology	infernal
catacomb	druidess	Jesuitic
canonize	druidism	Jesuitry
cathedral	ebionite	Judaizer
Catholic	elements	lay-clerk
cemetery	Ember Day	libation
cenobite	enthrone	literate
cenotaph	epiphany	lord's day
chasuble	episcopy	Lutheran
cherubim	epistler	lych-gate
chimere	Erastian	mass-book
chrismal	Essenism	mahayana
christen	Eternity	minister
ciborium	ethereal	ministry
cincture	Eusebian	minorite
clerical	evensong	miserere
compline	evermore	modalist
conclave	evildoer	Mohammed
confalon	exegesis	monachal
corporal	exegetic	monastic
covenant	exorcist	moravian
creation	faithful	nativity
credence	feretory	navicula
crucifer	foot-pace	Nazarene
crucifix	frontlet	nethinim
dalmatic	futurist	novatian
deaconry	God's acre	obituary
deifical	Hail Mary	oblation
demoness	heavenly	offering
devilish	hell fire	ordinary
devilkin	hierarch	orthodox
devotion	high mass	paganism

pantheon
papistry
pardoner
Passover
pharisee
pontifex
preacher
predella
priestly
prioress
prophecy
prophesy
Proverbs
psalmist
psalmody
Puseyism
Puseyite
quietism
quietist
Ramadhan
recollet
redeemer
religion
response
reverend
reverent
rogation
Romanism
Romanist
Romanize
sacristy
Sadducee
sanctify
sanctity
satanism
sequence
seraphim
sidesman
skullcap
Sunnites
superior
surplice
swastika

tenebrae
thurible
thurifer
transept
trimurti
triptych
unbelief
unbishop
unchurch
venerate
versicle
vestment
viaticum
vicarage
zoolatry

9

ablutions
alleluiah
allelujah
All Hallow
All Saints
alms bason
altar tomb
anchorite
anointing
antipapal
apocrypha
apostolic
archangel
archfiend
archiarcy
Ascension
athenaeum
atonement
Ayatollah
baptismal
beatitude
Beelzebub
beneficed
bishopric
bismillah
black mass

blasphemy
Calvinism
Candlemas
Carmelite
catechism
cathedral
celestial
cere-cloth
Christian
Christmas
churching
clergyman
co-eternal
communion
confessor
Cordelier
cremation
Dalai Lama
dalmatica
damnation
deaconess
dedicated
desecrate
diaconate
dissenter
dissident
dominical
eagle-wood
Easter day
Easter eve
Ember Days
Ember Fast
Ember Tide
episcopal
epistoler
eucharist
flabellum
eutychian
evangelic
gospeller
Gregorian
Halloween
hierarchy

hierogram
hierorlogy
high mass
holy ghost
holy water
incumbent
induction
interdict
interment
Islamitic
Jansenism
Jansenist
Jesuitism
joss-stick
Lammas Day
lay reader
Lazarists
Lazarites
Levitical
Leviticus
Low Church
Low Sunday
Mahomedan
Maronites
martyrdom
Methodism
Methodist
moderator
monachism
monastery
Mormonism
mundatory
Mussulman
Nestorian
obeisance
offertory
orthodoxy
ostensory
pantheism
pantheist
paraclete
Parseeism
patriarch

Pentecost
pharisaic
plainsong
prayer mat
prayer rug
preaching
precentor
presbyter
priestess
proselyte
prothesis
purgatory
pyrolatry
Quakerism
quasimodo
quicunque
reading-in
reconvert
red rubric
reliquary
religieux
religious
repentant
responses
reverence
ritualism
ritualist
rural dean
sabbatism
sabianism
sacrament
sacrifice
sacrilege
sacristan
salvation
sanctuary
Scripture
semi-Arian
sepulchre
shamanism
solemnity
solemnize
spiritual

sub-beadle
subdeacon
subrector
succentor
suffragan
suffrages
sutteeism
synagogue
synergism
synodical
teleology
Testament
theatines
theocracy
theomachy
theomancy
theopathy
theophany
theosophy
Theravada
tritheism
Vaishnava
Vajrayana
venerable
vestments
Waldenses
Yom Kippur

10

Abelonians
absolution
abstinence
aladinists
Albigenses
alkoranist
All Hallows
altar bread
altar cloth
altar cross
altar light
altar piece
altar steps
altar table

Anabaptism
Anabaptist
anointment
antichrist
apocalypse
apostolate
apotheosis
archbishop
archdeacon
archflamen
archimagus
archpriest
armageddon
assumption
Athanasian
baptistery
bar mitzvah
bas mitzvah
bat mitzvah
benedicite
benedictus
Bernardine
Bethlemite
bible class
biblically
black friar
Brahminism
Buddhistic
Carthusian
catechumen
Celestines
ceremonial
cherubical
chronicles
church army
churchgoer
church work
churchyard
Cistercian
confessant
confession
conformist
consecrate

consistory
cosmolatry
devotional
ditheistic
divination
Dominicans
doxologize
dragonnade
Eastertide
ecumenical
Ember Weeks
episcopacy
episcopate
epistolary
evangelism
evangelist
evangelize
free chapel
Free Church
Genevanism
gnosticism
Good Friday
gospel side
gymnosophy
halleluiah
hallelujah
hallowmass
heathenism
heaven-born
heliolater
heliolatry
heptateuch
hierocracy
High Church
high priest
holy orders
holy spirit
hylotheism
hyperdulia
iconoclasm
iconoclast
iconolater
iconolatry

idolatress
impanation
indulgence
infallible
invocation
irreligion
irreverent
juggernaut
lady chapel
lay brother
lectionary
magnificat
mariolatry
meditation
ministrant
missionary
Mohammedan
monotheism
monotheist
monstrance
omnipotent
ophiolatry
ordination
Palm Sunday
Pentateuch
pentecost
pharisaism
pilgrimage
prayer book
prayer flag
prebendary
presbytery
priesthood
prophetess
Protestant
puritanism
rectorship
redemption
repentance
reproaches
revelation
rock temple
rood screen

sacerdotal
sacrosanct
sanctified
sanctifier
schismatic
scriptural
septuagint
sepulchral
Sexagesima
Shrovetide
subdeanery
syncretism
tabernacle
temptation
39 articles
Tridentine
unanointed
unbaptized
unbeliever
uncanonize
unclerical
unorthodox
veneration
visitation
white friar
Whit Sunday
worshipper
Zend-Avesta

II

abomination
acephalites
agnosticism
All Souls' Day
altar screen
antepaschal
antependium
antiphonary
apotheosize
archdiocese
arches court
Arminianism
aspergillum

aspersorium
baldeochino
Benedictine
benediction
benedictory
bibliolatry
bibliomancy
black rubric
blasphemous
Bodhisattva
Catabaptist
Catholicism
chalice veil
celebration
chrismation
chrismatory
Christendom
christening
church house
commination
communicant
consecrator
convocation
crematorium
crucifixion
deification
desecration
devotionist
divine light
doxological
ecclesiarch
episcopalia
epistle-side
Erastianism
eschatology
eternal life
evangelical
evening hymn
everlasting
exhortation
fire-worship
freethinker
Geneva Bible

genuflection
hagiography
Hare Krishna
hierarchism
hierography
humeral veil
immortality
incarnation
inquisition
intercessor
investiture
irreligious
irreverence
Karmathians
Latin Church
Lord's supper
Lutheranism
miracle play
mission room
Mohammedism
Nicene Creed
oecumenical
parishioner
passing bell
passionists
passion play
Passion Week
paternoster
patron saint
Pedobaptism
pharisaical
Plymouthism
pontificate
pontifician
prayer wheel
priestcraft
procession
proselytism
proselytize
protomartyr
purificator
Reformation
religionary

religionism
religionist
religiosity
reservation
ritualistic
Roman Church
sacramental
sacring-bell
Sadduceeism
sarcophagus
scientology
scriptorium
Socinianism
theosophist
trinitarian
unbeneficed
uncanonical
undedicated
unorthodoxy
unrighteous
Wesleyanism
Whitsuntide
Zoroastrian

12

All Saints' Day
annunciation
altar frontal
archdeaconry
Ascension Day
Ash Wednesday
Augustinians
Bible Society
chapel of ease
choir service
Christianity
Christmas Day
Christmas Eve
church living
church parade
churchwarden
confessional
confirmation

Confucianism
congregation
consecration
consistorial
devil worship
discipleship
disciplinant
disestablish
dispensation
ditheistical
Easter Sunday
Ecclesiastes
ecclesiastic
ecclesiology
enthronement
episcopalian
evangelicism
exomologesis
frankincense
hot gospeller
image worship
intercession
interdiction
Low Churchman
metropolitan
mission house
New Testament
nunc dimittis
obedientiary
Old Testament
omnipresent
postillation
Presbyterian
purification
Quadragesima
reconsecrate
reconversion
red letter day
religionless
residentiary
Resurrection
Rogation Days
Rogation Week

Salvationist
sanctus bell
spiritualism
Sunday school
superfrontal
thanksgiving
Unitarianism
universalism
unscriptural
vicar general

13

All Hallowmass
All Hallows Eve
All Hallowtide
Anglican music
Anglo-Catholic
antichristian
antiepiscopal
Apostles' Creed
archarchitect
archbishopric
archdeaconate
baptismal
shell
beatification
bidding prayer
burial service
burnt offering
canonical hour
ceremoniarius
Christianlike
church service
confessionary
convocational
Corpus Christi
credence table
devotionalist
Eastern Church
excommunicate
glorification
High Churchman
holy innocents

incense burner
lord spiritual
miracle worker
mission church
Mohammedanism
Nonconformist
paschal candle
pastoral staff
pectoral cross
prayer-meeting
Protestantism
Quinquagesima
Roman Catholic
reincarnation
Sacerdotalism
Salvation Army
sanctuary-lamp
scripturalist
Shrove Tuesday
Swedenborgian
Tractarianism
Trinity Sunday
unconsecrated
unevangelical
way of the cross

14

antiscriptural
black letter day
burnt sacrifice
church assembly
communion table
crutched friars
Easter offering
ecclesiastical
Ecclesiasticus
ecclesiologist
evangelicalism
evangelization
extreme unction
fire-worshipper
fundamentalism
Gregorian chant

high priesthood
Maundy Thursday
Orthodox Church
Oxford Movement
psilanthropism
psilanthropist
reconsecration
redemptionists
Reformed Church
Rogation Sunday
sacramentarian
sanctification
sign of the cross
transmigration
trine immersion
Trinitarianism
vicar apostolic

15+

antievangelical
antiministerial
antitrinitarian
Athanasian Creed
cardinal virtues
Episcopalianism
excommunication
harvest festival
infernal regions
Jehovah's Witness
metropolitanate
Mothering Sunday
Presbyterianism
suffragan bishop
transfiguration

Books of the Bible

Old Testament

Genesis
Exodus
Leviticus
Numbers

Deuteronomy
Joshua
Judges
Ruth
1 Samuel
2 Samuel
1 Kings
2 Kings
1 Chronicles
2 Chronicles
Ezra
Nehemiah
Esther
Job
Psalms
Proverbs
Ecclesiastes
Song of Solomon
Isaiah
Jeremiah
Lamentations
Ezekiel
Daniel
Hosea
Joel
Amos
Obadiah
Jonah
Micah
Nahum
Habakkuk
Zephaniah
Haggai
Zechariah
Malachi

New Testament

Matthew
Mark
Luke
John
The Acts

Romans
I Corinthians
2 Corinthians
Galatians
Ephesians
Philippians
Colossians
I Thessalonians
2 Thessalonians
I Timothy
2 Timothy
Titus
Philemon
Hebrews

James
I Peter
2 Peter
I John
2 John
3 John
Jude
Revelation

Apocrypha
I Esdras
II Esdras
Tobit

Judith
The Rest of Esther
Wisdom
Ecclesiasticus
Baruch, with Epistle of
Jeremiah
Song of the Three
Children
Susanna
Bel and the Dragon
Prayer of Manasses
I Maccabees
II Maccabees

Biblical Characters

Old Testament

Aaron - elder brother of Moses; first high priest of Hebrews

Abel - second son of Adam and Eve; murdered by brother Cain

Abraham - father of Hebrew nation

Absalom - David's spoilt third son; killed after plotting against his father

Adam - the first man created; husband of Eve

Baal - fertility god of Canaanites and Phoenicians

Bathsheba - mother of Solomon

Belshazzar - last king of Babylon, son of Nebuchadnezzar; Daniel interpreted his vision of writing on the wall as foretelling the downfall of his kingdom

Benjamin - youngest son of Jacob and Rachel. His descendants formed one of the 12 tribes of Israel

Cain - first son of Adam and Eve; murdered his brother Abel

Daniel - prophet at the court of Nebuchadnezzar with a gift for interpreting dreams

David - slayed the giant Goliath

Delilah - a Philistine seducer and betrayer of Samson

Elijah - Hebrew prophet, taken into heaven in a fiery chariot

Elisha - prophet and disciple of Elijah

Enoch - father of Methuselah

Ephraim - son of Joseph; founded one of the 12 tribes of Israel

Esau - elder of Isaac's twin sons; tricked out of his birthright by his younger brother Jacob

Esther - beautiful Israelite woman; heroically protected her people

Eve - first woman; created as companion for Adam in Garden of Eden

Ezekiel - prophet of Israel captured by Babylonians

Gideon - Israelite hero and judge

Goliath - Philistine giant killed by David

Hezekiah - king of Judah (c 715—686 BC)

Isaac - son of Abraham and Sarah, conceived in their old age; father of Jacob and Esau

Isaiah - the greatest old testament prophet

Ishmael - Abraham's son by Hagar, hand-maiden to his wife, Sarah; rival of Isaac

Israel - new name given to Jacob after his reconciliation with Esau

Jacob - second son of Isaac and Rebekah. younger twin of Esau whom he tricked out of his inheritance. The 12 tribes of Israel were named after his sons and grandsons

Jeremiah - one of the great prophets; foretold the destruction of Jerusalem

Jezebel - cruel and lustful wife of Ahab, king of Israel

Job - long-suffering and pious inhabitant of Uz

Jonah - after ignoring God's commands he was swallowed by a whale

Jonathan - eldest son of Saul and close friend of David

Joseph - favourite son of Jacob and Rachel with his "coat of many colours"; sold into slavery by his jealous brothers

Joshua - succeeded Moses and led Israelites against Canaan. He defeated

Jericho where the walls fell down

Judah - son of Jacob and Leah; founded tribe of Judah

Lot - nephew of Abraham; he escaped the destruction of Sodom, but his wife was turned into a pillar of salt for looking back

Methuselah - son of Enoch, the oldest person ever (969 years)

Miriam - sister of Aaron and Moses whom she looked after as a baby; prophetess and leader of Israelites

Moses - Israel's great leader and lawgiver, he led the Israelites out of captivity in Egypt to the promised land of Canaan. Received ten commandments from Jehovah on Mt. Sinai Nathan - Hebrew prophet at courts of David and Solomon

Nebuchadnezzar - king of Babylon

Noah - grandson of Methuselah, father of Shem, Ham, and Japheth; built ark to save his family and all animal species from the great flood

Rebakah - wife of Isaac, mother of Jacob and Esau

Ruth - Moabite who accompanied her mother-in-law Naomi to Bethlehem. Remembered for her loyalty

Samson - Israelite judge of great physical strength; seduced and betrayed by Delilah

Samuel - prophet and judge of, Israel

Sarah - wife of Abraham, mother of Isaac

Saul - first king of Israel

Solomon - son of David and Bathsheba; remembered for his great wisdom and wealth

New Testament

Andrew - fisherman and brother of Peter; one of 12 Apostles

Barabas - Cypriot missionary; introduced Paul to the Church

Barabbas - robber and murderer; in prison with Jesus and released instead of him Bartholomew - possibly same person as Nathaniel, one of the 12 Apostles

Caiaphas - high priest of the Jews; Jesus brought to him after arrest

Gabriel - angel who announced birth of Jesus to Mary; and of John the Baptist to Zechariah

Herod -1. the Great, ruled when Jesus was born 2. Antipas, son of Herod the Great, ruled when John the Baptist was murdered 3. Agrippa, killed James (brother of John) 4. Agrippa II, before whom Paul was tried

James - 1. the Greater, one of 12 Apostles, brother of John 2. the Less, one of 12 Apostles 3. leader of the Church in Jerusalem and author of the New Testament epistle

Jesus - founder of Christianity

John - youngest of 12 Apostles

John the Baptist - announced coming of Jesus, and baptized him

Joseph - 1. husband of Mary the mother of Jesus 2. of Arimathea, a secret disciple of Jesus

Judas Iscariot - the disciple who betrayed Jesus

Lazarus - brother of Mary and Martha, raised from the dead by Jesus

Luke - companion of Paul, author of Luke and Acts

Mark - author of the gospel; companion of Paul, Barnabas, and Peter

Martha - sister of Mary and Lazarus, friend of Jesus

Mary - 1. mother of Jesus 2. sister of Martha and Lazarus 3. Magdalene, cured by Jesus and the first to see him after the resurrection

Matthew - one of 12 Apostles, author of the gospel

Matthias - chosen to replace the apostle Judas

Michael - a chief archangel

Nathaniel - see Bartholomew

Nicodemus - a Pharisee who had a secret meeting with Jesus

Paul - formerly Saul of Tarsus, persecutor of Christians; renamed after his conversion. Apostle to the Gentiles and author of epistles

Peter - Simon, one of 12 Apostles; denied Jesus before the crucifixion but later became leader of the Church

Philip - one of 12 Apostles

Pilate - Roman procurator of Judas; allowed Jesus to be crucified

Salome - 1. wife of Zebedee, mother of James and John 2. daughter of

Herodias; danced before Herod for the head of John the Baptist

Saul - see Paul

Simon - 1. Simon Peter see Peter 2. the Canaanite, one of 12 Apostles 3. one of Jesus' four brothers 4. the leper, in whose house Jesus was anointed 5. of Cyrene, carried the cross of Jesus 6. the tanner, in whose house Peter had his vision

Stephen - Christian martyr, stoned to death

Thomas - one of 12 Apostles, named 'Doubting' because he doubted the resurrection

Timothy - Paul's fellow missionary; two of Paul's epistles are to him

Titus - convert and companion of Paul, who wrote him one epistle

---

Bibles	Religious Buildings	
Authorised	**3**	convent
Bishop's	wat	deanery
Coverdale		minster
Cranmer	**4**	
Cromwell	cell	**8**
Donai	kirk	basilica
Geneva		cloister
Great	**5**	hounfort
Gutenberg	abbey	lamasery
Indian	bet am	
Itala	cella	**9**
Judas	duomo	badrinath
King James	hondo	cathedral
Kralitz	jingu	monastery
Matthew	jinja	synagogue
Mazarin		
Printers'	**6**	**12**
Revised	chapel	bet ha-knesset
Taverner	church	bet ha-midrash
Tyndale	mosque	chapter house
Vinegar	pagoda	meetinghouse
Wyclif	priory	
		13
	7	angelus temple
	chantry	

Religious Festivals

Date	Festival	Religion
Jan	Ephipany	Christian
Jan	Imbolc	Pagan
Jan, Feb	New Year	Chinese
Feb, Mar	Shrove Tuesday	Christian
Feb, Mar	Ash Wednesday	Christian
Feb, Mar	Purim	Jewish
Feb, Mar	Mahashivarati	Hindu
Feb, Mar	Holi	Hindu
Mar, Apr	Easter	Christian
Mar, Apr	Passover	Jewish
Mar, Apr	Holi Mohalla	Sikh
Mar, Apr	Rama Naumi	Hindu
Mar, Apr	Ching Ming	Chinese
Apr	Baisakhi	Sikh
Apr	Beltane	Pagan
Apr, May	Lailat ul-Isra wal Mi'raj	Islamic
Apr, May	Lailat ul-Bara'h	Islamic
Apr, May	Vesak	Buddhist
May, June	Shavuoth	Jewish
May, June	Lailat ul-Qadr	Islamic
May, June	Eid ul-Fitr	Islamic
May, June	Martyrdom of Guru Arjan	Sikh
June	Dragon Boat Festival	Chinese
June	Summer Solstice	Pagan
July	Dhammacakka	Buddhist
July	Eid ul-Adha	Islamic
Aug	Raksha Bandhan	Hindu
Aug	Lammas	Pagan
Aug, Sept	Janmashtami	Hindu
Sept	Moon Festival	Chinese
Sept, Oct	Rosh Hashana	Jewish
Sept, Oct	Yom Kippur	Jewish
Sept, Oct	Succoth	Jewish
Oct	Dusshera	Hindu
Oct	Samhain	Pagan
Oct, Nov	Diwalhi	Hindu, Sikh
Nov	Guru Nanak's Birthday	Sikh
Nov	Bodhi Day	Buddhist

Date	Festival	Religion
Dec	Christmas	Christian
Dec	Hannukah	Jewish
Dec	Winter Festival	Chinese
Dec	Winter Solstice	Pagan
Dec, Jan	Birthday of Guru Gobind Singh	Sikh
Dec, Jan	Martyrdom of Guru Tegh Bahadur	Sikh

Religious Orders

Augustinian
Barnabite
Benedictine
Brigittine
Camaldolese
Capuchins
Carmelite
Carthusian
Cistercian
Dominican
Franciscan
Hospitallers
Jeronymite
Minims
Poor Clares
Premonstratensian
Salesian
Servite
Sylvestrine
Templars
Theatine
Trappist
Trinitarian
Ursuline
Visitandine, Visitation

Religious Movements

3

Bon
I am
Zen

4

Ainu

5

Bosci
Islam
Kegon
Thags
Thugs

6

Babism
Parsis
Shinto
Taoism
Voodoo

7

Ajivika
Bahaism
Gideons
Jainism
Judaism
Jumpers

Lamaism
Mormons
Parsees
Quakers
Shakers
Sikhism
Wahabis
Zionism

8

Abelians
Abelites
Acoemeti
Adamites
Admadiya
Ahmadiya
Amarites
Baptists
Buddhism
Hinduism
Humanism
Mar Thoma
Nichiren
Nosairis
Studites

9

Calvinism
Chuntokyo
Frankists
Hicksites
Huguenots

Jansenism
Methodist
Pantheism

10

Abstinents
Adventists
Agonizants
Ambrosians
Buchanites
Calixtines
Puratinism

11

Abode Of Love
Abrahamites
Anabaptists
Anglicanism
Arminianism
Basilideans
Bernardines
Catholicism
Covenanters

12

Abecedarians
Benedictines
Christianity
Spiritualism
Unitarianism

13

Mohammedanism
Protestantism
Redemptorists
Salvation Army

14

Congregational
Fundamentalism

15

Presbyterianism

16

Christian Science
Plymouth Brethren
Roman Catholicism

17

Antipaedo-Baptists
Congregationalism
Jehovah's Witnesses

Clergy

Archbishop
Archdeacon
Bishop
Canon
Cardinal
Chaplain
Curate
Deacon
Dean
Elder
Minister
Parson
Pope
Priest
Rector
Vicar
Vicar-Forane

Popes

Pope (Date Of Accession)
St Peter (42)
St Linus (87)
St Anacletus (Cletus) (76)
St Clement I (88)
St Evaristus (97)

St Alexander I (105)
St Sixtus I (115)
St Telesphorus (125)
St Hyginus (136)
St Pius I (140)
St Anicetus (155)
St Soterus (166)
St Eleutherius (175)
St Victor I (189)
St Zephyrinus (199)
St Callistus I (217)
St Urban I (222)
St Pontian (230)
St Anterus (235)
St Fabian (236)
St Cornelius (251)
St Lucius I (253)
St Stephen I (254)
St Sixtus II (257)
St Dionysius (259)
St Felix I (269)
St Eutychian (275)
St Caius (283)
St Marcellinus (296)
St Marcellus I (308)
St Eusebius (309)
St Melchiades (311)
St Sylvester I (314)
St Marcus (336)
St Julius I (337)
Liberius (352)
St Damasus I (366)
St Siricius (384)
St Anastasius I (399)
St Innocent I (401)
St Zosimus (417)
St Boniface I (418)
St Celestine I (422)
St Sixtus III (432)
St Leo I (The Great) (440)
St Hilary (461)
St Simplicius (468)

St Felix III (483)
St Gelasius I (492)
Anastasius II (496)
St Symmachus (498)
St Hormisdas (514)
St John I (523)
St Felix IV (526)
Boniface II (530)
John II (533)
St Agapetus I (535)
St Silverius (536)
Vigilius (537)
Pelagius I (556)
John III (561)
Benedict I (575)
Pelagius II (579)
St Gregory I (The Great) (590)
Sabinianus (604)
Boniface III (607)
St Boniface IV (608)
St Deusdedit (Adeodatus I) (615)
Boniface V (619)
Honorius I (625)
Severinus (640)
John IV (640)
Theodore I (642)
St Martin I (649)
St Eugene I (654)
St Vitalian (657)
Adeodatus II (672)
Donus (676)
St Agatho (678)
St Leo II (682)
St Benedict II (684)
John V (685)
Conon (686)
St Sergius I (687)
John VI (701)
John VII (705)
Sisinnius (708)
Constantine (708)

St Gregory II (715)
St Gregory III (731)
St Zachary (741)
Stephen II (III) (752) *
St Paul I (757)
Stephen III (IV) (768)
Adrian I (772)
St Leo III (795)
Stephen IV (V) (816)
St Paschal I (817)
Eugene II (824)
Valentine (827)
Gregory IV (827)
Sergius II (844)
St Leo IV (847)
Benedict III (855)
St Nicholas I (858)
Adrian II (867)
John VIII (872)
Marinus I (882)
St Adrian III (864)
Stephen V (VI) (885)
Formosus (891)
Boniface VI (896)
Stephen VI (VII) (896)
Romanus (897)
Theodore II (897)
John IX (898)
Benedict IV (900)
Leo V (903)
Sergius III (904)
Anastasius III (911)
Landus (913)
John X (914)
Leo VI (928)
Stephen VII (VIII) (928)
John XI (931)
Leo VII (936)
Stephen VIII (IX) (939)
Marinus II (942)
Agapetus II (946)
John XII (955)
Leo VIII (963)

Benedict V (964)
John XIII (965)
Benedict VI (973)
Benedict VII (974)
John XIV (983)
John XV (985)
Gregory V (996)
Sylvester II (999)
John XVII (1003)
John XVIII (1004)
Sergius IV (1009)
Benedict VIII (1012)
John XIX (1024)
Benedict IX (1032)
Gregory VI (1045)
Clement II (1048)
Benedict X (1047)
Damasus II (1048)
St Leo IX (1049)
Victor II (1055)
Stephen IX (X) (1057)
Nicholas II (1059)
Alexander II (1081)
St Gregory VII (1073)
Victor III (1086)
Urban II (1088)
Paschal II (1099)
Gelasius II (1118)
Callistus II (1119)
Honorius II (1124)
Innocent II (1130)
Celestine II (1143)
Lucius II (1144)
Eugene III (1145)
Anastasius IV (1153)
Adrian IV (1154)
Alexander III (1159)
Lucius III (1181)
Urban III (1185)
Gregory VIII (1187)
Clement III (1187)
Celestine III (1191)
Innocent III (1198)

Honorius III (1216)
Gregory IX (1227)
Celestine IV (1241)
Innocent IV (1243)
Alexander IV (1254)
Urban IV (1261)
Clement IV (1265)
Gregory X (1271)
Innocent V (1276)
Adrian V (1276)
John XXI (1276)
Nicholas III (1277)
Martin IV (1281)
Honorius IV (1285)
Nicholas IV (1288)
St Celestine V (1294)
Boniface VIII (1294)
Benedict XI (1303)
Clement V (1305)
John XXII (1316)
Benedict XII (1334)
Clement VI (1342)
Innocent VI (1352)
Urban V (1362)
Gregory XI (1370)
Urban VI (1378)
Boniface IX (1389)
Innocent VII (1404)
Gregory XII (1406)
Martin V (1417)
Eugene IV (1431)
Nicholas V (1447)
Callistus III (1455)
Pius II (1458)
Paul II (1464)
Sixtus IV (1471)
Innocent VIII (1484)
Alexander VI (1492)
Pius III (1503)
Julius II (1503)
Leo X (1513)
Adrian VI (1522)
Clement VII (1523)

Paul III (1534)
Julius III (1550)
Marcellus II (1555)
Paul IV (1555)
Pius IV (1559)
St Pius V (1566)
Gregory XIII (1572)
Sixtus V (1585)
Urban VII (1590)
Gregory XIV (1590)
Innocent IX (1591)
Clement VIII (1592)
Leo XI (1605)
Paul V (1605)
Gregory XV (1621)
Urban VIII (1623)
Innocent X (1644)
Alexander VII (1655)
Clement IX (1667)
Clement X (1870)
Innocent XI (1676)
Alexander VIII (1689)
Innocent XII (1691)
Clement XI (1700)
Innocent XIII (1721)
Benedict XIII (1724)
Clement XII (1730)
Benedict XIV (1740)
Clement XIII (1756)
Clement XIV (1769)
Pius VI (1775)
Pius VII (1800)
Leo XII (1823)
Pius VIII (1829)
Gregory XVI (1831)
Pius IX (1846)
Leo XIII (1878)
St Pius X (1903)
Benedict XV (1914)
Pius XI (1922)
Pius XII (1939)
John XXIII (1958)
Paul VI (1963)

John Paul I (1978)
John Paul II (1978)
* Stephen ii died before consecration and was dropped from the list of popes in 1961; Stephen III became Stephen II

Archbishops Of Canterbury

Archbishop (Date Of Accession)

Augustine (597)
Laurentius (604)
Mellitus (619)
Justus (624)
Honorius (627)
Deusdedit (655)
Theodorus (668)
Beorhtweald (693)
Tatwine (731)
Nothelm (735)
Cuthbeorht (740)
Breguwine (761)
Jaenbeorht (765)
Aethelheard (793)
Wulfred (805)
Feologild (832)
Ceolnoth (833)
Aethelred (870)
Plegmund (890)
Aethelhelm (914)
Wulfhelm (923)
Oda (942)
Aelfsige (959)
Beorhthelm (959)
Dunstan (960)

Aethelgar (988)
Sigeric Serio (990)
Aelfric (995)
Aelfheah (1005)
Lyfing (1013)
Aethelnoth (1020)
Eadsige (1038)
Robert Of Jumieges (1051)
Stigand (1052)
Lanfranc (1070)
Anselm (1093)
Ralph D'Escures (1114)
William Of Corbeil (1123)
Theobald Of Bec (1139)
Thomas Becket (1162)
Richard Of Dover (1174)
Baldwin (1184)
Reginald Fitzjocelin (1191)
Hubert Walter (1193)
Reginald (1205)
John De Gray (1205)
Stephen Langton (1213)
Walter Of Evesham (1128)
Richard Grant (Wethershed) (1229)
Ralph Nevill (1231)
John Of Sittingbourne (1232)
John Blund (1232)
Edmund Rich (1234)
Boniface Of Savoy (1245)
Adam Of Chillenden (1270)
Robert Kilwardby (1273)
Robert Burnell (1278)
John Pecham (1279)
Robert Winchelsey (1295)
Thomas Cobham (1313)
Walter Reynolds (1314)
Simon Mepham (1328)
John Stratford (1334)
John Offord (1348)
Thomas Bradwardine (1349)
Simon Islip (1349)
Simon Langham (1366)
William Whittlesey (1369)
Simon Sudbury (1375)
William Courtenay (1381)
Thomas Arundel (1397)
Roger Walden (1398)
Thomas Arundel (1399)
Henry Chichele (1414)
John Stafford (1443)
John Kempe (1452)
Thomas Bourgchier (1454)
John Morton (1486)
Henry Deane (1501)
William Warham (1504)
Thomas Cranmer (1533)
Reginald Pole (1556)
Matthew Parker (1559)
Edmund Grindal (1576)
John Whitgift (1583)
Richard Bancroft (1604)
George Abbot (1611)
William Laud (1633)
William Juxon (1660)
Gilbert Sheldon (1663)
William Sancroft (1678)
John Tillotson (1691)
Thomas Tenison (1695)
William Wake (1716)
John Potter (1737)
Thomas Herring (1747)
Matthew Hutton (1757)
Thomas Secker (1756)
Frederick Cornwallis (1768)
John Moore (1783)
Charles Manners Sutton (1805)
William Howley (1828)
John Bird Sumner (1848)
Charles Thomas Longley (1862)
Archibald Campbell Tait (1868)
Edward White Benson (1883)
Frederick Temple (1896)
Randall Thomas Davidson (1903)
Cosmo Gordon Lang (1928)
Geoffrey Francis Fisher (1945)
Arthur Michael Ramsey (1961)
Frederick Donald Coggan (1974)
Robert Alexander Kennedy Runcie (1980)
George Leonard Carey (1991)
Dr Rowan Williams (2003)

Mythological Characters, Creatures, Places and Meanings

2 and 3

Aah
Aea
Ahi
All
Amt
Ana
Anu
Aon
As
Ate
Bel
Bes
Con
Cos
Dis
Ea
elf
Eos
Eru
fay
Fum
Ge
Gag
Heh
Hel
Ida
Ino
Io
Ira
Lar
Ler
Lif
Mab
Min
Neo
Nix

Nox
Nut
On
Ops
Pan
Pax
Ra
Ran
Roe
Set
Shu
Sol
Sua
Tiw
Tyr
Ule
Uma
Ve

4

Abae
Abas
Abia
Abii
Ads
Agni
Ajax
Amam
Amen
Amor
Amsi
Amsu
Anit
Ankh
Annu
Anpu
Apia
Apis
Area
Ares
Argo
Asia
Askr

Aten
Atys
Auge
Baal
Bakh
Bast
Beda
Bell
Bias
Bile
Bran
Buto
Ceyx
Chac
Chin
Clio
Core
Danu
Deva
Dice
Dido
Dino
Donu
Duse
Dwyn
Echo
Eden
Elli
Enna
Enyo
Eris
Eros
Esus
Fama
Faun
Frig
Fury
Gaea
gods
gram
Gwyn
Gyes
Hapi

Hebe	Nila	Yoga
Heno	Nubu	Yuga
Hera	Nudd	yule
hero	Odin	Zeus
Hest	ogre	Zume
Idas	Orc	
Ikto	Pasi	**5**
Ilia	Pen	Abila
Ilus	Pero	Acron
Iole	pixy	Actor
Iris	Ptah	Aedon
Irus	Puck	Aegir
Isis	Rahu	Aegis
Issa	Raji	Aegle
Itys	Rama	Aello
Iynx	Rhea	Aenea
jinn	Roc	Aesir
Jove	Roma	Aeson
Juno	saga	Aesop
Kali	Selk	Aetna
kama	Shai	Agave
Lear	Sita	Ahura
Leda	Siva	Alope
Leto	Sama	Amata
Llyr	Styx	Ammon
Lofn	Susa	Amset
Laid	tabu	Anava
Maat	Tadg	angel
Maia	Thia	Anher
Mara	Thor	Anhur
Mark	Tros	Anius
Mars	Troy	Antea
Math	Tupa	Anxor
Medb	Tyro	Anxur
Moly	Upis	Apepi
Mors	Vata	Arawn
muse	Vayu	Arete
Myth	Wasi	Argos
Nabu	Xulu	Argus
Naga	Yama	Ariel
Nebu	Yeti	Arimi
Nick	Yggr	Arion
Nike	Ymir	Armes

Artio	devas	ghoul
Ashur	Diana	giant
Asius	Dione	Gihil
Atlas	Dirce	gnome
Attis	djinn	golem
Aulis	Dolon	Gorge
Bacis	Donar	Grail
Barce	Doris	Gwyar
Belus	Dryad	Gyges
Bennu	Durga	Gymir
Beroe	dwarf	Hades
Bitol	Dyaus	Harpy
Biton	Dylan	Helen
Bogie	Edoni	Helle
Bogie	Egypt	Herse
Borvo	elfin	Homer
Bragi	elves	Honor
Butis	embla	Horae
Byrsa	Enlil	Horta
Cacus	Epeus	Horns
Cales	Epona	houri
Canis	Erato	Hydra
Capra	Estas	Hylas
Capys	Evius	Hymen
Carna	faery	Hymir
Ceres	fairy	Iamus
Chaos	Fates	Iapyx
Cilix	Fauna	Iason
Circe	Fides	Ichor
Coeus	fiend	Idmon
Creon	Flora	Idyia
Crete	Freya	llama
Cupid	Freyr	Ilium
Cyane	Friga	Indra
Dagda	Fulla	Ionia
Dagon	Gades	Iphis
Damon	Galar	Irene
Danae	Galli	Istar
Dares	Garme	Iulus
Delos	genie	Ixion
demon	genii	Janus
Deuce	Getae	Jason
Deuse	ghost	jotun

Jorth
Kaboi
Kabul
Ladon
Laius
Lamia
Lamus
lares
Lethe
Liber
Linus
Lludd
Lotis
Lugus
Lycus
Macar
Macha
Maera
Magog
Manes
Maron
Mazda
Medea
Medon
Melia
Metis
Midas
Mimas
Mimir
Minos
Mitra
Moira
Molus
Momus
Monan
Mothi
Mullo
Muses
naiad
Nanda
Nandi
Nemon
Niobe

Nisus
Nixie
Norna
norns
Nymph
Orcus
Oread
Orion
Paean
Pales
Panes
Paris
Pavan
Perse
Phaon
Phyto
Picus
pigmy
pisky
pixie
Pluto
Poeas
Preta
Priam
Pwyll
Remus
Rimac
Rudra
Sakra
Salus
santa
satyr
Sesha
Sibyl
Sinis
Sinon
Siren
Skuld
Sulis
Supay
sylph
Syren
taboo

Tages
Talos
Tanen
tarot
Ta-urt
Theia
Thoth
Thule
Thyia
Titan
Tohil
Tonan
Troll
Uazit
Uller
Urien
Urthr
Ushas
Vanir
Venti
Venus
Vesta
Woden
Wotan
Xquiq
Zamna
Zelia
Zetes

6

Abaris
Abdera
Abeona
Abydos
Acamus
Achaei
Achaia
Actaea
Admeta
Adonis
Aeacus
Aeetes
Aegeus

Aegina	Avalon	Cronus
Aegypt	Azazal	Cybele
Aeneas	Baalim	Cycnus
Aeneid	Bacabs	Cyrene
Aeolus	Balder	Daemon
Aerope	Balius	Damona
Aethra	Battus	Danaus
Afreet	Baucis	Daphne
Africa	Befana	Daulis
Agenor	Bendis	Daunus
Aglaia	Benshi	Delius
Agrius	Bestla	Delphi
Alecto	Bitias	Dictys
Aletes	Boreas	Dipsas
Aleuas	Brahma	Dirona
Aloeus	bunyip	Dodona
Althea	Bybils	Dragon
Amazon	Byblus	Dryads
Amen-Ra	Cabin	Dryope
Ampyse	Cadmus	Dumuzi
Amycus	Calais	Durinn
Amydon	Canens	Dybbuk
Anapus	Cardea	Echion
Andros	Caryae	Egeria
Angont	Castor	Egesta
Antium	Caurus	Elatus
Anubis	Celeus	Elymus
Anukit	Charis	Empusa
Aphaca	Charon	Eostre
Apollo	cherub	Eponae
Aquilo	Chione	Erebus
Araxes	Chiron	Erinys
Arctos	Chryse	Euneus
Arthur	Clotho	Europa
Asgard	Clytie	Evadne
Asopus	Codrus	Evenus
Athena	Comana	Faerie
Athene	Consus	Fafnir
Athens	Cratos	Faunus
Atreus	Creios	Febris
Augeas	Creusa	Fenrir
Aurora	Crissa	Fenris
Avatar	Crocus	fetish

Fidius	Iarbas	Mithra
Fimila	Iasion	Moccos
Fjalar	Iasius	Moirae
Foliot	Icarus	Moloch
Fornax	ilaira	Mopsus
Frigga	iliona	Munnin
Furies	Inferi	Mygdon
Furnia	Iolaus	Mythic
Galeus	Iphias	naiads
Ganesh	Ishtar	Narada
Gemini	Iseult	Natose
Genius	Isolde	Nectar
Geryon	Ismene	Neleus
Ghanna	Italus	Nereid
Glance	Ithaca	Nereus
Goblin	Ithunn	Nergal
Gorgon	Itonia	Nessus
Graces	kelpie	Nestor
Graeae	Kobold	Ninlil
Haemon	Kraken	Nireus
Haemus	Kvasia	Niskai
Hafgan	Latona	Nomius
Hamhit	Lilith	Nornas
Haokah	Lucina	nymphs
Hather	Lycaon	Oberon
Hecale	Lyceus	Oeneus
Hecate	Maenad	Oenone
Hector	Mamers	Oeonus
Hecuba	Mammon	Ogmios
Helice	Marica	ogress
Helios	Medusa	Ogyges
Hellen	Megara	Ogygia
Hermes	Meinnon	Oileus
Hesiod	Mentor	Olenus
Hestia	Merlin	Ophion
Heyoka	Merman	oracle
Hobbit	Merops	Ormuzd
Hroptr	Mestra	orphic
Huginn	Mictla	Orthia
Hyades	Milcom	Orthus
Hygeia	Miming	Osiris
Hyllus	Mintha	Palici
Ianthe	Minyas	Pallas

Pallos	Scyros	Undine
Panope	sea-god	Urania
Paphus	Selene	Uranus
Parcae	Semele	Utgard
Peleus	Semnai	Utopia
Pellas	Sestus	Vacuna
Pelion	Sethon	Valkyr
Pelops	Sibyls	Varuna
Peneus	Sigeum	Vishnu
Perdix	Simois	Vulcan
Peryda	Sinbad	Xangti
Phenix	Sirens	Xelhua
Pheres	Sirona	Xolotl
Phoebe	Somnus	Xuthus
Pholus	Sothis	Yaksha
Phylas	Sphinx	Zancle
Pirene	spirit	Zethus
Pistor	sprite	zombie
Plutus	Sthanu	
Polias	Syrinx	**7**
Pollux	Talaus	Abderus
Pomona	Tammuz	Acarnam
Prithi	Tarvos	Acastus
Prithu	Tellus	Acerbas
Pronax	Tereus	Acestes
Psyche	Tethys	Achaeus
Pulaha	Teucer	Achates
Pushan	Thalia	Acheron
Pyrrha	Theano	Acoetes
Python	Themis	Actaeon
Ravana	Thetis	Admetus
Rhenea	Thisbe	Aegaeon
Rhesus	Thunor	Aegiale
Rhodes	Thyone	Aenaria
Rhodos	Tiamat	Aepytus
Rumina	Titans	Aesacus
Safekh	Tityus	Aetolus
Samana	Tlaloc	Agamede
Sancus	Tmolus	Agyieus
Sappho	Triton	Ahriman
Saturn	Typhon	Alastor
Satyrs	Ulixes	Alcides
Scylla	Umbria	Alcmene

Alcyone	Bacchus	Coronis
Alpheus	banshee	Creteus
Aluberi	banshie	Curetes
Amathus	Belenos	Cyaneae
Amazons	Bellona	Cyclops
Ampelus	Beltane	Cythera
Amphion	Bifrost	Dactyls
Ampycus	bogyman	Daphnis
Amymone	Bochica	Delphus
Amyntor	Bona Dea	Demeter
Anaburn	Brahman	demi-god
Anagnia	Branwen	Diomede
Anaphae	Brauron	Dwynwen
Anaurus	Briseis	Echemus
Ancaeus	Bromius	Echidna
Angitia	Brontes	Ehecatl
Anigrus	brownie	Electra
Antaeus	Busiris	Elicius
Antenor	Caeneus	Elpenor
Anteros	Calchas	Elysian
Anthene	Calypso	Elysium
Antiope	Camelot	Epaphus
Antissa	Camenae	Epigoni
Aphetae	Camilla	Erigone
Aphytos	Canopus	Erinyes
Arachne	Capella	erl-king
Arcadia	Caranus	Eumaeus
Arestor	Carneus	Eumelus
Ariadne	Cecrops	Eunomia
Arsinoe	Celaeno	Euryale
Artemis	centaur	Eurybia
Asathor	Cepheus	Euterpe
Astarte	Cercyon	Evander
Asteria	Cessair	evil eye
Astraea	Chelone	Exadius
Ataguju	Chimera	Februus
Athamas	Chloris	Feronia
Atropos	Chryses	Formiae
Autonoe	Cinyras	Fortuna
Auxesia	Cleobis	Fylgjur
Avatars	Clymene	Galatea
Avernus	Cocytus	Galleus
Bacchae	Copreus	Gargara

Gelanor	Iztat Ix	Oeagrus
Glaucus	Jocasta	Oedipus
Gnossos	Jupiter	Ogygian
Goibniu	Juturna	Old Nick
Gordius	Krishna	Olympia
Gorgons	Laeradh	Olympus
Grannus	Laertes	Omphale
Gremlin	Laocoon	Onniont
grendel	Laodice	oracles
griffin	Larunda	Orestes
Grimnir	Latinus	Ormenus
Gryphon	Lavinia	Orphean
Gungnir	Leander	Orpheus
Halesus	Lemures	Ortygia
Hamoneu	Lorelei	Pandion
hanuman	Lothurr	Pandora
Harpies	Lynceus	Parvati
Helenus	Macaria	Pegasus
Helicone	Machaon	Penates
Hesione	Maenads	Perseis
Hilaira	Maponos	Perseus
Hor-Amen	Megaera	Petasus
Hun-Ahpu	Menippe	Phegeus
Hunbatz	Mercury	Phemius
Hurakan	mermaid	Phineus
Hydriad	Metylto	Phoebus
Hygeian	Michabo	Phoenix
Hylaeus	Midgard	Phorcus
Iacchus	Minerva	Phrixus
Ialemus	Mithras	Phyllis
Iapetus	Mordred	Pierian
Icarius	Morrigu	Pleiads
Idalium	Musaeus	Pleione
Idothea	Myrddin	Plouton
Iguvium	Nemesis	Pluvius
Inarime	Nephele	Polites
incubus	Neptune	Priapus
Inferno	Nereids	Procles
Iobates	Nokomis	Procris
Ioskeha	Nycteus	Proetus
Ismenos	Nysaeus	Proteus
Itzamna	Oceanus	Pryderi
Iztal Ix	Ocyrhoe	Purusha

Pylades	Tristan	Alberich
Pyramus	Troilus	Albiorix
Pyrrhus	Ulysses	Alcathoe
Pythias	unicorn	Alcestis
Qabanil	Unktahe	Alcimede
Racumon	vampire	Alcinous
Renenet	Veionis	Alcmaeon
Rhamnus	Venilla	Amaethon
Rhoecus	vestals	Amalthea
Rhoetus	Vintios	Ambrosia
Rig-Veda	Virbius	Anacreon
Robigus	Vitharr	Anatarho
Romulus	Walkyrs	Anchiale
Rubicon	Wayland	Anchises
Rukmini	Wieland	Anemotis
Samblin	wood god	Angharad
Scandea	Xanthus	Antemnae
Scaptia	Xibalba	Anthedon
Scheria	Xmucane	Anthemus
Scythia	Yakshas	Anthylla
Segesta	Yolcuat	Anticlea
Selleis	Zagreus	Antigone
Serapis	Zipacna	Antiphus
Setebos		Apaturia
Sicinus	_8_	Apidonus
Silenus	Abantias	Apollyon
Skirnir	Absyrtus	Appareus
Soranus	Academus	Arcesius
Spright	Achelons	Arethusa
sprites	Achilles	Argonaut
Stentor	Acidalia	Arianrod
Stimula	Aconteus	Ascanius
sylphid	Acontius	Asterion
Talarea	Acrisius	Astraeus
Telamon	Adrastia	Astyanax
Telemus	Adrastus	Ataensic
Temenus	Aeacides	Atalanta
Thaumas	Aegimius	Atlantis
Theonoe	Aegyptus	Avernian
Theseus	Aeneades	Baba Yaga
Thialfi	Agamedes	barghest
Titania	Aganippe	basilisk
Triopas	Aglauros	Bebryces

Bedivere	Dardanus	Hermione
behemoth	Deianira	Hersilia
Belisama	Dervones	Hesperus
bogeyman	Dionysos	Hyperion
Bolthorn	Dionysus	Iardanes
Branchus	Dioscuri	Ilithyia
Bubastis	Dodonian	Illatici
Bylazora	Doybayba	Iphicles
Caduceus	Draupnir	Jarnsaxa
Caeculus	El Dorado	Jurupari
Calliope	Elivager	Keridwen
Callisto	Endymion	Kukulcan
Camaxtli	Enigorio	Labdacus
Camazotz	Entellus	Lachesis
Capaneus	Enyalius	Lampetie
Carmenta	Epicaste	Lancelot
Castalia	Epidanus	Laodamas
Celaenae	Eriphyle	Laodamia
centaurs	Eteocles	Laomedon
Centeotl	Eteoclus	Lapithae
Cephalus	Eumolpus	Libertas
Cerberus	Euphemus	Libitina
Cercopes	Euryabus	Lupercus
Chalybes	Euryclea	Maeander
Chantico	Eurydice	Mama Nono
Charites	Eurynome	Marpessa
Chimaera	Faesulae	Megareus
Chryseis	Farbauti	Melampus
Cimmerii	Favonius	Meleager
Cipactli	folklore	Menelaus
Cocidius	Fornjotr	Merodach
Coroebus	Ganymede	Minotaur
Cretheus	Gigantes	Morpheus
Crommyon	Gilgames	Mulciber
Cyclades	good folk	Myrtilus
Cylopes	Govannon	Narayana
Cyllarus	Gucumatz	Nausicaa
Cynosura	Halcyone	Nephthys
Cytherea	Harmonia	Niflheim
Daedalus	Haroeris	Nin-Lilla
Damascus	Heliadae	Oceanids
Damastes	Heracles	Odysseus
Damocles	Hercules	Oenomaus

Olympian
Orithyia
Othrerir
Pacarina
Palaemon
Pandarus
Panopeus
Panthous
paradise
Parjanya
Pasiphae
Pasithea
Pelasgus
Penelope
Pentheus
Pephredo
Percival
Periphas
Pessinus
Phaethon
Philemon
Phintias
Phlegyas
Phoronis
Picumnus
Pierides
Pilumnus
Pisander
Pittheus
Pleiades
Podarces
Polyxena
Porthaon
Poseidon
Prithivi
Proximae
Psamathe
Pulastya
Queen Mab
Quiateot
Quirinal
Quirinus
Ragnarok

Rakshasa
Rhodopis
Rosmerta
Rubezahl
Sahadeva
Sarawati
Sarpedon
Schedius
Sciathus
Seriphos
Silvanus
Sipontum
Sisyphus
Sparsana
Srikanta
succubus
Summanus
Talassio
talisman
Tantalus
Tartarus
Tecmessa
Telephus
Terminus
Thamyri
Thanatos
Theogony
Thyestes
Tiresias
Tithonus
Tonatiuh
Tristram
Ucalegon
Valhalla
Valkyrie
Vasudeva
Vesuvius
Victoria
Virginia
Visvampa
Wakinyan
water god
Waukkeon

werewolf
Xpiyacoc
Yadapati
Zalmoxis
Zephyrus

9

Acherusia
Achilleum
Acmonides
Adsullata
Aegialeus
Aegisthus
Aethiopia
Agamemnon
Agathyrsi
Akha-Kanet
Alcathous
Alcyoneus
Amalivaca
Ambrosial
Amphrysus
Anaxarete
Andraemon
Androclus
Androgeus
Andromeda
Antandrus
Antevorta
Aphrodite
Areithous
Areopagus
Argonauts
Aristaeus
Ascalabus
Asclepius
Ashtoreth
Assoracus
Autolycus
Automeden
Aventinus
Bacchante
Bosphorus

Brunhilde	Hamadryad	Pirithous
Bucentaur	Harmakhis	Polydamas
Byzantium	Heimdallr	Polydorus
Cassandra	Hippolyte	Polynices
Cerberean	hobgoblin	Polyphron
Chalcodon	Holy Grail	Portumnus
Charybdis	Hypsipyle	Postvorta
Chthonius	Idacanzas	Pudicitia
Clitumnus	Idomeneus	Pygmalion
Coatlicue	Indigetes	Quahootze
Cockaigne	Iphigenia	Rakshasas
Concordia	Iphimedia	Rediculus
Cytherean	Ixiomides	Rigasamos
Davy Jones	Jotunheim	Robin Hood
Deiphobus	Lyonesse	Sagittary
Demophoon	manticore	Salmoneus
Dervonnae	Melanthus	Samavurti
Deucalion	Melisande	Saturnius
Diancecht	Melpomene	Scamander
Diespiter	Menoeceus	Scyllaeum
Dionysius	Menoetius	Sibylline
Domdaniel	Metaneira	Siegfried
Enceladus	Missibizi	Sthenelus
Epidaurus	Mnemosyne	Strophius
Eumenides	Mnestheus	Taranucus
Euphorbus	Nanahuatl	Tawiscara
Eurybates	Narcissus	Telchines
Eurypylus	Nibelungs	Telegonus
Eurysaces	Noncomala	Thersites
Excalibur	Nyctimene	Thymoetes
Fabia Gens	Oceanides	Tisamenus
Fairyland	Orgiastic	Tisiphone
fairy tale	Palamedes	Toutiorix
Faustulus	Pandareos	Uxellimus
Ferentina	Pandrosos	Valkyrean
Feretrius	Parnassus	Valkyries
Fjawrgynn	Patroclus	Vasishtha
Friar Tuck	Pelopidae	Vertumnus
Gagurathe	Periander	Walpurgis
Gargaphin	Philammon	white lady
Ghisdubar	Philomela	wood nymph
Gilgamesh	Phoroneus	Xbakiyalo
Guinivere	Pied Piper	Xbalanque

Yggdrasil
Zacynthus
Zerynthus

10

Abantiades
Achillides
Aetholides
Ahsonnutli
Ahura Mazda
Ambisagrus
Amisodarus
Amnisiades
Amphiaraus
Amphictyon
Amphitrite
Amphitryon
Andromache
Antilochus
Antitaurus
Arcesilaus
Archemoros
Berecyntia
Bussumarus
Callirrhoe
Cassiopeia
changeling
Cihuacoatl
cockatrice
compitalia
cornucopia
Corybantes
Cyparissus
Delphinium
Eileithyia
Eldhrimnir
Emathiades
Epimenides
Epimetheus
Erechtheum
Erechtheus
Erymanthus
Euphrosyne

fisher king
Galinthias
Gwenhwyvar
Hamadryads
Heliopolis
Hephaestus
Hesperides
Hippocrene
Hippodamia
Hippogriff
Hippolytus
Hippomedon
Hippothous
Horbehutet
Jabberwock
Juggernaut
Kaneakeluh
King Arthur
leprechaun
Lifthrasir
little folk
Maid Marian
Mama Quilla
Melanippus
Melanthius
Menestheus
mundane egg
Nausithous
Necessitas
Nilmadhava
Onocentaur
Pachacamac
Palladinus
Pallantias
Parnassian
Persephone
Phlegethon
Phosphorus
Pigwidgeon
Plisthenes
Polydectes
Polydeuces
Polyhymnia

Polymestor
Polyphemus
Porphyrion
Prajapatis
Procrustes
Prometheus
Proserpina
Qebhsennuf
Rhea Silvia
Round Table
Sakambhari
Salamander
Samothrace
Santa Claus
Saptajihiva
sea serpent
Strophades
Talthybius
Telemachus
Tlepolemus
Trophonius
Utgardloki
Visvakarma
Visvamitra
Vrihaspati
Vukub-Cakix
Wonderland
Yajneswara
Yoganindra

11

Aesculapius
Alaghom Naom
Alalcomenae
Amphisbaena
Amphilochus
Anna Perenna
Antaeopolis
Anthesteria
Aphrodisias
Apocatequil
Arimaspians
Atius Tirawa

Awonawilona
Bellerophon
Britomartis
Canopic jars
Cueravaperi
Dam Gal Nunna
Eileithyias
Enigohatgea
Erysichton
Eurysthenes
Ginnungagap
Gladsheimir
Harpocrates
Heracleidae
Hippocampus
mythologist
mythologize
Nantosvelta
Neoptolemus
Pandora's box
Penthesilea
Philoctetes
poltergeist
Polyphontes
Protesilaus
Rip van Winkle
Savitripati
Scamandrius
Scheherezade
Sraddhadeva
Symplegades
Terpsichore
Thrasymedes
Triptolemus
troglodytes
Ultima Thule

Vishnamvara

12

Acca Larentia
Achaemenides
Acroceraunia
Agathodaemon
Aius Locutius
Ancus Martius
Bandersnatch
Belatucadrus
Chrysothemis
Clytemnestra
Erichthonius
Gigantomachy
Golden Fleece
Hippocentaur
Hyperboreans
Hypermnestra
Jormundgandr
Kittanitowit
Mount Olympus
mythographer
mythological
Pallas Athene
Purushattama
Quetzalcoatl
Rhadamanthus
Tezcatlipoca
Theoclymenus
Trismegistus
Wandering Jew
white goddess
Xochiquetzal
Yohualticitl

Yudhishthira

13 and over

Abominable Snowman
(17)
Achilleus Dromos (15)
Apochquiahuayan (15)
Apple of Discord (14)
Augean stables (13)
Calydonian Hunt (14)
Colonus Hippius (14)
Damocles' sword (13)
Elysian Fields (13)
Father Christmas (15)
Halirrhathius (13)
Hermaphroditus (14)
Huitzilopochtli (15)
Itsikamahidis (13)
Jupiter Elicius (14)
Jupiter Pluvius (14)
Laestrygonians (14)
Loch Ness Monster
(15)
Llew Llaw Gyffes (14)
Mayan Mythology (14)
Never Never Land (14)
Oonawieh Unggi (13)
Phoebus Apollo (13)
Robin Goodfellow (15)
Quetzalcohuatl (14)
Tloque Nahuaque (14)
Tonacatecutli (13)
Tuatha de Danann (14)
Walpurgis night (14)
Yoalli Ehecatl (13)

Patron Saints

Name (Patron of)

Agatha (Bell-Founders)
Albert The Great (Students of Natural Sciences)
Andrew (Scotland)
Barbara (Gunners and Miners)
Bernard Of Montjoux (Mountaineers)
Camillus (Nurses)
Casimir (Poland)
Cecilia (Musicians)
Christopher (Wayfarers)
Crispin (Shoemakers)
David (Wales)
Dionysius (Denis) of Paris (France)
Dunstan (Goldsmiths, Jewellers, and Locksmiths)
Dympna (Insane)
Eligius or Eloi (Metalworkers)
Erasmus (Sailors)
Fiacre (Gardeners)
Frances Cabrini (Emigrants)
Frances of Rome (Motorists)
Francis de Sales (Writers)
Francis Xavier (Foreign Missions)
Frideswide (Oxford)
George (England)
Giles (Cripples)
Hubert (Huntsmen)
Jerome Emiliani (Orphans and Abandoned Children)
John Of God (Hospitals and Booksellers)
Jude (Hopeless Causes)
Julian (Innkeepers, Boatmen, Travellers)
Katherine of Alexandria (Students, Philosophers, and Craftsmen)
Luke (Physicians and Surgeons)
Martha (Housewives)
Nicholas (Children, Sailors, Unmarried Girls, Merchants, Pawnbrokers, Apothecaries, and Perfumeries)
Patrick (Ireland)
Peter Nolasco (Midwives)
Sava (Serbian People)
Valentine (Lovers)
Vitus (Epilepsy and Nervous Diseases)
Wenceslas (Czechoslovakia)
Zita (Domestic Servants)

Saints

Note: The numbers of letters mentioned do not include "St" or "Saint", for which allowances should be made when necessary.

3 and 4

Abb
Ann
Anne
Bee
Bede
Bega
Chad
Cyr
Ebba
Eloi
Gall
Jean
Joan
John
Jude
Just
Loe
Luce
Lucy
Luke
Mark
Mary
Paul
Roch
Zeno

5

Agnes
Aidan

Alban
Amand
Andre
Asaph
Barbe
Basil
Bavon
Bride
Bruno
Clair
Clara
David
Denis
Elias
Genny
Giles
Hilda
James
Kilda
Louis
Lucia
Marie
Olave
Paola
Peter

6

Albert
Andrea
Andrew
Anselm
Ansgar
Bertin
Brieuc
Claire
Cosmas
Fabian
Fergus
Gallus
George
Helena
Heiler
Hilary

Hubert
Jerome
Joseph
Ludger
Magnus
Martha
Martin
Maurus
Michel
Monica
Philip
Pierre
Thomas
Ursane
Ursula
Valery
Xavier

7

Ambrose
Anschar
Anthony
Austell
Barbara
Bernard
Bridget
Cecilia
Charles
Clement
Crispin
Dominic
Dorothy
Dunstan
Elsinus
Emidius
Etienne
Eustace
Francis
Germain
Gregory
Isodore
Joachim
Leonard

Matthew
Maurice
Michael
Nazaire
Nicolas
Pancras
Patrick
Raphael
Raymond
Romuald
Saviour
Stephen
Swithin
Swithun
Vincent
William

8

Aloysius
Augustus
Barnabas
Benedict
Bernhard
Cuthbert
Damianus
Denevick
Donatian
Eusebius
Ignatius
Lawrence
Longinus
Margaret
Nicholas
Paulinus
Placidus
Polycarp
Vericona
Walpurga
Waltheof
Winifred
Zenobius

9	10 and 11	
Apollonia	Apollinaris (11)	Symphorien (10)
Augustine	Athanasius (10)	Zaccharias (10)
Catherine	Bartholomew (11)	
Christina	Bernardino (10)	**12 and over**
Demetrius	Benhardino (11)	Anthony of Padua (14)
Eanswythe	Bonaventura (11)	Bridget of Sweden (15)
Elizabeth	Christopher (11)	James the Great (13)
Exuperius	Ethelburga (10)	James the Less (12)
Fredewith	Eustochium (10)	John the Baptist (14)
Hyacinthe	Gallo Abbato (11)	Louis of Toulouse (15)
Joan of Arc	Gaudentius (10)	Mary Magdalene (13)
Mamnertius	Hippolytus (10)	Nicholas of Bad (14)
Sebastian	Jeanne d'Arc (10)	Nicholas of Myra (14)
Servatius	Mercuriale (10)	Simon Stylites (13)
Sylvester	Peter Martyr (11)	Thomas Aquinas (13)
Valentine	Philip Neri (10)	Vincent Ferrer (13)
Walpurgis	Scholastica (11)	

Hindu Deities

Aditi - goddess of heaven; mother of the gods

Agni - god of fire

Ahi or Ihi - the Sistrum Player

Amaravati - city of the gods

Amrita - water of life

Bali - demon who became king of heaven and earth

Brahma - the Creator

Devi - a mother goddess

Diti - mother of the demons

Gandharvas - celestial musicians

Ganesha - god of literature, wisdom, and prosperity

Garuda - the devourer, identified with fire and the sun

Hanuman - a monkey chief

Indra - king of the gods; god of war and storm

Jyestha - goddess of misfortune

Kama - god of desire

Karttikeya - war-god; god of bravery

Kubera - god of wealth; guardian of the north

Lakshmi - goddess of fortune

Manasa - sacred mountain and lake

Prithivi - earth-goddess; goddess of fertility

Saranyu - goddess of the clouds

Sarasvati - goddess of speech

Shitala - goddess of smallpox

Shiva - the Destroyer

Soma - ambrosial offering to the gods

Sugriva - monkey king

Surya - the sun-god

Vayu - god of the wind

Visvakarma - architect for the gods

Vishnu - the Preserver

Yama - king of the dead

Varuna - god of water

Greek and Roman Mythology

Mythological Characters

Achilles - Greek hero; invulnerable except for his heel

Adonis - renowned for his beauty

Agamemnon - king of Mycenae

Ajax - Greek warrior

Atlas - bore heaven on his shoulders

Bellerophon - Corinthian hero who rode winged horse Pegasus

Boreas - the north wind

Cerberus - three-headed dog, guarded Hades

Charon - boatman who rowed dead across river Styx

Charybdis - violent whirlpool

Circe - sorceress who had the power to turn men into beasts

Cyclops - one of a race of one-eyed giants (cyclopes)

Daedalus - craftsman; designed and built the labyrinth in Crete

Gorgons - three sisters (Stheno, Euryale, and Medusa) who had snakes for hair and whose appearance turned people to stone

Hades - the Underworld

Helen Of Troy - famed for her beauty; cause of Trojan war

Heracles - famed for his courage and strength; performed the twelve labours

Hercules - Roman name for Heracles

Hydra - many-headed snake

Jason - led the Argonauts in search of the Golden Fleece

Lethe - river in Hades whose water caused forgetfulness

Midas - King of Phrygia whose touch turned everything to gold

Minotaur - monster with the head of a bull and the body of a man. It was kept in the Cretan labyrinth and fed with human flesh

Narcissus - beautiful youth who fell in love with his own reflection

Odysseus - Greek hero of the Trojan war

Oedipus - king of Thebes; married his mother

Olympus - a mountain; the home of the gods

Orpheus - skilled musician

Pandora - the first woman; opened the box that released all varieties of evil

Perseus - Greek hero who killed the Gorgon Medusa

Polyphemus - leader of the Cyclopes

Romulus - founder of Rome

Satyrs - hoofed spirits of forests, fields, and streams

Scylla - six-headed sea monster

Sibyl - a prophetess

Sirens - creatures depicted as half women, half birds, who lured sailors to their deaths

Styx - main river of Hades, across which Charon ferried the souls of the dead

Theseus - Greek hero who killed the Cretan Minotaur

Ulysses - Roman name for Odysseus

Greek Gods (Roman Equivalent)

Aphrodite - goddess of beauty and love (Venus)

Apollo - god of poetry, music, and prophecy (Apollo)

Ares - god of war (Mars)

Artemis - goddess of the moon (Diana)

Asclepius - god of medical art (Aesculapius)

Athene - goddess of wisdom (Minerva)

Charites - 3 daughters of Zeus: Euphrosyne, Aglaia, and Thalia; personified grace, beauty, and charm (Graces)

Cronos - god of agriculture (Saturn)

Demeter - goddess of agriculture (Ceres)

Dionysus - god of wine and fertility (Bacchus)

Eos - goddess of dawn (Aurora)

Eros - god of love (Cupid)

Fates - 3 goddesses who determine man's destiny: Clotho, Lachesis, and Atropos

Hebe - goddess of youth (Juventas)

Hecate - goddess of witchcraft (Hecate)

Helios - god of the sun (Sol)

Hephaestus - god of destructive fire (Vulcan)

Hera - queen of heaven, goddess of women and marriage (Juno)

Hermes - messenger of gods (Mercury)

Hestia - goddess of the hearth (Vesta)

Hypnos - god of sleep (Somnus)

Nemesis - goddess of retribution

Pan - god of woods and fields (Faunus)

Persephone - goddess of the Underworld (Proserpine)

Pluto - god of the Underworld (Pluto)

Plutus - god of wealth

Poseidon - god of the sea (Neptune)

Rhea - goddess of nature (Cybele)

Selene - goddess of the moon (Luna)

Thanatos - god of death (Mars)

Zeus - supreme god; god of sky and weather (Jupiter)

Roman Gods (Greek Equivalent)

Aesculapius (Asclepius)
Apollo (Apollo)
Aurora (Eos)
Bacchus (Dionysus)
Ceres (Demeter)
Cupid (Eros)
Cybele (Rhea)
Diana (Artemis)
Faunus (Pan)
Graces (Charites)
Hecate (Hecate)
Juno (Hera)
Jupiter (Zeus)
Juventas (Hebe)
Luna (Selene)
Mars (Ares)
Mercury (Hermes)
Minerva (Athene)
Mars (Thanatos)
Neptune (Poseidon)
Pluto (Pluto)
Proserpine (Persephone)
Saturn (Cronos)
Sol (Helios)
Somnus (Hypnos)
Venus (Aphrodite)
Vesta (Hestia)
Vulcan (Hephaestus)

Twelve Labours Of Hercules

The Nemean Lion
The Lernaean Hydra
The Wild Boar of Erymanthus
The Stymphalian Birds
The Ceryneian Hind

The Augean Stables
The Cretan Bull
The Mares of Diomedes
The Girdle of Hippolyte
The Cattle of Geryon
The Golden Apples of the
Hesperides
The Capture of Cerberus

The Nine Muses

Calliope (Epic Poetry)
Clio (History)
Erato (Love Poetry)
Euterpe (Lyric Poetry)
Melpomene (Tragedy)
Polyhymnia (Sacred Song)
Terpsichore (Dancing)
Thalia (Comedy)
Urania (Astronomy)

Norse Mythology

Aegir - god of the sea
Alfheim - part of Asgard inhabited by
the light elves
Asgard - the home of the gods
Ask - name of first man, created
from a fallen tree
Balder - god of the summer sun
Bragi - god of poetry
Eir - goddess of healing
Embla - name of first woman, created
from a fallen tree
Forseti - god of justice
Frey - god of fertility and crops
Freyja - goddess of and night
Frigg - Odin's wife; supreme goddess
Gungnir - Odin's magic spear
Heimdal - guardian of Asgard
Hel - goddess of the dead

Hodur - god of night
Idun - wife of Bragi; guardian of the
golden apples of youth
Loki - god of evil, trickster god
Midgard - the world of men
Norns - three goddesses of destiny
Urd (Fate), Skuld (Being), and
Verdandi (Necessity)
Odin - supreme god; god of battle
inspiration and death
Ragnarok - final battle between gods
and giants, In which virtually all life is
destroyed
Sif -wife of Thor; her golden hair was
cut off by Loki
Sleipnir - Odin's eight-legged horse
Thor - god of thunder
Tyr - god of war
Valhalla - hall In Asgard where Odin
welcomed the souls of heroes killed
in battle
Valkyries - nine handmaidens of Odin
who chose men doomed to die in
battle
Yggdrasill - the World Tree, an ash
linking all the worlds
Ymir - giant from whose body the
world was formed

Egyptian Mythology

Amon-Ra - supreme god
Anubis - jackal-headed son of Osiris;
god of the dead
Bes - god of marriage
Geb - earth-god
Hathor - cow-headed goddess of
love
Horus - hawk-headed god of light
Isis - goddess of fertility
Maat - goddess of law, truth, and
justice

Min - god of virility
Mont - god of war
Mut - wife of Amon-Ra
Neheh - god of eternity
Nun or Nu - the primordial Ocean
Nut - goddess of the sky
Osiris - ruler of the afterlife
Ptah - god of the arts
Ra – the sun god
Renpet - goddess of youth
Sekhmet - goddess of war
Set or Seth - god of evil
Shu - god of air
Tefnut - goddess of dew and rain
Thoth - god of wisdom
Upuaut - warrior-god; god of the dead

North American Mythology

Adlivun - Eskimo land of the unhappy dead
Aglookik - Eskimo spirit of hunters
Ahsonnutli - chief god of the Navaho Indians
Akycha - the Sun
Angakoo - Eskimo shaman
Anguta - Eskimo ruler of the underworld
Aningan - the Moon
Big Owl - cannibalistic monster of the Apache Indians
Coyote - trickster god
Dzoavits - Shoshone ogre
Glooskap - agent of good; made the earth, creatures and mankind
Hiawatha - legendary sage of the Iroquois Indians who founded the League of Five Nations
Hino - Iroquois god of thunder
Hinun - thunder spirit of the Iroquois Indians

Ictinike - trickster god of the Sioux Indians
Malsum - agent of evil; made the mountains, valleys, snakes
Nana Bozho (Mana Bozho) - trickster god of the Algonquins
Nanook - the Bear (the Pleiades)
Napi - chief god of the Blackfoot Indians
Natos - sun god of the Blackfoot Indians
Nayenezgani - hero of Navaho legend: name means 'slayer of evil gods'
Negafok - cold weather spirit
Sedna - the great Sea Mother; Eskimo goddess of the underworld and sea
Spider Woman - benevolent creature who helped Nayenezgani defeat the powers of evil
Tirawa - chief god of the Pawnee, who created the world and set the course of the sun, moon, and stars
Tornaq - familiar of a shaman
Tsohanoai - Navaho sun god, who carries the sun on his back across the sky
Wakonda - great god of the Sioux Indians whose name means 'great power above'
Wonomi - sky god of the Maidu Indians who was abandoned in favour of Coyote

Central And South American Mythology

Ah Puch - Maya god of death
Bachue - mother goddess and protector of crops
Bochica - Colombian founder hero;

appears as an old bearded man

Chac - Maya rain god

Cinteotl - Aztec god of maize

Coatlicue - Aztec earth goddess; a devouring goddess who was only satisfied by human flesh and blood

Cupay (Supay) - Inca god of death

Ehecatl - Aztec god of the winds who introduced sexual love to mankind

Guinechen - chief deity of Aruacanian Indians, associated with fertility

Huitzilopochtli - chief god of the Aztecs

Inti- sun god from whom Inca dynasty traced its descent

Itzamna - chief god of the Maya

Ixchel - Maya moon goddess

Ixtab - Maya goddess of suicide

Ixtlilton - Aztec god of medicine

Kuat - sun god of the Mamaiurans

Mixcoatl - Aztec god of the chase

Montezuma - Aztec god whose name was taken from the last emperor

Pachamama - Earth goddess of the Incas

Pillan - thunder god of Araucanian Indians

Quetzalcoatl - a priest-king of Central America; the snake-bird god or plumed serpent

Tezcatlipoca - Aztec god of summer sun; bringer of harvests as well as drought

Tlaloc - rain god of Central America, worshipped by the Toltecs and Aztecs

Tupan - thunder god of the Guarani Indians

Vaica - magician and medicine-man of the Jurunas

Viracocha - creator god of the Incas

Xipetotec - Aztec god of agriculture and self torture; his name means 'flayed lord'

XOCHIQUETZAL - Aztec goddess of flowers and fruits

Australian Mythology

Akurra - serpent god

Alchera - Dreamtime', primeval when the ancestors sang the world into existence

Arunkulta - Aranda spirit of evil

Bagadjimbiri - ancestral creator of gods

Biame - god of creation

Birrahgnooloo - chief wife of Biame

Bolung - serpent god; giver of life

Boomerang - symbolizes the rainbow and the connection of opposites (e.g. heaven and earth)

Bralgu - island of the dead

Bunjil - god of creation

Bunyip - monster and giver of mystic heating rites

Dilga - earth goddess

Djanbun - man who turned into a platypus after blowing too hard on a fire-stick Kapoo - ancestral kangaroo who gave cats their spots

Mangar-Kunger-Kunja - great lizard ancestor of the Aranda

Marindi - ancestral dog whose blood turned the rocks red

Pundjel - creator god who made the first human being

Wati-Kutjara - two lizard men of Central Australia

Yurlunyur - ancestor of the Murngin of the northern Australia, known as the great copper python or the rainbow serpent

African Mythology

Abassi - sky god of the Efik

Adroa - creator god of the Lugbara

Adu Ogyinae - first man of the Ashanti

Ala - mother goddess of the Ibo, eastern Nigeria

Amma - an egg, seed of the cosmos; god of creation

Anansi - West African trickster god

Asa - supreme god of the Akamba

Bumba -creator god of the Bushongo of the Democratic Republic of Congo

Chinaweji - serpent; founder of the universe

Chuku - supreme god of the Ibo, eastern Nigeria

Dxui - first god of creation

Eshu - messenger between High God and humans

Eshu - trickster god of the tribe who carried messages from the gods to mankind

Evening Star - wife of Mwetsi, bearer of animals and people

Faro - maker of the sky

Gu - heavenly blacksmith

Ifa - god of medicine and prophecy

Imana - supreme god of the Banyarwanda, Rwanda

Jok - creator god of the Alur

Kaang - creator god of the southwest African Bushmen

Leza - supreme god of the Bantu

Mawu-Lisa - twin creator gods

Mboom - god of creation

Minia - serpent; founder of the universe

Morning Star - wife of Mwetsi, bearer of grass, shrubs, etc.

Monya – hero who invented the bull-roarer

Mulungu – all-knowing sky god of the Nyamwezi

Mwari – High God

Mwetsi – the first man

Nana – earth goddess of the Yoruba

Ngaan – god of creation

Ngewo – sky god of the Miende

Nommo – a creator god

Ntoro – the soul, in the beliefs of the Ashanti

Nyame – mother goddess

Ogun – war god of the Yoruba

Pemba – maker of the earth

Ruhanga – high god of the Bangoro

Unkulunkulu – supreme god of the Zulus

Wele – chief god of the Abaluyia of Kenya

Wood – name of all the nine children of Mboom

Arthurian Legend

Agravain – younger brother of Gawain, helped expose Lancelot's and Guinevere's adultery to Arthur

Amfortas – Fisher King who looked after the Grail

Arthur – legendary British leader of the Knights of the Round Table

Avalon – wonderful island where Arthur was taken to be healed of his wounds

Bors – only knight to achieve the quest of the Holy Grail, and to survive and return to Arthur's court

Camelot – capital of Arthur's kingdom

Ector – foster father of Arthur, father of Kay

Excalibur – Arthur's magic sword
Galahad – son of Lancelot; purest of
the Knights of the Round Table;
succeeded in the quest of the Grail
Gawain – nephew of Arthur, son of
Morgan le Fay; searched for the Holy
Grail
Grail (Sangreal, The Holy Grail) –
said to be the vessel of the Last
Supper; in the custody of the Fisher
King
Guinevere – wife of Arthur, lover of
Lancelot
Igraine – wife of Uther Pendragon;
mother of Arthur and Morgan le Fay
Kay – foster brother of Arthur
Lady of the Lake – enchantress who
raised Lancelot and gave Arthur
Excalibur

Lancelot or Launcelot – knight and
lover of Queen Guinevere
Lucan – most trusted of Arthur's
friends
Merlin – magician and bard who
prepared Arthur for kingship
Mordred or Modred – son of Arthur
and his half-sister Morgause
Morgan le Fay – sorceress and
healer; half-sister of Arthur
Morgause – half-sister of Arthur;
mother of Mordred, Gawain, Gareth
and Agravain
Nimue – enchantress with whom
Merlin fell in love
Percival or Perceval – knight who
vowed to seek the Grail
Uther Pendragon – father of Arthur
Viviane – the Lady of the Lake

Science and
Technology

Agriculture

3

awn
bin
cob
cod
cow
cub
dig
ear
erf
ewe
far
feu
gid
hay
hep
hip
hoe
hog
ket
kex
kid
kip
lea
moo
mow
pig
pip
ram
ret
rye
sow
ted
teg
tup
vag
vat
zea

4

akee
aril
avel
bale
barn
bawn
beam
beef
bent
bere
bigg
boon
bran
bull
byre
calf
cart
clay
corn
cote
crop
culm
curb
drey
dung
farm
foal
gait
galt
gape
harl
haum
herd
hind
hink
holt
hops
hull
husk
kine
lamb
lime
loam

lyme
maim
mare
marl
meal
milk
neat
neep
nide
nout
nowt
oast
oats
odal
paco
peat
pest
pone
quey
rabi
rake
rape
resp
rime
root
roup
runn
rust
ryot
sand
scab
seed
sere
shaw
silo
skep
skug
slob
sock
soil
soya
span
stot

teff
toft
tope
tore
udal
vale
vega
weed
wold
yean
zebu

5

ammon
aphid
araba
baler
beans
bhyle
biddy
borax
bosky
bothy
braxy
briza
calve
carse
cavie
chaff
chum
clevy
closh
couch
croft
crone
crops
dairy
ditch
drill
drove
durra
ergot
ervum

farcy
fruit
fungi
gavel
gebur
glume
grain
grass
graze
guano
halfa
hards
haugh
haulm
hedge
hilum
hoove
horse
humus
kulak
lande
llano
lobby
maize
mower
mummy
ovine
plant
ranch
rumen
sewel
sheep
sheth
shoat
shuck
spelt
spuds
staig
stall
stead
stich
stipa
stock

straw
swill
tilth
tiver
tuber
veldt
vimen
vives
vomer
wagon
wheat
withe
withy
worms
yield

6

angora
animal
arable
arista
barley
basset
beeves
binder
bosket
bottle
butter
carney
cattle
cereal
clover
colter
corral
cowman
cratch
cutter
digger
disbud
dobbin
drover
earing
eatage

ecurie	pods	calving
enspan	polder	combine
fallow	porker	compost
farina	potato	Copland
fanner	punned	coinage
fodder	rage	coulter
forage	rancho	cowherd
furrow	realty	cowshed
gargol	reaper	demesne
garran	roller	digging
gaucho	run rig	dipping
gimmer	sheave	docking
gluten	silage	drought
grains	socage	droving
grange	swans	weanling
harrow	sowing	erosion
heifer	sprit	farming
hogget	stable	fee-tail
hogsty	steppe	foaling
hopper	Stover	foliage
huller	taints	foot rot
incult	tomand	forcing
inning	Travis	fox trap
inspan	trough	gasman
intine	turnip	granger
jument	turfs	grazing
linhay	warble	hillier
llanos	weevil	harvest
milking		hay cart
manger	**7**	hay rick
manure	acidity	hedging
mealier	aerator	herding
merino	alfalfa	hognose
mille	amandine	hop pole
millet	anthrax	hunkers
mislay	avenge	implant
mowing	binding	infield
nubbin	boscage	innings
pad nag	budding	kindling
pampas	belching	lamb-ale
piglet	bullock	lambing
pigsty	buttery	laniary
plough	cabbage	lay land

leas owe
lucerne
maizena
marlite
milk can
milking
misyoke
morling
multure
murrain
novalia
nursery
pabular
paddock
panicum
pannage
pasture
peonage
piggery
pinetum
pinfold
polders
popcorn
poultry
prairie
praties
predial
provine
pruning
pulping
pummace
radicel
raking
rancher
reaping
rearing
retting
rhizome
rokeage
rundale
rustler
ryotwar
sickled

slanket
spancel
stacker
station
stooker
stubble
stuckle
subsoil
swinery
tantony
tascall
tax cart
threave
thwaite
tillage
tilling
tractor
trammel
trekker
trotter
udaller
vaquero
vitular
wagoner
windrow
yardman

8

agronomy
branding
breeding
clipping
cropping
ditching
drainage
elevator
ensilage
farmyard
forestry
gleaning
grafting
hayfield
haymaker

haystack
haywagon
hopfield
kohlrabi
landgirl
loosebox
milkcart
pedigree
pig-swill
plougher
rootcrop
rotation
shearing
sheep-dip
vineyard
watering
wireworm

9

agrimotor
agroville
allotment
cornfield
dairy-farm
dairymaid
disc drill
fertility
fungicide
gathering
grassland
harrowing
harvester
haymaking
hop-picker
horserake
husbandry
implement
incubator
livestock
pasturage
penthouse
phosphate
pig trough

ploughing
rice field
screening
separator
shorthorn
sugar beet
sugar cane
swineherd
thrashing
threshing
trenching
winnowing

10

agronomist
battery hen
cattle cake
cultivator
fertilizer
harvesting
husbandman
irrigation
mould-board
plantation
rounding-up
self-binder
transplant
weed killer
wheatfield

11

agriculture
cake crusher
chaff cutter
chicken farm
crude plough
cultivation
fertilizing
germination
insecticide
motor plough
pastureland
poultry farm

reclamation
stock-taking
water-trough
weed control

12

agricultural
feeding-stock
fermentation
horticulture
insemination
market garden
smallholding
swathe turner
turnip cutter

Astronomy

Constellations

3

Ara
Leo

4

Apus
Argo
Crux
Grus
Lynx
Lyra
Pavo
Vela

5

Aries
Cetus
Draco
Hydra
Indus
Lepus
Libra

Lupus
Mensa
Musca
Norma
Orion
Virgo

6

Antlia
Aquila
Auriga
Bootes
Caelum
Cancer
Corvus
Crater
Cygnus
Dorado
Fornax
Gemini
Hydrus
Octans
Pictor
Pisces
Taurus
Tucana
Volans

7

Cepheus
Columba
Lacerta
Pegasus
Perseus
Phoenix
Sagitta
Scorpio
Serpens
Sextans

8

Aquarius
Circinus

Equuleus
Eridanus
Hercules
Leo Minor
Sculptor

9

Andromeda
Centaurus
Chamaelon
Delphinus
Monoceros
Ophiuchus
Reticulum
Ursa Major
Ursa Minor
Vulpecula

10

Canis Major
Canis Minor
Cassiopeia
Piscis Aust
Triangulum

11

Capricornus
Sagittarius
Telescopium

12

Horologium
Microscopium

13

Canes Venatici
Coma Berenices
Crux Australis

14

Camelopardalis
Corona Borealis
Musca Australis

15

Corona Australis
Piscis Australis
Sculptor's Chisel

General Astronomy Terms

2 and 3

Io
Sol
Star
Sun

4

belt
coma
Eros
halo
Juno
limb
Hebe
Moon
Node
nova
orb
pole

5

Ceres
comet
Digit
epact
epoch
error
flare
giant
label
lunar

nadir
orbit
phase
solar
space
stars
umbra

6

albedo
apogee
Apollo
astral
aurora
binary
Bolide
colure
Corona
crater
Dipper
domify
galaxy
gnomon
Leonid
lunary
meteor
moonet
nebula
octile
parsec
planet
pulsar
quasar
Radius
sphere
sun-dog
syzygy
vector
vertex
Viking
zenith
zodiac

7

apogean
auroral
azimuth
big-bang
Cepheid
cluster
cometic
eclipse
equator
equinox
gibbous
Mariner
metonic
mock sun
nebulae
nebular
new moon
perigee
radiant
sextile
spectra
sputnik
stellar
sunspot
transit

8

aerolite
aerolith
almagest
altitude
aphelion
asterism
asteroid
canicula
cometary
draconic
ecliptic
epicycle
evection
Explorer
fireball

free fall
full moon
Hesperus
latitude
meridian
meteoric
Milky Way
nutation
occulted
parallax
parhelia
penumbra
perigean
quadrant
quadrate
quartile
quintile
red giant
red shift
sidereal
solstice
spectrum
spheroid
starless
stellary
sublunar
systemic
tetragon
universe
Van Allen
Vanguard
variable
zodiacal

9

aerolitic
arc-en-ciel
ascendant
ascension
astrology
astronomy
azimuthal
black hole

canicular
celestial
cosmogeny
cosmology
Curtation
draconian
elevation
ephemeris
epicyclic
firmament
hour angle
light-year
longitude
lunisolar
magnitude
meteorite
meteoroid
meteorous
Minuteman
Nubeculae
novilunar
parhelian
planetary
planetoid
planetule
Ptolemaic
reflector
refractor
satellite
solar wind
star-gazer
starlight
sublunary
supernova
synodical
telescope
trioctile
uranology

10

aberration
altazimuth
apparition

asteroidal
astrologer
astrometer
astronomer
astronomic
atmosphere
brightness
cometarium
Copernican
cosmic rays
Crab nebula
depression
discoverer
dispositor
double star
earthshine
elongation
exaltation
extra-solar
hour circle
lunar cycle
lunar month
lunar probe
North Star
opposition
outer space
perihelion
precession
prominence
quadrature
refraction
retrograde
rudolphine
siderolite
star-gazing
supergiant
terminator
trajectory
uranoscopy
white dwarf

11

astrography

astronomize
blazing star
conjunction
declination
falling star
giant planet
last quarter
metemptosis
meteorolite
minor planet
neutron star
occultation
photosphere
observatory
planetarium
solar system
spectrology
terrestrial
uranography

12

astronautics
astronomical
astrophysics
chromosphere
doppler shift
eccentricity
first quarter
Halley's comet
intermundane
interstellar
lunar eclipse
lunar rainbow
Saturn's rings
shooting star
sidereal time
solar eclipse
spectroscope
spiral galaxy
uranographic
Van Allen Belt
variable star

13

constellation
meteorography
sidereal clock
zodiacal light

14

annular eclipse
Aurora Borealis
interplanetary
radio astronomy
radio telescope
right ascension
summer solstice
transit of Venus
vertical circle
winter solstice
zenith distance

15

armillary sphere
celestial sphere
Fraunhofer lines
meteoric showers

16

Alphonsine tables
astronomical unit
Magellanic Clouds

Popular names for constellations

3

Cup
Net
Ram

4

Bull

Crab
Crow
Hare
Lion
Lynx
Swan
Wolf

5

Altar
Arrow
Clock
Crane
Eagle
Tucan
Twins

6

Archer
Dragon
Fishes
Indian
Lizard
Octant
Scales
Square
Virgin

7

Airpump
Cepheus
Centaur

Dolphin
Furnace
Giraffe
Peacock
Phoenix
Sea goat
Serpent
Sextant
Unicorn

8

Great Dog
Hercules
Scorpion
Ship Argo
Triangle

9

Andromeda
Chameleon
Compasses
Great Bear
Little Dog
Noah's Dove
Ploughman
Sword-fish
Telescope

10

Cassiopeia
Charioteer
Flying Fish

Greyhounds
Little Bear
Little Lion
Microscope
Sea Monster
Watersnake

11

Hunter Orion
Little Horse
Southern Fly
Water-bearer
Winged Horse

12

Flying-dragon
Southern Fish

13

Berenice's Hair
Northern Crown
Painter's Easel
River Eridanus
Serpent-bearer
Southern Cross
Southern Crown

14

Bird of Paradise
Sculptor's Tools

Planets and Satellites

Main Planet	Named Satellite
Mercury	-
Venus	-
Earth	Moon
Mars	Phobos, Deimos
Jupiter	Metis, Adrastea, Amalthea, Thebe, Io, Europa, Ganymede, Callisto, Leda, Himalia, Lysithea, Elara, Ananke, Carme, Pasiphae, Sinope
Saturn	Mimas, Enceladus, Tethys, Telesto, Calypso, Dione, Rhea, Helene, Titan, Hyperion, Iapetus Phoebe, Janus, Pan, Atlas, Prometheus, Pandora, Epimetheus
Uranus	Miranda, Ariel, Umbriel, Titania, Oberon, Bianca, Cressida, Desdemona, Joliet, Portia, Rosalind, Belinda, Puck, Caliban, Sycorax
Neptune	Triton, Nereid, Naiad, Thassala, Despina, Galatea, Proteus, Larissa)
Pluto	Charon

Minor Planets

Achilles
Adonis
Agamemnon
Amor
Apollo
Astraea
Aten
Ceres
Chiron
Dactyl
Davida
Eros
Eunomia
Euphrosyne
Europa
Gaspra
Hebe
Hephaistos
Hermes
Hadalgo
Hygiea
Icarus
Ida
Iris
Juno
Mathilde
Pallas
Vesta

Comets

4

Faye

5

Biela
Encke
Kopff

6

Halley
Olbers
Tuttle

7

Bennett
D'Arrest
Vaisala
Whipple

8

Borrelly
Daylight

Hale-Bopp
Kohoutek
Westphal

9

Comas Sola
Crommelin
Hyakutake

10

Pons-Brooks
Schaumasse

11

Arend-Roland
Swift-Tuttle

12

Pons-Winnecke

13

Shoemaker-Levy
Stephan-Oterma

14

Bronsen-Metcalf

15

Giacobini-Zinner
Grigg-Skiellerup

Meteor Showers

6

Lyrids
Ursids

7

Cygnids
Leonids
Taurids

8

Cepheids
Geminids
Orionids
Perseids

10

Australids
Ophiuchids
Phoenicids

11

Quadrantids

12

Capricornids

Botany

3

awn
bud
bur
dig
eye
lax
lid
lip
mow
pod
ray
rib
sod
uva

4

apex
aril
axil
axis
barb

bark
bast
bole
bulb
burl
bush
cane
cell
claw
clay
coma
cone
corm
culm
cusp
cyme
disc
disk
duff
dust
form
free
gall
gene
head
heel
herb
hill
host
hull
husk
iron
keel
knee
knot
land
lawn
leaf
limb
lime
loam
lobe
male

marl	cross	mulch
mule	crown	ocrea
mull	crust	oxide
node	cycle	ovary
pale	downy	ovate
pest	drain	ovule
pore	drift	palea
root	drill	petal
seed	drupe	pinna
self	druxy	pistil
slip	eared	pulse
soil	erose	radix
spur	falls	raphe
stem	flora	rogue
tree	frond	rynia
tube	frost	sepal
tump	fruit	shrub
turf	fungi	shuck
vein	galea	sinus
vine	gemma	solum
	genus	sorus

5

acute	gland	spathe
ament	glans	spica
anion	glume	spike
attar	graft	spine
auger	grain	spore
auxin	guano	sport
beard	hardy	stalk
berry	hedge	sting
bifid	hilar	stipe
biota	hilum	stock
blade	hoary.	stoma
bloom	humus	stone
boron	jugum	stool
bough	keiki	stunt
bract	knurl	style
breed	larva	testa
brush	latex	theca
calyx	leach	thorn
chaff	level	tilth
clone	lingy	truss
crest	loess	tryma
	mucro	tuber

tunic
umbel
valve

6

achene
adnate
adsorb
aerate
Alpine
annual
anther
arbour
areole
balsam
banner
binate
blanch
blossom
bonsai
border
bosket
botany
branch
budding
buffer
burlap
cactus
callus
canker
carbon
carpel
catena
cation
catkin
caudex
chitin
cirrus
coccus
column
copper
cormel
corona

cortex
corymb
crocks
cupule
cyclic
cymose
defoil
dibble
disbud
dorsal
eddish
embryo
entire
escape
exogen
exotic
fallow
family
female
fimble
floral
floret
flower
foliar
fornix
fungal
furrow
gamete
gyroma
hamate
harrow
herbal
hispid
hotbed
hotcap
hybrid
inarch
kernel
labium
lacuna
lamina
lanate
lanose

lanugo
leader
lignum
ligule
linear
lobate
loment
lunate
lyrate
marrow
mentum
midrib
mildew
mosaic
oblong
obtuse
offset
oxygen
parted
pappus
pedate
pileus
pilose
pleach
pollen
raceme
rachis
ramose
replum
revert
rugose
runner
retuse
samara
secund
septum
setose
setula
shaggy
sheath
silica
single
sobole

spadix
species
sprout
squama
stamen
stigma
stipel
stirps
stolon
strain
stress
striate
striga
strike
struma
sucker
suture
terete
thyrse
torose
turgid
venous
villus
viscid

7

acantha
acidify
acidity
acrogen
aerator
aerobic
albumen
ammonia
ampulla
annulus
anterior
apatite
apicule
apogamy
aquifer
auricle
barbate

biotype
botanic
bristle
bulblet
bullace
calcium
caliche
cambium
capsule
caudate
chalaza
chimera
chipper
ciliate
cirrose
cladode
clavate
climate
climber
compact
compost
conical
conifer
connate
contour
cordate
corking
cornute
corolla
creeper
crenate
cullion
cuneate
cut back
cutting
cyathus
dehisce
deltoid
dentate
dieback
diffuse
discoid
divided

ecology
emersed
enation
endemic
endogen
epicarp
epigeal
erosion
erosive
étagère
exalate
exocarp
falcate
fernery
fertile
fimbria
firming
flaccid
floccus
foliage
foliate
foliole
foliose
forcing
friable
furcate
fuscous
galeate
gemmate
gemmoid
gemmule
generic
genesis
gibbous
globose
glochids
granule
guttate
habitat
haploid
hardpan
hastate
heaving

herbage	petiole	stupose
hirsute	piceous	stylate
hormone	pileate	subsoil
hydrous	pinnate	subtend
icterus	pinnule	sulcate
inbreed	pitcher	sulphur
incised	plicate	synacmy
ingraft	pollard	syncarp
jointed	prickle	taproot
labiate	process	tendril
laccate	profile	tension
lacinia	pruning	ternate
lamella	pustule	thallus
lateral	quinate	tigella
leafbud	radiate	tillage
leaflet	radical	topiary
leprose	radicle	top soil
lignify	ramulus	tussock
limbate	regular	utricle
lineate	residue	velamen
lituate	rhizoid	valvate
lobelet	rhizome	ventral
lopping	rosette	variety
macular	saccate	villous
meadow	sarment	
meiosis	sartage	**8**
midlobe	sectile	aberrant
mineral	septate	acephate
mitosis	septile	acervate
neutral	serrate	acicular
oblique	sessile	acid soil
obovate	sexfoil	additive
orchard	shrubby	adnation
organic	silicle	adnexed
osmosis	silique	aeration
palmate	sinuate	air plant
panicle	spicula	allogamy
pannose	spicule	alluvium
pappose	spindle	anthesis
pedicel	spinose	apomixis
peltate	spinule	aquatic
pendent	sterile	arborist
pericarp	stipule	arbuscle

aristate	digitate	furrowed
ascidium	dimerous	fusiform
atypical	division	galbulus
autogamy	dormancy	germ tube
axillary	drainage	glabrous
biennial	drowning	gladiate
biforate	drupelet	glaucous
bilobate	ecaudate	granular
biramous	echinate	grumrose
birimose	elliptic	gynobase
bisetose	elongate	hardwood
bisexual	endocarp	henequen
blastema	ensiform	homogamy
bleeding	epappose	homogony
blowball	epicalyx.	hothouse
bone meal	epiphyte	hydrogen
botryoid	episperm	hypogyny
burn lime	epispore	inarable
calyptra	ericetal	inarching
capitate	erodible	incanous
caruncle	espalier	included
catalase	etiolate	incubous
catalyst	eucyclic	incurved
cernuous	exanthem	indusium
chorisis	extrorse	inflated
clasping	farinose	inserted
cochlear	fasciate	introrse
columnar	fascicle	inverted
compound	filament	involute
coronule	filiform	irrigate
crispate	fish meal	labellum
cruciate	fixation	lacerate
cultigen	flexuous	lacinula
cultivar	floccose	landform
cyathium	floweret	layering
cytology	follicle	leaching
deflexed	frondage	leaf scar
defluent	frondent	lenticel
deforest	frondlet	lepidote
dendroid	frondose	ligneous
denshire	fructify	ligulate
didymous	fruit dot	lithosol
didynamy	fruitlet	littoral

liturate
lodicule
mericarp
meristem
mesocarp
molecule
monander
monocarp
muricate
mutation
mycelial
mycelium
mycology
obligate
obrotund
oogamous
opposite
panicled
papillae
parasite
pathogen
peduncle
petaloid
perianth
perigyny
phyllode
phyllody
phylloid
phyllome
pileolus
placenta
plantlet
plumose
polytomy
pomology
porosity
pot-bound
premorse
pruinose
punctate
pustular
pyriform
quadrate

rachilla
radicate
reaction
recurved
reflexed
reniform
retrorse
revolute
riparian
rivulose
root ball
root zone
rosarian
rotenone
sabulous
seed leaf
self-seed
sepalody
separate
setiform
setulose
softwood
speculum
spikelet
sporange
squamous
squamule
stalklet
standard
stellate
stem-leaf
stemless
stipular
strigose
striolate
strobile
strumose
subclass
subgenus
substrate
subulate
surculus
syconium

synacmic
synanthy
synsepal
terminal
terrarium
thalamus
thalloid
thyrsoid
transpire
tree ring
trichome
triploid
truncate
tubercle
tuberoid
tuberous
urceolus
vascular
venation
verticil
ramentum
ramicaul
tomentum
undulate

9

ablastous
accretive
aciniform
acuminate
adobe soil
adpressed
adsortion
adventive
aggregate
alternate
amendment
amino acid
anaerobic
anhydrous
appendage
applanate
arboretum

auxotonic	dehiscent	fragipans
backcross	depressed	fruticose
basifixed	dextrorse	fugacious
basifugal	diandrous	fungicide
bifarious	dichasial	funiculus
bifoliate	dichasium	galeiform
bifurcate	dichogamy	gemmation
bilabiate	dichotomy	gemmiform
bilocular	diclinism	geotropic
bipinnate	diclinous	germinate
biplicate	dicoccous	glandular
bispinous	dictyogen	glomerate
bracteate	dimidiate	glomerule
canescent	dioecious	glutinous
capillary	dipterous	graniform
capitulum	dissected	granulate
caryopsis	divergent	gumbo soil
cataphyll	drain-well	gynaecium
caudicle	dust mulch	gynophore
cephalium	ecarinate	heartwood
ceraceous	endostome	helobious
ciliolate	epicotyle	herbalism
cincinnus	epidermis	herbalist
circinate	epigenous	herbarium
colluvium	epigynous	herborist
connation	epixylous	hercogamy
convolute	epruinose	hispidity
corymbose	espathate	honeydew
cotyledon	evergreen	hybridize
cover crop	exfoliate	imbricate
creep soil	exogenous	imperfect
crenulate	exsuccous	impressed
cryptogam	falciform	incumbent
cuspidate	faveolate	inorganic
dactyloid	fertility	insertion
deciduous	film water	internode
declinate	fimbriate	involucel
decompose	flagellum	involucre
decumbent	floriform	irregular
decurrent	floscular	isandrous
decussate	foliation	isanthous
defluvium	foliolate	isogynous
defoliate	fornicate	isomerous

laciniate
lamellate
lanciform
landscape
leaf mould
leaf plant
leaf scorch
leafstalk
lineolate
macropore
magnesium
megaspore
mesochile
mitriform
monopodia
monosperm
monotypic
mucronate
musciform
monstrose
mycelioid
obcordate
obdeltoid
orbicular
osmophore
oxidation
papillary
pectinate
perennate
perennial
perignous
pesticide
petiolule
phenology
phenotype
pheromone
pinnatifid
pinnation
pinnulate
pollinium
potassium
propagule
prostrate

protogyny
pulverant
pulvinate
rachidian
ray flower
reticulum
rhipidium
rootstock
rostellum
sabadilla
sacciform
sagittate
saltation
sarcocarp
sebaceous
sedge peat
sericeous
serotinal
serrulate
setaceous
shrubbery
sigillate
spadicose
spatulate
spiciform
spicosity
spiculate
spiniform
spinulose
spore case
squamella
squarrose
staminate
staminode
staminody
sterilize
stipiform
stipitate
stipulate
stobiloid
subfamily
submerged
succubous

succulent
surculose
sympodial
sympodium
tigellate
tomentose
trigamous
trijugate
trilobate
trimerous
turbinate
uniparous
unisexual
urceolate
vegetable
vernation
verrucose
verrucous
versatile
viscidium
watershed

10

absorption
acinaceous
acinarious
activator
aerenchyma
aerial root
alkali soil
androecium
androphore
angiosperm
annual ring
anthophore
antibiosis
articulate
attenuate
auriculate
autogamous
buttonbush
caespitose
calcareous

calyptrate	fibrillose	indigenous
carpogenic	filiciform	indumentum
carpophore	flabellate	intake rate
caudiciform	flocculate	integument
caulescent	flocculose	intrazonal
coalescent	foliaceous	involucral
commissure	footstalk	irrigation
complanate	frutescent	isostemony
compressed	funnel form	lanceolate
coriaceous	furrow weed	lacinulate
cyathiform	gemmaceous	lacunulose
cytochrome	geniculate	lanuginous
damping off	geotropism	leaf cutting
decompound	glumaceous	lenticular
defoliator	gramineous	lignescent
dehiscence	greenhouse	lithophyte
desert soil	growth form	maculation
desorption	growth ring	mammillate
didynamous	gymnosperm	marcescent
dimorphism	gymnospore	microspore
dimorphous	gynandrous	monandrous
dipetalous	herbaceous	moniliform
diphyllous	heterogamy	monocarpic:
diplotegia	homogamous	monoecious
dispermous	homogonous	monomerous
dissilient	homostyled	monopodial
distichous	hose-in-hose	monotocous
divaricate	houseplant	morphology
dorsifixed	humid acids	mycorrhiza
drupaceous	hybridiser	paleaceous
ebracteate	hydrophily	palmatifid
ecalcarate	hydrophyte	paniculate
eluviation	hygrophyte	paraphysis
emarginate	hypanthial	parenchyma
embryotega	hypanthium	pediculate
endogenous	hypertrophy	percurrent
epichilium	hypochile	perfoliate
ericaceous	hypocotyl	perigynium
etiolation	hypogenous	persistent
fasciation	hypogynous	phanerogam
fastigiate	hypsophyll	phototaxis
ferric iron	immortelle	phyllotaxy
fertilizer	inbreeding	pistillate

pistilline
pistillode
polycarpic
polygamous
polygynous
polytomous
pomologist
procumbent
propagator
prophyllum
prothallia
pseudobulb
pseudocarp
puberulent
radiculose
receptacle
rest period
resupinate
reticulate
salverform
samariform
saprophyte
sarmentose
sebiferous
seed vessel
simple leaf
spadiceous
spinescent
sporophyll
sporophyte
squamiform
stove plant
subspecies
substratum
subvariety
synanthous
syncarpous
thalliform
topography
triandrous
tricostate
trifoliate
trifurcate

trioecious
tripinnate
tristylous
triternate
undershrub
uniflorous
unifoliate
variegated
vegetative
velutinous
ventricose
vespertine
virgin soil
water ratio
water table
viviparous

11

acaulescent
acinaciform
air layering
Alpine house
ammonium ion
amplexicaul
antheridium
antherozoid
anthocyanin
anthography
antholeucin
autocarpous
autotrophic
bacciferous
basal leaves
bifoliolate
bud mutation
bursiculate
calyptrogen
campanulate
chlorophyll
chromosomes
cladoptosis
cleistogamy
clinandrium

collenchyma
colloid soil
column-wings
conceptacle
concretions
conductance
consistence
consolidate
conspecific
crustaceous
deadheading
defoliation
degradation
dehydration
denticulate
diadelphous
dichogamous
dicotyledon
dissepiment
drepaniform
epipetalous
episepalous
esquamulose
everbloomer
extrafloral
facultative
ferrous iron
ferruginous
first bottom
floriferous
floriparous
flower heads
flower stalk
foliicolous
frondescent
fruticulose
gametophyte
geitonogamy
germination
germinative
glabrescent
glaucescent
glochidiate

glomerulate
glumiferous
graft hybrid
granulation
ground cover
ground water
guttiferous
gymnogynous
gynostegium
halophilous
heliophobic
heliotropic
hercogamous
hesperidium
heterodromy
heterotaxis
hispidulous
homomallous
homosporous
horizon soil
hydroponics
immarginate
indeciduous
indehiscent
induplicate
infrafoliar
insecticide
involucrate
iron chelate
isadelphous
lacrimiform
lance-linear
lentiginous
macropodous
mineral soil
monocarpous
monoclinous
monosporous
mottled leaf
mucronulate
odd-pinnate
odoriferous
orthostichy

orthotropic
palmatisect
papyraceous
paraphysate
parenchymal
pedicellate
pentamerous
pentandrous
perennation
pericarpial
phosphorous
photoperiod
phylloclade
phyllomania
phyllophore
pinnatisect
pollinarium
pollination
polyandrous
polymorphic
propagation
protogynous
pteridology
rhizanthous
salsuginous
saxifragous
self-sterile
semi-double
shelterbelt
soil climate
spadiciform
spinulescent
squamaceous
stem cutting
sternotribe
stipuliform
styliferous
stylopodium
subaxillary
subpetiolar
subspecific
subvarietal
subtropical

suprafoliar
symmetrical
sympetalous
synanthesis
ternatisect
terrestrial
tetragynous
tetramerous
tetrandrous
trimorphism
trimorphous
tripetaloid
tripetalous
triquetrous
tristichous
unguiculate
variegation
verruculose
water logged

12

adosculation
adventitious
alkaline soil
alluvial soil
angiocarpian
angiocarpous
anthoxanthin
antipetalous
antisepalous
assimilation
bactericide
bifollicular
bud variation
carbohydrate
caulocarpous
chestnut soil
cladocarpous
compound leaf
concrescence
conduplicate
conglomerate
contour basin

dasyphyllous
deflocculate
diageotropic
dialycarpous
dictyogenous
disboscation
disinfection
disk flower
divarication
dodecamerous
dolabriform
dorsiventral
ebracteolate
efflorescent
emargination
exalbuminous
exchangeable
fibrous roots
floriculture
foliage plant
frondescence
frondiferous
fructescence
fructiferous
fruiting body
furfuraceous
gamopetalous
gamophyllous
gamosepalous
growing point
gymnocarpous
gymnosporous
gynantherous
gynostemium
hardening off
heliophilous
heliotropism
heterauxesis
heterogamous
heteromerous
heterophylly
heterostyled
heterotactic

hexapetaloid
hibernaculum
homopetalous
honeydewed
horticulture
hortus siccus
hybridisable
hypophyllous
isostemonous
lateral lobes
laticiferous
lenticellate
ligniperdous
microclimate
microstylous
monadelphous
monopetalous
monosepalous
monospermous
monostichous
oblanceolate
orthotropism
orthotropous
polymorphous
polypetalous
productivity
pteridophyte
pterocarpous
radicicolous
ramentaceous
ramuliferous
rhizocarpous
semi-aquatic
seminiferous
sempervirent
soboliferous
soil analysis
somatotropic
spinulescent
squamuliform
suffruticose
synantherous
syngenesious

tessellation
thermotropic
tridactylate
tristachyous
unhumidified
unifoliolate
verticillate

13

angiospermous
anisophyllous
apheliotropic
arboriculture
asperifoliate
choripetalous
cyclospermous
deforestation
diageotropism
dialypetalous
dialyphyllous
dialysepalous
dichlamydeous
dicotyledoneae
dissepimental
doubly serrate
efflorescence
entomophilous
fertilization
field capacity
field moisture
foliar feeding
frumentaceous
geminiflorous
gymnospermous
gynodioecious
hermaphrodite
heterodromous
heteromorphic
heterosporous
horticultural
hybridisation
hypsophyllary
imparipinnate

indeterminate
inferior ovary
inflorescence
infrared mulch
infraspecific
insectivorous
interaxillary
involucriform
liguliflorous
macrophyllous
membranaceous
microphyllous
monocotyledon
monogynoecial
multiple fruit
orthostichous
pedicelliform
pentadelphous
pentastichous
phyllogenetic
polyadelphous
polycotyledon
polygynoecial
polystamonous
proteranthous
pteridologist
self-coloured
sodium nitrate
stenopetalous
stenophyllous
sterilization
stipulary buds
strobilaceous
subherbaceous
subirrigation
suffrutescent
tetradynamous
trace elements
trachycarpous
transpiration

tricarpellary

14

ammonification
amplexifoliate
androdioecious
anthoropic soil
circumnutation
circumscissile
dealkalization
desalinisation
diaheliotropic
drip irrigation
enantioblastic
floral envelope
fructification
heteromorphism
horticulturist
hydroxyapatite
infructescence
mineralization
obdiplostemony
photoperiodism
photosynthesis
polycarpellary
polycotyledony
polysporangium
pseudocehalium
pseudospermium
sinuate-dentate
stellate leaves
stigmatiferous
stratification
trachyspermous
tripinnatisect
verticillaster

15

acinacifolious
ammonium nitrate

calcium chloride
crumb structures
denitrification
diaheliotropism
epicotyledonary
infundibuliform
interfoliaceous
microsporangium
moisture tension
multicarpellate
open-pollinated
parthenogenesis
sedimentary rock
suprafoliaceous

16

adventitious buds
ammonium sulphate
calcium carbonate
calcium cyanamide
hypocotyledonary
obdiplostemonous
quinquefoliolate
verticillastrate

17

aluminium sulphate
dioeciopolygamous
lacustrine deposit
medicinal plants
self-fertilization

18

aluminium silicates
cross-fertilization
dolomitic limestone
evapotranspiration

Chemical Elements

Name	Symbol	Name	Symbol
actinium	Ac	hafnium	Hf
aluminium	Al	hassium	Hs
americium	Am	helium	He
antimony	Sb	holmium	Ho
argon	Ar	hydrogen	H
arsenic	As	indium	In
astatine	At	iodine	I
barium	Ba	iridium	Ir
berkelium	Bk	iron	Fe
beryllium	Be	krypton	Kr
bismuth	Bi	lanthanum	La
bohrium	Bh	lawrencium	Lr
boron	B	lead	Pb
bromine	Br	lithium	Li
cadmium	Cd	lutetium	Lu
caesium	Cs	magnesium	Mg
calcium	Ca	manganese	Mn
californium	Cf	meitnerium	Mt
carbon	C	mendelevium	Md
chromium	Cr	mercury	Hg
cobalt	Co	molybdenum	Mo
columbium	Cb	neodymium	Nd
copper	Cu	neon	Ne
curium	Cm	neptunium	Np
cerium	Ce	nickel	Ni
chlorine	Cl	niobium	Nb
dubnium	Db	nitrogen	N
dysprosium	Dy	nobelium	No
einsteinium	Es	osmium	Os
erbium	Er	oxygen	O
europium	Eu	palladium	Pd
fermium	Fm	phosphorus	P
fluorine	F	platinum	Pt
francium	Fr	plutonium	Pu
gadolinium	Gd	polonium	Po
gallium	Ga	potassium	K
germanium	Ge	praseodymium	Pr
gold	Au	promethium	Pm

Name	Symbol	Name	Symbol
protactinium	Pa	technetium	Tc
radium	Ra	tellurium	Te
radon	Rn	terbium	Tb
rhenium	Re	thallium	Tl
rhodium	Rh	thorium	Th
rubidium	Rb	thulium	Tm
ruthenium	Ru	tin	Sn
samarium	Sm	titanium	Ti
scandium	Sc	tungsten	W
selenium	Se	uranium	U
silicon	Si	vanadium	V
silver	Ag	xenon	Xe
sodium	Na	ytterbium	Yb
strontium	Sr	yttrium	Y
sulphur	S	zinc	Zn
tantalum	Ta	zirconium	Zr

Common Chemicals

4

alum
lime
urea

5

borax
ether
freon
furan
halon

6

baryta
cetane
cresol
dioxan
ethane
hexane
iodide
lithia

litmus
phenol
potash
quinol
silica
xylene

7

acetate
alumina
ammonia
aniline
benzene
borazon
bromide
calomel
camphor
chloral
cyanide
ethanol
heptane
pentane
quinone
realgar

red lead
soda ash
styrene
toluene

8

beryllia
catechol
chloride
cinnabar
corundum
cyanogen
fluoride
fluorite
formalin
magnesia
melamine
methanol
neoprene
peroxide
phosgene
plumbago
propanol
'soda lime

sodamide
strontia

9

acetylene
aqua regia
blanc fixe
boric acid
bromoform
ferrocene
iodic acid
limewater
phosphine
propylene
quicklime
saltpetre

10

capric acid
cyanic acid
formic acid
lactic acid
lauric acid
mustard gas
nitric acid
oxalic acid
picric acid
slaked lime
tannic acid
water glass
zinc blende

11

acrylic acid
benzoic acid
butyric acid
caproic acid
caustic soda
diphosphine
fumaric acid
iodomethane
laughing gas
malonic acid

nitric oxide
nitrous acid
prussic acid
sal ammoniac
stearic acid
sugar of lead
washing soda

12

acetaldehyde
benzaldehyde
benzoquinone
caprylic acid
carbolic acid
carbonic acid
decanoic acid
ethyl alcohol
fluorocarbon
formaldehyde
fulminic acid
green vitriol
hydroquinone
nitrobenzene
nitrous oxide
oil of vitriol
permanganate
phthalic acid
tartaric acid

13

isocyanic acid
methanoic acid
methyl alcohol
propranoic acid
silver nitrate
sodium cyanide
sulphuric acid
vinyl chloride

14

calcium carbide
carbon monoxide
chloral hydrate

copper sulphate
hydroiodic acid
methyl chloride
nitrocellulose
phosphoric acid
sodium chloride
sodium sulphate
sulphur dioxide
tetraethyl lead

15

absolute alcohol
bleaching powder
hydrobromic acid
hydrocyanic acid
hydrogen cyanide
nitrogen dioxide
phosphorous acid
sodium hydroxide
sulphur trioxide
tetrahydrofuran

16

calcium carbonate
calcium hydroxide
hydrochloric acid
hydrofluoric acid
hydrogen fluoride
hydrogen peroxide
hypochlorous acid
nitrogen monoxide

17

bicarbonate of soda
magnesium chloride
potassium chloride
sodium bicarbonate
vanadium pentoxide

18

chlorofluorocarbon
dimethyl sulphoxide
magnesium carbonate

19+

buckmaster-fullerene
carbon tetrachloride
potassium carbonate
potassium perman-
ganate

Elementary Particles

2

xi

3

eta
phi
psi

4

kaon
muon

5

boson
gluon
meson
omega
quark
sigma

6

baryon
hadron
lambda
lepton
photon
proton

7

fermion
hyperon

pion

neutron
tachyon

8

deuteron
electron
graviton
neutrino
positron

9

neutretto

12

antiparticle
beta particle

13

alpha particle

Alloys

4

alni – iron, nickel aluminium, copper
beta – titanium, aluminium, vanadium, chromium

5

alpha – titanium, aluminium, tin, copper, zirconium, niobium, molybdenum
brass – copper, zinc
invar – iron, nickel
mazac – zinc, aluminium, magnesium, copper
monel – nickel, cobalt, iron
steel – iron, carbon

6

alnico – aluminium, nickel, cobalt
Babbit – tin, lead, antimony, copper
bronze – copper, tin
cunico – iron, cobalt, copper, nickel
cunife – iron, cobalt, nickel

feroba – iron, barium oxide, iron oxide
pewter – tin, lead
solder – lead, tin (soft), copper, zinc (brazing)

7

alcomax – aluminium, cobalt, nickel, copper, lead, niobium
alumnel – aluminium, chromium
amalgam – mercury, various
chromel – nickel, chromium
columan – iron, chromium, nickel, aluminium, nobium, copper
elinvar – iron, nickel, chromium, tungsten
inconel – nickel, chromium, iron
kanthal – chromium, aluminium, iron
mumetal - iron, nickel, copper, chromium
nimonic – nickel, chromium, iron, titanium, aluminium, manganese, silicon

8

cast iron – carbon, iron
dowmetal – magnesium, aluminium, zinc, manganese
gunmetal – copper, tin, zinc
hipernik – nickel, iron
kirksite – zinc, aluminium, copper
manganin – copper, manganese, nickel
nichrome – nickel, iron, chromium
vicalloy – iron, cobalt, vanadium
zircaloy – zirconium, tin, iron, nickel, chromium

9

duralumin – aluminium, copper, silicon, magnesium, manganese, zinc
hastelloy – nickel, molybdenum, iron, chromium, cobalt, tungsten
permalloy – nickel, iron
peminvar – nickel, iron, cobalt
type mental – lead, tin, antimony

10

constantan – copper, nickel
misch metal – cerium, various
muntz metal – copper, zinc
Rose's metal – bismuth, lead, tin
superalloy – type of stainless steel
Wood's metal - lead, tin, bismuth, cadmium
cupronickel – copper, nickel
electrotype – lead, tin, antimony

supermalloy – iron, nickel
supermendur – iron, cobalt

12

ferrosilicon – iron, silicon
German silver – copper, nickel, zinc, lead, tin
silver solder – copper, silver, zinc

13

ferrochromium – iron, chromium
ferrotungsten – iron, tungsten
ferrovanadium – iron, vanadium

14

admiralty metal – copper, zinc
Britannia metal – tin, antimony, copper
ferromanganese – iron, manganese
phosphor bronze – copper, tin, phosphorus
stainless steel – iron, chromium, vanadium

Computers

Computer Languages

4GL
Ada
Algol
apl
assembler
assembly language
autocode
C
C++
Cobol
Comal
common lisp
coral
CPL
CSL
eulisp
Forth
Fortran
html
IPL
java
jovial
lisp
logo
Maclisp
Pascal
pilot
PL/1
PL/360
pop-11
pop-2
postscript
prolog
Quickbasic
RPG
SGML
snobal
UCSD Pascal
VBA
Visual Basic
Visual Basic for applications
Visual C++
Word Basic

Computer Terms

1 and 2

K
AI
BS
CD
CR
DP
LF
MB
NL
PC
UI

3

bit

bug
bus
CAD
cal
cam
CBL
CPU
DTP
DVD
gig
gui
ICR
ISP
job
key
meg
net
OCR
RAM
ROM
run
URL
VDA
VDU
wan
web
www

4

baud
boot
byte
chip
copy
data
disk
dump
edit
file
flop
goto
icon
loop

menu
node
prom
save wand

5

abort
block
cache
CD-Rom
crash
debug
e-mail
EPROM
erase
field
input
login
logon
macro
modem
mouse
octal
patch
pixel
queue
spool
virus
write

6

access
backup
binary
bitmap
bitten
boot up
branch
bridge
client
cursor
daemon
decode

delete
escape
filter
format
gopher
header
keypad
laptop
logoff
logout
memory
nybble
on-line
output
packet
parity
parser
raster
record
router
scroll
sector
spider
sprite
usenet
vector

7

address
archive
Arpanet
browser
channel
command
compile
counter
cracker
decimal
display
euronet
fidonet
hashing
hot spot

mailbox
monitor
nesting
network
newline
off-line
palmtop
parsing
plotter
printer
program
scanner
sorting
storage
toolbox
upgrade
wysiwyg

8

analyser
beta test
chat room
compiler
diskette
download
downtime
ethernet
gigabyte
graphics
halfword
hard disk
hardware
home page
internet
intranet
joystick
keyboard
kilobyte
language
light pen
linefeed
megabyte
notebook

password
quadword
real time
register
repeater
robotics

9

algorithm
backspace
bandwidth
benchmark
bootstrap
character
clock rate
data entry
decompile
digitizer
directory
downgrade
e-commerce
fixed disk
handshake
hash table
heartbeat
hypertext
interface
mainframe
processor
sound card
thesaurus
trackball

10

clock cycle
cyberspace
data tablet
diagnostic
encryption
file server
floppy disk
multimedia
peripheral

pre-process
programmer
serial port
source code
text editor
transistor
vacuum tube

11

accumulator
band printer
belt printer
compact disk
compression
coprocessor
cybernetics
drum printer
interpreter
line printer
motherboard
multiplexer
optical disk
programming
screen saver
semantic net
star network
time sharing
transceiver
Trojan horse
workstation

12

alphanumeric
assembly code
bubble memory
chain printer
character set
color printer
device driver
direct access
encryption
expert system

laser printer
minicomputer
multitasking
parallel port
program suite
search engine
user-friendly
worldwide web

13

authoring tool
bar-code reader
barrel printer
bulletin board
compatibility
cybercommerce
data structure
dot com company
dynamic memory
floptical disk
hypertext link
impact printer
ink-jet printer
microcomputer
neural network
primary memory
supercomputer
user interface
window manager
word processor

14

carriage return
data processing
electronic mail
flat-bed plotter
paper-tape punch
read-only memory
system software
theorem proving
utility program
volatile memory

15

acoustic coupler
batch processing
control sequence
cryogenic memory
database program
electronic brain
operating system
paper-tape reader
rule-based system
spelling checker
terminal display
wide-area network

16

bubble-jet printer
compiled language
dot-matrix printer
personal computer
solid-state memory
token ring network
turnkey operation
video display unit

17

daisywheel printer
desktop publishing
high-level language
parallel processor
personal organizer

18

ionographic printer
printable character
random-access memory
relational database
spreadsheet program

19

computer-aided design
perceptual computing
programming language
semiconductor

memory
touchstone software

20+

applications software
artificial intelligence
central processing unit
computer-aided
manufacture
computer-assisted
learning
computer-based
learning
erasable programmable
read-only memory
floating point operation
graphical user interface
hexadecimal character
hierarchical database
intelligent character
recognition
internet service
provider
modulator-demodulator
natural-language
processing
optical character
recognition
programmable read-
only memory
touchscreen hardcopy
device
what you see is what
you get

Electronic Components

3

FET

LED
RCD

4

chip
fuse
gate

5

choke
diode
igfet
relay
shunt
valve

6

bridge
dynamo
filter
jugfet
mosfet
switch
triode

7

ammeter
battery
counter
magneto
pentode
speaker
tetrode

8

armature
bistable
flip-flop
inductor
resistor
rheostat
solenoid
varactor

windings

9

amplifier
capacitor
gunn diode
microchip
rectifier
thyristor
voltmeter
waveguide

10

alternator
attenuator
microphone
oscillator
transducer
transistor
zener diode

11

electron gun
loudspeaker
silicon chip
transformer

12

electron lens
electron tube
galvanometer
logic circuit
oscilloscope
photocathode

13

semiconductor

14

circuit breaker
printed circuit

15+

electron multiplier
field-effect transistor
integrated circuit
light emitting diode
N-type semi-conductor
photomultiplier
P-type semi-conductor
thermionic cathode
Wheatstone bridge

Geometric Figures and Curves

3

arc

4

cone
cube
kite
line
loop
lune
oval
rose
zone

5

chord
conic
helix
locus
nappe
ogive
plane
prism
rhomb
sheet
solid
torus

wedge
witch

6

circle
conoid
folium
lamina
normal
octant
pencil
radius
sector
sphere
spiral
spline
square

7

annulus
cissoid
cycloid
decagon
ellipse
evolute
fractal
hexagon
limacon
octagon
perigon
polygon
pyramid
rhombus
segment
surface
tangent
trefoil
trident

8

cardioid
catenary
catenoid

conchoid
conicoid
cylinder
envelope
epicycle
excircle
frustrum
geodesic
heptagon
incircle
involute
parabola
pentagon
prismoid
quadrant
rhomboid
roulette
spheroid
tractrix
triangle
trochoid

9

antiprism
cruciform
directrix
dodecagon
ellipsoid
hyperbola
isochrone
Koch curve
loxodrome
multifoil
pentagram
pentangle
rhumb line
sine curve
strophoid
trapezium
trapezoid

10

acute angle

anchor ring
cylindroid
epicycloid
hemisphere
hexahedron
Kappa curve
lemniscate
octahedron
paraboloid
Peano curve
polyhedron
prismatoid
quadrangle
quadrefoil
right angle
semicircle
serpentine
trisectrix

11

Cornu spiral
epitrochoid
heptahedron
hyperboloid
hypocycloid
icosahedron
Klein bottle
latus rectum
Mobius strip
obtuse angle
pentahedron
reflex angle
tautochrone
tetrahedron

12

hypotrochoid
pseudosphere
rhombohedron
Sigmoid curve

13

circumference

cuboctahedron
parallelogram
parallelotope
pedal triangle
perpendicular
quadrilateral

14
snowflake curve

15
brachistochrone
scalene triangle

17
icosidodecahedron
isosceles triangle

19
equilateral triangle

Mathematics

2
Ln
p.c.
pi

3
add
arc
cos
csc
log
set
sum

4
area
axes

axis
base
cone
cube
edge
face
line
loci
math
mean
node
plus
ring
root
sine
term
unit
zero

5
acute
angle
chord
conic
cosec
cotan
cubic
curve
equal
field
focal
focus
force
graph
group
index
lemma
limit
locus
maths
minus
plane
point

power
proof
radii
range
ratio
slope
unity

6
centre
choice
circle
conics
conoid
convex
cosine
cuboid
degree
divide
domain
equals
factor
googol
height
matrix
maxima
median
minima
minute
module
moment
motion
normal
number
oblate
oblong
obtuse
origin
period
radial
radius
scalar
secant

series
sphere
square
subset
tensor
vector
volume

7

algebra
average
cissoid
complex
concave
conical
cycloid
divisor
formula
fractal
hexagon
indices
integer
inverse
maximum
minimum
modulus
nonzero
numeral
oblique
octagon
percent
polygon
product
prolate
pyramid
scalene
section
segment
tangent
theorem
unitary

8

abscissa

addition
analysis
binomial
bisector
calculus
circular
cosecant
cube root
cylinder
diagonal
division
elliptic
equation
exponent
fraction
function
fuzzy set
gradient
helicoid
identity
integers
integral
involute
Julia set
lie group
matrices
meridian
momentum
multiple
multiply
negative
operator
parallel
pentagon
positive
quadrant
quotient
rational
rotation
sequence
solution
subtract
symmetry

triangle
variable
velocity

9

algorithm
amplitude
asymptote
cantor set
Cartesian
conjugate
corollary
cotangent
expansion
factorial
factorise
frequency
hyperbola
identical
imaginary
increment
induction
inflexion
integrand
intercept
intersect
isosceles
iteration
logarithm
Napierian
numerator
numerical
parabolic
parameter
perimeter
primitive
recursion
remainder
resultant
set theory
sub-group
transform

10

arithmetic
concentric
continuity
derivative
difference
dimensions
eigenvalue
equivalent
expression
fractal set
game theory
googolplex
hypotenuse
inequality
irrational
kinematics
multiplier
percentage
percentile
polynomial
proportion
quaternion
real number
reciprocal
regression
square root
statistics
unit vector

11

aliquot part
approximate
associative
banach space
chaos theory
coefficient
combination
commutative
coordinates
denominator
determinant
eigenvector

equilateral
equilibrium
Galois group
group theory
integration
Klein bottle
magic square
Markov chain
möbius strip
permutation
power series
prime number
probability
real numbers
right angled
subtraction
translation
Venn diagram
whole number

12

acceleration
Bayes' theorem
decimal point
differential
eccentricity
gödel numbers
harmonic mean
Hilbert space
intersection
long division
multiplicand
number theory
Newton method
number theory
Simpson's rule
square number
substitution
Taylor series
trigonometry

13

antilogarithm

approximation
argand diagram
complex number
eigenfunction
Euclid's axioms
Euler's formula
extrapolation
fourier series
gauss's theorem
geometric mean
green's theorem
interpolation
mandelbrot set
ordinal number
perfect number
perfect square
power function
queuing theory
stokes' theorem

14

arithmetic mean
associative law
boolean algebra
cardinal number
cauchy sequence
commutative law
complex numbers
Euler's constant
hyperbolic sine
linear equation
multiplication
natural numbers
null hypothesis
proper fraction
rational numbers
root-mean-square
transformation
vulgar fraction

15

Bessel functions
binomial theorem

differentiation
dirichlet series
distributive law
fourier analysis
hermitian matrix
imaginary number
laplace operator
Leibniz's theorem
Maclaurin series
mersenne numbers
midpoint theorem
Pascal's triangle
Russell's paradox
stationary point

16

Bernoulli numbers
definite integral
de Moivre's formula
ibonacci numbers
Hilbert's problems
hyperbolic cosine
improper fraction
integral calculus
irrational number
Lagrange's theorem
Monte Carlo method
natural logarithm
polar coordinates
recurring decimal
remainder theorem
repeating decimal

17

Apollonius' theorem
catastrophe theory
common denominator
Euclidean geometry
hyperbolic tangent
partial derivative
point of inflection
significant figure
transfinite number

18

coordinate geometry
Fermat's last theorem
four-colour theorem
indefinite integral
least squares method
Napierian logarithm
Pythagoras' theorem
Riemannian geometry

19

Briggsian logarithms
diophantine equation
exponential function
harmonic progression
highest common factor
legendre polynomials
poisson distribution

20

arithmetic progression
Cartesian coordinates
Chinese remainder
theorem
differential calculus
differential equation
gaussian distribution
geometric progression
infinitesimal calculus
lobachevskian geometry
lowest common
denominator
lowest common
multiple
simultaneous equations
Stirling's approximation
trigonometric function
transcendental function

Physics

2 and 3

a.c.
bar
bel
e.m.f.
erg
gas
lux
mev
ohm
rpm
UHF
VHF

4

atom
cell
dyne
flux
foci
halo
heat
kaon
lens
mach
mass
muon
node
pile
pion
pole
rays
spin
tube
volt
watt
wave
work
X-ray

5

anode
curie
cycle
diode
earth
farad
field
fluid
focus
force
image
joule
laser
lever
light
lumen
maser
meson
motor
phase
pitch
power
prism
radar
radio
shell
solid
somc
sound
speed
valve
weber

6

ampere
atomic
baryon
camera
charge
corona
dipole
energy

fusion
impact
isobar
kelvin
lepton
liquid
magnet
moment
motion
newton
optics
period
photon
plasma
proton
quanta
torque
triode
vacuum
vector
weight

7

ammeter
aneroid
battery
beta ray
calorie
candela
cathode
Celsius
circuit
coulomb
crystal
current
damping
decibel
density
dry cell
elastic
element
entropy
fission

gaseous
gravity
hyperon
impulse
inertia
machine
maxwell
neutron
nuclear
nucleon
nucleus
nuclide
optical
orbital
pi-meson
quantum
reactor
rontgen
spectra
statics
thermal
torsion
voltage
voltaic

8

adhesion
aerofoil
antinode
beat note
betatron
brownian
cohesion
duo-diode
dynamics
electric
electron
emission
free fall
friction
graviton
half-life
infra-red

isogonic
kilowatt
kinetics
klystron
magnetic
magneton
molecule
momentum
negative
negatron
neutrino
overtone
particle
pendulum
polaroid
positive
positron
pressure
rest mass
roentgen
solenoid
spectrum
subshell
velocity

9

acoustics
adiabatic
amplifier
amplitude
antimeson
barometer
black body
bolometer
capacitor
coherence
condenser
conductor
cyclotron
electrode
frequency
gamma rays
generator

gyroscope
harmonics
impedance
induction
insulator
isoclinic
Leyden jar
magnetism
magnetron
manometer
mechanics
plutonium
potential
radiation
radio wave
real image
rectifier
resonance
spark coil
vibration
viscosity
voltmeter

10

aberration
absorption
achromatic
antilepton
antimatter
antiproton
atomic bomb
atomic mass
ballistics
binoculars
cathode ray
Centigrade
conduction
convection
cosmic rays
dielectric
dispersion
electrical
Fahrenheit

heavy water
horsepower
inductance
ionization
kinematics
latent heat
microscope
omega meson
oscillator
precession
reflection
refraction
relativity
resistance
ripple tank
scattering
shunt-wound
supersonic
thermionic
thermopile
transistor
vacuum tube
wavelength

11

accelerator
band spectra
capacitance
capillarity
centrifugal
centripetal
compression
conductance
declination
diffraction
electricity
falling body
focal length
gravitation
hypercharge
newton-metre
oscillation
positronium

radioactive
resistivity
restitution
series-wound
solar energy
spectrogram
statcoulomb
synchrotron
temperature
transformer
transuranic

12

acceleration
angstrom unit
antiparticle
atomic number
atomic weight
beta particle
centre of mass
cloud chamber
conductivity
critical mass
diamagnetism
eccentricity
electrolysis
electroscope
interference
kilowatt-hour
oscilloscope
permittivity
polarization
specific heat
spectrograph
wave equation

13

alpha particle
bubble chamber
chain reaction
critical angle
discharge tube
elastic impact

electric field
electric motor
electric power
electromagnet
electromotive
electron shell
electrostatic
Geiger counter
gravitational
induction coil
kinetic energy
magnetic field
magnetic poles
paramagnetism
photoelectric
quantum number
quantum theory
radioactivity
rectification
scintillation
semiconductor
standing waves
thermal capacity
transmutation

14 and over

electric energy (14)
electrostatics (14)
ferromagnetism (14)
nuclear reactor (14)
thermodynamics (14)
thermoelectric (14)

15

centre of gravity (15)
electric current (15)
electrification (15)
electromagnetic (15)
Planck's constant (15)
potential energy (15)
specific gravity (15)

16

terminal velocity (16)
Wheatstone bridge (16)

Poisons

4

bane
coca
drug
upas

5

acids
agene
dwale
ergot
fungi
lysol
nitre
opium
toxin
venom

6

alkali
brucia
cicuta
curare
heroin
iodine
ourali
phenol

7

aconite
alcohol
ammonia
aniline
arsenic
atropia

atropin
bromine
brucina
brucine
cadmium
calomel
caustic
chloral
coal gas
cocaine
gamboge
henbane
hyoscin
hypoxia
markuri
veronal
violine
vitriol
woorali
woorara
woralli
wourali

8

antidote
antimony
atropina
atropine
botulism
chlorine
chromium
ergotine
morphine
nicotine
oenanthe
paraquat
pearl ash
phosgene
ptomaine
ratsbane
selenium
soap lees
sulfonal

veratrum

9

amanitine
antiarine
baneberry
beryllium
chromates
colchicum
colocynth
croton oil
echidnine
grapewort
hellebore
herbicide
lead ethyl
mercurial
monkshood
nux vomica
potassium
rat poison
spit venom
strychnia
toadstool
white lead
wolf's bane
zinc ethyl

10

antiseptic
aqua fortis
belladonna
chloroform
cyanic acid
mustard gas
nightshade
nitric acid
oxalic acid
phosphorus
picric acid
salmonella
snake venom
strychnine

thorn apple
weed-killer

11

blue vitriol
boracic acid
caustic soda
dog's mercury
insecticide
lead acetate
luna caustic
prussic acid
snake poison
sugar of lead

12

barbiturates
bitter almond
carbonic acid
fool's parsley
pharmacoilte
water hemlock
white arsenic

13

carbonic oxide
caustic alkali
caustic potash
meadow saffron
sulphuric acid
yellow arsenic

14+

allantotoxicum (14)
carbon monoxide (14)
carbonate of lead (15)
deadly nightshade (16)
hydrocyanic acid (15)
irritant poisons (15)
narcotic poisons (15)

Sciences

5
logic

6
augury
botany
conics
optics

7
algebra
anatomy
biology
cookery
ecology
farming
finance
geodesy
geogony
geology
gunnery
history
hygiene
myology
orology
otology
pandect
phonics
physics
poetics
science
statics
surgery
tanning
trivium
weaving
zoology
zootomy

8
aerology
agronomy
analysis
atmology
barology
bio-assay
biometry
breeding
bryology
calculus
commerce
cytology
dairying
dosology
dynamics
ethology
etiology
eugenics
forestry
genetics
geometry
glyptics
horology
kinetics
medicine
mycology
nosology
ontology
penology
pharmacy
politics
pomology
posology
rheology
rhetoric
sinology
sitology
spherics
taxonomy
tidology
tocology
topology
typology
virology
zymology

9
acoustics
aerometry
aetiology
agriology
aitology
allopathy
altimetry
anemology
annealing
areometry
astronomy
barometry
biometrics
bleaching
cartology
chemistry
chiropody
chorology
cosmology
dentistry
dietetics
diplomacy
economics
embalming
emetology
engraving
ethnology
gardening
geography
gnomonics
harmonics
histology
horometry
husbandry
hydrology
hygrology
hymnology
ichnology
lithology

mammalogy
mechanics
micrology
neurology
ophiology
orography
osteology
otography
pathology
petrology
philology
phonetics
phonology
phytogeny
phytology
phytotomy
radiology
sitiology
sociology
surveying
taxidermy
telephony
uranology
zoography

10

actinology
aerography
aesthetics
apiculture
archaeology
arithmetic
ballistics
bathymetry
biophysics
cardiology
catoptrics
cell biology
chromatics
clinometry
conchology
craniology
demography

dendrology
docimology
Egyptology
embryology
energetics
entomology
entomotomy
enzymology
eudiometry
game theory
gastrology
geophysics
homeopathy
hydraulics
hydrometry
hydropathy
hygrometry
hypsometry
immunology
kinematics
lexicology
metallurgy
microscopy
morphology
nematology
nephrology
nosography
obstetrics
odontology
oneirology
organology
osteopathy
pedagogics
pediatrics
phlebology
photometry
phrenology
physiology
planimetry
pneumatics
potamology
psychiatry
psychology

relativity
seismology
selenology
semeiology
somatology
spasmology
spermology
splenology
splenotomy
statistics
technology
telegraphy
teratology
topography
toxicology
trepanning
typography

11

aeronautics
aerostatics
agriculture
anemography
arachnology
archaeology
arteriology
arteriotomy
campanology
carcinology
cartography
chondrology
chronometry
climatology
cosmography
craniometry
criminology
cupellation
cybernetics
dermatology
dermography
desmography
diacoustics
electricity

electronics
engineering
entozoology
ethnography
foundations
games theory
geomedicine
gynaecology
haematology
heliography
homoeopathy
hydrography
hyetography
ichthyology
ichthyotomy
lichenology
linguistics
mathematics
methodology
micrography
myodynamics
neurography
ornithology
osteography
paleography
petrography
photography
phytography
probability
prophylaxis
pteridology
radiography
sericulture
skeletology
spectrology
stereometry
stereoscopy
stethoscopy
stratigraphy
thanatology
uranography
ventilation
watch-making

12

aerodynamics
amphibiology
anthropology
architecture
astrophysics
atomic theory
auscultation
biochemistry
biogeography
brachygraphy
chronography
cometography
cytogenetics
econometrics
electropathy
epidemiology
epirrheology
floriculture
geochemistry
horticulture
hydrostatics
lexicography
lymphography
microbiology
nephrography
neuroanatomy
neurobiology
number theory
oceanography
orthalmology
organography
ornithoscopy
palaeography
pharmacology
physiography
pisciculture
pneumatology
protozoology
real analysis
seismography
silviculture
spectroscopy

spermatology
stratigraphy
sylviculture
syndesmology
synosteology
trigonometry
zoophytology

13

anthropometry
arboriculture
arteriography
bioenergetics
cephalography
chondrography
chrematistics
climatography
combinatorics
crustaceology
endocrinology
geochronology
geomorphology
helminthology
hydrodynamics
hydrokinetics
ichthyography
land measuring
land surveying
lichenography
linear algebra
marine biology
matrix algebra
meteorography
palaeontology
pharmaceutics
psychophysics
psychotherapy
quantum theory
saccharometry
sedimentology
splanchnology
stoichiometry
wave mechanics

zoophysiology

14

architectonics
bioclimatology
chromatography
cinematography
electrobiology
electrostatics
fluid mechanics
hippopathology
hydrophytology
macroeconomics
microeconomics
natural history
natural science
parapsychology
photogrammetry
phytopathology
psychonosology
radiochemistry
symptomatology
syndesmography
thermodynamics

15

computer science
crystallography
electrodynamics
electrokinetics
material science
neurophysiology
psychopathology
thermochemistry

Tools

3

awl
axe
bit

die
fan
gad
gin
hod
hoe
jig
loy
saw
zax

4

adze
bill
bore
brog
burr
cart
celt
crab
file
fork
frow
gage
hink
hook
jack
last
loom
mall
maul
mule
nail
pick
pike
plow
rake
rasp
rule
sock
spud
trug
vice

whim

5

anvil
auger
beele
bench
besom
betty
bevel
blade
borer
brace
burin
chuck
churn
clamp
clams
clasp
cleat
cramp
crane
croom
croze
cupel
dolly
drill
flail
flang
forge
gauge
gavel
gouge
hoist
incus
jacks
jemmy
jimmy
knife
lathe
level
lever
mower

paper
plane
plumb
preen
prose
prong
punch
quern
quoin
ratch
razor
sarse
screw
spade
spike
spile
spill
swage
temse
tommy
tongs
tromp
trone
wedge
winch

6

barrow
bender
blower
bodkin
borcer
bow-saw
brayer
broach
burton
chaser
chisel
colter
crevet
cruset
dibber
dibble

doffer
dredge
driver
fanner
faucet
ferret
folder
gimlet
graver
hackle
hammer
harrow
jagger
jigger
jig saw
ladder
mallet
mortar
muller
oliver
pallet
pencil
pestle
pitsaw
planer
pliers
plough
pontee
pooler
rammer
rasper
reaper
riddle
ripsaw
rubber
sander
saw-set
screen
scythe
segger
shears
shovel
sickle

sifter
skewer
sledge
slicer
square
stiddy
stithy
strike
tackle
tenter
trepan
trowel
tubber
turrel
wimble
wrench

7

boaster
bradawl
capstan
catling
cautery
chamfer
chip-axe
chopper
cleaver
coulter
crampon
crisper
crowbar
cuvette
derrick
diamond
dog-belt
drudger
fistuca
forceps
fretsaw
fruggin
gradine
grainer
grapnel

grub axe
hacksaw
handsaw
hatchet
hay fork
jointer
mandrel
mattock
nippers
nut hook
pickaxe
piercer
pincers
plummet
pole axe
pounder
pricker
salt-pan
scalpel
scauper
scraper
screwer
scriber
seed lop
spaddle
spanner
spittle
sprayer
strocal
tenoner
thimble
trestle
triblet
T-square
twibill
twister
whip-saw
whittle
woolder

8

bark mill
bar shear

beakiron
bench peg
bill hook
bistoury
bloomary
blowlamp
blowpipe
boathook
bowdrill
bull nose
butteris
calipers
canthook
crow mill
crucible
die stock
dowel bit
drill bow
edge tool
filatory
fire kiln
flame gun
flax comb
gavelock
gee cramp
handloom
handmill
hand vice
hay knife
horse hoe
lapstone
lead mill
mitre box
molegrip
muck rake
nut screw
oilstone
paint pad
panel saw
picklock
pinchers
plumb bob
polisher

power saw
prong-hoe
puncheon
reap hook
saw wrest
scissors
scuffler
slate axe
stiletto
strickle
tenon saw
throstle
tooth key
tweezers
twist bit
watercan
water ram
weed hook
windlass
windmill

9

belt punch
bench hook
bolt auger
boot crimp
canker bit
cannipers
can opener
centre bit
compasses
corkscrew
cotton gin
cramp iron
curry comb
cutter bar
dog clutch
draw knife
draw-plate
excavator
eyeleteer
fillister
fining pot

fork chuck
gas pliers
hammer axe
handbrace
handscrew
handspike
holing axe
hummeller
implement
jack-knife
jackplane
jackstraw
lace frame
lawnmower
nail punch
nut wrench
pitch fork
plane iron
planisher
plumbline
plumb rule
screwjack
scribe awl
shearlegs
sheep hook
steelyard
sugar mill
tin opener
try square
turf spade
turn bench
turnscrew
watermill

10

bush harrow
claspknife
clawhammer
cold chisel
crane's bill
cultivator
dray plough
drift bolts

drillpress
drillstock
emery wheel
firing iron
grindstone
instrument
masonry bit
masticator
mitre block
motor mower
mould board
paintbrush
perforator
pipe wrench
pointed awl
screw press
sleek stone
snowplough
spokeshave
steam press
stepladder
tenterhook
thumbscrew
thumbstall
tilt hammer
trip hammer
turf cutter
turnbuckle
watercrane
watergauge
waterlevel
wheel brace

11

brace-and-bit
breast drill
chaff cutter
chain blocks
chain wrench
cheese press
countersink
crazing mill
crisping pin

crosscut saw
drill barrow
drill harrow
drill plough
fanning mill
grubbing hoe
helvehammer
jagging iron
machine tool
monkey block
paint roller
ploughshare
pruning hook
rabbet plane
reaping-hook
sawing stool
screwdriver
single-edged
skim coulter
snatch block
spirit level
squaring rod
steam hammer
stone hammer
straw cutter
strike block
stubble rake
sward cutter
swingplough
tape measure
turfing iron
two-foot rule
warping hook
warping post
weeding fork
weeding hook
weeding rhim
wheelbarrow

12

barking irons
belt adjuster

branding iron
breastplough
caulking tool
counter gauge
cradel scythe
cramping iron
crimping iron
crisping iron
curling tongs
drill grubber
driving shaft
driving wheel
emery grinder
flour dresser
glass furnace
hydraulic ram
mandrel lathe
marline spike
monkey wrench
pruning knife
pulley blocks
running block
scribing iron
sledge hammer
sliding bevel
socket chisel

stone breaker
straightedge
swingle knife
touch needles
trench plough
turfing spade
turning lathe
water bellows
weeding tongs

12

chopping block
chopping knife
cylinder press
electric drill
grappling-iron
hydraulic jack
packing needle
scribing block
sewing machine
soldering bolt
soldering iron
sowing machine
spinning jenny
spinning wheel
stocking frame

subsoil plough
two-hole pliers
weeding chisel

14

blowing machine
carding machine
draining engine
draining plough
pneumatic drill
reaping machine
smoothing plane
swingling knife
thrusting screw
weeding forceps

15

carpenter's bench
crimping machine
dredging machine
drilling machine
entrenching tool
pestle and mortar
pump screwdriver
weighing machine

Sports and Recreation

Games, Pastimes and Sporting Terms

2

eo
go
by

3

ace
art
bat
bet
bob
bow
box
bye
cue
cup
die
fun
gym
hux
jeu
lap
lie
lob
nap
oar
out
pam
peg
put
rod
set
ski
sod
tag
taw
tie
tig

tir
top
toy
win
won

4

arts
bait
ball
bias
bite
boat
club
crib
dice
dive
draw
epee
faro
foil
fore
foul
gala
game
goal
golf
grab
hunt
I-spy
jack
jazz
judo
king
knar
knur
love
ludo
luge
main
mate
meet
mime

miss
mora
Oaks
odds
pace
pato
pawn
play
polo
pool
punt
quiz
race
ride
ring
rink
ruff
shot
sice
side
skip
slam
slip
solo
spar
suit
swim
team
toss
tote
trap
trey
trip
trot
turf
vole
volt
walk
whip
wide
xyst
yoga
yo-yo

5

amuse
arena
baign
bails
bandy
basto
batik
bingo
bogey
boule
bowls
boxer
caddy
capot
cards
caves
chase
cheat
chess
clubs
craps
dance
darts
Derby
deuce
dicer
diver
dormy
drama
drawn
drive
dummy
extra
field
fives
fluke
glaze
halma
hobby
joker
joust
kayle

kendo
knave
lasso
links
lists
loser
lotto
lucky
match
monte
mount
music
opera
paced
pacer
party
piste
pitch
point
prize
queen
quits
racer
rafia
rally
reins
relay
revel
rider
rifle
rodeo
roque
rugby
score
shogi
skate
skier
slice
slide
slosh
spade
spoof
spoon

sport
spurt
stalk
start
stump
stunt
swing
tarot
throw
touch
track
train
trial
trump
vault
veney
wager
yacht

6

aikido
archer
ballet
banker
basset
battue
bewits
boules
bowler
bowman
boxing
caddie
casino
cinque
Cluedo
clumps
cobnut
cockal
course
crafts
crambo
crease
cup tie

dealer
defeat
discus
diving
domino
driver
dyeing
falcon
finish
fluker
flying
gambit
gamble
gammon
guile
gobang
go-kart
googly
gully
gymnic
hammer
hazard
header
hiking
hockey
hoopla
hunter
hurdle
huxing
jetton
jigger
jigsaw
jockey
karate
kicker
knight
kung-fu
lariat
loader
lobber
manege
marker
mashie

masque
maying
no-ball
not-out
outing
outrun
pacing
Pac man
paddle
peg-top
pelota
pistol
player
poetry
punter
putter
puzzle
quoits
rabbit
racing
racket
raffle
rattle
recite
record
revoke
riddle
riding
rowing
rubber
rugger
runner
savate
scorer
second
see-saw
shinny
shinty
single
skater
skiing
slalom
slider

soccer
soiree
squash
stroke
stumps
Tai chi
tarocs
tarots
tenace
tennis
tierce
tip-cat
toss-up
travel
trophy
umpire
unfair
venery
victor
vigaro
winner
xystos

7

agonism
agonist
allonge
amateur
ambs-ace
ames-ace
angling
archery
athlete
auction
average
bathing
batsman
batting
beagles
benefit
bicycle
boating
bone ace

bowling	glazing	picquet
bran-pie	gliding	pitcher
bruiser	golf bag	play day
carving	gunning	playing
cassino	gymnast	play off
century	hunting	pottery
charade	hurling	potting
checker	innings	pushpin
chicane	javelin	putting
codille	joy-ride	rackets
collage	ju-jitsu	reading
concert	jumping	referee
contest	kabaddi	regatta
cookery	karting	reversi
cooking	keep fit	ringtaw
cricket	last lap	rinking
crochet	leaping	roadhog
croquet	loggats	running
curling	lottery	sailing
cycling	love all	saltant
cyclist	love set	scooter
dancing	low bell	scoring
decider	macrame	scratch
diabolo	mahjong	sculler
dice-box	marbles	sea trip
discard	matador	shot put
dobbers	may-pole	shuffle
doddart	misdeal	singing
doubles	montant	singles
drawing	mosaics	skating
dribble	netball	ski jump
driving	oarsman	sliding
etching	oarsmen	snooker
fencing	off-side	St. Leger
fielder	origami	stadium
fishery	outdoor	starter
fishing	outride	sub-aqua
fluking	pageant	surfing
forward	pallone	tilting
fowling	pachisi	tinchel
fox hunt	pastime	tombola
gambler	pat ball	top spin
glasses	pharaoh	tourney

trained
trainer
trapeze
'vantage
vaulter
wagerer
walking
wargame
weaving
weights
whip top
winning
wrestle
writing
yahtzee

8

all-fours
antiques
applique
aquatics
baccarat
baseball
biathlon
bird cage
boat race
boundary
canoeing
carnival
carolina
catapult
ceramics
champion
charades
cheating
chessmen
climbing
commerce
contract
counters
coursing
cup final
daddlums

dead heat
deck golf
dominoes
doublets
drag-hunt
draughts
dressage
duelling
eurythme
eventing
exercise
face card
fair play
falconry
fielding
flat race
football
foot race
forfeits
fox chase
full back
game laws
goal line
golf ball
golf club
gymkhana
handball
handicap
harriers
high jump
hurdling
jiu-jitsu
jousting
juggling
knitting
korfball
lacrosse
leapfrog
liar dice
long jump
love game
lucky-dip
marathon

may games
Monopoly
motoring
movement
natation
ninepins
olympiad
olympics
out-field
outsider
painting
palestra
pall-mall
petanque
ping-pong
pole jump
pony race
pope Joan
printing
proverbs
pugilism
pugilist
pyramids
quatorze
racquets
rambling
roulette
rounders
sack race
Scrabble
sculling
shooting
sing-song
skipping
skittles
sledding
softball
somerset
spadille
sparring
speedway
sporting
stalking

stumping
swimming
teamwork
teetotum
tiny golf
toboggan
training
tray-trip
trial run
tricycle
trotting
tug of war
tumbling
turf club
umpiring
vaulting
vauntlay
walkover
wall-game
woodwork
yachting

9

advantage
adventure
agonistes
agonistic
amusement
archeress
athletics
aunt-sally
babyhouse
badminton
bagatelle
ball games
bandalore
bicycling
bilboquet
billiards
bob cherry
breakdown
broad jump
bull board

bull feast
bullfight
camelling
challenge
checkmate
cherry pit
chicanery
clock golf
close time
cockfight
cockmatch
conqueror
court-card
cricketer
cup winner
decathlon
deck games
decoy duck
dirt track
dog racing
drawn game
dumbbells
embrocado
engraving
entertain
equitancy
fairy tale
fancy ball
fish spear
frivolity
gardening
gate money
goal posts
golf clubs
grand slam
gymnasium
gymnastic
hatha yoga
hopscotch
horseplay
horserace
ice hockey
joy riding

lampadist
lob bowler
make merry
marooning
marquetry
megaphone
merrimake
merriment
merriness
moto cross
motorboat
newmarket
night club
nine holes
novelette
overmatch
pacemaker
pageantry
palestric
palmistry
parcheesi
pedalling
philately
plaything
pole vault
potholing
prize-ring
programme
promenade
quadrille
racehorse
racestand
reception
relay race
repasture
revelment
revel rout
river trip
rolly poly
scorching
scorecard
scrapbook
sculpture

showplace
shrimping
ski runner
sky diving
skylarker
sleighing
smock race
snake-eyes
spectacle
sportsman
springing
stalemate
stool ball
stopwatch
storybook
stroke oar
summerset
symposiac
symposium
tablegame
tabletalk
tae kwan-do
tie dyeing
tip and run
torch race
touch line
trap stick
trial game
trial race
trump card
untrained
victoress
vingt-et-un
wandering
water jump
water polo
whipper-in
whirligig
whistling
woodcraft
wrestling
yacht-race
yachtsman

10

acrobatics
agonistics
agonothete
backgammon
ballooning
basket-ball
bat and trap
bat-fowling
battledoor
battledore
bear garden
blind harry
challenger
chessboard
collecting
competitor
conundrums
cover-point
cricket-bat
cup-and-ball
deck quoits
deck tennis
derby sweep
doll's house
drag racing
dumb crambo
eel fishing
embroidery
enamelling
equitation
fancy dress
fast bowler
feathering
feuilleton
field games
fishing net
fishing rod
fisticuffs
fives court
flat racing
flop-dragon
fly-fishing

fox-hunting
goalkeeper
goalkicker
grandstand
greasy pole
groundbait
gymnastics
handspring
handy-dandy
hippodrome
hobby horse
hockey ball
hockey club
hotcockles
hucklebone
humming-top
hunting box
hurdle race
ice dancing
ice sailing
ice skating
kettle pin
lace making
lampadrome
landing net
lansquenet
lawn tennis
ledger line
lob bowling
masquerade
midget golf
Monte Carlo
needlework
opposition
palestrian
pancratist
pancratium
paper chase
pentathlon
philopoena
pony racing
pot hunting
prison base

prize fight
racecourse
raceground
recreation
real tennis
relaxation
riding pony
riding whip
rollicking
rotary club
roundabout
rowing club
rugby union
running out
saturnalia
scoreboard
scratch man
sea bathing
shovepenny
shuffle cap
silk screen
ski running
skylarking
slow bowler
snapdragon
somersault
spillikins
stirrup cup
strokesman
surf riding
sweepstake
switchback
table bowls
tap dancing
tarantella
tauromachy
team spirit
tennis ball
thimblerig
tomfoolery
tournament
travelling
trial match

trick track
tricycling
triple jump
trivia quiz
troumadame
victorious
volley ball
vulnerable
weighing-in
whirlabout
word making

11

agonistical
athleticism
barley-brake
bear baiting
blood sports
bobsledding
bull baiting
bumblepuppy
calligraphy
chariot race
chess player
competition
competitive
county match
cricket ball
croquet ball
deck cricket
Derby winner
dicing house
discus throw
disportment
diving board
fast bowling
field sports
fishing line
fiaconnade
fleet-footed
fluking-iron
folk dancers
free fishery

garden party
general post
grand circle
grass skiing
gymnasiarch
hammer throw
hang gliding
happy family
heavyweight
hide-and-seek
high jumping
high pitched
hockey stick
horse racing
horse riding
horse trials
hunt counter
hunting horn
ice yachting
Indian club
inter-county
lawn bowling
lightweight
lithography
long jumping
magic square
make-believe
martial arts
masquerader
merrymaking
minute watch
motor racing
oarsmanship
open-air life
parachuting
pentathlon
picnic party
pillow fight
pole jumping
prawning net
prize giving
prizewinner
promenading

protagonist
public stand
regatta card
riding horse
river sports
rouge-et-noir
rough riding
rugby league
sand sailing
schottische
sepak takraw
shovel board
show jumping
shuttlecock
sightseeing
single stick
skateboard
skating club
skating rink
skittle pool
slot machine
slow bowling
snowballing
soap bubbles
span-counter
spelling bee
springboard
stirrup lamp
stonewaller
summersault
sweepstakes
sword player
table tennis
tale telling
tennis court
tent pegging
theatre-goer
tobogganing
tiddlywinks
top-spinning
totalisator
toxophilite
trap-and-ball

trick riding
trolmydames
trout-stream
uncontested
unexercised
water skiing
whipping-top
wild fowling
winning crew
winning side
winning team
wood cutting
world record
yacht racing

12

bar billiards
bantamweight
billiard ball
bird's nesting
bobsleighing
bowling alley
brass rubbing
bullfighting
butterfly net
caber tossing
calisthenics
championship
club swinging
cockfighting
competitress
consequences
cricket match
curling stone
deer stalking
draughtboard
drinking bout
Eton wall game
field glasses
figure skater
first-nighter
flower making
glass blowing

googly bowler
hoodman-blind
horsemanship
housewarming
hunting-horse
huntsmanship
javelin throw
jigsaw puzzle
knur and spell
losing hazard
magic lantern
marathon race
marking board
medicine ball
merry-go-round
miss Milligan
mixed baffling
mixed doubles
nimble footed
novel reading
obstacle race
Olympic games
opera glasses
orienteering
parallel bars
parlour games
pigeon racing
pitch-and-toss
pleasure trip
point-to-point
pole vaulting
professional
prize fighter
prize winning
pyrotechnics
Pythian games
racing stable
rock climbing
roller skater
rope climbing
rope spinning
rope throwing
sand yachting

scotch-hopper
shove ha'penny
shrimping net
skipping rope
skittle alley
space invaders
span farthing
speed skating
starting post
state lottery
steeplechase
stilt walking
stirrup strap
storytelling
swimming gala
table croquet
table turning
tennis player
tennis racket
theatre-going
thoroughbred
tittle-tattle
winning horse
winter sports

13

alectoromachy
alectryomachy
aquatic sports
ballad singing
blindman's buff
bubble blowing
camera obscura
Christmas tree
chuck farthing
cribbage board
cricket ground
cricket stumps
croquet mallet
deck billiards
divertisement
double or quits
entertainment

equestrianism
featherweight
figure skating
fishing tackle
googly-bowling
ground-angling
hare-and-hounds
harness racing
horizontal bar
international
Isthmian games
jigsaw puzzles
jollification
kiss-in-the-ring
machine junket
model yachting
motor cruising
musical chairs
Olympian games
parlour tricks
pillion riding
prisoner's base
prize fighting
record breaker
roller skating
roulette table
skateboarding
speed merchant
spirit rapping
sportsmanship
squash rackets
stalking horse
starting point
steeplechaser
sword fighting
ten-pin bowling
track and field
vantage ground
vaulting horse
victor ludorum
weight lifting
wicket keeping
winning hazard

14

all-in wrestling
billiard marker
billiard player
bladder angling
children's party
coin collecting
discus-throwing
divertissement
double patience
downhill skiing
driving licence
ducks-and-drakes
football league
hunt-the-slipper
hunt-the-thimble
long-arm balance
mountaineering
record breaking
shove-halfpenny
stockcar racing
steeplechasing
thimblerigging
Trivial Pursuit
weight training

15

ballroom dancing
cinderella dance
consolation race
crossword puzzle
Derby sweepstake
dirt track racing
greyhound racing
javelin throwing
king-of-the-castle
Old English bowls
public enclosure
short-arm balance
stamp collecting
talking pictures
three-legged race
unsportsmanlike

youth hostelling	snakes and ladders	19
16	18	Association football
American football motorcycle racing	clay-pigeon shooting freestyle wrestling	20
		devil among the tailors

Specific Sports and Games Information

Angling Terms

3

dun
fly
net
peg
rib
rod
tag
tip

4

bait
barb
cast
gaff
hemp
hook
lead
line
lure
plug
pole
reel
shot
tail
worm

5

blank
creel

float
floss
joker
leger
paste
quill
spoon
whisk

6

caster
dry fly
hackle
maggot
marker
palmer
pinkie
priest
slider
spigot
squatt
strike
swivel
wet fly
zoomer

7

antenna
bale arm
bristle
dapping
dubbing
keep net

missile
plummet
rod rest
rod ring
spinner
waggler

8

back shot
dead bait
freeline
legering
line bite
specimen
stop knot
swingtip

9

bite alarm
bloodworm
blued hook
cloud bait
disgorger
gorge bait
micro shot
midge hook
quivertip
roach pole
tying silk
waggy lure
wire trace

10

bread flake
bread punch
caddis hook
coffin lead
double hook
flybody fur
ground bait
hair-and-fur
landing net
snap tackle
stick float
swim feeder

11

arlesey bomb
bait dropper
bubble float
devon minnow
dough-bobbin
foul-hooked
gallows tool
loaded float
paternoster
sparkle body
whip-finish
wing-cutter

12

barbless hook
detached hook
dry-fly hackle
parachute fly
sliding float

13

butt indicator
centre-pin reel
flexi-tail lure

14

blockend feeder
breaking strain
grub-shrimp hook

multiplier reel

15+

Danish dry fly hook
detached-body hook
flat-bodied nymph hook
parachute-fly hook
Swedish dry fly hook
Yorkshire sedge hook

Cards

Card Games

3

loo
pan
rum

4

brag
jass
klob
snap
spit
vint

5

bingo
boure
cinch
comet
darda
ombre
pedro
pitch
poker
poque
rummy
samba
whist

yukon

6

boo-ray
boston
bridge
casino
chemmy
ecarte
eights
euchre
fan-tan
gaigel
go fish
julepe
mau-mau
piquet
pochen
pokino
quinze
red dog
sevens
smudge
trumps
yablon

7

authors
belotte
bezique
bolivia
canasta
colonel
cooncan
old maid
pontoon
primera
primero
set-back
seven-up
snooker
solomon
spinado

triumph

8

ace-deuce
canfield
conquain
cribbage
gin rummy
imperial
Irish loo
klondike
last card
low pitch
napoleon
Oklahoma
patience
pinochle
rockaway
rollover
sixty six
slapjack

9

blackjack
draw poker
forty five
in-between
open poker
solitaire
solo whist
spoil five
stud poker
thirty one
wild jacks

10

draw casino
joker pitch
panguingue
pishe pasha
put and take
tablanette
thirty five

wellington

11

Boston whist
bridge whist
catch the ten
chemin de fer
closed poker
crazy eights
double rummy
five card loo
five hundred
German whist
humbug whist
klabberjass
racing demon
royal casino
Russian bank
scotch whist
slippery sam
spade casino

12

auction pitch
domino fan-tan
jack change it
Swedish rummy

13

auction bridge
concentration
old man's bundle
six spot red dog
straight poker

14

baccaret banque
Chinese bezique
contract bridge
French pinochle
frogs in the pond
racehorse pitch
rubicon bezique

six deck bezique
spite and malice

15

around the corner
auction pinochle
banker and broker
Hollywood eights

16

continental rummy
double dummy whist
eight deck bezique
trente et quarante
trump humbug whist

17

beat your neighbour
beggar-my-neighbour

18

five hundred bezique
round the corner
rummy

19

beggar your neighbour

Bridge Terms

3

bid
fit

4

acol
call
deal
game
lead
ruff
void

5

alert
dummy
entry
guard
rebid
table

6

double
gerber
honour
length
misfit
revoke
rubber
system
tenace
timing

7

auction
control
cue bids
discard
finesse
jump bid
partner
signals
stayman
stopper

8

contract
declarer
director
limit bid
Mckenney
overcall
over ruff
redouble
response

side suit

9

blackwood
doubleton
grand slam
lavinthal
major suit
minor suit
overtrick
part score
sacrifice
singleton
small slam
solid suit

10

convention
forcing bid
line of play
reverse bid
system card
unbalanced
under trick
vulnerable

11

double dummy
match points
opening lead
partnership
third in hand

12

balanced hand
biddable suit
bidding space
distribution
fourth in hand
intervention
jump overcall
playing trick
semi-balanced

13

communication
not vulnerable
pre-emptive bid
take out double
touching suits
two-suited hand

14

competitive bid
destructive bid
grand slam force
rebiddable suit

15

constructive bid
duplicate bridge
invitational bid
playing strength
three-suited hand

16

contested auction
negative response
phantom sacrifice
positive response
single suited hand

18

mirror distribution

Poker Hands

flush
four of a kind
full house
one pair
royal flush
straight
straight flush
three of a kind
two pairs

Dances

3

dog
hop
fan
hay
hop
jig
ole
pas

4

bail
bump
cana
clog
giga
haka
hora
hula
jive
jota
juba
juke
kola
pogo
polk
polo
reel
shag
step
vira

5

baris
bebop
bulba
caper
carol
conga
cueca

dansa
debka
fling
galop
gigue
haloa
hopak
kummi
l'ag-ya
limbo
loure
mambo
nazun
pavan
pavin
polka
rondo
rueda
rumba
salsa
samba
sarba
shake
sibel
sibyl
stomp
tango
trata
twist
valse
velal
waltz

6

Abuang
Almain
amener
Apache
atinga
batuta
bolero
boston
bouree

boogie
branle
calata
canary
cancan
carole
cebell
cha-cha
chasse
corant
djoged
eixida
gallop
gangar
gienys
hustle
jacara
jarabe
jarana
kagura
kalela
lavolt
minuet
morisk
morris
oberek
pavane
pessah
polska
redowa
reigen
rhumba
rondel
shimmy
tirana
valeta
watusi
yumari

7

abrasax
abraxas
ahidous

aparima
arnaout
baborak
ball pla
bambuco
banjara
batuque
beguine
bharang
bourree
boutade
cachuca
canarie
canario
choctaw
cinq pas
coranto
csardas
esardos
farruca
forlana
fox-trot
furiant
furlana
gavotte
glocsen
gombeys
gondhal
goshiki
hoedown
himinau
jabadao
lancers
landler
la volta
llorona
madison
maypole
mazurka
measure
morisco
one-step
muneira

pasillo
pericon
planxty
purpuri
rondeau
roundel
sardana
satacek
sikinik
tsardar
tantara
traipse
two-step
wakamba
ziganka

8

alegrias
a moleson
balztanz
bunny-hug
bull-foot
cachucha
cake-walk
canacuas
candiote
capriole
chaconne
charrada
cotillon
courante
danseuse
excuse-me
fandance
fandango
flamenco
galliard
gymnaska
habanera
hand jive
hay-de-guy
hoolican
hornpipe

hulahula
huapango
mailehen
mohobelo
moonwalk
murciana
mutchico
oxdansen
pericote
rigadoon
rigaudon
saraband
tap-dance
tsamikos

9

allemande
arabesque
baguettes
bailecito
barndance
bossa nova
boulanger
cardadora
cha-cha-cha
clog dance
cotillion
ecossaise
eightsome
farandole
folkdance
gallegada
gallopade
hajdutanc
horn dance
jitterbug
kolomejka
mistletoe
mokorotlo
paso doble
passepied
Paul Jones
pirouette

polonaise
poussette
quadrille
quickstep
renningen
rock 'n' roll
sarabande
sateckova
Siciliana
tamborito
turkey-trot
tripudiary
troyanats

10

atnumokita
bandltantz
baton dance
boston reel
chaniotiko
charleston
espringale
fackeltanz
farandoulo
furry dance
gay gordons
hey-de-guize
hokey-cokey
kyndeldans
lauterbach
locomotion
pooka-pooka
running set
saltarello

strathspey
strip tease
suruvakary
sword-dance
tambourine
tarantella
torch dance
trenchmore
tripudiary
turkey trot

11

baboraschka
blackbottom
contra-dance
dansuringer
dithryambos
floral dance
gharba dance
jolly miller
Lambeth Walk
line dancing
morris dance
palais glide
pamperruque
rock and roll
schottische
square dance
tewrdannckh
varsovienne

12

breakdancing
country dance

creux de vervi
damhsa nam boc
danse macabre
funky chicken
green garters
maypole dance
palais-glide
reel o'tulloch
state-lancers
tripudiation

13

eightsome reel
ghillie callum
Helston flurry
Highland fling

14

babbity bowster
country bumpkin
light fantastic
milkmaids' dance
strip the willow

15

military two-step
Sellinger's round

17

haste to the wedding

18

Sir Roger de Coverley

Cricket

First-Class Cricketing Counties

Derbyshire
Durham
Essex
Glamorgan
Gloucestershire
Hampshire
Kent
Lancashire
Leicestershire
Middlesex
Northamptonshire
Nottinghamshire
Somerset
Surrey
Sussex
Warwickshire
Worcestershire
Yorkshire

Cricketing Terms and Expressions

3

bat
bye
cut
l.b.w.
run
ton

4

bail
duck
hook
over
wide

5

bosie
cover
gully
mid-on
point
sweep

6

beamer
bowled
bowler
caught
crease
googly
howzat!
leg bye
long on
maiden
mid-off
no-ball
run out
scorer
seamer
umpire
wicket
yorker

7

batsman
bouncer
century
cow-shot
fielder
fine leg
flipper
innings
late cut
leg slip
leg spin

long hop
long leg
long off
off spin
shooter
striker
stumped

8

boundary
chinaman
hat-trick
hows that!
longstop
short leg
the slips
third man

9

batswoman
hit wicket
in-swinger
leg glance
mid-wicket
overthrow
square cut
square leg
sticky dog
test match
the covers

10

all-rounder
golden duck
non-striker
out-swinger
sight-screen
silly mid-on
silly point
top-spinner

twelfth man	stonewalling wicketkeeper	offside fielder
11 _____		**15** _____
daisy-cutter silly mid-off	**13** _____	body-line bowling leg before wicket
12 _____	batting crease deep square leg popping crease	**16** _____
return crease reverse sweep sticky wicket	**14** _____	leg-theory bowling
	leg-side fielder	

Football

British Football Teams

Team	Ground	Nickname
Aberdeen	Pittodrie Stadium	Dons
Airdrieonians	Broomfield Park	Diamonds; Waysiders
Albion Rovers	Clifton Hall	Wee Rovers
Aldershot	Recreation Ground	Shots
Alloa	Recreation Park	Wasps
Arbroath	Gayfield Park	Red Lichties
Arsenal	Highbury	Gunners
Aston Villa	Villa Park	Villans
Ayr United	Somerset Park	Honest Men
Barnsley	Oakwell Ground	Tykes; Reds; Colliers
Berwick Rangers	Shielfield Park	Borderers
Birmingham City	St Andrews	Blues
Blackburn Rovers	Ewood Park	Blues Whites: Rovers
Blackpool	Blommfield Road	Seasiders
Bolton Wanderers	Burnden Park	Trotters
Bournemouth	Dean Court	Cherries
Bradford City	Valley Parade	Bantams
Brechin City	Glebe Park	City
Brentford	Griffin Park	Bees
Brighton & Hove Albion	Goldstone Ground	Seagulls
Bristol City	Ashton Gate	Robins
Bristol Rovers	Twerton Park	Pirates
Burnley	Turf Moor	Clarets
Bury	Gigg Lane	Shakers

Team	Ground	Nickname
Cambridge United	Abbey Stadium	United
Cardiff City	Ninian Park	Bluebirds
Carlisle United	Brunton Park	Cumbrians; Blues
Celtic	Celtic Park	Bhoys
Charlton Athletic	The Valley	Addicks; Robins; Valiants
Chelsea	Stamford Bridge	Blues
Chester City	Sealand Road	Blues
Chesterfield	Recreation Ground	Blues; Spireites
Clydebank	Kilbowie Park	Bankies
Clyde	Firhill Park	Bully Wee
Colchester United	Layer Road	U's
Coventry City	Highfield Road	Sky Blues
Cowdenbeath	Central Park	Cowden
Crewe Alexandra	Gresty Road	Railwaymen
Crystal Palace	Selhurst Park	Eagles
Darlington	Feethams Ground	Quakers
Derby County	Baseball Ground	Rams
Doncaster Rovers	Belle Vue Ground	Rovers
Dumbarton	Boghead Park	Sons
Dundee	Dens Park	Dark Blues; Dee
Dundee United	Tannadice Park	Terrors
Dunfermline Athletic	East End Park	Pars
East Fife	Bayview Park	Fifers
East Stirlingshire	Firs Park	Shire
Everton	Goodison Park	Toffees
Exeter City	St. James Park	Grecians
Falkirk	Brockville Park	Bairns
Forfar Athletic	Station Park	Sky Blues
Fulham	Craven Cottage	Cottagers
Gillingham	Priestfield Stadium	Gills
Grimsby Town	Blundell Park	Mariners
Halifax Town	Shay Ground	Shaymen
Hamilton Academical	Douglas Park	Acces
Hartlepool United	Victoria Ground	Pool
Heart of Midlothian	Tynecastle Park	Hearts
Hereford United	Edgar Street	United
Hibernian	Easter Road	Hibees
Huddersfield Town	Leeds Road	Terriers
Hull City	Boothferry Park	Tigers
Ipswich Town	Portman Road	Blues; Town

Team	Ground	Nickname
Kilmarnock	Rugby Park	Killie
Leeds United	Elland Road	United
Leicester City	Filbert Street	Filberts; Foxes
Leyton Orient	Brisbane Road	O's
Lincoln City	Sincil Bank	Red Imps
Liverpool	Anfield	Reds; Pool
Luton Town	Kenilworth Road	Hatters
Manchester City	Maine Road	Blues
Manchester United	Old Trafford	Red Devils
Mansfield Town	Field Mill Ground	Stags
Meadowbank Thistle	Meadowbank Stadium	Thistle; Wee Jags
Middlesbrough	Ayresome Park	Boro
Millwall	The Den	Lions
Montrose	Links Park	Gable Enders
Morton	Cappielow Park	Ton
Motherwell	Fir Park	Well
Newcastle United	St James Park	Magpies
Northampton Town	County Ground	Cobblers
Norwich City	Carrow Road	Canaries
Nottingham Forest	City Ground	Reds; Forest
Notts County	Meadow Lane	Magpies
Oldham Athletic	Boundary Park	Latics
Oxford United	Manor Ground	U's
Partick Thistle	Firhill Park	Jags
Peterborough United	London Road	Posh
Plymouth Argyle	Home Park	Pilgrims
Portsmouth	Fratton Park	Pompey
Port Vale	Vale Park	Valiants
Preston North End	Deepdale	Lilywhites; North End
Queen of the South	Palmerston Park	Doonhamers
Queen's Park	Hampden Park	Spiders
Queen's Park Rangers	Loftus Road	Rangers; R's
Raith Rovers	Stark's Park	Rovers
Rangers	Ibrox Stadium	Gers
Reading	Elm Park	Royals
Rochdale	Spotland	Dale
Rotherham United	Millmoor Ground	Merry Millers
Scarborough	Seamer Road	Boro
Scunthorpe United	Glanford Park	Iron
Sheffield United	Bramall Lane	Blades

Team	Ground	Nickname
Sheffield Wednesday	Hillsborough	Owls
Shrewsbury Town	Gay Meadow	Shrews; Town
Southampton	Dell	Saints
Southend United	Roots Hall	Shrimpers
Stenhousemuir	Ochilview Park	Warriors
Stirling Albion	Annfield Park	Albion
St Johnstone	Muirton Park	Saints
St Mirren	Love Street	Buddies, Paisley Saints
Stockport County	Edgeley Park	County; Hatters
Stoke City	Victoria Ground	Potters
Stranraer	Stair Park	Blues
Sunderland	Roker Park	Rokerites
Swansea City	Vetch Field	Swans
Swindon Town	County Ground	Robins
Torquay United	Plainmoor Ground	Gulls
Tottenham Hotspur	White Hart Lane	Spurs
Tranmere Rovers	Prenton Park	Rovers
Walsall	Fellows Park	Saddlers
Watford	Vicarage Road	Hornets
West Bromwich Albion	Hawthorns	Baggies; Albion
West Ham United	Upton Park	Hammers
Wigan Athletic	Springfield Park	Latics
Wimbledon	Plough Lane	Dons
Wolverhampton Wanderers	Molineux	Wolves
Wrexham	Racecourse Ground	Robins
York City	Bootham Crescent	Minstermen

European Football Clubs

Austria

Rapid Vienna
Salzburg

Belgium

Anderlecht

Ekeren
FC Bruges
Royal Antwerp
Standard Liege

Croatia

Hajouk Split

Czech Republic

Slavia Prague
Sparta Prague

Denmark

Brondby

France

Auxerre
Bastia
Bordeaux
Le Havre
Lille
Lyons
Marseilles
Metz
Monaco
Montpelier
Nantes
Nice
Paris St Germain
Strasbourg

Germany

Bayer Leverkusen
Bayern Munich
Borussia
Monchengladbach
Brann Bergen
Cologne
Duisburg
Hansa Rostock
Karlsruhe
Munich
Werder Bremen
VFB Stuttgart

Greece

AEK Athens
Galatasaray
Olympiakos
Panathinaikos

Italy

AC Milan
AS Roma
Atalanta
Bologna
Cagliari
Fiorentina
Inter Milan
Internazionale
Juventus
Lazio
Napoli
Parma
Perugia
Piacenza
Sampdoria
Verona
Vincenza

Netherlands

Ajax
FC Volendam
Feyenoord
Fortuna Sittard
JC Kerkrade
PSV Eindhoven
RKC Waalwijk
Tilburg
Utrecht
Vitesse Arnhem

Portugal

Amadora
Benfica
Boavista
Braga
Farense

FC Porto
Setubal
Sporting Lisbon

Spain

Atletico de Bilbao
Atletico de Madrid
Barcelona
Espanol
Racing Santander
Real Madrid
Real Sociedao
Real Zaragoza
Sevilla
Sporting Gijon
Vallencia

Poland

Legia Warsaw

Romania

Steava Bucharest

Russia

CSKA Moscow
Spartak Mosco

Sweden

AIK Stockholm
IFK Gothenburg

Ukraine

Dynamo Kiev

American Football Teams

Atlanta Falcons	Indianapolis Colts	New York Jets
Buffalo Bills	Kansas City Chiefs	Philadelphia Eagles
Chicago Bears	Los Angeles Raiders	Phoenix Cardinals
Cleveland Browns	Los Angeles Rams	Pittsburgh Steelers
Dallas Cowboys	Miami Dolphins	San Diego Chargers
Denver Broncos	Minnesota Vikings	San Francisco 49ers
Detroit Lions	New England Patriots	Seattle Seahawks
Green Bay Packers	New Orleans Saints	Tampa Bay Buccaneers
Houston Oilers	New York Giants	Washington Redskins

American Baseball Teams

Atlanta Braves	Kansas City Royals	Pittsburgh Pirates
Baltimore Orioles	Los Angeles Dodgers	St Louis Browns
Boston Red Sox	Milwaukee Braves	St Louis Cardinals
Brooklyn Dodgers	Minnesota Twins	San Francisco Giants
California Angels	New York Giants	Texas Rangers
Chicago White Sox	New York Mets	Toronto Blue Jays
Cincinnati Reds	New York Yankees	Washington Senators
Cleveland Indians	Oakland Athletics	
Detroit Tigers	Philadelphia Phillies	

Games Positions

3	pivot	**7**
end		batsman
	6	catcher
4	attack	defence
post	batter	defense
slip	bowler	fielder
wing	center	forward
	centre	leg slip
5	long on	long leg
guard	mid-off	long off
gully	safety	offense
mid-on	tackle	pitcher

striker
sweeper

9

fullback
halfback
left back
left half
left wing
midfield
split end
tailback
third man
tight end
wingback

9

infielder
mid wicket
nose guard
number one
number two
right back
right half
right wing
scrum half
shortstop
square leg

10

centre back

centre half
cornerback
cover point
extra cover
goal attack
goalkeeper
inside left
linebacker
number four
outfielder
silly mid-on
wing attack

11

deep fine leg
flanker back
goal defence
goal shooter
inside right
left fielder
left forward
number three
outside left
quarterback
running back
silly mid-off
wing defence
wing forward

12

first baseman

outside right
left-wing back
right fielder
right forward
short fine leg
standoff half
third baseman
three-quarter
wicketkeeper
wide receiver

13

centre fielder
centre forward
popping crease
right-wing back
second baseman

14

left-centre back
left defenseman
short square leg

15+

forward short leg
left-wing forward
right-centre back
right defenseman
right-wing forward

Grand Prix Circuits

Grand Prix	Circuit	Grand Prix	Circuit
Australian	Melbourne	German	Hockenheim
Austrian	Spielberg	Hungarian	Hungaroring
Belgian	Spa-Francorchamps	Italian	Monza
Brazilian	Sao Paulo	Japanese	Suzuka
British	Silverstone	Malaysian	Kuala Lumpur
Canadian	Montreal	Monaco	Monte Carlo
European	Nurburgring,	San Marino	Imola, Italy
	Germany	Spanish	Barcelona
French	Magny-Cours	United States	Indianapolis

Hobbies and Crafts

3
DIY

5
batik
bingo

6
sewing
bonsai

7
collage
cookery
crochet
keep fit
macramé
mosaics
origami
pottery
reading
tatting
topiary

weaving

8
aerobics
appliqué
basketry
canework
fretwork
knitting
lapidary
painting
quilting
spinning
tapestry
woodwork

9
astrology
astronomy
decoupage
gardening
genealogy
marquetry
palmistry

patchwork
philately
rug making

10
bee-keeping
beer making
crosswords
embroidery
enamelling
kite flying
lace making
upholstery
wine making

11
archaeology
bark rubbing
book binding
calligraphy
dress making
hang gliding
lepidoptery
model making

photography
stencilling
vintage cars

12

beach combing
bird watching
brass rubbing
candle-making
flower drying
tropical fish

13

fossil hunting

jigsaw puzzles
model railways
train spotting

14

badger watching
cake decorating
coin collecting
flower pressing
glass engraving
pigeon fancying

15

flower arranging

lampshade making
shell collecting
stamp collecting

16

amateur dramatics
autograph hunting

19

butterfly collecting

Rugby

Major Rugby Union Clubs

3

GHK

4

Bath
Gala
Sale

5

Flyde
Leeds
Neath
Orrel
Otley
Rugby
Wasps

6

Currie
Exeter

Havant
Hawick
Morley

7

Bedford
Bristol
Cardiff
Clifton
Melrose
Moseley
Newport
Reading
Redruth
Shannon
Swansea
Walsall

8

Aberavon
Aspatria
Bridgend
Coventry

Ebbw Vale
Llanelli
Richmond
Saracens
Treorchy
Waterloo

9

Ballymena
Garryowen
Harrogate
Heriot's FP
Jedforest
Landsdowe
Leicester
Newbridge
Newcastle
Old Wesley
Rotherham
Wakefield

10

Blackheath

Gloucester
Harlequins
Instonians
Nottingham
Pontypridd
Watsonians

11
___

Abertillery
Boroughmuir
London Irish
London Welsh
Northampton
Rosslyn Park

12
___

Old Belvedere
Young Munster

14
___

London Scottish
Stirling County
West Hartlepool

16+
___

Blackrock College
Cork Constabulary
Edinburgh Academicals
Liverpool St Helens

Rugby League Clubs

4
___

Hull
York

5
___

Leeds
Wigan

6
___

Batley
Widnes

7
___

Bramley
Halifax
Swinton

8
___

Carlisle
Dewsbury
St Helens

9
___

Highfield

10
___

Castleford

Warrington
Whitehaven

11
___

Oldham Bears
Salford Reds

12
___

Barrow Braves
Huddersfield
Hunslet Hawks

13
___

Bradford Bulls
London Broncos
Workington Town
Chorley Chieftains
Doncaster Dragons
Featherstone Rovers
Hull Kingston Rovers
Keighley Cougars
Leigh Centurions
Rochdale Hornets
Sheffield Eagles
Wakefield Trinity

Aintree (horse racing)
Anaheim Stadium,
California (baseball)

Stadiums and Venues

Ascot (horse racing)
Azteca Stadium, Mexico City (Olympics, football)
Belfry, The (golf)
Belmont Park, Long Island (horse racing)
Bernabau Stadium, Madrid (football)
Big Four Curling Rink (curling)
Brands Hatch (motor racing)
Brooklands (motor racing)

Caesar's Palace, Las Vegas (boxing)
Cardiff Arms Park (rugby union)
Central Stadium, Kiev (football)
Cleveland Municipal Stadium (baseball)
Corporation Stadium, Calicur (cricket)
Croke Park, Dublin (Gaelic football, hurling)
Crucible, Sheffield (snooker)
Crystal Palace (athletics)
Daytona International Speedway (motor racing, motor cycling)
Eden Gardens, Calcutta (cricket)
Edgbaston (cricket)
Epsom Downs (horse racing)
Forum, The (gymnastics)
Francorchamps, Belgium (motor racing)
Hampden Park, Glasgow (football)
Headingly (cricket)
Heysel Stadium, Brussels (football)
Lahore (cricket)
Landsdowne Road, Belfast (rugby union)
Lenin Stadium, Moscow (football)
Lords Cricket Ground (cricket)
Louisiana Superdome (most sports)
Maracana Stadium, Brazil (football)
Meadowbank (athletics)
Memorial Coliseum, Los Angeles (most sports)
Moor Park, Rickmansworth (golf)
Munich Olympic Stadium (athletics, football)
Murrayfield (rugby union)
Newmarket (horse racing)
Nou Camp, Barcelona (football)
Odsal Stadium, Bradford (rugby league)
Old Trafford (cricket)
Oval, The (cricket)
St Andrews (golf)
Senayan Stadium, Jakarta (cricket)
Shanghai Stadium (gymnastics)
Silverstone (motor racing)
Stahov Stadium, Prague (gymnastics)
Texas Stadium (most sports)
Twickenham (rugby union)
Wembley Conference Centre (darts)
Wembley Stadium {football, rugby)

White City (greyhound racing)
Wimbledon (tennis)
Windsor Park, Belfast (football)

Trophies, Events and Awards

Admiral's Cup (sailing)
African Nations Cup (football)
Air Canada Silver Broom (curling)
All-Ireland Championship (Gaelic football)
All-Ireland Championships (hurling)
Alpine Championships (skiing)
America's Cup (sailing)
Ashes (cricket)
Badminton three day event (equestrian)
BBC Sports Personality Of The Year (all-round)
Benson & Hedges Cup (cricket)
Boat Race (rowing)
British Open Championship (golf)
Bronze Medal (most sports)
Camanachd Association Challenge Cup (shinty)
Cheltenham Gold Cup (horse racing)
Classics (horse racing)
Commonwealth Games (athletics)
Cornhill Test (cricket)
Davis Cup (tennis)
Daytona 500 (motor racing)
Decathlon (athletics)
Derby (horse racing)
Embassy World Indoor Bowls Crown (bowls)
Embassy World Profes-sional Snooker Championship (snooker)
English Greyhound Derby (greyhound racing)
European Champion Clubs Cup (football)
European Champions Cup (basketball)
European Championships (football)
European Cup Winners Cup (football)
European Footballer Of The Year (football)

European Super Cup (football)
Federation Cup (tennis)
Football Association Challenge Cup (football)
Football Association Charity Shield (football)
Football League Championship (football)
Football League Cup (football)
Full Cap (football, rugby)
FWA Footballer of the Year (football)
Gillette Cup (Cricket)
Golden Boot Award (football)
Gold Medal (most sports)
Gorden International Medal (curling)
Grand National (greyhound racing)
Grand National Steeplechase (horse racing)
Grand Prix (motor racing)
Guinness Trophy (tiddlywinks)
Harmsworth Trophy (powerboat racing)
Henley Regatta (rowing)
Henri Delaney Trophy (football)
Highland Games
Icy Smith Cup (ice hockey)
Indianapolis 500 (motor racing)
International Championship (bowls)
International Cross-Country Championship (athletics)
International Inter-City Industrial Fairs Cup (football)
Iroquols Cup (lacrosse)
Isle Of Man TT (motorcycle racing
John Player Cup (rugby league)
John Player League (cricket)
Jules Rimet Trophy (football)
King George V Gold Cup (equestrian)
Kinnaird Cup (fives)
Le Mans 24 Hour (motor racing)
Littlewoods Challenge Cup (football)
Lombard Rally (motor racing)
Lonsdale Belt (boxing)
MacRobertson International Shield (croquet)
Man of the Match (football)
Marathon (athletics)
Middlesex Sevens (rugby union)
Milk Cup (football)
Milk Race (cycling)

Monte Carlo Rally (motor racing)
Most Valuable Player (American football)
National Angling Championship (horse racing)
National Hunt Jockey Championship (horse racing)
National Westminster Bank Trophy (cricket)
Nordic Championships (skiing)
Oaks (horse racing)
Olympic Games (most sports)
One Thousand Guineas (horse racing)
Open Croquet Championship (croquet)
Oxford Blue (most sports)
Palio
Pentathlon (athletics)
PFA Footballer of the Year (football)
Prudential World Cup (Cricket)
Queen Elizabeth II Cup (equestrian)
RAC Tourist Trophy (motor racing)
Rose Bowl (American football)
Royal Hunt Cup (horse racing)
Rugby League Challenge Cup (rugby league)
Runners-Up Medal (most sports)
Ryder Cup (golf)
Scottish Football Association Cup (football)
Silver Medal (most sports)
Simod Cup (football)
Skol Cup (football)
South American Championship (football)
Stanley Cup (ice hockey)
St Leger (horse racing)
Strathcona Cup (curling)
Super Bowl (American football)
Super Cup (handball)
Swaythling Cup (table tennis)
Thomas Cup (badminton)
Tour De France (cycling)
Triple Crown (rugby union)
Two Thousand Guineas (horse racing)
Uber Cup (badminton)
U.E.F.A. Cup (Union Of European Football)
Uniroyal World Junior Championships (curling)
Walker Cup (golf)
Wightman Cup (sailing)

Wimbledon (tennis)
Wingfield Skulls (rowing)
Winners Medal (most sports)
Wooden Spoon! (most sports)
World Club Championship (football)
World Masters Championships (darts)
World Series (baseball)
Yellow Jersey (cycling)

Transport, travel and vehicles

Aviation and space travel

3 and 4

ace
air
bank
bay
bump
buzz
car
crew
dive
dope
drag
fin
flap
fly
fuel
gap
gas
hull
jet
kite
knot
land
lane
leg
lift
loop
mach
mig
nose
prop
rev
rib
roll
slip
span
spar
spin

tail
taxi
trim
UFO
veer
wash
wind
wing
yaw
york
zoom

5

aloft
apron
bends
cabin
cargo
chock
chord
cleat
climb
craft
crash
crate
ditch
drift
flaps
flier
float
glide
jumbo
pitch
plane
prang
pylon
radar
range
rev up
rigid
slots
stall
strut

stunt
valve

6

aerial
airbus
airman
airway
basket
beacon
bomber
camber
canard
cruise
cut out
drogue
fabric
flight
floats
flying
gas-bag
glider
hangar
intake
launch
module
nose-up
octane
piston
ram jet
refuel
rocket
rudder
runway
wash-in
yawing

7

aileron
air base
aircrew
airdrop
air flow

air foil
air lane
airlift
airline
airport
air-raid
airship
aviator
ballast
balloon
banking
biplane
birdman
bale out
bomb bay
capsule
ceiling
cellule
charter
chassis
chopper
clipper
cockpit
compass
contact
co-pilot
cowling
descent
ejector
fairing
fighter
flyover
flypast
gliding
gondola
helibus
inflate
landing
lift-off
Mae West
nacelle
nose-cap
on board

pancake
payload
re-entry
ripcord
rolling
sponson
sputnik
tail fin
take-off
taxiing
Trident
Tristar
twin-jet
wingtip

8

aerodyne
aerofoil
aeronaut
aerostat
air brake
airborne
aircraft
airfield
air force
airframe
airliner
air route
air scoop
airscrew
airspace
airspeed
airstrip
airwoman
altitude
anhedral
approach
autogiro
aviation
aviatrix
ballonet
bomb-rack
buoyancy

Concorde
corridor
cruising
decalage
dihedral
drip-flap
elevator
envelope
flat spin
fuel pipe
fuselage
grounded
gyrostat
heliport
in flight
intercom
jet pilot
jet plane
joystick
moonshot
non-rigid
nose-cone
nosedive
nose down
pitching
pulse-jet
radiator
seaplane
sideslip
spaceman
squadron
stopover
streamer
subsonic
tail-boom
tail-skid
tail unit
terminal
throttle
triplane
turbojet
twin-tail
volplane

warplane
wind cone
windsock
wing-flap
Zeppelin

9

aerodrome
aeroplane
air intake
air pocket
airworthy
altimeter
amphibian
astrodome
astronaut
autopilot
backplate
cabin crew
caravelle
carlingue
cosmonaut
countdown
crash-land
crow's-foot
delta-wing
dirigible
doodlebug
empennage
fuel gauge
fuel intake
gyroplane
jet bomber
launch pad
launching
lift-wires
longerons
low-flying
monocoque
monoplane
navigator
overshoot

parachute
power dive
propeller
rudder bar
sailplane
satellite
semi-rigid
spacecrew
spaceship
spacesuit
spacewalk
stability
stratojet
sweepback
tailplane
test pilot
touch down
turboprop
twin-screw
wind gauge

10

aerobatics
aero-engine
aeronautic
aerostatic
air balloon
air control
air defence
air hostess
air service
air steward
air support
air traffic
anemometer
ballooning
balloonist
cantilever
cargo plane
Challenger
dive bomber
flight deck

flight path
flight plan
flying boat
ground crew
helicopter
hydroplane
jet fighter
landing run
mach number
outer space
oxygen mask
pilot plane
robot plane
rudder-post
slipstream
solo flight
spacecraft
space probe
splashdown
stabilizer
stewardess
supersonic
test flight
V-formation

11

aeronautic
aerostatics
afterburner
air terminal
air umbrella
blind flying
combat plane
ejector-seat
flying speed
free balloon
ground speed
heat barrier
heavy bomber
kite-balloon
laminar flow
landing deck

landing gear
leading-edge
loop the loop
moon landing
mooring-mast
ornithopter
parachutist
retro-rocket
retractable
sesquiplane
slotted wing
soft landing
space centre
space flight
space rocket
space travel
stabilizers
stunt flying
vapour trail
weather-vane

12

aerodynamics
airfreighter
air-sea rescue
arrester gear
beacon lights
belly landing
control tower
crash landing
ejection seat
fighter pilot
flying circus
flying saucer
gliding-angle
jet-propelled
landing light
landing speed
landing wires
launching pad
maiden flight
manned rocket
night fighter

pilot balloon
pressure suit
pursuit plane
radar scanner
radial-engine
sound barrier
space capsule
space station
space vehicle
trailing-edge

13 and over

aircraft-carrier (15)
airworthiness (13)
control-column (13)
cruising speed (13)
decompression (15)
engine-mounting (14)
escape-velocity (14)
forced landing (13)
ground control (13)
heavier-than-air (14)
in-line-engines (13)
lighter-than-air (14)
looping the loop (14)
radio-location (13)
semi-retractable (15)
shock-absorber (13)
space traveller (14)
stalling-speed (13)
troop-transport (14)
undercarriage (13)
weightlessness (14)

Aircraft

3

jet

4

kite

5

plane

6

air car
bomber
glider

7

airship
balloon
biplane
clipper
fighter
jump-jet
shuttle

8

aerostat
airplane
autogiro
Concorde
jumbo-jet
rotodyne
sea-plane
triplane
turbo-jet
warplane
zeppelin

9

aeroplane
dirigible
mail-plane

monoplane
sailplane
turbo-prop

10

flying boat
gas-balloon
helicopter
hovercraft

hydroplane
fire-balloon

12

freight-plane

13

stratocruiser

14

flying bedstead
passenger plane

18

Montgolfier balloon

International Airports

Airport	City	Airport	City
Arlanda	Stockholm	La Guardia	New York
Ataturk	Istanbul	Leonardo da	Rome
Barajas	Madrid	Vinci (Fiumicino)	
Charles de Gaulle	Paris	Linate	Milan
Changi	Singapore	Lindbergh Field	San Diego
Chiang Kai-Shek	Taipei	Logan	Boston
Cointrin	Geneva	Luis Munoz Marin	San Juan
Dallas-Fort Worth	Dallas	McCarran	Las Vegas
Dorval	Montreal	Mirabel	Montreal
Douglas	Charlotte	Narita	Tokyo
Dulles	Washington	Ninoy Aquino	Manila
Echterdingen	Stuttgart	O'Hare	Chicago
Findel	Luxembourg	Okecie	Warsaw
Fornebu	Oslo	Orly	Paris
Gatwick	London	Pearson	Toronto
Hartsfield	Atlanta	St Paul	Minneapolis
Heathrow	London	Schipol	Amsterdam
Helsinki-Vantaa	Helsinki	Sheremetyevo	Moscow
Hongqaio	Shanghai	Sky Harbor	Phoenix
Hopkins	Cleveland	Soekarno Hatta	Jakarta
John F. Kennedy	New York	Stansted	London
(Benito) Juarez	Mexico City	Subang	Kuala Lumpur
Kimpo	Seoul	Tegel	Berlin
King Khaled	Riyadh	Tullamarine	Melbourne
Kingsford Smith	Sydney	Wayne County	Detroit

Airline Flight Codes

Code	Airline	Code	Airline
AAF	Aigle Azur	BAF	British Air Ferries
AAG	Air Atlantique	BAL	Britannia Airlines
AAL	American Airlines	BAW	British Airways
AAN	Oasis	BBB	Balair
ABB	Air Belgium	BBC	Bangladesh Biman
ABR	Hunting	BCS	European Air Transport
ACA	Air Canada	BEA	Brymon European
ACF	Air Charter International	BEE	Busy Bee
ADR	Adria Airways	BER	Air Berlin
AEA	Air Europa	BIH	British Intl Heli
AEF	Aero Lloyd	BMA	British Midland
AFL	Aeroflot	BRA	Braathens
AFM	Affretair	BWA	BWIA
AFR	Air France	BZH	Brit Air
AGX	Aviogenex	CAC	CAAC
AHK	Air Hong Kong	CDN	Canadian Airlines Intl
AIA	Air Atlantis	CFE	City Flyer
AIC	Air India	CFG	Condor
AIH	Airtours	CIC	Celtic Air
ALK	Air Lanka	CKT	Caledonian
AMC	Air Malta	CLH	Lufthansa CityLine
AMM	Air 2000	CLX	Cargolux
AMT	American Trans Air	CMM	Canada 3000 Airlines
ANA	Air Nippon Airways	CNB	Air Columbus
ANZ	Air New Zealand	COA	Continental Airlines
AOM	Air Outre Mer	CPA	Cathay Pacific
APW	Arrow Air	CRL	Corse Air
ARG	Argentina Airways	CRX	Cross Air
ATI	ATI	CSA	Czech Airlines
ATT	Aer Turas	CTA	CTA
AUA	Austrian Airlines	CTN	Croatia Airlines
AUR	Aurigny Aero Service	CYP	Cyprus Airways
AVA	Avianca	DAH	Air Algerie
AWC	Titan Airways	DAL	Delta Airlines
AYC	Aviaco	DAT	Delta Air Transport
AZA	Alitalia	DLH	Lufthansa
AZI	Air Zimbabwe	DMA	Maersk Air
AZR	Air Zaire	DQI	Cimber Air

Code	Airline	Code	Airline
DYA	Alyemda	KAC	Kuwait Airways
EGY	Egypt Air	KAL	Korean Air
EIA	Evergreen Intl	KAR	Kar-Air
EIN	Aer Lingus	KIS	Contactair
ELY	El Al	KLM	KLM
ETH	Ethiopian Airlines	KQA	Kenya Airways
EUI	Euralair	LAA	Libya Arab Airlines
EWW	Emery	LAZ	Bulgarian Airlines
EXS	Channel Express	LDA	Lauda Air
EXX	Air Exel UK	LEI	Air UK Leisure
FDE	Federal Express	LGL	Luxair
FIN	Finnair	LIB	Air Liberte
FOB	Ford	LIN	Linjeflyg
FOF	Fred Olsen	LIT	Air Littoral
FUA	Futura	LKA	Alkair
FXY	Flexair	LOG	Loganair
GBL	GB Airways	LOT	Polish Airlines (LOT)
GEC	German Cargo	LTE	LTE
GFA	Gulf Air	LTS	LTU Sud
GFG	Germania	LTU	LTU
GHA	Ghana Airways	MAH	Malev
GIA	Garuda	MAS	Malaysian Airlines
GIL	Gill Air	MAU	Air Mauritius
GNT	Business Air	MDN	Meridiana
GRN	Greenair	MEA	Middle East Airlines
HAL	Hawaiian Air	MNX	Manx Airlines
HAS	Hamburg Airlines	MON	Monarch Airlines
HLA	HeavyLift	MOR	Morefly
HLF	Hapag-Lloyd	MPH	Martinair
IAW	Iraqi Airways	NAD	Nobleair
IBE	Iberia	NAW	Newair
ICE	Icelandair	NEX	Northern Executive
IEA	Inter European	NGA	Nigeria Airways
INS	Instone Airlines	NSA	Nile Safaris
IRA	Iran Air	NWA	Northwest Airlines
IST	Istanbul Airlines	NXA	Nationair
ITF	Air Inter	OAL	Olympic Airlines
JAL	Japan Airlines	OYC	Conair
JAT	JAT	PAL	Philippine Airlines
JAV	Janes Aviation	PGA	Portugalia
JEA	Jersey European Airways	PGT	Pegasus

Code	Airline	Code	Airline
PIA	Pakistani Intl	THA	Thai Airways Intl
QFA	Qantas	THG	Thurston
QSC	African Safaris	THY	Turkish Airlines
RAM	Royal Air Maroc	TLE	Air Toulouse
RBA	Royal Brunei	TMA	Trans Mediterranean
RIA	Rich Intl	TOW	Tower Air
RJA	Royal Jordanian	TRA	Transavia
RNA	Royal Nepal Airlines	TSC	Air Transat
ROT	Tarom	TSW	TEA Basle
RWD	Air Rwanda	TWA	TWA
RYR	Ryanair	TWE	Transwede
SAA	South African Airways	TYR	Tyrolean
SAB	Sabena	UAE	Emirates Airlines
SAS	SAS	UAL	United Airlines
SAW	Sterling Airways	UGA	Uganda Airlines
SAY	Suckling Airways	UKA	Air UK
SDI	Saudi	UKR	Air Ukraine
SEY	Air Seychelles	ULE	Air UK Leisure
SIA	Singapore Airlines	UPA	Air Foyle
SJM	Southern Air Transport	UPS	United Parcels
SLA	Sobelair	USA	USAir
SPP	Spanair	UTA	UTA
STR	Stellair	UYC	Cameroon Airlines
SUD	Sudan Airways	VIA	Viasa
SUT	Sultan Air	VIR	Virgin Atlantic
SWE	Swedair	VIV	Viva Air
SWR	Swissair	VKG	Scanair
SXS	Sun Express	VRG	Varig
SYR	Syrian Arab	WDL	WDL
TAP	Air Portugal	WOA	World Airways
TAR	Tunis Air	ZAC	Zambia Airways
TAT	TAT	ZAS	ZAS Airline of Egypt
TCT	TUR European		

Motoring

2 and 3	bhp	cog
A.A.	cam	fan
c.c.	can	fit
air	cap	gas
	car	G.T.

hub
H.P.
jam
jet
key
lap
lug
map
M.O.T.
nut
oil
pin
pit
R.A.C.
rev
rim
rod
run
ton
top

4

axle
belt
body
bolt
boot
boss
bulb
bush
clip
coil
dash
disc
door
drum
flat
fuse
gear
hood
hoot
horn
idle

jack
lane
lock
nail
park
pink
plug
pump
road
roll
rope
seat
skid
sump
tail
tank
test
tire
tour
tube
tyre
veer
wing

5

apron
brake
cable
chain
chart
choke
clamp
coupe
cover
crank
cut in
drive
float
frame
gauge
joint
knock
lay-by

level
lever
model
motor
on tow
pedal
rally
rev up
rivet
rotor
route
scale
screw
sedan
servo
shaft
shift
spark
speed
spoke
squab
stall
start
ton up
tools
tread
U-turn
valve
wheel
wiper
works

6

adjust
big end
bonnet
bumper
bypass
camber
car tax
charge
clutch
cut out

damper
dazzle
decoke
de-icer
de luxe
detour
dickey
divert
driver
dynamo
engine
filter
fitter
flange
funnel
garage
gasket
grease
handle
heater
hooter
hot rod
hub cap
idling
klaxon
lock-up
louvre
mascot
milage
mirror
octane
oilcan
one-way
petrol
pile up
pinion
piston
rebore
saloon
signal
spokes
spring
stroke

swerve
switch
tappet
timing
torque
tuning

7

air hose
airlock
axle-box
battery
bearing
blowout
bollard
bracket
build-up
bus lane
bus stop
car park
carport
cat's eye
chassis
contact
control
cooling
dipping
drive-in
driving
dynamic
exhaust
fanbelt
flyover
gearbox
give way
goggles
gudgeon
hardtop
highway
joyride
L driver
L plates
licence

linkage
locknut
log book
luggage
magneto
map-case
mileage
misfire
missing
mixture
muffler
no entry
non-skid
offside
oil-feed
oil seal
parking
pillion
pinking
pull out
reverse
roadhog
roadmap
road tax
rolling
run into
seizing
service
skidpan
spindle
springs
starter
test run
toolkit
top gear
touring
towrope
traffic
trailer
viaduct
warning
wingnut

8

adhesion
air brake
air inlet
airtight
armature
arterial
Autobahn
backfire
back seat
bodywork
brake pad
brakerod
bulkhead
calliper
camshaft
cat's eyes
clearway
coasting
converge
coupling
crankpin
cruising
cross-ply
cul-de-sac
cylinder
declutch
delivery
dipstick
driveway
fastback
fast lane
feed pipe
feed pump
flat tyre
flywheel
foglight
footpump
freezing
friction
fuelpipe
fuel pump
fuel tank

garaging
gasoline
gradient
guide-rod
handpump
ignition
inlet cam
kick-down
knocking
live axel
manifold
missfire
motoring
motorist
motorway
mounting
mudguard
nearside
oil gauge
oncoming
open road
overhaul
overpass
overtake
overturn
pavement
prowl car
puncture
radiator
rattling
rear axle
rear lamp
ring road
roadside
road sign
road test
roof rack
rotor arm
rush hour
selector
side road
sideslip
silencer

skidding
skid mark
slip road
slow down
slow lane
small end
speeding
squad car
steering
stock car
tail gate
tail skid
taxi rank
throttle
tire pump
track rod
two-speed
tyre pump

9

air filter
alignment
anti-glare
autoroute
back wheel
ball-valve
batteries
brakedrum
brakeshoe
breakdown
bus driver
cab driver
car driver
car polish
chain-link
chauffeur
clearance
coachwork
concourse
condenser
cotter pin
crank axle
crankcase

crossroad
cutting in
dashboard
dashlight
defroster
dipswitch
direction
dirt track
disc brake
diversion
drum brake
estate car
filler cap
footbrake
framework
free-wheel
front axle
front seat
fuel gauge
gear lever
gear stick
generator
Grand Prix
grease-box
grease-gun
guarantee
half-shaft
handbrake
headlight
hit-and-run
indicator
induction
inner tube
insurance
limousine
lubricate
misfiring
motorbike
motorcade
motor show
nipple key
oil filter
overdrive

oversteer
passenger
patrol car
petrol can
piston rod
point duty
police car
prop shaft
racing car
radial-ply
rear light
reflector
revving up
road sense
road works
saloon car
sidelight
side valve
spare tire
spare tyre
spark plug
sports car
spotlight
switch off
tail-light
taximeter
third gear
tire lever
T-junction
tramlines
trunk road
two-seater
two stroke
tyre lever
underpass
underseal
wheelbase
wheel spin
white line

10
_____

access road
adjustment

air cleaner
alternator
amber light
anti-dazzle
antifreeze
bevelwheel
bottom gear
box-spanner
brakeblock
brake fluid
brake light
brake pedal
broken down
car licence
coachbuilt
combustion
commutator
crankshaft
crossroads
detonation
dickey seat
drive shaft
dry battery
four-seater
four-stroke
front wheel
gear casing
gear change
green light
gudgeon pin
headlights
horsepower
inlet valve
insulation
lighting up
low-tension
lubricator
motorcycle
overtaking
petrol pump
petrol tank
piston ring
private car

radial tire
radial tyre
rear mirror
rev counter
right of way
roadworthy
roundabout
safety belt
signalling
spare wheel
speed limit
streamline
suspension
tachometer
thermostat
third-party
three-speed
toll bridge
touring car
traffic cop
traffic jam
two-wheeler
understeer
upholstery
ventilator
wheelbrace
windscreen
wing mirror

11

accelerator
accessories
accumulator
anti-roll bar
blind corner
brake-lining
built-up area
carburetter
carburettor
carriageway
clutch pedal
compression
convertible

crash helmet
crossmember
decarbonize
de-luxe model
distributor
driving test
exhaust pipe
exhaust port
feeler-gauge
front lights
highway code
ignition key
interrupter
lorry driver
lubrication
luggage rack
motor spirit
needle-valve
number plate
oil pressure
overhauling
overheating
over-revving
owner-driver
petrol gauge
pre-ignition
racing model
radiator cap
request stop
reverse gear
reverse turn
rotary valve
screen-wiper
sell-starter
servo system
sliding roof
speedometer
sports model
streamlined
sunshine roof
synchromesh
tappet valve
thermometer

through road
ticking over
trafficator
vacuum brake
valve-timing
wheel wobble

12

acceleration
approach road
arterial road
ball-bearings
breakdown van
clutch-spring
coachbuilder
contact-screw
countershaft
cylinder head
diesel engine
differential
double-decker
driving-chain
driving-shaft
exhaust valve
float-chamber
freewheeling
fuel injection
gear changing
lock-up garage
miles per hour
motor scooter
motor vehicle
motorcyclist
parking light
parking meter
parking place
petrol filter
pillion rider
racing driver
ratchet-wheel
registration
repair outfit
road junction

running-board
single-decker
sparking plug
steering gear
supercharger
transmission
turbocharger
two-speed gear
viscous drive
warning light

13

admission-pipe
breakdown gang
chain-adjuster
connecting rod
cooling system
decarbonizing
driving mirror
fluid flywheel
fuel injection
hydraulic jack
induction pipe
inspection pit
licence-holder
overhead valve
pillion-riding
power steering
pressure-gauge
rack-and-pinion
roller-bearing
servo-assisted
shock absorber
shooting brake
slave cylinder
spark ignition
speed merchant
starting motor
steering wheel
traffic signal

14

adjusting-screw

circuit-breaker
compression tap
contact-breaker
double-declutch
driving licence
exhaust-cam axle
filling station
friction-clutch
four-wheel drive
grease-injector
lighting-up time
lubricating oil
luggage-carrier
miles per gallon
propeller shaft
reclining seats
reversing lights
service station
starting handle
steering column
third-party risk
three-speed gear
universal joint

15

carriage-builder
dual carriageway
front-wheel drive
hydraulic system
instrument panel
insurance policy
petrol injection
seating capacity
windscreen wiper

17+

automatic transmission
(21)
crown wheel and pinion
(19)
independent suspension
(21)
induction manifold (17)

power assisted steering
(21)
revolution counter (17)

Vehicles

2 and 3

BMX
BR
bus
cab
car
DAF
dan
fly
gig
GWR
jet
LMS
MG
mig
RY
SR
van

4

Audi
auto
bier
biga
bike
cart
drag
dray
duck
ekka
Fiat
Ford
hack
heap
jeep

limo
LNER
loco
luge
mini
Opel
pram
Saab
Seat
shay
skis
sled
tank van
taxi
tram
trap
tube
wain

5

araba
artic
bandy
bogey
bogie
brake
brett
buggy
caddy
chair
coach
coupe
crate
cycle
dandy
dilly
dooly
float
lorry
metro
moped
motor
palki

plane
pulka
Rover
sedan
sulky
tonga
train
truck
Volvo
wagon

6

Austin
banger
barrow
Berlin
calash
chaise
dodgem
dennet
diesel
doolie
drosky
engine
fiacre
gingle
go-cart
hansom
hearse
hotrod
hurdle
Jaguar
jalopy
jitney
Lancia
landau
limber
litter
maglev
model-T
Morris
oxcart
pochay

pulkha
rocket
saloon
sledge
sleigh
snocat
spider
surrey
tandem
tanker
tender
tricar
troika
waggon
weasel
whisky

7

amtrack
autobus
autocar
balloon
bicycle
bob-sled
britzka
Bugatti
caboose
cacolet
caleche
caravan
caravel
cariole
caroche
chariot
chopper
Citroen
coaster
Daimler
dogcart
droshky
flivver
fourgon
growler

gyrocar
hackery
hackney
hard-top
haywain
helibus
kibitka
mail car
mail-van
minibus
minicab
minicar
off-road
omnibus
open-car
pedrail
phaeton
pullman
railcar
railbus
Renault
scooter
shunter
sidecar
Sputnik
tally-ho
taxi-cab
tilbury
tipcart
tonneau
tractor
trailer
tramcar
trishaw
Triumph
trolley
trundle
tumbrel
tumbril
turnout
two-door
unicorn
vis-à-vis

voiture
whiskey

8

barouche
brakevan
branchard
britzska
brougham
cablecar
Cadillac
cape-cart
carriage
carriole
carrycot
clarence
curricle
cycle-car
dead cart
dormeuse
dustcart
four-door
equipage
goods van
handcart
horse-bus
horse-cab
horse-van
ice-yacht
jetliner
jump-seat
kibitzka
mail-cart
milk-cart
monorail
motorbus
motorcar
motorvan
old crock
pony-cart
pushbike
pushcart
quadriga

rickshaw
roadster
rockaway
runabout
sociable
staff car
stanhope
steam-car
tarantas
toboggan
tricycle
Vauxhall
victoria
zeppelin

9

aeroplane
ambulance
amphibian
applecart
bandwagon
bath-chair
boat-train
bob-sleigh
box-wagon
bubblecar
buckboard
bulldozer
cabriolet
char-a-banc
Chevrolet
diligence
dining car
dodgem car
dormobile
estate car
funicular
guard's van
hansom cab
hatchback
horse-cart
ice skates
landaulet

land rover
limousine
mail-coach
mail-train
milkfloat
motorbike
motorcade
muletrain
palankeen
palanquin
prison van
racing car
Rolls-Royce
saloon car
sand yacht
sports car
streetcar
stretcher
tarantass
tin lizzie
wagonette
water-cart

10

automobile
bail gharry
beach wagon
Black Maria
boneshaker
chapel cart
conveyance
donkey-cart
fire-engine
four-in-hand
glass coach
goods train
goods truck
hackney cab
hand-barrow
hovercraft
invalid cab
jinricksha
knockabout

local train
locomotive
motorcoach
motorcycle
motor lorry
night train
outside car
paddywagon
pedal cycle
pony engine
post-chaise
pullman car
rattle trap
sedan chair
shandrydan
Sinclair C5
smoking car
snowplough
spacecraft
spring-cart
stagecoach
stage wagon
state coach
timwhiskey
tip-up lorry
touring car
tramway-car
trolley-bus
trolley-car
two-wheeler
velocipede
waggonette
war chariot
wheelchair

11

armoured car
bone breaker
brewer's dray
bullock cart
caterpillar
convertible
delivery van

diesel train
fire balloon
four-wheeler
goods waggon
gun-carriage
horse-litter
jaunting-car
jinrickshaw
landaulette
mail phaeton
quadricycle
sit-up-and-beg
sleeping car
souped-up car
state landau
steam engine
steamroller
thika-gharry
three-in-hand
waggon train
wheelbarrow
whitechapel

12

baby carriage
coach-and-four
coach-and-pair
desobligeant
double-decker
express train
freight train
furniture-van
hackney-coach
horse and cart
invalid chair
luggage train
magic carpet
motor scooter
pantechnicon
perambulator
puffing billy
railway train
single decker

station wagon
steam omnibus
three-wheeler
through train
watering-cart

13

ambulance cart
cycle rickshaw
electric train
electric truck
governess cart
horse carriage
mourning-coach

penny-farthing
people carrier
racing chariot
shooting-brake
state carriage
steam-carriage
wheel-carriage

14

ambulance wagon
bathing-machine
four-wheel drive
luggage trailer
passenger train

riding carriage
traction-engine

15

hackney carriage
invalid carriage
prairie-schooner
railway carriage

16+

horseless carriage (17)
motorized bicycle (16)
travelling carriage (18)
underground train (16)

IVRs (Vehicle Registration)

Registration Letter	Country	Registration Letter	Country
A	Austria	CR	Costa Rica
ADN	Yemen	CS	Czechoslovakia
AL	Albania	CY	Cyprus
AND	Andorra	D	Germany
AUS	Australia	DDR	E. Germany
B	Belgium	DK	Denmark
BDS	Barbados	DOM	Dominican Republic
BG	Bulgaria	DY	Dahomey
BH	British Honduras	DZ	Algeria
BR	Brazil	E	Spain
BRG	Guyana	EAK	Kenya
BRN	Bahrain	EAT	Tanzania
BRU	Brunei	EAU	Uganda
BS	Bahamas	EC	Ecuador
BUR	Burma	ET	Egypt
C	Cuba	F	France
CDN	Canada	FJI	Fiji
CH	Switzerland	FL	Liechtenstein
CI	Ivory Coast (Cote d'Ivoire)	GB	Great Britain
		GBA	Alderney
CL	Sri Lanka	GBG	Guernsey
CO	Columbia	GBJ	Jersey

Registration Letter	Country	Registration Letter	Country
GBM	Isle of Man	PI	Philippines
GBZ	Gibraltar	PO	Poland
GCA	Guatemala	PY	Paraguay
GH	Ghana	R	Romania
GR	Greece	RA	Argentina
GUY	Guyana	RB	Botswana
H	Hungary	RC	China
HKJ	Jordon	RCA	Central African Republic
I	Italy		
IL	Israel	RCB	Congo
IND	India	RCH	Chile
IR	Iran	RH	Haiti
IRL	Ireland	RI	Indonesia
IRQ	Iraq	RIM	Mauritania
IS	Iceland	RL	Lebanon
J	Japan	RM	Madagascar
JA	Jamaica	RMM	Mali
K	Kampuchea	ROK	South Korea
KWT	Kuwait	RSM	San Marino
L	Luxembourg	RU	Burundi
LAO	Laos	RWA	Rwanda
LAR	Libya	S	Sweden
LB	Liberia	SD	Swaziland
LS	Lesotho	SF	Finland
M	Malta	SGP	Singapore
MA	Morocco	SME	Surinam
MAL	Malaysia	SN	Senegal
MC	Monaco	SU	Soviet Union
MEX	Mexico	SWA	South West Africa
MS	Mauritius	SY	Seychelles
MW	Malawi	SYR	Syria
N	Norway	T	Thailand
NA	Netherlands Antilles	TG	Togo
NIG	Niger	TN	Tunisia
NL	Netherlands	TR	Turkey
NZ	New Zealand	TT	Trinidad and Tobago
P	Portugal	U	Uruguay
PA	Panama	USA	U.S.A
PAK	Pakistan	V	Vatican City
PE	Peru	VN	Vietnam

Registration Letter	Country	Registration Letter	Country
WAG	Gambia	WS	Western Samoa
WAL	Sierra Leone	YU	Yugoslavia
WAN	Nigeria	YV	Venezuela
WG	Granada, Windward Islands	Z	Zambia
		ZA	South Africa
WL/WV	Windward Islands (St Lucia and St Vincent)	ZR	Zaire
		ZW	Zimbabwe

Boats and ships

3 and 4

argo
ark
bac
bark
boat
brig
buss
caic
cog
cot
dhow
dory
dow
duck
four
gig
grab
hoy
hulk
junk
keel
koff
pair
pram
proa
punt
raft
saic
scow
ship
snow
sub
T.B.D.
trow
tub
tug
yawl

5

aviso
balsa
barca
barge
batel
boyer
canoe
caper
casco
coble
craft
crare
dandy
E-boat
eight
ferry
fifie
fleet
float
funny
kayak
ketch
kobil
liner
nobby
oiler
P-boat
praam
prahu
prove
Q-ship
razee
R-boat
saiok
scull
shell
skiff
sloop
smack
tramp
U-boat
umiak
whiff

xebec
yacht

6

argosy
banker
barque
bateau
bawley
bireme
bug-eye
caique
carvel
coggle
cooper
crayer
cutter
decker
dinghy
dogger
droger
dugout
galeas
galiot
galley
gay-you
hooker
hopper
kumpit
launch
lorcha
lugger
masula
oomiak
packet
pedalo
pirate
puffer
pulwar
puteli
PT boat
randan
saique

sampan
sealer
settee
slaver
tanker
tartan
tender
tosher
trader
trough
vessel
wafter
whaler
wherry

7

airboat
almadie
budgero
bumboat
caravel
carrack
carrier
catboat
clinker
clipper
coaster
cockler
collier
coracle
corsair
cruiser
currach
dredger
drifter
drogher
dromond
eel punt
felucca
flyboat
four-oar
frigate
galleon

galliot
gondola
gunboat
gunship
hog-boat
ice-boat
jangada
lighter
man-o'-war
minisub
mistico
monitor
mudscow
muletta
pair-oar
permagy
pinnace
piragua
pirogue
polacca
polacre
pontoon
rowboat
sculler
sea-sled
shallop
shoaler
spy boat
steamer
tartane
tonkong
tow boat
trawler
trireme
tugboat
warship

8

baghalak
bilander
car ferry
coalship

cockboat
corocole
corvette
crumster
dahabeah
dahabiya
derelict
eight-oar
fireboat
fireship
flagship
foldboat
galleass
galliass
gallivat
hoogarts
hoveller
ice yacht
Indiaman
ironclad
johnboat
keelboat
lifeboat
longboat
mailboat
mailship
man-of-war
Noah's ark
netlayer
outboard
sailboat
schooner
showboat
smuggler
steam-tug
tilt-boat
trimaran
waterbus
well-boat
woodskin

9

bomb-ketch

bucentaur
cable ship
canal boat
cargo boat
catamaran
container
cris-craft
crocodile
depot ship
destroyer
ferryboat
fire-float
freighter
frigatoon
funny-boat
guard boat
guard ship
herringer
horse-boat
house boat
hydrofoil
jollyboat
lightship
minelayer
motorboat
motorship
mud-hopper
oil tanker
outrigger
peter-boat
pilot boat
pilot ship
powerboat
privateer
prize ship
river boat
rotor ship
sand yacht
sheer-hulk
ship's boat
slave dhow
slave-ship
speedboat

steamboat
steamship
storeship
submarine
swampboat
transport
troopship
tunny-boat
two-decker
whaleboat
wheelboat

10

advice boat
barge-yacht
banana boat
barkentine
battleship
bomb vessel
brigantine
cattleboat
chain-ferry
cockleboat
Deal lugger
flying boat
four-master
hovercraft
hydroplane
icebreaker
monkey-boat
motor yacht
narrowboat
nuclear sub
ocean liner
ore-carrier
packet-boat
paddleboat
patrol boat
picket boat
pirate-ship
quadrireme
repair-ship
rescue boat

rivercraft
rowing boat
royal barge
sloop-of-war
small craft
submarine
supply ship
survey ship
target ship
tea-clipper
train-ferry
turret ship
victualler
Viking ship
windjammer
watercraft

11

barquentine
capital ship
chasse-maree
cockleshell
double-canoe
dreadnought
fishing boat
galley foist
hopper-barge
hydroglider
mail-steamer
merchantman
minesweeper
motor launch
motor vessel
mystery ship
naval vessel
penteconter
pilot cutter
prize vessel
quinquereme
racing shell
Rob-Roy canoe
sailing boat
sailing ship

sardine boat
slavetrader
steam launch
steam vessel
submersible
three-decker
three-master
torpedo boat
victual ship

12

cabin cruiser
coasting boat
coasting ship
despatch boat
East Indiaman
escort vessel
ferry steamer
fishing smack
heavy cruiser
hospital ship
landing barge
landing craft
light cruiser
merchant ship
motor drifter
motor trawler
pirate cutter
pleasure boat
police launch
pontoon crane
river gunboat
sailing barge
sailing craft
sculling boat
square-rigger
steam gondola
stern-wheeler
survey vessel
Thames bawley
training ship

13

battlecruiser
Bermuda cutter
Canadian canoe
container ship
double-sculler
four-oared boat
herring fisher
hovelling-boat
motor lifeboat
paddle-steamer
passenger-boat
passenger-ship
sailing vessel
ship-of-the-line
trading vessel
transport ship

14 AND 15

aircraft-carrier (15)
cable-laying ship (15)
cable-repair ship (15)
channel steamer (14)
coasting vessel (14)
despatch cutter (14)
eight-oared boat (14)
electric launch (14)
floating palace (14)
flotilla leader (14)
ocean greyhound (14)
seaplane tender (14)
submarine chaser (15)
topsail schooner (15)
torpedo-gunboat (14)
Yorkshire coble (14)

Nautical Terms

2 and 3

A.B.
aft
A1

bay	back	haul
bow	bale	haze
box	beam	hazy
cat	beat	head
cay	bend	helm
C.I.F.	bitt	hold
con	boom	hove
cox	bows	hulk
ebb	brig	hull
fay	bunk	jack
fid	bunt	junk
F.O.B	buoy	keel
fog	calk	knot
guy	calm	land
H.M.S	coak	last
hog	comb	lead
jaw	cott	leak
jib	crew	line
lee	deck	list
log	dive	load
man	dock	loof
nut	down	luff
oar	dune	lute
ply	east	mast
ram	eddy	mate
rig	fake	mess
R.M.	fend	mine
R.N.	flag	mist
rum	floe	mole
run	flow	moor
sag	foam	navy
sea	fore	neap
set	foul	oars
SOS	frap	peak
tar	furl	pier
top	gaff	poop
tow	gale	port
way	gang	prow
yaw	gear	punt
	girt	quay
4	grog	raft
ahoy	hank	rail
alee	hard	rake

rank	wind	cadet
rate	wing	canal
rear	yard	cargo
reef	yarn	caulk
ride		chain
roll	**5**	chart
rope	aback	check
rove	abaft	chock
rung	abeam	clamp
sail	afore	cleat
scud	afoul	craft
seam	after	crank
ship	ahead	cuddy
sink	ahull	davit
skid	aloft	depth
slip	apeak	diver
slue	aport	douse
spar	atrip	downs
stay	avast	dowse
stem	awash	draft
step	beach	drift
surf	belay	embay
swab	belee	entry
swig	bells	fanal
tack	below	flake
taut	berth	fleet
tend	bibbs	float
tide	bight	fluke
tilt	bilge	foggy
toss	bilts	gauge
trim	bitts	grave
trip	blirt	gusty
vang	block	hands
veer	board	hatch
voya	bosun	haven
waft	bower	hawse
wake	bowse	hitch
wapp	brace	hoist
warp	brail	horse
wave	bream	jetty
wear	briny	jutty
west	cabin	kedge
whip	cable	kevel

lay-to	siren	bonnet
lay up	skeet	bridge
leach	sling	bumkin
leaky	sound	bunker
leech	spars	burton
ligan	spoom	cablet
liner	sprit	canvas
lobby	steer	careen
lurch	stern	carina
metal	storm	comber
misty	surge	convoy
naval	swell	course
north	swing	crotch
oakum	thole	cruise
ocean	tidal	debark
order	trice	diving
orlop	truck	double
panch	truss	driver
pitch	waist	earing
prick	watch	embark
prize	weigh	engine
prore	wharf	ensign
radar	wheel	escort
radio	winch	fathom
range	windy	fender
refit	woold	fo'c'sle
rhumb	wreck	for'ard
right		fother
roads	*6*	funnel
ropes	aboard	furled
route	adrift	galley
rower	afloat	gasket
royal	anchor	gromet
sally	armada	gunnel
salve	ashore	halser
salvo	astern	hawser
sands	aweigh	hounds
screw	awning	hove-to
sheer	balker	inship
sheet	batten	jetsam
shelf	beacon	jetson
shoal	becket	jigger
shore	billow	kedger

lading	reefed	vessel
lateen	reefer	voyage
launch	rigged	yawing
lay-off	rigger	
league	rocket	**7**
leeway	rudder	admiral
Lloyd's	sailor	aground
locker	saloon	athwart
manned	salute	backing
marina	salvor	bale out
marine	sculls	eye-bolt
marker	sealer	ballast
maroon	seaman	beached
marque	seaway	bearing
masted	sheets	beating
mayday	shroud	bilboes
mid-sea	signal	blister
mizzen	sinker	boarder
moored	sinnet	bobstay
mutiny	splice	bollard
nautic	squall	boomkin
neaped	square	bowline
needle	stocks	bow wave
offing	stormy	boxhaul
on deck	strake	bracing
outfit	strand	breaker
paddle	stream	bulwark
patrol	tackle	bunkage
pay off	tender	buntine
pay out	thwart	bunting
pennon	tiller	buoyage
Pharos	timber	caboose
pillow	toggle	calking
pintle	towage	can-buoy
piracy	unbend	capsize
pirate	unbitt	capstan
piston	uncoil	captain
pooped	undock	cast off
poppet	unfurl	catfall
purser	unlade	cathead
raider	unload	cat's-paw
rating	unmoor	catwalk
ratlin	unship	channel

charter	go about	listing
claw off	go below	loading
coaling	grapnel	logbook
coaming	grating	logline
cockpit	graving	logreel
compass	grommet	lookout
conning	gudgeon	luffing
cordage	gun-deck	lugsail
corsair	gunnage	maintop
counter	gun-port	mariner
cresset	gun-room	marines
cringle	gunwale	marline
cyclone	guy-rope	marling
deadeye	half pay	matelot
deep-sea	halyard	mistral
degauss	harbour	monsoon
dismast	harpoon	moorage
dockage	haul off	mooring
dog-vane	head off	mudhook
dolphin	head sea	oarsman
drabler	headway	oceanic
draught	heave to	offward
dry-dock	horizon	old salt
dunnage	iceberg	on board
ease off	icefloe	outport
ebb-tide	inboard	oversea
embargo	inshore	painter
fairway	Jack Tar	pennant
fishery	jib boom	pooping
flotsam	jibstay	port-bar
flotson	keelage	quarter
fogbank	keelson	quayage
foghorn	landing	rafting
foretop	laniard	rations
forward	lanyard	ratline
founder	lashing	reefing
freight	lastage	reeming
freshen	latches	ride out
freshet	leaking	rigging
frogman	lee-gage	rollers
futtock	lee side	rolling
gangway	lee tide	rope-end
gimbals	leeward	rostrum

rowlock
rundown
sailing
salvage
scupper
scuffle
seacard
seafolk
sea-lane
sea-legs
sea mile
seamark
sea-ooze
sea-room
seasick
seaward
set sail
sextant
shallow
shelves
shipper
shipway
shrouds
sick-bay
sinking
skipper
skysail
slipway
spanker
spencer
squally
stand-by
steward
stopper
stowage
tacking
tackled
tackler
tactics
tempest
thimble
tonnage
top deck

top mast
topping
topsail
topside
tornado
torpedo
towline
towpath
towrope
transom
trysail
typhoon
unladen
unsling
unslung
veering
waftage
ward off
warping
watches
wavelet
waveson
wet dock
whistle
wrecked
wrecker
yardarm

8

anchored
anteport
aplustre
approach
armament
at anchor
aweather
backstay
backwash
barbette
bargeman
barnacle
beam-ends
bearings

becalmed
berthage
berthing
binnacle
boat-deck
boathook
bolt-rope
bowsprit
broach to
bulkhead
bulwarks
buntline
castaway
caulking
claw away
club-haul
coasting
coxswain
crossing
cruising
cutwater
dead slow
deadwood
deckhand
derelict
disembay
ditty-bag
ditty-box
dockyard
dogwatch
doldrums
doubling
downhaul
drifting
driftway
easterly
eastward
even keel
fife-rail
flag-rank
floating
flotilla
fogbound

foot-rope	lifebelt	portoise
forefoot	lifebuoy	portside
foremast	lifeline	pratique
forepeak	load-line	pumproom
foresail	loblolly	put about
foreship	logboard	put to sea
forestay	long haul	quarters
forewind	low water	ratlines
free-port	magazine	reef-knot
gaffsail	mainboom	re-embark
go aboard	main deck	ride easy
go ashore	mainmast	ride hard
halliard	mainsail	roadster
halyards	mainstay	sail-loft
hard-alee	mainyard	sail-room
hatchway	make sail	sail-yard
headfast	maritime	salvable
head into	martinet	salvager
headwind	masthead	sandbank
helmless	mastless	scudding
helmsman	messmate	scuppers
high seas	midships	seaborne
high tide	moorings	sea-chest
hornpipe	moulinet	seafarer
hull-down	mutineer	seagoing
icebound	mutinous	sea-rover
icefield	nauscopy	shallows
iron-sick	nautical	shark-net
jackstay	navigate	sheer off
jettison	neap tide	ship ahoy
jury mast	ordnance	shipmate
keelhaul	outboard	shipment
keel over	overrake	ship oars
land ahoy!	overseas	shipping
landfall	paravane	sounding
landmark	periplus	splicing
landsman	picaroon	spy-glass
landward	pierhead	squadron
land wind	pilotage	standard
larboard	pitching	stand off
lead-line	plimsoll	staysail
leeboard	poop deck	steerage
lee shore	porthole	sternage

sternway
stowaway
stranded
streamer
stunsail
submerge
tackling
tafferel
taffrail
thole-pin
timoneer
tranship
traverse
unbuoyed
uncoiled
underset
under way
unfurled
vanguard
wall-knot
wardroom
waterman
water-rot
waterway
waveworm
welldeck
westerly
westward
west wind
windlass
wind-rode
wind-sail
windward
woolding
wreckage
yachting

9

about-ship
admiralty
affreight
afterdeck
air-funnel

all aboard
alongside
amidships
anchorage
anchoring
back-stays
bargepole
barnacles
beaconage
below deck
bilge-keel
bilge-pump
blue peter
boardable
boat drill
broadside
bunkering
captaincy
careenage
chartered
chartroom
close haul
coastwise
companion
corposant
crossjack
crosstree
crosswind
crow's nest
Davy Jones
dead-water
deck cargo
demurrage
departure
disanchor
discharge
disembark
doggerman
dogshores
dress ship
drift-sail
driftwood
Elmo's-fire

false keel
firedrill
floodmark
flood-tide
flying jib
foreshore
foundered
freeboard
gangboard
gangplank
gather way
groundage
half-hitch
hard aport
high water
hoist sail
holystone
house-flag
houseline
hurricane
jack-block
jack-staff
jack-stays
kentledge
land ahead
lobscouse
lower deck
maelstrom
mainbrace
mainsheet
manoeuvre
midstream
minefield
minute-gun
mizzentop
naumachia
navicular
navigable
navigator
neptunian
northerly
northward
north wind

ocean lane
orlop deck
outrigger
overboard
parbuckle
periscope
press-gang
privateer
prize-crew
promenade
quicksand
recharter
reckoning
red ensign
reef-point
refitment
revictual
rhumb-line
roadstead
rockbound
royal mast
Royal Navy
rum-runner
sailcloth
seafaring
sea-letter
sea-robber
seaworthy
semaphore
sheething
shipboard
shipowner
ship's bell
ship's crew
shipshape
shipwreck
shoreward
sick-berth
sight land
sidelight
southerly
southward
south wind

sou'wester
spindrift
spinnaker
spritsail
stanchion
starboard
stateroom
steersman
sternfast
sternmost
sternpost
stokehold
storm-beat
stormsail
stormstay
stretcher
tarpaulin
telescope
tide-table
tophamper
trade wind
twin-screw
two-decker
unballast
uncharted
unharbour
unlighted
unsounded
upper deck
water-line
water-sail
whirlwind
wind-bound
wring-bolt
yachtsman

___10___

A1 at Lloyd's
aboard ship
after-guard
after-hatch
after-sails
alongshore

anchorable
anchor buoy
anchor hold
astarboard
ballasting
batten down
Bermuda rig
bilgewater
blue ensign
bluejacket
breakwater
bootlegger
breastfast
bridge deck
cargo space
cast anchor
casting-net
catch a crab
chain-cable
chain-plate
charthouse
coal-bunker
cork-jacket
cross-piece
crosstrees
deadlights
deadweight
degaussing
diving bell
dockmaster
downstream
drop anchor
drop astern
embarkment
engine room
escutcheon
fathomless
fiddlehead
figurehead
first watch
fore-and-aft
forecastle
forge ahead

freightage
freshwater
frostbound
full-rigged
gaff rigged
harbourage
heavy-laden
high-and-dry
hollow-mast
jigger-mast
Jolly Roger
jury-rigged
jury rudder
landlocked
landlubber
lateen sail
lateen yard
lay a course
liberty-man
life-jacket
lighterage
lighthouse
lookout-man
loxodromic
manoeuvres
marine soap
marker buoy
martingale
middle deck
midshipman
mizzenmast
mizzensail
mizzenstay
navigating
navigation
night-watch
ocean-going
orthodromy
parcelling
pilothouse
pipe aboard
port of call
powder-room

prize-court
prize-money
quarantine
raking fire
reduce sail
rendezvous
reshipment
rope-ladder
round-house
rudderless
rudder post
Samson post
seamanlike
seamanship
ship-broker
shipmaster
shipwright
signalling
skyscraper
slack-water
spring-tide
square-sail
stanchions
stay-tackle
stern-board
stern-frame
sternsheet
submariner
supercargo
take in sail
tally-clerk
tidal basin
tidal river
tiller-rope
topgallant
unfathomed
unfordable
upperworks
water-borne
waterspout
watertight
wheel-house
wring-staff

11

abandon ship
beachcomber
belaying pin
captainship
centreboard
chafing-gear
close-hauled
compass card
compass rose
contact mine
debarkation
depth-charge
dismastment
diving-bell
diving suit
dock charges
echo-sounder
embarcation
embarkation
escape hatch
foam-crested
fore-topmast
foul weather
gallows-tops
get under way
go alongside
graving-dock
ground-swell
harbour dues
harness-cask
hug the shore
innavigable
keelhauling
landing deck
lifeboatman
loblolly-boy
loxodromics
maintopmast
maintopsail
make headway
marine store
mess steward

middle watch
mizzen course
monkey-block
naval rating
orthodromic
overfreight
paddle wheel
port charges
port of entry
press-of-sail
quarter-deck
range-finder
reconnoitre
riding-light
sailing date
Samson's-post
searchlight
seasickness
sheet anchor
shipbreaker
ship's doctor
ship's papers
sliding-keel
snatch-block
sounding-rod
south-wester
spanking boom
spring a leak
standing off
station-bill
steerage-way
stern-chaser
sternsheets
storm signal
three-masted
thwartships
tidal waters
torpedo tube
unballasted
unchartered
under canvas
under-masted
unnavigable

unnavigated
unsheltered
unsoundable
waistcloths
waterlogged
weather-gage
weathermost
weather-roll
weather side
weigh anchor
white ensign

12

air-sea rescue
between-decks
bill of lading
breeches- buoy
cable's-length
canvas length
caulking iron
change course
collision-mat
companionway
conning tower
counter-brace
displacement
double-banked
double-braced
double-manned
equinoctials
fishing fleet
floating dock
futtock-plate
ground-tackle
hard-aweather
jack-o'-lantern
jacob's ladder
lateen-rigged
line of battle
longshoreman
magnetic mine
maiden voyage
man overboard

marine boiler
marine engine
marline-spike
measured mile
minesweeping
nautical mile
naval command
navigability
orthodromics
outmanoeuvre
outward-bound
Plimsoll line
Plimsoll mark
privateering
recommission
ride at anchor
ship-chandler
shipping line
ship's husband
slack in stays
square-rigged
starboard bow
stream anchor
studding sail
tourist class
training ship
transhipment
Trinity House
undercurrent
unfathomable
war-insurance
weatherboard
weatherbound
weather cloth
weatherglass
weatherproof
westerly wind
will-o'-the-wisp

13

affreightment
cat-o'-nine-tails
close quarters

compass signal
dead reckoning
deck passenger
fishing-tackle
floating light
grappling-iron
high-water mark
hurricane deck
life-preserver
mizzen rigging
naval dockyard
naval ordnance
navigableness
north-east wind
northerly wind
north-west wind
order-of-battle
quartermaster
re-embarkation
royal dockyard
ship-of-the-line
south-east wind
southerly wind
south-west wind
spilling-lines
starboard beam
starboard side
steering-wheel
weather report

14

circumnavigate

compass-bearing
disembarkation
futtock shrouds
hard-astarboard
letter-of-marque
Lloyd's Register
mushroom-anchor
naval architect
powder magazine
prevailing wind
running-rigging
schooner-rigged
screw-propeller
ship's-carpenter
superstructure
swivel-rowlocks
topgallant mast

15

Admiralty Office
circumnavigable
command of the sea
companion ladder
Davy Jones' locker
marine insurance
mariner's compass
operation orders
victualling yard

Shipping areas named in weather forecasts

Bailey
Biscay
Cromarty
Dogger
Dover
Faeroes
Fair Isle
Fastnet
Finisterre
Fisher
Forth
Forties
German Bight
Hebrides
Humber
Irish Sea
Lundy
Malin
Plymouth
Portland
Rockall
Shannon
Sole
South-East Iceland
Thames
Tyne
Viking
Wight